SCORCHED EARTH

HUMAN RIGHTS AND CRIMES AGAINST HUMANITY

Eric D. Weitz, Series Editor

Scorched Earth

ENVIRONMENTAL WARFARE AS A
CRIME AGAINST HUMANITY
AND NATURE

EMMANUEL KREIKE

PRINCETON UNIVERSITY PRESS

PRINCETON & OXFORD

Published by Princeton University Press
41 William Street, Princeton, New Jersey 08540
6 Oxford Street, Woodstock, Oxfordshire OX20 1TR

press.princeton.edu

ISBN 9780691137421
ISBN (e-book) 9780691189017

British Library Cataloging-in-Publication Data is available

Editorial: Brigitta van Rheinberg, Eric Crahan, Priya Nelson, Thalia Leaf
Production: Danielle Amatucci
Publicity: Alyssa Sanford (US) and Kate Farquhar-Thomson (UK)
Copyeditor: Kelly N. Clody

Jacket Image: Soldiers of an Australian 4th Division field artillery brigade on a duckboard track passing through Chateau Wood, near Hooge in the Ypres Salient, October 29, 1917

This book has been composed in Arno

Printed on acid-free paper ∞

Printed in the United States of America

10 9 8 7 6 5 4 3 2 1

Voor Nora Kreike-Martin

CONTENTS

ACKNOWLEDGMENTS

THE INSPIRATION for the book comes from deeply personal stories from survivors of war and displacement who rebuilt homes and livable environments in the aftermath of traumatic violence. My grandparents and parents lived through the Second World War, experiencing destruction of their homes (on the maternal side) and hunger (on the paternal side). As a college student, I had the privilege to meet and talk with former members of the Dutch Resistance and concentration camp survivors while I worked at the Dutch National War and Resistance Museum at Overloon, the Netherlands. Particularly influential was Harry van Daal, the secretary of the museum board and a former member of the resistance. My next formative experience was conducting fieldwork in northern Namibia in the early 1990s, in the immediate aftermath of the end of the liberation war against Apartheid South Africa. The women and men who shared their life histories with me were victims of wars and displacement that had transformed their villages, farms, and fields into smoldering ashes, yet they rebuilt lives and livelihoods among ruins and graves with an incredible energy and determination that inspired their children and grandchildren. All these strong women and men opened my eyes to the challenges of postwar rebuilding of communities and habitats.

As a child I spent much of my summers with my grandparents in Holland and Brabant, two Dutch provinces that feature large in the book. My father's family is from Halfweg ("halfway" between Haarlem and Amsterdam), straddling the Haarlem Lake and the northern sea dike discussed in chapter 1. My father grew up on one of the farms that was established in the Haarlem Lake after it was drained in the 19th century. My mother's family is from the area of Steenbergen and

ix

Hoeven in the Brabant polder lands west of Breda. I was impressed but a bit puzzled by the ubiquitous dikes and drainage canals. I especially recall the oddity of the steep downward decline of the road while driving from Zwanenburg to my grandparents' house in the Haarlem Lake polder and traveling over a high dike between Hoeven and Steenbergen miles away from any seaboard, two singular aberrations in an otherwise comfortably flat landscape. At the time, I had no perception of the historical significance of these features, and my research for the Dutch content chapters made for a fascinating journey as I peeled back the layers of history in places filled with childhood memories. Before undertaking this book project, I never would have imagined that my professional interest in the history of war, society, and environment, which took me to from the Netherlands to Africa, would eventually lead me back to my grandparents' homes.

The book owes much to the encouragement of Eric Weitz and Brigitte van Rheinberg, who first proposed that I should go global with my concerns about environmental warfare. I also received much support from my colleagues in the history department at Princeton University, including Bob Tignor, Anson Rabinach, Shel Garon, Jan Gross, Vera Candiani, Jacob Dlamini, Paul Miles, John Haldon, Bill Jordan, and Jeremy Adelman. I am particularly grateful to Petra van Dam, who not only introduced me to Dutch water management history but also took me on a bicycle tour along the northern sea dike of Holland, including the sluices and the wheel at Halfweg, and organized a visit to the monumental former Rijnland water board headquarters in Leiden. Henk Beijers provided expert guidance in unlocking the rural archives of Brabant and generously shared his transcripts. Rich comments from two anonymous readers for the Princeton University Press were very helpful in turning the manuscript into a book, as was the professional assistance of Eric Crahan, Thalia Leaf, and Kelly Clody also of the press. The maps owe much to the expert assistance of Tsering Shawa, GIS and map librarian at Princeton University.

A year of leave at the Netherlands Institute for Advanced Study (NIAS) as a fellow-in-residence, Royal Netherlands Academy of Arts and Sciences (KNAW), at Wassenaar, the Netherlands in 2012–13 and an Old Dominion Professorship at the Society of Fellows in the Liberal Arts of the Humanities Council at Princeton in 2016–17 were instrumental in writing the book. Funding from the Princeton University History Department and the Princeton University Committee for Research in the Social Sciences and Humanities made possible the field and archival research in Angola, the Netherlands, France, and Italy that was central to the research project.

I am grateful for the generous assistance and professional advice from the archivists and staff of numerous archival collections. In the Netherlands: The Nationaal Archief (National Archive), the Hague; The Archives of the Water Boards of Rijnland in Leiden, of Delfland in Delft, and Schieland in Rottterdam; Historisch Archief Westland in Naaldwijk; Regionaal Archief Leiden, Leiden; Noord Hollands Archief, Haarlem; West-Brabants Archief, Bergen op Zoom; Brabants Historisch Informatie Centrum, 's-Hertogenbosch; Zeeuws Archief, Middelburg; Tresoar Archief Friesland, Leeuwarden; Regionaal Historisch Centrum Eindhoven; and Nederlands Instituut voor Militaire History, the Hague. In France: Archives Départementales du Nord, Lille; Archives Municipales de Lille; and Archives Départementales des Alpes-Maritimes, Nice. In Italy: Archivio di Stato di Napoli, Naples; Archivio di Stato di Imperia, Imperia; and Archivio di Stato di Imperia, Sezione di Sanremo, Sanremo.

I presented ideas and chapters and received valuable feedback at various venues, including the African Studies Association annual meetings, the American Society of Environmental History annual meetings, and the American Historical Association annual meetings, the latter on a National History Center/AHA Panel organized by William Tsutsui. I was fortunate to be invited to present a paper at the 2012 conference of the Netherlands Institute for War, Holocaust, and Genocide Studies (NIOD), Amsterdam, honoring the work of Wichert Ten Have, the director of the Centre for Holocaust and Genocide Studies, who taught me at the University of Amsterdam and first suggested that I consider PhD studies. I was also privileged to present drafts at the University of Leiden, the Free University of Amsterdam, the University College of the University of Maastricht, the University of Antwerp, Wageningen

University, and the 2014 Second World Congress of Environmental History (WCEH), hosted by the University of Minho and The International Consortium of Environmental History Organizations, Guimarães, Portugal.

At Princeton I presented draft chapters to the Shelby Cullom Davis Center for Historical Studies, the Princeton Environmental Institute Associated Faculty Seminar, the American Studies Seminar, the Latin American Studies Seminar, and the Colonial America Workshop. I also received valuable feedback from my students in History 507 (World and Comparative Environmental History) and History 432 (War and Environment) in 2018, 2019, and 2020.

An earlier version of chapter 9 appeared as "Genocide in the Kampongs? Dutch Nineteenth-Century Colonial Warfare in Aceh, Sumatra," *Journal of Genocide Research*, 14, nos. 3–4 (2012), Special Issue, *Mass Violence and Decolonization of the Netherlands East Indies*; and in Bart Luttikhuis and A. Dirk Moses, eds., *Colonial Counterinsurgency and Mass Violence: The Dutch Empire in Indonesia* (London: Routledge, 2014). An earlier version of part of chapter 10 appeared as "Environmental and Climate Change in Africa: Global Drought and Local Environmental Infrastructure," in *Environmental Change and African Societies*, edited by Ingo Haltermann and Julia Tischler, 73–97 (Leiden: Brill, 2020). I am grateful to the presses for allowing the use of these materials for the book. All translations and errors are mine, unless otherwise indicated.

I am especially grateful to my spouse Carol Lynn Martin for helping me to bring this work to fruition, and to Manus and Nora for their moral support. I dedicate the book to Nora.

SCORCHED EARTH

Introduction

ENVIRONCIDE, SOCIETY, AND TOTAL WAR

MOST BOOKS about total war *begin* with the First World War in the fields and forests of Flanders. This book about the impact of total war on society and the environment *ends* with the First World War in the woodland savannas of Angola and Namibia. In fact, by 1914, total war had been central to the practice of war across the globe for at least four centuries. The scorched landscape in Flanders depicted on the cover is an iconic photo that to many captures the devastation caused by war much better than a thousand words. But, like similar images, the photo typically is taken to symbolize the impact of total war as an entirely new 20th-century Western phenomenon, a product of the dark side of modern industrial society, science, and technology. The First World War, however, was not the first conflict that transformed the idyllic fields and forests of Flanders into a muddy and charred chaos, nor was such an experience unique to Flanders. Rather, total war as the indiscriminate and simultaneous destruction of society *and* environment marked armed conflict throughout the 16th and 17th centuries, from the Spanish conquests of the Aztec and Inca Empires to the Iroquois Wars, the War of Flanders/Dutch Revolt, and the Thirty Years War. The Age of Reason with its credo of limited war offered no respite from the practice of total war. To the contrary, such conflagrations as the Wars of the Spanish, Austrian, and Javanese Successions; the French and Indian Wars; and the American Revolutionary War demonstrate a high degree of continuity in the ways of war across the globe. In many respects, 18th-century warfare actually constituted a bridge between 16th- and 17th-century so-called primitive or uncivilized war and 19th- and 20th-century modern war, including the French Revolutionary and Napoleonic Wars; the colonial wars in Latin America, Asia, and Africa; and the First World War.

This book revisits select early modern and modern era conflicts by examining the impact of war on the environment-society nexus. Nuclear proliferation, a resurgence of the Cold War, and escalating conflicts in the Middle and Near East, Eastern Europe, and Africa raise troubling concerns about the consequences of total and genocidal war, while climate change, pollution, emergent diseases, and extinctions raise the specter of global ecocide. Scholars, however, have rarely studied total war, ecocide, and genocide in constellation. Studies of the war-environment nexus and the war-society nexus remain largely separate: war *and* environment *and* society as an interrelated trinity has been relatively neglected.

War affects environment and society simultaneously because humans are shaped by and in turn shape the environments they inhabit. The human-shaped environment constitutes environmental infrastructure because it is neither fully Nature (thence the anthropocentric *infrastructure*) nor entirely an artifact of Culture (thence the qualifier *environmental*). Rather, environmental infrastructure, which includes homes and stables, fields, fences, soils, crops and weeds, granaries and food stores, animals, orchards, wells, dams, canals, and sluices, is a coproduction of human ingenuity and labor on the one hand and nonhuman actors (animals, insects, microbes, and plants) and forces (physical, chemical) on the other. Moreover, maintaining, repairing, and (re)producing environmental infrastructure is a process that can perhaps more easily be imagined as a verb: *environing*. Environing denotes that humans shaping their environment is a perennial project that is subject to and dependent on continuous investments of energy, capital, and knowledge in the face of ever changing conditions. It both grafts on and competes with biological, climatic, chemical, and geophysical dynamics. War interrupts environing, increasing societies' vulnerability to human-made and natural disasters.

Environcide consists of intentionally or unintentionally damaging, destroying, or rendering inaccessible environmental infrastructure through violence that may be episodic and spectacular (e.g., genocide or mass killing) or continuous and cumulative (e.g., everyday war violence). The unholy alliance between war, famine, and disease has been noted from biblical times to the present: the Four Horsemen of the Apocalypse often ride together. Targeting an opponent's environmental infrastructure, either directly by destroying homes, fields, orchards, food and seed stores, reservoirs, and dams or indirectly through population displacement, constitutes environcide because it undermines livelihoods and ways of life, increasing a society's vulnerability to drought and disease, and triggering epidemics and famines.

The concept highlights the how and the why of the simultaneous and interactive impact of war on environment and society. Environcidal strategies and tactics aim to deny the use of environmental infrastructure to the opponent through scorched earth tactics, sieges, and strategic bombing; by living off the enemy's land and making war pay through conquest and booty; and by weaponizing fire and water. Environcide typically manifests as total war because human societies and their environmental infrastructures are at once the object, the subject, and the instrument of war. Belligerents mobilize all available military and civilian resources for war through recruitment of soldiers and labor; war taxes and tribute; requisitions of food, animals, and shelter; and outright pillage and plunder. Premodern and modern heads of state, generals, and soldiers did not merely wage war about and in abstract and empty state territory. Rather, they fought wars about, with, and in what animates, fills, and enriches space: the environmental infrastructure that sustains populations, states, and armies. Combatants and noncombatants alike enacted and were affected by the deprivation of environmental infrastructure.

The four main arguments of this book are laid out in the sections that follow and are accompanied by an outline that explains how the various chapters contribute to the larger argument. The first section (*War, Environmental Infrastructure, and Environcide*) argues that the impact of war on the environment-society nexus is more comprehensively framed by highlighting *how* belligerents depend on, target, and weaponize environmental infrastructure. Armies and soldiers undermine and destroy rural livelihoods and ways of life, effectively waging environcidal war. The second section (*Genocide, Ecocide, and Environcide*) explains how environcide is both derived from and different from genocide and ecocide. Genocide and other crimes against humanity are categories of legal action, rather than merely descriptive or analytical concepts. Ecocide is considered a heinous act against nature with an ambiguous legal status in international law. Environcide highlights how mass violence simultaneously affects environment and society: environmental warfare is a crime against humanity and a crime against Nature. The third section (*Perpetrators, Victims, and History*) focuses on *who* is involved in and affected by mass violence and addresses the implications for historical agency. Typically, the literature on mass violence identifies discrete categories of active perpetrators and passive victims, attributing the former's agency to a historically determined development of a specific way of waging (total) war, for example, a German *Sonderweg* or a Western way of war. But the practices of war discussed in this book suggest a much more dynamic positioning and repositioning of perpetrators and victims. The fourth section (*Environcide, Total War, and Resource Wars*) explains *why* environcide constitutes total war. Environcide treats a group's environmental infrastructure as a subject, object, and instrument of war, increasing the entire population's vulnerability to drought, flooding, hunger, thirst, predators, plagues, and pests, with the attendant risk of mass killing, ecocide, and genocide. Each chapter emphasizes different combinations of how environcide and other forms of mass violence were practiced and experienced in different eras and regions.

War, Environmental Infrastructure, and Environcide

Concerns about nuclear, biological, and chemical holocaust in the 1970s and 1980s, fueled by the fallout of Agent Orange in Southeast Asia and the global escalation of the Cold War, drew attention to the devastating direct impact of war on the environment and human health. The First Gulf War, with its blackened skies and soils, unexploded ordinance scattered across the landscape, and exposure to nerve gases and low-grade nuclear ammunitions, renewed the debate.[1] Environmental historians turned to the study of conflict, while military historians highlighted the impact of war mobilization and warfare on ecosystems. The destruction of such environmental resources as forests during conflicts as a result of scorched earth tactics and the cratered moon-like landscapes of WWI Flanders and northern France battlefields dramatically illustrate the destructive impact of war on environment and society. Landscapes have been and continue to be "militarized" across the globe as they are drained of their natural resources or biodiversity to support military buildup during times of war and peace, from the deforestation caused by the construction of wooden warships to the massive mobilization of such resources as oil, metals, timber, and food during the World Wars and the Cold War.[2]

Frequently, however, the impact of war on human society and culture, as well as its impact on the environment as an ecosystem, are studied in isolation, reflecting the long shadow of the Nature–Culture dichotomy. Theoretically, the Nature–Culture paradigm has been rejected in the field of environmental history; in practice, however, it has proven to be tenacious. The Nature–Culture dichotomy is both embedded in and expressed through a closely overlapping and nested set of binaries: the non-Western/premodern versus the Western/modern. Presumed to be largely living in and by Nature, premodern and non-Western societies consequently are thought of as highly vulnerable to the caprices of undomesticated Nature. In Western/modern societies, however, science and technology are perceived to have domesticated Nature, replacing it with human artifact, that is, Culture.[3] In modern and Western perceptions, mass violence against human culture constitutes a crime against humanity or a war crime. War against Nature, for example, the destruction of forests, is considered an environmental crime at best, rather than a crime against humans.[4]

But war's impact on Nature and Culture can't be separated. What often is described as either Nature or a natural resource on the one hand and as Culture or technology on the other is, in fact, usually something in between, that is, a dynamic mixture of Nature and Culture:

environmental infrastructure. Environmental infrastructure sustains and facilitates human (and nonhuman) lives, livelihoods, and ways of life, but it is neither solely a gift from Nature nor exclusively a human Cultural artifact. It is the product of both human and nonhuman (including biological and geological) agency and processes. In the past as well as the present, most of the earth has been shaped by human use and management, resulting in, for example, the maintenance of savannas and prairies through fire regimes, domestic animals and plants, anthropogenic forests and soils, polder lands, mounds and terraces, irrigated and "cultivated" landscapes, and the "built environments" of villages, towns, and cities. Human shaping of the earth's environment often was and is a coproduction involving nonhuman animate and inanimate agency. For example, humans deployed the force of water and the principle of gravity to drain or irrigate lands or to generate energy. They also mined carbon deposits, including wood, peat, coal, and oil as fuel, and employed animals as companions, protection, and sources of power, food, fur, hides, and medicine. In turn, select animals, microbes, and crops and weeds exploited, shared, shaped, and thrived in the environmental infrastructures that sustain human societies.

Moreover, the discussion about global climate change highlights the fact that despite the greatly increased human mastery of science and technology in the Anthropocene, modern society remains embedded in and dependent on ecosystem earth, just as the future of ecosystem earth depends on humanity. The concept of environmental infrastructure explicitly acknowledges the role of human agency and nonhuman forces in managing and shaping the (natural) environment. The concept accepts that humans have neither conquered Nature nor replaced it by cultural artifact, and recognizes that having shaped premodern or traditional societies, Western and non-Western alike, the environment continues to shape modern societies as well.[5]

The indirect impact of war on human societies and the environments upon which they depend has received little attention.[6] Yet, the indirect impact of environmental warfare may be spatially and temporally even more significant than the intentional destruction effected by conscious scorched earth tactics or the "collateral damage" caused by actual armed combat. The massive population displacements caused by war forcibly removed refugees from their homes and the environmental infrastructure that sustained them. These displacements affected not only the war zone but also the refugee safe havens as well as the corridors between home and refuge. In addition to being spatially significant, the population movements are also temporally significant given their long-term and cumulative effects. Human and nonhuman shaping of the environment is an ongoing process: in order to sustainably support lives, livelihoods, and ways of life, environmental infrastructure must be continuously maintained, repaired, re-created, and reinvented in the face of decay and ever changing circumstances, including global climate change. Otherwise, the environmental infrastructure deteriorates and collapses: animals go feral, crops re-wild, canals and wells silt up; orchards and plantations are swallowed by the forest; and villages and cities are overgrown by weeds and bush or covered by surging seas or sweeping desert sands. Although damaged or destroyed environmental infrastructure can be recovered and reconstructed, the costs are often enormous and sometimes prohibitive.

Genocide, Ecocide, and Environcide

In the context of poor sanitation, malnutrition, and exposure, armies constituted mobile and self-replicating arsenals of biological warfare. Mongol armies spread the plague to a medieval Europe wracked by famine and war, and the First World War unleashed the Great Influenza of 1918.[7] War caused famine and deadly diseases in 1940s Warsaw, Leningrad, Holland, and Bengal.[8] Typhus and rinderpest are known as "war plagues."[9] Nevertheless, although war, famine, and disease often feature in accounts of genocidal and mass violence, rarely are they identified as major factors.[10]

This is especially marked in the 15th- through 19th-century Americas, where distinct bodies of literature focus on the wars of conquest, the impact of epidemic diseases, and environmental transformations as largely isolated events. The conquest approach focuses on the politico-military dimensions and the attendant political, social, and cultural destruction.[11] The disease approach emphasizes the virgin-soil epidemics that resulted in the indigenous American demographic collapse. Because the demographic collapse is attributed to ecological agency through contagion, the near extermination of these indigenous populations remains largely disconnected from the violence and displacement caused by military and political conquest.[12] The environmental transformation approach highlights the impact of invasive species, institutions, practices, and ideas. Buffalo and beaver were virtually hunted into oblivion following the introduction of guns, horses, and capitalism, and virulent alien plants unchecked by natural enemies overwhelmed vulnerable endemic species. The consequences of species extinctions and ecosystem collapse through habitat loss and overexploitation at times have been framed as ecocide.[13] Relatively recently, the concept of genocide has been invoked to understand the impact of the destruction of indigenous American populations (effectively linking mass violence to demographic collapse), but its use is highly contested. Moreover, the genocide argument focuses on direct (mass) killing without highlighting the context of the interaction between war, displacement, and disease.[14]

In legal terms, genocide, or the eradication of an entire population group, and ecocide, the destruction of one or more species or entire ecosystems, are both modern concepts dating from the post-Second World War era.[15] As practices, however, genocide and ecocide are much older. A key legal requirement for genocide is proof of the *intent* to exterminate a group. A perspective that segregates humanitarian atrocities from intentional environmental destruction, even if that environment sustains a specific population, would thus be considered *indirect* genocide, at best.[16] The premeditated destruction of environmental infrastructure, or displacing a population that depends on it, could constitute genocide if it imposes upon a population "conditions of life calculated to bring about its physical destruction," such as depriving people of food and homes. The destruction of the "environment," however, is one degree removed from the destruction of the group, complicating the requirement of genocidal intent: the environmental destruction is merely a tool to accomplish the premeditated physical annihilation of the group.[17]

Nevertheless, in depriving a group of such environmental infrastructure as shelter, agricultural lands, and food supplies, thereby exposing people to cold and hunger during a freezing winter, the perpetrator consciously and intentionally takes the risk that the exposed group might be exterminated. Moreover, for non-Western or premodern societies, an additional issue is the pervasive perception that they exist in and by Nature, that is, they lack environmental infrastructure. From such a perspective, displacing a group from one "natural" environment to another might not necessarily be deemed as an imposition of fatal "conditions of life," making it even more difficult to argue that extermination was the ultimate objective.[18]

Yet, some human rights scholars have argued that the intent to commit genocide can be derived from the acts of explicitly depriving a population of food, water, shelter, and other key resources that willfully exposes a group of people to cold, heat, hunger, or insecurity. The situation may result in circumstances that endanger human lives, health, and sanity, and ultimately jeopardize a group's ability to survive. The perpetrators can be expected to understand that their reckless use of such deadly weapons as scorched earth or the separation of a population from its environmental infrastructure might risk a group's extermination.[19]

Deploying the concept of environcide evokes both genocide and ecocide. Genocide is first and foremost a legal category. Ecocide is not currently acknowledged as an international crime, but it is under consideration to be defined as such, and several individual states have defined ecocide as a crime.[20] Moreover, ecocide resulting from human greed and abuse may involve a structural violation of ecosystems in the form of slow or silent violence that is gradual, cumulative, and almost imperceptible, in contrast to the highly visible and immediate impact of spectacular and dramatic acts of mass violence.[21] Finally, although large-scale environmental destruction and the obliteration of civilian infrastructure during mass conflict constitute war crimes, such concerns are frequently subordinated to and legitimized by the principle of military necessity.[22]

Environcide may employ the same spectacular acts of extraordinary mass violence that mark genocide. Unlike genocide, however, and like ecocide, environcide may involve the everyday violence of war. These different forms of violence need not be compartmentalized, and spectacular and episodic violence, everyday war violence, and structural violence may occur simultaneously.[23] Kings and generals extorting annual war taxes, officers demanding monthly protection money, and soldiers exacting meals and money, as well as stealing a chicken or two every day, could bring farmers and villagers to the brink of despair even without overt deadly violence.

Perpetrators, Victims, and History

Highlighting humans as creators and destroyers of environmental infrastructure, as well as perpetrators and victims of genocide, ecocide, or environcide, raises the issue of historical agency. While victim agency is limited and constrained by perpetrator violence and the forces of Nature, the outcomes are neither predetermined nor linear. Moreover, a disregard for human agency in the perpetration of environcide privileges such structural and ahistorical defaults as human nature and the nature of war, as though these causal factors require little or no further explanation. One influential structuralist argument contends that a German culture of mass violence that developed during the 1870–71 Franco-Prussian War subsequently was refined during the German colonial experience in Namibia and East Africa, creating a distinctively German way of war that shaped the World Wars and caused the Holocaust.[24] Yet, British, Portuguese, French, British, North American, and Dutch colonial warfare were very similar to the German way of war.[25]

Settler colonialism in Africa and the Americas constituted a major source of genocidal violence. Yet, the Rwandan case in Africa suggests that while the context of colonial settlers was commonly a facilitating factor, colonial settlers were not necessarily always the perpetrators. The 1990s Rwandan genocide was a case of subaltern genocide in which Hutu groups launched a "pre-emptive" first strike at the minority Tutsi after repeated Tutsi "settler" mass killings of Hutu subjects. Colonial education and practices constructed the Tutsi as a race of alien Hamitic settlers who had conquered Rwanda.[26] Acknowledging the experience of subaltern genocidaires, that is, acknowledging that fearful potential or actual past victims of mass killings may turn into mass killers themselves, as occurred in Rwanda, suggests that the division between perpetrators and victims is not clear cut.[27]

Nonsettlers were often perpetrators in exterminatory mass violence, and genocidal violence occurred in nonsettler colonial contexts, too. During the 1950s Mau Mau revolt in Kenya, British boots on the ground were few, and the colonial forces relied heavily on indigenous Kikuyu loyalists in a ruthless and inhumane counterinsurgency campaign.[28] Similarly, the perpetrators of the 1871 Camp Grant Massacre against a group of Apache, included not only Euro-American settlers but also indigenous American O'odham and Mexican American *vecinos* who had long suffered Apache raids.[29]

During the Rwandan genocide, neighbors and "upstanding" citizens, including clergymen, doctors, and intellectuals, frequently were among the perpetrators.[30] Similarly, the perpetrators of the Holocaust were not solely fanatic German SS but also "common" German fathers, Ukrainian guards, and at times even the victims' neighbors.[31] Perpetrators and victims of genocide are often constructed as "others" in racial, religious, cultural, political, social, or economic terms, but they can also be intimates. This discussion in the field of genocide studies is highly relevant for understanding environcide as a historical practice. Indeed, the chapters that follow demonstrate that even where outsiders practiced environcidal warfare, local allies frequently played a key role as facilitators and sometimes even as instigators. In addition, victims themselves sometimes perpetrated environcide.

Can victims of mass violence speak? Certainly, survivors can, however mediated and shaped by memory- and history-making their narratives might be. The history of the Holocaust relies on the limited and fragmented sources of survivors' and perpetrators' testimonies.[32] Chapter 10 is based heavily on oral histories of the survivors of two decades of war, famine, and deadly epidemics before, during, and following the First World War in southern Africa. Although introduced in the last chapter, the interviewees' experiences with environcidal war and their postconflict struggles to rebuild their communities and a viable environmental infrastructure are the model and inspiration for the book. Other chapters similarly draw on testimonies by farmers and villagers—often submitted orally to local officials, detailing the impact of war on their lives, livelihoods, and ways of life—and offer a viable alternative to oral history and the court and inquisition records that inform social history.[33]

Throughout Western and Southern Europe, local, regional, and state administrations collected detailed accounts of the cost incurred by town and countryside as a result of the imposition of special cash war taxes ("contributions") and military requisitions of provisions, fuel, lodging, and transport; extortions of bribes and gifts; and the damage caused by soldiers to property. These documents served to support individual and community claims for tax reductions or restitution, submitted as oral or written testimony. Restitution cases often dragged on for years, sometimes even decades, creating a specific type of archive. These records ended up in a special subcategory of pre-Napoleonic-era local archives often labeled with the equivalent of the English term "war damage."

The records, of course, have their own biases.[34] For one, they are selective because war destroyed an incalculable number of documents. Moreover, because the documents served to support claims for restitution, the potential exists that they inflated losses, misidentified the perpetrators of the inflicted damage by attributing losses to soldiers as opposed to drought or disease, and emphasized the damage and the value of the losses of the rural elite who did the reporting. The war damage records thus understated the losses of the poor and marginalized (and illiterate) who had little or no wealth to lose beyond such ordinary possessions like a loaf of bread, a ham, a few chickens, or perhaps a mule or cow. In addition, women's testimonies are underrepresented overall and predominantly concern widows because only the death of their husband made them legible in the records as default heads of households. Last, but not least, the "war damage" records seem to underreport the occurrence of severe physical violence in the countryside. Accounts of soldiers inflicting serious bodily harm, including torture, rape, and murder, are relatively rare in the archive. Two factors may account for this. First, the documents seek restitution for losses of and to movable and immovable "property" and do not relate to compensation for bodily harm. Second, the reports often were submitted to the (military) authorities that controlled the area during the war while the perpetrating soldiers and their commanders were still present, and the petitioners may have feared retaliation for making accusations of what were capital crimes.

Four chapters (1, 3, 5, and 6) are heavily based on such local "war damage" archives. To compensate for a Low Countries' environmental and historical bias, chapters 5 and 6 each compare the practices and experiences in the Low Countries with those of a different theater of war: eastern coastal Spain (the Kingdom of Valencia) and the Riviera coast of France and Italy, respectively. The rationale for a heavy reliance on Dutch archives is that, in comparison to other Western European sources, Dutch archival sources have been used relatively less frequently for publications in English. Still, the emphasis on Dutch sources does not mean that the chapters specifically highlight Dutch war practices. During the Dutch Revolt, the Thirty Years War, and the Wars of the Spanish and Austrian Successions, the Low Countries were the theater of transnational wars that drew in armies, generals, and soldiers from across Europe and were in many ways European wars.[35]

Histories of war, histories of societies, and environmental and climate histories tend to emphasize the larger abstract, structural, and conjunctural forces of history and reflect the views of the elite. History, however, operates at different scales simultaneously, though they are not necessarily in sync. This phenomenon is brought into sharp focus by the debate surrounding the Crisis of the 17th Century, an age of upheaval that marked the beginning of the modern world. Perhaps no case highlights the challenges and contradictions of the era more than that of the Dutch Republic. Despite being deeply embroiled in existential and destructive conflict, the Dutch Republic simultaneously experienced a Golden Age with a booming economy and a global empire that spanned the seven seas. It seems difficult to reconcile the Golden Age moniker with the fact that many people who lived in Dutch territories were subjected to the brutal destruction of the Thirty Years War. The paradox is partly attributable to scale. Studies of the Dutch Republic heavily weigh the thriving economy of Holland, which was by far the largest of the provinces of the United Netherlands. Holland and most of the provinces of the republic did not experience the direct impact of war in the 17th and 18th centuries, while the inhabitants of Dutch Brabant and Dutch Flanders bore the brunt of the war's devastation. Because aggregating the economic output of the republic averages out the decline in Dutch Brabant and Dutch Flanders, the glare of Holland's Golden Age hides the destruction and trauma of war in the republic's periphery. Moreover, the Dutch Republic forced occupied enemy or neutral territories in the Spanish or Austrian Low Countries and France to sustain its armies and soldiers in the field through the exaction of contributions (the name used for special war taxes) and the requisition of provisions, supplies, labor, and transport, reducing the burden of war on its core economy and society.

Environcide, Total War, and Resource Wars

Environmental infrastructure was not only a tool and subject of war but frequently also an object and a prize of war. The product of continuous investments of capital, labor, and knowledge, and the means for sustaining lives, livelihoods, and ways of life, environmental infrastructure was a highly valuable resource, and capturing or exploiting it was as essential in war as it was in peace.[36] During war, in addition to pillaging, plundering, stealing, damaging, destroying, and alienating environmental infrastructure, armies and soldiers lived off the land; sheltered in farms, villages, and towns; and extorted food, drinks, forage, livestock, valuables, and money. France's revolutionary and Napoleonic armies lived off the land, as did the German army in Belgium and Northern France during the First World War.[37] It was only during the second half of the 19th century that armies developed their own logistical apparatus and consequently became less dependent upon foraging and pillaging.[38] In theory, modern armies no longer directly live off the countryside's environmental infrastructure through plunder, extortion, or tribute. In practice, of course, this has not always been true. Moreover, the importance of the strategy of denying access to and use of environmental infrastructure to "the enemy" remains unchanged. In this sense, modern strategic bombing, however 20th-century the technology might be, echoes 16th-century scorched earth.

Resource wars are not merely a modern phenomenon. Across time, belligerents fought wars not only to destroy enemy resources but also to gain them.[39] Nazi soldiers and policemen as well as local police, civilians, and even neighbors pilfered Jewish victims' dead bodies, lands, homes, money, valuables, and clothes.[40] Confiscated royal domains and impounded Catholic church and loyalist properties were a key source of income for rebel authorities during the Dutch Revolt.[41] Having armies live off the opponent's land transferred part of the cost of waging war to the enemy: in that sense, war paid for itself. Extorting contribution (war tax) and tributes, as well as pillage and territorial conquest for resources, especially environmental infrastructure, made war profitable or at least helped defray its enormous cost. In fact, war was a business to many until at least 1700: colonels who commanded regiments were also entrepreneurs who used their own funds to raise and maintain the regiments that constituted early modern armies.[42] The profitability mechanism operated not only at the institutional level but also at the individual level: soldiers and civilians benefited through wages, plunder, booty, and black marketeering. Both ancient Rome and the early modern United States commonly used confiscated conquered land to pay its veteran soldiers.

Because humans were its cocreators, the destruction or alienation of environmental infrastructure constitutes a loss of proprietary resources rather than simply a loss of unimproved and bountiful natural resources. The fact that indigenous peoples' resources are often seen as natural and therefore as nonproprietary or communal complicates the prosecution of pillage as a war crime because pillage is defined as stealing the personal and individual property of civilians.[43]

The perception of an existential threat imposed by challenging material or immaterial conditions can also lead to environcide, ecocide, or genocide: famished refugees displaced from their own environmental infrastructure might use extreme violence against other people, animals, and plants in order to survive, and in the process, shape-shift from victims to perpetrators.[44] The act of burning homes, fields, fences, villages, and towns, and the subsequent re-wilding of the landscape, erased all evidence of the violent appropriation and, in effect, created terra nullius. Killing former owners or driving them away, preferably beyond the territorial, social, political, or cultural space of the perpetrator, removed not only the owners but also contemporary witnesses and future claimants who could file for property restitution, damages, or justice. Writing the former owners out of history erased them from memory. Historical claims of genocide, extermination, and demographic collapse, or its denial, by both victims and perpetrators may constitute active memory cleansing, even if unintentional.[45]

Total wars are unrestrained resource wars: they target and employ all resources, both human and nonhuman. Total war sometimes is portrayed as a quintessential modern phenomenon that evolved from modern institutions, ideas, and technology.[46] But, total war and mass killings are not dependent on modern technologies. While many victims of the Holocaust perished in industrial gas chambers, numerous others were killed by regular firearms and villagers wielding improvised weapons. Similarly, the 1990s Rwandan genocidaires killed many of their victims with machetes.[47]

What defines total war is that anything and everything is the object, subject, and means of war. It involves the total mobilization of a society's resources to destroy the opponent, and the deployment and targeting of any people and resources by any and all means necessary. During the Second World War and the planning and practice of conflict during the Cold War, strategic bombing aimed to destroy the enemy's military and civilian infrastructure, including housing, energy, communications, water, and food production and processing, in order to deprive the enemy of all resources and break its will and capability to fight.[48] Scorched earth warfare, war taxes and tributes, and armies living off the land had the same intent and impact in premodern wars. Mass mobilization for the military may have been an 18th-century innovation, but the mass mobilization of civilian resources for war predated the French Revolution by far.[49]

Moreover, instigating massive population displacement is perhaps the most powerful weapon of total war in the past and present. Displacement deprives a population of its environmental infrastructure, exposing it to the elements, affecting the abandoned areas as well as taxing the host area's resources.[50] As illustrated by the current refugee crises in Europe and North America, a massive influx of refugees poses a severe challenge for any state, ancient or modern.

In brief, throughout human history, environcidal warfare has had a highly destructive impact on rural populations and landscapes, directly through murder, maiming, rape, plunder, and the destruction of homes, crops, and food stores, and indirectly through population displacement and the ensuing loss of access to key environmental infrastructure. Total war and environcide were common ways of war in the premodern era of the 16th, 17th, and 18th centuries. For armies that lacked a logistical apparatus, securing such rural resources as labor (to construct or undermine fortifications and transport army supplies), shelter, construction materials, food, and livestock, while denying the same to the opponent, was essential. For many peasants, farmers, hunters, and gatherers, securing lives and livelihoods, even under peaceful conditions, was a daily struggle with very narrow margins. Individually or as a group, the effects of exactions or plunder by passing, billeted, or camped soldiers and armies, and displacement or flight from the environmental infrastructure that sustained them, could easily spiral into catastrophic destruction, disease, and death.

War, Society, and Environment: Chapters and Cases

The argument for environcide is presented in ten chapters that navigate between different temporal and spatial scales. Six chapters (1, 3, 5, 6, 9, and 10) dissect the processes of interactions between war, society, and environment at the level of the lived experience in hamlets and villages over several years. Four chapters (2, 4, 7, and 8) operate at regional or continental levels across time periods ranging from multiple decades to a century or so. Chapters 1–2, 3–4, and 7–8 work in pairs: one chapter is a detailed case study and the (New World) partner chapter offers a broader macroscale overview that demonstrates how the dynamics identified at the microscale may have played out elsewhere over much larger units of space and time. The trio of chapters 5, 6, and 7 demonstrate that total war as environcidal war was a global phenomenon, exposing the myth of the 18th century as an age of limited, rational, and scientific war. Total war did not emerge at the *end* of the 18th-century Age of Reason; rather, it *defined* the Age of Reason, despite being intellectually rejected as a relic of a bygone and primitive era. The last three chapters (8, 9, and 10) demonstrate that 19th- and early 20th-century conflicts in North America, Southeast Asia, and Southern Africa were not marked by a set of separate "petite guerre" practices of war. Rather, the wars shared fundamentally environcidal strategies and tactics with one another, through premodern 16th- through 18th-century warfare in general and contemporary European and "Western" warfare in particular, and therefore constituted total war.

The structure of this book's argument is largely chronological to allow for the identification of both continuity and change. The case of the late 16th-century Dutch Revolt precedes the chapter about the early 16th-century Spanish conquest of the Americas because it exposes in more detail how war, environment, and society interacted. Environcidal warfare did not originate in late 16th-century Holland. Rather, the Spanish conquistadors used it as a tactic and strategy in early 16th-century America. Many indigenous American societies in Central and South America relied on environmental infrastructure that included dikes, dams, polders, irrigation canals, and drainage works that equaled or surpassed that of contemporary 16th-century Holland. Living off the land through taxation, forced contributions, plunder, and scorched earth marked the Spanish campaigns in the Old and New Worlds alike, giving rise to the Black Legend that broadcast the ruthless and unbridled violence of the Spanish war machine.

Bringing the wars of conquest in the Americas in conversation with environcidal wars elsewhere suggests that war, environmental change, and societal transformations in the New World may have been much more intimately connected than has been acknowledged. War and dislocation did not merely expose American indigenous populations to new diseases, as per the contagion model of the virgin-soil epidemics. Rather, war rendered indigenous human, animal, and plant species highly vulnerable to human and nonhuman invaders because it destroyed key indigenous environmental infrastructure or displaced indigenous Americans from their resource base.[51] War refugees exposed to cold, heat, hunger, and thirst were easy prey to invaders, be they human, animal, plant, or microbiological. To survive, desperate refugees intensified the exploitation of whatever resources were available, including animals (beaver, bison, horse) and humans (captives, slaves). In the process, neighbors often turned against one another, which triggered further displacement and destruction.[52] Displaced from their home environment and their social, economic, political, and cultural moorings, traumatized refugees were highly receptive to experimentation with new practices, beliefs, technologies, flora, fauna, and institutions, some creative, some destructive. The conditions provided an opening to introduce slave trading, wage labor, Christianity, guns, horses, livestock, wheat, commodity production, and commercial hunting. Physical and psychological displacement thus literally and figuratively opened the flood gates to invasive practices, mentalities, institutions, and species, including deadly microbes.[53]

The first chapter offers an in-depth case study of the late 16th-century Dutch Revolt, a conflict that blended with the Wars of Religion and that unveils the face of war in early modern Europe. Troops loyal to the Spanish Habsburg crown as well as rebel forces maneuvered to maximize opportunities to requisition or to raid for shelter, food, fodder, and other supplies, while simultaneously employing a scorched earth strategy in areas that they could not control in order to force the enemy to withdraw.[54] The chapter sketches an apocalyptic image of how environcide and total war transformed the heavily human-shaped polder lands of the County of Holland into a desolate swamp, crowding the survivors into urban islands where hunger and the Black Death ruled. Farms, fields, and entire villages were lost to the raging flood waters for three centuries. The close-up of the interaction between war, society, and the environment between the late 1560s and the early 1580s serves to help identify the drivers and outcomes of similar dynamics at the macroscale of the 16th-century Spanish conquest of the New World. Thus, the elements and processes identified in chapter 1 serve to reframe the narrative of the Spanish conquest of the Americas in chapter 2.

Chapter 2 uses the rich literature on the conquest to trace how processes of environmental and societal change played out at macroscales of time and space in the first half of the 16th century. Spanish conquistadors targeted the larger societies of Central and South America because the elaborate and monumental environmental infrastructure, which included irrigation works and expansive agricultural terraces, could sustain their invading forces. Exploiting indigenous American environmental infrastructure through conquest, tribute, and pillage was essential to Spanish settlers in the Americas. In Central America, indigenous allies played a key role in the "Spanish" conquest, which raises a question about the extent to which some indigenous Americans were responsible for environcidal and genocidal warfare against other indigenous Americans. Spanish and indigenous conquerors alike were motivated by and rewarded with land grants. Deadly epidemics accompanied and followed the massive destruction and displacement caused by the wars of conquest.

Chapter 3 focuses on Brabant in the Low Countries from 1621 to 1648, when it was a major battleground for the Thirty Years War. The Thirty Years War has long been regarded as the last barbaric premodern war before the military-fiscal-political revolution that changed the face of violent conflict. The chapter highlights the everyday practices and experiences of war in the countryside. The major campaigns and sieges that occurred in Brabant during the 1620s, 1630s, and 1640s involved Spanish forces and their German Imperial allies on one side and the Dutch army and its German, English, Swedish, and French allies on the other. From the mid-1620s onward, both the Dutch state and their Spanish opponents tried to limit the extent of scorched earth campaigns, as well as exactions and extortions by officers and soldiers in the field, to prevent large-scale flight and the collapse of the rural tax base. The attempts, however, were only partially successful because armies continued to live off the land.

Chapter 4 shifts to the macroscale of 17th-century eastern half of North America and draws on the expansive literature on European and indigenous American contact. The history of the Dutch, English, and French conquest of North America's Atlantic Rim demonstrates that what their leaders rejected as a barbaric "Spanish Habsburg" way of war describes a widespread set of practices that they used themselves. Many settlers in 17th-century North America survived by exploiting indigenous American environmental infrastructure, either directly or indirectly emulating the Spanish conquistadors. Most European settlers were not so much after "land" as territory. Rather, they sought to appropriate indigenous American village and town sites, croplands, water sources, and hunting grounds, that is, cleared and fertile environmental infrastructure.[55] Dutch West India Company (WIC) officials and settlers destroyed indigenous American lives, livelihoods, and ways of life with the same methods and facility that had rendered their own Old World ancestors into refugees only a few generations earlier. Indigenous Americans responded in kind, and moreover, as in Latin America, seem to have drawn on a precontact suite of indigenous environcidal practices. The latter casts doubt on the extent to which a "Western" way of war simply crossed the Atlantic as perpetrators and victims of environcidal war migrated from Europe to the New World.

The trio of chapters 5, 6, and 7 offers a comparative and global sweep of war practices in the 18th century that demonstrates the enduring characteristics of environcide and total war. While publications and manuscripts about the art or science of war increasingly presented 18th-century "limited war" as the norm for war between "civilized" European states, the notion was far removed from the everyday lived experience of warfare. The rules of civilized war in the Age of Reason made such episodes of spectacular violence as the sacking and burning of towns and the massacring of garrisons and civilians after sieges less acceptable and thus they happened less frequently. But the rules of war did little to mitigate the cumulative erosive effects of the everyday violence of armies and the impact of soldiers' exactions and extortions on key environmental infrastructure. Based on local and regional archives in the Netherlands, France, and Italy, chapter 5 focuses on the early 1700s War of the Spanish Succession in the Low Countries, northern France, and Spain. Chapter 6 focuses on the 1740s War of the Austrian Succession in the Low Countries, southern France, and northern Italy. Chapter 7 discusses 18th-century warfare in the Americas, Ghana, Sri Lanka, and Indonesia.

Because the prevalence of total war in modern Europe is uncontested, the last three chapters (8, 9, and 10) focus on wars fought outside of Europe. Chapter 8 ascends to the macrolevel of 19th-century North America, emphasizing how and why the indigenous populations in the North American West should be understood as war refugees. Western indigenous Americans overwhelmingly are depicted as living in, off, and by Nature as virtual primordial hunters and gatherers. For many groups, however, hunting, gathering, and raiding was a response to the loss of their homes and other environmental infrastructure. Many Western indigenous American groups had been displaced by war and were forced to create new and often dramatically different lives and livelihoods in challenging and alien environments west of the Mississippi River. Some groups created large empires based on commercial buffalo hunting and trade as well as raiding and tributes exacted from Spanish settlers and indigenous neighbors. For indigenous Americans and settler Europeans alike, however, and within the Spanish empire and beyond, living off the land often meant exploiting or alienating other societies' environmental infrastructure, as opposed to living off Nature's bounty.

The Aceh War on Sumatra, Indonesia, is the topic of chapter 9. The Dutch sought to add the Aceh sultanate to their southeast Asian empire, but met with fierce and sustained resistance. In response, Dutch forces systematically burned Aceh villages, driving the indigenous population into the mountains and forests of the interior and using hunger as a weapon of war, eerily echoing the US Army campaigns fought in the West during the same period. In conjunction, chapters 8 and 9 strongly suggest the existence of a wider consensus about the practices of war. Moreover, although 19th- and 20th-century armies by and large abandoned the custom of living directly off the land, the environcidal scorched earth and population displacement that marked 19th-century wars in North America and Indonesia were fundamentally identical to the methods of warfare of the preceding centuries.

Focusing on the Portuguese and South African colonial conquest of the Ovambo floodplain in Southern Africa during the early decades of the 20th century, chapter 10 demonstrates that environcidal practices continued unabated into the modern era. Based on oral histories as well as colonial and missionary reports, the chapter reveals the human scale of environcide by identifying human and nonhuman historical agents, victims, and perpetrators. Taken together, the ten chapters provide a more comprehensive analysis of the interactive constellation of structures, processes, and individual and collective human and nonhuman dynamics that impact war, the environment, and society.

1

The Dogs of War and the Water Wolf in Holland

ENVIRONCIDE DURING THE LATE 16TH-CENTURY DUTCH REVOLT

To the Lion of Holland

Chasing foreign enemies
Waving your tail courageously at sea
Is futile if your lungs are consumed
Perishing from inside out and with a weak heart you

Sigh and cough terribly and vomit in large pieces
Waves of rotting organ from the throat
What use is your claw seizing everything East and West
If you do not bite in the heart this cruel Water Wolf
That seeks in time to defeat you

O land's lion rise and awake with a roar
All the Kennemer[land] peatmen, the old lords of Rijnland
With the Amsterlanders, to make them come to their lion's aid
Enclose with a dike this animal that plagues you
That the prince of the winds flies there on his [wind]mill's wings
The fast prince of winds knows how to chase the Water Wolf
To the sea, whence he came, ever voracious[1]

IN THE POEM, Joost van den Vondel, the most famous poet of the 17th-century Dutch Golden Age, celebrates rebellious Holland's military successes against its Spanish Habsburg overlord, but warns against the enemy from within that saps its strength: the water wolf. The water wolf refers to the Haarlem Lake, which from the early 16th century onward gobbled up increasing amounts of precious productive land in the heart of Holland, devouring its environmental infrastructure and weakening its society and economy. The polder landscapes of Holland relied on a high-maintenance hydraulic system of dikes, drains, sluices, and windmills to keep the seas at bay and was highly vulnerable to human-made and natural disasters. Vondel's poem championed radical proposals to dike and drain the Haarlem Lake, with the aim of eradicating the water wolf once and for all. Focusing on the impact of war on environment *and* society in late 16th-century southern Holland demonstrates that the belligerents knowingly and intentionally sought to capture, control, and exploit Holland's environmental infrastructure to provide food, shelter, money, construction materials, fuel, water, transport, and other services and resources to sustain their soldiers, armies, and war effort, while seeking by all means to deny the use of the same by their opponents. In the process, the soldiers killed, raped, maimed, and traumatized people, robbing them of their livelihoods; displacing them from their communities, homes, fields, and food supplies; and exposing them to hunger, thirst, disease, and death. Many soldiers were mercenaries, "dogs of war," but all depended for their wages and sustenance on the legal and illegal business of war. Sixteenth-century war affected anyone and anything in its wake: it constituted total war.

War engulfed the Low Countries in the late 16th century as resistance against its overlord the Spanish King Philip II turned violent in 1568. The year marked the beginning of a drawn-out conflict known as both the Dutch Revolt and the War of Flanders, which lasted until 1648.[2]

During the 1560s, the centralizing policies of the Catholic Habsburg Philip II ran into opposition from the Low Countries' nobles and urban elites, who sought to protect their economic, political, and religious privileges. Full-blown war hit the county of Holland in 1572 as King Philip II ordered his army to squash the rebellion that had spread to various towns in Holland, including Alkmaar, Haarlem, and Leiden. Amsterdam remained loyal to the king. The huge royalist army and the troops mobilized by the rebels, including many mercenaries from across Europe, weighed heavily on town and countryside. Flooded earth followed pillage and scorched earth as the rebels, unable to hold their own against the Spanish army on the battle field, inundated the countryside to break the royalist sieges of their towns. Such tactics displaced the rural populations to the towns, leaving the countryside bare, barren, and subject to the tides, storms, wild animals, and weeds. The destruction and displacement wrought by the dogs of war opened the floodgates to massive ruin, resulting a "re-wilding" of and a subsequent collapse of Holland's polder lands, which is symbolized by the image of the (water) wolf, the Low Countries' most fearful predator.

The Dogs of War and Environcide

The Dutch Revolt (also known as the War of Flanders) was both a civil war and an international imperial war with religious overtones. Although the conflict was fought in the Low Countries between loyalists and rebels, it involved not only the king's Spanish and Italian soldiers but also drew in princes and soldiers from England, Scotland, France, Sweden, and the German Empire. Rebel leaders including Prince William of Orange, a favored intimate of King Philip II's father, the Emperor Charles V, were overwhelmingly Protestants.

Political tensions between officers of the Habsburg crown and local leaders in the Low Countries escalated in 1568, when Protestant refugees turned to raiding the coasts of Holland from English ports. The king's governor in the Low Countries, the Duke of Alva, responded by organizing a coastal defense system in Holland that included signal beacons, garrisons, and a fleet of warships to patrol the coast and protect the herring fleets.[3] The rebels' capture of the small town of Den Briel in April 1572 culminated in open war. With a permanent base in the Low Countries, the Protestant rebels grew more audacious. Rebel fleets repeatedly attempted to blockade the bustling city of Amsterdam, and its crewmen raided for cattle right up to the city walls.[4] Subsequent to the rebel successes, many of Holland's towns publicly sided with the rebels, causing loyalists and Catholic clergy to seek sanctuary in Amsterdam, Utrecht, and other towns that continued to support the king.

Rebel prospects soon turned dim. In August 1572, the French Huguenots, ideological allies of the Dutch rebels, were decimated in the St. Bartholomew Massacre. In December, King Philip II's mighty army marched into Holland and captured and sacked rebel-held Naarden, massacring the surviving defenders before advancing to rebel Haarlem. Haarlem fell after a brutal siege in July 1573; the royalist soldiers executed the defenders en masse. Next, the king's army marched on rebel Alkmaar, north of royalist Amsterdam. Intentionally released flood waters drove the king's army back to southern Holland, where it advanced on the key rebel stronghold of Leiden. The fall of Leiden would have made Delft, Rotterdam, and the remaining rebel towns highly vulnerable.

The troop movements and the war affected rural society and the environment both directly and immediately. Armies, groups of soldiers, and armed gangs roamed the countryside to exact money, food, forage, fodder, labor, transportation, and shelter. The royalist and the rebel authorities alike imposed special war taxes. They held the local officials, including burgomasters, sheriffs, and aldermen, personally accountable for raising the required funds and goods. In 1572, for example, Willem van Berendrecht, the secretary of the Delfland regional water board, was charged with raising a special war tax to feed the royalist garrisons guarding the Maasland and Vlaardingen sluices on the southern sea dike.[5]

Officers and common soldiers also personally profited from the war, extorting, robbing, and pillaging on their own account. Taxation blended into and was accompanied by outright plunder. This was not a coincidence because the collection of the official war taxes in conflict zones was premised on the threat of violence. "Brandschatting," literally "fire tax" or "fire tribute," a special Dutch term of the time, conveyed that nonpayment of war taxes and other demanded supplies was punished by outright plunder of a community, followed by torching its homes and barns. The royalist chronicler Wouter Jacobsz claimed that in February 1573 the rebel commander-in-chief, Prince William of Orange, demanded that the inhabitants of the rural district of Waterland, north of royalist Amsterdam, pay a 2,400-guilder war tax within eight days or see their villages put to the torch.[6]

Although plunder was sometimes sanctioned by the higher military commanders, often it was not. In September 1574, a dozen soldiers of the King's army were put on trial in royalist Amsterdam because, disguised as rebels, they had robbed farmers of their cattle for their personal profit.[7] Roaming individual or groups of soldiers tortured, raped, and killed farmers and travelers. A refugee from Waterland witnessed a group of royalist soldiers rob a farmer. After the soldiers tortured the farmer and his wife and threatened to kill the latter, the farmer indicated where he had buried his life savings. The soldiers still executed the farmer, despite having unearthed a small fortune amounting to 300 golden crowns and silver dollars.[8]

The logistical capabilities of late 16th-century armies were practically nonexistent. Armies lived off the land. Typically, generals forcibly "quartered" their soldiers in homes in towns and the countryside, where the host families provided shelter, bedding, heating, and food. When and where armies were concentrated, as during the 1570s sieges of Naarden, Haarlem, Alkmaar, and Leiden, the strain on local resources multiplied. Enemy raids threatened supply lines, and when subsistence stores on nearby farms had been depleted, especially during the winter, armies and soldiers became ever more desperate in their attempts to secure food, fuel, and shelter. Villagers and farmers sometimes resisted the soldiers' exactions, which led to more violence. In February 1573, royalist soldiers burned down the village of Crommenie after its inhabitants had killed several plundering soldiers in self-defense. The destruction of the village turned its inhabitants into homeless refugees in the middle of a severe winter.[9]

While the royalist army besieged Haarlem during the same 1573 winter, its armed foragers scoured the countryside all the way south to the gates of Leiden and as far north as Alkmaar for food, fuel, and other supplies. One raid on the surroundings of Alkmaar netted the royalist army 2,000 head of cattle. To the south and southwest of loyalist

Amsterdam, the main supply depot for the royalist army besieging Haarlem, rebel raiders reduced the countryside to ashes. At night the burning farms and homes were visible in the city.[10] On July 27, 1573, shortly after Haarlem had fallen to the royal army, Wouter Jacobsz traveled from Amsterdam to Haarlem: "On the way I saw the terrible destruction in the countryside. . . . I encountered very few unburned houses between Haarlem and Amsterdam. . . . The countryside was in many places entirely deserted and devoid of animals. I observed many animal carcasses spread out on the road and also a naked human body that was entirely mummified by the sun and flattened and pressed into the wagon tracks."[11] Although the fighting concentrated around Haarlem and Leiden, even the far south of Holland was not safe. In 1573, Maerten Pietserszn and his wife and children fled to the town of Delft. When he returned to his village of Monster just before Christmas 1573 to secure his home and to pick up some belongings, royalist soldiers captured him and imprisoned him in The Hague. He died in March 1574, mere days after his release when the bulk of the royalist army temporarily decamped from Holland.[12] Despite the tragic death of her husband, Maerten Pietserszn's widow took her children back to Monster and with tremendous will and effort endeavored to put her farm and land back into production. In April 1574, to restore order and peace, Delft expanded the town's provost force by 40 men to better patrol the countryside and protect such farmers as Maerten Pietersz's widow.[13] But the provost's men were powerless when the royalist army returned to Holland in May 1574 and resumed the siege of Leiden. Maerten Pietserszn's widow and her children fled back to Delft. En route, royalist soldiers robbed her of nine of her cattle, and she only managed to bring two of her cows to safety behind Delft's walls.[14]

Billeting troops with households in the towns and countryside was the norm and constituted a heavy burden on the civilian population.[15] In May 1574, the village of Naaldwijk, south of The Hague, fed and housed a company of soldiers. Naaldwijk's aldermen appealed to the inhabitants of the nearby village of Monster to share the cost of sustaining the soldiers. Monster's aldermen initially refused, arguing that they were already effectively maintaining the soldiers quartered at Naaldwijk because the soldiers roamed through its territory by day and night, knocking at doors, demanding food, and even entering homes to break open storage chests and steal valuables and money. When Naaldwijk's magistrates threatened to send the entire company to Monster, however, the aldermen relented and agreed to contribute 250 guilders.[16]

Soldiers often stole anything of value. In 1576 Warmond, a village north of Leiden, the offending soldiers were "friendlies," and since the plundering took place during a lull in the fighting, the soldiers may have been less demanding than they would have been during midwinter sieges. The pillagers took a cow valued at 50 guilders, cash, bread and butter, bedsheets, cloth, clothes, and copper wares. Dirck Cornelissz, a 34-year-old carpenter, lost his bed, a kettle, a copper pot, three tin plates, four tin spoons, five adzes, and four loaves of rye bread. The widow Marije Wouters's losses valued three guilders and included a couple of barrels filled with various goods, a loaf of white bread, a loaf of rye bread, and her new slippers. These losses, while seemingly trivial, constituted the victims' meager wealth, the tools of their trade, and their daily bread, and their loss deeply affected their livelihoods and quality of life.[17]

Scorched earth was a conscious strategy in which warring parties used and consumed all they could in an area to sustain their own forces while destroying everything they could not control so that no shelter, food, forage, or anything of value was left for the opponent. Scorched earth was also used to terrorize a population or to punish it for supporting the enemy. In the fall of 1573, the Duke of Alva, governor of the Spanish Netherlands and the supreme commander of the royalist army, ordered the destruction of the countryside throughout Holland. The aim was to force rebel towns, which were dependent on the food produced and stored in the surrounding rural areas, to abandon the rebel cause.[18] Royalist and rebel soldiers typically punished failure to comply with orders to supply money, food, forage, shelter, or other services by plundering and burning homes, farms, and entire villages. The same fate awaited villagers and farmers suspected of collaborating with the enemy. On January 16, 1573, royalist soldiers burned the village of Uitgeest to the ground and executed many of its male inhabitants because the villagers had sounded the alarm bell when the unit approached the village;

the soldiers suspected that the villagers had intended to betray their presence to the rebels and thus punished them accordingly.[19]

Scorched earth tactics also served to deplete the countryside around threatened rebel towns of any food, forage, construction materials, shelter, or other means to sustain an enemy siege. Homes and barns could serve a besieger for shelter and cover. Windmills close to the city walls provided the enemy with potential observation points to spy on a besieged town. Buildings surrounding a town could also be mined for materials to construct fortifications, siege engines, and shelter, and to provide fuel for cooking and fires for warmth. Trees provided timber and branches for siege equipment and shelter. In preparation for sieges, rebel commanders in the 1570s ordered the rural populations to move to the nearest rebel towns with their livestock, food supplies, and all other precious goods and resources that could be used to assist the besieged. Anyone who refused to comply with evacuation orders could be hung, and their homes and farmsteads were torched. Hendrick Pietersz from the village of Schalkwijck consequently hastened to nearby Haarlem with his animals when told to evacuate his home on the eve of the siege. Threatened by sieges in 1572 and 1573, respectively, the town authorities of Haarlem and Leiden ordered the destruction of all houses, churches, windmills, orchards, and trees within a large perimeter outside the cities' walls. On July 13, 1573, after the fall of Haarlem, the town council of Leiden issued an order to carry all salt, peat, wood, branches, dairy, hay, and forage located within a two-mile radius around the city into the town. The penalty for noncompliance was that any such goods that remained at a property would be impounded.[20] In the same month, the Leiden rebels burned all villages, castles, and landed estates directly west and northwest of Leiden, including the convents and the commoners' houses at the village of Warmond.[21]

The Water Wolf and Environcide

The royal army's control over the northern sea dike between Amsterdam and Sparendam (just north of Haarlem) and its sluices was a key factor in the battle for Haarlem. With the capture of the rebel fort at Sparendam in December 1572, the royalist army effectively occupied the entire northern sea dike.[22] The royalist army, including its train of heavy siege cannons, moved to Haarlem across the dike after forcibly recruited local civilian labor from town and countryside (referred to as pioneers) had flattened the top. After only a few weeks of heavy traffic, however, the dike became impassable to horse-drawn transport, and the army forced the Amsterdam guilds to organize its members to hand-carry sacks of bread from the city in order to feed the besiegers of Haarlem.[23] In February 1573, pioneers opened a passage for royalist ships in the dike at the sluices at Halfweg, where ships could enter directly onto the Haarlem Lake.[24] This secured a reliable supply route between Amsterdam and the besiegers' camps around Haarlem, and royalist warships could cut off the rebel supply lines across Haarlem Lake. In May 1573, the royalist fleet gained full control over the lake itself, leading to the surrender of Haarlem two months later.[25]

After the fall of Haarlem, elements of the royalist army moved south toward The Hague and from there east and southeast toward the rebel towns of Leiden, Delft, and Rotterdam, while the bulk moved north to Alkmaar.[26] In early August 1573, rebels from Gouda, to the east of The Hague, torched all houses outside of their city walls and opened a major sluice to flood the town's surroundings.[27] On August 21, the royalist army surrounded Alkmaar, but the rebels cut the local dikes around the town and the sea dike at Waterland north of Amsterdam. By early October, the rising waters around Alkmaar forced the besiegers to retreat to the south, although foragers continued to plunder the Waterland district.[28]

The royalist army moved its powerful siege train to Leiden south of Haarlem, and its soldiers roamed the countryside west and southwest of Leiden, exacting war taxes, food, and money. They reoccupied The Hague and the forts they had established earlier along the southern sea dike at the Vlaardingen and Maasland sluices.[29] The forts served to protect the besiegers from attacks from Delft and Rotterdam and acted as bases from which to raid for taxes, supplies, and labor in the countryside. Moreover, the forts also guarded a series of major sluices in the southern sea dike, west of rebel-held Rotterdam, which could serve to inundate the southwest of Holland. The latter must have figured prominently in the minds of both the rebels and the royalists. The lesson of Alkmaar's successful incursions against the seemingly invincible royalist army was not lost on the leadership of either side, as is also suggested by a rumor that circulated in early February 1574 Amsterdam. Allegedly, the rebels planned massive flooding by "breaching all dikes and using the interior as waters to get from one city to another without taking into consideration the enormous damage they would cause just to protect their rebellion."[30]

In January 1574, expecting an assault by the royalist army, the Leiden rebels tried to emulate the Alkmaar flooded earth tactics. A contingent of civilian laborers protected by three companies of soldiers razed the Steenenveld and Zijlhof brick mansions and used the debris to dam the Rhine River northeast of the town, flooding the countryside on the eastern approaches to Leiden.[31] The dam, however, does not appear on the 1580s Lanckaert Tapestry that depicts the story of the flooding and the rebel relief of Leiden in the form of a map, suggesting that the rebels removed the makeshift dam after the king's army temporarily raised the siege. In March 1574, the king's army marched south and successfully repelled a rebel invasion near Maastricht, then resumed the siege of Leiden in May. Almost immediately, heavy fighting erupted over control of the dike at the Boshuizen sluice directly west of Leiden; the sluice and dike held the potential to flood the western approaches to the city.[32]

Royalist commanders were well aware of the possibility that rebels would use such tactics as a weapon of war. As early as 1568, the king's governor, the Duke of Alva, issued orders to guard carefully the dikes and sluices of Delfland (the water board region south of Leiden) against attempts to flood the area. This order came before Delfland sided with the rebels, and the territory complied right away, boasting that its segment of the southern sea dike (the Maas dike) was so massive and strong that it could only be breached with the help of a huge labor force. In 1569, the royalist authorities stationed military contingents along the Maas dike to protect the sluices that served to drain excess water into the Maas River. Pioneers constructed forts at the sluices, probably after the rebels took the small town of Den Briel on the opposite bank of the Maas River in April 1572. Early during the siege of Leiden, royalist units took up positions in several villages along the Rhine River dike east of Leiden. The royalist forces temporarily abandoned most of their positions along the Maas and the Rhine dikes in March 1574 to repel the rebel invasion force near Maastricht. When the king's army returned, however, it not only reoccupied the positions along the Maas and Rhine dikes but also posted units along the Yssel dike further east. The Yssel dike was the extension of Delfland's Maas dike in the Schieland regional water board's territory and part of the southern sea dike, which stretched deep into the interior of Holland. One of the units took up positions at Capelle aan de Yssel, where the rebels later would make the first breach. Moreover, on July 23, 1574, a large contingent of the royalist army was sent to occupy the Dordtse Waard polder in response to rumors that the rebels planned to cut the southern sea dikes.[33]

The royalist control over the northern sea dike and its sluices between Haarlem and Amsterdam prevented the rebels from breaching it in order to inundate the surroundings of Leiden. For the waters to reach Leiden from the southern sea dike, the territories of the Delfland and Schieland regional water boards would have to be flooded. For them to make it north to Leiden, the main interior dike separating the three water board regions (the Landscheijding) would have to be breached too. Meeting on July 30, 1574, in Rotterdam, the rebel leadership, moved by the desperate pleas from besieged Leiden, agreed to inundate a large part of southern Holland. At best, the rebel leadership hoped that the inundation waters would force the king's army to withdraw, or that the rising waters would allow the rebel fleet to break through to Leiden to reinforce the garrison and resupply the famished, pest-ridden city. If all else failed, the rebel leaders trusted that the inundations would utterly destroy the countryside and deny the besieging army any prospect of living off the land, thereby starving the king's soldiers into ending the siege. [34]

Two days later, on August 1, 1574, the rebel leaders ordered the evacuation of the countryside of the Rijnland, Schieland, and Delfland water boards' territories: all villagers, farmers, and their livestock had to relocate to the nearest rebel town.[35] Even as the rebel leadership made these fateful decisions, Leiden seemed so close to surrender that the royalist

MAP 1.1. Holland with northern and southern sea dikes and the extent of the inundations in 1574.

army's commanders grew complacent, or their soldiers derelict in their duties. The royalist units stationed along the (Holland) Yssel River dike in Schieland abandoned their posts, and although they maintained their positions along the Maas dike in Delfland, they left the sluices at Vijfs-luizen unguarded.[36] Quick to exploit the opportunity, on August 2, rebel commander William of Orange met with the Schieland water board on the southern sea dike at Cappelle aan de Yssel to assess where the dike could best be breached.[37] The next day, the rebels opened sev-eral breaches in the dike between the abandoned royalist fort at Capelle and the Kralinger Lake. They limited the breaches to the top segment of the dike to allow water to pass through it at high tide, rather than cutting the dike down its entire height. The idea was to minimalize dam-age to the dike and better control the flooding: water would only enter the polder lands at high tide and the waters would not drain back into the Yssel River at low tide.[38]

By August 21, the inundation waters stood 3.5 feet high against the Landscheijding dike that separated Schieland (where the breaches had been made) and Rijnland, where Leiden was located.[39] The Landschei-jding dike and the royalist forts crowning it blocked both the flood waters and the rebel fleet's advance. Behind the Landscheijding dike was a second line of defense with forts on the Voorweg, a smaller dike that controlled access to the Zoetermeer Lake, which was the gateway to the canal that ringed Leiden. The rebels needed the waters to accu-mulate against the entire Landscheijding dike so that they could ma-neuver their ships close enough to bombard the royalist forts and pro-vide cover to the pioneers cutting the breaches. They also worked out a secret alternative plan to outflank the royal army's defenses. Rebel leaders met in Delft with a select group of people who had intimate knowledge of the terrain and waters, and set up a special committee to decide exactly where and what additional interior dikes to breach, if necessary.[40]

At issue was that many more breaches in the exterior and interior dikes were required than the rebel command had envisaged. For one, the inundation waters rose far more slowly than anticipated. Second, the two rings of fortifications on the Landscheijding and the Voorweg dikes blocked the most direct route to Leiden. In fact, the fortifications had been erected on the advice of a loyalist water board councilor in anticipation of a rebel waterborne offensive from the south. To increase the water level, the rebels propped open the unguarded sluices in the Maas dike at Vijffsluizen, inundating Delfland and allowing more water to accumulate against the Landscheijding dike.[41] The rebels took advantage of a storm that brought heavy rain and pushed the floodwaters high enough against the Landscheijding dike to bring their cannons to bear on the royalist forts, allowing their pioneers to breach the dike and their ships to ride the waves through the Spanish defenses.[42]

But the second royalist defensive line on the Voorweg dike held, preventing waterborne access to Leiden. A day later, on September 19, the rebel fleet executed the secret plan that had been formulated in August to outflank the royal army's defenses at Zoetermeer: they backtracked through Schieland via the Zegwaard sluice, exploiting new breaches made further north in the Landscheijding dike.[43] A second heavy storm on September 29 pushed the inundation waters deeper into Rijnland.[44] The next day, after the royalist forces abandoned their forts on the Maas dike, the rebels opened the remaining sluices in the lower southern sea dike to increase the extent and depth of the inundations.[45] The rebels also breached dikes and opened sluices further east along the Yssel at the rebel towns of Gouda and Oudewater.[46] As the countryside flooded on October 3, 1574, the royalist army hastily retreated west via the dikes to the coastal dunes around The Hague while the rebel fleet entered Leiden in triumph.

Deadly Urban Sanctuaries

Most villagers and farmers had heeded the rebel orders to evacuate the countryside, hastening to nearby towns with all they could carry. The largest forced removal occurred on the eve of the inundations in early August 1574, when the rebel leaders ordered the evacuation of all of the countryside territories of the Rijnland, Schieland, and Delfland water boards. Announced first on August 3, the evacuation was slow to materialize and the order was repeated on August 7, when the deadline to

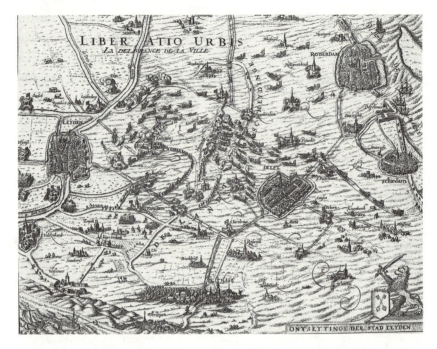

FIGURE 1.1. Inundations to relieve the Spanish siege of Leiden in 1574 with rebel ships sailing across flooded polder lands. Rotterdam and Delft are entirely enclosed by the inundations. Spanish troops retreat to the Hague (Hage) across the narrow dikes to the higher dune lands along the coast at the bottom of the image. On the left in the middle is Leiden (Leyden). In the right top corner near Rotterdam, the breaches are depicted. (Liberatio Urbis/La Delivrance de la Ville 1574, TU Delft Beeldbank, Delft University of Technology, J. Jnz. Orlers, *Beschryvinge der Stadt Leyden* [Leiden: H. Haestens, J. Jzn, Orlers, J. Maire, 1614], accessed online at https://repository.tudelft.nl/view/MMP/uuid%3A5a2d4de5-5d81-42f3 -9fbe-eaf8ef6f2378).

abandon the countryside was extended by another eight days.[47] In some areas, the waters rose slowly, and many were hesitant to abandon their homes and lands. Cattle owners may have been particularly reluctant to evacuate because August and September were prime months for grazing and haymaking. Moreover, they were vulnerable to soldiers' harassment en route to the towns, and once within a town's walls, their cattle might be impounded by the authorities to stock up for a siege. The rising waters, however, left them no choice. Farmers who had been hiding their cattle had to move their animals either to a town, or trek west to the narrow higher coastal dune strip between The Hague and Haarlem, which was not prone to flooding. So many beasts were crammed into the narrow streets of Gouda that it looked like a cattle market.[48] A large group of refugees who reached Amsterdam with their cattle on September 13, 1574, was part of the exodus triggered by the rising waters. Their escape from the floodwaters was particularly traumatizing because rebels and royalist soldiers alike preyed on them during their journey, robbing them of their cattle and other possessions and killing anyone who resisted.[49] The refugees may have originated in the region to the southeast of Leiden, including the Waddinxveen area, which was inundated only in September 1574.[50] Gouda, the town nearest to Waddinxveen, decided to severely restrict its intake of rural refugees so as not to burden the town in case of a siege. Only those who could demonstrate that they had enough money to feed themselves for a year gained entrance to the town. This stipulation caused heartbreaking dramas at the city's gates and may explain why many ran the gauntlet all the way to Amsterdam.[51]

Before the onset of the massive inundations, some farmers had chosen to take their chances in the countryside. During the winter of 1573, while the siege of Haarlem was in full force, however, these diehards had had to abandon all semblance of normal life. For fear of roaming soldiers, families remained on their farms during the day only. At sundown, they hid in their fields or among the reeds that lined the waterways.[52] Some of the displaced themselves became predatory bandits. In April 1574, Wouter Jacobsz witnessed the offloading of a ship full of captured rebels. He noted that they were "mostly men from the countryside who because of the horrible circumstances made the mistake to become freebooters, robbing and stealing anything they could find."[53]

The rural refugees who sought safety behind a town's walls often found themselves caught in a death trap. Even in peacetime, mortality in the towns was high as a result of endemic and epidemic diseases. Due to flight and the forced evacuations, the urban populations ballooned overnight. Delft saw its population swell from 20,000 to 80,000 people.[54] The refugees' precious cattle flooded the urban streets, adding to the congestion and pollution. In 1574, Haarlem may have sheltered 6,000 head of cattle. Because pasturing the cattle outside of the town walls was extremely hazardous, the animals were stall-fed, and grass and hay were stacked everywhere, literally and figuratively transforming the towns into tinderboxes. After the siege, disease, poverty, and violence killed over 3,300 people in Haarlem during 1574. This figure was in addition to the huge losses the town suffered during the 1573 siege when one in ten civilians residing in the town had died. The mortality was highest among the refugees.[55] After the city fell to the king's army, a garrison of German mercenaries prevented other royalist and rebel soldiers from plundering those sheltering in the town, but at a heavy price. In return for their protection, the town's inhabitants and the refugees paid debilitating war taxes and housed and fed the mercenaries and their families. At night the town's streets were extremely dangerous as roaming soldiers robbed and raped passers-by at will.[56]

Royalist Amsterdam was the only other safe haven for rural refugees who tried to evade the rebel towns. In Amsterdam, too, refugees were those most vulnerable to plagues, famine, and death. Many refugees were already exhausted, traumatized, sick, and starving before they staggered through the city's gates. The town authorities housed rural refugees in convents and other church properties that soon became overcrowded.[57] Impoverished refugees who were ill were often not admitted to Amsterdam's hospitals. Erstwhile well-off refugees, including Catholic priests who were not welcome in the rebel towns, roamed Amsterdam's streets as common beggars.[58] As was the case in other towns, food prices were exorbitant. In Amsterdam in September 1573, only meat was affordable because of the large number of stolen cattle that were being brought to market.[59] Rural refugees residing in the towns had little or no rights because they were not town citizens, and during a siege, the town authorities often impounded any livestock the refugees had saved from their farms.[60] To many rural refugees, the town walls provided immediate physical security, but as the food and sanitation conditions in the towns deteriorated, they were among the most vulnerable to the plague and other threats.

The Water Wolf: Voracious Wild Seas

Much of southern Holland remained flooded for at least four years, until 1578. With the countryside abandoned and submerged, and the rural tax base eliminated, the regional water boards could not raise the labor and resources to repair the dikes and drainage infrastructure. Nor could farmers raise crops or pasture their animals. Illegal peat mining damaged lands and dikes. The tides, winds, and storms had free play, causing heavy erosion. Moreover, continued violence prevented repairs and reconstruction. On September 8, 1574, when the full extent of the rebels' inundations could not yet have been known to them (because the Landscheijding dike protecting Rijnland and Leiden had not yet been breached), the royalist water board councilors exiled in Utrecht stressed that all of Schieland and a large part of Delfland already had been flooded. Schieland's rural populations fled across the Maas River with their animals, or, in the case of Delfland, to the higher western coastal dunes region around Noordwijck. The councilors feared that the salt water would soon flood the remainder of Delfland, all of Rijnland, the Woerden region, part of Kennemerland (north of Haarlem), all of Amstellant (the region around Amsterdam), and even part of the province of Utrecht. Emphasizing that if the existing breaches were not repaired before the winter, the tides would erode the dikes, mills, bridges, and other drainage works as well as the houses that had escaped being torched, the councilors warned that once this infrastructure had been destroyed, reconstruction would be daunting.[61]

Less than a month later, the royalist water board members sent an urgent report to the king's new governor of the Netherlands, Luis Requesens. Dated October 4, 1574, one day after the end of the siege of Leiden, it stated that 85,000 hectares (210,000 acres) of land were inundated with water. Its authors appealed to Requesens to pursue an alternative course to brute military conquest because the rebels had demonstrated that they preferred "to flounder with the land rather than be overpowered by his majesty's soldiery." The loyalist councilors feared that the rebels would cut more dikes if the king's army advanced, endangering Delft, Rotterdam, and Gouda, and ruining large numbers of farmers.[62] Requesens, however, rejected the loyalists' urgent appeal for funds to repair the breaches before the onset of the winter storm season.[63]

The worst fears of the loyalist councilors soon materialized. Attempts in Rijnland to repair the dikes and sluices in the northern sea dike came to naught, and the tides continued to surge through the breaches. More-over, for fear of royalist army attacks the rebels not only maintained the existing inundations, but as predicted, they breached additional dikes, inundating more land to protect Gouda, Woerden, and other rebel towns on the new frontline along the border with the Spanish-held province of Utrecht east of Holland.

The effect of the wartime inundations was fundamentally different from the seasonal flooding that occurred annually throughout the pol-der lands of Holland.[64] The violence and displacement caused by the war prevented any repairs and drainage of the waters. The tides ripped through the dikes and polder lands, and the onset of the winter storm season raised the specter of the wild seas devouring the low lands. Here-bert Stalpaert, a royalist member of the Rijnland water board, made valiant attempts to repair the northern sea dike before the onset of the 1574 winter by using personal loans. Stalpaert compared the raging flood waters with a voracious wolf, and by repairing the breaches, he sought "to turn the wolf back to the forest."[65]

Early in 1576, the extent of the inundations had almost tripled to 212,000 hectares (523,800 acres), encompassing fully two-thirds of the total surface of the province of Holland south of the northern sea dike. The expansion was partly the outcome of intentional further inunda-tions caused by the rebels and partly the result of the combined agency of tides and storms multiplying the erosive forces of the accumulated water.[66] The flooding was cumulative; the inundation waters could not be extracted because the drainage infrastructure of sluices and wind-mills had been damaged or destroyed. The royalist water board mem-bers warned that the worst was still to come. They feared that sea water would feed the interior lakes, in particular the Haarlem Lake via the Rhine River through the breaches in the Schieland dikes. More apoca-lyptically, they predicted that through the large breaches, the Maas, Merwede, Lek, and Yssel Rivers would be redirected into the interior, with the rivers abandoning their old channels and cutting out new ones in the lower polder lands. Not only Holland's physical existence was at stake, but neighboring Gelre (Gelderland) and the Betuwe were also threatened. Only immediate repairs, they warned, would save Holland and the adjacent regions from this doomsday scenario.[67]

Attempts to repair the dikes only got under way in 1576 when military operations in the heart of Holland died down after widespread mutinies in the ranks of the king's army (in 1575 and 1576), and peace talks culminated in the Pacification of Ghent. Pre-1576 repairs were makeshift in nature. During the summer of 1576, much of the royalist army was in a state of open mutiny. Its soldiers refused to fight the rebels and decamped from Holland to Brabant to plunder its rich towns and villages. With the lull in the fighting brought by negotiations and the retreat of the royalist army, the countryside became accessible again, a precondition for reconstruction.

In April 1576, the Rijnland, Schieland, and Delfland water boards requested permission from the rebel government to dam the Rhine River to facilitate the extremely complicated task of closing what was probably the most dangerous breach in the southern sea dike: the cut made at the Wolfferdike (Wolves' dike) near Gorinchem.[68] War debris, however, blocked access to the countryside. An April 1576 ordinance issued by the Delfland water board instructed the village aldermen to make all roads and waterways passable to allow for an inspection of dikes and drainages. The regional water boards prioritized restoring dikes to prewar heights and widths, and cleaning out drainage canals. Breaches that had been hastily backfilled were especially vulnerable and in need of urgent attention. Workers reinforced such sites by compacting the earth filling and constructing protective woodwork to shield the dikes from the erosive forces of the seas. Locations where the warring sides had constructed forts atop the dikes were among the most challenging projects because the dike sections on either side of the forts had been narrowed and breached, weakening the dike, yet the forts simultaneously needed to be kept fully operational.[69] In May 1576, the rebel government ordered that the holes in the Rhine River dike should be closed. In June, representatives of Schieland and Delfland met to plan closing the breaches in a series of low interior dikes shared between the two water boards.[70] That same month, the rebel government issued orders to close or barricade the holes in the Kinderdijk at Alblasserdam and Papen-drecht in the Alblasserwaard polder. The rebel government instituted a committee that was authorized to borrow money in the town of Dor-drecht and mobilize the resources required for the task. Three months later, however, with winter on the way, the holes remained open.[71]

By the end of 1576, Schieland had not been able to seal the remaining holes in the Yssel River segment of the southern sea dike or the breaches in its interior dikes. The situation, in turn, delayed the next required step: draining the inundating waters with gravity and windmill power.[72] In June 1577, Wouter Jacobsz visited the interior town of Gouda and commented that it had the appearance of a seashore town. Indeed, to travel from Gouda to Schoonhoven, he had had to take a boat in order to cross the submerged polders between the towns.[73]

Large stretches of Holland remained inundated through June 1577: "Many lands in Holland . . . are unprotected by dikes and can't be freed from the waters."[74] The floods stretched from the region east of Delft and north of Rotterdam up to the Landscheiding dike that seperated Rijnland from Schieland. Makeshift dike repairs proved unable to with-stand heavy storms. A June 21, 1577, storm caused multiple dike breaches throughout the region. At Schoonhoven, the storm undid all the dike repairs in a single stroke, and the Verhoeck Polder in Voorne was but one of several polders that flooded that day. Schieland, in particular, suffered during the storm because a lack of funds had paralyzed repair efforts.[75] Most of southern Holland remained inundated well into 1578, that is, four years after the breaching of the dikes to relieve the siege of Leiden.[76]

Whereas much of southern Holland remained inundated, in the higher dune region along the coast that had remained dry, a semblance of regular life returned. Many villagers commuted to their pastures by day to graze their cattle, harvest hay, or cultivate crops, but retreated to the relative safety of Haarlem's town walls with their animals when the sun set. The 1575 harvest was modest. The October 1575 Haarlem ox market proved a poor reflection of its prewar glory: only 33 oxen were on offer, and what little cheese and butter was available commanded exorbitant prices. Butter sold for a staggering 42 guilders per barrel. Not long after the ox market event, arson caused a large part of Haarlem to go up in flames, destroying homes, property, and food, and further impoverishing the inhabitants of the town. The 1576 harvest brought an abundant quantity of hay and good yields of barley, wheat, hemp and oats. The rye staple, however, fared poorly.[77]

On December 8, 1576, the proclamation of the Pacification of Gent was read in public in Haarlem.[78] Formal peace, however, did not mean immediate security because the news of the end of the hostilities caused the royalist garrison in the town to mutiny. The town's residents had to raise a considerable sum for the soldiers to prevent them from plundering and burning Haarlem.[79] Upon hearing the news of the pacification, many refugees who had sought sanctuary in Amsterdam returned home. Others, however, remained.[80]

A proclamation issued by the rebel high command on December 20, 1576, ordering soldiers to cease robbing travelers seemed to promise increased security, but the rebels surrounding Amsterdam and Haarlem ignored the orders.[81] Until Haarlem and Amsterdam joined the rebel cause in March 1576 and May 1578, respectively, rebel raids, roadblocks, and ambushes made the countryside between and around the towns highly dangerous, inhibiting reconstruction and the return of the displaced.[82] From late August 1577, Amsterdam was effectively under siege as the rebels surrounded the city, raided cattle pasturing outside the city walls, and blocked the waterways. A rebel force even attempted to take Amsterdam through a ruse. In response, at the end of December 1577, Amsterdam opened its sluices for two days to inundate the surrounding countryside. On January 25, 1578, the city cut the dike in front of the Haarlem Gate to further expand its defensive inundations. In early 1578, flight from Amsterdam reached dramatic proportions, but most people returned to the city by March, after the city government reached an agreement with the rebels.[83]

The Amsterdam region aside, most of Holland became relatively safe after the mutinous royalist army retreated to the southern Netherlands. The army's looting in Brabant and Flanders and the resumption of the war after the collapse of the short-lived Pacification of Ghent, however, unleashed another flood in southern Holland, but this one was a flood of war refugees from the Southern Low Countries. Some sought refuge in the dune ridges along the coast, but the remaining long-suffering villagers had little to offer the refugees. Jasper Pieterszn, a linen weaver, had fled to rural Monster from war-torn Flanders around Christmas of 1576 with his sick wife and his children. Six months later, the hospitality of the Monster farmers reached its limit because in addition to feeding the Flemish refugee family, they were burdened by many other poor.[84] Refugees from Brabant and Flanders generally arrived with empty hands; a few, however, managed to bring their precious weaving looms. Craftsmen with or without the tools of their trade were sought after in the depopulated towns of Holland. Between 1576 and 1603, Leiden welcomed almost 2,000 refugees from the southern Netherlands as full legal town citizens and 500 more from the war-torn northern Netherlands. Available housing soon ran out, and many refugees lived in great poverty. Leiden's total population increased from 12,016 inhabitants in 1582 (after it had already absorbed refugees) to 44,745 in 1622. Of the latter, 30,000 may have been war refugees from the southern Netherlands.[85] The refugee influx compensated for the terrible demographic loss caused by the war.

The Challenges of Reconstruction:
Draining the Polder Lands

Draining the inundation waters in the interior constituted a tremendous challenge because the drainage infrastructure had been destroyed or abandoned to the erosive waters and winds. Southern Holland relied on two methods of drainage. The most important was gravity drainage through the sluices in the northern and southern sea dikes. The second was mechanical drainage through windmills that pumped the water from the low-lying polders to the main canals that led to the sluices. The belligerents had destroyed or dismantled most of the drainage sluices. In 1575 and 1576 the sluice openings had been temporarily dammed to prevent new water from entering the interior. Many drainage mills also had been destroyed, dismantled, or damaged.

The drainage sluices had horizontally pivoting doors covered with a low roof that prevented the passage of larger ships. Even under normal conditions, the sluices were vulnerable to storm damage and required constant maintenance and repair. The sluices' double doors, which were mounted in a V-shape with the point of the V facing toward the sea, locked against one another when the waters on the seaside of the sluice were higher than the water levels in the interior. When the interior water levels were higher than the exterior water levels, the force of the water pushed the doors open toward the sea and the surplus water drained outward. Most of the sluices in the southern sea dike in 1574 and 1575 were opened to let water into the interior. To do so, the doors had to be propped open to let the water in; otherwise, the high tide would simply close them. Alternatively, the doors were removed. The former solution left the sluice doors and the sluice housing vulnerable to tides and storms. The latter dismantled the sluice. Soldiers stationed near the sluices in both the northern and southern sea dikes damaged the sluice doors and housings to source easily accessible construction and fuel-wood, especially during the long cold winters of 1573 and 1574. They also willfully damaged the sluices and woodwork that protected the sluices and the dike to extort money and goods from the local population.[86]

Repairing the sluices was exceptionally costly because it required imported, high-quality heavy timber, specialist craftsmen, and large numbers of laborers, boats, and horse-drawn carts. The water boards, however, were short of funds, staff, and labor as the inundated country-side remained flooded, depopulated, and unable to provide revenue, labor, or equipment. At Halfweg, Sparendam, and Vijffhuizen, little was left of the sluices, and the sluice openings had been provisionally closed with low semicircular earthen dams.[87] The alternative costly drainage outlet for Rijnland to the North Sea at Katwijk that had been completed in 1572 no longer functioned by 1574, and no attempts were made to repair it.[88]

Thus, after the damaged sluices were dammed, which in most cases may have been accomplished in 1575, no new water entered through the sluices. The already accumulated inundation water, however, could not be drained through the dammed sluices, and rain and seepage water further increased the polder water levels. By 1579, two drainage sluices at Halfweg (the old wooden Middle Sluice and the wooden Great or Eastern Sluice) had been brought back on line. The two sluices constituted approximately one-third of the total prewar drainage capacity of Rijnland through the northern sea dike. The four drainage sluices located at Sparendam all remained dammed until the early 1580s. The two Woerden Sluices at Sparendam were not functioning until 1580 at the earliest, and its Great Haarlem sluice did not work until 1583. Thus, Rijnland's drainage capacity was not restored to its prewar complement of six drainage sluices until 1584 when the new stone Middle Sluice at Halfweg, which replaced the wooden sluice that collapsed in 1582, was completed. Even before the war, when Rijnland had all six drainage sluices in the northern sea dike on line, its water board had felt that the drainage capacity was entirely insufficient. That sentiment legitimized the extremely costly project to establish direct drainage into the North Sea at Katwijk, which critics at the time decried as utter madness.[89]

The rebels had opened most of the sluices in the southern sea dike to create the inundations for Leiden, including the sluices at Gouda and Oudewater.[90] The Delfland water board initiated preparations to undertake a damage assessment inspection in April 1576; hence, it is unlikely that any major repairs to the sluices in the Maas dike section of the southern sea dike had been completed before the spring of 1576.[91] The gravity drainage sluices in the southern sea dike were probably open to the tides in 1574, provisionally dammed during 1575 or 1576, and repaired to allow for drainage between 1577 and 1580. In May 1575, William of Orange threatened the councilors of the village of Monster with being subjected to exemplary punishment as rebels if they did not immediately send 15 pioneers to assist at the Maesland [Maasland] sluice, probably to dam the sluice opening, after having ignored an order to do so a month earlier.[92] Drainage sluices in the southern sea dike would therefore have only come on line in 1577, and it is unlikely that the entire sluice drainage capacity of Schieland, Delfland, and adjacent areas draining through the southern sea dike would have been restored to its prewar capacity until 1580 at the earliest. The Arkel sluice near

Gorinchem, for example, was only repaired in the second half of 1580 when carpenters installed two new doors.[93]

Windmill power was important for interior drainage within the water boards' territories and critical to removing the inundation waters. Windmills could pump surplus water from the lower polders a few feet up into the surplus water storage bodies that were drained by the gravity sluices. Before the war, the Haarlem Lake functioned as the overflow for surplus water in Rijnland. The domain of Montfoort and the West-eijnde of Weerden (or vande Waerder) polders near Woerden in the far southeast of Rijnland, for example, pumped their surplus water into the Rhine River through a series of windmills.[94] The Rhine River, in turn, guided the water to the Haarlem Lake, draining it into the sea through the sluices at Halfweg and Sparendam.

Polders that were dependent on mechanical pump drainage were too low to be drained through the sluice gravity technique. Moreover, because many of the interior dikes had been breached and eroded during the war, the water from higher polders drained to the low-lying mill polders even if, when, and where gravity drainage for the higher polders had been partially or entirely restored after the hostilities ended. The belligerents intentionally had destroyed a number of windmills long before the 1574 Leiden inundations, in particular in the countryside around Haarlem and Leiden.[95]

Moreover, in Schieland, the millers had been ordered to hand over the sails that propelled the mills to the rebel commanders to power the shallow draught vessels that liberated Leiden. It is unlikely that these sails were returned speedily, if ever. Without sails, the mills could not operate and no water could be pumped out.[96] Most if not all the mills in Rijnland, Schieland, and Delfland may have been inoperable in 1574 and 1575, with many destroyed or damaged.[97] For comparison, only one of three food processing windmills at Gravenzande south of The Hague survived the hostilities; two mills were burned to the ground.[98] In Schieland, drainage mills that had survived the war or that had been repaired in the meantime did not become operational until December 1576 at the earliest.[99] The inhabitants of Heemskerk north of Haarlem negotiated an agreement in 1577 with a neighboring village to jointly build windmills to drain the area.[100] The windmills that drained the polders in Pijnacker may have been repaired and so were functioning from 1577 onward, but the inhabitants of the polder had to pay a high special annual tax to underwrite the repair of the windmills for 15 years, until 1592.[101] In 1578, the Rijnland water board claimed that 300–400 private larger drainage mills (smock mills) and numerous smaller post-mills were in operation in Rijnland. In early 1579, when the rebel government of Holland requested that the regional water board and local village magistrates and councilors assess the war damage at the village level, the questionnaire included a query about whether the village windmill had been burned during the conflict.[102]

Environcide's Aftermath

Rebuilding the dike and drainage infrastructure of southern Holland was a precondition to postconflict reconstruction. Rural refugees could not return to their farms and villages to rebuild their homes, barns, fields, and other environmental infrastructure until the land had been reclaimed from the water. Land reclamation, however, required the labor, expertise, and taxes that only a repopulated and productive countryside could supply. The Catch-22 impeded rural reconstruction, and the resulting delay, in turn, led to more sustained loss of environmental infrastructure. The rebel government and the water boards pursued different strategies to escape the dilemma. In 1574, when the rebel government of Holland took the fateful decision to flood southern Holland, it promised that the entire province would contribute to the costs of postwar reconstruction: "It is understood, that although the costs and the damage caused by the said inundation, breaches, and damage caused to sluices, dams, or dikes, as well as its repairs, would be for the account of the Lands involved [that is the water boards and rural communities] [but] will be equally shared by the general Land [the government of Holland], and the towns of Holland, as are all general costs of this war."[103]

No doubt the promise was a concession to getting the water boards and their rural constituencies to agree to the massive inundations. The rebel leaders also promised to fund the repairs for the additional defensive inundations that had been ordered in 1575 and 1576.[104] The rebel leadership failed to honor the pledges, however, leaving the water boards to implode. The Rijnland water board had already fallen apart in June 1572 when its royalist members fled to Utrecht. The rebel sympathizers in turn sought refuge in rebel-held Delft. The full Rijnland water board did not meet again until September 1577.[105] The Schieland water board had been virtually defunct from 1570 to 1574 and by the end of 1576 it was on the verge of bankruptcy.[106]

The water boards tried to collect current and back taxes, a measure that proved not only unsuccessful but even counterproductive. Unable to pay because their lands were submerged or overgrown and their homes, tools, livestock, and other property burned or pillaged, many surviving farmers and villagers never returned to their lands. By 1577, most of the once-wealthy farmers on the northern sea dike, each of whom personally had been responsible for the repair and maintenance of the dike segment that abutted their land, were either dead or bankrupt. The smaller farmers in the interior proved equally unable to meet their obligations toward dike maintenance and repair. A 1577 Rijnland attempt to raise funds failed "because many lands in Rijnland are unused and desolate and some villages and polders are still submerged as a result of the burning down of the drainage mills." The Rijnland councilors feared that if they pressed the farmers they "would stick the spade in the dike," the legal formula used to indicate that they would abandon their farms for good, surrendering all rights and obligations.[107] In 1575, the Delfland water board was frustrated in its attempts to raise taxes from the rural districts responsible for the repair of the Maas dike sluices "because all of Delfland remained inundated and many of the land owners and tenants had either perished or had scattered to different places."[108] The situation was no better in early 1576, when the rebel government granted the villages of Delfland an exemption from all water board taxes and contributions to prevent the total and permanent abandonment of the countryside.[109] In April 1576, the rebel government decided to sell the right to levy a tax in Rijnland that consisted of a regular rate on productive lands and a discounted rate on unused inundated lands. The entrepreneur who bought the right to collect the tax would be allowed to sell the lands, animals, and other property of land owners and tenants who were unable to meet the tax obligation.[110] The rebel government "found that many lands are being abandoned every day, and remained unused, because of the burdens and taxes . . . imposed because of the war"; however, it added a provision that all land users and tenants subject to the taxation could deduct part of the tax from the first land rent due to the owner of the land.[111]

Many villages may not have been repopulated and rebuilt until well into the 1580s, as was the case in Aalsmeer and Heemskerk. Located in Rijnland on the eastern bank of the Haarlem Lake between Amsterdam and Leiden, in 1580, one quarter of Aalsmeer's (farm) properties still lay abandoned. Many other properties were only partially being used and their owners received tax discounts.[112] Heemskerk, north of Haarlem, lay entirely abandoned for at least five years. Many of its inhabitants had perished, the livestock had been stolen, and most of the houses lay in ruins. Moreover, parts of Heemskerk remained submerged in 1577.[113] A decade later, only a few houses in the village had been restored to a habitable state. Most returnees still lived in makeshift shacks and were too poor to restore their homes or repair the fences that had protected their lands and crops against plagues of rabbits and deer. In addition, the low-lying lands remained waterlogged because the sluices no longer drained the land. The returnees petitioned the rebel government to be granted forgiveness for half of the back taxes from the previous seven years so that they could invest in constructing a large windmill to drain their lands and restore them to productivity.[114] In 1577, the rebel government granted the inhabitants of Bommenée (Bommenede) in the far south of Holland a ten-year postponement of all its debt repayments and taxes to allow the inhabitants to rebuild their burned and destroyed homes. Bommenede "and adjacent polders were abandoned, unused and laying fallow because many of the tenants and its users were dead, lost, impoverished or displaced."[115]

With the countryside unable to supply the taxes needed to rebuild the rural drainage infrastructure, the rebel government turned to the towns. New special levies taxed urban trade and consumption of both beer and peat, amounting to an urban subsidy of rural reconstruction. The beer tax was introduced in October 1576 to raise funds to repair the sea dikes. In recognition of the desperate state of Rijnland, the rebel government diverted part of the beer tax returns to the repair of the northern sea dike and its sluices, something it previously had refused to allow.[116]

In July 1577, the rebel government of Holland authorized a special tax to be raised in Leiden and Rijnland to repair the northern sea dike, provided that the fort on the dike at Halfweg would be maintained.[117] Simultaneously, it announced a general one-time 1 percent property tax to be levied throughout rebel-held Holland to finance the repairs of sluices and dikes that had been cut for defensive inundations. The tax revenues would be used partly to repair existing forts and to erect new ones; the remainder was reserved for the sluices and dikes. Half of the tax would be paid by the tenants and users of the land and half by the owners of the land.[118]

Early in 1578, the Rijnland water board was determined to collect its taxes, threatening to impound the possessions of all noncompliant village aldermen. The latter were held personally responsible for raising the arrear contributions for their constituencies for 1572, 1576, and 1577. The village aldermen, however, argued that most of the lands in their villages had remained unoccupied and unused from 1572 to 1578 and that the land owners had been so impoverished that they could not pay any contributions. The aldermen pleaded for the contributions to be forgiven or the payment postponed. The water board subsequently appointed a special committee to conduct a hearing with the village aldermen of Rijnland to assess the situation.[119]

Rijnland was not an outlier. Villagers throughout southern Holland proved unable to pay current and arrear rents, taxes, and contributions. Early in September 1578, the rebel government reluctantly agreed to postpone all sales by execution of property and land for any rent arrears on unused land and properties until January 1, 1579. Earlier it had threatened to sell any land on which back taxes were due. The government relented because it became aware of "the enormous damage, the inability [by people] to use [land and property], and the heavy burdens that many inhabitants of the said Land [Holland] and others suffered and had to bear in their lands and other immovable properties during the recent wars, both through the violence used by the enemy and as a consequence of the defense of the said Land." Anyone in arrears with their rent payments was ordered to go to the nearest town to explain their situation to special committees that were appointed by the town magistrates. The committees assessed on a case-by-case basis whether forgiveness was justified for any rents or other payments owed up to and including 1577.[120]

With so many rural land users unable to pay rents, individual and institutional landowners, in turn, were unable to pay their taxes, duties, and other contributions. Based on what must have been a flood of requests to the committees, the rebel authorities concluded that the extent of the rural devastation far surpassed their worst fears. Subsequently, they required all dike counts (the water boards' executive officers) and revenue collectors (usually local rural councilors or magistrates) to submit a report about all the individual villages that had been granted tax forgiveness to explain "how long they [the villages] have been inundated, and if their mills were burnt down, and [report on] all other villages and hamlets that might have suffered comparable damage."[121]

Any request for tax exemption or reduction had to be accompanied by proof in the form of a copy of the village's tax register. In 1579, a considerable number of villages received exemptions after submitting their tax registers. In 1580, the rebel government employed pairs of local deputies (each of whom came from a different rural constituency) in 29 locations in Holland to assess the tax registers to evaluate whether the exemption requests were justified.[122] Based on the assessment, in 1580, the rebel authorities generally forgave the arrear taxes and contributions throughout southern Holland for the years 1574, 1575, and 1576. Taxes for additional years were also partly or entirely forgiven upon the provision of written proof that lands had been unused for additional years, though typically their testimony came in the form of oral statements that supplicants made under oath to rural magistrates. From 1580 on, however, the rebel authorities authorized the water boards to forfeit and sell any lands with arrears for which no exemption had been granted.[123]

Yet, even during the 1580s it was not uncommon that villages and towns were unable to meet their tax responsibilities. In 1580, the aldermen of Haarlemmerliede and Spaarnwoude, both near Haarlem, identified neighbors who not only were unable to pay their 1580 taxes but also had not yet paid their taxes for 1579.[124] In practice, therefore, the rebel government authorized tax exemptions on a case-by-case basis well into the 1580s, suggesting that the rural areas involved still lay in ruins.

It is likely that the resumption of the war in 1578 caused the rebel government to decide to cut its losses and grant nearly wholesale exemption for the 1570s arrears. The decision resulted in a dramatic decrease of tax revenues in the short run, which was compensated by renewed access to the revenues from impounded Catholic church and royalist properties. But it had become clear that without granting substantial exemptions, the repopulation and reconstruction of the countryside would stall. The rebel government of Holland also may have felt more secure after March 1578, when Amsterdam, the last royalist bastion in Holland, changed sides and acknowledged its authority.[125]

One of the few ways that remained to make a living in the war-torn and devastated countryside was through peat mining, but the practice made the flooding worse, effectively feeding the water wolf. Peat was the main source of fuel for cooking, heating, and industrial activities, in particular, beer- and brick-making. Before the war, the water boards of Rijnland, Delfland, and Schieland had sought tight control over peat mining to limit its economic and environmental impact. Peat mining resulted in the loss of tax revenue for the water boards because it literally stripped lands of their agricultural value, and in the long run, it also led to land loss. Dryland peat strip mining had been prohibited long before the war. Only wet peat mining from relatively narrow holes or strips using a large spoon-like contraption to scrape the peat from water-filled holes was allowed.[126]

From 1572 onward, however, violence, flooding, and the collapse of the water boards rendered the restrictions utterly unenforceable. Under the dire circumstances, peat mining was the only rural productive activity possible. Even where the land was inundated with water, all that was required was a small boat (although peat mining from a boat formally was prohibited), one or two men or women, and some simple tools. The rewards were great, especially since the demand for peat skyrocketed as soldiers and civilians faced brutal winters in forts, shacks, or overcrowded towns. Peat prices continued to surge into the 1580s.[127]

Peat mining was very lucrative not only for peat land owners or those who organized strip mining on abandoned lands but also for the laborers who actually dug the peat.[128] Rural officials, including sheriffs and village aldermen, were often complicit in illegal peat mining.[129] The towns encouraged peat mining because peat was the main urban household and industrial source of energy. Moreover, the rebel government of Holland also had a stake in the peat war economy: peat taxes were a steady source of revenue even if or because the depopulated and devastated countryside yielded no regular taxes or rents.[130] The rebel government taxed peat mining, peat consumption, and the export of peat from Holland.[131] The peat tax revenues were substantial: in 1578, the rebel government sold the tax rights on the peat trade in the town of Geertruydenberg for 5,400 pounds, more than Haarlem's regular tax contribution for 1579.[132]

Already a major problem before the war, peat mining during and directly after the war greatly accelerated the process of land loss. Extractive peat mining may have become more critical to the rural economy of Holland from the mid-1570s onward, during and immediately following the destruction of the countryside. Many villages along the Haarlem Lake in the 1580s and 1590s submitted requests to decrease their tax-assessed land surface due to land loss to the water wolf. In many cases, Rijnland granted all or part of the reductions after surveyors had confirmed the actual land loss.[133]

The case of Hillegom, a village rich in peat deposits on the western side of the lake is illustrative of the correlation between the war and land losses along the Haarlem Lake. During a 1643 meeting of the Rijnland water board, the inhabitants of Hillegom testified that the village had lost a great deal of its best lands on the banks of the lake during the last 50–60 years. The villagers emphasized that "in the past when her lands stretched to the lake, Hillegom flourished ... but after the *w[ater]wolf* ate them [the lands] it descended into its present state of poverty."[134]

The Impact of Environcidal and Total War

The 1570s war profoundly shaped Holland's society, economy, and environment. Nationalist history has stressed the positive: Holland fought off the powerful Habsburg royalist army and became a leader in the rebellion that eventually led to the founding of the Dutch Republic and the Dutch nation. Moreover, during the late 16th and early 17th century, Holland emerged as a global economic powerhouse, and the 17th century is regarded the Dutch Golden Age. Its towns, in particular Amsterdam, attracted large numbers of migrants and refugees, making Holland one of the most urbanized regions in the world. In the process, Holland paid a heavy price: the mass killings at Naarden and Haarlem; starvation and the plague in Leiden; and the harrowing liberation of Leiden through massive inundations are central themes in Dutch history. What soon was erased, however, is that the countryside's destitution was much more sustained, and its postconflict recovery far more challenging than most contemporary or modern observers have recognized. Much of the countryside remained inundated with flood waters from 1574 through 1578 and depopulated until the 1580s; some regions never recovered, and the loss of valuable farm and village lands due to lakeside erosion accelerated during and after the war. The balance of economic and thence political power consequently shifted in favor of the towns. Urbanization in late 16th-century Holland therefore was as much the outcome of a countryside torn asunder by total war as a product of economic growth. As the focus of the war shifted to Flanders and Brabant in the second half of the 1570s, increasing numbers of refugees from the Southern Low Countries flooded the relatively safe towns of Holland.

Many rural war refugees never returned to their villages and farms in the countryside of Holland. In the aftermath of war, urban institutional and private land owners captured increasing amounts of rural land as the towns appropriated religious and royalist properties and town financiers bought up abandoned farms. In addition, urban elites increasingly controlled the reconstituted water boards that simultaneously became more centralized, with the principal members dominating the commoners. Peat mining to meet urban demand for fuel soared at the expense of agricultural production and caused further land losses. The prewar rural society and environment thus changed radically. An entire class of farmers who had maintained dike segments or sluices individually or collectively, and who had had a significant voice on the water boards, vanished as the water wolf swallowed their fields, farms, and entire villages, and as they themselves succumbed to violence or disease, or washed up in the towns as urban poor. The wartime floods not only swallowed the land, but with it also extinguished an entire way of life. The countryside shrank both physically and economically. Lands that had been gobbled up by the Haarlem Lake or mined for peat were no longer productive, constituting lost livelihoods for farmers and lost revenues for local (village), regional (water board), and state (the rebel government) institutions. Rural southern Holland emerged from the war less an agricultural economy marked by independent and tenant farmers and more an exploitative and unsustainable peat mining periphery that served an urban core of private and industrial consumption.

The enormous loss of lives, lands, and livelihoods, and the collapse of rural society triggered by the flooded earth strategy, ultimately were attributed to the random violence of Nature, rather than the strategists of total war. Yet it was conscious acts of environcidal war that decimated and displaced Holland's population while burning and flooding the environmental infrastructure that sustained urban and rural lives, livelihoods, and ways of life. Holland's population rebounded and its environment recovered, thanks to a massive influx of refugees from the southern Netherlands as the war shifted to Flanders and Brabant, but the Haarlem Lake remained a festering wound in Vondel's Lion of Holland's side long after the war was over, causing the loss of fertile lands well into the 19th century.

2

Scorched Earth, Black Legend

ENVIRONCIDE AND THE EARLY 16TH-CENTURY SPANISH CONQUEST OF AMERICA

Although there was such a large [Inca] army at Cajamarca, one could see their [the local population's] lovely fields, slopes and valleys—how they were sown and well cultivated because they retained and assiduously observed the laws of their elders, which mandated that they [the Inca soldiers] should eat from the deposits [the food storage depots] without destroying the fields. The villages were filled with supplies of precious cloth and other riches, and herds of sheep.[1]

THE SPANISH chronicler Piedro de Cieza de León ascribed the preceding comment relating to the 1532 fateful meeting between Inca Emperor Atahualpa and Spanish conquistador Pizarro to an eyewitness. It expressed a Spanish soldier's utter disbelief that a large army could have been encamped in the densely populated Cajamarca Valley without having plundered and destroyed the inhabitants' villages, crop fields, livestock, and other possessions. Indeed, the subsequent Spanish army's occupation of the valley was devastating. The disbelief was because the environcidal violence of living off the land and scorched earth described in the previous chapter on Holland was dead(ly) common throughout the 15th and 16th centuries. In fact, Spanish King Philip II's enemies

59

argued that massacres; burning down villages; forcibly extracting food, goods, and labor; plundering; and pillaging were part and parcel of a Spanish way of war. The Black Legend holds that the Spanish conquest of the Americas caused the death or enslavement of millions and the eradication of entire ways of life. To Spain's rivals, the legend served to contest Habsburg rule in both the New World and the Old. Rebel towns in the late 16th-century Low Countries played a prominent role in the dissemination of the Black Legend propaganda in print. Pamphlets compared the Spanish massacres of indigenous Americans in the New World with the mass killing of Protestant rebels in the Low Countries. They depicted Spanish officials and their king as tyrannical and barbarous oppressors, and compared Spanish soldiers to "savage war dogs" that tortured and pillaged Dutch and indigenous American peasants alike. The Dutch rebel renunciation of Spanish rule in 1581, known as the Act of Abjuration, stressed that the Spanish had trampled the "native privileges and rights" in the Americas, waging a war of extermination against its indigenous populations. The rebel grievances emphasized the ruthless nature of the Spanish way of war and the infringements on age-old rights and privileges in the Low Countries. The rebels drew heavily on the work of Bartolomé De Las Casas, whose *The Devastation of the Indies* was published in 1552, translated into Dutch in 1578, and widely quoted in Dutch texts. Dutch rebel leader William of Orange argued that only the denunciation of the Spanish king would save the Low Countries from suffering the same disastrous fate as befell the indigenous societies in the Americas.[2]

The aforementioned quote from Piedro de Cieza de León's 16th-century chronicles suggests that the Dutch rebels' accusations were not mere propaganda. Based on his experience in Spanish America, Spanish Bishop De Las Casas stressed that during the first four decades of the conquest, Spain's soldiers butchered and enslaved indigenous Americans en masse, pillaged and burned their towns, robbed their food stores, and hunted down the survivors as the latter sought refuge in inaccessible mountains and forests. De Las Casas claimed that four million indigenous Americans perished, that Cuba was transformed into a desert, and that the soldiers had razed 800 indigenous American towns in the Jalisco region of Mexico alone. He emphasized that Spanish soldiers indiscriminately massacred indigenous Americans, or simply starved or worked them to death. In contrast to the modern literature that attributes indigenous Americans' demographic and societal collapse to virgin-soil epidemics, both De Las Casas's and Cieza de León's contemporary critiques of the conquest singled out its murderous violence and the brutal exploitation of indigenous American men and women as porters and slaves.[3] Indeed, the epidemics that caused the demographic collapse of America's indigenous populations cannot be separated from the context of the environcidal wars of conquest. The epidemics were not merely caused by invasive microbes and ecological or biological imperialism.[4] Rather, destroying or damaging indigenous American environmental infrastructure or displacing populations from it—both through mass killing, enslavement, sacking, burning, and pillaging as well as incessant requisitions of food, labor, livestock, and tribute—broadcast famine and trauma, exposed survivors to the elements, made people vulnerable to disease, and facilitated epidemics.

Various indigenous sources from Central America seem to downplay the Spanish conquest as one more invasion in a region marked by waves of imperial conquests rather than a dramatic historical break. In some ways, the image of the Spanish conquest as the end of indigenous American history is overdrawn, and narratives of conquest, extermination, and genocide serve to erase indigenous history and inscribe the history of the conquerors on the land, legitimizing their claims of political sovereignty and economic property. The descendants of indigenous American allies of the Spanish who produced the indigenous sources, however, who derived much of their status, privileges, land, and labor as coconquerors not surprisingly created more "positive" memories about the conquest and its impact.[5]

The origins of the Black Legend predated the Dutch Revolt, stemming from the violence of the Spanish conquest in the Americas and Italy. The excesses initially had been regarded as aberrations committed by individual rogue commanders. During the war in the Low Countries, however, the atrocities were reimagined as being intrinsic to Spanish imperial rule. Spanish soldiers, in general, and the Spanish King Philip II, in particular, were held directly responsible for the destructive nature of Spain's wars, even though the American conquests took place under King Philip's predecessor, Emperor Charles V, during the first half of the 16th century.[6] Moreover, there are limitations to applying the label "Spanish" to the conquest, as the role of Charles V suggests. While most of the conquistadors were from modern Spain, some were from other parts of Charles's empire, including the Low Countries and Germany.[7]

The Spanish conquest was environcidal almost from the day Columbus set foot in the Americas in 1492: indigenous environmental infrastructure was the object, subject, and tool of war. As did 16th-century Dutch farmers, indigenous Americans critically depended on their homes and granaries, farms and fields, orchards, food and water stores, drains and canals, and other forms of infrastructure. In turn, the environmental infrastructure that provided resilience to episodic droughts and climate fluctuations was sustained through incessant maintenance and repairs. The bulk of the environmental infrastructure was in or near settlements to optimize access and maximize labor and other inputs. The systematic destruction of environmental infrastructure through scorched earth and the displacement of indigenous Americans from their settlements through massacres, enslavement, flight, and forced removals exposed the population to trauma, famine, disease, and death. As during the Dutch Revolt, the boundaries between perpetrators and victims, at times, blurred. Forced to abandon their homes and hearths, indigenous American men and women tenaciously sought to shape their destinies, however constrained their choices. Many refugees fled into the forests, swamps, and mountains in the vast interior of Central and South America that remained beyond Spanish control and rebuilt not just a life, but even entire societies. Conquest and colonialism deeply victimized indigenous American women in the regions under Spanish control: as soldiers invaded towns, villages, and farms, they raped and enslaved women on a massive scale. In addition, Spanish colonialism and Christianity imposed patriarchal structures, formally disempowering women as land and property owners and political and religious office holders. But as conquistadors killed or conscripted most of the men (and some women as well) as soldiers, porters, and labor in faraway lands, women ran the villages and farms, and maintained the environmental infrastructure that provided the food, provisions, and labor that sustained the Spanish conquest and colonization as well as the survival of their own communities.[8] Moreover, much like the Dutch rebels who flooded most of southern Holland, indigenous Americans themselves employed environcide and total war against their opponents, irrespective of whether they were indigenous neighbors or European invaders. In fact, the early 16th-century "Spanish" conquest and pacification depended heavily on indigenous American allies. Moreover, as the previous chapter demonstrated and the subsequent chapter will confirm, environcidal warfare was neither an invention of the Spanish, nor a Spanish monopoly; to the contrary, it was deeply embedded in the practices of war of the period and deployed throughout the Old and New Worlds in the 16th and 17th centuries.

Whereas the previous chapter focused on a small place (Holland) and a short time frame (a decade) to bring into focus the specifics of the who, what, and how of the process of interaction between war, environment, and society, this chapter zooms out to a macrolevel of analysis (the Americas occupied by the Spanish) over a longer timeframe (the first half of the 16th century). This allows for the identification of wider patterns, but, because of the larger scale, scarcer data, and a reliance on a selection of (mainly secondary) literature, the causal relationship of how war and displacement affected populations and their environmental infrastructure are somewhat blurry. Essentially, this chapter rereads the early 16th-century conquest through the environcidal framework. As in the Dutch Revolt where belligerents sought to make war pay for itself or even make a profit, Spanish conquistadors in the New World fought for gain: their eyes were on the big prize of El Dorado. But in the meantime, they settled for extorting tribute, food, and labor even if in the process they caused the collapse of indigenous American societies and the environmental infrastructure that sustained them. The crown rewarded both Spanish soldiers and their indigenous American allies with *encomiendas*, grants of land and indigenous labor, as well as other privileges. The short-term search for pillage by the conquistadors caused the destruction of environmental infrastructure and displacement of indigenous communities, which clashed with the long-term goal of the Habsburg crown to develop the newly conquered territories and provide revenues. The crown attempted to limit soldiers' violent pillaging through ordinances and the New Laws, but with limited impact.

Environmental Infrastructure

Environcidal warfare was widespread because armies and soldiers lived off the land in more than one way. Armies literally marched on their stomachs because they lacked a logistical apparatus. The other side of the same coin was the strategy to deny the enemy access to any environmental infrastructure through scorched earth, with the aim of wearing the enemy population and army down, ultimately forcing them to withdraw, flee, or surrender. Rulers, generals, and soldiers shared the sentiment that war had to pay for itself and for them. Campaigns were often the landlubber equivalent of naval privateering ventures, intended to enrich states, generals, and soldiers through the capture of booty. For the Americas, the ruler of Spain typically issued a charter for the conquest of a region and a title (i.e., governor, captain-general) to an individual who organized and financed the expedition; assembled an army, equipment, and supplies; and executed the conquest. The soldiers received no salary, but instead pillaged for their own account during the expedition and received a share in the army's loot, although the commander granted select officers and soldiers administrative offices and *encomiendas*, grants of land and labor.[9]

The conquistadors relied entirely on indigenous American environmental infrastructure during their quest for El Dorado. The extent to which indigenous American landscapes constituted environmental infrastructure is obscured because it typically did not manifest itself through the monumental size canals or dams of the Aztec, Inca, Maya, and Pueblo societies. Yet, indigenous farmers shaped soils, flora, fauna, and entire ecosystems through clearing, burning, terracing, mounding, and ditching, creating "dark earths" in the process. Large swaths of the

Americas were "cultivated" or "mosaic" landscapes shaped by human use and management.[10]

The environmental infrastructure of dams, dikes, canals, raised fields, agricultural terraces, and storage facilities that marked Aztec, Inca, Maya, Pueblo, and other societies throughout the Americas more than matched with the contemporary Low Countries' polder landscapes and was equally vulnerable to war and dislocation. Water management for irrigation, drainage, or both was a key component of the environmental infrastructure of many indigenous American societies. The Spanish conquerors marveled at the Aztec empire's canals. Bounded by terraced hillsides, the Aztec empire's Valley of Mexico was filled with farms, orchards, villages, towns, and, at its center, an expansive dike-and-sluice-controlled wetland with polders.[11] Up to 20,000 hectare may have been under irrigation in the Valley of Mexico alone.[12] Spanish observers equally admired the intricate irrigation systems that sustained the lush valleys along Peru's arid coast.[13] The elaborate environmental infrastructure required enormous and continuous labor, capital, and intellectual inputs to construct, maintain, operate, and update. As a result, it was highly sensitive to any substantial decline in investments. The population collapse and displacement resulting from the Spanish conquest was so dramatic that sediment buried many pre-Columbian irrigation canals, erasing any sign of the intricate hydraulic features that marked different regions.[14]

Less spectacular forms of environmental *infrastructuring* were even more widespread. Flood-recession agriculture and various forms of water harvesting were widely practiced in the floodplains of the Mississippi, the Colorado, and the Sacramento Rivers, and among the indigenous societies of the North American Southwest. Zuni and Pueblo farmers located fields at the mouth of runoff lines or channels below mesas or plateaus. They also used rock fields to reduce evaporation and preserve soil humidity.[15] Shallow waterholes, deeper wells, or the use of natural or human-made water cisterns, including collapsed sinkholes or cenotes, were common sources of drinking water and manual irrigation in the North American Southwest and the Great Basin, the

Mexican Highlands, Mexico's Oaxaca Valley, and areas throughout Central America and in Peru.[16]

Indigenous environmental infrastructure extended beyond the dikes, dams, canals, and irrigated fields to the very soil where they settled and farmed. Draining or irrigating served to manipulate soil as well as water. Indigenous American farmers shaped soils through clearing, terracing, mounding, and ditching. These, too, were not one-time "fire-and-forget" investments that changed the earth forever; maintaining, repairing, and clearing the features were time- and labor-intensive and continuous processes. Many precontact and early contact indigenous societies used terraced fields, which facilitated hillside agriculture and downhill drainage, providing irrigation and erosive materials from uphill that fertilized the soil further down.

Andean terraced fields are difficult to date because of disturbances caused by soil erosion, cultivation, and a history of maintenance and repair, but many have pre-Columbian origins. Andean farmers used small-scale irrigation on these fields.[17] Terracing and the use of field walls were also widespread practices in Yucatan.[18] Many Meso-American terraces had already been abandoned by the late 16th century but seem mostly associated with the early contact period.[19] In North America, terraced fields, often linked with some form of irrigation or water harvesting, were limited to the Southwest regions that, too, were subjected to Spanish warfare.[20]

Indigenous farmers prepared fields by literally building up the soil into small mounds, larger raised beds, or more elaborate raised fields. Mounding added planting depth, mitigated flooding, and improved the soil available to the crops.[21] Cultivation mounds and raised fields occurred in many forms and sizes. Some of the largest measured approximately 3,000 by 80 feet in size. Sixteenth-century Mojo raised fields included small mounds that were 4–5 feet long, 2–3 feet wide, and 1–3 feet high. The remnants of tens of thousands of Mojo raised fields still dot Northern Peru's Amazon floodplain. They also were common in Ecuador, Mayan Mexico, and the Caribbean.[22]

Raised fields rendered flood-prone wetland environments or soils subject to waterlogging more suitable to crops. Raising fields or cultivating mounds effectively extended the growing season in wetlands because farmers did not have to wait until the floodwaters or rainwaters had completely drained or evaporated before seeding or planting. Moreover, a great advantage of cultivating flooded or waterlogged lands is that the soil can be more easily worked when it is wet and soft.[23] Indigenous farmers also drained waterlogged soils by digging ditches, as in the case of the Karinya swamps in the Orinoco Llanos of Venezuela. The ditches needed to be cleaned annually before the fields were planted to ensure the excess water drained properly.[24]

By mounding, ridging, and terracing, indigenous Americans not only physically shaped the earth, but they also changed the soils' chemical properties, producing so-called dark earths that are increasingly acknowledged as anthropogenic soils. Villagers and farmers enriched soils around settlements (including fields) by incorporating organic matter.[25] Soil conservation and soil fertilization were widespread and deliberate practices used, for example, by the Aztecs who built their *chinampa* fields from fertile lake bottom mud and human or animal manure.[26] "Shifting" cultivation on thin tropical soils often involved the periodic incorporation of organic materials and minerals.[27] The deep debris buildup that marks the dark earths at precontact Amazonian settlement sites indicates that the inhabitants were not typical shifting cultivators but that their villages, farms, and fields remained in situ for extended periods. The sites are significantly higher in organic matter and select minerals than surrounding soils as a result of garbage disposal, human waste products, and burials.[28]

The postcontact demographic collapse caused by the Spanish conquest brought an end to the active creation of dark earths by 1700, suggesting that violence and depopulation dramatically decreased investment in environmental infrastructure.[29] Population displacement removed people from the fertile dark earth soils that they had built up through significant and sustained investments, which negatively affected food production. In addition, the decline or discontinuation of human investment in the dark earth soils often led to their deterioration; erosion had free play as runoff and landslides crumbled the retaining walls of terraced fields, and rains and floods washed away mounds and raised fields. In Central Mexico, sun, wind, and water conspired to leach the organic matter and nutrients from deserted indigenous American fields.[30]

Across the Americas, indigenous societies constructed and maintained large settlement mounds. In the Amazonian floodplain, farmers often located settlements and fields on natural bluffs, and sometimes on mounds. Over time, settlement deposits built up the soils on the bluffs, blurring the distinction between natural and anthropogenic mounds.[31] Ecuador contains several thousand earth mounds that were used for habitation, ceremonial buildings, or burials that are often associated with precontact- or early contact-era raised fields.[32] Hispaniola (modern Haiti and the Dominican Republic) contained large indigenous earthworks, and temples crowned mounds throughout Central America.[33]

Homes, granaries, farms, villages, and towns in and of themselves constituted critical environmental infrastructure that provided protection and shelter against drenching rains, scorching heat, howling winds, and freezing cold as well as human and animal predators, pests, and plagues. The loss of dwellings and their precious contents proved disastrous. In the early 16th-century Coosa kingdom in what would become the southern US, the inhabitants constructed elaborate adjacent winter and summer quarters with sunken floors. Exterior wall posts supported thatched roofs. During the winter, the huts were the locus of many household activities, including cooking and tool making. Each residential structure boasted separate "public" areas (hearths) and private quarters. The private quarters consisted of beds that lined the walls. The corners served to store food.[34] Early Spanish invaders survived harsh winters in North America only because of the shelter offered by Coosa homes and villages. The Hopi, the Zuni, and other Southwestern Pueblo communities quarried the locally abundant stone to construct their homes and villages. Dwellings often contained multiple stories and frequently shared walls. Villagers used mud mortar to stabilize the stone walls, but the mortar eroded quickly and had to be reapplied regularly. Because of the heavy maintenance requirements, dips in population size and the subsequent loss of labor investments in repair and maintenance greatly affected the pueblos. For example, while the Orayvi pueblo may have been occupied for 800 years, the pueblos clearly reflect periods of population contraction in historical and prehistorical times, leading to repeated abandonments and reoccupations.[35]

Homes often offered physical and spiritual protection for the living and the dead. Indigenous communities in early colonial Mexico buried the ashes of deceased family members and the umbilical cords of newborns under the floor of their homes. The grinding stone that was key for preparing the staple maize meal occupied a central place in the home. In addition to shelter against the elements, homes also offered protection against sorcery. The protective home, however, was always a work in progress and required constant cleansing to keep dirt and disorder at bay.[36]

Homes and settlement sites also contained the precious food and seed stores needed to survive inevitable seasons of scarcity. The towns that the Spanish De Soto expedition encountered in the 1540s southern parts of North America contained large stores of food, kept either in the homes or in separate granaries.[37] Spanish sources mentioned mud-plastered granaries in the fields of the Lacandon Mayan highlands in Central America. Underground plastered storage chambers in the Mayan lowlands of Northern Yucatan may have served to store food or water. Mayan and Aztec leaders maintained facilities to store tribute. A single state storage center at Texcoco had the capacity to hold 10 million liters of maize.[38] Veracruz's indigenous leaders supplied the conquistador Hernán Cortés with large quantities of food for his initial march on the Aztec capital of Tenochtitlán. Central American pictograms and hieroglyphic documents also frequently refer to food storage, underscoring its importance.[39] In early colonial Mexico, maize granaries (cuexcomatl) were common in household compounds and were referenced in inheritance cases.[40] Indigenous Central Mexicans stored food in large wattle baskets; in other parts of Mexico, small log or plank granaries were common.[41]

Inca authorities maintained an empire-wide storage system. They collected food and other tribute and stored it in regional centers to sustain the court, to feed and lodge armies on the march, and to provide

FIGURE 2.1. Depiction of Inca storage facilities with an official reporting the inventories on a knot record or *quipu*. (Drawing by Felipe Guamán Poma de Ayala from *El primer nueva corónica y buen gobierno*. Courtesy, Library Services Department, American Museum of Natural History, New York [Neg. No. 321546]).

food in case of shortages and famines. They deliberately located food storage centers to exploit environmental features to optimize storage conditions. Many sites were situated in the highlands and on mountain slopes to take advantage of lower temperatures and to facilitate drainage. Sealed jars protected shelled corn and other foods, limiting fungal damage and allowing the corn to be safely stored for up to four years. At each center, rows of small round or square huts with an average capacity of 60 cubic meters housed the food jars and other products. In the 1540s, six such small storage huts contained 180,000 liters of maize, as well as potatoes and quinoa. The city of Huánuco Pampa was a major node in the Inca storage system, and 500 of its total 4,000 structures may have been storehouses. Inca state storage infrastructure contained 16,000–30,000 storehouses, with a total capacity of up to 1–2 million cubic meters.[42] When the Inca Empire expanded into modern Ecuador in the 15th century, the system of storehouses was introduced there as well.[43]

Overwhelmingly indigenous American societies stored their food reserves in their homes. In Western coastal Mexico and the Caribbean Basin, families often suspended food stores from the roof rafters.[44] In 1540s Paraguay, a conquistador observed large vessels filled with maize in a large hut.[45] Pre-Columbian villages in Oaxaca dating from 1000 BC are associated with bell-shaped, cylindrical, or bottle-shaped excavated underground storage pits for maize and other foods both within and outside the contours of residential huts. The inhabitants sealed the food stores airtight with rocks to minimize insect predation.[46] The Pueblo societies dried food supplies on their rooftops before storing them in a dedicated room.[47] After drying it, the Navajo packed unshelled corn in elk- or goat-skin leather bags in pits that were 5–6 feet deep with fire-hardened walls lined with cedar bark. The Navajo covered the storage pits with branches or rocks topped by a foot of dirt to hide their location. They located the pits in the fields or in or near the homes. Corn could be stored in this manner for up to two years. They also stored beans, squash, and melons in pits or in unused homes.[48]

Many plants used by indigenous populations were effectively maintained as environmental infrastructure. That is, rather than gifts of Nature that simply could be gathered freely and at will; the plants were cofostered by humans through planting, seeding, cultivation, management, and use that resulted in higher yields. South America is a major center for plant domestication. Manioc, potato, and sweet potato are all among the top dozen domesticated food plants today and originated there as cultivars. Peru is a domestication hotspot with 4,400 plants that people used, 1,700 that they cultivated, and 182 native domesticates of which 58 are (fruit) trees.[49] Elsewhere, indigenous Americans cultivated amaranths or pigweed and many other plants.[50] Losing access to plant environmental infrastructure as a result of displacement from the home environment, therefore, negatively impacted the availability of food (fruit, nuts) and other products (plant oils and fibers, medicine, leaves, branches, poles) and services (shade). As was the case with other environmental infrastructure, managed plants were concentrated at the sites of permanent or seasonal homes and settlements or at the locations of former settlements.

Trees and bushes were particularly important environmental infrastructure, providing not only building materials and fuel but also nuts, berries, and fruits—all high-nutrition and vitamin-rich foods that often ripened during the hungry season (before the field crops harvest) and that could easily be stored as dry season and famine foods. Many of the New World's indigenous fruit and other trees were or are cultivated or otherwise managed. Spanish conquistadors highlighted the abundance of fruit and other trees in or near indigenous villages and fields, no doubt sensitized by the importance of trees to humans and livestock in the semiarid south of Spain. In the New and Old Worlds alike, trees were a source of food to the soldiers and a source of forage to the herds of horses, mules, cattle, and pigs that accompanied the Spanish expeditions.[51]

Trees constituted long-term investments: most fruit and nut trees only start producing five to ten years after they have been seeded or planted, and require weeding, pruning, shading, fencing, and sometimes watering. Meso-America alone counted 41 cultivated and protected species of plants, mostly trees or bushes, including ramón, white and black sapote, agave, Pacapay palm, pineapple, Coyol palm, soursop, cacao, and vegetable pear.[52] The ramón or breadnut tree (*Brosimum alicastrum*) is so highly valued for its nuts that in one indigenous American language it is called the maize tree. The tree is abundant in the Maya lowlands and beyond, and it is found in especially high concentrations on old abandoned indigenous settlement sites.[53]

Fruit trees grown in Honduran home gardens included mammees, sapodillas, papaws, *jocotes* (*Spondia purpirae*), calabash tree (*Crescentra cujete*), and the ubiquitous guava, avocado, pineapple, pomegranate, and sapote.[54] Many managed fruit and nonfruit trees were located on-farm in gardens and orchards next to the homesteads, but they also occurred off-farm. Indigenous farmers grew agave in home orchards as well as in fields and stabilized terraces, intercropped it with maize, and planted it as border markers between fields and orchards. Indigenous Americans cultivated both *Nopal* (prickly pear) and *Nopal de Granas* (the host plant for the dye-producing cochineal insect). Managed tree species also included mesquite, copal, and possibly vanilla. Aztec Nahuatl language precontact vocabulary relating to trees included a set of words for seedbeds, transplanting, pruning, shading, and perhaps grafting, suggesting an extensive history of tree management and cultivation. The illustrations in the Mapa de Cuauhtlantzinco (written in Nahuatl) contains an image of what seems to be a tree with several large branches lopped off that is still growing, suggesting coppice management.[55] In the southern Valley of Mexico, indigenous Americans coppiced their ancient oak trees (*Quercus rugose*) so that they retained their vigor and supplied poles and wood fuel. The Huastec of San Luis Potosí and adjacent Veracruz actively managed tree stands. The handflower tree (*Chiranthodendron pentadactylon*) and kapok were considered sacred and were planted on the eve of contact.[56] That capulin (native cherry tree) features in indigenous American inheritance cases brought before early Spanish colonial courts in Mexico suggests that they were seen as farm improvements and property, that is, as environmental infrastructure rather than a gift of Nature.[57]

Postconquest, the range of plants used and cultivated in Mexico dramatically decreased: early colonial era chronicles listed 150 edible plants of which only 15 are eaten today and the variety in maize cultivars narrowed after 1500. Various trees cultivated by indigenous Americans in the early contact period, including Brazil nut, American oil palm, and sapodilla, re-wilded as they were no longer managed.[58] Entire stands of fruit and other trees that mark abandoned indigenous American settlement sites in the Amazon basin are thought to be semi-domesticated, semiwild, or feral. Agroforestry (i.e., the cultivation of trees and bushes) was widespread in Amazonia. Secondary forest or long-term (bush) fallows often contain high numbers of "semi-domesticated" plants, especially fruit and palm trees. Amazonia contains 138 cultivated or managed "crops," including 86 that have been identified as "incipient domesticates and semi-domesticates." The latter are overwhelmingly trees and woody vines, mostly fruit- and nut-bearing.[59] Significantly, most of the 138 crops are indicator species for dark earth patches associated with past concentrated or sustained settlement, including Brazil nut, Babassu palm, cocoa, and American oil palm.[60]

Conquistador accounts relating to the 1530s and 1540s conquest in Paraguay and the neighboring districts of Argentina and Brazil reported on the abundance of "wild" fruit trees in the region's river valleys that sustained indigenous populations and invaders alike. Although the accounts may have exaggerated the region's fertility and its wealth of fruit tree, it is notable that the occurrence of the fruit trees was usually associated with current or past human settlement.[61] Brazil's Atlantic forests and woodland savannas equally contained a large variety of trees that indigenous Americans protected, managed, and transplanted.[62] In Northern New Mexico, plants that are often associated with abandoned indigenous American settlement sites include Parry's agave (*Agave parryi*), Cholla cactus (*Opuntia imbricate*), wolfberry (*Lycium pallidum*), squawbush (*Rhus trilobata*), and sagebrush (*Artemesia tridentate*).[63]

In the Andean region's *Campina* landscapes, trees that demarcate fields and pastures are testimony to the resilience of precontact tree planting practices. Early colonial documents attested to Inca practices of distinguishing cultivated trees (*mallko*) from those that were not planted (*sacha*). Two trees that were especially important in the late Inca period were the proper Quishuar (*Buddleja incana*) and colle or puna quishuar (*Buddleja corracea*); indigenous Americans reproduced the trees through cuttings and routinely irrigated them.[64]

The high and repeated investment in the creation and maintenance of environmental infrastructure is reflected in terms of "ownership" notions. Among the Aztecs, community leaders allotted land to extended families. Sons inherited their fathers' crop fields.[65] In the Inca and post-Inca Andes region, planted trees were privately owned, at times fenced, and their ownership in some instances was accounted in knot records or *quipus*.[66] Inca farmers highly valued crop fields because they were the product of substantial investments of labor (terracing) and other resources, including llama dung, guano, ashes, and fallows, which were used to increase soil fertility. Although many highland indigenous American farmers were removed from their farms and concentrated in new towns in 16th-century colonial Spanish America, they frequently continued to cultivate their old fields, even if the fields were far away, suggesting that they saw them as critical infrastructure.[67] Moreover, fields that had been established by indigenous farmers in the 16th-century North American South were still in use in recent times, eliciting an agricultural historian to comment "[that] the Indian farmers whom De Soto discovered tending fields . . . had picked their lands well, for the Indian fields of the mid-sixteenth century have become part of the fertile [settler] farmlands."[68]

Many indigenous Americans by the 15th and 16th centuries were, therefore, not merely exploiting natural resources but (co)creating and maintaining environmental infrastructure. Moreover, the environmental infrastructure was heavily concentrated at settlements, homes, and seasonal camps because it required continuous investments to maintain and incessant vigilance to protect, and livelihoods, lives, and ways of life depended on it. Dwellings sheltered people, seeds, tools, and food stores. Sources of water were close to the settlements, as was hydraulic infrastructure. Indigenous farmers produced dark earths at and around settlements and homes. Destroying settlements and displacing people from their homes therefore left them deprived of the environmental infrastructure that sustained them, making them highly vulnerable to human and nonhuman invaders and pests.

War, Displacement, and Environmental Infrastructure

The conflict and population displacement that tore people from their environmental infrastructure were not post-1492 phenomena. The hundreds of abandoned hilltop forts that marked the Andean highlands in the pre-Inca period (1000–1450 CE) demonstrate that the era was one of war and insecurity, causing the inhabitants to abandon fertile valleys and thousands of hectares of terraced fields to seek sanctuary on the barren hilltops. Tuberous crops (which could be dried and stored) and pastoralism with llama and alpacas that provided meat, dung, and wool in the highland grasslands became the main products for the hilltop villagers, supplanting the irrigated crops from the valley floors. The inhabitants invested considerable labor and other resources in constructing and maintaining the fortifications even as access to key resources (fertile land, water) deteriorated.[69]

During the Spanish invasion, destroying or capturing environmental infrastructure and displacing the indigenous Americans from it dramatically undermined the means and the will to resist European conquest. European invaders in the Americas lived off the "land," that is, indigenous environmental infrastructure, by pillaging or taxing indigenous food stores. Bereft of their homes and sources of sustenance, indigenous Americans on the run were highly vulnerable to predation by humans and nonhumans, including microbes that spread such new diseases as smallpox. Moreover, appropriating or plundering the indigenous Americans' environmental infrastructure supplied the invaders with the resources to sustain the war until the indigenous populations surrendered, fled, or succumbed.

War in the Caribbean

The invasion of the Caribbean was marked by intense violence. When Columbus landed, most of the indigenous inhabitants of the Caribbean islands practiced mound agriculture, with manioc and sweet potato or arrowroot as the main crops grown in fields near their villages. The manioc staple was drought resistant. Moreover, the harvest could be staggered (i.e., it could be left in the mound), and the crop could be easily preserved in the form of baked cassava loaves. Manioc also yielded a high caloric value for the labor investment of growing it, although that labor savings was largely offset by the elaborate processing that was required to remove the cyanic acid it contained. In addition to the *conuco*

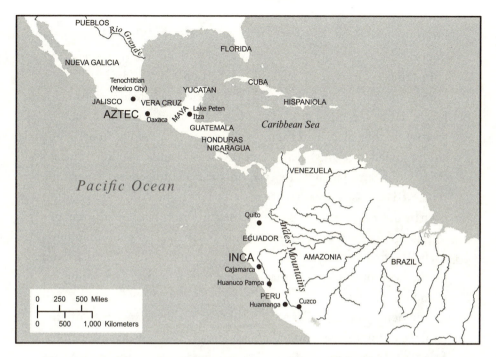

MAP 2.1. Central and South America in the early 16th century.

fields, indigenous Caribbeans maintained gardens and orchards at their homes that contained guava and pineapple. The Arawak-speaking communities also hunted, fished, and gathered. They used a range of palm trees, including the *Mauritia flexuosa* or *Aguaje* (known to the Spanish as the tree-of-life) that served as a source of "emergency food." On the eve of contact, the indigenous Caribbeans enjoyed a balanced diet and produced food surpluses. Spanish sources from the early contact era report no food or nutritional shortages, and at the time, Hispaniola contained many villages with populations of 1,000–2,000 people residing in more than 50 timber-walled homes built around a central square.[70]

Estimates of the early contact period indigenous population of Hispaniola (Haiti and the Dominican Republic) range from as low as 100,000 to as high as 7–8 million people. Spanish census figures date from after the virtual extermination of the indigenous populations that accompanied and resulted from the violent 1492–96 conquest of the

island. The Spanish enslaved most of the Caribbean Islanders who survived the onslaught. Many fled their villages and fields, and food production declined rapidly, causing hunger and famine. By force of circumstances, survivors increasingly relied on hunting and gathering.
During the early 1500s, forced cultivations (cassava to feed the Spanish),
forced labor (to mine gold), and forced removals (to new Spanish
towns) further displaced the population of Hispaniola. Acute labor
shortages led to Spanish slave raids on other islands, including Puerto
Rico, Cuba, and Jamaica. By 1518, only 11,000 indigenous Americans
remained on Hispaniola, a mere 10 percent of its precontact population
even by the lowest estimates. In 1518, the colonizers resettled the remaining indigenous Americans in small towns with 400–500 inhabitants
each. The first smallpox epidemic recorded in the New World arrived
on the heels of this forced villagization project, further decimating the
island's population.[71]

The demographic collapse radically changed the landscape of Hispaniola. Many villages and their fields already had been abandoned before the 1518 smallpox epidemic. Short of indigenous labor, many Spanish settlers left to try their luck on other islands. With far fewer people
and the remaining indigenous Americans unable to invest in maintaining and cultivating their fields because of the heavy colonial labor and
tribute demands, weeds and bushes invaded more and more fields.
Guava, shrub acacias, sage, and other indigenous plants overran Hispaniola and other islands, joined by free-ranging or semiferal Spanish
livestock that spread Old World seeds. By the 1570s, the indigenous
populations on most of the Caribbean islands had been destroyed and
their former villages, fields, and clearings had been retaken by the forest.
On Hispaniola, some of the former indigenous American fields had
been diverted to sugar cane plantings.[72]

Mainland Central America

The conquest of the mainland started in the 1520s when Spanish armies,
reinforced by local allies, invaded the Aztec and the Inca Empires. Local
indigenous leaders supplied large quantities of provisions thereby

facilitating Hernán Cortés's march on the Aztec capital of Tenochtitlán.[73] This was not unusual. Pre-Columbian armies in Central America
had also lived off the land. During campaigns, towns in subject and allied territories supplied passing Aztec armies with food and other supplies. Oaxaca towns in the 1520s and 1530s provided supplies, warriors,
and porters to the Spanish forces marching southward.[74] The protracted
war against the Aztecs consisted mainly of confrontations between
armies on battlefields, sieges, and raids, culminating in the long siege of
Tenochtitlán in 1521. More than weapon technology and smallpox, the
aid by indigenous American allies was decisive in the success of the
conquistadors in the Valley of Mexico and throughout Mesoamerica.
The Spanish armies of conquest had Spanish soldiers in the hundreds,
but its allied indigenous warriors, porters, servants, and slaves numbered in the thousands and even tens of thousands. Cortés's consort
Maria, or Malintzin, was not only the conquistador's interpreter and
guide but also a key advisor: she made him aware of the divisions in the
Aztec empire and brokered his alliances with the Totonacs and the
Tlaxcalans.[75] The army marching on the Aztec capital in 1521 consisted
of 800 Spanish soldiers and 200,000–300,000 indigenous American allies, including a sizable number from the Valley of Mexico. Many in the
army of Cortés's Tezcuco ally Ixtlixochitl had close relatives among the
besieged in the Aztec capital. The tens of thousands of conscripted indigenous American laborers build siege works and dismantled
defenses.[76]

Before commencing the siege of Tenochtitlán, Cortés and his indigenous allies occupied the towns surrounding the capital, capturing food
supplies and depriving the Aztecs of the same as well as denying them
reinforcements. Meeting fierce resistance in the Valley of Mexico in
April and May 1521, they plundered and burned several towns, including
Tepotzlan, Tlacopan, and Xochimilco. They narrowly escaped disaster
when the inhabitants of Ixtlapalapan coaxed the Spanish army into their
polder town and cut the dikes, flooding its streets. In May 1521, Cortés
and his Spanish and indigenous American host destroyed the capital's
aqueduct, took control over the causeways leading to the island capital,
and launched ships onto the lake surrounding the city to prevent any

food, supplies, and reinforcements from reaching the besieged—the very same tactics the Spanish deployed against the Dutch rebel towns of Haarlem and Leiden five decades later. The violence, dislocation, and continued mobilization of the region's indigenous farmers as soldiers and porters in the opposing armies prevented crop cultivation and harvest. The fighting took place in the middle of the agricultural season and the previous planting season had been equally affected by the violence between the Spanish and their allies as well as forces loyal to the Aztecs. The besiegers destroyed the city's irrigated gardens, and systematically tore down buildings and burned down houses as they fought their way deeper into the city, using the debris to fill the canals. Famine and epidemic disease caused the resistance to crumble. In August 1521, Aztec emperor Cuauhtémoc surrendered. Ordered to leave the city, the survivors filed past the Spanish and their allies, who robbed them of their possessions and took the strong young men and beautiful women as slaves.[77]

After the fall of the Aztec capital, indigenous American allies not only supplied the backbone of the fighting forces in the conquest of central America but also served as scouts and foragers, and exacted food and supplies by force or the threat of force. Sacking, plundering, and burning towns that resisted demands for supplies, continued to fight, or whose population fled into the mountains was common practice in Mesoamerica in the 15th and 16th centuries, even before the arrival of the Spanish invaders. After the siege of Tenochtitlán, the Spanish, their allies, and their opponents sacked towns and cities. In 1522, rebels in Totopec fighting against Cortés's ally Ixtlixochitl sacked 20 towns in his domain, and the Spanish and their allies in turn went on a killing and plundering spree in the rebellious Pánuco province, burning the houses and executing any captured lords and captains. Pillaging served to intimidate surrounding towns into submitting to the conquerors without resistance, a tactic that was often successful. Plunder also compensated soldiers for their service: indigenous American soldiers fought for loot, status, land, lordships, and captives. Before the Spanish defeat of the Aztec empire, indigenous American allies mainly used the Spanish to end Aztec overrule. After the fall of Tenochtitlán and the capture of the emperor, Spanish-allied warriors were often motivated by the prospect of lordships and land grants or by revenge.[78]

Spanish expeditions during the 1530s and early 1540s into Nueva Galicia, northwest of Tenochtitlán, relied heavily on indigenous American allies and porters who foraged and plundered to supply the expeditions with food, water, and other resources, and systematically burned all towns that did not immediately submit. The atrocities in the conquest and pacification of Nueva Galicia were yet another inspiration to De Las Casas in formulating his critique of the Spanish conquest. Large-scale resistance only subsided after the viceroy of Mexico, Antonio Mendoza, marched a massive army, including 30,000 indigenous allies, into the region, burned down several settlements, and slaughtered or enslaved the rebels in the early 1540s. To force recalcitrant opponents into submission, Mendoza's indigenous allies systematically uprooted *magueys* in the fields, cut the mesquite trees, and threatened to destroy the nopal cacti. Epidemics followed hot on the heels of Mendoza's campaign. By the 1550s, the populations of many pueblos had been greatly reduced through death and flight; some fertile valleys lay entirely abandoned. Indigenous allies, both recruited locally and in central Mexico served as local militias to maintain colonial order and suppress rebellions, receiving political and economic privileges in return, including the reduction of tributes.[79]

Epidemic disease accounted for the steep decline in the population of the Oaxaca Sierra of Mexico further south. Between 1548 and 1622, the population dropped from 95,000 to 20,000 inhabitants. The context of war, displacement, and ruthless exploitation is telling. The steepest population decline, which occurred between 1520 when the population was estimated at 346,000 people and 1548 when it had been reduced to 90,000, coincided with the years of conquest.[80] Whereas most of Oaxaca fell quickly to Spanish conquerors in 1521, the conquest of the northern Sierra in 1529–31 was so brutal that the higher Spanish authorities excommunicated one of the Spanish commanders involved and severely reprimanded another. The commanders attacked indigenous American towns without provocation and killed or enslaved hundreds. Again, indigenous allies from central Mexico were the main component of the conquest army. A fair number settled on the Oaxaca Sierra and constituted the backbone of the militias that maintained Spanish rule thereafter. Rewarded with land grants and exemptions from tribute payments, they shared responsibility for the environcidal violence their Spanish commanders meted out. Higher-level Spanish officials routinely were granted exemptions from a formal ban on using indigenous Americans as porters because horses and mules could not be used as pack animals on the steep slopes of the highlands. The region was remote from the major centers of administration, and lawlessness and violence prevailed. Spanish officials received low salaries, and settlers and local officials abused the indigenous population. The settlers in the single Spanish outpost in the Oaxaca Sierra were entirely dependent on their indigenous subjects for their subsistence and on their indigenous allies to enforce their rule, to collect exactions, and to mete out punishment.[81]

Similarly, the 1520s–40s conquest of Yucatan in southern Mexico heavily relied on indigenous allied fighters, porters, and slaves. The porters carried supplies to sustain the expeditions, and the allied warriors foraged for food and water as Maya villagers who fled before the advancing conquistadors hid their food stores and water supplies. Francisco de Montejo's brutal conquest of Yucatan and his exploitation and enslavement of its populations was one of inspirations for Bartolomé de las Casas's critique of the Spanish conquest. After the completion of the conquest and throughout the early colonial period, the Spanish settler population in Yucatan sustained themselves by exacting food and labor from the local populations, causing many of the exploited indigenous Americans to flee into the interior.[82] The Itza kingdom in the lowland tropical forest around remote Petén Itzá Lake in modern northern Guatemala was a haven for refugees that the Spanish only brought under their control in the early 1700s. The kingdom's Kowojs neighbors had originally moved to the area from Yucatan during the 1530s Spanish invasion.[83]

The Spanish conquest of the Cuchumatán Highlands in modern western Guatemala in the 1520s was equally violent. Disease and demographic decline followed on the heels of conquest. Several illnesses struck the Guatemalan highlands in 1520, four years before the arrival of Pedro de Alvarado's invasion force, including smallpox and plague, or typhus, killing up to one-third of the population. Pedro de Alvarado relied heavily on indigenous allied soldiers and porters from central Mexico, many forced, some attracted by the prospect of land and labor grants. A number of the indigenous central Mexican conquerors remained as colonists, founding Ciudad Vieja. More epidemics followed the conquest: measles struck in 1532–34 in the direct aftermath of the conquest, and plague accompanied further displacement in the 1540s.[84]

After wreaking havoc in Guatemala, Pedro de Alvarado recruited local soldiers and porters then invaded modern-day Honduras. Although his men responded with great brutality to the fierce resistance they encountered, they failed to bring western and central Honduras under Spanish control until 1539, and resistance in eastern Honduras continued throughout the colonial period, decimating the population. Pedro de Alvarado's campaign was only one of many that eventually led to the conquest of the region. In all, the conquest may have cost the lives of 30,000–50,000 people. Resistance and revolts were excuses for slave raids, and recalcitrant eastern Honduras became a main source for slaves.[85]

The preconquest 1520 smallpox epidemic that originated in Central Mexico affected Honduras as did the early 1530s smallpox epidemics that struck Guatemala and Nicaragua. The indigenous populations not only suffered greatly from exotic diseases but also from such commonly occurring intestinal diseases as typhoid, amoebic dysentery, and hookworm. To consolidate their control, the conquerors founded towns and missions where they concentrated the populations, exposing the indigenous Americans to abuse and disease. Here, too, forced recruitment of indigenous Americans as porters for further campaigns and enslavement were major factors in the demographic decline. In 1527, a Spanish expedition to Nicaragua forcibly recruited 4,000 men as porters; only 6 men returned.[86]

The Inca Empire and Mainland South America

The smallpox epidemic that brought the Aztec empire to its knees and spread through the Central American isthmus, also, ravaged the Inca Empire in 1524–27 while its armies fought a war of conquest in Ecuador.

Inca massacres, scorched earth, and large-scale population displacement may have killed more than 10 percent of Ecuador's population during the conquest. Smallpox claimed the life of Inca Emperor Huanya Capac as he returned home from the campaign. His death triggered a protracted succession war during the 1520s and 1530s, facilitating the Spanish conquest and another deadly epidemic in 1530–31.[87]

The succession war provided Francisco Pizarro with the opportunity to establish bases in coastal northern Peru and recruit local indigenous allies. Sustaining Pizarro's army with provisions and accommodation for months, however, strained the relationship with his allies. Explained a chronicler: "Because in war it is difficult to keep soldiers well disciplined certain offences were committed which Pizarro did not punish." No doubt eager to have their demanding guests move on, his Tumbez allies showed Pizarro the Inca highway leading south and provided him with guides and porters. En route, the small Spanish army exacted or pillaged local towns and villages for food: "It was said [among the indigenous Americans] that the bearded strangers [the Spanish invaders] did not plant, but went from place to place eating and stealing whatever they found." One of the contenders for the Inca imperial throne, Atahualpa, marched to Cajamarca in the north to forestall the raising of forces by his opponent, Huascar, and to prevent the later from seeking an alliance with the Spanish invaders. En route, Atahualpa's men pillaged regions loyal to his opponent. After his main army defeated Huascar, Atahualpa invited Pizarro to meet him in Cajamarca in November 1532. When Pizarro's men descended into the Cajamarca valley, they were stunned that it had not been devastated by the presence of the Inca army's large encampment. Atahualpa housed the Spaniards in the imperial residence of Cajamarca, a lodging and food depot complex. But, when the new Inca emperor visited Pizarro's lodgings, the Spanish treacherously captured him after massacring his entourage.[88]

Pizarro used the Inca emperor as a hostage to exact a huge ransom and gain nominal control over the empire. After killing Atahualpa in August 1533, Pizarro marched along the main inland Inca highway (in the highlands) southward with many conscripted indigenous porters, requisitioning or pillaging supplies as he advanced, and fighting off several attacks. The invaders mainly relied on the Inca imperial lodgings and storage complexes that lined the highway at intervals. Although Inca resisters attempted to burn the storage complex in the Jauja Valley to starve the Spaniards, the invaders salvaged 100,000 fanegas of maize and a large quantity of fine stitched cloth. Pizarro arrived in Cuzco in November 1533. His advance guard found the city practically abandoned, and the main temple and other buildings on fire. The Spaniards managed to douse most of the fires only to pillage the city for gold and silver.[89]

The Spanish capture of the Inca capital did not end the war. The new emperor, Manco Inca, besieged Spanish-held Cuzco. Only with the arrival of reinforcements that included Nahua and Maya warriors and servants from Mesoamerica was the siege broken.[90] To suppress the Manco Inca-led revolt in Callejou de Huaylas in 1539, Spanish forces sacked houses, plundered fields, and massacred men, women, and children.[91] Manco Inca's men raided the Huamanga region that neighbored their mountain stronghold. The Huamanga, in turn, pillaged the local imperial state storehouses.[92] During the Spanish invasion, at several occasions Inca resisters used scorched earth tactics against the Spanish, destroying or hiding their own stores of food (including livestock) and burning bridges as well as dwellings that the Spaniards could use as shelter.[93]

Veteran conquistadors looking for more spoils and newly arrived soldiers eager for a share were difficult to control even when and where the crown's officials sought to enforce the ordinances meant to limit Spanish soldiers' destructive pillaging and killing. In 1549, the governor of Quito issued orders to prohibit robbing or severely punishing indigenous Americans and land seizures. He got rid of the worst offenders by organizing an expedition to conquer new lands, of which Pedro de Ciezo de León was a participant. The expedition lived off the land, robbed and pillaged, recruited porters, and employed several thousand indigenous American allies.[94]

But the destruction and pillaging were not caused only by the actions of undisciplined and greedy individual soldiers. Commanders abetted pillaging to keep their soldiers' loyalty and, moreover, they consciously and systematically used the looting and burning of villages to terrorize communities into submission and to coerce them into suppling their forces with food, supplies, and services (including shelter). Continued resistance and noncompliance with Spanish demands led to the sacking and burning of villages. These same practices were used by the Spanish commanders and their rebel opponents three decades later in the Low Countries and were generally accepted under the rules of war. The rules of war had been entirely ignored during the initial conquest and the subsequent civil wars because the Spanish invaders considered the indigenous Americans to be hostile devil worshippers and cannibals. The New Laws of Habsburg Emperor Charles V, however, redefined the indigenous Americans as Spanish subjects, making them subject to the rules of war—thence the critique against unnecessary violence by such conquistadors and authors as Cieza de León and Vargas. A full member of the 1549 Robledo expedition (sharing in the loot and for which Robledo awarded him with an *encomienda* and other spoils of war), Cieza de León described it as a model and legitimate war of conquest, largely free of random violence. Indigenous Americans who submitted peacefully to the conquerors and who heeded their demands for war booty, taxes, and labor were treated as any other subjects of the crown, but resistance and any form of noncooperation unleashed the dogs of war. In 1549, the population of the unconquered province of Carrapa agreed "in order to escape being wounded by swords or torn to pieces by dogs, to admit them [Captain Jorge Robledo's expedition] to their territory and supply them with provisions." In the province of Picara, the inhabitants fled and hid, and only the threat that "he [Captain Robledo] would wage war with ruthless cruelty" made its leaders pay homage to the invaders. When the inhabitants of the adjacent province of Pozo refused to surrender and took a stand on a hill, the Spaniards and their indigenous allies killed all the men and many women and children, taking any survivors captive.[95]

Open warfare between different Spanish armies over the division of the spoils intensified and prolonged the violence, and displacement and constituted "a great pestilence, both to the Indians and to their flocks."[96] During the civil wars, all factions ruthlessly exploited indigenous

Americans as guides, scouts, spies, servants, slaves, concubines, porters, and soldiers. Francisco Pizarro's nemesis and one-time partner Diego de Almagro deployed 6,000 Inca warriors led by Inca Paulo, a brother of the rebel Manco Inca.[97] During the second half of the 1530s and 1540s, opposing Spanish armies marched up and down Peru, exacting food, pressing indigenous men and women into porter service and slavery, slaughtering and capturing llamas, pillaging gold and silver, and burning temples, homes, and villages. The armies were larger than Pizarro's initial invasion force, comprising 700 Spanish soldiers each, and "in those days the Indians suffered great oppression so that many died; for the soldiers were numerous and they had no mercy." After Francisco Pizarro's forces in 1538 defeated and killed Diego de Almagro, the victors went on a raping and plundering spree first in Cuzco and next in the provinces, torturing indigenous Americans who hid their flocks of llamas. Despite pleas by indigenous leaders to stop the marauding, Pizarro did not intervene. Almagro's supporters, robbed of their spoils of conquest after their defeat, struck back in 1541, murdered Governor Pizarro, and briefly took control of part of Peru. Loyalist troops defeated the rebels in 1542, but factional violence continued. Soldiers proved especially difficult to control during the Spanish infighting, because if captains tried to maintain discipline, their men would desert to the opposition. As a result, soldiers could rob and pillage practically unhindered.[98] Next to killing and flight, porter recruitment was an important factor in population decline. Thousands of men were press-ganged as porters for Spanish war bands within and beyond the Inca territories, and few of the porters ever returned.[99]

Cieza de León, who traveled through the vice royalty of Peru during the late 1540s, noted that the coastal valleys along the Inca highways were severely depopulated. He observed abandoned and overgrown fields and ruined imperial lodgings and storage facilities along the highways, which had constituted the favored march routes for the Spanish armies. He stressed that crop and tree cultivation in the arid coastal valleys of Peru were entirely dependent on local irrigation systems, which harvested water that rivers and streams brought from the interior highlands. His descriptions of irrigated valley fields overgrown by thickets indicate bush encroachment and recent decline or collapse of irrigation infrastructure management, measured in decades at most rather than centuries, suggesting that the abandonment is associated with contact and the Spanish invasion, and not a general pre-Columbian phenomenon.[100]

Throughout the Andes region, during the conquest era, Spanish logistics relied heavily on the regional Inca state storage infrastructure that continued to function in some places into the 1550s and even 1560s. The inhabitants of Peru's Xauxa Valley replenished the state storage facilities for 20 years after the conquest to keep the Spanish from raiding their villages. During the early 1540s, Governor Vaca de Castro (the successor of the murdered Francisco Pizarro) ordered the local indigenous leaders to maintain the imperial lodgings and supply storage facilities along the highways as had been the custom under the Incas. From the mid-1540s, however, most storehouses remained empty, and by the late 1540s, they were abandoned and in ruins. Often the infrastructure was maintained by indigenous settlers from elsewhere in the Inca empire who lived at the storage complex.[101] As the state storage system collapsed, Spanish armies, officials, and settlers became entirely dependent on indigenous American village food stores and standing crops.

Massive depopulation marked the first decades of Spanish conquest. Violence and disease killed, while birth rates declined. With the exception of the 1524–28 smallpox epidemic preceding Pizarro's invasion and the 1531–33 epidemic that partly preceded and partly accompanied it, the records are silent on any further major epidemics until the 1540s.[102] Devastating outbreaks of disease occurred in the late 1540s, including possibly typhus or plague and a double whammy of an epidemic and an epizootic that killed large numbers of llamas and alpacas (in 1549).[103] During the rebellion of Gonzalo Pizarro in 1547 "a great pestilence spread over the whole kingdom of Peru, which . . . pervaded the whole country. People without number died. The illness consisted of a headache accompanied by raging fever, and presently the pain passed from the head to the left ear, when it became so great that the patient did not last more than two or three days." It killed most of the afflicted and instilled great terror.[104]

In the Peru's early 1530s Colca Valley, a deadly mix of smallpox and measles accompanied the Spanish invasion. Late 1540s epidemics spared neither indigenous Americans nor Spanish settlers. The second half of the 1550s witnessed further epidemics. Up to half of the Colca Valley population may have succumbed to disease during the first three decades of contact. Peru's Huamanga highlands suffered less from the epidemics because many of its inhabitants lived in isolated herding communities in the mountains; roughly 20 percent of the population succumbed to disease. But labor exactions increased in Huamanga with the opening of silver and gold mines in the 1540s–60s.[105] Huamanga had a population of 200,000 early during the Spanish occupation, but only counted 120,000 souls in 1570.[106] Massive exactions and scorched earth marked the 1572 campaign against the rebel exile Inca state of Vilcabamba. The Spanish not only commandeered a large force of indigenous auxiliaries and llamas to carry supplies into the rebel territory but also devoured the large food stores they captured in rebel forts. The population of Vilcabamba's capital fled as the Spanish approached, and the city fell without a fight. Before they fled into the forests, however, the refugees burned all the food supplies they were forced to leave behind.[107]

The pattern of environcidal conquests was similar beyond the territories of the Inca empire and its immediate neighbors. The 1535–50s Spanish invasion of the Paraná River basin of northern Argentina, Paraguay, and southern Brazil heavily relied on indigenous allies: typically, several thousand indigenous warriors supported several hundred Spaniards. The invaders were entirely dependent on food and supplies extorted from indigenous American villages and motivated by stories about an El Dorado ruled by the Amazons, a tribe of female warriors, and the prospect of plunder and captives. Without indigenous allies or faced with opponents who burned their own fields and villages, hid their provisions, and fled into the interior, the conquistadors succumbed to famine, disease, and ambushes. After the initial leader of the expedition, which included a contingent of German and Flemish participants, was killed in the fighting, Alvar Nunez Cabeza de Vaca arrived as the new governor of the region in 1540. Cabeza de

Vaca's account is heavily colored by his attempt to exonerate himself after his own officers sent him back to Spain in chains. In doing so he tried to ride the wave of the criticism De Las Casas shared with Charles V and that subsequently led to the 1542 New Laws abolishing the *encomienda* system and prohibiting the enslavement of the indigenous Americans. Cabeza de Vaca's *Commentaries*, first published in 1555, portrayed the author as a defender of the indigenous American subjects of Spain in accordance with the requirements of the New Laws. He emphasized that he had carefully paid for all the provisions he requisitioned during his long overland voyage from the mouth of the River Plata to Asunción. He had forbidden his soldiers and his indigenous allies from entering the villages and homes of subject communities and stealing their possessions. He had used his own wealth to pay for the expedition's weapons, provisions, and other equipment, and he had always sought to compel indigenous Americans to subject themselves to the crown and Christianity through peaceful means. Yet, the details presented in his *Commentaries* rehearsed the same familiar practices that marked the Spanish conquest elsewhere. Mentions of payment for provisions soon disappear; indigenous Americans had to supply food, provisions, warriors, porters, scouts, and translators; and soldiers' rewards consisted of booty and captives. Any resistance by allies or enemies resulted in the massacre and enslavement of villagers and the burning of homes and fields. Cabeza de Vaca suggests he freed indigenous American men and women that his soldiers had illegitimately enslaved, yet by his own account, his own officers bribed his men to mutiny by offering to give them Cabeza de Vaca's "Indian girls," furniture, and other property.[108]

Bernardo de Vargas Machuca, who served as a soldier and official in the Spanish Americas in the late 1500s and early 1600s, argued that the brutal warfare De Las Casas condemned was justified to punish indigenous Americans who committed cruelties when they resisted Spanish rule, or in expeditions in unconquered territories, that is, against rebels and in hostile territory. In friendly territory that was subject to the crown of Spain, Vargas stressed armies should march without causing harm, in contrast to what he acknowledged as usually occurs, taking the son, the wife, or the daughter, and taking from the neighbor the services most freely given, such as use of acculturated [ladino] Indian servant girls and boys, taking horse or mule from their owners along the road or from the field, and causing harm in the farmhouses where they eat, raping and committing many other offenses, disrupting everything, bringing upon themselves a million curses. . . . And clearly the commander neither desires nor gives permission for this; however, the bad . . . soldiers commit these acts with no fear of God or justice, confident that they are soldiers and that they go to serve the king. Shame upon those whose lack of consideration causes them to commit such unmerited acts, lacking honor and not considering the risk they run, so soullessly they throw themselves into committing robbery, rape, and abuse.

Nonetheless, Vargas advised strongly against sanctioning the soldiers who committed such heinous acts "for if he [the commander] should wish to settle these outrages by punishment before they set forth, he will be left with few soldiers." Instead, to prevent marauding in friendly territory, the commander of the expedition should establish a well-supplied assembly camp in the remotest parts of the friendly territory, warn the soldiers not to harm anyone, have them travel only in small groups, and only if supervised by an officer. Any damages committed by the soldiers should be reimbursed by the commander.[109]

Spanish Conquests and Expeditions in North America

The 1539–42 De Soto expedition that snaked through much of the present-day southern US on a 4000-mile quest for El Dorado sustained itself through the capture and plunder of indigenous American food supplies and the use of indigenous villages and towns as winter quarters and camps. In classic scorched earth fashion, De Soto's men often destroyed anything they could not use, carry, or control. In most cases, when the Spanish approached, the inhabitants hastily abandoned their towns. When the De Soto expedition backtracked, it directly and physically experienced the impact of its own scorched earth practices: returning to the Mississippi River Valley after the death of their leader, they found little food or shelter in the areas to which they previously had laid waste. The indigenous Americans who had survived the earlier encounter with the expedition hid whatever food they had left. Only a few indigenous towns had been rebuilt and contained substantial supplies. In other areas, the indigenous Americans had not even planted their fields for fear of a Spanish return. What saved the expedition from oblivion was the well-stocked indigenous town of Aminoya, where the Spanish found 9,000 bushels of stored maize as well as dried fruits and nuts. The expedition used the town as its quarters during the winter of 1542–43 and survived on the food stores. Throughout the winter, starving indigenous Americans begged the Spanish for food. Despite being sheltered against the cold and well-fed, the Spanish nonetheless were struck by a disease that caused high losses.[110]

Yet, the information provided by indigenous guides about unscathed Aminoya was key to the De Soto expedition's survival, as were the hundreds of porters and slaves accompanying the De Soto expedition. The Spanish forced their slaves to kill their neighbors to make sure that they could never return to their homes, a practice widely used during the late 20th-century civil wars in Liberia and Sierra Leone to assure the loyalty of child soldiers.[111] At times, indigenous Americans guided the expedition to their enemies, using the Spaniards to settle scores. The role of guides and porters to the De Soto expedition is illustrative of a much wider dependence of Spanish conquistadors on indigenous American guides, interpreters, porters, auxiliaries, and allies throughout the Americas during and after the conquest, culminating in the key role of indigenous leaders in the colonial administration.[112] The involvement highlights that indigenous Americans were not only victims but also historical actors and sometimes even (co)perpetrators in mass violence.

Archaeological evidence supports that the impact of the De Soto expedition was disastrous: between 1550 and 1650 the southern chiefdoms experienced sharply declining populations. Entire regions were abandoned. The level of ritual and artistic elaboration decreased, and the construction and maintenance of platform mounds ceased by the end of the 16th century. In 1559, when the conquistador Tristan de Luna sent scouts to an indigenous American town close to Old Mabila, "the people complained that they once had been great, but they had suffered terribly from Spaniards who had been there years before Luna arrived." In 1567, when Juan Pardo's expedition reached Satapo on the Tennessee River, the indigenous American inhabitants told him that a Spaniard had been there earlier and had killed many.[113] The Little Egypt archaeological site in Northwest Georgia is likely the location of the capital of the indigenous Coosa kingdom that the De Soto expedition descended upon in the summer of 1540. The kingdom collapsed in the early 1600s, and its inhabitants migrated to new sites in Alabama.[114] Cherokee groups later reoccupied the site, which was known as Coosawattee Old Town. In 1830 it was taken over by white settlers.[115] Significantly, while, the inhabitants abandoned their towns and mounds in the southern part of North America in the 16th century, by the 18th century, new societies had emerged with new towns that were based on a system of agriculture that had the same staple crops, tree crops, and food storages as those that had been described two centuries earlier by the Spanish chroniclers.[116] This outcome highlights both the destructive impact of war and victimhood, and the societal and environmental resilience and agency of indigenous Americans.

While much of the North American South seems to have made a remarkable recovery between the 16th and 18th centuries, the situation in Florida, which sustained continuous colonization attempts by the Spanish, was different. Human remains in the Spanish colony of La Florida demonstrate that the impact of Spanish colonization on diets and livelihoods was dramatic. Postcontact, the share of marine foods declined, and mission populations shifted to a heavily maize-based and nutritionally poor diet. Early mission populations in modern-day Georgia show increased bone strength and a decline in differentiation in bone strength between men and women, suggesting a heavier manual workload, with both men and women involved in agriculture. Dental caries and declining health accompanied the introduction of maize in the region around 1000 AD, but overall health declined further following contact in the late 16th century. Late mission populations in Georgia and Florida display a large increase in tooth enamel defects, indicating deteriorating health. Nutritional stress affected infants after weaning, and the biggest killer was likely diarrheal disease rather than such diseases as smallpox. No comparable evidence for agricultural intensification exists for upland Georgia, where Spanish colonization did not occur. Spanish masters demanded that their indigenous subjects produce maize to feed themselves and to pay tribute. In addition, increased Spanish labor demands and restrictions on indigenous mobility forced people to rely increasingly on maize in their diets. Thus, diets during the contact period in the Spanish territories further undermined indigenous health. The combination of a heavier workload and a less nutritionally balanced diet resulted in Floridian mission populations becoming increasingly vulnerable to old and new pathogens.[117]

In 1540 Francisco Vásquez de Coronado encountered over five score villages along the Rio Grande River and six settlements along the Zuni River. The Zuni villages were well-stocked with water preserved in cisterns and maize stored in pits. The Spanish chose one of the pueblos along the Rio Grande as their winter quarters and forced the other villages to supply them with food throughout the winter. When the other pueblos refused to comply, Spanish soldiers destroyed a couple of villages and laid waste to numerous crop fields to set an example. The Spanish force of 500–600 men remained in the region for two years, living entirely on the food extorted from the villagers. In desperate attempts to prevent destructive raids on villages and crop fields, indigenous Americans invariably provided large offerings of food to subsequent expeditions that passed through the area. Spanish reports in the 1580s and 1590s described irrigated and dryland crops and canopy style huts in remote fields that provided shade and shelter, marveling at the large quantities and the variety of food stored at the villages. The villagers stored corn for up to two or three years and kept stores of beans, herbs, chilies, and squash. The violent Spanish exactions triggered food shortages among the indigenous populations and caused flight into the mountains. Franciscan friars complained that the Spanish soldiers robbed the indigenous communities of all their food supplies, exposing them to hunger and feeding resistance. The friars also reported an incident that involved the mass killing of 800 indigenous Americans and the destruction of three entire villages. By 1601, many pueblos lay deserted, as did many Spanish settler farms. Spanish livestock owners literally had a field day: their animals freely pastured in indigenous American crop fields, damaging irrigation canals in the process. One soldier drove his herd intentionally into the cotton fields of indigenous owners adjoining his land and brazenly built his corrals and barns in the middle of the cotton crop.[118] The archaeological record shows that the Pueblo population's nutritional health deteriorated rapidly during the 17th century, increasing susceptibility to such diseases as tuberculosis.[119] The region counted 110–150 pueblos in 1539, 130,000 people in 61 pueblos in 1581, but only 17,000 inhabitants residing in over 46 pueblos in the 1680s.[120]

Environcide and the Black Legend

Contemporary sources identify the joint impact of conquest, disease, and the ruthless exploitation by the Spanish in the 16th century as the main causes of a demographic collapse. Qualitative sources and quantitative data support such a conclusion, although the extent of the collapse is in dispute because of disagreements about the size of the preconquest indigenous populations. Putting numbers on the demographic collapse is a challenge because Spanish officials gathered census data on the eve of the massive mid-to-late 16th-century resettlement projects, thus leaving out the population changes caused by the actual conquest, the first epidemics, and large-scale flight.[121]

Nevertheless, while the Black Legend may have been Protestant propaganda, it was not a myth. The Spanish waged environcidal and total war in the New World and the Old, targeting their opponents' lives and livelihoods. Aided by indigenous American guides, forcibly conscripted porters, auxiliaries, and allies, the Spanish soldiers massacred those who resisted, enslaved many of those who survived, and pillaged and burned indigenous towns, villages, food stores, crops, and livestock. In the process, they damaged and destroyed environmental infrastructure or displaced indigenous communities from it, exposing the survivors to the elements, hunger, and deadly old and new diseases, causing a demographic collapse. Spanish invaders literally lived off the land during the prolonged period of war that included the conquest, civil wars among the invaders, rebellions, and pacification campaigns that lasted well into the 1550s. Effectively, the Spanish maintained a military occupation in what they treated as hostile territory, extorting war taxes and tributes, provisions, labor, and services, largely ignoring the New Laws that stressed that indigenous Americans were subjects of the crown and therefore protected against random violence, exactions, and pillaging by military commanders and their soldiers. One illustration of Spanish conquerors' total dependence on indigenous Americans' environmental infrastructure is that although contemporary Spanish authors hailed wheat as a super food and expressed their discomfort with indigenous foods, indigenous American maize quickly became the Spanish settlers' and soldiers' staple food and maize stalks their livestock's main fodder. In brief, the Spanish conquest during the first half of the 16th century was entirely dependent on the direct or indirect exploitation of indigenous populations and their environmental infrastructure.[122]

3

Environcide in the Dutch Golden Age

THE THIRTY YEARS WAR IN BRABANT, 1621–48

We sadly and humbly inform Your Princely Lord [Prince Maurice, the Dutch commander-in-chief] that his desolate subjects the inhabitants of Etten in the Barony of Breda . . . in this extreme emergency of war and contagious diseases have sought refuge with others in some 30 houses, on the cemetery between the moat dug around the village and the Leur [River], where they have stayed in great poverty until the present and [that] they hope that with the grace of God they may survive there . . . [and they] request [Prince Maurice] to permit them to provide to the [Spanish] king's army and the Count of Isenburgh [a general in the Spanish service] . . . food and small gifts . . . to be liberated from pillaging by their men, that they [the Spanish soldiers] would otherwise take it without orders and in large quantity anyway and also that the supplicants may use the furnaces [brewing kettles] . . . to brew small beer for the sick, passers-by and prisoners (who violently want to drink) . . . to prevent total ruin of your domain . . . and prey that your princely lordship order the surrounding [Dutch] garrisons . . . to leave them unmolested because they [the Dutch soldiers] raise the people from their beds at night without good reason, dragging them through hedges . . . [and] woods and in other ways treat them badly.[1]

THE PETITION from the magistrates of Etten illustrates the devastating impact of 17th-century conflict on a rural community, causing displacement, the loss of homes and livelihoods, and dramatic increases in levels of poverty and epidemic disease. The villagers and farmers of the rural district of Etten were caught between the siege lines during the protracted Spanish siege of Dutch Breda from August 1624 to June 1625. This left them subject to demands for provisions, forages, cash, and other goods by both Dutch and Spanish senior commanders, officers, and soldiers. Both sides threatened to sack and burn Etten's homes and farms for sustaining the opposing army. Early in 1625, the desperate magistrates appealed to Dutch Commander Prince Maurice of Orange-Nassau to be allowed to provide the Spanish besiegers with provisions to prevent wholesale punitive pillaging and the destruction of Etten. The quote also demonstrates how war victims sought to survive the onslaught of war through petitioning and bribing senior officers in attempts to lessen the exactions by the soldiers. Moreover, the magistrates also tried to exploit an opportunity created by the siege conditions to earn some income: meet a demand for beer "for the sick, passers-by and prisoners."

The image of the Thirty Years War as a conflict of murderous barbarity and absolute destruction with (foreign) mercenaries pillaging, burning, and raping their way through a divided and defenseless Germany served nationalistic state-building agendas, not in the least those of Nazi Germany. Even without the exaggerations, however, the conflict constituted a deep human tragedy. As during the first half of 16th-century Spanish wars of conquest in the Americas, the first half of the 17th-century war in Europe caused a demographic collapse. Although the conventional estimate of a 60 percent or more decline in the Holy Roman Empire's population is no longer accepted, the revised lower figure of 15–20 percent still far surpasses the 12 percent losses in the WWII Soviet Union as a result of modern total war.[2] The impact of the Thirty Years War varied dramatically in time and place. Brabant and Bavaria were exposed to war almost continuously, whereas Austria and Bohemia witnessed long periods of relative "peace" interspersed with episodes of dramatic violence.[3] The intermittent occurrence of spectacular acts of violence, however, does not mean that populations were free of the everyday violence of war in the form of exactions by armies and extortions by soldiers.

While the impact of the 1618–48 Thirty Years War in Germany has perhaps been magnified, in the Low Countries, it has been downplayed. Whereas the Thirty Years War marks the culmination (and end) of premodern uncivilized war in the West, the contemporary 1621–48 Dutch-Spanish war is seen as distinct and a precursor of 18th-century limited war. According to this narrative, the Dutch and the Spanish deployed professional soldiers who were controlled and paid by the state rather than mercenary armies in search of pillage and plunder. The Dutch Republic is portrayed as an early modern military-fiscal state with civilian control over its soldiers. By providing regular pay, the republic could maintain a well-drilled and highly disciplined standing army that did not directly prey on the civilian populations. Excesses committed against civilians conveniently are ascribed to German, Swedish, Croat, or French soldiers.[4]

The argument that the republic could afford to wage a limited war because of the golden age's thriving economy shrouds both the gains and losses of the 1620s–40s war. Although fighting a limited war spared the urban and rural productive and tax base of the republic, the argument plays down the economic contribution of Dutch war profiteering from the arms trade, smuggling, and pillage and plunder at sea and on land. Instead, the Golden Age is constructed as a linear outcome of a prewar long-term economic growth trend.[5] Moreover, the negative effects of the war are averaged out by an overemphasis on Holland and the core provinces of the republic. If the impact of the three decades of war are differentiated by place and time, it becomes clear that whereas Holland was shielded from actual violence, Brabant, Flanders, and Gelderland/Limburg were exposed to continuous warfare. By the late 1640s, large areas in Dutch and Spanish Flanders and Brabant lay abandoned, with homes and farmsteads in ruins and crop fields and pastures overtaken by weeds or inundated by water.[6]

The 1620s–40s war in the countryside of the Low Countries constituted environcidal and total war. Increased civilian control, drills and discipline, and regular pay did not immunize Dutch armies and soldiers from living off the land, practicing scorched earth tactics, or extorting food, shelter, and money from villagers and farmers.[7] Dutch soldiers and sailors in overseas operations plundered and pillaged Spanish, Portuguese, indigenous American, African, and Asian settlements and ships in the same way as the soldiers and sailors of any other nation.[8] Senior Dutch and Spanish commanders repeatedly tried to limit the exactions of their soldiers in the countryside for fear that rural societies and environments would collapse and, in the process, erase their tax base.[9] The imposition of articles of war to control soldiers' excesses, however, had little effect: as long as soldiers refrained from public acts of murder, rape, and torture, the articles were rarely enforced.[10] In fact, the governments, generals, regimental colonels, lower officers, soldiers, and camp followers all sought to make war profitable and shared a willingness to do so through violence.[11] The province of Holland's success in commercializing warfare at home and abroad was a boost to its thriving Golden Age economy.[12]

The Thirty Years War was not merely a "German" war; the Holy Roman Empire encompassed much of modern Central and Western Europe, including the Low Countries.[13] The Habsburg Holy Roman emperors were closely allied with their Spanish Habsburg cousins, and their armies often operated jointly throughout their territories, with soldiers and generals moving between the various fronts.[14] The leading commander of the German-Austrian emperor's armies, Johan Tserclaes Tilly, was born in the Spanish Southern Low Countries and first served in the Spanish army of Flanders against the Dutch. Henri Turenne, one of French King Louis XIV's field marshals, earned his spurs as an officer serving in the Dutch army against the Spanish. The republic supplied soldiers, arms, and funding to the enemies of the emperor, thus exchanging not only men and materials but also military know how, technology, practices of war, and germs between the theaters of the Thirty Years War.[15]

Although the spectacular violence of the sacking of such towns as Magdeburg captured the imaginations of contemporary observers and modern historians alike, the everyday violence of armies living off the land and soldiers exacting food, money, and services in the countryside was far more widespread and destructive because of its cumulative social and environmental effects.[16] The everyday violence of war in the countryside is less visible and occupies a space between the spectacular violence of massacres and genocide on the one hand and the silent and slow structural violence inflicted through impoverishment and environmental degradation. Spectacular violence is immediate and public, and while episodic, it often defines the memory of events because of its dramatic nature. Structural violence is long-term, incremental, and internal to processes and institutions; it operates below the surface and, therefore, is often slower and more silent than spectacular violence. The idea of structural violence as slow also highlights the temporal dimension of such violence: it is only perceptible in its full impact over time and after the exposure of its underlying dynamics.[17]

The everyday violence perpetrated by soldiers while extorting food, services, and money may be less visible to a historian than episodes of spectacular violence, yet it is no less real to its victims, even if it was disguised by euphemistic language. Although extortions were termed "contributions" and "gifts," suggesting a voluntary element, nonpayment resulted in military punishment, which typically consisted of sacking and burning.[18] Soldiers always intimidated villagers and farmers, and they routinely took hostages. Moreover, the threat of spectacular violence was always present: noncompliance with soldiers' demands could result in authorized torture, rape, and (mass) killing, as in the case of Haarlem in the late 16th century and Magdeburg in the early 17th century. Soldiers living off the land and their attempts to make war profitable had a devastating cumulative impact on the rural populations because they suffered the loss of homes, food, tools, utensils, clothes, and other property essential for their survival, health, and welfare, thus weakening the environmental infrastructure they depended on.

Brabant at the Outbreak of the Thirty Years War

After the environcidal warfare in 1570s Holland, the fighting between the Dutch rebels and their Spanish Habsburg overlords shifted to the southern provinces of Brabant and Flanders as well as the eastern provinces. By the 1590s, the Spanish generals had secured most of Flanders

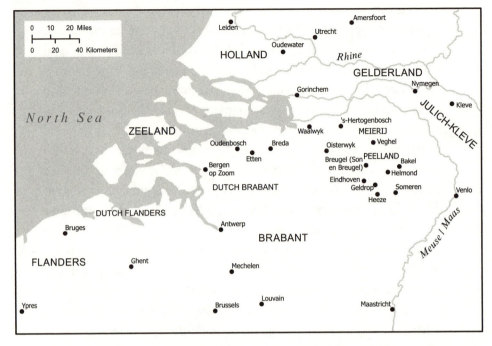

MAP 3.1. Brabant during the early 17th-century Thirty Years War.

and Brabant for the king and had confined the rebels to the provinces north of the Rhine and Maas Rivers. In 1609, Spain signed a temporary 12-year truce with the rebel Dutch Republic after having failed to conclude a peace agreement. In 1618, the Spanish Habsburgs intervened in the Thirty Years War to support their Habsburg cousins who held the Imperial throne of the Holy Roman or German Empire based in Vienna. Neither the Spanish Habsburgs nor the Dutch leaders renewed the truce in 1621, which drew the republic into the Thirty Years War.

Brabant became the main theater of war during the 1620s–40s Spanish-Dutch war in the Low Countries. Its northern half, the modern province of North Brabant boasted a dense population that was supported by an elaborate environmental infrastructure, which required a massive and continuous investment of labor and resources. Polders dotted the western seaboard and the banks of the major rivers along its northern boundary. Sustained by a system of dikes, drains, and sluices, the polders' rich soils supported livestock and dairy production. In select areas with fertile soils on the upper banks of rivers, hops (for beer brewing) was a major crop grown in special gardens close to the homes. The bulk of North Brabant's arable land consisted of poor sandy soils, which farmers transformed into raised fields with fertile black or brown (*plaggen*) soils comparable to the black earths created by indigenous Americans. In 1630, the magistrates of the Meierij (the countryside of eastern North Brabant) argued that their region was (poor) heathland "or land reclaimed from it requiring continuous investments and labor to cultivate." In fact, even the "natural" heathlands that covered much of the sandy soils resulted from human management. Continuous cropping in the medieval era impoverished the soils, while farmers actively maintained the heath for sheep grazing by preventing bush and tree encroachment.[19]

Farmers kept horses for plowing and transport, cattle for dairy and manure, and sheep for wool and manure, in addition to pigs and poultry. The farmers captured livestock droppings by keeping their animals stabled as much as possible. After mixing the droppings with sand, tree leaves, straw, heath or grass sods, and peat, they carried the fertilizer to their fields, creating the so-called *plaggen* soils of northwestern Europe. In terms of the required investments, the *plaggen* soils were second only to polder lands and irrigated lands, and in the same league as the indigenous terraced fields and raised field systems in the New World. The *plaggen* soils in North Brabant and inland Flanders were often continuously cropped, whereas elsewhere in Western Europe half or more of the arable land lay fallow each year to restore soil fertility. The *plaggen* soil supported the annual cropping of the rye staple, sown in the fall as a winter crop. A second (semi)annual crop was corn spurrey (*Spergula arvenis*), which doubled as livestock fodder and green manure. The heavy manuring allowed the inclusion of rotations with barley, buckwheat, and such commercial crops as turnip, rapeseed (for oils), and flax (for linen) as well as beans, fruit, and timber and coppice woodlots. Oats, a key source of forage for farmers' and soldiers' horses were a minor crop in the region. In North Brabant, up to one-third of the sandy soils is classified as old agricultural lands on modern soil maps and identified as human-made, as compared to 10 percent in the other provinces of the modern Netherlands, highlighting a long history of dark earth creation. These soils are generally higher and deeper, with a top layer of humus-rich earth resulting from the import of organic materials. In many cases, the soils have late medieval to 16th-century origins. Grass turf or sods were a main component of the *plaggen* soils in riverine environments, whereas west of Breda, heath sods dominated. The enriched *plaggen* soils are associated with high population density and intensive agriculture.[20]

An English traveler observed the use of *plaggen* fields around Antwerp in 1644, noting lush fenced islands of fertile, arable soil in a sea of barren heath.[21] What he described was actually a war-scarred landscape as is suggested by the abundance of heath: the region was a major theater of war and pillage during the Thirty Years War. As a result, many farmlands had been abandoned and recolonized by heath. *Plaggen* soils constituted elaborate environmental infrastructure that was less vulnerable to immediate destruction than polder lands with their precious drainage works, but without a continuous infusion of large amounts of manure and labor, weeds and shrubs quickly invaded the fields. Rural households were also often involved in such small-scale home crafts as spinning and weaving (wool and linen) and beer brewing.[22] Thus, because the production, processing, and storage of food and many other products was located on farms and in villages, the loss of homes, barns, fields, animals, agricultural and trade tools and equipment, orchards, and pastures had an immediate and dramatic impact on livelihoods, lives, and ways of life.

Even in peaceful times, production margins in the countryside were narrow. Seventeenth-century farmers were especially vulnerable because of the Little Ice Age that led to more frequent harvest shortfalls.[23] Harvest failures in turn caused hunger and famines, but the combination of war and harvest failure proved yet more disastrous.[24] Similar to the 16th-century Americas, in 17th-century Europe, epidemic disease was not simply a biological force that was spread by armies in contagion-like fashion.[25] Rather, the chaos, congestion, destruction, and displacement of war actively created more favorable conditions for plagues. Populations deprived of shelter, food, and clean water, and traumatized by violence, were highly vulnerable to epidemic diseases. War, displacement, exposure, nutritional stress, and disease were thus intimately connected and mutually reinforcing. A song from 1625 appears to implore God to relieve the Dutch Republic from the three heavy plagues to which it was subjected: "intense war . . . that robs countryside and towns, and destroys many beautiful fruits [of the earth, i.e., crops] . . . causing everywhere sorrow, crying, and sighing . . . fiery pest that daily increases . . . [and] [t]he suffering imposed on the animals [by hunger and the winter]." Instead, the song appealed to God to direct the wind and rain to defeat the Spanish onslaught.[26]

When the Spanish-Dutch war in the Low Countries resumed in 1621, major sieges and campaigns caused the most visible and immediate rural destruction and trauma. Encamped in the field, soldiers were difficult to control, especially since conditions in the camps were often extremely challenging, with the soldiers at best living in improvised huts that offered little protection against the cold and rain.[27] North Brabant was a major strategic gateway between the Republic and the Spanish Netherlands on the one side and the Low Countries and the German Empire on the other. It was densely populated and offered relatively decent (dirt) roads lined by towns, villages, and farms that could sustain large numbers of soldiers. Brabant was a front and a frontier zone for the Dutch and the Spanish alike. The Dutch regarded North Brabant more as an occupied territory than as a full part of the United Provinces.[28]

Throughout three decades of seesaw warfare in North Brabant, neither side could offer the countryside effective protection against the other's exactions. Therefore, villagers and farmers remained continuously subjected to exploitation by both armies. Even as the intensity of actual fighting in the heartland of North Brabant decreased during the late 1630s and 1640s, the belligerents continued to exact war taxes, money, food, and other goods. During the major sieges and in their direct aftermath, the exertions of the belligerent administrations, their armies, and their soldiers repeatedly brought rural communities and their livelihoods to the brink of collapse, as illustrated by the 1625 petition from Etten that opened this chapter. Numerous villages and farms were temporarily abandoned; many villages and hamlets were plundered.[29]

In 1621, North Brabant had not recovered from the previous 1568–1609 war years. The 1580s were characterized by particularly devastating scorched earth campaigns. The eastern Brabant Meijerij (the countryside around 's-Hertogenbosch) lost 70 percent of its population. Some of the rural flight was temporary as villagers and farmers sought refuge behind the city's walls. But 900 rural families migrated from eastern North Brabant to Haarlem in Holland, constituting 10–15 percent of the region's prewar total. The town of Eindhoven was reduced from 267 to a mere 80 households.[30] The belligerents forced the inhabitants of Brabant to continue to pay war contribution throughout the 1609–21 truce. By 1615, the 102 villages of the countryside around 's-Hertogenbosch were paying a Dutch contribution of 18,552 guilders per month.[31] Villages and towns borrowed heavily in order to meet the contribution payments and other exactions. In 1618, the 120 households of Breugel carried a crushing debt of 53,000 guilders, or an average of 440 guilders per household. Some rural communities fared even worse. Heeze, Zesgehuchten, Geldrop, Lieshout, and Nederwetten were not only deep in debt but also counted numerous burned, ruined, and abandoned homes and farms. The church in Gerwen along with 138 houses and numerous barns, sheds, sheep cots, and breweries lay in ruins or ashes, and 57 farmsteads were abandoned.[32]

Habsburg Spain massively intervened in the Thirty Years War from the beginning. Led by Ambrosio Spinola, the army of Flanders invaded the German Rhine Valley fiefs of Frederick of the Palatinate, the leader of the Protestant Union that had rebelled against the Catholic Habsburg emperor. By early 1621, almost 40,000 Spanish troops were fighting alongside the Imperial forces in the empire. Using Spanish reinforcements, Imperial Commander Tilly defeated the Bohemian rebels at the White Mountain in November 1620.[33] Meanwhile, the Spanish army of Flanders prepared for war in the Low Countries. In 1619, the Spanish requisitioned hundreds of horse carts and wagons from the countryside around 's-Hertogenbosch to move cannons and gunpowder to their Antwerp and 's-Hertogenbosch strongholds. Villages along the route fed and lodged the passing convoys and their military escorts, which cost the local populations thousands of guilders.[34]

As the truce ended in 1621, the Dutch and the Spanish reimposed trade restrictions and restored wartime defenses. Inundations to protect the Spanish stronghold of 's-Hertogenbosch caused the River Aa in Schijndel to flood pastures and hay lands on its banks, causing heavy losses among farmers' cattle and sheep. At the same time, Schijndel's grain lands on the sandy ridges above the flood level suffered from drought. The area's most valuable croplands were covered with hedges to support the cultivation of hops for beer brewing. But, hop prices were low, and with the renewal of the war, the supply of hops to the breweries in either Dutch or Spanish territory was again subject to a special war tax levied on any products exported to enemy territory. Schijndel and other such villages as Veghel that produced hops were dependent on the demand of beer brewers in Antwerp, Holland, and the German Rhineland, but with the renewal of the war, the roads became perilous.[35]

Spanish Commander Spinola's first direct act of war against the Dutch Republic occurred outside of the Low Countries, when he besieged Dutch-occupied Julich (in Germany), which capitulated in January 1622. The town and the surrounding Julich-Kleve region were of great strategic value to control the riverine Rhine trade between the Republic and the German interior, and provided the Spanish with a bridgehead north of the Rhine and Maas Rivers from which they could launch attacks on the Republic's eastern provinces.[36]

In May 1622, the soldiers of Dutch General Frederick Hendrick of Orange-Nassau, the half-brother of Dutch Supreme Commander Maurice of Orange-Nassau, sacked, pillaged, raped, and burned in Flanders and Brabant. The objective of the raid was to force the enemy Spanish-Netherlands countryside to pay contribution (war taxes) to the Dutch. In July 1622, reinforced with a German Imperial army, Spinola invaded Dutch Brabant, taking the fortress-town of Steenbergen and laying siege to nearby Bergen op Zoom. The threat of a Dutch relief army, reinforced with a German Protestant Union army led by Count Ernst von Mansfeld, caused the Spanish to abandon the siege three months later.

In August 1623, the joint Spanish and Imperial armies defeated the Protestant Union's army of Duke Christian of Brunswick at Stadtlohn in Germany, close to the Dutch border. During the severe winter of 1624, Spinola took advantage of the frozen rivers to invade the northern Dutch province of Groningen, burning numerous villages.[37]

During the early 1620s campaigns and sieges in Brabant, Dutch and non-Dutch soldiers alike extorted food, lodging, and bribes from the rural populations. Dutch officers not only failed to protect civilians or punish abuses by their men, but they also demanded money and gifts from mayors and aldermen. Soldiers mercilessly harassed the inhabitants of the few occupied houses and farms remaining in Geldrop at the end of 1621. Throughout 1621–22, passing soldiers demanded and stole food and money in Liempde and Heeze. Early in 1622, horsemen from Grave and Nijmegen (a Dutch bulwark) extorted food, lodging, and money in Son. The Nijmegen horsemen also stole goods from the villagers. In August 1622, ten Dutch companies invaded Erp, left an unpaid bill of 1,000 guilders for lodging and food, and marched off with a "contribution" of 422 guilders. Nuenen and Gerwen in 1622 and 1623 incurred 500 guilders in losses caused by soldiers from the nearby garrisons.[38]

During their failed July–October 1622 siege of Bergen op Zoom, Spanish soldiers freely extorted food and money in the countryside, although both the Dutch and the Spanish authorities had warned the villagers and farmers not to supply any food or goods to the enemy.[39] With the prohibitions on trade with the enemy, the inhabitants of the countryside of west Brabant were literally caught in the middle: "These days due to the change to times of war the quarters [rural districts] and the communities are heavily burdened by the heavy extortions by the garrisons."[40] During 1623 alone, the inhabitants of Etten, a series of hamlets wedged between Bergen op Zoom and Breda, spent 775 guilders on food, drinks, and gifts to passing Dutch and Spanish soldiers.[41]

In December 1622, Prince Maurice, the Dutch commander-in-chief, prohibited the Dutch garrisons in West Brabant from all further extortions in the Barony of Breda, which was his patrimony. The prince was appalled at the destruction caused by his own soldiers: "Our subjects are severely molested on an almost daily base and burdened by lodging and provisioning and indeed have never been more badly treated as at present by the horsemen and soldiers from the aforementioned garrisons who ride and march back and forth through the said Barony under the pretext to seek out the enemy so that these subjects of ours would soon be corrupted." Henceforth, ordered the prince, soldiers had to be accompanied by an officer who would be held personally responsible for making sure lodging or provisioning was done in good order and without molesting or harming any of his subjects.[42] A few months later, the prince urged the rural magistrates of the Barony of Breda to supply food and services only to soldiers who presented written orders signed by him personally. After proper accounting, documented expenses that resulted from fulfilling demands by parties bearing the signature of the prince would be deducted from the monthly contributions. Any abuses were to be immediately reported to the prince.[43]

The orders had so little impact that in March 1623, Prince Maurice authorized the magistrates and inhabitants of the Barony of Breda to arm themselves and arrest marauding soldiers and deserters. The prince also warned his officers and men not to interfere with the magistrates' actions against marauders. The prince explained that the rampant pillaging warranted these exceptional measures: "It is feared that the . . . inhabitants [of the Barony of Breda] will be entirely ruined unless they are for the time being given other means to act against the excesses of the aforementioned soldiers."[44]

Marauding went entirely unchecked in eastern Brabant. Toward the end of 1623, soldiers' extortions in the Peelland region added hundreds of guilders to the costs of the regular contributions. The inhabitants of Bakel contemplated fleeing their homes to escape the soldiers' incessant demands. Lierop was pestered by soldiers of both armies who broke into inns and private homes at all hours of the day and night to demand food and money. In Mierlo, soldiers took 172 guilders in cash, torched several houses, and beat up the hapless owners when they protested. The King's garrisons at 's-Hertogenbosch, Heeswijk, Weert, and Venlo exacted food and bribes amounting to over 300 guilders at Son and over 500 guilders at Veghel.[45] Tongelre had the misfortune of being forced to host the king's general, Hendrik van de Bergh, with his escort of 420 men for the Easter holiday of 1623. Hosting another large group of 250 horsemen from the Grave garrison led by a lieutenant and 17 other larger and smaller groups cost the villagers another 450 guilders.[46] Local garrison commanders also resumed the practice of selling high-priced safeguards to civilians to allow them to travel through the area unmolested by their soldiers.[47] The resumption of the Spanish-Dutch conflict in the Low Countries thus had an immediate impact on the countryside of North Brabant, multiplying the peacetime burden to sustain both the Spanish and Dutch armies.

The Spanish Siege of Breda and Its Aftermath

During the summer of 1624, Spanish Commander Spinola campaigned both in Brabant south of Breda and in Julich-Kleve in Germany. The latter tricked the Dutch into sending reinforcements to their eastern Provinces for fear of a repeat of the previous year's invasion of Groningen. With the Dutch army divided, the Spanish army laid siege to Breda on August 28. Spinola's troops immediately created large-scale inundations to prevent the Dutch army from reinforcing Breda.[48] The inundations came after the grain crop harvest but may have spoiled hay lands and pastures, diminishing livestock winter feeding supplies.

A month earlier, Justinius of Nassau, the Dutch governor of Breda, had ordered the magistrates of the villages of Etten and Leur to encourage their farmers to sell their harvest surpluses in Breda.[49] The siege placed Etten on the frontlines. After obtaining a safeguard from the Spanish commander, the inhabitants of Etten sought refuge at the parish church with all they could carry. The safeguard pertained to "the village parish church with the cemetery and the home of the priest as well as all the inhabitants, their movable property, grains, livestock and whatever else except for forages. We order . . . all Quartermasters, Colonels, Captains, officers and soldiers in the service of his Majesty under our command . . . to not cause any suffering or . . . exactions . . . in any way subject to the common punishment and to be punished as broachers of the safeguard."[50]

Before and during the siege, soldiers lodged, ate, and drank freely in Leur's inn, demanded oats and hay for their horses without paying, and extorted bribes and gifts to boot, costing the innkeeper 1,400 guilders. Before the siege, the Inn's overbearing and insolvent clients were from the Dutch garrison of Breda; as the siege tightened, Spanish soldiers replaced them.[51] During the early days of the siege, in September 1624, Prince Maurice ordered the Etten magistrates to secretly smuggle the village's beer brewing kettles to Dutch-held Oudenbosch to prevent their capture by the king's men. The prince promised that the assets, along with the kettles of the other villages, would be kept safe under his personal protection.[52] The prince's actions were part of a larger strategy to deprive the Spanish besiegers of any of Breda's resources. Because Spinola had initiated the siege by surprise, the Dutch defenders of Breda had been unable to remove key resources from the surrounding countryside to the city and destroy what could not be carried away. This left the Spanish besiegers in control of local rural supplies of provisions, forage, and wood. In mid-September, soldiers from the garrison of Grave cut down over 600 trees in the villages and estates in the Land of Cuijk to collect wood for the fort's defense and prevent the Spanish from capturing the timber.[53] In early October, the Dutch governor of Bergen op Zoom repeated an earlier demand that the magistrates of Etten "remove the ironwork from your grain mill," warning them to comply or "[the ironwork] will be taken at your cost."[54]

Both sides forbade all trade with the enemy and neutrals, and blocked overland and riverine trade routes as the Spanish besiegers sought to starve the garrison and the Dutch army sought to starve the besiegers.[55] A Dutch public notice issued on September 2, 1624, reiterated the prohibition against supplying food, ammunition, weapons, or any other goods to the king's armies. Anyone who breached it would be treated as a hostile: their villages would be burned and destroyed, and all individuals involved would be taken captive and prosecuted.[56] The Dutch garrison at Bergen op Zoom used the notice as an excuse to abduct and ransom villagers and farmers.[57] The inhabitants of Etten wanted to flee but had nowhere to go to because they were literally caught in the no-man's-land between the two opposing armies. Fortunately, Dutch

General Count Ernst Casimir took pity on them and ordered his men to cease abducting and ransoming Etten's inhabitants for supplying livestock and food to the enemy, arguing that the village was under the effective control of the Spanish, and the inhabitants had no choice in the matter. The count also instructed his men to suspend any exactions, plunder, and acts of violence in Etten for two months.[58] The following month, Count Isenburg, the commander of a Spanish fort at neighboring Leur, also granted a safeguard to Etten. Isenburg prohibited his men from taking the standing grain in the fields or letting their horses forage in the crop fields. He also ordered his men to refrain from breaking into people's houses or causing damage, and threatened to arrest any trespasser and punish them.[59]

Dutch morale had sagged after the death of Dutch Supreme Commander Prince Maurice in April 1625, and Breda capitulated to Spinola on June 5, 1625. A significant number of the surviving inhabitants of the town subsequently left.[60] Plague spread into the countryside following the siege. Originating in France, the epidemic migrated north in 1625–26 with Wallenstein's Imperial army. The village of Klundert, north of Breda, imposed severe restrictions in June 1625 on the movement of people to stop the disease from spreading. Households with a contaminated member had to isolate themselves in their home for two weeks, and if a sick person died of the plague, everyone living in the house had to remain isolated there for six weeks with all doors closed. That the magistrates resorted to recycling a plague ordinance from 1603 testifies to the urgency and despair of the times.[61]

The long siege left the countryside around Breda devastated. Threatened with execution for failure to pay the contributions to the Spanish, the Etten magistrates petitioned to have the royal taxes for 1624 forgiven and to be granted a safeguard against soldiers' exactions, explaining that Etten's wealthier inhabitants had fled. Having nothing to lose to the marauders and no means and place to flee, only the poor remained, and they did not have the money to pay for the contribution. The (royalist) Brabant Estates supported a postponement until after the siege and the inhabitants' return, but the king's tax collector granted Etten only a two-month stay.[62] Both Frederick Hendrick, the new Dutch commander-in-chief and the Baron of Balançon, the governor of Spanish-occupied Breda, issued pardons to the inhabitants of the countryside for having supplied the enemy. To prevent further pillaging, Governor Balançon ordered his men not to cause Etten any further harm.[63]

Many villages in the region were in the same dire straits as Etten and asked for reductions on the royal tax. The Baron of Balançon, concerned that the countryside would otherwise be deserted, forgave the villages half of the taxes for the siege years of 1624 and 1625. Although Dutch soldiers during the siege of Breda did not engage in large-scale and systematic scorched earth, burning and sacking villages, the continuous extortions of money and goods greatly impoverished the countryside, leading many to abandon their homes and other environmental infrastructure and flee elsewhere. Large-scale rural displacement and the total collapse of the countryside was narrowly averted because the commanders of both armies reduced their impositions and prevented their soldiers from sacking villages as punishment for failing to pay contributions or for trading with the enemy. The commanders' actions demonstrate that the daily grind of the everyday war violence—even without mass murder, torture, and rape—could fatally damage environmental infrastructure and displace people from it. Moreover, the fate of the countryside around Breda during the siege also highlights how blurred the boundary between wartime everyday violence and episodic spectacular violence could be. It was only the successful appeal of the village aldermen to the two local army commanders that saved their communities from the fire and the sword.

Military Buildup and the Dutch Siege of 's-Hertogenbosch

A public notice issued by the Republic in 1625, and reissued in April 1629 on the eve of the Dutch siege of 's-Hertogenbosch, demonstrates that such abuses as marauding were continuous and widespread. None of the rules and prohibitions listed in the notice were new. It complained that soldiers were committing daily extortions in neutral territories or areas that were paying contribution to the Dutch authorities: illegal acts subject to corporal punishment. Officers were reminded not to requisition horse carts or funds for the repair or maintenance of fortifications in lands under safeguards (by having paid contribution) or neutral lands without written orders from the General Estates, the highest authority of the Republic. The notice prohibited soldiers and officers from entering any civilian houses unless they were billeted there, and it made the officers personally responsible for the behavior of their men when passing through villages or farmsteads. Soldiers billeted in private houses were not to steal or damage their hosts' cattle, small stock, furniture, or any other property. Wronged civilians were encouraged to lodge complaints with the governors of the nearest garrison so that any offenders could be prosecuted. The notice reiterated that soldiers required a pass in order to leave their garrison and that it was illegal for officers to extort goods, money, or services from civilians for personal gain. The placard also expressly condemned civilian abductions, citing frequent reports that officers and soldiers had forcibly "recruited" children as hostages to extort money or food from the parents.[64]

With its resources depleted after the siege of Breda, the need to support Imperial allies in Germany, and the threat of French invasions, the Spanish army of Flanders went on the defensive in the second half of the 1620s. Even in the absence of episodes of spectacular mass violence in Dutch Brabant until 1629, the presence of large concentrations of soldiers and repeated troop movements imposed a heavy burden on the countryside. In 1627, Tilly's Imperial army invaded and took up winter quarters in Germany's East Friesland, threatening the neighboring Dutch territory of Groningen. In March 1628, over 10,000 Spanish troops were stationed in garrisons across Brabant and another 19,000 in Flanders, Limburg, and neighboring Germany. In addition to the garrisons, the Spanish army of Flanders had a field army of 25,000–30,000 men. The Spanish troops alone in or near the Low Countries totaled 60,000 men, and the Dutch army was of comparable size.[65]

The countryside was forced to sustain not only the permanent garrisons but also troop movements as they marched back and forth across the region, in addition to field armies in their winter quarters and in their summer camps. The military buildup was clearly felt throughout the eastern Brabant countryside. Although the entire region was under contribution to both belligerents, which in theory should have freed the villagers and farmers from further depredations by soldiers, reported losses increased. Liempde, a village halfway between Eindhoven and 's-Hertogenbosch spent 838 guilders on food and extortions in less than a year. The miller of the watermill at Kasteren fed a contingent of 70 soldiers, who were responsible for guarding the nearby sluice through which inundations could be controlled. In the hamlet of Boxtel, soldiers extracted five barrels of beer, which they consumed on the nearby heath, away from the preying eyes of their commanding officers.[66] Between January 1628 and Easter of 1629, the aldermen of Tongelre recorded a loss of 1,524 guilders to provisions, beer, and "gifts" for passing soldiers from as far away as 's-Hertogenbosch, Breda, Mechelen, and Venlo. Individual losses were substantial: the widow Peterken Jacobs Verbeeck supplied soldiers with 70 guilders in meals and beer; Hanrick Bartels van der Waarden dispensed 35 guilders on food and another 34 guilders in bribes; and a captain from the Eindhoven garrison carried off three barrels of beer, 200 pounds of bread, and 75 pounds of butter worth 50 guilders.[67] In the first three months of 1629, Lierop's innkeepers and mayors provided Spanish soldiers with 181 guilders worth of food, drinks, and bribes.[68]

As had occurred during the siege of Breda, the belligerents prohibited all trade and blocked overland and riverine trade routes. Dutch Captain-General Frederick Hendrick of Nassau very successfully kept his real target a secret: 's-Hertogenbosch. The city was held to be impregnable because it was defended by a series of forts, extensive swamps, and water inundations. In April 1629, with Spain preoccupied with its war in Italy and financially damaged by the Dutch capture of the Mexican silver fleet, Frederick Hendrick seized the opportunity. After spreading rumors about an impending Dutch attack on Antwerp in the southwest and a feint on Wesel in the east, the Dutch army surrounded 's-Hertogenbosch and immediately built a massive circumvallation reinforced by inundations to ward off any attempts to relieve the city.[69]

In June 1629, to sustain his troops during the siege, Prince Frederick Hendrick ordered the villages in the region to report on their grain stores. Unfortunately for his plans, the villages were all running low on grain. The responses made crystal clear that the war had caused widespread insecurity, loss of livelihoods, impoverishment, and displacement. The 19 villages and the lone town (Helmond) that responded to the prince's request emphasized that their grain stores would be depleted before the next harvest, requiring people to buy rye at the grain markets of Eindhoven, Mechelen, or further away. Only some of the more remote farms had enough grain to last until the harvest. The previous harvest in 1628 had been poor, and many villagers were craftsmen who relied on purchasing grain or food. In some villages, the aldermen attributed the grain shortages to the high rents demanded by absentee landlords. Other villages faced shortfalls because they had sold their grain in order to pay the war contributions. Many of the poorest villagers were in dire straits. In Lierop, more than half of the population had to purchase grain to survive until the next harvest; many families with small children had descended into "bitter poverty." In Geldrop, most of the inhabitants were craftsmen who had no food, work, or income; they would have had to flee their homes if soldiers had been sent to forcibly collect provisions. The 1,600 inhabitants of Veghel too soon would have no choice but to purchase food grains from beyond the village because most of the district's crop land lay abandoned and uncultivated. In Helmond, many households had less than half a cup of rye. In Vlierden, inhabitants lived in terror because the hamlet was "a mere chapel without any ditches or other defenses to seek shelter with some of our property." That precious grain stores and other valuables were stored in strong houses or the attics of churches rather than in people's own homes or farms illustrates the pervasive sense of insecurity.[70]

Both the Spanish defenders and the Dutch besiegers destroyed a large number of farms, fields, and pastures in a large radius around the city of 's-Hertogenbosch to create inundations and siege works. In Vugt, pioneers razed or inundated 150 farms and their fields and orchards. Rosmalen suffered a similiar fate. The Geefhuis convent in 's-Hertogenbosch lost much of its income for 1629 and 1630 because its farms, fields, and pastures were flooded. Frederick Hendrick mobilized thousands of pioneers to drain the Spanish defensive inundations to prepare for his attack. Postsiege recovery was slow. Farmers returning to their lands after the waters had receded initially lived in straw huts until they could rebuild their farmsteads. No compensation was offered for the losses caused by the inundations, and 20 years later, one-third of the agricultural lands in the countryside around 's-Hertogenbosch still lay abandoned.[71]

Even with reinforcements from the Habsburg Imperial army, the new commander of the Spanish army of Flanders, Hendrik van den Bergh, was reluctant to assault head-on the Dutch defenses that circumvallated the city. For two weeks, he tried to taunt the Dutch army into breaking the siege while sustaining his troops by draining the countryside of horses and supplies. Dutch Prince Frederick Hendrick threatened the rural magistrates into resisting the Spanish troops' demands: "We understand that when required by the enemy the villages of your district do not fail to assist him with horses and other needs for his use. . . . We can no longer condone this because it contradicts the neutrality and service of the land. With this [letter] we urge you to issue orders so that it no longer occurs, or else we will be forced to take measures against the villages collectively and you personally."[72] But obeying the Dutch prince's orders resulted in violent reprisals by the Spanish troops. In July 1629, Spanish soldiers sacked Vlierden, causing "very great damage . . . in people's houses . . . robbing[ ] pot, kettle, [and] carrying away beds . . . and all sorts of household items and both woolen and linen clothing . . . and they also ripped the clothes off peoples' backs in the street." The villagers' total losses amounted to 2,000 guilders, but they were fortunate that the soldiers did not burn their homes.[73]

When Frederick Hendrick did not take the bait, Hendrick van den Bergh marched his army east across the Rhine to Wesel. Assisted by an Imperial army, the Spanish invaded the Republic's eastern provinces, burning villages along the way and occupying Amersfoort, deep in Gelderland. Hasty and extensive defensive inundations caused additional damage. The Dutch surprise capture and sacking of van den Bergh's supply base at Wesel made the Spanish and their Imperial allies withdraw from Dutch territory. 's-Hertogenbosch capitulated to the Dutch besiegers soon thereafter, following a heavy bombardment that left the city in ruins.[74]

Soldiers' robberies increased in the chaotic aftermath of the siege. At the end of 1629, the villages and hamlets of Peelland complained that following the fall of 's-Hertogenbosch "they are very heavily plagued by soldiers roaming the countryside in bands and groups, most without being in the employ of either side and only as vagabonds . . . submitting the good inhabitants and all free passers-by to great violence and nuisance by day and night, on roads and paths [and] in their homes invading with entire groups [taking] loot, plunder and also taking the good people for ransom without the inhabitants daring to resist or assist one another." Referring to the earlier ordinances and public notices issued by the republic, the inhabitants of Peelland requested permission to arrest such "vagabonds" and "servants of the nightingale" by force of arms and escort them to the nearest garrison. M. Huijgens of the Dutch Republic's Council of State granted the request.[75]

A contemporary ordinance issued by the Spanish Governess Isabella at Brussels indicates that Spanish soldiers (and their officers) also widely abused rural populations, even if they paid contribution. Isabella issued the 1630 *Ordinance on the roaming, passages and lodging of soldiers in the countryside under contribution* "because of the many complaints we received about the infringements and taxing by [the threat of] fire occurring at the expense of the inhabitants of the countryside." The ordinance stipulated the conditions under which soldiers could request lodging and food in the countryside and the quantity of allowable beer, food, and forage. Officers were required to show their travel orders to the village aldermen, who recorded the date of their stay. Village aldermen who sought to bribe soldiers into bypassing their village risked the draconian fine of 500 guilders. Finally, the ordinance authorized villagers to apprehend any of the king's soldiers who misbehaved and escort them to their garrison to be punished.[76]

The Dutch conquest of 's-Hertogenbosch did not liberate the eastern Brabant countryside from Spanish contributions, but it may have emboldened its rural magistrates to petition for a reduction of the royal tax.

FIGURE 3.1. Soldiers, including a soldier's wife or female sutler and a child soldier plundering a farm during the Thirty Years War (Painting by Sebastiaen Vrancx, Soldiers Plundering a Farm [1620], Commons Wikipedia.org: Deutsches Museum).

Referring to Spanish Governess Isabella's ordinance's lamenting the heavy extortions by Spanish soldiers, the magistrates complained that their contribution was much higher than that in neighboring districts, causing population flight to the places with lower war taxes.[77] The concern about people fleeing between different territories to avoid war contributions was significant enough that the governor of 's-Hertogenbosch in early 1630 requested that the Etten magistrates submit a list of recent immigrants to the district. Ensuring that refugees were properly listed in the tax registers would facilitate the Dutch authorities in imposing war contributions. Only the heads of households were counted for tax purposes. Refugees in Etten included a nobleman and his family from Spanish Brabant, five refugees from Breda, and 13 others from unknown origins, for a total of 19 refugee households out of a total of 449 households.[78] Etten thus counted only a small percentage of refugees, but because of its location just outside of heavily contested Breda and its history of devastation and suffering during the early 1620s siege, it seems somewhat surprising that people would use it as a place of refuge at all. Perhaps Etten's liminal status as a contested no-man's-land was attractive to refugees trying to remain under the radar and off the tax registers of the authorities on both sides of the conflict.

After the fall of 's-Hertogenbosch, the Spanish withdrew many of their garrisons on the lower Rhine in Germany to strengthen the army of Flanders in the Low Countries. After receiving reinforcements and a new commander from Italy, the Spanish launched a failed combined naval and overland offensive against Tholen, west of the Dutch fortress-town of Bergen op Zoom.[79] The regrouping and consolidation of the army of Flanders in 1630 and 1631, and the military campaigns in Brabant and Flanders in 1631, maintained heavy pressure on the countryside, especially in West Brabant. Military campaigns required requisitioning and storing enormous quantities of provisions. Breda served as the main Spanish base in Brabant, and after the 1630 harvest, the Spanish governor issued orders to the villages to supply rye and other grains as well as carts and wagons to move soldiers and goods.[80]

Overwhelmed by the exactions, the representatives of the Barony of Breda petitioned Spanish Governor Balançon to intervene and limit private exactions because their cost equaled the amount of the annual war contribution and made it impossible to provide both. The petitioners explained that despite the dearly purchased safeguards,

> parties of [Spanish] soldiers move from village to village and one hamlet to the other as if they are engaging with the enemy to have themselves provided for free with food and drinks as if there was a party. . . . [We] humbly request that these exactions [by the Spanish soldiers] be ended or become less excessive. Also if these parties [of soldiers] come out [from their garrison in Breda] that their sergeant or commanders be charged to prevent the soldiers from molesting anyone on the roads or in their houses or straw hut or to extort something on the backroads or woods under some pretext of [military] action.

The petitioners also asked the governor's permission to freely import and export products and goods to enemy territory "or else it is impossible to obtain money to pay for the [war] taxes or to repair the[] burned-down houses."[81] Governor Balançon responded favorably, permitting the region's farmers to continue marketing their crops at Vugt, which technically had become enemy territory after the Dutch conquest of 's-Hertogenbosch. In doing so, he acknowledged that selling their products at Vught allowed the farmers to earn money to pay the war contribution, repair environmental infrastructure, and forestall their total ruin.[82]

In 1631, the Spanish authorities in West Brabant introduced a "plow tax," which effectively constituted a special war tax on the wealthier. Households rated as having a full plow had to pay two Karolus guilders. The assessors designated households with less than a plow as "paupers," who paid a much lower fee or were exempt. Jacob Piersz and his wife were together rated as half a plow because he was "very poor and broke"; he was designated a "pauper" and charged 24 Stuivers.[83] For the village of Etten and the surrounding hamlets and individual farms, the new plow tax register listed 449 names of household heads, including 31 households headed by women, all of whom except one were widows. Local parish priest Desernitoir, whose wealth was assessed at three plows, was at the top of the list, together with Sheriff Van Broecke, who was charged for ten plows. The May 1631 register compiled by the sheriff and aldermen of Etten identified 119 households as paupers, almost all of which were exempted from the tax. Most widow-headed households were not taxed either. In the 48 cases that included a male servant, the household was required to pay an extra Karolus guilder. In ten additional cases, the original annotation indicating the presence of a male servant had been struck out and no charge was added. In 69 cases, the original full plow (two horses) or half plow (one horse) assessment was struck out and the tax adjusted. Ultimately, the total assessed "plow tax" for Etten was 450 Karolus guilders.[84] The reevaluated assessments expressed in the corrections might reflect changes in the wealth and status of households due to the siege-time exactions. The magistrates corrected 79 out of 449 households downward by half their wealth in the final assessment, suggesting that the households recently had been dramatically impoverished, probably during the siege and its aftermath.

The 79 "new paupers," along with the 119 existing paupers, reveals that by 1631, almost half of households in Etten were designated as very poor, with the 1629 siege conditions and their aftermath accounting for an increase in the pauper population by over 60 percent.

In September 1631, the belligerents forged a highly unusual ad hoc collaboration. The Spanish authorities granted a "living" safeguard to the villages of Etten, Sprundel, and Leur in the Barony of Breda *and* the Dutch army agreed to honor the Spanish safeguard. On behalf of the Dutch Council of State, Christiaan Huygens issued orders at the Dutch army camp at Halsteren:

> To protect their animals and goods [the inhabitants of the above-mentioned villages] may collect twenty soldiers from the army of the King of Spain and keep them there as living safeguard provided the foresaid soldiers do not come closer to this army [the Dutch army at Halsteren] than one-and-a-half hour's distance [and on the condition that] they do not do anything to the detriment of the united Netherlands or its army. . . . [We] therefore order everyone . . . in the service of this land [the United Netherlands] and present in its territories to not in any way molest or damage the fore-mentioned twenty soldiers that may be positioned there subject to . . . punishment.[85]

Even as the belligerents tried to control their soldiers' unauthorized private extortions, they continued to exact products and services in western Brabant. In December 1631, the governor of Breda ordered the delivery of hay to his garrison.[86] This and other orders requisitioning transport for the army diverted horses, carts, and drivers from rural household production and maintenance activities. In 1631, Etten supplied 2,385 guilders worth of transport services to the Spanish army. The amount included supplying four wagons to carry Governor Balançon from Breda to his new residence at Antwerp. In 1632, Etten was reimbursed the entire 2,385 guilders for the transport services over 1631, an exceptional occurrence that most likely can be attributed to the personal intervention of Balançon, who on several previous occasions had been particularly solicitous of the countryfolk of the Barony.[87]

Lives, livelihoods, and ways of life in eastern Brabant were similarly affected by the grinding environcidal impact of the day-to-day exactions of generals and soldiers. In 1630, the villages and hamlets of the quarter of Peelland petitioned the Dutch authorities for a reduction of cash contribution payments, asserting that the billeting and extortions by the Republic's soldiers left them poor and desolate and unable to pay the regular war taxes referred to as "contribution." Concerned, the Republic's Council of State ordered the sheriffs and alderman of Peelland to submit accounts of what they had paid in contribution and the type and amount of the other costs (including requisitions of food, forage, and bribes) they had incurred.[88]

The reports demonstrated that between September 1629 and March 1631, the Peelland communities had expended almost 40,000 guilders in official and unofficial contribution payments, as well as requisitions, extortions, and pillage. Six communities, including Geldrop, Heeze, Mierlo, and the only town (Helmond), lost the equivalent of between 2,000 and 3,000 guilders each, and St. Oedenrode over 4,000 guilders. The aldermen from Geldrop and Zesgehuchten petitioned to be relieved of all contribution payments and other impositions: during the siege of 's-Hertogenbosch, they had spent 1,781 guilders on constructing and then subsequently breaking down siege works, in addition to providing forage and oats for the horses; carts, horses, and drivers; pioneer salaries; and cash gifts. The extortions by the postconquest Dutch garrison were even higher and included the ransom to free their mayor. Rightly expecting that the financial losses resulting from Spanish demands would be disallowed, the Peelland sheriffs and aldermen reported only the costs inflicted by Dutch soldiers in their submission to the Dutch Council of State.[89] The total losses of the Peelland communities during the siege year were thus substantially higher than the 40,000 guilders they reported.

Everyday War Violence and Environcide

No major episode of spectacular large-scale mass violence occurred in Dutch Brabant between the 1629 siege of 's-Hertogenbosch and the 1636 second siege of Breda. The major armed confrontations occurred in Flanders, Spanish Brabant, Limburg, Gelderland, and neighboring Germany. In 1632, a Swedish offensive in Germany diverted part of the

Spanish Army of Flanders from the Low Countries, creating an opportunity for the Dutch Republic. While a smaller Dutch army feigned an attack on Antwerp, the main Dutch army took Venlo and Sittard, and in June surrounded Maastricht, all in modern Limburg. Although reinforced by an Imperial army, the army of Flanders was unable to break the siege, and Maastricht surrendered to Frederick Hendrick on August 23, 1632.[90] Soon after the surrender, a devastating Black Plague epidemic broke out in the city, killing thousands and spreading across the Low Countries. Spanish reinforcements for the army of Flanders had carried the plague from Italy, via the Spanish Road to Germany.[91]

Even without major sieges or battles in North Brabant, the belligerents' exactions continued to damage and destroy environmental infrastructure, inhibit its maintenance and repair, and displace people who relied on it. The cost of sustaining the armies and soldiers of both the belligerents may have amounted to at least four times the peacetime taxes. The contribution (war tax) payments to each side were based on (and usually surpassed) peacetime taxation, and the exactions by soldiers in the form of lodging, transport services, provisions, forage, and gifts often exceeded the amount of the annual contribution payments. Villagers and farmers consequently had no funds to invest in their farms, fields, equipment, or tools. Requisitions left them short of produce to sell, food for their families, and forage for their livestock. Labor and transport chores for the army robbed farmers of animals, carts, and men during peaks in the agricultural season, leaving uncultivated lands, weed infestation, and substantial harvest losses.

In the aftermath of the 1632 fall of Maastricht, a Dutch army commanded by Hendrick Casimir of Nassau, Stadholder of Friesland, and a cousin of Dutch Commander-in-Chief Frederick Hendrick of Orange-Nassau marched through eastern Brabant. A two-day stay of his army in Helmond cost the town over 4,000 guilders. While encamped at Heeze and Leende, Hendrick Casimir and his men mercilessly exacted provisions and money from the surrounding villages. Even a decade later, Leende's inhabitants still vividly recalled the violent episode.[92] Other villages, including Veghel, Aarle Rixtel, and Breugel, incurred losses of hundreds of guilders to feed and bribe Spanish and Dutch soldiers who marched through during the last months of 1632. One group of soldiers threatened to hang a Breugel inhabitant in his own chimney in order to force him to borrow money from his neighbors to pay them a bribe.[93] In November, a two-day stay by Count John of Relafroy's cavalry cost Bakel 1,805 guilders, an amount that far surpassed its quota of 733 guilders.[94] The damage suffered by the Peelland villages during the single month of November 1632 approximated the costs incurred for the entire six-month period that followed the Dutch siege of 's-Hertogenbosch in 1629. Someren's aldermen stated that the village had already had to borrow 100,000 guilders because of the war and that under the circumstances "it is impossible that the poor inhabitants of Someren can remain residing [in their homes]."[95]

Another scion of the House of Nassau, Hendrick Casimir's cousin, Count John of Nassau-Siegen, left a trail of devastation in western Brabant. John of Nassau served the Habsburgs in both the Spanish and Imperial armies:

> The count John of Nassau just recently crossed through various rural quarters with the enemy cavalry and did heavy exactions in the villages that were under contribution of this side [the Dutch side] therefore her High Powers [the Estates General of the United Netherlands] asks (since the same [the exactions] are in contradiction to the freedom [of exactions] of the safeguards of this side ...) to ... inform me what each village had to provide to Count John and his troops and also what damage each suffered.[96]

The sheriffs and aldermen of 19 villages (including Oosterhout, Etten, Roosendaal, Ginneken, and Gilze) subsequently reported their losses to the Dutch government, hoping to get some tax relief. Four of the villages—Leur, Hage, Sundert [Zundert], and Rijsbergen—also petitioned the (royalist) Brabant Estates for the same reason. The villagers had hosted a large unit of Spanish cavalry for three days and nights, during which time the latter had consumed food, beer, wine, oats, hay, and enormous amounts of firewood to maintain large fires during the long, cold winter nights. In addition, the riders stole and extorted money "against the prohibition or [without the] knowledge of the general." The episode was so costly that the villages could no longer sustain the regular daily extortions.[97]

Despite the careful accounts that accompanied the petitions, there is no evidence to suggest that either the Spanish or the Dutch authorities subsequently permitted any reductions in the contribution payments as compensation. Instead, the Dutch authorities simply condoned trading with the enemy. In April 1633, the Dutch General Estates granted the inhabitants of much-plagued Etten and Leur permission to seasonally and freely move their beehives between Brabant (contested territory) and Holland. The beekeepers were also permitted to market their bee products in Holland (Dutch territory) or Breda (Spanish territory), as an acknowledgement that the sales constituted the only opportunity for the villagers to earn money to pay their contribution.[98]

Major military operations recurred in Brabant in the summer of 1633. Early in 1633, with a smaller Dutch army threatening Spanish Flanders, the main Dutch army targeted the remaining Spanish positions in the Rhine Valley in Germany. Meanwhile, a Spanish army in the Maas Valley took Maaseik, Weert, and other positions in modern Limburg before moving to Brabant in the summer of 1633. The Spanish army, however, frequently moved camps to evade a battlefield confrontation with the Dutch main force that shadowed it across the region.[99] During these operations, Prince Frederick Hendrick of Orange-Nassau burned homes in Leende (near Heeze).[100] Dutch and Spanish troops extorted food, drinks, and bribes in Liempde, Someren, and other villages in eastern Brabant.[101]

In June 1633, to build up a food supply for a siege, the garrison at recently Spanish-occupied Weert demanded that the villages of Peelland supply the town with 100 *mudden* (30,000–43,000 liters) of rye within the next ten days, which drained household grain stores in the area.[102] In September 1633, Dutch and Swedish troops camped at Gemert for ten days, burned down several homes, including the Catholic parish house, and consumed all hay, grain, and straw, causing the villagers' livestock to starve.[103] Someren provided an unidentified army camping at Boxtel with 4,000 guilders worth of wagons, horses, forages, and bread.[104] In the fall, to interdict the movement of enemy troops and better defend Steenbergen and Willemstad northwest of Breda, the Dutch authorities inundated a polder at Klundert. The inundations preceded the September harvest and destroyed the standing crop of rye and buckwheat, the rapeseed fallows, and the pastures, resulting in the death of 34 cattle and 4 horses.[105]

In June 1634, when the Spanish invested Maastricht, the Dutch surrounded Breda, but retreated when the Spanish marched north after abandoning their siege of Maastricht.[106] The sieges and the concentration of the armies immediately increased soldiers' exactions, despite reissued orders to curtail the worst abuses. In June 1634, the navy commander of Spanish Antwerp urged his men to limit their demands on the rural population while they marched back and forth to Breda. He reminded his men "[to] be satisfied with the food that they are offered there and one pot of beer for each man in the evening by day or night, without demanding or taking any money or anything else, nor threatening the residents or causing violence or nuisance in any way punishable with the gallows, or other corporal punishment depending on the case."[107] On July 2, the governor of Breda ordered his soldiers to adhere strictly to the public notice or be subjected to exemplary punishment. The governor's order followed reports that some of his soldiers had systematically gone from village to village to extort bribes and excessive quantities of food and beer.[108]

Rank-and-file soldiers, however, remained seemingly unimpressed by the threats of exemplary punishment. In September of the same year, the magistrates of Etten and Hoeven (west of Etten) offered a gift of 50 Rhenish guilders and game meat to the governor of Breda to persuade him to end the ongoing extortions by his soldiers.[109] The Spanish government in Brussels considered the failure to control the soldiers to be a wider disciplinary problem: in July 1634, a public ordinance ordered all soldiers to report back to their units within eight days or face "rigorous" punishment.[110]

Late in 1634, the Infante Ferdinand arrived in the Low Countries with 11,000 Spanish and Italian soldiers after an overland march from Italy. En route in Germany, the Infante had joined the Imperial army to defeat the Swedes at Nordlingen. With the Infante Ferdinand assuming command of the reinforced army of Flanders, and with the Swedes defeated, the tide of war momentarily turned against the Dutch and their allies, but France's declaration of war on the Habsburgs in May 1635 leveled the playing field. In June 1635, the Dutch and French armies jointly invaded the Spanish Netherlands from Maastricht, sacking Tienen on the road to Brussels and pillaging the countryside. After a failed attempt to besiege Louvain, the Franco-Dutch army marched via Weert to Kleve for a standoff at the Schenckenschans fort. In the meantime, the Spanish Infante Ferdinand secured his supply lines between Kleve and Spanish Brabant by occupying a string of towns in Kleve and fortifying Gennep, Helmond, and Eindhoven.[111]

The 1634 exactions in the countryside during the failed sieges of Breda and Maastricht once again highlighted the detrimental impact of soldiers' excesses on the belligerents' ability to sustain their armies in the field. During the early 1630s, soldiers' private and unauthorized extortions had been repeatedly so exacting that entire rural communities were on the verge of fleeing their homes because they could not pay their contributions. The situation provided the context for another unusual arrangement between the belligerents. The military governor of Dutch Maastricht, Henri Turenne, permitted the inhabitants of Leur (next to Breda) to supply eight wagons of locally produced food weekly to Spanish-held Antwerp in order to satisfy their contribution payments.[112]

The Dutch Siege of Breda

In 1636, the main confrontations took place across the border in Germany and in France. In May 1637, Prince Frederick Hendrick of Orange-Nassau feigned an attack on Dunkirk in Flanders, but rapidly disembarked his army at Bergen op Zoom and deployed it around Breda. The Spanish were unable to dislodge the Dutch besiegers in a direct assault and instead marched east and took Venlo after firebombing the town and subsequently occupying Roermond. Frederick Hendrick persevered with the siege, and Breda capitulated in October.[113] In 1636, the eastern Brabant village of Someren had supplied 429 guilders worth of forages to Frederick Hendrick's army camped at Waalwyk, in the Lang-straat north of Breda.[114] On October 7, 1637, after the capitulation of Breda, Frederick Hendrick ordered the region's villagers and farmers to provide wagons and carts to carry his soldiers' military accoutrements into the town.[115]

In June 1638, the Dutch suffered a bloody defeat after advancing on Kallo and the ring of forts that were defending Antwerp. In July, a Spanish-Imperial army broke Frederik Hendrick's siege of Geldern east of Venlo. Oisterwyk had provided horse wagons to 's-Hertogenbosch to transport supplies in preparation for the siege. In the following year, the Dutch army kept a close eye on the Spanish and Imperial forces near Kleve. In 1640, the Dutch army advanced on Bruges while their French allies were laying siege to Arras, only to be repulsed by the army of Flan-ders. With Breda and 's-Hertogenbosch under firm Dutch control and the French threat from the south, the main terrain of operations shifted increasingly to Antwerp, Flanders (with amphibious operations by the Dutch army), and the Rhine-Maas region, including Venlo and Kleve. While no major sieges or battles recurred in Dutch-controlled Brabant during the 1640s, smaller-scale encounters persisted, including the Spanish reoccupation of Eindhoven in 1644.[116]

Located right in the middle of these hot zones of the war, North Brabant served as a base of operations for the Dutch army. Even though most of the actual fighting occurred outside of the region, the cam-paigns continued to directly affect North Brabant's countryside. In the early 1640s, the armies traversing Brabant caused so much damage that villages throughout the region protested that they would not be able to pay contribution to either party. The magistrates of Etten asserted that many people had lost their crops and property and lived with their neighbors, who supported them.[117] In 1642, Geldrop requested an ex-emption from the annual contribution, given the severe losses that sol-diers had caused between 1629 and September 1641. Geldrop's expenses for the 12-year period totaled over 15,000 guilders. Because many inhab-itants were already heavily in debt, with some having pawned their property, and numerous households having fled their homes, the village was unable to raise the funds for the contribution payments.[118] The magistrates of Someren feared that unless the contributions were for-given, the village's inhabitants would have to abandon their homes. By the early 1640s, Someren's debt had risen to a staggering 100,000 guil-ders. The contribution to the Spanish king over the previous 12 years had amounted to 1,000 guilders per annum, while the contribution to the republic during the same period was 12,384 guilders. In addition, the unauthorized "consumptions" and taxes imposed by nearby Dutch gar-risons and passing Dutch cavalry amounted to 8,000 guilders while other costs included unpaid transport services.[119] The aldermen of Heeze and Leende in their turn argued that their villages had never re-covered from when the prince's army had burned their homes in 1633.[120]

In response to the petitions for exemptions from the contribution payments, the Dutch authorities merely issued yet another ordinance to remind its soldiers that they were not allowed to exact food from vil-lages that paid their monthly contribution installments. Exactions were only permitted if soldiers had written authorization from their com-mander, and even then, they could only take the stipulated amounts. The ordinance warned the soldiers that if they took more than their rightful share or caused any damage, their commanding officers would deduct the cost from their wages.[121]

The Spanish authorities showed equally little compassion to the plight of the rural population. Dr. Jorge Mendes de Andrade, the Span-ish military auditor based in Antwerp, was dismissive of Etten's magis-trates' accounts that Spanish soldiers had abducted people from their very homes in order to extort ransoms. Acceding that the practice violated the royal ordinances, he warned the magistrates that their case was weak because the soldiers had let the abductees go free. Among the abducted was Cornelis Hendrix, the skipper of an intercepted boat. Eleven Spanish soldiers on leave from their regiment had taken Hendrix captive on the pretext that he was not carrying a proper toll letter signed by a royal officer. Demonstrating little respect for the articles of war, the military auditor added that he thought the abductions were merely a tool to extort money and a very common practice that therefore was impossible to prevent. Instead, the military auditor was far more con-cerned about a nightly home invasion by a group of unidentified men who locked up and tortured the inhabitants and assured the magistrates that he was investigating the "murderous and violent" incident.[122]

In the light of the highly formalistic and evasive responses by the Spanish and Dutch authorities, it is little wonder that the soldiers' practices continued unabated. In the summer of 1644, the magistrates of the quarters of Peelland and Kempenland again complained about the heavy cost of continued unauthorized extortions. Don Andreu Cantelmo and his soldiers pillaged St. Oedenrode in 1643, allegedly causing more damage than His Highness "would with his whole army in an entire month." Cantelmo's men "robbed the good people of their movables, livestock and all they owned, so that many are left with nothing [after] having suffered [the loss of] thousands of guilders."[123] During the winter of 1643–44, the Dutch cavalry took up winter quarters in "Waalwijck [Waalwyk] . . . and the other principal villages of the quarter of . . . Oisterwijck [Oisterwyk] and as a result all the villages' (winter) forages had been consumed."[124] In December 1644, a least three large units of cavalrymen based in Maastricht, Breda, and Nijmegen, respectively, traveled through eastern Brabant and adjacent regions, requiring lodging for up to three days at a time and extorting the inhabitants. The sheriff of the quarter of Peelland testified that it was obvious "that these voyages do not serve any real state purpose . . . but only [serve] to exact private contribution [by the officers] which is in contravention of the public notices of the . . . [General Estates] . . . that no villages or any other places can be forced to pay anything to the soldiers beyond the impositions ordered by her High Potentates [the General Estates] . . . not even when ordered by the governor [or] officers." Emphasizing that it was not legitimate for Dutch soldiers to "tax with [the threat of] fire" a region that already was under contribution to the Republic, the Peelland magistrates proposed deducting the cost of the extortions from the Dutch contribution and suggested that the government recoup the shortfall from the officers of the soldiers involved.[125]

Official transport requisitions remained especially burdensome because the military campaign season coincided with the summer and early fall agricultural season, when horses and carts were most needed for the harvest. Moreover, the farmers were not compensated for providing the transport services.[126] During his 1646 campaigns, Frederick Hendrick's army camped near Breda early in the summer before embarking via Bergen op Zoom for Flanders for an assault on Antwerp from the south. Changing his plans, he subsequently disembarked at Bergen op Zoom again and marched across Brabant east to besiege Venlo. Etten and other villages supplied the horse-drawn wagons and carts that transported the prince's soldiers from Breda to the ships in Bergen op Zoom in July, and that carried the army's supplies from Bergen op Zoom to Venlo in October 1646. Providing the drivers, carts, and horses for the prince's 1646 campaigns cost Etten 1,130 guilders and the villages of the rural quarter of Oisterwyk 6,000 guilders.[127]

Peace in 1648 brought only partial relief to the long-suffering Brabant countryside: the republic not only maintained its war contribution but actually increased it by the amount of the contribution that the rural communities had been forced to pay to the Spanish government.[128] In brief, even though the hostilities had ended, rural North Brabant remained responsible for paying the combined Dutch and Spanish contribution taxes to the republic.

Environcide in the Republic's Golden Age

Dutch soldiers were perhaps more subject to state and civilian control, more regularly paid, and more disciplined and drilled than most of their other contemporaries. Yet, they, too, routinely extorted food, goods, and money from villagers and farmers, frequently pillaging and burning the countryside, and repeatedly bringing entire regions to the brink of collapse. The sackings, massacres, and systematic and large-scale killing, raping, and torturing of civilians in towns appear to have been less common in the wartime Low Countries during the 1620s–40s than during the 1570s–80s. The combined impact of the spectacular violence (related to sieges) and the everyday war violence perpetrated by soldiers from Dutch, Spanish, German Imperial, and German Protestant Union armies nevertheless constituted environcide and total war. Soldiers' authorized and unauthorized exactions damaged or rendered inaccessible such key environmental infrastructure as farms, houses, barns, fields, dark earth *plaggen* soils, crops, food stores, livestock, orchards, wood-lots, polders, canals, and dikes.

Attempts in the 1620s to limit the destructive impact of war on the countryside in Brabant were not motivated by any Christian or humani-tarian concerns. Rather, the objective was to preserve a minimally pro-ductive countryside that could fund and feed armies. At issue was that soldiers, officers, and the colonels in charge of the army's regiments competed with state administrations and superior army commanders over the same rural resources. Soldiers' private and unauthorized extor-tions in the 1620s equaled and sometimes even surpassed the "official" contributions exacted by the state authorities and the army command-ers. The unofficial demands from soldiers and officers lodging, camping, or garrisoned in the countryside or marching en route to a military tar-get constituted the most immediate threats, consequently villagers en-deavored to meet them first.

As a result, rural communities frequently could not meet their obliga-tions to the state or occupying army, leading to episodes of spectacular violence that included sacking and burning villages and farms, and sub-sequent rural flight, which created fiscal and logistical deserts that could no longer sustain armies. When villagers and farmers were unable to pay the contributions, fear of being abducted, raped, and tortured often made them flee with whatever they could carry. Articles of war promul-gated through public notices, ordinances, or field orders sought to con-trol and limit soldiers' private and unauthorized extortions, but had little effect. Because soldiers, officers, and garrison and regimental com-manders only partially and indirectly benefited from the official cash war contribution raised by the state authorities, anything that they could extort themselves constituted supplementary in-hand income, and sometimes it was their only income if they had not been paid. Of-ficers therefore had little incentive to enforce the articles of war that limited soldiers' exactions.

There is little evidence to suggest that individual soldiers or officers were in any systematic way held financially or criminally responsible for unauthorized exactions of food, lodging, goods, services, or money, as long as no civilians had been publicly tortured, raped, or killed. In considering damage accounts from pillaged villagers and farmers, state and occupation authorities, at best, granted forgiveness of part of the contribution payments that were in arrears. Moreover, articles of war only applied to armies when they were operating in their home territory. In contested, neutral, or enemy territory, articles of war were only considered applicable to communities that were current with their contribution payments and protected by safeguards. Communities that provided supplies to the opposing army, even under duress, forfeited the safeguards and legitimized being treated as the enemy.

The impact of three decades of war in the 1620s–40s was comparable in Germany and the Low Countries. In Germany, up to one-third of the countryside lay abandoned at the end of the war; the same was true for the eastern North Brabant. The situation in the western half of North Brabant was hardly any better. The challenges of postwar recovery in North Brabant and in the German Empire were also similar. Although restocking with animals occurred relatively rapidly in Germany after the end of the war, reclaiming the overgrown abandoned lands took 15–20 years, in part because the fertility of the land had to be restored.[129] In many parts of North Brabant, flooded lands had to be reclaimed, a costly and laborious undertaking, as the 1570s and 1580s history of Holland demonstrates. Abandoned *plaggen* soils in North Brabant would have required labor-intensive clearing and new infusions of manure-enriched organic soil collected from stables, sheep cots, pastures, and heath fields.

With the advent of peace in 1648, the republic's central government lost substantial revenue because it could no longer impose contributions on the enemy territories of Spanish Brabant and Flanders. The deficit was only partially addressed by the ruthless decision to effectively double the amount of the contribution payments imposed on Dutch Brabant and Dutch Flanders by requiring the territories to pay both the wartime Dutch contribution payments and the similar payments they had been making to the Spanish king. The main reasons for the overall decrease in the amount of wartime and postwar taxes and fees between 1630 and 1650, however, were depopulation and reduced agricultural production.[130] The heavy wartime debts, the continued state exactions (through war contribution taxes) imposed by the Republic, and the population and wealth losses constituted major obstacles in rebuilding environmental infrastructure and rural society in Brabant.

As in the German empire, the impact of the war in the Low Countries was differentiated, temporally and spatially. The far north and the far south of the Low Countries that were under the firm control of the Republic and Spain, respectively, were shielded from the direct impact of the war. North of the Rhine and Maas Rivers, only Groningen and Gelderland were directly affected by episodes of mass violence. But Brabant, Flanders, modern Limburg, Julich-Kleve, and to a lesser extent neutral Liège were on the frontlines of the war throughout the three decades. The large-scale and protracted sieges of Breda and 's-Hertogenbosch were periods of intense and often spectacular violence and destruction in the countryside. In between the episodes of spectacular violence, the everyday wartime extortions and pillaging by garrisoned soldiers and marching armies gradually accumulated as a slow form of environcide that in the long run was equally destructive. As in the Thirty Years War in Germany, some profited from the war: arms dealers in Holland and Liège, war lords, and perhaps even some individual soldiers. The Liège region directly southeast of North Brabant endured significant destruction, but industry, crafts, and the mining sector profited from the war, and wealthier, land-owning farmers proved to be resilient.[131] In the north, the provinces of Holland and Zeeland thrived, while the interior provinces fared less well, and Dutch Brabant and Flanders were devastated.[132]

While some regions lost population, others gained. In general, Holland's population rapidly increased following the 1570s war because of a massive influx of refugees from Flanders and Brabant. The rapid urbanization of Amsterdam, Leiden, Haarlem, and other towns in the republic typically are attributed to the effects of urban pull caused by a growing Golden Age economy. But the large-scale migration from Brabant and Flanders to Holland resulted from push factors, specifically, the displacement caused by the war in the south. In other words, the Golden Age and the environcidal Thirty Years War were, to an extent, opposite sides of the same coin. Finally, the transformation of Holland's towns from victims of environcidal and total war in the 1570s to thriving Golden Age cities in the 1630s highlight both the dynamic positionality of perpetrators and victims as well as the agency of refugee-victims. War refugees from Brabant and Flanders gained prominent positions in Holland, and their labor, capital, knowledge, and passion helped rebuilt Holland's towns and contributed to the republic's war efforts against the Spanish enemy on the North Brabant front. Thus, ironically, from the 1620s to the 1640s, victims from the 1570s environcidal war in Holland collaborated with victims of the 1580s-to-early-1600s environcidal war in the southern (and eastern) Low Countries to wage environcidal war in Brabant and the Southern Low Countries.

4

Raiders and Refugees

ENVIRONCIDE, DISPLACEMENT, AND DISEASE IN 17TH-CENTURY EASTERN NORTH AMERICA

The [French] Governor of Canada will come here [Onondaga in the Iroquois Five Nations] when the Indian corn grows ripe, to destroy you all.[1]

After they [the Iroquois Five Nations] had purchased from the Christians Good Arms they conquered their Enemies and rooted them out so that where they then inhabited has now become a Wilderness.[2]

We too have abandoned our lands and fields on which we depended for a large share of our food and we are now in a forest, more deprived of aid than we were when we first arrived in this country . . . and consequently he [the enemy] threw us in a famine more horrible than the war itself. The Hurons . . . too have fled their lands and now it is necessary to build defenses for themselves and they and we have to build houses or rather huts and if we want to harvest grain next year, it will be necessary to cut the forests to create fields and open countryside. These works, hindered by the fear for the enemy, are very difficult, not in the least because the poor people have neither hunted nor fished, have no grain, and move around here and there to search for acorns and roots.[3]

THE FIRST STATEMENT is ascribed to an elderly Iroquois man who moved back from a French Catholic mission village in New France to his Five Nations (home) town in the 1690s, warning his neighbors. The second statement is attributed to an orator of the Five Nations in 1712. Whether they are indeed literally the words spoken by two Iroquois men or not, the statements can serve to illustrate key traits of 17th-century conflicts in eastern North America. Indigenous American and European men of war alike readily deployed scorched earth tactics, synchronizing their attacks with the harvest to capture the maximum amount of food supplies and at the same time deny such necessities to their opponents. Casting the enemy into a wilderness state by destroying the environmental infrastructure that sustained lives, livelihoods, and ways of life, or displacing the communities that depended on and sustained this environmental infrastructure was both the objective and the tool of war.

The third quote highlights the effects of environcidal warfare: famine and fear consumed those displaced from their villages, homes, food stores, and crop fields. Taken from a 1649 letter by a French Jesuit Missionary, it recounted how famine decimated Huron refugees in their forest hideouts after the Five Nations of the Iroquois sacked and burned their towns. Clearly the devastating wars condemned in the Black Legend narratives were not confined to the Habsburg realms in Europe or the Americas. French, Dutch, English, and other colonists and indigenous Americans in eastern North America systematically sought to live off the land to sustain their war effort while mercilessly denying their opponents the opportunity to do the same, resulting in famines, pests, and plagues that decimated and uprooted populations.

European sources describing indigenous North American societies as primitive hunter-gatherers or as seminomadic, shifting cultivators typically dated from long after initial contact.[4] In fact, the precarious and wilderness-based livelihoods the sources described were frequently the *outcome* of war and violence caused by conflict between indigenous Americans or as a result of the European encounter. Depicting indigenous Americans as living in and by Nature also legitimized the European alienation of their lands: in Lockean terms, indigenous Americans' alleged failure to improve the land was a precondition to establishing both (economic) property and (political) territorial claims by the European settlers.[5]

As in South and Central America, eastern indigenous North Americans relied on an elaborate environmental infrastructure that typically included homes and food storage facilities, fields with mounds and fertile dark earth soils, orchards and fruit trees, fishing and game traps, and towns and villages. Indigenous American environmental infrastructure became a target of aggression and violence because it was a precondition for survival for war refugees and newly arrived and ill-prepared European fortune-seekers, missionaries, and migrants. Losing the use of environmental infrastructure and the concentration of settlements left populations more vulnerable to devastating epidemic diseases, and subsequent depopulation and displacement offered invasive organisms, institutions, technologies, and ideas easy entry into the New World.

Protestant Conquistadors and the Black Legend

English and Dutch Protestant, French Calvinist, and French Catholic soldiers, explorers, and settlers deployed the same environcidal practices in the New World as their Spanish enemies. During the 16th and early 17th centuries, Dutch rebels fighting the Spanish crown sympathized and identified with the indigenous Americans, whom they regarded as natural allies in a common war against Catholic Spain. Willem Usselincx, one of the founders of the Dutch West India Company (WIC), a privateering enterprise committed to waging war on the Spanish empire for profit, argued that the WIC should ally with the indigenous Americans and liberate them from the Spanish yoke. Willem Usselincx was a war refugee from the Spanish-occupied Southern Low Countries who had escaped to rebel Holland during the Dutch Revolt. WIC soldiers joined English privateers in mercilessly sacking Spanish and Portuguese settlements in the Americas. Indigenous Americans, however, were not exempt from the depredations of Dutch soldiers and settlers for long. By the mid-17th century, Dutch critics argued that the WIC practiced the same cruel oppression in its North American possessions that had made the Dutch rebels rise up against the Spanish crown less than half a century before.[6]

The English encounter with the indigenous Americans also quickly soured and turned deeply violent. The first generations of English settlers were not only inspired by and led by men who had participated in the brutal wars on the British Isles and the continent (English, Scottish, and Irish soldiers participated in large numbers in the Dutch Revolt and the Thirty Years War), but the new settlements were mired in violence, misery, and failure. In the face of crisis, Puritan and other Protestant conquistadors sometimes shared with their Catholic enemies a crusading outlook that increasingly saw indigenous America as a false paradise peopled by satanic cannibals who needed to be destroyed materially and spiritually, thereby legitimizing exterminatory violence and scorched earth tactics.[7] Yet, Dutch, English, and French conquistadors also often heavily relied on indigenous American allies in both war and diplomacy. The Iroquois Five Nations were key allies for the Dutch and subsequently the English. The Huron and their allies provided staunch support for the French.

The demographic collapse of the North American indigenous population largely is attributed to Old World diseases that accompanied European settlers and African slaves. Absent immunity to such diseases as smallpox, measles, and malaria, indigenous American populations quickly and "naturally" succumbed to deadly virgin-soil epidemics. Traders, warriors, and refugees carried the pestilences deep into the interior, causing epidemics that paved the way for subsequent European westward expansion.[8] Some Spanish, English, and French migrants saw the hand of God in the indigenous American population collapse.[9]

According to the virgin-soil epidemics argument, the near-extermination of the indigenous North Americans did not constitute genocide because the European invaders did not intentionally cause the epidemics with the objective of exterminating the indigenous population.[10] Rather, the microbes that carried new diseases to the Americas were stowaways. This depiction suggests that the decimation of indigenous Americans was not only natural but also inevitable, and thus reduces the indigenous Americans to passive victims. Moreover, the emphasis is on the agency of the vector and contagion, excluding the importance of local environmental conditions that facilitated the spread of the disease or the social and political factors that rendered indigenous American populations vulnerable to disease.[11]

As in the case with the conquest of Spanish America, the extent to which war and displacement rendered indigenous North Americans more vulnerable to disease is underestimated. Continuous warfare and militarization triggered destructive raids and counterraids, and the vacillating movements of people facilitated the spread of diseases by opening a pathway for the invasive germs to enter new human communities.[12] Indigenous American and settler populations alike were affected by hunger, thirst, cold, famine, and displacement conditions that lowered their resistance.[13] Concentrating populations in larger and denser villages for defense in and of itself made people more susceptible to disease, creating death traps comparable to the 16th-century forced resettlement villages in the Spanish Americas and the refugee-packed rebel towns in Holland.[14] Thus, although a powerful tool, the virgin-soil contagion model does not on its own account for the dramatic indigenous American demographic collapse.

Eastern Indigenous Americans and Environmental Infrastructure

The literature often depicted eastern indigenous Americans as shifting cultivators who moved their fields and abodes every couple of years to a new virgin forest plot. Villagers cleared the new site through slash-and-burn techniques that left behind tree stumps. They seeded maize in the ashes between the stumps. Except for clearing and burning, these cultivators supposedly made no real investments in the land, that is, they practically lived in and by Nature. Indigenous American "shifting cultivators," however, typically engaged in labor-intensive mound agriculture that required heavy and sustained investments of labor and other resources.[15] When Dutch traders first encountered the Lower Hudson Valley Munsee in the early 1600s, they considered them to be nomadic hunter and gatherers. Only later did Dutch settlers become aware that the Munsee inhabited permanent villages with round or longhouses, abundant maize and bean stores, and elaborate fields that were located deeper inland.[16] The large majority of eastern indigenous Americans lived in (semi)permanent villages, but (a part of) the inhabitants moved seasonally between a main fixed village site and one or more fishing or hunting or gathering camps.[17]

In the Northeast of North America, entire villages moved at decades-long intervals to new sites, seemingly within a bound village territory and ultimately often returning to near their original sites. The pattern suggests that the number of suitable village sites within a territory was limited and that the movement followed a cyclical pattern.[18] The fields were shifted to the new location as well. The abandoned village site and its surrounding fields would then lay fallow.[19]

Iroquoian villages remained in the same locations for 20–50 years before they rotated to a new site within a limited territory; old and new village sites were rarely more than ten miles apart from one another. In the case of Mohawk villages, the successive sites occupied by a single village were only a few miles apart. Decaying wood from longhouses and palisades, charcoal and ashes from hearths, and household debris enriched the soils of abandoned village sites with organic matter, making them choice locations for fields. A French Jesuit returning to the Huron-Wendat territory in 1634 after a three-year absence found that his village had metamorphosed into maize fields. Only one longhouse remained on the old location, and the villagers had built new houses on a site one mile away. During the 17th century, Iroquois villages occurred in tight clusters with the larger towns and villages only a few miles apart from one another. Smaller hamlets and individual longhouses dotted the countryside around the larger villages and on the edges of each nation's territory to offer shelter to hunters, fishermen, and travelers.[20]

Huron village site occupation archaeology offers an archive of the upheavals in the late 16th and early 17th centuries. Before 1580, a village site was occupied for an average of 30 years, but during the turmoil of the early 1600s, the occupation duration first halved and finally was reduced to only ten years during the 1630s and 1640s wars between the Huron and the Five Nations. Village site occupation was no longer based on environmental conditions (soil fertility, availability of wood) but was primarily a reflection of the apprehension about violence and disease.[21] In the Mohawk River Valley, optimal locations for village site selection were more limited. Villagers located their homes and fields on the higher ground directly adjacent to the narrow floodplain to prevent flooding. Successive village sites were almost without exception adjacent to the river's floodplain (sometimes just across the river) and rarely were relocated deep into woodlands.[22]

Northeastern indigenous Americans grew maize on mounds, although the cultivation mounds were smaller in size than in Central or South America. The fields generally took the form of the "corn hills" found throughout the Midwest and East. The narrow ridges or garden beds in Wisconsin and Michigan in the Midwest may have been abandoned before European travelers entered the region in enough numbers to report on their use.[23] In 16th-century Virginia, John Smith reported active indigenous use of mounds, observing indigenous Americans weeding around the crop mounds three to four times a season.[24] The remnants of thousands of such mounds have survived, all still relatively high in organic matter and constituting dark earths that are more fertile than the surrounding soil.[25]

The use of fire to clear new fields and to prepare existing fields for the cultivation season contributed to the dark earth formation. Carbonized organic matter figures prominently in old indigenous American settlements and field sites, and account for its dark hue. Initial land clearing for fields and homesteads was through slash and burn. Eastern indigenous Americans in North America ringbarked the larger trees one year and burned the desiccated vegetation the next. Although European observers condemned slash and burn as primitive and a waste of timber, faced with a shortage of labor, settlers widely adapted the practice. Indeed, the 18th-century *Natural History of Virginia* highly recommended the method to planters because it was far less expensive than clear cutting and processing the wood as timber.[26]

Indigenous American farmers used fire to clear their existing fields of plant debris and weeds for the cropping season. In 16th-century North Carolina, indigenous men and women cultivated the soil by tearing out weeds and old corn stalks, allowing the weeds to dry in piles before burning them.[27] They also carried the ashes from household and cooking fires to the fields. Mohawk farmers prepared their fields with fire, and Huron farmers also maintained their fields' soil fertility by burning. In April 1637, a raiding party traveling through Iroquois territory reported that "the land was everywhere on fire and the smoke hid those who burned . . . their fields as was customary."[28]

Indigenous North Americans not only used fire on fields but also deployed it to shape the landscape beyond their farms. The practice was so widespread that it had deeply transformed the American environment on the eve of contact, creating open park landscapes that attracted wildlife and facilitating hunting.[29] Not all fire, however, was anthropogenic. Managing fire—let alone controlling it—was and continues to be challenging and often impossible. Moreover, fire management did not affect all of the Americas, and the practice did not uniformly impact land.[30]

Fire had a major impact on tree vegetation, and fruit- and nut-bearing trees were key resources for eastern indigenous Americans. Most acorn-producing oaks are relatively fire tolerant and resprout after fires. In contrast, the hickory nut tree of the North American south is highly fire intolerant. The ubiquitous occurrence of the hickory implies that fire was used judiciously. Human-caused clearing with fire and other management impacts were highly localized and concentrated around settlements, along paths, and in hunting areas, reflecting population densities and occupation intensities.[31]

The middle and eastern regions of North America contain thousands of large mounds and earthworks. Some in Michigan were built for defense. Several of the larger earthen enclosures in southern Michigan had palisades and contained household debris, indicating inhabitation, especially when they were close to water supplies. Other mounds contained little or no household debris, suggesting that they served a ceremonial function, while others still were far from surface sources of water and so are associated with burial mounds.[32] The mounds of the Mississippi culture and the Great Lakes region generally are regarded as artifacts intended to physically or spiritually "domesticate" the environment. Communities in the lower Mississippi region seem to have practiced flood-recessive agriculture, cultivating crops in the flood-plain after the floodwaters receded. The floodwaters would have carried silt onto the fields, fertilizing them. Mounds protected people, habita-tions, stores, property, and shrines from seasonal flooding. Even where mounds show no evidence of residential occupation, they may have served as temporary refuges during floods, as is common elsewhere in flood-prone environments.[33]

Indigenous American dwellings constituted invaluable infrastructure that protected people and their property against the elements. Without these dwellings, it is doubtful that indigenous Americans and their pre-carious food and seed stores would have survived blistering summers, freezing winters, or soaking rains. The maize cultivators of eastern North America inhabited permanent dwellings grouped into fortified towns. Each longhouse contained benches and sleeping platforms to accommodate many people. In May 1637, the villagers of a large Huron-Wendat town labored for three weeks to build a medium-size longhouse for French missionaries, a task that took more time than usual because most of the young men were away. In 1639, the larger Huron-Wendat longhouses each contained four to five hearths, accommodating eight to ten families. The longhouse's pole framework was fixed in the ground and bent together to form the roof. Depending on the region, bark mats (in the Atlantic region), grass (for Arkansas's Wichita), or rushes (for Lake Michigan's Ojibwa and Menominee) covered the frame.[34] In cold weather, the Chesapeake Bay region's oval bark or reed mat-clad houses were kept comfortably warm by continuously burning fires in the hearths. Smoke filled the homes and exited though holes left in the roofs.[35]

Although all indigenous American societies stored food, food storage has received little systematic attention.[36] Dwellings often doubled as storage barns. The longhouses of the eastern and the Great Lakes's in-digenous Americans sheltered people as well as food stores.[37] Food and seed stores had to be kept dry and protected from fungi, insects, and animals. Depending on the region, the winter (in temperate climate regions) or the summer (dry season) was the time of scarcity, when little

FIGURE 4.1. Algonquian village of Secotan on the Pamlico River with (long) houses surrounded by fields and trees (Library of Congress Rare Book and Special Collections Division Washington, DC 20540 USA, aquarel by John White, published in Theodor de Bry, *Americae Pars Decima* [Oppenheimi: Typis H. Galleri, 1619]).

or no food was available beyond what had been preserved and stored. Households stored food attached to the roof rafters, in discrete compartments or rooms, or in subterraneous pits. The Iroquois stored their bulk food supplies inside and outside their homes in aboveground granaries and storage pits. A Dutch traveler who visited several Iroquois Mohawk and Seneca villages during the 1634–35 winter noted large stores of grain, beans, and dried salmon and venison in the longhouses, and his hosts shared preserved nuts and berries with him as well.[38]

Villagers also stored provisions outside the houses in specially designed huts, pits, and caves, or on platforms. In Michigan, food cache pits, which typically are found in clusters of 50–60 pits, are a commonly occurring archaeological feature. The cache pits primarily date 1000–1600 or later.[39] The Menominee hunter-gatherers of Wisconsin stored surplus wild rice in pits.[40] In what would become the Southeast in the United States, granaries consisted of a pole frame with wattle or mud-wattle walls covered with a thatch or bark roof.[41] Indigenous Americans elaborately processed food before it was sealed in containers and stored. Once processed and dried, many foods, including corn, beans, pumpkins, fish, nuts, and berries could be safely stored for long periods.[42]

Food stores could be very substantial: the plunder from the town of Ocale (in the modern US South) fed the Spanish conquistador De Soto's 600-plus member expedition for over three months, and the food stores pillaged in and around modern Tallahassee sustained the conquistadors throughout the entire winter. The bulk of the captured stores consisted of maize, beans, and smaller quantities of dried deer meat, nuts, berries, and fruit.[43] With their concentrations of people, dwellings, crop fields, food stores, tools, weapons and other valuables, villages and settlements were bound to attract raiders, especially in conditions of scarcity and insecurity. Sixteenth-century Iroquoian villages consequently were located on hilltops and ringed by palisades. The use of palisades predated contact in many parts of the Americas but spread rapidly as insecurity increased.[44]

Eastern indigenous Americans cultivated a variety of plants. By the early contact period, maize had become the main staple in eastern North America. Maize and other starches alone, however, do not make a healthy diet. Even under conditions of peace, a maize-rich diet might render a population nutritionally vulnerable to disease.[45] To balance their diet, indigenous American communities relied on the fruits and nuts of a range of cultivated, semidomesticated, or "wild" trees and shrubs. Fresh and stored tree fruit, nuts, and berries were important sources of food, especially during lean seasons and years, and they served as critical sources of vitamins and minerals to supplement nutrient-poor stored staples. In most cases, the trees were associated with human settlements, occurring in or near villages, towns, farms, or fields.[46]

French missionaries residing in Huron-Wendat villages in the 1630s frequently reported about the importance and abundance of fruit and nuts, and in the 1640s Huron war refugees depended heavily on acorns for their survival.[47] Members of the 16th-century De Soto expedition noted abundant fruit and nut trees near indigenous American towns and on and near fields, including pecan, hickory, chestnut, mulberry, and wild plum.[48] In 1773, William Bartram noted a variety of fruit and nut trees in or near indigenous American villages or crop field sites during his travels in the same region, concluding that the Chickasaw plum only occurred on old indigenous American fields and never grew wild in the forests.[49] Trees and bushes were, of course, a type of immobile environmental infrastructure that was lost when populations fled their villages.

Indigenous North Americans actively protected, managed, and seeded or planted a range of berry- and nut-producing vegetation, including blackberry, pecan, chestnut, oak, maple, Californian black walnut (*Juglans spp.*), wild crab apples, Kentucky coffee tree (*Gynnocladus Canadensis*), and American plum.[50] The archaeobotanical record of eastern North America confirms the presence of hickory nuts, walnuts, and acorns at most of the known settlement sites, as well as hazelnuts, chestnuts, and *chinqua* pines (*Castanea pumili*). Numerous indigenous fruits occurred at the same sites, notably persimmons, plums, cherries, sumac, blueberries, strawberries (*Fragaria virginiana*), and blackberries.[51] Several of the berry species that indigenous Americans used, as well as pecan and wild rice, have been domesticated and today are grown as commercial crops. The domestication of plants typically is a very slow process, stretching over hundreds of years.[52] European colonists may have seemingly rapidly domesticated these plants because they already had been cultivated or (semi)domesticated by indigenous Americans. Thus, at the time of contact, indigenous Americans relied to a critical degree on environmental infrastructure that was concentrated in and immediately around the settlements and difficult or impossible to move. Displacement from their villages and farms therefore meant the loss of key resources, including shelter, food, food stores, cleared and fertile fields, and orchards.

War, Displacement, and Disease in the Northeast

Climate change caused displacement and conflict independent of European contact. The onset of the Little Ice Age rendered crop cultivation a less secure livelihood in what would become the Canadian–US border region. Although there is evidence of maize cultivation as far north as Manitoba, Canada, before the onset of the Little Ice Age in the 14th century (see Map 8.1), by the late 18th century, the Mandan and Hidatsa villages on the Missouri River had become the northernmost crop cultivators west of the Great Lakes.[53] Climate change made crop cultivation more precarious in the northern latitudes, heightening competition over existing environmental infrastructure. In the summer of 1635, famine conditions prevailed in Huron country because late snowfall and frost in the spring had forced farmers to reseed their maize fields three times, resulting in the loss of seed maize as well as a shortened agricultural season and probably a reduced harvest.[54]

Conflict between Iroquois groups predated the earliest contact in the 1530s, leading the indigenous American populations of the Northeast to concentrate in fortified hilltop villages. Pre-1600 conflicts between Iroquois groups have been characterized as "mourning wars" with limited objectives. The main purpose was to take captives, some of whom were ritually killed for revenge. Other captives were adopted into families to replace relatives killed in war. A growing dependence on guns, iron weapons and tools, and other European trade goods escalated the raids by the 1640s, affecting large regions of eastern North America and with repercussions well into the 18th century as far west as the Great Plains.[55]

Devastating epidemics accompanied the violence. French Jesuit missionaries based in the eastern Great Lakes area and the St. Lawrence Basin reported dramatic depopulation among their indigenous allies

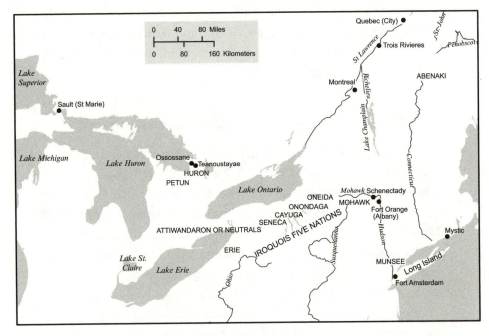

MAP 4.1. The Northeast of North America in the 17th century.

caused by measles in conjunction with an intestinal ailment that occurred in 1634–35. Epidemic disease continued to cause widespread
sickness and death into 1638, although it is unclear if the same diseases
were responsible and smallpox struck in 1639. The Jesuits' friends and
foes alike were convinced that the missionaries manipulated the new
deadly diseases. Indeed, the Jesuits, who founded their first mission in
the Huron-Wendat territory in the southeast corner of Lake Huron in
1634 may have unintentionally spread the first contagions among their
hosts. Frenchmen and indigenous Americans alike fell ill after the arrival of a French fleet in Quebec in that year, but whereas the former
recovered, most of the latter died. Several Jesuits subsequently traveled
to Huron-Wendat where the disease spread after their arrival. Neither
the onset of winter nor prayers offered by the French missionaries and
Huron healers stopped the epidemic, although the Jesuits acknowledged that a Huron healer's root-based concoctions did help them recover. Jesuits attended a Huron-wide council in August 1637 when

Huron leaders enumerated the losses their villages and families had suffered. One elder lamented that all the longhouses in his village had been
affected and that only two members of his own family had survived. He
stressed that never in his life had he experienced such a disease that had
lasted longer than two or three moons. Jesuits and Huron healers alike
were held responsible. Two months later, the Jesuits' newly constructed
longhouse at Ossossané town mysteriously burned down. Two Huron
healers fared worse, having turned up dead. Delegates of the Petun-
Tionontate Nation to the southwest of Huron-Wendat implored the
Jesuits to stop the disease from ravaging their country.[56]

In 1639, two men, a Huron trader and a French Jesuit servant, inde-
pendently carried smallpox from Quebec to the Huron towns and villages. As smallpox raged, the missionaries baptized 1,000 Huron on
their deathbeds. Most died, including 360 children under the age of
seven. An additional 100 small children who had been baptized before
the epidemic also perished. The epidemic had subsided by the summer
of 1640 when the Jesuits conducted a census in the Huron and neighboring Petun villages, counting 12,000 people in 700 longhouses divided over 32 towns and villages.[57] For comparison, in 1634, the Jesuits
had estimated that the 20 Huron settlements alone contained 30,000
inhabitants. While that number may have been exaggerated to highlight
the potential of missionizing in the region, the 1630s Jesuit reports suggest that the population losses caused by the epidemics had been dramatic. Moreover, the Huron's neighbors did not escape the 1630s and
subsequent plagues. Ironically, Huron, Algonquian, and French war
captives taken back to the Iroquois villages may have been the main
source of spreading the contagions to the Iroquois. Epidemics affected
Iroquois Mohawk villages in 1634 (smallpox or measles), 1636 (possibly
pneumonia), 1637, and 1639–40 (smallpox), and the Iroquois Seneca in
1640–41. Not all diseases were exotics. Even before contact, tuberculosis
was rampant in the densely inhabited Iroquois hilltop villages.[58]

Microbes spreading through human contact were only part of the
story of the devastating 1630s and subsequent epidemics. It was war that
paved the way for the invasive and indigenous microbes at times aided
by a higher incidence of droughts or frost brought about by the Little

Ice Age. The St. Lawrence Valley Algonquian Nations and their Huron allies had been at war with the Iroquois Five Nations since the early 1630s. Iroquois attacks and ambushes in the Lawrence River Basin severely hampered trade and hunting. The St. Lawrence River was the major conduit to the French settlements at Trois Rivieres and Quebec for the beaver pelt trade. Iroquois attacks displaced Algonquian hunting camps, and less productive hunting made them more dependent for their sustenance on maize supplied by Huron farmers. Mid-1630s droughts depressed maize harvests, interfered with hunting, and increased the risk of uncontrolled fires. Even under normal conditions, the bark-clad longhouses were fire-prone. Three out of 20 Huron villages and numerous isolated cabins burned down during the droughts, causing the loss of significant winter food stores as well as other valuable possessions that had been kept in the longhouses. In 1634–35, the Five Nations Iroquois virtually closed off the St. Lawrence trade after destroying an Algonquin fortified village at Trois Rivieres and defeating a Huron company that had sought to fight its way through to Quebec. Displaced from their hunting village, and with no access to Huron maize supplies and, the St. Lawrence Algonquians suffered famine. In the meantime, the French, allied to the St. Lawrence Algonquians and the Huron and keen to restore the St. Lawrence beaver pelt trade, fortified their settlements at Quebec and Trois Rivieres.[59]

Environcide and the Destruction of the Huron Homeland

War, displacement, drought, and frost continued to provide fertile ground for disease in the second half of the 1630s. During the summer of 1635 and the winter of 1635–36, Huron villagers were left virtually defenseless with most of the men away to fish, hunt, trade, or raid. Rumors about imminent Iroquois attacks, made villagers loath to leave the protection of the palisaded villages to tend their crops, and many were packed and ready to flee at the slightest alarm.[60] In the spring of 1636, frost, disease, and ceremonial reburials delayed the onset of the cultivation season in the Huron region to late May, leaving a very narrow time frame for the maize to ripen. To restore morale, the Huron Captain Andahia visited all the longhouses in his village to exhort the women not to allow themselves to be overcome by the loss of their relatives and to announce that the Huron-Wendat would take the war to the Iroquois Five Nations lands so that the Huron women could safely cultivate their crop fields.[61]

Making farmers feel safe proved difficult. Continued Iroquois Five Nations raids spread fear and hindered crop cultivation, hunting, and trading, which reduced access to food and other resources. In June 1636, Iroquois raiders attacked a group of Huron warriors right next to the eastern-most Huron village of Contarea.[62] In April 1637, a company of Tadoussac, Huron allies, met disaster in the Five Nations territory, bad news that only increased the sense of insecurity. In August 1637, the Iroquois ambushed two Huron trading canoes near Trois Rivieres, causing panic among the Algonquians camped next to the French fort; the women and children fled to Quebec, and the men sought shelter in the fort.[63] In 1638, people remained constantly on their guard for the Iroquois, which distracted them from more productive endeavors.[64]

The late 1630s influx of Wenro (Weanohronon) refugees boosted depleted Huron numbers, but also compromised food security and health. The Wenro constituted the eastern-most of the Iroquois Neutral Nations, closest to the Iroquois Five Nations border. When the Five Nations attacked the Wenro, the other Neutrals refused to come to their aid. The Wenro subsequently broke with the Neutrals and federated with the Huron. The 600 Wenro men, women, and children and their Huron escort carried their possessions on the 80-mile trek north. Several of the migrants died en route and "almost all arrived sick or became sick after they arrived." The Huron leaders distributed the migrants over the main towns, and the Jesuits noted with surprise and satisfaction that the refugee families were given the best places in the longhouses that hosted them. It took the new arrivals two months to recover from the exhaustive migration. The Wenro soon built their own town, which was included in the 1640 Jesuit census.[65] The Huron's Petun neighbors also suffered the impact of war and displacement, but more directly. In 1639, the Iroquois burned most of the longhouses of Ehwae, the main town of the Petun. The loss of homes containing food, clothes, pots, and other precious goods left many ill-prepared for the winter, resulting in heavy losses to hunger, cold, and smallpox.[66]

Raids continued to affect food production after the smallpox epidemic subsided. In 1640, a man was killed near his crop fields in the Huron region. Hungry, L'Isle Algonquians once again sought refuge in the French fort at Trois Rivieres, abandoning the seasonal hunt and their fields. It took a French sloop of war to drive back 500 well-armed Iroquois from Trois Rivieres.[67] An Iroquois raid on Montreal in the following year caused the L'Isle Algonquian (Ekonkeronon) to abandon both their island and Trois Rivieres altogether and flee to Quebec. They sent their hunters deep into the interior to evade enemy interference, but an Iroquois Five Nations' war party found their tracks and pillaged their hunting camp. The Iroquois Five Nations also captured 12 Huron trading canoes returning from Quebec to the Huron villages and mounted a fierce attack on French soldiers erecting the new Fort Richelieu along the river of that name south of Trois Rivieres.[68]

In the early 1640s, the Five Nations changed their strategy, dividing their forces into smaller bands to cover more ground and to be able to sustain operations not only throughout the summer but year-round. They based their war bands in small forts along the St. Lawrence riverbanks near Montreal to ambush trading canoes and harass the French forts. In response, the St. Lawrence indigenous Americans left the valley three months earlier than usual to hunt in the interior, but early hunting and fishing was risky because thick ice could prevent fishing and game may not have returned for the season.[69] Having lost confidence in the French's ability to protect them, the St. Lawrence Algonquians moved their winter camps near the Huron towns and villages in the early 1640s, which brought them closer to their sources of maize.[70] But, they were not safe in Huronia either. In 1642, the Iroquois Five Nations attacked a border village in the far southeast of the Huron territory, killed or captured the inhabitants, and burned the homes.[71] With a decline in hunting, an increase in the demand for maize by the displaced and refugees, the loss of an entire village's food stores, and farmers fearful of tilling their fields, maize and other foods became scarcer, leading to a regional famine. Indigenous farmers hoarded the little maize they had to ensure seeding their fields in the spring. Most villagers consequently subsisted on pumpkins, acorn, and roots dug up in the woods.[72] More concentrated populations, bringing together destitute war refugees who had been exposed to hunger and disease, however, also increased the likelihood of contagion.

Despite high hopes, the new French Fort Richelieu proved unable to seal off the Lawrence Valley from attacks by the Five Nations war bands. In 1644, the Five Nations besieged the fort, preventing its garrison from leaving the fort even to collect firewood without suffering casualties.[73] Hunting and trading in the St. Lawrence Valley bordered on the impossible. Iroquois Five Nations success, however, came at a high price. One of its four Mohawk towns, Ononjoté, lost nearly all its men during the 1640s conflicts, leaving it a place of widows and orphans. Subsequently, the town lost its status as a full member of the Mohawk Nation, shrinking the Nation from four to only three towns.[74] The Mohawk losses may have set the stage for negotiations between the warring parties that provided a brief and partial respite. The diplomacy, however, was punctuated by an early spring abduction of a group of Huron women and children preparing their fields and an incident in which a Huron company repelled an Iroquois raiding party. With a cease fire, however, the Huron farmers saw their maize crops reach full maturity almost everywhere for the first time in years, Huron fishermen netted an abundant catch on the shores of Lake Huron, and 60 Huron canoes filled with beaver pelts made it down the St. Lawrence to Quebec.[75] When the peace talks collapsed in the fall, full-scale war resumed with a raid on Montreal late in 1646 and multiple attacks on different parties of hunters and hunting camps early in 1647. In October 1647, a French sloop of war patrolling the St. Lawrence found that the Five Nations had reestablished their base along the St. Lawrence River.[76]

The arrival of a fleet that brought a new governor to New France introduced yet another disease-carrying suite of microbial newcomers. French sailors and soldiers were the carriers and the first victims, filling the small Quebec hospital to capacity. Several died. The author of the

1648 report despondently noted that "everything that kills people has travelled through this region," explicitly including war and disease.[77] From their base on the banks of the St. Lawrence, the Five Nations launched a bold attack on a party of Frenchmen who were clearing the vegetation around the fort to reduce the risk of ambushes on Montreal Island. The attackers were routed by the unexpected arrival of a party of 250 Huron traders and warriors en route to Quebec. Having taken an alternative, much longer route to Quebec via the River of the Prairies, the traders had evaded the Five Nations lookouts and ambushes.[78]

The absence of so many of their fighting men because they were traveling to Quebec made the Huron villages once again vulnerable to attack. In the aftermath of repulsing an Iroquois Five Nations raiding party early in 1647, the eastern-most of the four Huron Nations, the Arendahronon, abandoned their main town (St. Baptiste) and a smaller village, retreating to the larger towns further west, and losing their homes and fields in the process.[79] This left the large towns of Teanoustayaé (christened St. Joseph by the Jesuits) and St. Ignace, both boasting large Christian populations and resident missionaries, on the frontline. In the winter of early 1648, raiders attacked a hunting camp in the woods at two days' travel from St. Ignace, killing 7 and capturing 24 of the residents. When a few days later a party of 300 from St. Ignace went to the camp to bury their dead and carry its meat stores home, Iroquois Five Nations ambushers fell upon the stragglers five miles from their hometown, killing or capturing 40 people. In the following spring, attackers captured a girl working in her maize field. At the end of the summer, another raiding party guided by a long-time Huron captive adopted by the Five Nations stormed a small and well-hidden fishing camp and killed or captured 11 of its residents.[80]

More devastating attacks followed in 1648 and 1649, turning Huron-Wendat's towns, villages, and farmlands into charred ruins. In the summer of 1648, the Iroquois assaulted and burned Teanoustayaé (St. Joseph), the main town of the Huron and nearby La Chaudiere, while most of the men were away on hunting or raiding expeditions. After the attacks, the inhabitants of St. Ignace decided to move their town to a new location on the western side of the nearby creek. The new location was only half a mile away from the old location, but the move was a slow process because they first had to construct longhouses at the new site. In early spring of 1648, 400 families still resided at the old location, protected by a 15-foot-high palisade and a deep moat. The palisaded town morphed into a death trap, however, when a large force of 1,000 Five Nations Iroquois rushed the gate at daybreak, killing or capturing the sleeping inhabitants. Only a few escaped to sound the alarm. Leaving a garrison at the occupied town, the main body of the invaders hastened to invade the Huron town of St. Louis three miles to the northwest. Forewarned, 500 of its inhabitants fled, leaving 80 or so defenders. The attackers soon prevailed and burned the longhouses before returning to their new temporary base at occupied St. Ignace. The next day, 300 Huron Bear Nation warriors from the main western towns of Ossossané (la Conception) and Arenté (la Magdaleine) fell upon the Five Nations advance guard that retreated behind the palisade of St. Louis. When the main body of the Five Nations army joined the battle, the Bear Nation warriors were overwhelmed. Arriving too late and reluctant to engage the large Five Nations army, reinforcements from the other Huron towns stood by as the attackers loaded captives with pillaged provisions and other war booty, torched St. Ignace, and marched away.[81]

Fearful of renewed attacks, the Huron abandoned their remaining 15 towns and villages, scattering into the forests or hiding on the many islands off the coast in Lake Huron. Many sought sanctuary in the neighboring mountain villages of Petun. Before evacuating their towns and villages, the Huron set fire to their homes to prevent the Iroquois from using them. The destruction, displacement, and loss of food stores (the towns taken by the Iroquois included most of the largest and wealthiest towns of the Nation) meant that food was already scarce before they abandoned their settlements and the farmlands that surrounded them. The displacement from the environmental infrastructure located at the abandoned towns and villages came at a key time in the agricultural season, when farmers would normally prepare their fields for seeding.[82]

The island refuges were densely forested, and the priority of the displaced was to construct shelters surrounded by heavy defenses for protection from further Five Nations attacks. On one of the islands, rechristened St. Mary's, the Jesuits built a strong fort. Adjacent to the fort, the Huron built a palisaded town of 100 longhouses, each of which held eight to ten families totaling 60–80 persons, which suggests a refugee community of 6,000–8,000 people. The disorderly displacement and the construction efforts, however, consumed precious time and energy that was diverted from hunting and fishing as well as clearing, mounding, and seeding fields. Only one in every ten families on the island had been able to carve out a maize field in the heavy forest cover. Combined with the earlier loss of much of the food stores, the situation spelled famine followed by a disease that proved especially fatal to children. Very few people had any maize left, and the poorest were reduced to roaming the forest to gather roots. With the onset of winter, the lakes and rivers froze solid, preventing fishing. Unlike most of their fellow refugees, the missionaries had the means to purchase a large quantity of acorns and dried fish before the first snow of winter, which they shared piecemeal with the core of their Christian flock.[83]

The Huron refugees who had sought sanctuary in the Petun towns and villages did not escape war, which compounded the loss of environmental infrastructure and famine. In December 1649, a Five Nations Iroquois army outmaneuvered a Petun force sent to intercept them and burned the main Petun border town of St. Jean. Most of St. Jean's men had joined the interception force, leaving the town poorly defended. Given the earlier massive intake of Huron refugees and the loss of a major town and its food stores, it is not surprising that famine overtook the Petun towns, too.[84] With Petun under siege and the famine decimating their flock, the Jesuit missionaries at St. Mary's reluctantly heeded the advice of the Huron elders to seek sanctuary at remote Quebec. With only 300 remaining Christians of the original 3,000, they marched through the devastated Huron country "as if through enemy terrain" and past the "skeletons" of longhouses, miraculously reaching Quebec undetected by any enemy scouts. In Quebec, the survivors received rations from the main Jesuit mission and built new longhouses. Five Nations raids, however, once again made hunting and agriculture beyond the French forts hazardous.[85]

In the 1650s, Five Nations attacks against the Huron mission colonies in the St. Lawrence Valley continued. The Five Nations also forced the Neutrals (Attiwandaron) and the Erie (Cat) Nations to abandon their towns, villages, and fields to the north and east of Lake Erie. The victorious Iroquois made their captives carry the loot back to the Five Nations villages, where most were adopted into Iroquois families. In the 1660s, emboldened by their success, the Five Nations warred with almost all the indigenous American nations in the northeast, as well as with the French in search of beaver pelt stores, captives, and other booty. The beaver pelt business boomed, leaving the Five Nations warriors well supplied with guns and powder by their Dutch allies even as it raised fears that the heavy hunting might exterminate the beaver as well as deer and other game.[86]

The success of the Iroquois Five Nations constituted an existential threat to the population of much of the Northeast. Five Nations environcidal warfare destroyed lives and livelihoods. It caused massive population displacements from homes, villages, food stores, and crop fields, which fueled the famines and plagues that exacted a terrible price from friend and foe alike. The Five Nations had not been immune to the 1630s epidemics that had decimated their enemies, and further plagues visited the Mohawk in 1647 and the Onondaga in 1656–57. Smallpox killed thousands in the Oneida, Seneca, and Cayuga villages in 1661–63, an unidentified contagion hit the Mohawk in 1673, and the Seneca suffered from influenza in 1676.[87]

The long-distance movements of refugees, captives, raiders, and traders exposed traumatized and famished refugees to opportunistic microbes. Many refugees from the northeastern wars resettled in the Great Lakes region in dense, interethnic villages that offered shelter but were also rife with famine and disease. Against the odds, these refugees rebuilt communities and environmental infrastructure, often aided by and in alliance with local groups.[88]

Bringing Environcidal War to the Iroquois Five Nations

In the 1660s, with their indigenous American allies dispersed and their inland missions destroyed, the French took the war directly to the Iroquois Five Nations heartland. French regular troops, seasoned in the practices of total war in Europe, and their indigenous American allies spearheaded New France's environcidal campaigns against the Five Nations. The campaigns demonstrate that war practices on either side of the Atlantic, that is, those used by New World indigenous and settler militia soldiers on the one hand and Old World professional soldiers on the other, were very similar in that they targeted environmental infrastructure and therefore the communities that relied on it. The campaigns against the Five Nations towns were neither an adaption to indigenous American warfare nor a backslide to uncivilized war. Rather the French commanders and soldiers carried on in the tradition of environcidal warfare, with practices that were well known to New World indigenous Americans and European colonists alike.

In 1665, the French king sent the veteran Carignan-Saliere regiment to New France with orders to "exterminate" the Five Nations. Upon their arrival, all the Five Nations, except for the Mohawk, made peace with France. Ordered to engage, the newly arrived French regulars failed to locate the Mohawk villages, narrowly escaping a Mohawk ambush before reaching the Anglo-Dutch settlement of Schenectady. As was common in Europe, the French commander demanded that villagers care for the wounded and provide his troops with provisions. The inhabitants of Schenectady hastened to comply. Satisfied that their demands had been met, the French soldiers marched back to New France, leaving the Anglo-Dutch settlement otherwise unharmed. At the time, the French soldiers were unaware that France and England were already at war. Had they known, the inhabitants of Schenectady might not have been let off so lightly. In September 1666, the French returned to the Mohawk River Valley. The inhabitants fled, and the invaders found the towns "devoid of people, but full with grain and provisions" and after taking what they wanted, they burned the longhouses, palisades, and all the remaining food stores in the three Mohawk towns. Next, they systematically destroyed everything of any value in the countryside around the towns, with the stated objective to bring famine to the Mohawk survivors.[89]

With the Mohawk pacified, New France's settlers and indigenous farmers could resume cultivating their fields. The royal regiment returned to France, leaving 400 of its soldiers residing in New France as settlers. The Jesuits who established several missions among the Five Nations Iroquois noted in 1667 that the Mohawk village of Tionnontoguen had already been rebuilt merely a quarter of a mile from the blackened remains of the original village. The high mortality (especially among children) and the general poverty the missionaries witnessed, however, bespoke of the recent destruction of homes and fields and the impact of continued war with the Wolf Nation (Mahinga) as well as other indigenous nations. The missionaries even freed a captive by threatening the Five Nations Iroquois with future attacks from the French army: "Your land will be devastated, your fields, your homes, your villages will be ruined." In August 1669, the Mohawk repelled a Wolf Nation attack on Gandaouagué, the easternmost of the three Mohawk towns. In the winter of 1669–70, smallpox once again spread inland from Quebec with the arrival of 150 girls sent from France. With one exception, none of the local French settlers was seriously affected by the epidemic, but losses among the Christian indigenous Americans of New France and among the Five Nations were high.[90]

The French victory over the Mohawk encouraged the emigration of Catholic Iroquois (many of whom were Huron captives taken in the 1640s and 1650s wars) from the Five Nations towns to French indigenous American mission settlements in New France, including La Prairie de la Madeleine, Sault, Notre Dame de Lorete near Quebec (the main Huron refugee colony), and Montreal Island. Unable to stop the exodus, the Five Nations leaders allied with the British, who had occupied New Netherland. As part of the agreement with the English, the Susquehannock, who had been driven out in previous wars, could return and either be adopted into Five Nations towns or resettled in their former prewar settlement sites in the Susquehanna River Valley. Reinforced with the returnees and at peace with the French and the English, the Five Nations launched new raids during the 1670s against the indigenous American Nations to their west, including the Fox, Miami, and Illinois. Epidemics hit the Mohawk in 1673, the Seneca in 1676, and smallpox returned to wreak havoc in the towns of the Five Nations, the Hudson Valley, and New York in the late fall and early winter of 1679.

By the early 1680s, raiding parties of up to 1,000 men netted the Five Nations hundreds of captives, which at the time was more than their towns could easily absorb. In 1686, a large Seneca army destroyed the Miami village at the base of Lake Michigan, capturing 500 women and children at once.[91]

The Five Nations successes in the West and tensions between Iroquois non-Christian anti-French and Christian pro-French factions led to renewed open conflict with France in 1684. A French expedition launched across Lake Ontario with 1,400 regulars, militia, and indigenous Americans. They established a base on the lake's southern shore close to the Five Nations towns in September 1684 but were paralyzed by fevers and food shortages, and ultimately withdrew without attacking any targets. In the summer of 1687, however, a French force of 2,000 regulars, militia, and indigenous allies (including Wyandot-Huron and Miami) looted and burned the Seneca villages, the standing crops, and the corn caches after the inhabitants hid in the forest or sought sanctuary in the neighboring Five Nations Cayuga villages. The French and their allies destroyed an estimated 400,000 bushels of corn. Food aid from the other Five Nations villages saved the displaced Seneca from starvation during the subsequent winter, and in the spring of 1688, they started rebuilding their villages. Dutch Prince William of Orange's conquest of England in the same year dragged the English colonies into the war between the Dutch Republic and France.[92]

In 1689, Albany (formerly Fort Orange) requested and received troops from Connecticut to better its defenses against attacks from New France, and the inhabitants of Schenectady committed to bearing a portion of the quartering and other costs involved in housing the troops. Twenty soldiers led by an officer subsequently billeted in the Schenectady blockhouse. In the second half of 1689, a Five Nations raiding party attacked two indigenous American mission settlements, Lachine and La Chesnaye, killing and capturing scores of inhabitants. In the wake of the raids, the French forced the indigenous American inhabitants of the French mission at Sault to burn their own village, fort, and church, and retreat to Montreal, but they returned to Sault in the spring of 1690. In retaliation, French Governor Frontenac contemplated the conquest of

Albany (Fort Orange) and New York, with strict royal orders that the two towns should be occupied and added to New France rather than pillaged and destroyed. In this scenario, however, Schenectady and other small settlements served as sources of provisions that, if necessary, could be plundered to sustain the French invading forces. The grandiose plans of conquest did not materialize. Too small to attack Albany, a French force struck at Schenectady instead, but met with fierce resistance from the 20 Connecticut soldiers quartered in the town and some of the inhabitants, costing the French two of their own. In a European theater of war, an enemy town resisting a superior force typically received no quarter. Such, too, was the fate of Schenectady. Afterward, the remains of 60 inhabitants lay among the ash-covered ruins of homes and barns that had stored the community's possessions and winter food supplies. The French and their allies took 27 people and 50 horses as war booty, and French soldiers tortured Schenectady's Protestant minister to death. The total damage inflicted was estimated at a value of 400,000 livres.[93]

The burning of Schenectady was no exception in the wars of the late 1600s and early 1700s that scorched the Northeast. French and allied indigenous American raiders similarly burned and pillaged the English settler villages at Salmon Falls (New Hampshire) and Casco/Falmouth (Maine) in 1690 and Deerfield (Massachusetts) in 1704, each time resulting in dozens killed and captured. Thus, French regulars employed the same practices as French and English militias and indigenous American fighters, irrespective of whether the villages were European or indigenous Americans settlements. As on previous occasions, a smallpox epidemic spread in the immediate aftermath of the French raid, delaying an English response. In June 1691, New York militiamen reinforced by Mahican and Mohawk warriors raided the indigenous American mission settlement of La Prairie in New France, killing up to 100 of its inhabitants. In January 1693, a French force of regulars, militia, and indigenous allies took the three principal Mohawk villages by surprise, capturing 300 of the inhabitants. The French commander had orders to kill all enemy warriors, but the French-allied Catholic Iroquois among the assailants prevailed on him to spare most of the captured warriors because they shared family and clan ties. The New France mission villages along the St. Lawrence River contained many religious refugees from the Five Nations who had participated in the French raids in large numbers, and former inhabitants of the Mohawk towns among them must have been instrumental in planning and executing the devastating French surprise attacks on the Mohawk settlements. A Mohawk leader lamented after the disaster: "We are a poor people and have lost all by the Enemy."[94]

The French returned to the Five Nations heartland in the summer of 1696. The inhabitants of the Onondaga town burned their own homes as they fled, abandoning their ripening corn, which the French destroyed. Next, the invaders burned the houses and fields of the main Oneida town. A winter of hunger followed, despite pledged food aid from the English governor of New York. Raids by the Miami and other western indigenous Americans interrupted winter hunting, leaving the Iroquois with few beaver pelts to trade for precious weapons and goods. The end of the war between France and England in 1697 did not bring much relief to the Five Nations. Considering them to be rebellious subjects, the French encouraged their indigenous allies to raid the Five Nations and to deny the latter access to the beaver hunting grounds north and west of Lake Ontario. Some of the raiding parties killed people right next to Seneca villages that had only been recently rebuilt after having been destroyed in 1687. The three Mohawk villages had gone unscathed during the violence of the last two decades of the 17th century, but by 1703 the Mohawk population had consolidated into just two villages.[95]

Almost 20 percent of the population of the Five Nations may have been killed or captured, or succumbed to disease and famine during the late 1680s and 1690s. The losses among the Iroquois-speaking populations in the French-allied mission villages in New France were also high: at least three of their villages had been burned during the same period.[96] The Five Nations practice of welcoming refugees also demonstrates how some indigenous American societies successfully resisted being written out of history through (demographic) "collapse" or "genocide." Still, the losses that indigenous Americans societies suffered as a result of the environcidal warfare that destroyed villages and other environmental infrastructure or displaced the people who relied on it were dramatic and real.[97]

Environcide by Despair: Competition between Refugees

Whereas Spanish conquerors successfully established themselves throughout the Americas in the 16th century, similar attempts by non-Spanish European settlers on the East Coast of North America were much more prone to failure. During the "starving period" of the early 1600s, the few existing European colonies were precarious, as illustrated by the high losses of life suffered by the settler populations.[98] Jamestown and other early European settlements that survived did so because of indigenous American aid. As in the Spanish Americas, the North American colonists' diets became increasingly "indigenized" with the adoption of a maize staple and turkey.[99] European colonists often located their settlements and fields at or near the sites of actual or abandoned indigenous American villages and fields.[100]

Moreover, European settlers depended heavily on indigenous American communities for food and other resources. From the 1620s onward, the number of settlers grew rapidly as a result of flight from war and prosecution in Europe. The increased number of settlers translated into a growing dependency on indigenous Americans and their resources, leading to conflict as settlers encroached on indigenous lands. Virginia's settler population grew from 1,000 people in 1624 to 20,000 in 1637, while New England witnessed the influx of 20,000 Puritan and other Protestant settlers fleeing violence in Europe between 1630 and 1660. A century later, Greater Virginia alone counted 400,000 European settlers and African slaves.[101] Not only did the settlers arrive in larger numbers from the 1630s onward, but they also included increasing numbers of children, a demographic that is highly susceptible to harboring and spreading infectious diseases.[102]

War in the East of North America in the 17th and 18th centuries contested "land" in the form of environmental infrastructure, that is, land with crop fields, fruit trees, shelter, and food stores, as much as land as (political) territory. Settler propagandists painted North America as a naturally rich wilderness paradise, overlooking the fact that indigenous Americans created, maintained, and controlled the infrastructure that unlocked the so-called "natural" abundance.[103] It proved difficult for settlers to survive in the "wilderness" areas beyond the border of indigenous American settlements. Rather, European settlers sought out mature indigenous American settlement sites and fields because the land had already been cleared of vegetation and made fertile through the creation of black earths. As a settler in the tidewater region of Virginia observed: "Wherever we meet an Indian old field or place where they have lived, we are sure of the best ground."[104] English settlers in both 18th- and 19th-century Virginia and New England similarly sought out and appropriated old indigenous American fields.[105]

The existential conflict between indigenous Americans and settlers, between competing settler groups, and between different indigenous groups escalated in the 17th century; the increasing number of settlers tapped into indigenous American infrastructure ever more intensively, either indirectly through trade, barter, gifting, patronage, tribute, or plunder, or directly by taking ownership through purchase, alienation, or conquest. The settlers included substantial numbers of war, political, or religious refugees and ex-soldiers from Europe's destructive late 16th- and 17th-century conflicts. Like the French Huguenots who tried to establish colonies in Florida in the 1560s and 1570s, the European refugees were desperate and determined to create new lives in the colonies. The first Dutch WIC settlers at Fort Orange (later Albany) in the 1620s were from the war torn Southern Low Countries.[106] Plunder, pillage, the extortion of food and other resources, scorched earth, torture, murder, and mass killing were commonplace in the settlers' previous experience of 16th- and 17th-century war in Europe. Moreover, the successful Spanish conquests and the rich tribute they extracted from indigenous American subjects in their colonies may have served as a model for settlers and their sponsors. In turn, the East Coast indigenous Americans, who were as equally scarred by war, had everything to lose and responded in kind to the settlers' intrusions.

Faced with a growing settler population that increasingly encroached upon their environmental infrastructure, some indigenous American societies appear to have understood the high stakes from the start. In the 1620s and 1640s, the Powhantan sought to exterminate the English settlers in Virginia, killing a full quarter of the 1,000 colonists in the area in 1622 alone. The mass killing was a heavy blow to Virginia's settlers, but ultimately not a fatal one. In retaliation, the settler militias sacked indigenous American villages. The settlers continued the hostilities for another eight years, timing their raids to capture or destroy the largest possible share of the annual indigenous American crop harvests. The settlers thus lived off the captured food while denying the crops to their opponents—standard tactics in 16th- and 17th-century European wars. The settler war bands similarly targeted indigenous American fields and crops during a resurgence of the conflict in the 1640s that followed another Powhantan attempt to deal a mortal blow to the settlers, this one leaving 400 of 8,000 settlers dead.[107] The infamous 1637 massacre of hundreds of indigenous American men, women, and children at the village of Mystic was by no means exceptional in 16th- and 17th-century warfare in America or Europe. In fact, John Mason, who led the English soldiers and their indigenous allies in the sack of Mystic, was a veteran from the wars in the Low Countries. The Dutch WIC settlements, which went to war with the Munsee in the 1640s, hired the same Captain John Underhill who had assisted Mason during the Mystic massacre. Underhill led the 1644 Dutch counterattack that killed 1,600 Munsee men, women, and children.[108]

The violence was triggered by the WIC's imposition of contributions on the indigenous American villages located in what it considered to be the colony's territories in 1639, to be paid in maize, beaver pelts, and wampum beads. Contributions were special war taxes imposed on subject or enemy populations to fund the defense or occupation of a territory, a common practice in the wars in the Low Countries at the time. New Netherland's Governor Willem Kieft introduced the contributions to induce the Munsee to pay for the maintenance of Fort New Amsterdam and its garrison. When a Raritan village refused to comply with the demand for contributions, WIC soldiers burned the village and massacred its inhabitants as was the custom during the contemporary wars in the Low Countries. Other factors that soured the relationship between the WIC and Munsee groups included the Dutch settlers' maltreatment of indigenous American men and repeated acts of sexual violence against indigenous American women.[109]

The brutal violence between Dutch settlers and indigenous Americans in New Netherland was not merely a matter of settler aliens on the one hand versus indigenous "others" on the other. In fact, Dutch settlers and their indigenous American opponents often had intimate knowledge of one another. The grievances that triggered the violence in part derived from Dutch and indigenous American neighbors perceiving one another as dishonoring or breaching those intimate relationships.[110] Levying contributions, sacking and burning of villages, and abusing villagers, and damaging cropfields were standard wartime practices in enemy lands, common in wartime neutral territory, but not permitted in friendly territory. The Munsee therefore read the signs correctly: the Dutch treated and exploited them and their land and other property in exactly the same way that a wartime hostile would when occupying a new territory.

Like the Powhantan with their blitz wars, Munsee groups waged total war on the Dutch when and where hostilities broke out. Munsee raids wreaked havoc in the Hudson Valley, killing many settlers and displacing even more, which left the Lower Valley deserted. Many of the displaced left the Dutch colony altogether, and the remaining traumatized settlers strongly distrusted the indigenous Americans, laying the groundwork for a future of more violence.[111]

Various Munsee groups started negotiations with the Dutch in April 1644 with the aim of securing a respite to cultivate their crops and to fish in order to stave off starvation. The 1650s saw a deadly epidemic that killed many indigenous Americans as well as violence from indigenous American raiders who burned 28 settler farms and 9,000 bushels of grain. Hostile Munsee warbands in 1655 killed 150 New Netherland settlers, took others captive, razed their settlements, and slaughtered their livestock. Other settlers abandoned their fields and plantations, leaving their lands uncultivated for at least a year. The violence flared up again in the early 1660s. The Dutch and their Long Island Munsee allies attacked Esopus Munsee villages and systematically destroyed their crops and food stores, causing famine and disease. Throughout the recurrent episodes of violence, trade with friendly and allied Munsee villages continued. New Netherland's settlers and soldiers depended on the maize grown by Munsee farmers, and food trade was as essential to the survival of the Dutch colony as the acquisition of beaver pelts. As additional settlers arrived in the 1660s, the conflict against the hostile Munsee increasingly came to be seen as a just war, and the settlers escalated to offensive warfare with raids on indigenous villages.[112] Ironically, the Dutch atrocities were described and criticized in the Netherlands using images derived from Las Casas, which compared the Dutch settlers' savageries against indigenous Americans to the cruelties that had been committed against Dutch rebels by the notorious Spanish Governor Alva during the Dutch Revolt barely a century earlier.[113]

The recurrent violence, destruction, and displacement left the indigenous Americans vulnerable, and many Munsee fell victim to disease in the late 17th century. Survivors fled as far west as the Ohio Valley during the 18th century, and few Munsee were left in the Hudson Valley by 1800.[114] Dutch reports from New Netherland noted instances in which fallowed or abandoned indigenous American cornfields were overgrown with small trees and shrubs in a matter of one or two decades; the forest subsequently reclaimed fields abandoned for longer.[115]

The use of massacres was not limited to the Dutch colony. During the rebellion that bears his name, Nathaniel Bacon and his fellow settlers indiscriminately killed or enslaved indigenous Americans on sight. Up to 10 percent of New England's European settlers and 40 percent of their indigenous neighbors perished during the King Phillip's 1670s war, and scores of settler and indigenous American towns were sacked and destroyed. Oral and written accounts of the horrors of the wars circulated widely among the settlers, deepening the perceived cultural chasm between indigenous Americans and New England's European colonists, and giving rise to further violence.[116]

Indigenous Americans not only perished in war, raids, famines, and epidemics, but warring parties also sold captives into slavery. In many ways, the indigenous American slave trade fueled war in eastern North America. As elsewhere in the Americas, not only settlers engaged in the indigenous American slave trade; increasingly, indigenous Americans violently enslaved other indigenous Americans.[117] In the southeast of North America, the European demand for slaves at the end of the 17th century fueled the indigenous American slave trade. Slave wars compromised the health of indigenous American populations and facilitated the spread of diseases along the trade paths into the interior, resulting in the devastating Great Southeastern Smallpox Epidemic of 1696–1700.[118]

Capturing indigenous Americans and selling them was highly lucrative and provided the means to purchase guns, ammunition, horses, and other goods. Moreover, the slave wars also constituted ethnic cleansing with a valuable material reward; the wars simultaneously removed indigenous Americans as a threat while freeing up indigenous American environmental infrastructure: settlement sites, fertile fields, and cleared forest land. During King Philip's war in 1670s New England, European colonists sold indigenous American war captives for 30 shillings a piece to slave traders who shipped them to the Caribbean.[119]

Endemic violence to the south of the Hudson River Valley predated contact but intensified in the mid-17th century, displacing much of the population and exposing them to disease. Beginning in the 1500s, Iroquoian settlers pushed southward because of climate cooling. The violence and displacement caused by the Iroquoian invasion, combined with a large influx of European settlers who introduced new diseases, accelerated the decline of the indigenous Algonquian populations in the basin.[120]

The colonial settlement of Maryland declared war on the expansionist Five Nations in 1664. In 1675, Maryland offered sanctuary to the Susquehannock, who were under attack by the Five Nations. A year later, the Marylanders joined the Virginia militia in driving the Susquehannock out of the colony's territory, causing their dispersal. New European settlers arriving in the region took advantage of the turbulent times to simply force indigenous American villagers off their lands or to take over village sites and fields that recently had been abandoned.

Even when epidemic malaria hit the Potomac Basin in the early 1660s, smallpox in the late 1660s, and influenza in the second half of the 1670s, raids continued throughout. In February 1681, a midwinter raid by a Five Nations Seneca band virtually exterminated the Potomac Mattawoman in a single blow. The raiders marched the survivors north as captives. In the early 1690s, Shawnee, Delaware, and Miami refugees flooded the Potomac Valley to escape violence in Ohio, fueling the crisis in the valley and causing further displacements. In 1696–97, a smallpox outbreak in the dead of a severe winter proved disastrous. By mid-April 1697, the bulk of the remaining indigenous population in the Potomac Valley, including the Piscataways, Mattawoman, Pamunkys, and Chopticos, had fled their homes to seek refuge south of the Potomac River.[121]

With many indigenous Americans on the East Coast from New England down to Virginia displaced or on the defensive, their environmental infrastructure, damaged or intact, increasingly fell to the settlers. Taking over indigenous American environmental infrastructure therefore gave the European settlers a critical head start: they did not need to invest the enormous amount of labor and time required to clear the land, fertilize the soil, or plant fruit- and nut-producing trees. The first settlers around Fort Amsterdam during the 1610s encountered land "quite suitable for use cleared in former times by the savages, who tilled their fields there." Near Fort Orange (Albany) good arable land was scarce, but here, too, the colonists found choice crop land previously tilled by indigenous Americans.[122]

Environcide in the Northeast: A Weapon of the Weak and the Strong

The literature about the European conquest of North America highlights the characteristic mass violence, displacement, and scorched earth tactics that accompanied it, but glosses over how these phenomena affected indigenous American environments and societies beyond their collective existence and identity. Rather than viewing indigenous villages and towns, irrigated or dryland fields, fences, traps, hunting and fishing grounds, water sources, drainage works, and fruit and nut trees as critical environmental infrastructure that the indigenous Americans created and maintained, such resources were recast as *natural* resources, free for the taking. Moreover, the extent to which the destruction and loss of environmental infrastructure constituted a major challenge to societies' livelihoods, and therefore their health and survival, is largely ignored. At the time, however, European settlers steeped in environcidal and total war acknowledged the value of indigenous fields and clearings as sources of survival and means of livelihood, and intentionally targeted indigenous environmental infrastructure as an object, subject, and instrument of war. The early Columbian Exchange literature highlights the independent (ecological) agency of invasive animals and plants. But in the postconquest Valley de Mesquital, sheep flourished not only because of ecological and biological dynamics but also because European colonists and their African slave shepherds actively defended their flocks against indigenous farmers who sought to prevent the animals from damaging their crops and irrigation ditches. In the same way, European colonists in North America actively defended their livestock even as their animals damaged indigenous American fields. Bioecological processes thus operated hand in hand with force and violence, and military and political conquest literally cleared the way for human, animal, plant, and microbial invaders.[123]

The literature also glosses over how indirect exploitation (through trade, taxation, tribute, and pillage) and the alienation and use of (indigenous American) environmental infrastructure provided indigenous American refugees with the means to rebuild communities. These same processes also provided European settlers (many of whom were also displaced by war in Europe or the Americas) with the resources to survive and subsequently gain a foothold in North America and gave some refugees, colonists, and others the means to build lucrative commercial or political empires. Environcide and total war were weapons of the weak as well as the strong and wielded by indigenous Americans and Europeans alike. Overall, however, all indigenous Americans who found themselves in the 17th-century cauldron of war and displacement suffered dramatic and traumatic personal and collective losses.

5

(Un)Limited War and Environcide in the Age of Reason

THE LOW COUNTRIES, FRANCE, AND SPAIN DURING THE WAR OF THE SPANISH SUCCESSION, 1701–14

The great desolation and cruel wasstation, of windmille once standing hei [high]. Al[l] round the toun [town of Lille] are brunt [burnt] and broke down, the houses of these villages so sadly annoyed and pairtly destroyed are the bouers [peasants] of these tillages . . . and hugrie [hungry] dogs for lack of food, Found eating the dead in the ground. Likeways the destruction . . . that armies did make in the fields. Al[l] sorts of grains destroyed by them, And al[l] fruits that the earth yealds [yields]. In marching and camping and rough foradging [foraging], [a]nd bringing in things that they need. And that milrodding [marauding] and houses dounrouging [rough up], Occasioneth the dearth of our bread. The cruell sidgeings [sieges] of fortified touns. Causseing armies together lay long.[1]

THE VETERAN soldier John Scot here offers an apocalyptic image of a depopulated countryside filled with the charred skeletons of windmills, ruined villages, desolate and barren fields, and roaming dogs digging up human corpses. Scot attributes the devastation to marauding and pillaging armies, echoing similar accounts from the Dutch Revolt, the Spanish-Aztec War, the Thirty Years War, and the Huron-Iroquois Five Nations War. But John Scot does not refer here to an episode from a premodern 16th- or 17th-century "uncivilized war." Significantly, his lamentation relates to the impact of a model 18th-century "limited war" (the War of the Spanish Succession) on French Flanders in 1708.

The 18th century was considered the age of limited war, when warfare became practiced by professional, disciplined armies led by enlightened kings, princes, and generals in a closely choreographed effort to gain a strategic and tactical advantage before engaging the enemy.[2] War was limited not only in terms of its objectives and tools (the enemy army and one's own army) but also in space (battlefields) and time (formal declarations of war, truces, and peace treaties). Rules and laws of war sought to limit the excessive violence that characterized the 16th- and early 17th-centuries, when armies and soldiers indiscriminately destroyed rural society and environment.[3]

Although the rules of war may have dampened the frequency and intensity of soldiers' propensity to inflict grievous physical violence (torture, rape, and murder) on prisoners of war and civilians, an appeal to military necessity legitimized the continued use of organized spectacular violence authorized by senior military commanders in the form of "military execution." During the 18th century, the rules of war did not ban scorched earth, sacking and burning, or marauding. Rather it institutionalized and formalized such tactics in the form of war taxes/ contributions, provisioning, foraging, billeting (winter quarters), and requisitioning. Spectacular violence was to be the exception—a threat and punishment for disobeying army demands. The cumulative effect of the everyday war violence of exactions and extortions by armies and soldiers, however, could be as destructive and deadly as chapter 3 highlighted.

Knowledge about the impact of unrestrained scorched earth, pillaging, exactions, massacres, and population displacement was widespread. During the Age of Reason in the late 17th and 18th centuries, rules or articles of war were widely circulated in Western Europe. The articles of war imposed capital punishment on marauders and sought to regulate the actions of armies living off the land in order to prevent the complete devastation of the rural tax base, which would render states utterly incapable of paying their soldiers. The articles of war, however, were poorly enforced, widely breached in practice, and increasingly challenged even as they found their way into military manuals, memoirs, diaries, correspondence, and tax records.[4]

In many respects then, 18th-century limited war was a lofty ideal, not a lived experience. In theory, armies only exacted war taxes or contributions from enemy territory, and communities that met the obligations supposedly were relieved of any other exactions in money or in kind.[5] During the War of the Spanish Succession, however, the Dutch and the French imposed contributions on hostile, neutral, and friendly territories, without distinction.[6] Moreover, although it became less acceptable to sack towns, selectively pillaging a few villages or hamlets in order to terrorize an entire region into paying contributions was common practice. Military execution against villages or hamlets was less public and conspicuous, with fewer and less literate witnesses. Meanwhile, unconstrained scorched and flooded earth remained standard strategies to defend forts, towns, and entire regions, which denied key resources to the enemy army, and the extortion of money, food, goods, and supplies sustained one's own war effort.[7]

The logistical sophistication suggested by armies' reliance on pioneer detachments, military magazines, and supply convoys was misleading. Farmers were in fact forced to provide labor as pioneers during sieges, they had to stock the military supply depots with food and forage, and they had to provide the carts, horses, and drivers for the "military" convoys. That is, armies and soldiers still systematically targeted rural communities' environmental infrastructure by requisitioning labor, livestock, and homes; robbing provisions, forages, tools, utensils, goods, and money; destroying barns, crops, fields, orchards, and woodlots; and displacing people from their farms and villages. Using rules and manuals of war to both institutionalize and rationalize scorched earth and living off the land appeared to domesticate the bloody and messy business of war into an art and science. Given that environmental infrastructure and the people that shaped it and depended on it remained the object, subject, and tool of 18th-century warfare, in essence, environcidal and total war persisted even during the 18th-century Age of Reason and Limited War. During the late 17th- and 18th-century wars against France, the civilian and military authorities of the Dutch Republic of the Northern Low Countries employed a highly standardized set of rules of war that aimed to regulate the behavior of the armies within its territories. The rules sought to maintain army discipline and prevent the destruction of the countryside; the Dutch Revolt and the Thirty Years War had left the republic's rural population destitute, eroding its tax base and economy. A 1694 pamphlet, which reiterated a 1673 pamphlet issued by the republic's ruling body, the General Estates, emphasized that Dutch soldiers' robberies, extortions, and abuses impoverished the inhabitants of the countryside, leaving the latter incapable of paying the taxes required to maintain the republic's armies or to pay their land rents.[8]

The rules obligated rural communities to lodge, feed, and support Dutch soldiers in the republic's territories during times of war in return for fair and prompt payment. A 1703 set of regulations, for example, valued a simple straw bed with sheets and blankets and access to a fire and water in the host's house at four stuivers per week, per soldier.[9] Moreover, commanding officers were held responsible for the costs, damage, and violence perpetrated by their troops. All abuses and excesses committed by individual soldiers, including pillage, theft, and extortion, collectively referred to as marauding, were punishable by death.[10]

The rules of war were widely distributed through pamphlets issued to military commanders and civilian magistrates, with orders to publicly announce their contents. Soldiers and officers also learned about the regulations via their marching, billeting, and camping orders, as well as military manuals. Even rural magistrates in small communities were familiar with them. Notably, surviving village archives frequently contain pamphlets with the rules of war, sometimes accompanied by correspondence that indicates the magistrates had requested the copies to support their war damage claims.[11]

The republic also disseminated rules of war applicable to allied armies operating in its territory.[12] The 1694 pamphlet referenced earlier had been issued by William III in his capacity as Prince of Orange, Commander-in-Chief of the Dutch Republic's armed forces, and King of England.[13] In 1708, the Republic's commanders incorporated the rules in contracts with the local magistrates of occupied French territory.[14] The French subsequently imposed similar contracts on the local magistrates of French-occupied Dutch Flanders in the early 1700s.[15] The rules also found their way into the military orders written by a high-ranking Dutch staff officer.[16] In a 1714 treaty with the King of Prussia, the Dutch imposed the rules on Prussian troops passing through the republic's territories and Dutch troops marching through Prussian lands.[17] The codification of the rules of war into the laws of war during the Age of Reason, however, had a limited impact on the practice of war. Enforcement of the rules was lax, the rules only applied to friendly territory, and military thinkers publicly contested their value as local civilian leaders increasingly used the rules to demand compensation for losses caused by armies and soldiers.

The War of the Spanish Succession (1701–14) in the Low Countries and Northern France

In February 1701, to support his grandson Philip V's claims to the Spanish throne, French King Louis XIV's armies invaded and occupied the Spanish Southern Low Countries. Dutch garrisons controlled the so-called Barrier towns there, but the French forces quickly overran them. The king placed 30 or so battalions in winter quarters in the occupied territory, making the local communities responsible for their sustenance.[18] On May 15, 1702, England, the Dutch Republic, Denmark, Brandenburg, and the allied northern German states declared war on France in support of Archduke Charles III, the Austrian rival claimant to the Spanish crown.[19]

War preparations affected the Dutch Republic's countryside long before any actual hostilities. Defensive inundations flooded fields and pastures, and farmers who resisted saw their lands confiscated.[20] Some farmers' fields remained inundated even after the war ended because draining them was laborious and costly.[21] The defensive preparations also diverted valuable rural labor, horse carts, wagons, and even wheelbarrows away from crop cultivation, harvesting, and the maintenance and repair of environmental infrastructure. In the late summer of 1701, when Dutch Flanders's farmers asked to be excused from months of backbreaking work building defensive positions for the army to harvest their ripening crops, the Dutch army commander flatly refused. To prevent further escalation and minimize delay in constructing the defensive works, the republic's officials hastily intervened, promising the farmers that they would be properly paid for their labor.[22]

Horses and carts were critical means of transport for soldiers and farmers alike. Armies relied on horse-drawn carts and drivers requisitioned in the countryside to move men and supplies. In March 1702, the republic authorized an allied English officer to press-gang 320 horse carts in Dutch Brabant to transport the ammunition and supplies of the 12 English regiments that had arrived to reinforce the Dutch army.[23] Providing transport services in a war zone was risky. Horse theft was common among friendly and enemy soldiers, and raiders considered the supply convoys' horse carts to be high-value targets. In August 1702, the French intercepted an allied supply convoy of 700 wagons; two of the horse carts they captured were from the village of Rucphen. In 1703, five of Moerstraten's inhabitants lost their horses when the French attacked a small Dutch army led by General Obdam. The army narrowly escaped annihilation by abandoning all its heavy equipment, including the 150 horse carts that the general had requisitioned from villagers and farmers in Dutch Brabant.[24]

The impact of the war on the southern districts of the Dutch Republic was the most dramatic between 1702, when the French armies took control of the adjacent Spanish Southern Low Countries, and 1706, when the French army retreated. For four years, the Dutch countryside bordering the Spanish Southern Low Countries sustained both the Dutch-allied and French-allied armies: up to 200,000 men plus tens of thousands of horses. The armies not only exacted food, forage, contributions, and services as allowed under the rules of war but also extorted money and robbed, pillaged, raped, and killed, actions that constituted marauding. Even Dutch-allied soldiers in friendly territory routinely

FIGURE 5.1. Soldiers attack a convoy. The convoy may consist of refugees or a supply train of civilian carts requisitioned by the army. Among the attacked are women, children, and infants, and the defenders of the convoy are only lightly armed and bear no armor (Painting by Jan Brueghel the Elder and Sebastiaen Vrancx, *Assault on a Convoy*, circa 1612, Kunsthistorisches Museum, Vienna, Austria), accessed online at https://commons.wikimedia.org/wiki /File:Jan_Brueghel_(I)_and_Sebastian_Vrancx_-_Assault_on_a_Convoy.jpg).

broke the rules that, moreover, their officers seldom enforced. Indeed, in 1702, the colonel commanding a Dutch cavalry regiment garrisoned in Dutch Flanders openly disputed the validity of the rules of war. Acknowledging that his men had used violence to confiscate straw from farmers' carts and barns, the colonel justified the actions as a wartime necessity: his regiment's horses had been without proper fodder for two weeks, incapacitating many animals and eroding his unit's fighting capacity. The colonel refused to reimburse the farmers, arguing that it would be unfair to make his men pay while the entire army enjoyed free forage. The colonel similarly dismissed the "uppity peasants" who complained that his soldiers had underpaid them for their lodgings.[25]

As was customary, wartime governments imposed contributions or special war taxes to finance their armies. Belligerents commonly compelled the inhabitants of frontier zones and regions along the front lines to pay contributions to both sides, as occurred in Dutch Brabant and in French Flanders during the War of the Spanish Succession.[26] During the prolonged war with the French in the 1680s and the 1690s, the republic had strictly prohibited the villages and towns of Dutch Brabant from paying any contribution to the enemy.[27] Soon after the War of the Spanish Succession engulfed the republic in mid-1702, however, the French demanded contributions from the southernmost Dutch frontier districts in Brabant, threatening military execution for noncompliance. Military execution meant pillage and plunder, a fate that befell Diessen in 1702 and Waelre in 1703, and which the inhabitants of the village of Eersel only narrowly escaped.[28] Instead, the French took hostages and imposed a ransom and fine of a total of 275 guilders on the inhabitants of Eersel.[29] Boxtel's inhabitants paid the French a total of 20,000 guilders in contributions for four years between 1702 and 1705, while the neighboring village of Udenhout paid the French 2,000 guilders per year from 1702 to 1708.[30]

Ignoring the rules of war, Dutch-allied troops generally failed to pay for food or services in the republic's countryside. In 1701, English troops owed the villagers of Oisterwyk 10,000 guilders for requisitioned oats, straw, and the use of their horse carts. At the request of the magistrates of Oisterwyk, the General Estates adopted a resolution in 1702 to raise the matter with the allied army commander, the English Duke of Marlborough.[31] No records have been found to suggest that the duke resolved the matter in favor of Oisterwyk.

Enemy French and Spanish soldiers never paid for food, billeting, or transport services while operating in the territories of the republic. Feeding or billeting French soldiers typically veered into theft, extortion, and outright pillage.[32] On January 12, 1703, a group of enemy soldiers at the village of Oistelbeers in Dutch Brabant not only failed to pay their hosts 6 guilders for the food they had consumed but also extorted an additional 48 guilders in cash. Three more groups of soldiers that passed through Oistelbeers in April and May exacted meals only, but a fourth extorted cash as well.[33]

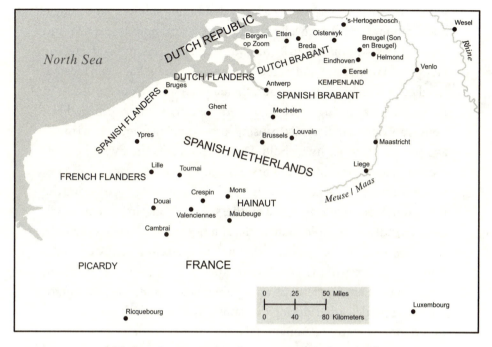

MAP 5.1. The Low Countries and northern France during the early 18th century.

The occasional depredations of small groups of enemy soldiers that drained households and villages, however, paled in comparison to the devastation wrought by entire armies marching through a district, or worse, making camp. Military encampments translated into thousands of soldiers roaming the countryside by day and night. During the summer and fall of 1702, the 60,000-strong Anglo-Dutch army and an equal-sized French army attempted to outmaneuver one another, without coming to blows.[34] Still, the impact on the Dutch Brabant countryside and the adjacent territories of the Spanish Southern Low Countries was dramatic. In the fall of 1702, both the Anglo-Dutch and the French armies established temporary camps in Dutch Brabant's Kempenland. Estimates of the damage caused by the French and Spanish troops to each of the thirty-odd towns, villages, and hamlets in the Kempenland district varied from 1,000 to over 10,000 guilders. Tongelre, Westerhout, Aelst, Diessen, and Waelre were among the worst affected communities, with homes and barns picked clean by marauding soldiers. Not a single home among Aelst's 80 dwellings and Waelre's 120 houses was safe, and the total losses amounted to 8,000 and 28,000 guilders, respectively. The villages of Westerhout and Bergeijk, where the camp had been located, fared even worse: in Westerhout, the damage was 46,000 guilders; in Bergeijk, a staggering 77,000 guilders. Enemy soldiers pillaged 303 houses and farms in Bergeijk, causing losses ranging from 14 to as much as 2,500 guilders per household. Dutch-allied and enemy French soldiers pillaged Tongelre in the first six months of the war, costing the villagers 13,000 guilders. Eersel reported the highest damage during the 1702 French occupation: 92,628 guilders. As in Tongelre and other villages, friendly and hostile soldiers alike plundered Velthoven repeatedly, with the heaviest damage occurring not as a result of enemy depredations but courtesy of the Dutch army and its allies. Eleven Dutch regiments razed Eersel's orchards and grain fields to make their camp for the night, while earlier during the same day, the English vanguard extorted money by threatening to take the villagers' small stock. In 1702 and 1703, the village of Wintelre paid safeguards to passing Dutch-allied English troops three times to stave off pillaging.[35]

In 1703, the French raided Wouw in retribution because the villagers had supplied 40 palisade poles to the Dutch army. They took Wouw's sheriff hostage and stole 44 horses and 1,000 guilders worth of food, clothes, and bedding, even ripping the silver buttons off people's shirts in the process.[36] The Dutch Republic condemned the French raid on Wouw as excessive and "against the law and practices of war."[37] Meanwhile, Dutch-allied raiders wrought havoc in the French-occupied Spanish Low Countries. A senior Dutch staff officer reported in March 1703 that "the hussars pillage as far as Luxembourg and beyond [and] the peasants fear them more than any other groups."[38]

In 1704, the center of gravity of the fighting briefly shifted southward to the German Rhine Valley, offering a brief respite to the Low Countries' countryside.[39] But long-range French raiding parties continued to plague Dutch Brabant as a conscious strategy to force rural communities to pay contribution to the French authorities.[40] Cornelis Vermicx from the village of Middelbeers fed groups of French or Spanish soldiers

5 times in 1703 but 11 times in 1704. One group of six men claiming to be French soldiers knocked at his door in the dead of night, but he hastily bought them off by offering them all the cash he had at hand.[41] Pillaged households remained destitute for years, as is illustrated by the fact that the Dutch Republic granted the Kempenland district villages tax restitutions for 1702, 1703, and 1704.[42]

Environcide in Northern France

In May 1706, the Dutch Republic and its allies soundly defeated French Field Marshall Villeroi's army at Ramillies, leaving most of the Spanish Southern Low Countries under allied control. The Dutch immediately imposed war contributions on the "liberated" Spanish Southern Low Countries. Yet, because the territory had been reconquered on behalf of Archduke Charles III of Austria, the Anglo-Dutch-supported Habsburg claimant to the Spanish throne, the area subsequently was considered friendly rather than hostile, and as such subject to the rules of war. The Dutch and allied commanders consequently ordered that any marauding or theft was prohibited and any such actions that occurred thereafter were punishable by death. The soldiers henceforth were required to pay for food and beer at set prices.[43]

The Dutch deemed Tournai to be enemy territory, however, and imposed a war contribution retroactive to the beginning of the war in 1702, with a total of 248,200 guilders payable before the end of 1707. In return, as per the Republic's contract with the Estates of Tournai, the region would not be subject to any further demands for contributions, provisions, livestock, or other goods by Dutch troops. Dutch soldiers would be required to pay for any provisions, commanding officers were prohibited from exacting gifts, and the residents could defend themselves against marauders with the force of arms. The republic and Tournai renewed the contract for May 1707 to May 1708 with the additional provision that the inhabitants of Tournai were permitted to supply labor and transport services to their sovereign, the King of France.[44] As a result, like the population of Dutch Brabant, the villagers and farmers of Tournai had to meet the demands of both sides at the same time.

In July 1708, the French main army counterattacked, retook Ghent and Bruges, and invaded Dutch Flanders. The French soldiers went on a pillaging spree, robbing and burning farms and barns in several of the polders in Dutch Flanders and imposing a large contribution of 55,000 guilders on what was a relatively small district.[45]

With the Anglo-Dutch siege of Lille in the summer and fall of 1708, however, the weight of the war shifted to French Flanders and Spanish Flanders. French Field Marshall Louis François Boufflers, who led the Lille defense, had played a prominent role in the French campaigns in the 1680s German Palatinate, razing towns, burning the countryside, and displacing the inhabitants.[46] Boufflers demonstrated the same ruthless total war attitude in his defense of Lille. On the eve of the siege, he ordered everything and everyone removed from the countryside or destroyed. The order created abundant opportunities for plunder and theft.[47] In the city, billeted soldiers stole and damaged the property of their hosts. Officers meanwhile lived on credit at the expense of Lille's citizens, racking up debts that they never repaid.[48] Rural refugees streamed into Lille, trying to save their precious grain stores to ensure their families' survival and to preserve enough seed grain for the next agricultural season.[49] To improve their defenses, the French troops cut 10,000 palisade poles, 40,000 fascines (bundles of wood), and 60,000 picket poles from the forests of the local abbeys, deforesting the Lille countryside in the process.[50]

What could not be removed was razed so that nothing of value would be left to the besiegers.[51] A large number of houses, windmills, and hedges around and on the outskirts of the town were demolished to clear fields of fire in front of gates and embankments. The value of the lost infrastructure was staggering: the bill to repair a single razed windmill was more than 5,000 livres.[52] Having begun in the harvest month of August, the siege must have caused great loss of field and tree crops as well as hay and straw throughout the countryside. Dominique Couplain lost his field of wheat valued at 300 livres; 500 livres of standing oats; a field with carrots, kohlrabi, and shallots worth 200 livres; and a 60-livres plot with herbs. Rolf Blancher, a tenant on a farm owned by Lille's St. Nicolas Hospital, lost his hay crop just as it was ready to be harvested.[53] With the loss of at least part of the standing crop, grain soon grew scarce during the siege. As the misery and poverty among the inhabitants and refugees in the town increased, Field Marshall Boufflers nevertheless requisitioned more grain and cattle to feed his garrison, and his men continued to consume beer on credit.[54]

The siege of Lille dragged on into the 1708 winter months while allied foragers exacted contributions, food, forage, and pillage in much of northwestern France and the Spanish Southern Low Countries.[55] The Anglo-Dutch army requisitioned thousands of farmers' wagons in the Spanish Southern Low Countries to carry provisions to the besiegers of Lille, forcibly recruited 35,000 pioneers in France and the Spanish Low Countries, and gathered 1 million picket poles and 200,000 bundles of branches to construct the siege works.[56] That the Spanish Low Countries and northern France were sustaining both Marlborough's Anglo-Dutch army as well as the Prince d'Eugene's allied army, which joined the siege of Lille in July, multiplied the burdens on the countryside.[57] In July 1708, Dutch-allied scouts and foragers ventured deep into France's Picardy, plundering and burning villages and hamlets. When local farmers killed some of the foragers, a unit of light cavalry reinforced by 600 grenadiers brutally retaliated, advancing to Ruquebourg (Riquebourg) halfway between Lille and Paris to strike terror in the population and to ensure that no one would ever dare to resist Dutch-allied demands again. The locals fled their homes and farms, hiding in the forests or seeking refuge in the towns.[58]

The town of Lille capitulated in November. Boufflers and his garrison held out in Lille's formidable Vauban-designed citadel for another month. November also marked the beginning of an unusually severe winter across Europe; the heavy snow and ice killed many trees and kept the swamps frozen, making it impossible to mine peat, which was a main source of fuel.[59] The victorious Dutch showed little compassion for the survivors of the siege. Instead, they tried and failed to confiscate whatever grain was left in the city. They requisitioned pioneer labor to repair damaged barracks, confiscated homes to house their troops, and billeted soldiers with individual citizens. They also imposed a large war contribution, which the Lille town officials were unable to raise.[60]

With Lille's town and countryside bled dry, supplies for the allied army and grain for the occupied city had to be shipped in all the way from the republic. Stormy weather in January and February 1709 hindered the shipments and aggravated the defensive inundations along the Flemish coast, drowning entire villages and causing heavy damage to beast and human. Famine and disease subsequently engulfed Lille and the surrounding countryside. Louis-Martin Lepetz and Marie-Francoise Logelent, tenant farmers of the abbey of Loos in the Ancoisne hamlet, barely survived the war winter. Two of their six children, eight-year old Jean-Francois and seven-year old Pierre-Francois, did not.[61]

The harshness of the allied exactions drew protests from King Louis XIV. By the close of 1708, France was destitute as a result of years of heavy taxes to finance the war and the extremely cold weather that destroyed crops and livestock in a war-torn countryside. Soldiers went unpaid. France's armies consequently relied even more heavily on the countryside, even as farmers' resources plummeted in the face of environcidal war and the freezing weather.[62]

Requisitions and pillaging before, during, and after the siege of Lille had laid waste to the regions of Douai and Tournai.[63] Cambrai, south of Lille, therefore bore the brunt of supporting the French troops concentrated in the area to defend France against the allied advance. Residents suffered from plundering Dutch parties, in addition to providing winter quarters to an exorbitant number of French soldiers; supplying wagons, horses, and pioneers to the French field army; and rushing 1,000 bags of wheat to the royal magazines at Valenciennes. When the king increased the wheat requisition to 4,000 bags, Cambrai's officials and farmers balked, protesting that the incessant demands for their carts and labor during the siege had impeded their harvest work.[64]

Left without wheat to seed, Cambrai's farmers carefully preserved their stocks of oats and other grains during the winter to ensure that they could cultivate their fields for the coming season. When in April 1709, the king's army sought to requisition more oats for its horses, the farmers refused to comply. Angry peasants mobbed the king's intendent in Cambrai: "[They] complained strongly that our repartition [the quantity of oats demanded] will rob the[ir] cattle of the oats they need to subsist and also prevent the seeding of the fields [required] to ward off a threatening famine in this province." The peasants emphasized that they needed their horses "to sow, but they [the horses] are extremely tired because of the chores that they have done and are still performing [for the army], transporting forages and straw." The intendent emphasized that the requistions combined with the contributions were ruining the region. He proposed that the oats requisition be reduced, because a demand

> that will distress everyone while the people in the countryside already are starting to die of famine because of a lack of grain and without any prospect that the land will yield any harvest in coming August because of the fact that the farmers do not clear the wheat [stalks] on their lands to once more protect them in the coming [winter] season it is clear that the lands will remain fallow and barren instead of serving the world ... that You [the King] will be filled with compassion for the poor inhabitants of this province ... and if god wants that the world dies of hunger and misery we are grateful for his justice which we have offended by our sins.[65]

Early in 1709, the Anglo-Dutch armies retook Bruges and Ghent. On September 5, Tournai surrendered to the Dutch and their allies after a two-month siege. A week later, they defeated the French army at Malplaquet near Mons, pushing the French armies back into their destitute country. The unusually cold weather lasted into mid-March 1709, depressing grain yields and tripling the prices of wheat and oats in northern France.[66] The inclement weather had the most devastating impact on arboriculture. Frost and snow killed many trees and the surviving olive, grape, fruit, and nut trees yielded but a fraction of the average harvest.[67] Even along the Italian Riviera, snowfall and strong winds in early January killed citrus trees and severely damaged hillside olive trees.[68]

Yet, in the spring and summer of 1709, French provinces in the frontline, such as Cambrai, sustained ever larger concentrations of troops and supplied increasing numbers of wagons and pioneer labor to the military campaigns. Bernieres, the newly appointed intendent apologized to the General Estates of Cambrai for the excessive demands but refused to compromise.[69] In fact, in the late summer of 1709, Cambrai began to pay war contributions to the Dutch Republic under a contract that was similar to the one that Tournai had agreed to in 1707. Urged by the French Intendent Bernieres, Cambrai's deputies even managed to negotiate a modest reduction in the contribution to the republic: 28,000 guilders instead of 30,000.[70]

The passions of Cambrai's farmers flared once more however, when French cavalrymen feasted their horses on the standing grain crop. Bernieres promised to issue orders to prevent further damage but added discouragingly that "such orders are difficult to execute when the troops suffer," suggesting he was unwilling to enforce the measures. The king's intendent dismissed claims that marauding was more than an incidental problem and entirely ignored the effect of the exactions on the farmers' harvest peak labor and equipment needs. He doubled the number of requisitioned wagons and carts and instructed the deputies of Cambrai to send immediate replacements for the escalating number of deserters among Cambrai's pioneers. Bernieres threatened individual deserters with a life sentence on the galleys and the Cambrai region with a sacking if the inhabitants did not immediately supply the demanded winter forages. Replacement pioneers suffered terrible mistreatment. In October, conceding that the province already was overburdened, Field Marshall Boufflers nevertheless personally ordered Cambrai to provide another 150 horse carts in addition to the 150 already employed by his army.[71]

In 1710, the Dutch and allied armies laid siege to the towns of Douai, Ypres, and Aire. Food and forage shortages plagued the besiegers and the besieged alike. Epidemic disease struck the Anglo-Dutch army at Aire and spread rapidly to the rural population, killing many.[72] Having little choice in the matter, the General Estates of Cambrai renewed the war contribution treaty with the Dutch Republic for 1710–11. Once again, Cambrai was now compelled to sustain both belligerent parties in cash and in kind. French Hainaut also signed a contribution treaty with the republic in the summer of 1710, thus at least limiting Dutch pillaging. The republic issued orders to the commanders of raiding parties en route to France that no extortions were permitted in the Cambrai villages, that commanding officers would be held personally responsible for any damages, and that soldiers' abuses would subject them to "exemplary punishment."[73]

The Cost of War in the Dutch Republic

In November 1710, the bulk of the Dutch-allied army once again took up winter quarters in the Spanish Low Countries.[74] With the burden of the war having shifted into the Spanish Low Countries and northern France, exactions on Dutch Brabant and adjacent districts lessened significantly, although the countryside continued to pay war contributions to both the republic and the French king. Passing Dutch and allied troops also continued to extort food, forages, shelter, and transport.[75] The French king's collector of contributions proved to have a remarkably long reach. In 1708, the magistrates of Eersel in the east of Dutch Brabant, far beyond the French lines, paid a French lieutenant-colonel 1,000 guilders to save their village from the firebrand. The officer had orders to reduce Eersel and other villages to ashes, so as to terrorize Dutch villages into continuing to pay the French contributions.[76] In August 1712, French raiders caused 35,000 guilders of damage to over 100 households in the village of Hoogeloon in western Dutch Brabant, looting food stores, livestock, horses and carts, money, woolens and linens, beds, chests with clothes, and other furniture, and thus leaving people ill-prepared for the coming winter.[77]

The 1708 Dutch and French contribution treaties with local magistrates that guaranteed the application of the rules of war were easily set aside when the practice of war demanded it. The French broke an agreement after mere weeks when they ordered the countryside of Aerdenburgh in Dutch Flanders to supply forage to the French army.[78] The Dutch army in northern France foraged around Ypres in breach of the 1708 agreements, and only after a French retaliatory raid in Dutch Flanders in September 1712 did the republic order its commanders in occupied French Flanders to adhere to the agreements.[79]

The postwar era was marked by deep economic and financial crises for the republic and the other belligerents. The war dramatically increased state expenses and decreased state income, requiring costly loans to balance the budget.[80] The republic's central and local authorities and the populace in the war-affected regions were mired in debt. Any compensation to rural communities for war damages came from the republic's central government in the form of forgiving taxes and land rents, further reducing state revenue. Only one recorded case in 1711 held military officers responsible for unpaid bills in the countryside, as stipulated in the rules of war. These concessions, however, did not result from the intervention of princes, generals, or state officials. Rather, the rural magistrates of the village of Woensel in Dutch Brabant employed a lawyer who invoked the rules of war to compel the commanding officers of two Dutch regiments to pay a modest lump sum for the damages their men had caused.[81]

Epidemic disease closely tracked the war. The doctors who narrowly contained an unidentified epidemic in the village of Hilvarenbeek in 1719 attributed the outbreak to the deep poverty that ran throughout the eastern half of Dutch Brabant, where many villagers and farmers had been ruined by the war.[82] Another plague, rinderpest, raged uncontrolled between 1713 and 1727, decimating cattle herds and prolonging the republic's postwar economic crisis. Rinderpest outbreaks were closely associated with invasions, wars, and their aftermaths, especially in 18th-century Europe, where it killed millions of cattle.[83] The Brabant village of Etten, which had been the locus of destructive raids during the war, was severely affected by the epizootic.[84] During the war and up to 1716, when Dutch forces remained mobilized in Brabant, forage resources, including pastures, hay, clover, and straw, had been primary targets for friendly and enemy soldiers alike and consequently remained scarce throughout the war. The shortage of forage weakened the cattle, and the movement of armies with their horses and stolen livestock facilitated the spread of the disease.[85]

The Spanish Theater of War

By joining the Grand Alliance of the Dutch Republic, England, and Austria in 1703, Portugal turned the Iberian Peninsula into yet another theater of the War of the Spanish Succession. The republic and its allies

launched several invasions into Spain, over land and by sea, before retreating and leaving behind an impoverished countryside.

In 1704, a Franco-Spanish army invaded Portugal. During this time,
the French army was only partially successful in its objective of living
off the land; a shortage of forage decimated the army's horsepower. In
1705, soldiers sacked several towns as the border war became a stalemate. The Dutch and their allies opened a second front in Spain when
they landed an army of 7,000 men near Barcelona, inciting a revolt in
Catalonia. Local militiamen, known as Migueletes, supported the invaders, who took Barcelona in October 1705 after a short siege. The
Grand Alliance forces opposing King Philip V and his French backers
captured Madrid in 1706 but were forced to withdraw to the coast to
establish winter quarters in Catalonia and Valencia. The Portuguese,
Dutch, and English allies resumed their offensive in the interior in 1707
but met with defeat. As a result, the Dutch and English troops found
themselves confined to Catalonia and a few besieged outposts. In 1708,
Austrian Field Marshall Guido of Starhemberg took command of the
expeditionary forces in Spain, which included Dutch, German-Austrian
Imperial, Italian, and Palatinate troops. The soldiers often went unpaid,
and although the British-Dutch navies controlled the seas, only limited
supplies reached the troops after the Grand Alliance lost Valencia in
1707. The Grand Alliance retook Madrid in 1709, but in November 1710
French-supported King Philip V regained control of the capital. Most
of the Dutch-allied expeditionary forces withdrew in 1711, and from 1712
onward, Catalonia was on its own, capitulating to the army of King
Philip V in 1714.[86]

Although large armies campaigned throughout much of Spain and
often lived off the land, the war in Spain conventionally is considered to
have been a limited war. Severe harvest failures occurred simultaneously,
but they were rarely seen as connected to the war.[87] Yet, the war severely
affected rural populations and their environmental infrastructure, and
the harvest failures likely are associated with the displacement caused
by the conflict. Both sides sacked towns. In 1702, British soldiers ran
amuck in a town near Cadiz, looting and raping while their officers stood
idly by. The British authorities charged several officers, including two
generals, but they ultimately went unpunished.[88] The correspondence

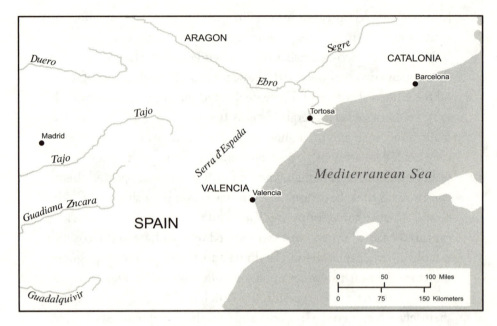

MAP 5.2. The Northeast of Spain during the early 18th century.

of Francisco de Caetano y Aragon, a general from Naples in the service of King Philip V of Spain, demonstrates that French and Spanish soldiers often went unpaid and hungry and that they extorted food from villagers and farmers in very much the same way as soldiers did in the war theater in the contemporary Low Countries and northern France.[89]

Although the armies of both sides lived off the land in Spain, the army commanders of French-supported Spanish Bourbon King Philip V and his Habsburg contender King Charles III initially tried to limit the exactions on the local populations so as not to lose their support. The repeated issuing of ordinances to regulate his troops' requisitions alone implies that excesses were common. Moreover, Philip V's ordinances often explicitly mentioned infringements. In 1707, Charles III's army purchased part of its provisions, forages, and other materials.[90] In 1709, Philip V's army carefully planned an advance, deploying the army along three different routes to minimize the impact on the rural communities.[91] In July 1709, on the eve of the harvest season, King Philip V prohibited all pillaging of grain and ordered his officers to punish all infringements, large or small, to the full extent of the law. In practice, both sides commonly pillaged grain to feed their armies.[92] Philip V's advisers also standardized the regulations on billeting and the costs allowed for food and services provided to soldiers to prevent the types of abuses that had occurred earlier in the war.[93]

Philip V's winter quarters ordinance noted that civilian hosts had suffered a great deal. To redress the situation, he mandated that the commanding officers were required to pay their men's salaries and cost of living or service allowances in cash. The king also stipulated that citizens who wished to be exempt from lodging soldiers in their home were required to pay a new fixed tax. Soldiers were to be quartered in empty buildings as much as possible, and one bed was to be provided for every two soldiers. Only officers could command a house for themselves, and officers and cavalrymen would be billeted in the villages while common infantrymen would be located beyond the village centers, toward the scattered homes and farms in the mountains.[94]

That same year, following a wealth-based assessment, Philip V's government imposed an extra one-time war tax on the villages and towns of Aragon and Valencia.[95] Despite protests, Philip V refused to relieve French subjects residing in Spain from the obligations to pay contributions and billet soldiers.[96] In the wake of serious abuses, the homes of priests and religious orders were exempt from having to billet soldiers unless all the homes in a community were already full. Even in the latter case, under no circumstances were the priests, monks, and nuns required personally to serve the soldiers.[97]

The rules had little practical impact. Officers were unwilling and unable to enforce them. Although preventing desertion was a high priority because it directly affected the cohesion of the army, Spanish military justice in 1709 did little to stop it.[98] Extortions by hungry and unpaid soldiers were likely much lower on the list. Philip V's government was constantly out of funds in 1709 and 1710, and could neither pay its soldiers nor reimburse communities for any requisitioned provisions, services, or goods. Soldiers were therefore entirely dependent for their survival, food, and income on the local population, and the lack of pay led to more desertions.[99] By November 1709, numerous garrisons had not been paid for nine months and relied entirely on requisitions and extortions of goods and money.[100] In December 1709, King Philip V ordered his governors to confiscate all horses suitable for the cavalry in the region, with the caveat that the owners would be compensated at the end of 1710.[101] The army also confiscated grain and cattle.[102]

With rules and regulations left unenforced, communities could no longer sustain the combined burden of the King's contributions and the soldiers' incessant exactions. In the Kingdom of Valencia, numerous villages and small towns emptied out as the inhabitants fled to Aragon for fear of military execution, which could include the imprisonment of local magistrates and the sacking and burning of towns, villages, and farms. Only the poorest remained, "and with the calamities of the war they are in the most deplorable misery."[103] In December 1709, the small towns of Cartala, Onil, Ibri, and Tiby begged the king to forgive the regular royal contribution.[104] The Almoradi University also petitioned the king to have its contribution payment reduced. The supplicants argued that the university had become impoverished because it had had to provide officers and soldiers with winter quarters, lodging, provisions, and gifts, in addition to purchasing extremely expensive safeguards from commanding officers, all of which cost the venerable institution many thousands of pounds.[105] Early in 1710, Castellano de Mamposta similarly petitioned to have the district's contribution reduced because many inhabitants had fled, and those who remained had had to perform incessant pioneer labor in addition to transporting supplies for the army.[106]

The situation deteriorated even further in 1710. The small town of Ribarroja (in Catalonia's Ebro River Valley) protested that Captain Francisco de Meto y Rocaberti, the commander of the troops quartered there for the winter, had confiscated six horses after the rebel Migueletes had stolen six of the captain's horses. Neither the hapless owners of the horses nor the community could afford the loss because the excessive contributions had "consumed their inheritance." Appealing to the king as "the universal Father of all his subjects," the town elders begged him to order the captain to return the six animals "so that they could work and cultivate their fields with them."[107]

The king reprimanded the superior of another Spanish officer, calling on him to curb his subaltern's "violations and extortions not only because they prejudice the rights and assets of the concerned order but also are contrary to his royal cause and inflict damage on these vassals."[108] Governors routinely extorted extra money from villagers by requisitioning pioneer service on local fortifications that the selected persons could then buy off. To counter such practices, all subsequent fortification projects were required to be approved by the king.[109]

The king also launched an inquiry into the winter quarters conditions to end "the disorders [caused] by the troops in the villages of this kingdom [of Valencia]." He ordered that any abuses be severely punished.[110] The investigation found that soldiers and their officers had in fact routinely demanded much more from their hosts and the neighboring farmers than permitted by the king's regulations.[111] Moreover, the opposing army also sent out raiding parties to exact grain and other provisions. In October 1710, one of the enemy's foraging parties was attacked and its booty of 1,000 fanegas of grain recaptured.[112]

In December 1710, the defeated Dutch-English army and their allies retreated north of the Ebro River, thereby making the territory of Valencia less subject to enemy raids.[113] Still, the war damage in the countryside caused severe shortages of grains and provisions for the army early in 1711 and forced the commanders to move their winter quarters outside of the Kingdom of Valencia.[114] To prevent further destruction in the countryside, King Philip V ordered his entire army out of Valencia.[115] Yet, as in the previous year, the army was so short of horses that the king once again instructed the army to confiscate as many horses as possible in Valencia "by all means possible."[116] In March and April 1711, the army demanded all town and rural authorities in Valencia to provide any and all forms of transport to carry grain to its military supply depots in the region so that it could sustain the army for the next campaign season.[117]

In May 1711, King Philip V ordered his troops to abandon their winter quarters. It seems that the troops had been remaining in winter quarters in the countryside throughout the year, which not only was contrary to the rules of war but had proved an impossible burden to bear for the rural populations.[118] In 1711, Orihuela requested reduced contributions because, alongside the regular contributions, the community also had incurred the cost of lodging and feeding passing soldiers.[119] In Tortosa, the military garrison had effectively usurped control over the town from the civilian administration to facilitate its incessant exactions.[120] Officers of four of the king's regiments had been held awaiting trial for crimes that had been committed in the small town of Secuellamos.[121] Wanting to set an example in this case, the king asked that the victims be paid compensation; however, in the course of awaiting a final decision on whether to punish the officers, and if so, how to do so, the officers were set free.[122]

Whereas King Philip V attempted but failed to limit his soldiers' violence against the population at large, he ordered his supporters to fight a war of extermination against the rebel Migueletes. He dismissed the Migueletes operating in the Kingdom of Valencia as Catalonian rebels, although their leaders were primarily from Valencia.[123] The Migueletes remained a problem in Valencia even after British and Dutch troops abandoned the region in 1709. The Migueletes lived off the land, conducting raids against those loyal to King Philip V and ambushing convoys. They operated throughout the kingdom, but their main bases were in the mountainous Serra d'Espada, northwest of the town of Valencia.[124] By 1710, the rebels had spread throughout the region, imposing a reign of terror that made people fearful to leave their homes, which in turn prevented tax collection. To quell the rebellion, Philip V ordered the "extermination" of the rebels and the confiscation of their properties.[125] Regular French and Spanish soldiers stationed in the mountain villages (and lodged and fed at the villagers' expense) proved unable to combat the Migueletes effectively. Valencia's governor and military commander, Don Francisco de Caetano y Aragon, subsequently resorted to using militias recruited from local loyal rural communities. The militias sought to isolate the rebels in the remote mountains, cutting off their access to the villages in the valleys and starving them of food, supplies, and information.[126] In 1711, the Catalonian rebels from Barcelona called for a general revolt against the Bourbon King Philip V, recruiting entire regiments of Migueletes and promising them loot as payment, thus operating in the same way as naval privateers.[127] In response, Philip V ordered his troops to kill any captured Migueletes.[128] Despite these measures, by mid-1711 the roads throughout the region were unsafe because of Migueletes ambushes.[129]

Although most of the anti-Philip V Grand Alliance troops withdrew from Spain in 1711, in 1712, Barcelona remained in the hands of the Catalonian rebels, supported by a small contingent of foreign troops. A large force of Migueletes led by Colonel Armengol was based in the mountains of Montseny, north of Barcelona, while the town was under siege by Philip V's army. Abandoned by their allies, the Catalan rebels defended Barcelona until finally capitulating in September 1714, after the English and the Dutch had made peace with France.[130]

As early as 1712, the situation in the Valencia countryside was so dire that its magistrates felt compelled to petition King Philip V for an extension of the deadline to pay the region's contribution of 8,000 livres.[131] In addition, individuals appealed directly to the king for relief from the many demands imposed by the army and its soldiers. The widow Juana Baup[is]ta Monrreal asked the king to be exempted from the obligation to lodge and feed soldiers because the war had impoverished her: partisans of the Habsburg usurper Charles III had pillaged her farm when they occupied the Kingdom of Valencia in 1706. After King Philip V's forces regained control over Valencia in 1707, rebel Migueletes had abducted her daughter and son-in-law for ransom. General Antonio del Valle, the governor of Valencia, vouched for the veracity of the account and the widow's loyalty, and recommended that her family and her village be exempted as requested.[132] In another case, in 1713, Don Juan Bautista Rosa complained that soldiers repeatedly had been quartered at both his homes in the town of Valencia and in the small town of Villa Nueva de Castellón since 1706, causing significant damage to the land and the houses. He requested that he no longer be singled out to quarter soldiers and that henceforth soldiers be more evenly divided over the communities.[133]

Limited War Theory and Environcidal Practice

The War of the Spanish Succession had a devastating impact on the countryside of French Flanders, which endured scorched earth tactics before the siege of Lille and the destructive effects of two invading armies that sought to sustain themselves off the land before, during, and after the siege. Dutch and English detachments foraged over a large part of Northern France, pillaging and sacking villages and farms to terrorize the rural population into supplying contributions, provisions, and other goods. As a result, hunger and disease already reigned in French Flanders before the onslaught of an exceptionally cold 1708–9 winter that decimated tree crops and livestock. As a result, in northern France and the adjacent Spanish Flanders, war had made rural societies and environments much more vulnerable to the impact of climate dynamics.

The terrible suffering in the countryside, however, did not limit the impositions of the belligerents because their soldiers still needed food, shelter, transport, and fuel. French, Spanish, and Dutch Flanders; Spanish and Dutch Brabant; and Spanish Hainaut not only sustained large armies but also paid massive war contributions to *both* the French and the Dutch. The Dutch forced the local authorities in French Flanders to sign treaties with the Republic, pledging to pay tribute in return for being exempt from any further requisitions or extortions by the Dutch army. The treaties allowed the local authorities to also meet their obligations toward the French king, including providing pioneer labor and transport to the French army. Louis XIV's officials used the same procedure to exact contributions from the republic's southern territories.

Significantly, the agreements were often preceded by extreme violence and pillaging to terrorize communities into submission, in particular in French Flanders in 1709 and 1710. Communities that defaulted on payments risked being sacked. Several villages in Dutch Brabant experienced the long arm of the French army's raiders, who traversed the Dutch-English–occupied Spanish Low Countries and neutral Liège to reach the republic. The village of Eysden in neutral Liège is illustrative of the heavy demands made by the belligerents. It was required to raise four to six times its peacetime tax revenues to cover the wartime contributions as well as the requisitions and billeting costs. This inflated bill could only be met through loans and aid.[134] Many of the communities in the Low Countries and northern France similarly would have experienced at least a doubling of their peacetime taxes as a result of paying the general official contribution payments imposed by both the

French and the Dutch. In addition, they would have incurred at least the equivalent of one or even two contribution payments through official in-kind requisitions of provisions, forages, and the like. Last, but certainly not least, there were informal "private" exactions (prohibited as marauding) by soldiers and their officers, and accompanying damage to environmental infrastructure.

Spain similarly experienced the impact of invading Dutch, English, Portuguese, and allied armies that twice marched deep into the interior to occupy its capital of Madrid, forcing French-allied Bourbon King Philip V to flee. To maintain his tax base and retain or gain the favor of the Spanish countryside, Philip V initially drew on the rules of war to limit and regulate his armies' exactions. He prohibited his generals from obliging the population to provide troops year-round room and board facilities. Technically, soldiers were expected to sleep in tents or other forms of improvised shelter during the campaign season; the local communities were expected to accommodate them in their homes only during the winter months. The king had several of his officers detained to await trial for breaking the rules of war, although he ultimately set them free, and it is doubtful that they were ever prosecuted or punished.

In brief, Philip V's good intentions soon floundered in the face of financial reality: unpaid troops resorted to fending for themselves at the expense of their rural hosts and thereby effectively revoked the rules of war that sought to limit soldiers' exactions and extortions. Although his forces liberated the Kingdom of Valencia in 1707, the local population continued to suffer a double war burden until at least 1712. In addition to sustaining Philip V's troops that were guarding the frontline with neighboring Catalonia and Barcelona, which served as a base for separatists allied with his adversaries, the inhabitants endured raids and exactions by the rebel Migueletes allied with Barcelona. By 1712, five long years of environcidal war had left the inhabitants of the Kingdom of Valencia with a severely damaged environmental infrastructure, unable to sustain their prewar livelihoods or ways of life.

The lived experience of environcidal and total war in the Low Countries, northern France, and eastern Spain in the early 1700s was not exceptional. English General Marlborough's army looted the countryside of Bavaria in 1704 to force the Bavarians to break their alliance with the French. Charles XII's Swedish army lived off the land in Saxony in 1706 and 1707, and Villar's French army extorted contributions and supplies in rural Germany in 1707.[135]

The model of limited war pervaded conversations, but even as an idea and ideal, it remained contested in the early 18th century. In 1703, the Dutch Republic condemned a French "military execution" in a Dutch village as excessive and contrary to the law and practices of war. Yet some commanders in the field openly rejected the very notion of rules of war, including the colonel of a Dutch Cavalry regiment in 1702 after he was reprimanded by a Dutch official for his excessive impositions on Dutch farmers. The verbal contestations of kings and generals about the laws of war, however, had little or no practical or moral impact on the ground: the laws did not significantly reduce the overall impact of war in terms of requisitions, extortions, and pillage in the countryside. Rather, villagers and farmers nonetheless paid the high price of sustaining enlightenment sovereigns' wars, armies, and soldiers. War cost the rural populations at least three or four times the taxes and fees that they were required to pay to their governments in peacetime. Moreover, these staggering numbers exclude the toll wrought by damaged and pillaged homes, barns, food stores, livestock, and equipment, and the physical and mental traumas caused by the accompanying violence, hunger, displacement, disease, and death.

6

Total War and Environcide
in the Age of Reason

THE LOW COUNTRIES, FRANCE, AND ITALY DURING THE WAR OF THE AUSTRIAN SUCCESSION, 1740–48

Of all the communities of the Riviera di Ponente there are none that have suffered greater damage and travails than the community and people of Oneglia; either by the incursions and demands done by the soldiers such as the heavy and continuous billeting of the soldiery or by the many heavy cost[s] caused by the hardships of the past war by which they were reduced to [a state] of great disaster and misery, [so] that [they] could not support [their] life, nor could their poor families survive and [consequently] they have abandoned their homeland, leaving their fields uncultivated, barren, and degraded, as the soldiers robbed . . . the wood that supports the vineyards and in addition they were deprived of their own homes and forced to move into inferior places; [in order] to accommodate their [the army's] officers and [the] soldiers resulting in the majority of the houses being so destroyed and ruined that they are inhabitable.[1]

AS THIS LATE 1740s supplication by the aldermen of Oneglia in northern Italy illustrates, the incessant everyday war extortions and pillaging by armies and soldiers destroyed people's livelihoods and forced them to flee their farms and vineyards, leaving their towns and villages in ruins and the countryside abandoned and barren. The impact of the War of the Austrian Succession was very similar in Northern and Southern Europe, despite attempts by rulers, generals, and town and village magistrates to uphold the rules of war in an effort to limit the destruction and displacement inflicted by friendly and hostile armies and soldiers.

During the 1740–48 War of the Austrian Succession, Dutch officials incorporated the rules of war in the treaties between the republic and its allies, Great Britain and Austria. Allied troops operating in Dutch territory "were not to cause any damage or discomfort to the population." The treaties and rules were widely distributed to Dutch local town and village officials in 1747.[2] The English commander-in-chief operating in the Low Countries, the Duke of Cumberland, ordered his officers to adhere to the rules of war to ensure that "exact discipline should be kept amongst our forces, and due care taken for preventing all violences, excesses, disorders, outrages and robberies being committed upon the inhabitants of this country [the Dutch Republic], which if not timely prevented will hinder our army from being duly supplied with necessary provisions." Offenders, warned the duke, were to be summarily executed.[3] Contemporary French military codes imposed the death sentence on rape and stealing food and household goods from civilians, and corporal punishment for cutting down trees, shooting domestic animals, and damaging mills, cages, and ponds.[4] In 1750, when the war ended, the Dutch Republic's military commander-in-chief, the Prince of Orange, published a pamphlet against marauding and other excesses.[5]

The rules, however, had a limited impact on the practice of war, since absent a specific treaty, they only applied to allied forces operating in friendly territory. More importantly, military and civilian authorities rarely enforced the rules of war even in friendly territories. King William III's 1694 pamphlet outlining the laws of war rebuked governors, field commanders, and captains for ignoring complaints and the infrequent use of exemplary punishment.[6] In *The Military Guide for Young Officers*, which was largely based on the 1740s war practices in the

Low Countries, Thomas Simes stated that the death penalty proscribed in the rules of war for marauding (which included murdering, raping, and stealing) was actually counterproductive. He argued that the severe punishment made fellow soldiers reluctant to report their comrades and caused senior officers to look the other way: "[Marauders] are rarely discovered; because every one is unwilling to occasion the death of a poor wretch, for only having been seeking perhaps to gratify his hunger."[7] Rape, too, was a capital crime in military courts but equally rarely executed to the full extent of the law in British and French armies.[8]

In his mid-18th-century memoirs on the art of war, the French Field Marshall Maurice of Saxony not only condemned the death sentence for marauders as overly harsh and counterproductive but also rejected the entire concept of binding laws of war. Instead, he argued that commanding generals should be given the latitude to be guided by the necessities of war. He lamented the deteriorating discipline among French soldiers since 1700 that resulted in marauding and pillaging, but warned against the proliferation of regulations and rules that were inefficient, complicated, and seldom enforced by the officers.[9] Maurice of Saxony developed his critique of the rules of war during his 1740s campaigns in the Low Countries and northern France. Army operations in the Low Countries, France, and Italy during the first half of the 18th century demonstrated that environcide and total war continued to characterize the practice of war.[10] Indeed, Maurice of Saxony's memoirs and *The Military Guide for Young Officers* suggest a systematic rejection of the very idea of limited war among war practitioners.

Up to half a million people may have perished as a direct consequence of the military operations during the Austrian Succession War. Overwhelmingly, the victims were civilians whose deaths have been too easily attributed to Nature's agency: microbes and the weather/climate. As with the virgin-soil (ecological) agency argument in the Americas, overemphasizing ecological, biological, or climate dynamics shrouds how the destruction, displacement, and trauma of war critically and fatally increased the vulnerability of human populations and their infrastructure to environmental and climate dynamics.

The War of the Austrian Succession, 1740–48

In 1740, war engulfed Europe once again, triggered by the contested accession of Maria Theresa to the Austrian throne. The war pitted Bourbon France, Bourbon Spain, and Prussia against Britain, Austria, and the Dutch Republic with their allies.[11] During the negotiations that ended the early 1700s War of the Spanish Succession, the Austrian Habsburgs conceded the Spanish throne to the Bourbon Philip V after the latter accepted the transfer of the Spanish Southern Low Countries and the Spanish possessions in Italy to the Austrian Habsburgs. During the War of the Austrian Succession, Bourbon France and Bourbon Spain sought to regain the former Spanish territories in the Low Countries and northern Italy. As a result, northern Italy and the Low Countries were among the main theaters of the war. Full-blown war erupted in Italy in 1742, while large-scale hostilities in the Low Countries commenced in 1744.

Living off the land and sacking villages and farms was standard practice for armies during the War. The Prussians and the Austrians savagely pillaged the countryside in Moravia and Bavaria, respectively; British troops engaged in looting and burning in the Rhineland; and Spanish armies ruthlessly exploited Savoy and the Bologna region as their winter quarters. The French army's pillaging while overwintering in Piedmont in 1744 and the burden of supplying the Austrian army in southern France in 1746 led to bloody retribution by angry farmers, which in turn triggered more violence. French soldiers looted Bergen op Zoom in the Dutch Republic, and Austrian soldiers sacked Velletri in southern Italy after taking the towns by storm. Spanish and French soldiers sacked Demonte in Piedmont after it had surrendered. Austrian troops savagely wrecked the countryside of Liguria during a six-month siege of Genoa in 1747 that cost the lives of 24,000 people, mostly civilians.[12]

In northern Italy, French and Spanish armies faced off against the combined forces of Austria and its ally, Piedmont-Sardinia. Britain supported the Austrians and Piedmont-Sardinians with subsidies and a fleet. The Genoese Republic and other Italian states also entered the fray. Lombardy and its capital Milan were the main axis of contestation:

it was claimed by Spain, Austria, and Piedmont-Sardinia. A major challenge to the French and Spanish was how to reinforce and resupply the Spanish forces based in Italy. Early during the conflict, the British navy established control over the western Mediterranean, making it hazardous to send reinforcements by sea. Piedmont-Sardinia controlled the easily defendable passes through the Alps between France and Italy. The alternative overland route, from Nice via Liguria to Genoa along the narrow coastal plain of the Riviera, followed the old Roman Via Aurelia, which by the 18th century was no longer passable for animal-drawn wagons or carts. Only mules and human porterage could be used.[13] Of key strategic value to the French and Spanish war effort in northern Italy, the coastal plain between Nice and Genoa became a major locus of military operations during the war.[14]

The War Front on the French-Italian Riviera

Such small port towns as Ventimiglia, Sanremo, and Savona in the Italian Riviera were located where steep river valleys intersected with the coast. Villages and hamlets were scattered in linear fashion higher up in the valleys. Mountain ridges separated the neighboring valleys, leaving the interior villages and hamlets relatively isolated from the settlements in the next valley. The villages and hamlets in each valley constituted the countryside and hinterland of the coastal town to which it was connected. Around 1700, the larger town of Ventimiglia had 3,000 inhabitants, whereas a smaller town like Bordighera had only 700. The coastal towns relied on fishing and trade. Farmers cultivated food crops, wine grapes, and olive trees on terraced hillsides. They produced wine, chestnuts, nuts, potatoes, and various grains primarily for local consumption, while the olive oil was an export commodity that found its way as far north as the Dutch Republic. Only the wealthier farmers kept cattle.[15]

The large armies campaigning in the Riviera in the 1740s moving back and forth across the region exacting cash war contributions, in-kind provisions, forage, and lodging, imposed a heavy burden on the countryside. Getting food, firewood, and other supplies for the armies down from the interior mountain villages and hamlets was difficult because

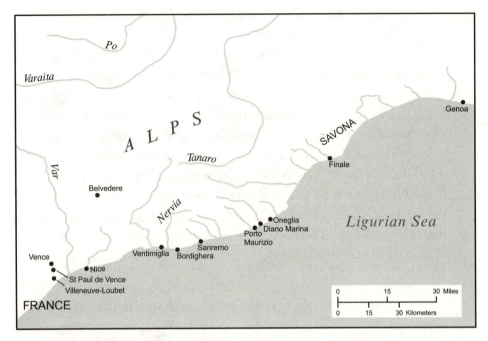

MAP 6.1. The French and Italian Riviera during the 18th century.

farmers had to carry the goods on their backs or use donkeys or mules.[16] The dispersed and relatively low population density also shaped the armies' recruitment of civilians as pioneers. Whereas pioneer labor was exclusively male in the Low Countries, on the Riviera, women were often among the laborers forced to work on military construction projects. Moreover, soldiers operating or quartered in the remote villages were largely unsupervised by senior officers, and even if the latter had been willing to prevent marauding, their orders had limited effect.

Fighting in the Riviera erupted in 1744 when the combined Franco-Spanish army crossed the border Var River on April 1 and swiftly occupied Piedmont-Sardinian Nice. The invaders fought their way east along the Via Aurelia to Ventimiglia, meeting fierce resistance from the Piedmont-Sardinian army along the way. In June 1744, leaving a few small garrisons behind in the Riviera, however, the main Franco-Spanish army withdrew to Nice, marched north to the Dauphiné, and crossed the Alpine passes into the Piedmont-Sardinian heartland.

Despite a promising start, the Franco-Spanish advance into Piedmont across the Alps soon faltered.[17]

Meanwhile, the Franco-Spanish forces garrisoned in the Riviera lost no time exploiting the occupied Piedmont-Sardinian Nice region, requisitioning supplies, lodging, food, and transport, while officers and soldiers stole for their own profit, threatening the local populations with military execution. In addition, both the French and the Spanish armies exacted a general contribution or war tax in cash.[18] Bouyon's town and countryside's share in the war contribution imposed on the Nice region was substantial: 128 livres in October 1744, 884 livres in 1745, and 883 livres in 1746. Maintaining the Fiandres Regiment in its winter quarters cost the inhabitants of Bouyon another 3,500 livres.[19] In September 1744, the officer commanding the French occupation forces in the area warned the consuls of Alpine Belvedere that their failure to provide the demanded provisions and pioneer laborers was "akin to mutiny." He ordered the consuls to personally and promptly bring him the requested pioneers, plus a cash fine. The community of Belvedere also supplied hay, straw, and cattle from its Alpine pastures. The farmers expected payment for the animals they provided, but it is doubtful they ever received it.[20]

In addition to the formal exactions of war tax contributions and supplies demanded by senior commanders, junior officers and soldiers sought to personally benefit. Small groups of soldiers wandered through the countryside of Bouyon demanding bread and flour, and an unidentified armed gang stole 30 mules and 3 donkeys.[21] Bands of Vaudois soldiers were such an affliction throughout the region that a French military commander felt compelled to assure the village consuls that he would "apply to the fullest the laws of war" in punishing the culprits.[22]

The French territories adjoining Nice were also compelled to lodge Franco-Spanish troops and deliver supplies to the military supply depots, although French farmers and villagers were not required to make a cash war contribution. The town and countryside of French Villeneuve provided long-term lodging and food for a unit of cavalrymen, in addition to supporting larger or smaller groups of soldiers merely passing through its territory. A large French army camp had a particularly severe impact on Villeneuve's lands. The soldiers demanded firewood and supplies and damaged vineyards and other agricultural lands to the tune of 2,000 livres. Soldiers camping in the vineyards of Joseph Giraud and his neighbors tore down the frames that supported the grape vines, severely damaging the precious plants. The soldiers also demolished fences, chopped down apple trees, and dug holes everywhere to serve as latrines or garbage disposal pits. A regiment of Dragoons camped on Villeneuve's hay fields, thereby spoiling the harvest.[23] In 1745, the town of St. Paul-de-Vence, north of Villeneuve, fed seven companies of the Languedoc Regiment of Dragoons and supplied grain to the army, though not always voluntarily. Soldiers forcibly took 3,800 pounds of grain from at least one uncooperative farmer's barn.[24]

Although the Spanish troops stationed in southern France were operating in allied territory and consequently were expected to abide by the same rules as the French soldiers, Spanish officers and soldiers readily abused the French villagers. In October–November 1746, Spanish soldiers camping near St. Paul-de-Vence caused 2,700 livres of damage. The camp housed 18 battalions returning from the war in Italy. Although the village consuls duly delivered provisions, firewood, and straw to the camp, the soldiers wandered into fields, vineyards, orchards, and woodlots, where they cut branches and trees, stole hay and straw from sheds, tore out fences and the frames supporting the grape vines, ransacked barns and a dove cot, and stole planks, ironwork, and pigeons.[25] On Bernardy's farm alone, soldiers cut down 9 timber oaks, 179 timber pines, and hundreds of small pines for firewood. They stole the hay and straw from his sheepfold and uprooted his grapevines to make room for their tents. The damage to his lands amounted to 1,443 livres.[26]

The experience left the inhabitants of St. Paul-de-Vence unable to provision the French army and on the brink "of falling into a state of total destitution." The community's consuls petitioned the French crown to be reimbursed for the damage, as was allowed in cases where enemy troops were responsible. The French provincial authorities, however, were uncooperative and argued that because the Spanish troops had marched under their own orders, they did not have the same rights to free supplies as the French troops and should immediately have paid for their requisitions. The losses, therefore, were neither the responsibility of the local communities nor the provincial authorities; rather "[If] such damage is very considerable it should be included in the reports sent to the [royal] court, . . . if the demand . . . was met [by the Provincial authorities,] there will be an infinite number of similar cases that will entirely ruin the province." Suche, the village consul or alderman at the time, agreed, but noted that if the inhabitants had not cooperated, the Spanish soldiers would have certainly sacked the countryside.[27] At the end of the war, the St. Paul community treasury reimbursed a total of 1,874 livres to a number of inhabitants for the cost of lodging Spanish and French soldiers in 1746. It is likely that this reimbursement at least in part related to expenses incurred because of the Spanish camp. Only townspeople who had been issued receipts by the Spanish officers, however, were eligible. Farmers and villagers who had not dared to ask the soldiers who had banged on their doors for a receipt appear to have been excluded.[28]

The French-Spanish Occupation of the Riviera

In May 1745, after the Genoese Republic openly sided with France and Spain, the Franco-Spanish army marched from Nice across the Riviera di Ponente to Genoa. The Franco-Spanish advance briefly concentrated 87,000 soldiers in the Riviera before they marched north toward the Po Valley, defeating the Piedmont-Sardinian army at Bassignana and taking Paiva. The French army established winter quarters in the Po Valley and the Riviera while their Spanish allies advanced on and took Milan in December 1745.[29]

Although much of the Riviera east of Nice was friendly Genoese territory, the Franco-Spanish army imposed a cash war contribution using the pretext that the local communities had failed to properly organize the delivery of provisions and other supplies. French and Spanish commanders warned that any refusal to pay the war contribution would result in military execution.[30] In practice, then, the Spanish and French commanders treated the entire Riviera from Nice to Genoa as occupied enemy territory. They ordered local officials to conduct a census of all the available livestock and to supply their troops with provisions, hay, straw, pack animals, chickens, and doves. Men and women alike were required to repair roads. Punishment for delays in the delivery of requisitioned goods, however, was milder in the allied Genoese territories and consisted of billeting soldiers in the homes of delinquent local officials. In addition to feeding and lodging the soldiers, however, the host had to pay their unwelcome guests a daily fine until the community had fulfilled its obligations.[31]

The exactions overwhelmed the inhabitants of the coastal village Luogo del Mare. Village officials pleaded with the commander of Oneglia for a reduced share in the general war contribution of 4,147 lire (equivalent to 1,382 Dutch guilders or 1,612 French livres).[32] They explained that although they comprised just 90 households, the village lodged the officers and provided hay, straw, candles, oil, cattle, and cash to the men of the entire Africa Regiment. The soldiers had severely damaged the villagers' olive trees, which were the villagers' main source of income. Moreover, the previous year's crop and olive harvests had failed, and the villagers were entirely dependent on the next harvest. The aldermen feared that unless the war contribution was reduced, the villagers would flee their homes and lands, creating a tax and requisition desert. After an investigation, the Spanish War Commissioner at Oneglia agreed to a reduction, and the village paid the outstanding sum with a loan secured by one of its inhabitants.[33] Many other villages in the area also resorted to borrowing money in order to pay the imposed war contribution. In 1747, war debts varied from 300 lire for Terzero di Prela (Prelà), high up in the valley, to 3,850 lire for Pontedassio just a kilometer or so upland from Oneglia.[34]

Castelvecchio, Oneglia-Costa, and the village of Borgonella (Borgovalle) struggled to meet the demands of the Africa and Granada Regiments while the soldiers they sustained damaged their environmental infrastructure. Soldiers dug trenches in fields and vineyards and their horses foraged freely in fields, pastures, and orchards. Out of despair, some farmers tried to sell their livestock and flee elsewhere.[35] They would have had great difficulty in selling their animals for a good price:

the occupation authorities prohibited the export or sale of provisions, livestock, or forage except to agents appointed by the army commander of Oneglia. Those found in breach of the prohibition were subject to a fine of 100 lire for the first offense and the confiscation of their livestock for a repeat offense.[36]

Rinderpest presented another reason that selling livestock would have been challenging. Requisitioned or captured livestock that accompanied the invading armies like a mobile commissariat spread the disease across Europe in the 1740s, much as occurred during the early 1700s War of the Spanish Succession. Heavy requisitions of grass, hay, straw, and grains to fill military supply depots and supply passing armies caused severe shortages of forage for farmers' own cattle. Malnutritioned animals were highly susceptible to infection, in particular during the winter when animals consumed little beyond hay and straw and were stabled in close quarters.[37] Notified of the outbreak of rinderpest in the Riviera in January 1746, Fernando de Caxigal, the region's Spanish military commander, immediately ordered that animals that died of the disease be burned and buried in a deep trench. Moreover, handling or eating infected meat was subject to a fine of 100 lire and three months' incarceration.[38]

The Austrian and Piedmont-Sardinian Occupation of the Riviera

In June 1746, the tide of the war turned as the Austrian and Piedmont-Sardinian armies crushed the Franco-Spanish army at Piacenza, sending the French and Spanish into a headlong retreat to France via the Riviera. The Austrian army and their Piedmont-Sardinian allies followed hot on their heels, overrunning Genoa, Savona, Finale, and Ventimiglia. Isolated by the retreat of its allies, Genoa surrendered and Savona fell after a short but destructive siege, exposing it to pillaging. The Austrians forced the Genoese Republic to pay an enormous war contribution and to supply them with provisions and goods. After recapturing Nice, the Austrian and Piedmont-Sardinian forces crossed the Var River into French territory where they spread havoc. Without supplies and his soldiers unpaid,

Austrian commander Browne and his men lived entirely off the land in the French Provence during the winter of 1746–47.[39]

Piedmont-Sardinian King Charles-Emmanuel III in turn imposed a war contribution that included the funds to pay his officers and soldiers a bonus, rewarding them for their service during the conquest. Savona's share in the royal war contribution was 127,121 lire out of a total of 1 million lire for the Riviera di Ponente as a whole. The villages of the Oneglia region responded to the new impositions by petitioning the king for a reduction in their share in the contribution payment, citing the impoverishment that had resulted from the extortions by the previous Franco-Spanish occupation forces.[40]

In September 1746, the bulk of the Piedmont-Sardinian army was camped at Bordighera just east of Ventimiglia. Provisioning the concentration of soldiers was an enormous undertaking, and the Piedmont-Sardinian King used a combination of threats and incentives, including repeated references to the laws of war. On September 27, the king's intendent requisitioned 320 barrels of wine and 32 oxen to be delivered by 10 p.m. the next day under the threat of military execution "by the laws of war."[41] The King personally ordered the aldermen of Porto Maurizio and Sanremo to provide his camp with weekly contributions of 5,280 pounds of pasta, 950 pounds of flour, 176 pounds of beechnuts and other vegetables, 50 pigs, 3,520 pounds of lard and cured meat, 400 barrels of wine, and 3,520 pounds of cheese. All provisions had to be offered for sale at the camp on Sundays at reasonable prices, and noncompliance would result in punitive billeting and a fine of 50 scudi in gold.[42]

In addition, the villages and hamlets in the valleys received orders to supply hay, straw, and firewood, and transport the materials to the camp by the next day using "men, women, and all other means of transport."[43] The army also required communities to supply pickets to construct the camp's defenses. Apologizing for a delayed delivery, village elder Giacomo Rosso explained that his community only counted 30 households; few villagers had the strength to cut and prepare the picket poles, and they were short of animals to deliver the poles to the coast. Moreover, foraging soldiers harassed his people.[44] But the king was unrelenting; in early October, when contrary winds inhibited sea transport toward the west, he ordered Sanremo to mobilize 200 men and women and every available pack animal to carry hay from the town's military supply depot to the Bordighera camp within a day or face the maximum punishment under the "rights of war."[45]

The councilors of Sanremo protested that different officers bombarded them with verbal orders and that they rarely received proper written orders for requisitioned goods, notes of credit, or cash payments for transporting the goods to the camp. After a personal meeting with the councilors, the king issued an ordinance and appointed special royal representatives to regulate his army's requisitions and contributions. The king's newly appointed representative in Sanremo was the high-ranking Conde de Gubernatis, no less than a former ambassador to Portugal, suggesting that the king took the matter very seriously. Drawing on the same articles of war in use elsewhere, De Gubernatis and his colleagues introduced preprinted orders that specified the product and the quantity of forage, firewood, and other goods that troops could requisition from their civilian hosts in their winter quarters.[46]

The Sanremo *Libro del Magistrate di Guerra* (Book of the War Magistrate) for 1745 and 1746 lists reimbursements that compensated individuals for providing goods, services, or funds supplied to the army in the name of the community above a certain quota. The local officials repartitioned taxes, war contribution payments, and other impositions among the taxpayers of their community, making everyone responsible for a specific share based on their wealth. Wealthier members of the community were expected to pay a larger percentage of the collective expenses, but were compensated if they contributed significantly more than their share. The more affluent community members also frequently advanced the money to meet part or all of a war contribution payment, provided compensation to the men and women who dug trenches for the army, and purchased the expensive oil and candles required for the officers and detachments on guard duty.[47]

By January 1747, the Piedmont-Sardinian king had moved his headquarters to his liberated Nice domains. There, he triumphantly announced the subjugation of the entire Riviera di Ponente. He ordered his military commanders to maintain strict discipline and informed all local officials to ensure "that our troops quartered in the Riviera like our forces in the [French] Province are provided with the necessary provisions."[48] The king made no exceptions for the Nice region, but late delivery or noncompliance in his own domains (and the Riviera domains he hoped to annex) was sanctioned by the milder punitive billeting of soldiers.[49] Complying with the king's instructions, Sanremo provided winter quarters from January to June to the Infantry Regiment La Regina and to the Regiments Monfour and Pinevolo in 1747 and again in 1748.[50]

But the king was not the only one to impose demands on the Riviera. His Austrian ally expected the countryside to sustain its troops and stock its military supply depots, as well.[51] The Austrian army's brutal exactions in the countryside of Genoa in the far east of the Riviera di Ponente reduced farmers to starvation, causing them to flee into the city, their despair contributing to the eruption of an urban revolt in December 1746. The Austrian army thereupon laid siege to Genoa while its British ally blockaded the port. Yet, the defenses held and the French smuggled several thousand soldiers into the city to reinforce the rebels.[52]

In December 1746, Browne's Austrian army settled into winter quarters in the conquered French Provence. As was customary in occupied territory, the Austrian intendant directed local officials to compile an inventory of all wheat, barley, rye, hay, and straw stores, as well as all livestock and vehicles.[53] Based on the inventory, the intendent compelled Villeneuve and neighboring communities to deliver specific quantities of flour, firewood, hay, straw, and oil within a day or risk "be[ing] reduced to fire and ashes."[54] In addition, the Austrian army established a military hospital in St. Paul-de-Vence, north of Villeneuve, making the town responsible for feeding and maintaining the patients, the hospital staff, and the Austrian garrison that guarded it. The inhabitants of St. Paul consequently expended 9,628 livres in firewood, oil, and wine for the hospital and 8,724 livres in food and wine for the garrison. The Austrian occupation cost St. Paul almost 40,000 livres, in addition to provisioning food and other services to passing units.[55]

In January 1747, a 50,000-men strong French army expelled the 30,000 Austrian and Piedmont-Sardinian men.[56] During its retreat, the Austrian army briefly established a camp near Villeneuve, and the soldiers robbed everything that the inhabitants could not carry as the latter ran for the hills. In the process, the Austrian soldiers "entirely destroyed all the houses ... the inhabitants ... had no grain to seed, lost their olive trees, and in general all Hope [because of] the misery of the inhabitants and the destruction of their homes and fields."[57] The losses included tools, agricultural implements, barrels with stored food, storage trunks, furniture, tables, chairs, planks, and the ironwork on doors and windows. Austrian officers who had been accommodated at Villeneuve's castle pillaged the wine cellar and all the ironwork, including key components of the wine and oil presses. Soldiers stripped the barns of all the remaining hay and ripped out all the wooden frames and sticks that supported the grapevines in the vineyards, a total of some 24,000 pieces of wood. The estimated damage to the castle, its vineyards, mills, oil and wine presses, and barns amounted to 6,100 livres.[58]

The Villeneuve consuls stated "[that] the invasion of the enemy has been so destructive since their arrival in this province [Villeneuve] having been the first to be attacked and [again] pillaged during their retreat so that this poor place has been almost entirely destroyed even the homes and buildings in the countryside which has left its inhabitants in the utmost misery." In an unusual gesture, the French army intendent lent Villeneuve's consuls 1,000 livres to buy grain to feed the destitute population after French control was restored.[59] The devastation so shocked French Field Marshall Belle-Isle that he sent a letter to his Austrian opponent, Field Marshall Browne, condemning the excessive violence.[60] St. Paul-de-Vence narrowly escaped the same fate as Villeneuve. St Paul's consul, Suche, offered Austrian General de Larche eight oxen and a calf as a gift thus "evading the sacking that threatened the town." The real savior of St. Paul, however, was not Consul Suche. Based on Suche's assurances that she would be compensated, the widow Marianne Giraud volunteered to immediately supply the animals. After the Austrian forces hastily evacuated the town during the dead of the night and the danger had passed, Suche coldly refused to reimburse her for her losses.[61]

The French authorities' compassion for the victims of Villeneuve's sacking did not last long. Its villagers and farmers had to provide labor to repair the roads and the bridge over the Var River, which the retreating Austrians had destroyed.[62] In May, Villeneuve was among the villages ordered to deliver hay to the French king's military supply depots.[63] French army Intendent Laborde urged the consuls of Villeneuve to deliver the supplies on time, even if it meant carrying them on their backs in the middle of the night. Laborde warned that if there was any delay, he would send a party of grenadiers or dragoons to their homes to be lodged and paid at the village's expense.[64] In addition to the regular requisitions and impositions by the army intendents, St. Paul-de-Vence and neighboring communities were compelled to host larger and smaller groups of soldiers traveling to the front.[65]

The Riviera Divided

In retaliation for the brutal Austrian sacking of Villeneuve, French Field Marshall Belle-Isle ordered his men to exact food and forage without mercy as they reoccupied the enemy Piedmont-Sardinian possessions west of the Var River in early February 1747. Without concern for the farmers' winter fodder requirements for their livestock, the colonel who commanded the French Regiment Condé threatened the consuls of Vence with military execution if they did not immediately provide his officers with forage for their horses.[66] As soon as he occupied the Piedmont-Sardinian village of Bouyon, French Colonel Danferret similarly demanded the delivery of 900 rations of bread for his men, and wine and meat for his officers by 6 a.m. the following day. Ominously, he added: "The punishment for disobedience is to be pillaged and burned." The colonel issued the same warning to other villages.[67] Fortunately for Bouyon, when the village fell behind in meeting subsequent French demands, other regimental commanders proved more lenient, forcing the villagers to lodge, feed, and pay a couple of grenadiers until the requisitions had been fully satisfied. The cost of such punitive billeting was high, but obviously sacking and burning would have been dramatically more costly.[68]

Community leaders frequently sought reimbursement for the costs incurred during the war. The boldest were perhaps the consuls of Bouyon, located in Piedmont-Sardinian territory and thus occupied enemy territory to the French. Still, in the summer of 1747, Bouyon's consul, Jean Baptiste Michelis, asked the French official Muraire if the community could be paid for the labor that 15 of its farmers and eight oxen had performed for a month because "consequently the poor community today finds itself unable to carry the burden of the daily expenses, not even being able to borrow money at acceptable terms."[69] The consuls tried again in 1748, after the end of the hostilities. They submitted a detailed accounting of everything they had supplied to the French and Spanish armies from 1744 through 1747, mostly by orders of high-ranking army officers. The cost to the community for the delivered provisions, goods, and services from February 3 to August 21, 1747, alone amounted to 3,428 livres. They requested reimbursement of 926 livres to 38 of its inhabitants, mostly former or current village consuls.[70]

Not surprisingly, the French commissioner of war flatly refused, "because as you know it is not the custom to pay for forages in conquered lands for any reason. I do not see how one could provide for the payment of these supplies."[71] In contrast, some well-documented demands by French troops in French territory were approved for reimbursement. Two sets of 1745 instructions specified that the costs of transporting timber to repair the bridge over the Var River and to provide forages for a cavalry unit on the personal orders of the French Field Marshall de Mallebois should be reimbursed to the communities.[72]

On June 3, 1747, French Field Marshall Belle-Isle's army crossed the Var River into the Riviera, capturing Nice. The French advanced virtually unopposed along the Riviera coast to Ventimiglia, which surrendered after a short siege. Rather than advancing further along the narrow coastal plain, the Franco-Spanish alliance once again opted for a direct invasion of the Piedmont heartland across the Alps. The campaign led to a crushing French defeat at Assietta on July 19, 1747, creating a stalemate in the war. The Riviera war front stabilized on the Nervia

River west of Bordighera until September 1747, when the frontline was marginally redrawn with the Piedmont-Sardinian recapture of Ventimiglia.[73]

Even without any major military campaigns in the Riviera, its communities were still required to sustain 50,000 to 80,000 French, Spanish, Austrian, and Piedmont-Sardinian soldiers. The Piedmont-Sardinian domains west of Ventimiglia were under French control for the rest of the war, providing cash contributions, provisions, supplies, lodging, and transport to the French and Spanish armies under the threat of military execution and sack and burn.[74]

The continued Franco-Spanish occupation from May 1747 to July 15, 1748, cost the Alpine community of Belvedere 200,000 Piedmontese lire. Two companies of the Salis Regiment stationed at the Belvedere village throughout the two last years of the war consumed provisions, firewood, and oil, and at least 36 cows, 2 oxen, and 15 goats. The soldiers also caused 2,500 livres in damage to fields and gardens. In addition, the occupation forces regularly made Belvedere's inhabitants transport supplies and soldiers back and forth to Nice and Antibes, and the garrison commander extorted a total of 71 livres as gifts. By April 1748, increasing numbers of farmers and villagers were abandoning their homes and lands for fear of reprisals because they lacked the cash or credit to pay the regular and extraordinary war contributions to the French army.[75]

East of Ventimiglia, the Piedmont-Sardinian army and allied Austrian units similarly continued to live off the Riviera's lands. King Charles-Emmanuel requisitioned labor from Sanremo to repair and upgrade the road between Sanremo and his camp in order to improve his supply lines.[76] Sustaining the large number of troops at the Bordighera camp stressed the capabilities of the neighboring Riviera communities to the limit. When the councilors of Sanremo failed to supply the required quantities of bread and forage, causing "suffering for the troops," Piedmont-Sardinian Commander Baron Leutrum cynically proposed that the king ask his Austrians allies to borrow one of their Croatian regiments, implying that the mere mention of the fearsome Croatians, who had a reputation for burning and pillaging, would inspire the communities to pay up at once.[77] The quantity of hay demanded for the Bordighera camp was so massive that the king's representatives requisitioned all boats "big and small" as far east as Porto Maurizio and Diano Marina to transport it to the camp.[78]

Whereas the King of Piedmont-Sardinia tried to centralize his requisitioning, Austrian commanders' demands were uncoordinated and resulted in contradictory, competing, and confusing orders. Mules and donkeys were in short supply, and the muleteers were constantly on the road to transport men and goods for different military commanders and officers.[79] The situation also caused tensions between the allies because the Piedmont-Sardinian and Austrian armies competed for the same scarce resources.[80]

In the late summer of 1747, the Austrian forces' demand for hay entirely overwhelmed the region's farmers, who complained that their scarce stocks had dwindled because of heavy foraging by passing cavalry and because individual soldiers requisitioned and sold hay for their own profit. The recently imposed hay quotas that were intended to stock the Austrian military supply depots at Oneglia, they argued, would make farmers unable to feed their own livestock and consequently go without the animal power to cultivate their lands or transport supplies for the military.[81] That the demands of the occupation armies drained rural stocks is also suggested by an increase in the use of punitive billeting as fines for late deliveries.[82]

Another indication that farmers' supplies were exhausted is that military commanders began to accept tree leaves for bedding because there simply was not enough straw available. In December 1747, Sanremo alone hosted no less than two Piedmont-Sardinian and three Austrian battalions, which required the villagers and farmers in the neighboring valleys to supply 58 tons of hay and 184 tons of firewood within two weeks.[83] The quantity demanded in the December order alone surpassed the entire winter hay store of one of Sanremo's valley communities. The said village's winter stock totaled 42 tons divided over 278 households and sustained a total of 80 head of cattle and 23 mules. Most households had only 88–176 pounds of hay each.[84]

By the end of the year, the army requisitions may have depleted more than half of the entire Sanremo valley's winter stores of hay: one

Sanremo community lost 10 of its 14.5 tons to the army in December alone. Anyone who had harvested hay was likely to have had to surrender most of it: Pietro Maria Palmare was only allowed to keep less than half of his original 528 pounds of hay, and Bartolomeu Bracco was left with only 35 pounds of his initial store of 704 pounds.[85] The demands did not stop there. In January 1748, an officer compelled the aldermen of Porto Maurizio to supply the battalion quartered in Sanremo with two head of cattle every week or risk having to lodge ten soldiers at the aldermen's personal expense. Failing that, the commander threatened to resort to "arbitrary" military billeting, which in practice meant having to contend with a large group of soldiers and no rules.[86] As the war dragged on, these and other exactions continued unabated during the first half of 1748.[87]

Everyday War Violence in Peacetime

Peace in June 1748 provided no relief from the relentless everyday burden of cash contributions and in-kind requisitions. The opposing armies remained in their positions in the territories they had occupied, exacting war contributions, provisions, and supplies until early 1749, eight to nine months after the war ended.[88] The Piedmont-Sardinian army actually stepped up its exploitation of the Riviera's town and countryside because the peace treaties stipulated that the Genoese territories it had coveted would revert to the republic's control. The Piedmont-Sardinian king thus lost any incentive to exercise restraint. Mere days after the fighting in Italy had ended in the summer of 1748, the king dispersed his army throughout the Riviera, allocating battalions to communities and requiring them to provide the soldiers with "bed, light, and fire," a practice that typically occurred only at the end of the campaign season, when troops were assigned to winter quarters. One battalion each took up quarters in Diano (Diano Marina), San Pietro (Diano San Pietro), Dolcedo, and Porto Maurizio, and two battalions in Sanremo. The Piedmont-Sardinian soldiers' wages were in arrears, implying an empty treasury, and moving troops into winter quarters transferred the maintenance cost of the army from the crown to the host communities.[89]

In addition, in the preceding months, the army had ordered the communities of the Riviera to deliver large quantities of firewood, hay, and straw to fill the supply depots before the approaching winter.[90]

In July 1748, the king of Piedmont-Sardinia ordered local officials to submit an account of the goods and services that had been provided to the armies of the king and his allies since September 1, 1746. The officials were required to provide details of the cost, what unit was involved, and when the exactions occurred for the extent of the reimbursement to be considered.[91] Complying with the king's demand, Porto Maurizio claimed that from 1746 through August 1748 it had supplied 560 tons of hay, 176 tons of straw, 832 tons of (fire)wood, half a ton of oil, 250 pounds of candles, and 12 tons of charcoal in the king's name. In addition, it had incurred the cost of 27,000 lire for lodging soldiers, spent 7,707 lire on provisions for soldiers, and was due 3,144 lire in unpaid transport expenses. Soldiers also had caused 7,607 lire of property damage, and contribution and other cash payments alone amounted to an average of 15,000 lire per year over the last three years.[92]

Detailed accounting kept by local officials specified who had paid for and/or supplied what quantity of which goods to the army in Porto Maurizio on a daily basis. On January 21, 1748, for example, lodging a sergeant and eight soldiers for four days amounted to 52 lire, and the delivery of a quantity of hay cost a muleteer 40 lire. Indeed, the cost of transporting hay or firewood from the villages in the valley to the port in town was the most frequently mentioned item.[93] During 1746, 1747, and 1748, the small village of Caramanga supplied seven tons of hay, one ton of straw, two-and-a-half tons of firewood, mules and donkeys to carry the materials to the military depot, and four beds to lodge soldiers in 1746 and three beds in 1747. Two soldiers usually shared a single bed. Cutting the delivered firewood involved a total of 18 human days.[94] In addition, the officials identified a total of 25,832 lire that the Porto Maurizio communities had spent sustaining the troops from January 1 to July 18, 1748.[95]

The share of Porto Maurizio and its rural valley hinterland in the war contribution for 1748 was 16,565 lire.[96] The cash war contribution was usually roughly based on prewar regular tax assessments and would therefore have been approximately 16,500 lire. The cost of the exactions and requisitions by armies and soldiers per year (25,832 lire for Porto Maurizio for January through July 1748) thus surpassed the official war contribution of 16,565 lire. Wartime extortions totaled 28,832 plus 16,565 lire, for a total of 45,397 lire, which more than doubled peacetime exactions. In addition, the requisitions radically reduced available food, livestock fodder, and other resources, undermining human and animal nutrition and opening a gateway to such diseases as rinderpest and displacing people from their homes and their environmental infrastructure. The cash contribution payments sucked any wealth out of the Riviera communities and households, loaded them with debts, and left them unable to invest in the repair or maintenance of all but the most critical environmental infrastructure, lowering productivity and leaving households and communities ill-prepared for such challenges as droughts, flooding, and other natural or human-made disasters. Thus, even when kings, generals, and soldiers did not directly kill, maim, or sack and burn, their actions often were environcidal.

Even as the war came to an end in June 1748, Piedmont-Sardinia imposed an extra contribution of 300,000 lire on the Riviera di Ponente to maintain its army. The order was met with such resistance that the king felt compelled to repeat the order in August and October and reduce the amount by half, protesting that despite being a conqueror, he had always treated the region with clemency.[97] In January 1749, the Piedmont-Sardinian occupation army tried to extort yet another 18,608 lire from the Riviera communities, carefully avoiding the use of the term "contribution."[98]

Punitive billeting of soldiers appears to have become more frequent in 1748, especially after the cessation of hostilities in the midsummer.[99] Officers and soldiers on their own initiative abused the system to extort even more from the Riviera's communities. Between June and September 1748, the officers of a battalion of the Swiss Keller Regiment (in the service of the Piedmont king) and a battalion of the Regina Regiment exacted part of their hay allocations (generally used for bedding) in cash, netting a total of 4,590 lire in four months. A battalion of the Say Regiment quartered in Dolcedo also extorted cash in this manner, and

the practice continued at least into October.[100] Piedmont-Sardinia's remaining troops continued to exact lodging, firewood, hay, livestock, and
cash (fines) in the Riviera until the last of its soldiers abandoned Savona, Sanremo, and Porto Maurizio in early February 1749.[101]

The Franco-Spanish forces in the occupied Piedmont-Sardinian territories in the Riviera similarly continued their exactions throughout
1747, 1748, and early 1749, doubling the cash war contribution in 1747
and tripling it in 1748. The town and countryside of Bouyon paid 883
livres in 1746, 1,523 in 1747, and 4,255 in 1748. In the peace year of 1749,
the occupation forces exacted another 1,075 livres.[102] Well after the end
of the war, the Spanish garrison commander of Nice demanded hay,
firewood, and other supplies for "winter quarters" in cash or in kind and
a monthly cash payment of 16,000 lire. The Spanish official threatened
the "total evacuation of the current city" and a 100,000 lire indemnity
for any refusal to pay, and punitive military billeting and the incarceration of the town councilors for any delay.[103] In October 1748, the town
and countryside of Belvedere not only owed the additional cash war
contribution payments but also carried the burden of maintaining six
French battalions that had been encamped in the area since the end of
the war. Belvedere's consuls contrived to present the French commander with a gift of two gamebirds, assuring him that the required 120
livres and straw was forthcoming and imploring him in the meantime
"to pay the fullest attention to the discipline of the soldiers."[104]

The Riviera sustained armies and tens of thousands of soldiers
throughout the 1744–48 conflict and for at least another six to eight
months after the declaration of peace. More than one military officer
may have returned home from service in the occupied Riviera with a
handsome pocket of money obtained as "gifts" from terrified villagers.
Several soldiers may have returned home with a bag of valuable tools or
ironwork pillaged from a farm, castle, workshop, or mill. Some of Savona's town officials and merchants may have profited from the war
economy by supplying garrisons with grain, firewood, hay, and other
goods. Yet, as late as 1755, the Savona community still owed 180,000 lire
to some of its inhabitants for having supplied firewood and mule transport to the Piedmont-Sardinian occupation army on behalf of the

community.[105] Some of the town and village authorities and others involved in managing the requisitions for the armies may have gained through fraud or corruption.[106] But overwhelmingly, the episodes of such spectacular violence as sacking and burning along with the grinding everyday violence of war deeply impoverished communities. The violence directly destroyed and damaged environmental infrastructure, and displaced and deprived people of their homes and fields. Moreover, the ruthless extortion of cash, food, forage, transport, and other goods and services by generals, officers, and soldiers prevented investment in the maintaining, repairing, and reproducing of environmental infrastructure, thereby endangering people's health and well-being, livelihoods, and ways of life.

The War of the Austrian Succession in the Low Countries

The war did not spread to the territory proper of the Dutch Republic until 1747. From the beginning, however, the war indirectly affected the countryside in Dutch Brabant because of military mobilization, troop movements, inundations, and the construction of defensive works. The Southern or Spanish Low Countries abutting Dutch Brabant had come under Austrian rule after the end of the War of the Spanish Succession in 1714 and the so-called Barrier forts in the now Austrian Low Countries had been restored to Dutch control. When the French invaded the Austrian Low Countries in 1744, however, the Dutch Barrier forts were soon overrun. In the last two years of the war, huge armies once more maneuvered, camped, and took up winter quarters in the southern territories of the Dutch Republic, living off the land, exacting food and goods, and requisitioning civilian labor and transport. Inundations and scorched earth warfare destroyed or damaged environmental infrastructure or rendered it inaccessible. French soldiers pillaged, burned, and razed Bergen op Zoom and the surrounding countryside, and also plundered farms and villages in Dutch Flanders (see map 5.1).

Contemporaries and modern historians depict the sacking of Bergen op Zoom as an aberration, a throwback to an earlier, primitive way of war. Lowendahl, the French commander who took Bergen op Zoom, allegedly apologized, and "informed European opinion was staggered."[107] But in a biography of Lowendahl published in 1749, there is no mention of any sort of apology, and accounts of a massacre are rejected as Dutch propaganda. Morerover, Lowendahl did not punish any of his officers or soldiers, or offer restitution for the damages that his men had caused.[108] In fact, the garrison at Bergen op Zoom had refused to surrender and had continued to fight in the town's streets after French soldiers scaled the walls. The garrison and inhabitants of a fortified town that resisted after its defenses had been breached normally received no quarter. Finally, the pillaging in the town and countryside of Bergen op Zoom and Dutch Flanders was not exceptional by the standards of the contemporary fighting on the French and Italian Riviera or when compared to the practice of war during the War of the Spanish Succession a generation earlier.

Not only were the rules of war ignored yet again in 1740s warfare, but the norms of war themselves were openly contested. A Dutch officer held the Dutch commander of the Barrier Fortress of Ypres in the Austrian Flanders personally and directly responsible for its fall to the French. The Ypres garrison commander had deployed his own soldiers to requisition palisades in the countryside rather than pressing local farmers into service as was common, and the soldiers were cut off from their base when the French advanced, weakening the garrison. The commander also had failed to raze and burn the homes, farms, orchards, and trees beyond Ypres's walls, which subsequently were used as shelter and cover by the besiegers. Finally, the commander had hesitated too long to flood the countryside around the town, which made it easier for the besiegers to gain entry.[109] In brief: the Dutch officer faulted the Ypres commander for having been so fixated on minimizing damage to the civilian population of Ypres and abiding by the articles of war that he had failed in his military duties.

In the spring of 1744, the French launched an army of 87,000 men into the Austrian Low Countries under the command of King Louis XV and Field Marshall Maurice of Saxony against a combined army of 65,000 Dutch, British, Hanoverian, and Austrian troops led by the Duke of Cumberland. While no major pitched battle between the two main armies occurred, the French outmaneuvered the allies and captured several Dutch Barrier forts, including Ypres, leaving the French in control of Austrian Flanders.[110]

During the summer of 1744, French and Austrian frontline commanders in the disputed Hainaut region initially tried to constrain their soldiers' extortions in the countryside, seeking to fight a limited war. French commanders even formally complained to their Austrian counterparts, the Duke of Aremberg and his deputy, the Count of Nava, that Austrian hussars were committing excesses. The hussars daily robbed French Hainaut farmers and villagers of meat, bread, beer, livestock, "and other things necessary for life," as well as linen and other cloth. Nava assured the French that he had reported the complaint to his superior "so that he could give the necessary orders to prevent similar excesses" and promised to do everything to alleviate the French concerns "to the extent that the service to her majesty, the queen [of Hungary, i.e., the Austrian Empress] will permit."[111] Aremberg had more than a passing interest in the Mons region because he had personal domains there, and he conspicuously deployed his small Austrian field force to defend the area.[112] On orders of his superior, a French official conducted research in the archives of French Hainaut, where he uncovered copies of war contribution agreements between Dutch and French authorities from the early 1700s War of the Spanish Succession. The archival documents subsequently served as models for the French imposition of war contribution in occupied Austrian and Dutch territories, presumably with the knowledge of French Field Marshall Saxony, who kept his headquarters at Hainaut.[113]

The French mounted counterraids in the countryside in the Austrian northern part of Hainaut around Mons, causing almost 6,000 livres of damage. Large detachments of French hussars, chasseurs, and other troops conducted the forays on explicit orders from Field Marshall Saxony in retaliation and "compensation" for past and continued excessive extortions by Austrian soldiers. The past extortions probably referred to the Dutch pillaging of northern France during and after the siege of Lille during the War of the Spanish Succession, which was revealed through the discovered archival documents. A dozen or so villages fell prey to the raiders, some repeatedly so, as the soldiers took not only food, forages, beer, and liquor but also silver, clothing, cloth, ducks, geese, and hens, and drove their horses through ripening wheat fields, damaging the crop. One group of foot soldiers that assaulted a village in the dead of night may have acted on its own initiative, leaving with cash, liquor, and beer after threatening to burn down the houses.[114] Even as the raids targeting people and their environmental infrastructure intensified, senior commanders continued to communicate about limits:

> The favorable disposition that this general [Aremberg] has for the rest [here: peace, well-being] of the inhabitants of the lands under the dominion of my master the King [of France] and for those of the Queen [of Hungary, i.e., Austrian lands] are very much in line with the thinking of his excellency . . . the Marshall of Saxony, he has provided sufficient proof of that by the strict discipline he has made the French armies observe after they entered the Austrian Low Countries. . . . He [Saxony] had wanted to confer with M[onsieui]r the Duke of Aremberg before ordering retaliation but they [the retaliatory raids] are entirely justified and equitable.[115]

Field Marshall Saxony proposed that each side keep accounts of the damage caused so that the parties could be reimbursed, if necessary.[116]

The raids actually escalated at the end of September, however, as Austrian hussars pillaged the Condé region, causing villagers to flee to the nearest fortified town with their cattle and all the property they could carry. When the displaced villagers returned to their homes, they found that their clothes, chickens, and provisions had been stolen, and their doors and windows smashed. In the village of Vieux-Condé, 30 inhabitants reported losses and damage varying from a value of 3 to 72 livres, while total losses for the region as a whole amounted to almost 2,500 livres.[117] Austrian commanders claimed that some of the troops' pillaging was punishment for French communities having failed to comply with their legitimate demands or that orders had originated from subaltern officers without proper authorization from their superior commanders.[118]

Yet, Austrian commanders did little to rein in their soldiers. Austrian hussars continued to rob farmers of their sheep, lambs, pigs, chickens, bottles of wine, clothing, and cash, causing 5,600 livres of damage in the Bavaij countryside alone.[119] During the months preceding the 1744 harvest, Austrian hussars systematically rode through and severely damaged wheat, rye, oats, and barley fields throughout French Hainaut, causing 12,500 livres of losses to farmers and the abbeys of St. Sauve and Crespin.[120] The preharvest destruction of standing crops; the postharvest loss of food, forage stores, and livestock; and the damage caused to homes and household goods left farmers and villagers ill-prepared to face the long and challenging winter and spring seasons of want. Moreover, 1745 brought only more destruction and losses.

In May 1745, the French defeated the Dutch and their allies at Fontenoy, near Tournai, thereby bringing most of the western half of the Austrian Low Countries under French control.[121] Dutch commanders hastily expanded the defensive inundations in Dutch Flanders, flooding precious fields of standing crops and consequently causing severe harvest losses.[122] The French victory, however, did not free their country from Austrian raids. Based in the formidable fortress at Mons in Austrian Hainaut, Austrian detachments continued to terrorize and impoverish the population, to the great chagrin of Field Marshall Saxony. Some villages suffered comparatively light losses of several hundred livres, but most communities lost 2,000–5,000 livres, with others losing more than 20,000 livres.[123]

Indeed, by the summer of 1745, French Hainaut had descended into a state of total anarchy, as "partisans," Austrian hussars, deserters, and bandits roamed and pillaged the countryside at will. One "partisan," calling himself the Chevalier de La Rive, sent threatening handwritten notes to various villages to deliver "bread, meat, and wine" or "be burned the next day at noon." De la Rive ambushed an officer of the king traveling on the road between Maubeuge and Valenciennes, causing widespread panic in the region. The officer might have been one of Field Marshall Saxony's personal couriers stationed at his Maubeuge headquarters. Austrian hussars also abducted the mayor of Barbencon in broad daylight. The inhabitants of many villages reportedly feared they would be attacked next and contemplated fleeing to the neutral region of Liège. In an effort to forestall a rural exodus, the military commander of Valenciennes resolved to ask Field Marshall Saxony for an independent company to patrol the area and to burn down the Roesin forest between Maubeuge and Valenciennes, which the raiders had been using as a base.[124]

Local witnesses recognized the grandiosely named Chevalier de La Rive as a man called Fezu, a cashiered soldier or deserter, who in 1744 had served in the company of Captain Fisener, garrisoned in Maubeuge.[125] It was difficult to distinguish the actions of friendly French troops from enemy actions and robberies committed by bandits. French soldiers equally exacted supplies and goods from the countryside and sometimes intentionally misled their victims about their identity to avoid prosecution. A detachment that claimed to be from French Field Marshall Saxony's army demanded that a large quantity of meat, bread, beer, wine, liquor, tobacco, and salt be handed over within 2.5 hours to avoid "military corporal punishment." The men presented written orders by a Bouval of the Godemeaux Company. But Captain Godemeaux had no one in his company with that name, and he was deeply offended: "[If] I had had the honor to know the gentlemen [the duped magistrates], you would not have judged my company capable of such an unusual action, the more so because my objective as captain is to maintain the strictest discipline and I do not permit any 'refreshments' [a euphemism for soldiers forcibly taking food] beyond those that are necessary for the horses." Captain Godemeaux vowed to take up the matter with Field Marshall Saxony personally and request that the culprits be severely punished.[126]

If the field marshal had indeed intervened, the effect had worn off by September 1745, when no less than three companies of Austrian soldiers pillaged Barbencon, causing over 22,000 livres in damage and losses of property. The soldiers demanded contributions in the name of their Captain Mertena for his senior commander the Marquis de Warmes. This instance did not involve just a band of hussars or partisans acting on their own. Rather, it was an organized attempt by a senior Austrian army commander to terrorize the countryside of French Hainaut into paying cash war contribution and sustain his troops with food and forage. The hussars accompanying the three Austrian companies badly wounded one of the inhabitants of Barbencon when he claimed to have no money. Five hussars attacked François Thomas, slashing his hat and his back with their sabers and plundering his house. Even the convent of Crespin was not safe: the Austrian soldiers robbed the abbey of 4,200 in cash and stole the abbot's cross, rings, his habits, and sheets, as well as linens and clothing from the convent's residents, which amounted to an additional 4,500 livres of damage.[127]

By November 1745, many villages and towns in French Hainaut had been forced to pay contribution to the Austrian empress, enduring pillaging by Austrian soldiers meant to hasten the payments. Barbencon paid a cash war contribution of 7,200 livres, and its inhabitants lost 15,669 livres to pillaging; Bossu paid 2,400 livres as war contribution and lost 200 livres to plundering; Renlies paid 1,882 livres as war contribution while soldiers marched off with loot valued at 2,000 livres. No doubt terrorized by their neighbors' fates, other villages promptly paid the contribution, barely escaping being pillaged, as well.[128]

With his preference for retaliatory raids over negotiations to end Austrian raids, Field Marshall Saxony demonstrated a lack of concern if not an outright contempt for the laws of war. Indeed, at the end of 1745, he publicly rejected another customary tenet of limited war: a winter cease-fire to allow the belligerents' troops to disperse to their winter quarters and subsist off the land without interference from the opponent. When Waldeck, the commander of the Dutch field forces asked Saxony for a cessation of hostilities on condition that his troops could forage in French territory, the French field marshal flatly refused. He was loathe to allow his opponent any opportunity to accumulate stores of forages and provisions, or to exact cash war contributions, especially not at the expense of the French countryside, which constituted his own primary source of supplies.[129] Saxony's surprise attack on Brussels during the dead of winter demonstrated to the great detriment of his opponents a few months later that he was beyond professing to play by the rules of "civilized war."

For the inhabitants of the neutral territory of the Bishopric of Liège in the southeastern Low Countries, the 1740s so-called limited war proved far more devastating than the previous conflicts affecting the region, including the Thirty Years War.[130] In 1745, when a French army camped briefly in the Liège region during its advance from France into the Republic, French soldiers pillaged a castle and several farms. As the owner recounted "contrary to all orders, the marauders utterly pillaged his castle . . . maltreating his wife and his children who could not escape loss." Another 20–30 households living in various parishes near the French camp each suffered losses of up to 500–1,000 livres. The orphans of Lambert Rousseau endured the theft of a golden cross valued at 15 livres, a book embellished with silver worth 12 livres, clothes, hats, bed-sheets, iron plates, and a chamber pot. One Jean Huou's losses included bread, cheese, butter, bedsheets, and cash, and his neighbor Lambert Marchand had 19 hens and his rooster stolen, all of which constituted devastating losses to the individuals and the households concerned. In compiling the reports of the damages, French Intendent Seychelles crossed out the loaded word "maraudes" (acts of marauding) in the heading. Local officials had identified French soldiers as the marauders, but French Field Marshall Saxony was in denial that his troops engaged in unauthorized pillaging and plunder.[131] Seychelles, perhaps for fear of Field Marshall Saxony's wrath, did not want to acknowledge that French troops engaged in marauding, especially not in neutral territory. Yet, after peace returned, the French authorities agreed to pay for the damages their troops inflicted on Liège communities, in effect acknowledging their armies had indeed broken the rules of war. The reimbursements varied from 2,000 to 25,000 guilders per case, indicating the severity of the marauding and pillaging. Liège based the requested reimbursement on 36,000 individual claims, which demonstrated the extent to which the damage was widespread. The French authorities paid part of the claims between 1746 and 1755.[132]

At the end of January 1746, with the allied army still dispersed over its winter quarters, French Field Marshall Saxony took Brussels by surprise, dispensing with the customary winter cease-fire and campaign stop. Saxony's army took Antwerp in early June, and in September 1746, the French imposed war contributions on Dutch Brabant.[133] Until its surrender on July 11, 1746, Mons had served as a base from which to launch Austrian raiding parties deep into the countryside of French Hainaut, French Flanders, and Cambrai.[134] After the loss of Mons, Austrian raids on French territory became less frequent, although to Field Marshall Saxony's great annoyance, they never fully ceased. After one such Austrian raid in French Hainaut in 1747, Saxony threatened to burn all the villages that the Austrian hussars had passed through as punishment for the inhabitants having failed to alert his commanders.[135]

By the winter of 1746, the French armies, counting a total of 200,000 men, could draw on the occupied Austrian Low Countries for sustenance and shelter, relieving the pressures on the French countryside, while the 80,000 soldiers of the Dutch-English armies and their allies had no choice but to seek winter quarters in the republic.[136] The burden of maintaining tens of thousands of troops fell heavily on the countryside of the republic's southern territories. In 1746 alone, the Dutch Brabant town of Eindhoven and the four surrounding villages supplied the allied armies with 802 barrels of oats, 53,600 pounds of hay, 2,311 bundles of straw, and 9,800 bundles of tree branches, for a total value of 1,600 guilders. Transport provided to the soldiers added another 3,000 guilders in unpaid fees. The republic's central government later compensated Eindhoven for at least part of these expenses.[137]

Getting costs reimbursed, however, was a slow and torturous process, even if successful. The republic's authorities only partially reimbursed the village of Gestel for transport services that its inhabitants had supplied to allied Austrian troops in 1747, and waited until 1750 to do so. Gestel had no such luck being reimbursed for the firewood, straw, and hay that had been supplied to English and Hanoverian units. British officers of the elite Third Guards Battalion commanded in person by the British-Dutch forces supreme commander, the Duke of Cumberland, paid for their expenses in accordance with the rules of war; but other British units did not.[138] With the French armies positioned on their borders, the Dutch set up a series of military magazines in the southern districts with fodder rations for the cavalry and draught horses. The countryside of Maastricht and Bergen op Zoom provided the largest supplies of forage, respectively, 700,000 and 400,000 rations, each of which consisted of a combination of hay, straw, and oats. The country-side of Dutch Brabant, Guelders (Gelderland), and Limburg supplied a total of 1.5 million rations to stock the magazines in support of the approaching campaign season.[139] Supplying such quantities of hay, straw, and oats undoubtedly severely depleted rural households' key resources for their own livestock and livelihoods.

The French Invasion of the Dutch Republic

In the spring of 1747, a French army led by Lowendahl invaded and oc-cupied Dutch Flanders.[140] French soldiers pillaged and plundered the villages and farms in the western half of the region, causing over 5,400 guilders of damage to 375 households. One of the affected farmers lost six milk cows, two other cattle, three calves, pigs and piglets, his food stores, blankets, tin and copper objects, and his entire supply of hay and straw. The soldiers also tore planks from his barns and chicken coop, and cut down trees from his woodlot, leaving him and his family trau-matized and destitute. In June 1747, French soldiers launched a second plundering spree in the Dutch Flanders countryside, taking food, cloth-ing, valuables, and money.[141] Many inhabitants of Dutch Flanders aban-doned their homes and lands, and fled deeper into the republic to the province of Zeeland, where their arrival caused widespread panic.[142]

The French subsequently imposed a heavy cash war contribution on occupied Dutch Flanders and exacted forages for the king's magazines, as well as food, lodging, and transport services. In addition, the French king ordered an extra cash war contribution to be levied in the occupied Austrian Southern Low Countries and Dutch Flanders to raise funds to repair the fortifications of Lille that had been destroyed three decades earlier during the Dutch siege. The extra contribution included a gratu-ity to allow his military officers to purchase furniture and other needs for their winter quarters in the occupied territories. The magistrates of Dutch Flanders protested against the imposition of the extra war con-tribution and the requested forages, explaining that they already had lost everything they owned and that the further exactions would leave their horses famished and too weak to plow their fields.[143] In June 1748, they capitulated, however, taking out massive loans to pay the war contribution after the French took several magistrates hostage and following reports that two French regiments of dragoons had been dispatched to Dutch Flanders to perform military execution.[144]

After the French capture of Dutch Flanders in 1747, the army of the Dutch and their allies marched continuously between Dutch Brabant and Limburg, determined to prevent the French army from laying siege to either the key fortress town of Bergen op Zoom in Brabant, which anchored the western defenses of the Republic, or the city of Maastricht, the key to its eastern defenses. The large concentrations of marching soldiers weighed heavy on the land because the villages and towns they passed through had to sustain them. During the fall of 1747, the entire allied army camped three times in the moors of Woensel and Stratum. The town and country folk in the region supplied the camps with large quantities of food, oats, hay, straw, and wood for fuel and construction. These supplies were in addition to the food and services that already were being provided to support the war. Horse carts requisitioned in Eindhoven, for example, had to carry army supplies to Maastricht in the southeast and as far west as Oudenbosch and Steenbergen, near Bergen op Zoom. Their weeks-long absences from the villages constituted violations of the rules of war and meant that farmers and villagers were deprived of their transport and horses for extended periods. The region also provided pioneers, guides, and messengers, diverting precious labor resources from agriculture as well as repair and maintenance of key rural infrastructure. At the war's end, the total owed to Eindhoven and the surrounding countryside was almost 20,000 guilders. Three years later, the republic had only partially reimbursed the outstanding bills, leaving the inhabitants impoverished and their magistrates pleading for compensation through tax remissions.[145]

On July 2, 1747, the main French army defeated the Dutch-allied army at the village of Laffeld, near Maastricht. The allied army withdrew intact, but the French victory enabled a second, smaller, Flanders-based French army led by General Lowendahl to besiege Bergen op Zoom. The Dutch garrison had thoroughly scorched the immediately surrounding countryside, razing all houses, barns, sheds, orchards, trees, and hedges to deprive the French besiegers of any shelter, cover, and resources. Even so, the key link in the Dutch defensive line fell in September 1747 after a bloody siege.[146] As the French soldiers stormed the walls, the defenders continued to offer fierce resistance as they retreated toward nearby Steenbergen. This instigated the French troops to massacre any defenders they caught and sack and burn Bergen op Zoom.[147] The town's destitute population subsequently sought refuge in the republic, where they remained for two years, living in deep misery. Four hundred houses lay in ruins; the estimated repair costs amounted to a staggering total of 500,000 guilders.[148] Only massive tax remittances over some 20 years combined with commercial loans allowed for the reconstruction of the town, which was still incomplete in 1766, a full generation later.[149]

The victims of the French sacking of Bergen op Zoom included refugees from the surrounding countryside and men from villages farther afield who had been pressed into service as pioneers or horse cart drivers and who subsequently were trapped in the besieged town. An exploding cart with gunpowder killed Lucas van Eeck's farm horse during the siege, and the horses and carts of two other farmers from Wouw were lost when the French captured Bergen op Zoom. The farmers from the countryside around the town lost all their livestock, which a group of cavalry had driven into the town just before the French attack.[150] The French war booty from Bergen op Zoom included 1,500 mules and horses, as well as 140,000 bags of flour and grain, all requisitioned from rural Dutch Brabant before the siege.[151]

During and after the siege, General Lowendahl's French army lived off the countryside of western Dutch Brabant. Because the Dutch Republic had prohibited supplying any food, forage, or services to the enemy, the French took rural magistrates hostage and threatened to sack and burn the villages to force the inhabitants to comply with their demands.[152] Most farmers and villagers experienced losses in kind or in cash varying from several guilders to 1,000 guilders each. The occupation army forced many of the men to work as pioneers for days or even weeks on end. The locals also provided transport and supplies to French soldiers, including wood and cattle.[153] The villagers received no compensation from the French, but after the war, the republic's central government provided some compensation to the villages around Bergen op Zoom by forgiving the regular 1749 taxes.[154]

To hold the line after the fall of Bergen op Zoom, the Dutch and their allies reinforced Breda and fortified their positions at Oudenbosch while waiting for reinforcements to arrive from England. The army employed pioneers and horse carts from as far away as the Eindhoven region at the defensive works.[155] The impact of the large concentrations of soldiers evoked images reminiscent of the biblical plagues of Egypt. Dutch and Dutch-allied soldiers that were camped at Rucphen, near Breda, picked clean farms and fields like a swarm of locusts. Marijnis Wouters Brant was one of many victims. Soldiers ravaged his coppice forest and hedges to clear the land for their camp. They also dug wells and a pond, stole his standing crops and his single cow, and ransacked his home, taking his woolens and linens, spoons, knives, and butter. A group of hussars and female sutlers forcibly expelled the renters in the widow Wouter van Overvele's house, severely damaging the dwelling and the adjacent barn, and thereby causing 1,100 guilders in damage.[156] The panic that followed the fall of Bergen op Zoom triggered a breakdown of all order and discipline, providing ample opportunity for theft and plunder, even right in the Dutch and allied military encampments.[157]

In October 1747, the French and Dutch-allied troops dispersed to their respective winter quarters. The countryside of the southern republic and the Austrian Low Countries reeled under the burden of having to support 200,000 men and their horses throughout the winter.[158] Civilians and soldiers suffered alike. A Bavarian battalion commander in the allied army garrisoned at the Dutch town of Grave complained in November 1747 that three soldiers occasionally had had to share a single bed (two was the norm) and that their thin blankets provided little protection against the biting cold.[159] The demand for fuel to keep the soldiers warm was enormous. The town of Eindhoven supplied a general and his staff with six carts of chopped wood blocks and over 9,000 bars of peat during January, February, and March 1748. The general left without paying. The Count of Bath, a Dutch-allied field marshal, left an even larger unpaid bill of 500 guilders for firewood, peat, and transport for May–June 1748.[160] Etten, between Rucphen and Breda, incurred tens of thousands of guilders in damage by feeding, billeting, and paying off allied soldiers and providing peat, and fire and construction wood to the army during the winter of 1747–48.[161]

Despite the initiation of peace negotiations at Aix-en-Chapelle in March 1748, the French army besieged Dutch Maastricht in April, forcing the city to capitulate in May.[162] In total, the French-occupied districts of the Dutch Republic and the Austrian Low Countries had to sustain 200,000 French soldiers and tens of thousands of horses.[163] Billeting the army in the occupied Low Countries not only relieved France of much of the cost of maintaining the troops in the field but was also convenient because France was bankrupt by the end of the war.[164] The French armies continued to live off the land in the occupied territories for up to six months after the June 15, 1748, armistice ended the war in the Low Countries.[165]

A 1748 letter from Dutch Flanders provides an impression of the everyday impact of the French occupation. According to the author, billeted French soldiers extorted their hosts and took hostages to ensure that communities paid their war contributions. The countryside lay abandoned, fields fallow because farmers had sought refuge in the towns. Only the prospect of peace had prevented many from fleeing Dutch Flanders altogether. Poverty and hunger reigned: those used to eating three slices of bread now ate only two, and those who had eaten two were now reduced to just one.[166] The slow retreat of the French in turn delayed the withdrawal and demobilization of the allied troops, which continued to be a burden in the Dutch Republic's territories. English and Scottish troops quartered in Willemstad, north of Bergen op Zoom, cost the small town almost 6,000 guilders in food, forage, and damages during the winter months of 1748–49. The soldiers ripped out doors, windows, and fences for fuel and stole valuables from their hosts.[167]

FIGURE 6.1. Depiction of the deadly impact of rinderpest (Royal Collection Trust, UK, Wenceslaus Hollar, Cattleplague, 1654), accessed online at https://www.rct.uk/collection /801996/cattle-plague).

The resurgence of rinderpest, the killer cattle disease that had plagued the republic in the aftermath of the early 1700s war, exacerbated the deprivation and chaos in the countryside. To contain the outbreak, the republic ordered an absolute and immediate prohibition on the import of any kind of cattle. Infractions were punishable with a fine of 1,000 guilders or a whipping, perpetual banishment, and the extermination of the cattle, with the meat to be donated to the church or to the local poor. The disease festered well into the 1760s, and the loss of returns from cattle products caused widespread poverty in the countryside that depressed land rents and the republic's tax revenues.[168] The decimation of livestock herds impacted nutrition and health and reduced income and revenue, as well as the availability of manure to restore and maintain soil fertility. The epizootic's correlation with the war is especially obvious in the region of Etten, between Bergen op Zoom and Breda, placing it right in the frontlines. Etten households suffered the highest cattle losses in 1747, when all-out war surged in West Brabant, and then immediately following the war. As during the early 1700s War of the Spanish Succession, the fierce competition between soldiers and farmers for forage was a major factor, leaving livestock malnourished and with weakened resistance to disease.[169]

The war damages wrought in the countryside by undisciplined soldiers and officers were highlighted in two pamphlets issued in 1750, one by the republic's military commander-in-chief, the Prince of Orange, and the other by the republic's highest assembly, the General Estates. The first pamphlet rehearsed the rules of war. The timing of its release suggests it was an attempt to restore a semblance of postwar order as Dutch and allied soldiers roamed the countryside in large numbers, stealing and pillaging to make a living. The second pamphlet reflected the reality of the war's destruction in the rural areas; the republic promised significant tax relief in Dutch Brabant in an attempt to stimulate the reconstruction of rural society and environmental infrastructure, which the war had severely damaged.[170] Published years later, the 1776 English *Military Guide for Young Officers*'s section on "Marauding and Oppression" may be read as deep embarrassment concerning the systematic violations of the rules of war by English troops in the allied Low Countries during the 1740s and the devastation it caused:

> Not to murder or steal, is a precept as binding in the field, or winter quarters, as it is in the camp or city. Marauders are a disgrace to the camp, to the military profession, and deserve no better quarter from their Officers than they give to poor peasants; nor should they find more mercy, than they shew [show] in rifling of villages. The rapes and violences of soldiers, rebound on their indulging Commanders. Licentious armies, spread a plague, instead of giving protection; and where terror and desolation march before the camp, a thousand imprecations of undone peasants follow. More purses are plundered than towns stormed; hen-roosts and sheep-cotes are assaulted, more than counter-scarps; and where the lawless soldier scatters ruin with fire and sword, there Commanders spread desolation with safeguards. Protection from these, is more expensive than the avarice of those; and kindness and fury prove equally cruel. The remedy is applied, when the country can lose, and the army gain no more. Yet these are the pranks sometimes played among friends and allies. Friendship so expensive, is unworthy of purchase; and it may be more tolerable to be at the mercy of a foe, than thus to suffer by the avarice of a friend; since to be hug'd or pistol'd to death, are equally destructive. We read, that mortality, for these offences, has swept off whole companies without remedy, and buried, in oblivion, regiments without honour."[171]

In brief, the *Guide* openly criticized the systematic and flagrant breaches of the rules of war of English soldiers in friendly territories: war had been neither limited nor civilized.

The merciless French exactions and pillaging in Dutch Brabant in turn were in part a reaction to the fierce resistance encountered at Bergen op Zoom. The French also sought revenge and compensation for the terrible destruction the Dutch and British armies had inflicted upon Lille and northwestern France a generation earlier during the War of the Spanish Succession. A third factor, however, was Field Marshall Maurice of Saxony's rejection of the rhetoric and practices of limited war, however incomplete and symbolic the latter had been applied. His first-hand experiences with the merciless raids by the Austrian hussars in French Hainaut only strengthened his disdain for waging war bound by strict rules, giving rise to his conviction that the only effective way to limit enemy raids on one's precious countryside was by seeking retaliation and compensation through pillage and plunder. Far from being innovative, Saxony's ideas were in fact a continuation of the environcidal and total war practices that were standard operating procedure during the wars of conquest in the Americas, the European wars of religion, and the Thirty Years War.

The 18th-century laws or rules of war sought to increase military discipline and limit the damage of military operations and requisitions on the countryside. But the everyday reality of the war interfered: armies needed to be paid and fed, and when kings and generals failed to do so, officers and soldiers in the field took matters into their own hands. Despite the existence of military contractors, the depots or magazines, supply columns, and barracks, military logistical capabilities during the mid-18th century were quite limited, and armies consequently relied overwhelmingly on requisitions. It was the farmers and villagers who supplied military contractors with provisions and forages; filled the military depots; provided the wagons, horses, and drivers for the supply columns; and lodged and fed soldiers and officers at their homes. Moreover, scorched earth remained a ubiquitous strategy to deny food, forage, supplies, cash, and shelter to the enemy and terrorize reluctant neutral and hostile villagers and farmers into sustaining one's own army. Each practice specifically targeted rural environmental infrastructure and the communities that depended on it. Even when armies and soldiers did not systematically deploy such spectacular violence as sacking and burning or mass killings, the cumulative impact constituted environcide because the everyday extortions and requisitions eroded the environmental infrastructure, preventing repair and maintenance, and displacing populations from the source of their sustenance. Scorched earth, armies living on their stomachs, and the everyday violence that accompanied such conditions endangered lives, undermined livelihoods, and exposed populations to hunger and disease.

After the War of the Austrian Succession, the Dutch Republic avoided war in its home territory until it was drawn into the revolutionary wars at the end of the 18th century. In the 1790s, French troops once again invaded the Low Countries, this time occupying its entire territory and abolishing the Dutch Republic. War damage that resulted from living off the land and scorched earth resurfaced and was framed in the same terms as in previous centuries: to the villagers and farmers affected, there was nothing new in the revolutionary soldiers' exactions and extortions. Rucphen, a village in Dutch Brabant that had suffered greatly during the wars in the first half of the 18th century, reported in 1793 that French troops once again had inflicted heavy damage on crops and property. Enemy soldiers forced the villagers to supply money, food, forage, transport, pioneer, and guide services, while their own Dutch generals had subjected them to the effects of defensive inundations that damaged trees, crops, and fields. Allied English and Hessian troops that entered the village in July and August 1794 after driving out the French behaved little better, and they, in turn, destroyed the crops and hay harvests and demanded food and transport at a cost to the villagers of 4,800 guilders.[172] The first half of the 18th century thus demonstrates continuity with earlier wars more than discontinuity, with similar environcidal war tactics targeting rural environmental infrastructure and robbing or displacing people from their homes and the sources of their existence: total war was not a late 18th-century innovation brought by the troops of revolutionary France.

7

A Global Way of War in the Age of Reason

ENVIRONCIDE AND GENOCIDE
IN 18TH-CENTURY AMERICA,
AFRICA, AND ASIA

[Asante and allied Wassa forces] from all sides drove them [the Denkyira] from their towns and villages, taking them captive and killing many.[1]

And [the indigenous attackers will] massacre all [Dutchmen], without exception as if they are finches caught in a net and [they will] also throw the earth on which [Dutch] fort Masure stands into the sea.[2]

If they fled and turned disloyal once more, they [the inhabitants of Waru] will be subjected to rigorous punishment, prosecution, and the demise of land and people . . . [while] under the Company [the Vereenigde Oost-Indische Compagnie (VOC) or Dutch United East India Company] they had enjoyed the fruits of a peaceful land and people. Alternatively [if they refused to obey], they would wander here and there like the birds because the product of their labor, the plantations, trees, and crops would be destroyed and their homes burned, and if they were caught they would even be killed.[3]

THESE QUOTES serve to illustrate that mass violence in Ghana in West Africa, Sri Lanka in South Asia, and Indonesia in Southeast Asia constituted total war and suggest that no one held a monopoly over it. The armies of the West African kingdom of Asante and its allies displaced, captured, and massacred the inhabitants of neighboring Denkyira in 1707; indigenous Sri Lankan rebels threatened to exterminate the Dutch on the island and raze their settlements in 1760; and the Dutch VOC governor of Ambon in Indonesia in 1784 vowed to burn the Waru settlements, their fields, crops, and orchards to the ground and kill any captives if they abandoned their villages again.

The main argument here is that when comparing the ways of war in 18th-century Europe with warfare in the Americas, Africa, and Asia, the similarities are as salient as the differences.[4] The previous two chapters demonstrated that in terms of the impact of war on society and environment, the continuities in the practices of war in Europe between the 17th century and the 18th century are as important as the changes. Taken together, chapters 5, 6, and 7 highlight that at the local, regional, and global levels, 18th-century war constituted environcidal warfare—fought over, with, and through the control or destruction of rural environmental infrastructure. Such warfare directly and indirectly affected the local environmental infrastructure and the civilian populations that maintained and depended on it sometimes even resulting in ecocide or genocide, or both.

Yet there was a growing sensitivity about the dissonance between the ideal of rational, civilized war and the primitive uncivilized war of the 16th and 17th centuries. Eighteenth-century pamphlets, treaties, and orders condemned marauding. During the early 1700s, French King Louis XIV and the Dutch Republic's General Estates accused one another of excessive exactions that breached the conduct prescribed by the rules of war. The sacking of Bergen op Zoom in 1747 consequently was imagined as an exception and a regression to more primitive war. Critics of limited war, principally European senior military officers, however, at times openly contested the rules of war as being ineffective or even counterproductive given that they were seldom enforced, or unenforceable, or because they seemingly prolonged wars, making them more costly economically, politically, militarily, and socially.

In the Americas, General George Washington and his British superiors (and subsequent adversaries) are sometimes portrayed as propo-
nents of limited war. Yet, before and during the Revolutionary War in
North America, living off the land, scorched earth, and plunder were
common practices. For rebel American soldiers, for example, loyalist
Tory property was a favorite target to pillage.[5] The prominent French
Field Marshall Saxony became one of the most notable critics of limited
war. He argued that military commanders should be allowed to freely
improvise rules depending on the circumstances, rather than being
bound by a fixed and universal body of articles of war. Effectively he
opposed the conversion of the rules of war into binding laws of war.
In his 1770s military manual, Jacques Antoine Hippolyte de Guibert
rejected limited war as being too slow and too costly. Instead, he urged
a return to a more aggressive and decisive way of war in which armies
lived entirely off the land in enemy territory, making war pay for itself,
as exemplified by the campaigns of Field Marshall Saxony and the ancient Romans.[6] In other words, Saxony and Hippolyte de Guibert argued for total war, and in light of the discussion of the practices of war
during the Wars of the Spanish and Austrian Succession in the last two
chapters, this was not a call for a fundamental change in how wars were
actually fought but a reflection of the everyday face of war for those who
lived it as perpetrators and as victims.

Uncivilized, or small war (*petite guerre*), in the 18th century that targeted civilians, towns, villages, crop fields, and orchards did not diverge
from the essential practices of conventional Western civilized war.
Rather, armies and soldiers in both conventional war and *petite guerre*
within and beyond Europe continued to live off the land and to extort
money, labor, transport, shelter, food, and other services from the civilian populations. The compartmentalization of conventional war and
petite guerre was artificial, cosmetic, and utilitarian. Mid-18th-century
colonial newspapers in North America justified unlimited warfare
against indigenous Americans by arguing that they posed a deadly
threat to civilization *because* they did not fight by the rules of war. European observers accused indigenous Americans and indigenous Asians

of uncivilized warfare, even as they themselves and their indigenous allies routinely sacked and pillaged towns and villages. In general, 18th-century European armies increasingly relied on so-called "light" forces who specialized not only in scouting and skirmishing but also engaged in scorched earth, raiding, foraging, and marauding. In the Americas, Africa, and Asia, the Spanish, British, Dutch, and French relied on indigenous allies or settler militias and rangers. In Europe, armies deployed units of hussards and pandoers, or ad hoc small independent units, referred to as "partisans."[7]

This is not to say that "othering," based on existing or emerging concepts of religious, racial, ethnic, or other essentializing markers of civilization (or lack thereof) did not play an important role. Heretics, Papists, pagans, and cannibals received no mercy during the religious wars, the Dutch Revolt, the Habsburg and Puritan Conquistas, and the Thirty Years War. Yet, whereas it appears to have been less common for soldiers to inflict severe bodily harm on noncombatants beyond battlefields, sieges, or military punishments in the 18th century in the Low Countries, France, and Italy, in the Americas, Africa, and Asia, neither European nor non-European combatants showed such restraint. Rather, the crux of the argument here is that important continuities in the practices of war across of time and space have been underemphasized. For example, settlements that refused to surrender and had to be stormed were sacked and burned (i.e., Dutch Bergen op Zoom). The same principle guided the sacking and burning of indigenous American towns and indigenous Indonesian villages when their populations fought back or fled into the mountains, forests, or swamps. Flight in and by itself was considered an act of resistance. Moreover, environcidal tactics and strategies were key to destroying an opponent who refused to fight conventional battles or sieges: destroying the homes, food stores, tools, fields, and sources of food and water of such elusive enemies, or displacing them from such environmental infrastructure, were part and parcel of war throughout the 16th to the 20th centuries.

The following sections provide an impressionistic and episodic overview of a selection of conflicts across the Americas, Africa, and Asia during the 18th century in order to highlight some of the features that made environcidal warfare and total war a global phenomenon. Placed in the context of chapters 2 and 4 on the 16th-and 17th-century wars in the Americas, this chapter suggests that there is also more continuity in the practices of war beyond Europe than has been acknowledged.

Environcide in the Americas

Despite the declining indigenous American populations, which Bartolomé de las Casas and others had attributed to the destructive violence of conquest and its accompanying ruthless and immoral exploitation, Spanish authorities in the Americas adhered to unlimited war practices in order to maintain or expand their control. In 1695, the Spanish located and invaded the indigenous American kingdom of Itzá around the northern Guatemala Lake Itzá, a haven for refugees from the Spanish territories (see Map 2.1). Spanish soldiers and their Mayan auxiliaries took the Itzá capital Nojpeten in 1697. Still, the war dragged on in the form of raids and counterraids. Spanish forces tracked down the Itza settlements one by one, but the inhabitants fled ever deeper into the interior. The Spanish troops lived off the land, sometimes bartering for food but often pillaging indigenous American food stores and standing crops as well as raiding for slaves. With the Itza population retreating into the forest, however, the availability of food decreased rapidly. Even a group of Spanish settlers who arrived with a herd of livestock for sustenance went hungry soon after arriving in 1699, and half of their number succumbed to disease.[8]

The invaders frequently found the indigenous American settlements empty as the Itza responded with a scorched earth strategy, denying the Spanish soldiers and their allies, food, supplies, loot, and shelter. In one case, villagers subjected to a night raid narrowly escaped, but not until setting fire to their own fields, granaries, and houses. Another Spanish foraging party encountered an abandoned 15-dwelling settlement that had sheltered many refugees displaced by the invasion. Before fleeing into the forest, the inhabitants not only destroyed their fields but also broke all the pottery that they could not carry. The Spanish and Mayan soldiers often did not even find enough food during the raids to feed themselves, let alone to support their dependents or the settlers. In a counterproductive effort to force refugees to return to the Spanish-occupied towns by making survival in the forest hideouts impossible, the Spanish governor ordered the systematic destruction of all maize stores and fields. Accused of using excessive force and disobeying royal instructions, the governor contended that his actions aimed to subdue cannibals who deserved no mercy.[9]

Diseases that had first struck Spanish soldiers and settlers also decimated the indigenous American populations, beginning with their children. Flight continued to cause population decline in the Spanish mission towns until at least 1750. Early in the 18th century, the Spanish concentrated the remaining indigenous Americans in several missions located along Lake Itzá, triggering renewed outbreaks of epidemic diseases. Indeed, the poverty and the danger of flight from the missions were so acute that the authorities exempted the Peten Maya from tribute. A 1765 census reported only 1,450 people in the region outside of the capital and revealed an unusually low ratio of less than one child per two adults in the four towns enumerated, suggesting low infant and child survival rates.[10]

In 1680, the Pueblos in the North American Southwest revolted, nearly exterminating the Spanish colonists in their midst; the survivors fled. When the Spanish sent an expedition to squash the rebellion, they found that most pueblos were deserted, and that the inhabitants had carried off all they could into mountain hideouts. The soldiers plundered and burned the villages, destroying vast supplies of food that had been left behind. In 1692, when the Spanish regained control over the area, they captured large fields of maize, melons, and squash but again found the villages deserted. Four years later, another revolt erupted. The soldiers burned the cornfields at two rebellious villages, and by the end of the year, starvation drove the resisters to surrender.[11]

Many of those who had fled the Spanish invasions of 1680 and 1692 never returned. Entire villages relocated into the highlands. Others settled among the Hopi or sought refuge among the Great Plains populations to the north. By the 18th century, the remaining Zuni occupied a single village. The impact of the heavy demographic losses due to the population displacements was devastating to the region's environmental infrastructure: irrigation canals and fields that had been maintained over centuries lay wasted, although some fields and ditches had been taken over by Spanish settlers. Disease, drought, and raids contributed to the further demographic decline, and by the mid-18th century, the Spanish settlers outnumbered the indigenous population.[12] By 1780, only 19 of the 66 pueblos that had dotted the Rio Grande Valley in the 1540s were still inhabited.[13]

From their regained base in the Pueblos region in the early 1700s, the Spanish raided the Navajo, causing the latter to migrate westward into the mountains. In the process, the Navajo became increasingly dependent on agriculture, and they also adopted the use of sheep and horses. The Navajos welcomed many refugees from the Pueblos, but they were also subject to Spanish slave raids. In response to the Spanish aggression and subsequent increased conflict with the expanding Comanche and Ute, the Navajo invested heavily in masonry fortifications known as pueblitos, diverting labor and other resources from more productive endeavors. By the mid-1750s, the old Navajo homeland was significantly depopulated, and most pueblitos had been abandoned.[14]

In eastern North America, in the wake of 1670s warfare, Abenaki refugees rebuilt their lives and livelihoods around Lake Champlain (see Map 2.1). Although their fortified town of Missisquoi was largely abandoned during the Anglo-French wars in the late 17th and early 18th centuries, its infrastructure remained largely intact, which allowed the inhabitants to return after the wars had ended. Many, however, moved further north to the region around the St. Francis Mission. During the war winter of 1704–5, smallpox struck the refugees at St. Francis. Disease struck again in the 1730s, which led to the final abandonment of Missisquoi and its surrounding villages. Temporarily sheltered by relatives, the displaced continued to hunt in the Lake Champlain area from the safety of their St. Francis base.[15]

During the wars in the 1740s, constant retaliatory raiding caused the English settlers in Vermont to abandon their farms and fields, even as the Abenaki retreated from the Lake Champlain region. The American War of Independence brought yet another round of violence, dislocation, and famine. As before, some Abenaki tried to survive locally by hiding in the wilderness and stealthily hunting or planting crops at their deserted villages. Doing so, however, was dangerous and, at best, earned them a meager livelihood. Those who attempted to return home during intermittent times of peace frequently found their villages and farmlands occupied by white settlers and displaced Iroquois. White settlers continued to encroach upon Abenaki lands throughout the 18th century, occupying ever more indigenous American croplands and orchards. The surviving Abenaki increasingly turned to hunting, gathering, and trading to survive, although no recognizable Abenaki village-size settlements appear to have remained in Vermont. The resulting dispersed and subterfugeous settlement pattern left the European settlers with the erroneous impression that the western Abenaki had entirely disappeared from Vermont and New Hampshire.[16]

Destructive pillaging and scorched earth tactics equally marked the 1750s–60s French and Indian Wars. In 1760, the British forces torched 15 Cherokee towns. Before the attacks, the inhabitants of the targeted Lower Cherokee towns had sought refuge in the Middle Cherokee towns that had escaped the same fate. The refugees constructed temporary villages and intensified hunting to supplement the food aid that their host towns offered them. After the British forces retreated, refugees from the towns that had been torched managed to harvest the corn crops in their own fields, which miraculously had survived unscathed, and some even rebuilt their homes. In the summer of 1761, however, the British forces returned and burned many of the remaining towns. This time, the soldiers ruthlessly cut down the standing corn crops and the peach tree orchards, and they ripped out the pea and bean plants by the roots. British units also scoured the town's surroundings for isolated farms and fields, and systematically destroyed them. Having evacuated their towns before the British attack, the Cherokee hid in the mountains. After the British withdrew, the displaced Cherokee crowded into the western-most towns, which had been the only ones to survive the consecutive invasions. Threatened by famine after having been deprived of their homes, crops, orchards, and food stores, the Cherokee sued for peace, giving up a substantial part of their territory, including its

environmental infrastructure.[17] The war marked a turning point: traumatized English settlers in the region now often routinely executed indigenous American prisoners, and English officers began to cast indigenous Americans as vermin. Settler intellectuals subsequently felt
compelled to provide a justification for waging total war during the Age
of Reason, with its credo of limited, rational, and civilized war. In newspapers, settler intellectuals argued that indigenous Americans not only
stood outside civilization but that they were also a threat to it, thereby
providing a rationale for rejecting the articles of war as inappropriate.[18]

During the first half of the 18th century, refugees from the wars further
northeast found a new home in Ohio. Shawnees fleeing from Iroquois
raids in Pennsylvania as well as displaced Delaware and Wyandot
(Huron survivors) were among those who resettled in Ohio. Arriving
in groups, they constructed new towns and villages, clearing land for
corn, beans, and pumpkins, and storing the surplus in their homes. War,
however, overtook the Ohio refugees yet again in the 1760s, and settler
militias systematically destroyed indigenous American crops. In the
aftermath of war and destruction, 1762 brought a devastating combination of famine and smallpox to the Ohio Valley, forcing indigenous
Americans to survive only on what they could hunt, fish, or gather. In
1764, British colonial forces issued a warning that indigenous Americans
should release all European captives, or their villages would be burned
and they would be "in danger of being destroyed as a people."[19]

During the American Revolutionary War, living off the land and
scorched earth were common practices during the campaigns between
the British and the rebels as well as in the fighting between the rebel
forces and indigenous Americans allied with the British. In 1777, the
rebels burned crops and bridges, and requisitioned horses, cattle, and
carts to prevent their capture by British forces advancing south into the
Hudson Valley. They also defeated a large British foraging party attempting to capture cattle, horses, and carts in Vermont. Prevented from
living off the land after being surrounded by the rebels, the British surrendered at Saratoga. Rebel Commander George Washington, fearing
the loss of support of the rural population, was reluctant to forcibly
exact food and transport from them. Given a shortage of funds and the

experience of two near-starvation successive winter quarters at Valley Forge and Morristown, respectively, however, Washington had little choice (see Map 8.1). During the winter of 1779–80, the rebels shifted to a system of in-kind war contribution of food and forage organized by each state, but provisioning the army remained a huge problem. In May 1780, continued food shortages caused a Continental army unit to mutiny, and the soldiers threatened to pillage the countryside. Early in 1781, the British landed a force led by Benedict Arnold in Virginia that systematically destroyed food stores, crops, and animals. When the Marquis de Lafayette marched to Virginia to expel Arnold in May, he quickly found himself short of supplies and forced to live off the land.[20]

Rebel forces systematically used scorched earth in desperate attempts to neutralize the British indigenous American allies. During the 1770s, the Ohio indigenous Americans raided settler farms, driving the affected households to near starvation. In turn, rebel militias attacked indigenous American settlements, killing inhabitants on sight. In 1779, revolutionary forces marched through Iroquia, destroying every indigenous American village they encountered. Several revolutionary soldiers even boasted in their diaries that they had torched crop fields to ensure that indigenous Americans would starve during the approaching winter. The settlers' environcidal violence against the Ohio indigenous Americans continued throughout the 1780s and 1790s, resulting in the destruction of scores of settlements and the surrounding crop fields. During the 1780 summer, settler militias destroyed the Shawnee town of Pica and its well-built log cabins, plundering the graves and burning the corn fields that surrounded the town. Deprived of homes and food, the inhabitants narrowly survived the winter through hunting and British handouts.[21]

Although the American War of Independence ended in 1783, the war against the Ohio indigenous Americans continued unabated. In October 1786, the Kentucky militia burned eight villages and 15,000 bushels of corn, depriving the villagers of their entire winter food supply. In 1790, another settler expedition burned several abandoned villages and destroyed 20,000 bushels of corn before being ambushed and defeated. A new expedition returned in 1791 to exact revenge and wreak "utter destruction" on indigenous Americans, but once again met defeat. In 1792, the US army organized a winter expedition with the expectation that the indigenous Americans would be "tied to the food supplies in their villages." Although the expeditionary army endured influenza and smallpox, it managed to establish a fort in the middle of the contested territory that served as a base from which to systematically destroy indigenous American settlements and their food supplies. Late during the summer of 1794, many indigenous American villages lay abandoned, although they were surrounded by bountiful fields; the army subsequently burned both the villages and the crop fields. That same year, the British Fort Miami functioned as a refuge for displaced indigenous Americans. American settler forces pursuing the refugees, however, destroyed the refugees' dwellings and the fields around the fort before retreating.[22] Here, again, the widespread and calculated destruction and plunder targeted environmental infrastructure, with the expressed intent of sabotaging the indigenous Americans' ability to survive.

Environcide in West Africa: The Gold Coast

Raiding for slaves and livestock, scorched earth, and pillaging towns and villages was just as common in warfare throughout Atlantic Africa during the 16th through the 18th centuries as in North America.[23] Large-scale displacement of populations from their environmental infrastructure marked 18th-century warfare on the West African Gold Coast and its interior (modern Ghana). Much of the interior of the Gold Coast was thickly forested, and clearing the vegetation to establish villages, towns, and fields was an enormous labor investment, making such lands highly prized. By the early 18th century, the interior forest was home to dozens of larger and smaller polities concentrated around towns connected by forest paths to one another, to the coast, and to the northern savannas.[24] Farmers grew maize, yams, groundnuts, and palm oil in forest fields and orchards, and kept cattle and goats—all livelihoods that required clearing forest patches and keeping them open through the use of labor and burning.[25] Populations deprived of their lands were not only exposed to the elements (heat and rain) but also could not sustain themselves in a forest environment without dispersing or raiding another community's villages and crops.

War refugees displaced from their lands and their environmental infrastructure took to raiding and selling prisoners to European slave traders in a bid to survive, creating yet more violence, displacement, and disruption of lives and livelihoods. In 1705, Wassa refugees who had been chased from their homeland raided Denkyira traders, triggering hostilities between Wassa and Denkyira. Allied to Wassa, Asante intervened, driving much of the Denkyira population from their towns; some fled north, while others hid in forests and caves in their homeland. Deprived of homes and livelihoods, the Denkyira refugees turned to raiding Asante lands and traders. In 1707, Denkyira raiders penetrated deep into the Asante heartland and attacked the gold miners who were working for the Asante King Osai Tutu. In retaliation, the king ordered a massacre of the Denkyira living in his realm, and his army and his Wassa allies invaded Denkyira, sacking its towns and villages, displacing the population, and capturing and killing many.[26]

In 1713, an Asante army subdued a small district wedged between Asante and the neighboring Aowin polity. Loaded with plunder, however, the entire Asante army deserted to Aowin, where they received sanctuary in return for a share in the loot. During the next few years, Aowin became a haven for refugees from Asante and Denkyira who are likely to have been primarily servants, slaves, and hostages. The population flight from Asante to Aowin intensified so substantially that it "obliged Osai [Tutu, the Asante king] to prepare himself for war to prevent his country from depopulation."[27] In 1715, Asante invaded Aowin. Many Aowin fled to nearby Cabo Appolonia, which subsequently was laid to waste by an Asante army.[28]

In August 1717, the Asante army invaded Akyim after the end of the agricultural season. On the advice of and guided by their ally, the king of Akwamu, part of the Asante army took a circuitous route through the forest to attack the Akyim forces from behind. The Akwamu king, however, betrayed and abandoned his allies. Since armies typically lived off the land, the soldiers had carried little food, and the scarcely populated forest could not sustain them. Facing starvation, the flanking force fell

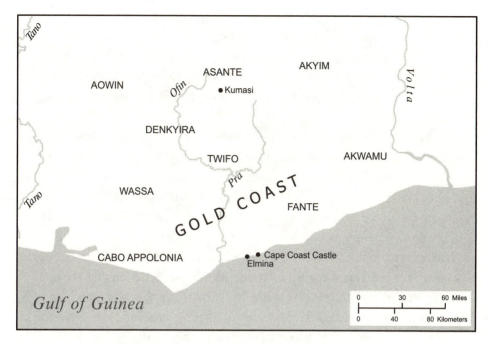

MAP 7.1. The Gold Coast (Ghana) during the 18ᵗʰ century.

apart and dispersed south toward the coast to forage for food in the Fante lands. In the process, they were overpowered by the hostile Annamabo, who sold most of them to European slavers.[29] Short of food and weakened by smallpox, the main Asante army repulsed an attack by the Akyim army, with heavy losses on both sides.[30] Rumors that the Asante army had been defeated encouraged Aowin and Wassa to send raiding parties deep into Asante to pillage and burn its towns, plunder the rich royal graves, and enslave the women and children.[31] While the Akyim army waged its campaign against the Asante army, Akwamu bands raided Akyim, capturing women and children left unprotected in the villages.[32]

The succession to the Asante throne of King Opoku Ware and the rebuilding of their homes, villages, and towns preoccupied the Asante for several years. Consequently, it was only in 1721 that the Asante army marched on Wassa and Aowin in retribution for having pillaged the Asante heartland a few years earlier. The Wassa initially retreated into

Aowin, but as the Asante army invaded the country, the Wassa refugees fled to the coast to seek sanctuary near the European trade forts. The Aowin fled westward to escape the invading Asante and most never returned to their original lands. During the invasion, the Asante army freed many of their own who had been captured during the 1718 raids.[33]

In 1726, when the Wassa King Intuffer incurred the wrath of the Asante king, the Wassa rose against him, fearful that the Asante would lay waste to their villages and farms once more. King Intuffer and several thousand followers subsequently fled southward across the Pra River to seek the protection of the English forts and their Fante allies on the coast. Along the way, they raided the Asante tributary Twifo in a failed attempt to seize part of the harvest, which was in season.[34] In 1730, Asante invaded Wassa again, scattering its inhabitants. Many fled to the coast to seek protection near the WIC fortresses, but the Dutch and their allies handed the refugees over to the Asante so as not to harm their trade relations.[35] War also resumed between the Akyim and the Akwamu, with the result that the Akyim came to occupy much of Akwamu, displacing much of the population. The Fante captured a large number of the Akwamu refugees and sold them to European slavers on the coast. With the Akwamu capital under siege, many Akwamu surrendered while others fled into the forests. Groups of refugees crossed the Volta River and built a new society, which required the arduous task of clearing the land and constructing new homes, fields, and other environmental infrastructure from scratch.[36]

As the violence and destruction continued, mining became too dangerous and gold exports declined. Around 1700, the Gold Coast's total annual export of gold may have valued 2.3 million guilders, with the Dutch WIC's share amounting to half a million guilders per annum.[37] In 1720, the head of the WIC on the Gold Coast, William Butler, warned that the gold trade had decreased by half during the last 12 years, a situation that he blamed on the high prices that traders received for slaves. Butler noted that selling slaves had become much more profitable because they could be easily "produced" through raids and war: "A lucky slave raid can make a black man rich in a single day, thus they engage themselves more with warfare, stealing, and robbing, than with their old practice of mining gold, or collecting it ... and ... in time, if the price of slaves rises even more, the Gold Coast will turn entirely into the Slave Coast."[38] Butler's complaint was not inspired by any humanitarian or Christian concerns. On the Gold Coast and elsewhere, the WIC was very deeply involved in the slave trade. Butler simply expressed that the gold trade was more profitable. Moreover, the WIC very quickly adapted to the "new normal" on the Gold Coast and expanded its local share in the slave trade. By 1730, a mere decade later, the destruction and displacement caused by unlimited warfare had indeed transformed the Gold Coast into a slave coast.[39]

Environcide in Asia

VOC officials in Asia described warfare in the 18th century in terms of scorched earth, soldiers living off the land, massive refugee movements, hunger, disease, and death. These officials witnessed and took part in wars on Java in western Indonesia in the 1740s and 1750s, Sri Lanka in the 1760s, and the Molucca islands (Maluku) in eastern Indonesia in the 1770s and 1780s. While VOC records contain obvious biases and inaccuracies, and reflect mainly the views of outsiders, occasionally they provide insights into indigenous perceptions and experiences, given VOC officers' heavy reliance on local indigenous oral and written sources.[40]

Environcide and Genocide on Java

Violence was so pervasive in Java between 1676 and 1755 that the entire period has been called Java's "Eighty Years War." By the 1720s, entire districts lay depopulated, transforming abandoned fields and villages into wilderness.[41] Mass violence escalated during the 1740s and 1750s with VOC forces as well as their allies and adversaries extorting food and tribute in the countryside, burning crops and razing villages, and displacing the population into the mountains and forests.[42] In 1740, the Chinese rebelled against the VOC and, sensing an opportunity, the king

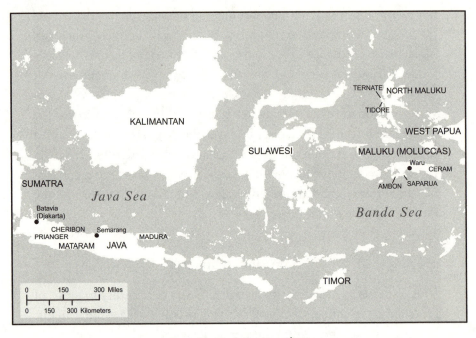

MAP 7.2. Indonesia during the 18th century.

of Mataram came to the aid of the Chinese rebels in 1741, resulting in a protracted and devastating war on Java that lasted until 1755. VOC Governor-General Valkenier of the Indies and Ferdinand de Roy, his commissioner of native affairs, bear much of the responsibility for escalating localized violence into a Java-wide environcidal and genocidal war. Two prominent Chinese witnesses, the sugar cane miller Tsjoeki-etko and the planter Tsjoet Jienko, claimed that abusive and corrupt associates of Ferdinand de Roy had triggered a relatively minor Chinese insurrection in the Javanese countryside south of the colonial capital of Batavia that subsequently resulted in the massacre of thousands of Chinese. It all started when De Roy dispatched inspectors to the sugar plantations south of Batavia to round up undocumented surplus Chinese laborers. Instead, the inspectors detained all the Chinese laborers, irrespective of whether they had passes, and demanded a bribe in exchange for freedom. At the same time, a nightmarish rumor circulated that the detained Chinese laborers would be transported to Sri Lanka to be drowned en masse at sea. Fearing that "with such treatment no

TABLEAU de la Partie de BATAVIA, où s'est fait proprement le terrible MASSACRE des CHINOIS, le 9 Octob. 1740
AFBEELDING van dat Gedeelte van BATAVIA, alwaar eigentlyk de schrikkelyke SLAGTING der CHINEZEN geschied is, den 9 Octob. 1740

FIGURE 7.1. Massacre of the Chinese in Batavia 1740 (Rijksmuseum, Amsterdam, etching by Jakob van der Schley [1715–79] after the original by Adolf van der Laan [1690–1742], Tableau de la Partie de Batavia, ou s'est fait proprement le terrible Massacre des Chinois, le 9 Octobre 1740, accessed online at https://commons.wikimedia.org/wiki/File:Tableau_de_la_Partie _de_Batavia,_ou_s%27est_fait_proprement_le_terrible_Massacre_des_Chinois,_le_9 _Octob.jpeg).

one could be assured to live in peace[,] the Chinese mobilized and gathered agitatedly because they preferred to die in other ways than to innocently suffer to be deported or be drowned at sea."[43] The concerns about deportations were real, as the VOC indeed had intended to ship Chinese plantation workers from Java to its Sri Lankan possessions.[44] The panicked Chinese laborers destroyed the sugar mills, halting sugar production.[45] Short of food, a large group of Chinese armed with cutlasses, pikes, and guns pillaged the village of Tuhu and burned its church, causing the villagers to flee into the forests.[46] Distraught by the destruction of the sugar works, Valkenier retaliated against the inhabitants of the Chinese quarter in Batavia, leading to mass arrest, pillaging and burning of Chinese residences, and killings.[47]

By early October 1740, the arbitrary arrests of Chinese residents of Batavia left so many Chinese in custody that they could not be properly processed. The Council of the Indies, an advisory body to the governor-general, decided that further arrests should be highly selective, with special care to avoid taking "good citizens," but the situation instead escalated into an indiscriminate massacre among Batavia's Chinese population. The council made a half-hearted attempt to stop the killing spree from spreading beyond Batavia by proposing an amnesty for any Chinese who surrendered and vowed to return to their agricultural pursuits. The amnesty excluded anyone who had committed crimes and all Chinese caught while bearing arms. The latter would be considered hostile and killed or imprisoned. Those eligible for the pardon would be issued a pass and resettled on a site outside of Batavia.[48]

The governor-general, however, disagreed with the council's proposals, contending that rather than pardoning the Chinese, they should be considered rebels and all their property confiscated and sold. The council protested that Chinese goods and money already stored at Batavia's town hall should remain under the control of the judge, rather than being immediately sold off. To remedy the pressing shortage of rice and to revive the economy, however, the council consented to declaring void all Chinese-held commercial licenses for the trade in rice, vegetables, meat, and fish, and for shipping and innkeeping in and around Batavia. The licenses were to be sold to others instead, with a preference for Christian Javanese who, furthermore, would not have to pay any rent.[49]

Chinese lives, livelihoods, and property became open targets. A few days after the council's deliberations with the governor-general, Commissioner of Native Affairs De Roy's men confiscated a boatload of fish and other goods from one Chinese trader and a boatload of rice from another. De Roy's men took the fish trader's pass, stole his silver tobacco box, and locked him up. The rice trader, Nio Owacko, was less fortunate. Early in the morning of the day after the rice had been unloaded from the boat, a fire consumed the vessel, killing the owner and one of his companions. The VOC subsequently appropriated the proceeds of the sale of the rice.[50] The deadly fire may not have been an accident. It very conveniently removed the owner and key witnesses that could sue for restitution. In the context of such incidents, it is not difficult to imagine why some Chinese leaders who escaped the mass killings in Batavia feared the VOC's amnesty offer was a trap. Although a group of refugees at Caliaban "live[d] in great fear and misery," they were suspicious because the amnesty placard they were shown lacked the VOC's official seal.[51] The VOC council in Batavia in turn interpreted the refugees' hesitation to mean that "the Chinese" were not interested in amnesty and ordered that any Chinese who continued to "murder, rob, and burn" in the countryside be "prosecuted and killed" as "public enemies." The council consequently ordered all VOC officials on Java to shoot on sight any armed Chinese person they encountered and to summarily execute all armed Chinese who had been taken alive.[52]

Despite the continued violence and the ruthless killing of Chinese prisoners, 4,000 Chinese did apply for amnesty before the November 22, 1740, deadline. The notes of the council meetings revealed the dark calculations of Governor-General Valkenier and his supporters: they expressed the hope that not too many more Chinese would apply for amnesty and recommended that the amnesty requests be slowly processed to prevent too many applicants from being pardoned before the deadline.[53] Those who had not been granted a pardon before the deadline could be freely killed, or deported and robbed of their possessions and property. Moreover, while the VOC leadership was preoccupied with suppressing the Chinese rebellion outside of Batavia, it made no attempt to stop the anti-Chinese violence in Batavia, where sacking, pillaging, and burning Chinese properties continued unabated.[54]

The complicated amnesty process required that rural Chinese obtain a reference from their landlord, but this was not always easy to do. Laauw Tjeeko was a Chinese tenant on VOC-owned lands, but his Chinese landlord, Lim Hongsaaij, disappeared during a visit to Batavia, likely a victim of the mass killings. With only days remaining before the amnesty deadline, Laauw Tjeeko appealed to the neighboring Dutch farmer, Jan van Thoff, who had helped several other Chinese apply for the amnesty. Jan van Thoff, however, was hesitant to offer a reference for someone he did not personally know. After a month-long precarious wait at van Thoff's farm, the locals chased Laauw Tjeeko away. Forced to hide in the forest, he survived on sugar cane, wild vegetables, and rice that his wife secretly supplied. When Laauw Tjeeko was constructing a small hut in his hideout, a Buginese man who came across him convinced him to surrender. The man took Laauw Tjeeko to Commissioner for Native Affairs De Roy to claim the Chinese bounty. Suspecting that Laauw Tjeeko might be a rebel, De Roy sent him to Batavia for interrogation. During two days of interrogation and torture, Laauw Tjeeko denied any involvement with the rebellion, an assertion that the Dutch farmer Jan van Thoff later confirmed.[55]

Greed was a key motivation for Governor-General Valkenier, De Roy, and the militiamen and civilians who attacked, robbed, enslaved, and murdered Chinese men, women, and children in 1740 and 1741. Chinese businessmen controlled the sugar cane production, processing, and trade on Java and in Southeast Asia, as well as the rice trade and tax collection. Moreover, Chinese planters and businessmen preferred to employ Chinese migrant laborers and brought many into the Dutch colony. Individual Dutch officials and colonists and their Javanese associates consequently had much to gain from eliminating the Chinese. In December 1740, the Batavian alderman Godlieb Johan Adolph van Trabe took over the lucrative *arak* (sugarcane-based brandy) distillery of the Chinese businessman Tjo Tjanko who had "perished" during the Batavian massacres.[56]

On December 6, 1740, Governor-General Valkenier staged a coup d'état with the aid of a group of garrison soldiers, arresting and jailing the three members of the Council of the Indies that had opposed his hardline policy against the Chinese.[57] The remaining council members supported Valkenier's strategy to wage total and genocidal war against the Chinese. To determine the strength of the rebels at their Bacassy base, the council approved the proposal by the governor and Commissioner De Roy "to ignore the customary practices of war" (e.g. the rules of war) and use torture to interrogate prisoners of war.[58]

One of the tortured prisoners, 24-year-old Lim Sinko, who had been living with his relative Lim Kienko in the *arak* distillery of Passenburg in Batavia when the mass killings erupted, narrowly escaped death by hiding in the empty distillery for three days before fleeing the city. He sought refuge in Bacassy at the Tuluk Bujang sugar mill owned by the VOC-appointed "captain" of the Chinese, Ni Hoikong. Lim Sinko told his torturers that he had never heard that any notable Chinese such as Captain Ni Hoikong had called for an armed uprising against the VOC. He explained that early during the uprising, two of their leaders had urged the refugees assembled in Bacassy to save the Chinese in Batavia, but they had refused. Although Governor-General Valkenier claimed that up to 10,000 rebels had assembled in Bacassy, Lim Sinko said there were only 3,500 men and that 500 had died of disease or had been killed in the fighting. Food was in short supply and many were hungry and sick at Bacassy. When some of the refugees wanted to surrender, Kle Panjang, their leader, had beheaded an envoy from Batavia for carrying the VOC amnesty proclamation and had threatened to kill anyone who would even talk about laying down their arms.[59]

Lim Sinko's testimony undermined allegations of a Chinese conspiracy between the Chinese elite in Batavia and the Chinese sugar plantation workers south of the city. The purported existence of such a conspiracy was the legitimization for Valkenier's declaration of total war against Java's Chinese community. Yet, in fact, the sugar mills owned by the Chinese elite had been the first and principal target of the Chinese plantation workers' wrath. The mass killing of the Chinese in Batavia therefore targeted people who had nothing to do with the laborers, whose actions, moreover, never threatened the city directly. Indeed, none of the laborers engaged in the revolt ever seem to have come near the city. A large group of rebels that attacked the VOC militia camp south of the city at Pondok Malatty had done so only because the soldiers had cut off the rebels' food supply from a rice-producing area, and this was in late December, long after the massacres in Batavia started.[60]

The height of the rebellion coincided with the January 1741 rice planting season, paralyzing agriculture and food production. Chinese rebels captured Javanese farmers, spreading fear and interfering with the seasonal clearing and planting of the paddy rice fields. The rebels forced their captives to extort rice and water buffalo from Javanese villagers and bring the goods and animals to their base at Bacassy. Sura Marta was a tenant of the Chinese landowner Djamko at Pulo Kitjil, half a day from Batavia. Having abandoned his farm and village in December in fear of the roaming rebels, he was pressed into their service to requisition rice, cows, horses, arms, and recruits from Javanese villages deep in the interior. Sura Marta estimated there were over 14,500 rebels (including Chinese and Javanese), armed with snaphance firearms, spears, and swords. Sura Marta and his fellow foragers, in turn, ordered 40-year-old Gabok of Bakalonga to stop planting rice and help them to carry rice and bananas to provision the rebels.[61] Sakria, a free Javanese tenant farmer at Caliam, half a day from the rebel stronghold at Bacassy and a day's travel from Batavia, was also abducted by Chinese rebels while tending to his paddy rice field. The rebels took him to Bacassy, trained him in the use of weapons, and provided him with a lance. His captors then forced him to participate in an attack on a VOC military camp. The VOC soldiers captured him, and he subsequently was interrogated and tortured. Sakia similarly stressed that the rebels lived off the land, stealing Javanese farmers' water buffalo and other possessions and damaging environmental infrastructure or displacing farmers from their homes and fields.[62]

On March 10, 1741, the VOC Council received a letter translated from Chinese and signed by the rebel leaders at Bacassy. The letter expressed the rebels' willingness to submit to the company, although they stressed that it would be difficult to provide a list of names of the refugees in advance as the VOC demanded. The rebel leaders explained that the refugees were scattered among the villages, sugar mills, and forests around Bacassy. They emphasized that no misdeeds had been committed by anyone under their care. Rather, they had merely fled to Bacassy in order to escape certain death at the hands of the VOC and their local allies. They begged the VOC for a pardon and for safe passage to China.[63] Governor-General Valkenier calculatingly ignored the offer, ordering instead an offensive to "exterminate" the rebels.[64] Commissioner De Roy recruited indigenous militiamen for the purpose, with the promise that they could keep any booty they captured, including Chinese serfs.[65]

Meanwhile, the Chinese rebellion spread across Java. In May 1741, 4,000 Chinese rebels assembled at Semarang on eastern Java and took control over the main rice-growing region, cutting off the supply to the VOC settlements and raising fears that they would destroy the rice crop ripening in the fields. To ensure its ability to feed its soldiers and sailors, the VOC ordered rice from its overseas posts in Malacca, Bengal, Siam, and elsewhere.[66] In July 1741, the Chinese rebels laid siege to Semarang supported by troops and cannons sent by Mataram King Pakubuwana II. Famine threatened as the rebels cut off access to the rice-producing regions, and the rebellion escalated into a Javanese-wide war. The head of the VOC at Semarang requested 300 indigenous soldiers as reinforcement to protect the district's Javanese farmers from the rebels "[who were] threatening the total ruin or neglect of the beautiful padi crop in the field."[67]

When the VOC forces finally occupied the rebel base of Bacassy in western Java in July 1701, Governor-General Valkenier rewarded his allied Javanese militiamen with the Chinese rebels' captured wives, children, and slaves.[68] The gesture transformed at least 175 Chinese men, women, and children into slaves of the soldiers.[69] The VOC also reimbursed local leaders in the Bacassy area for 93 water buffalo that the indigenous militiamen had requisitioned during the final campaign against the rebel stronghold.[70] The water buffalo were essential for plowing the rice fields and transporting the harvest and goods, and thus very highly valued.

As the rebels continued the siege of Semarang and captured several villages in the Cheribon region, threatening the key rice-producing region of Prianger (Preanger), the VOC was in dire need of reinforcements, and impressed the soldiers and crews of several East Indiamen about to sail back to the Netherlands. The VOC also escalated recruitment of indigenous soldiers on Ambon and Ternate in the Moluccan archipelago (Maluku) of eastern Indonesia.[71] Rice continued to be scarce, and it was imported from as far away as Bengal. Still, by the end of September, famine threatened to envelope Java.[72] In desperation and in a bid to weaken Mataram King Pakubuwana II, the VOC offered generous bribes to any of his vassals who switched sides, further escalating the war.[73] Bolstered by the reinforcements from the delayed VOC ships, the Dutch broke the siege of Semarang and massacred the Chinese in the region. The VOC's Maduran ally, Cakraningrat IV, defeated the remaining rebels in eastern Java.[74] When the Dutch refused to acknowledge Cakraningrat IV's conquests as his own, however, fighting erupted with their erstwhile ally and continued until company soldiers captured Cakraningrat IV in 1745.[75]

Peace did not return to Java with the capture of the Maduran king, however, because in 1746, Mataram Prince Mangkubumi joined the long-time rebel Mas Said in his fight against the Mataram king and his Dutch allies. In 1748, the rebels even threatened to overrun the royal capital, Surakarta. The death of Mataram King Pakubuwana II, who after his capture had been heavily dependent on the VOC, triggered the Third Javanese War of Succession, which lasted until 1755. Maduran armies played a prominent role in the 1740s and 1750s fighting on Java, mostly as allies of the VOC, but at times fighting against the Dutch. The Madurans not only were known for their military prowess, according to a VOC official, but also were infamous for "destroying everything according to their usual way of waging war."[76] The Enlightenment-era VOC official who wrote these words may have been attempting to "externalize" scorched earth as a throw-back specialty of the barbarous Madurans. Yet, the Dutch practice of war in the very same conflict was no different. The Dutch, their allies, and their opponents alike lived off the land and employed scorched earth warfare to deny food and supplies to their opponents. The Dutch invaded rebel-held lands; deprived the local population of their environmental infrastructure, including homes, crops and fields, food stores, and livestock; caused villagers and farmers to flee into remote forests, mountains, and caves, and thereby exposing them to hunger and disease.

In 1752, the rebels twice defeated Dutch-led forces, which encouraged several important Javanese leaders to join the rebels. Once again, environcidal warfare was unleashed in the VOC-controlled coastal lowlands, which still were recovering from the early 1740s depredations by the Chinese rebels. Many Javanese farming households fled the countryside to seek sanctuary in Semarang and other towns. Military tactics included not only pillaging villages and robbing livestock but also burning the paddy rice drying in the fields, which caused widespread hunger and a deadly unidentified epidemic. The war cost the VOC 4.2 million guilders, and the destruction in the countryside can be gauged through a disastrous decline in coffee production. In 1741, just before the war affected the region, the VOC generated 21,000 pikol (1,260 tons) from its local coffee suppliers. In contrast, during the height of the violence and displacement in 1742 and 1743, the VOC acquired no coffee at all, and in 1744 it received only 4,000 pikol (24 tons). It would not be until 1756 that the countryside had recovered sufficiently enough that coffee production would reach the 1741 prewar levels again. Indeed, the official VOC report on the rebellion estimated that the recovery of the war-affected regions of Java would take more than 20 years.[77]

In 1743, the VOC removed Governor-General Valkenier from office in the Indies because of his mishandling of the Chinese rebellion and detained him along with Commissioner De Roy for their role in the torture and extrajudicial killing of prisoners of war. Both the governor's accusers and his defenders referred to the laws of war, the former arguing that he had broken them and the latter using the laws to legitimize his actions. During the inquest preceding the governor's trial, one of his defenders conceded that executing prisoners without trial and issuing standing orders to shoot any armed Chinese person on sight were illegal under normal circumstances. The unusual conditions under the "state of war" brought about by the Chinese armed rebellion, he argued, rendered permissible Governor-General Valkenier's decision to outlaw the Chinese as a "nation" and to set a bounty of one ducat on every Chinese person's head to "incentivize" the population to defend the VOC's rule. While noting that it was regrettable that Governor-General Valkenier's orders led to the massacring of the Chinese population of Batavia, the defense argued that the outcome was unintended. Valkenier escaped a trial because he died in custody, and the VOC did not pursue the case further.[78]

Spice Wars and Scorched Earth on Sri Lanka

At the end of 1760, as the VOC was still recovering from the Java wars, a rebellion erupted on Sri Lanka, the source of cinnamon, the precious spice that constituted the primary reason for the company's presence on the island. The rebellion rapidly descended into environcidal and total war as the rebels sought to expel the Dutch from the island or exterminate them. The rebels also threatened the lives of the indigenous allies and subjects of the VOC and their families. They burned and sacked their homes, farms, and fields, displacing many into the interior forests and exposing them to famine and disease.

One of the causes of the rural rebellion was the VOC monopoly over the ownership and protection of cinnamon trees: the trees were not to be cut down, and land with cinnamon trees could not be burned to clear new land or prepare existing fields for crop production.[79] Although cinnamon production in the VOC territories had been declining since the late 1650s, the king of the interior Kandy state had increased cinnamon production and processing in his realm in the interior of the island. The VOC, however, controlled the main seaports and tried to monopolize the cinnamon trade by any means necessary. The king and the rebels therefore allied to drive the VOC from the island at any cost.[80]

Most VOC settlements quickly found themselves under siege. The rebels captured three Dutch forts and massacred 350 VOC soldiers in the process, forcing the company to mobilize all available Dutch civilians and recruit and arm any local volunteers, including "Moors, Chittijs [Chetties], washers, and other *castas*." The rebels burned the houses around the forts they besieged and brought up cannons, seeking to starve the garrisons.[81] Significantly, the VOC reports do not identify the massacring of the Dutch garrisons or the scorched earth around the forts as a marker of uncivilized war or a breach of the laws of war. That the forts seem to have been taken by storm appears to have legitimized sacking, burning, and massacring as in the case of Bergen op Zoom during the 1740s War of the Austrian Succession.

In a written order captured and translated by VOC staff, the king of Kandy warned that any indigenous Sri Lankans who did not immediately join the rebel cause "would soon know what would be done to their bodies as well as those of their wives and children."[82] The rebels pillaged and burned homes and destroyed crop gardens. They also cut off the rice supply to the coast where the VOC settlements were located and requisitioned rice, cattle, goats, pigs, dried fish, oil, and other foods to sustain their troops.[83]

In an ultimatum directed to the Dutch commander of one of the besieged forts, the rebel leaders boasted that even if every Dutchman killed 1,000 of their men, that would not stop them massacring all the Dutchmen and razing the fort. The rebels offered the besieged Dutch garrison the opportunity to retreat to the VOC ships, threatening that if they continued to defend the fort "they will be cut down like their people at Hakman [Hakmana], Cattoene, and Pangala [other Dutch forts that had been taken by the rebels] . . . because they wanted to wage war."[84] In the face of such resolve, only timely reinforcements from the VOC settlements at Cormandel and Malabar from the Indian mainland saved the company on Sri Lanka from annihilation.[85]

VOC subjects who had remained loyal to the company lost their homes and possessions, and fled into the remaining Dutch-held fortified towns. Devoid of income and food, the VOC supported them with money or gifts of rice. It was only in April 1761 that the VOC broke the sieges of its outposts. The inhabitants of the villages surrounding the forts subsequently pleaded with the VOC for a pardon, claiming that the rebels had forced them to join their ranks. The VOC accepted, on the condition that the villagers cooperate in driving out the remaining rebels.[86] In July, when the rebellion still had not been fully suppressed, famine and such diseases as chickenpox, shaking fever, dysentery, and dropsy caused high losses among the indigenous population.[87]

Unwilling or unable to side either with the rebels or the VOC, a number of leaders and their followers fled into the interior forests. In a translated letter sent to the VOC by the villagers of Calanie [or Salanie], Pammeloewille, and Goenehenne in the Hima Corte, the supplicants explained that the rebels' threats of violence had made them "abandon and sacrifice their homes and gardens" and flee into the forests where they were exposed to disease, want, and suffering, "[and] death had snatched away many of them, leaving the survivors drowning in extreme poverty." They asked to be allowed to return "to their pillaged settlements and accept the loss of their former possessions," requesting to be

pardoned and accepted again as loyal subjects.[88] In the Kandy Kingdom, the Dutch faced continued fierce resistance and only managed to
take and then sack the capital during a second expedition in 1765. A 1766
treaty left the VOC in control of the coastal regions and the outlets for the
cinnamon trade, with the Kandy Kingdom locked in the interior.[89]

Spice Wars and Environcide in Maluku

Whereas the rebels systematically targeted the VOC's precious cinnamon trees on Sri Lanka in the 1760s, in eastern Indonesia's Maluku archipelago, it was the VOC that deployed ecocidal violence to eradicate
spice trees. Although destroying spice trees was the official objective, in
practice, the VOC forces destroyed all environmental infrastructure it
encountered near spice tree stands, including fruit trees, crops, homes,
fields, and entire villages, and its soldiers killed all men who resisted.
Since the 16th century, Dutch campaigns to gain control over the spice
islands were marked by scorched earth, mass killings, and population
displacement. By the second half of the 17th century, the spice wars between the Spanish with their Tidore ally and the VOC with its ally Ternate had decimated the Maluku population. The Spanish retreat from
Maluku in the 1660s left the VOC as the only European actor in the
archipelago. The VOC allied with both the Ternate and Tidore sultan-
ates and enlisted them in systematic campaigns throughout the archipelago to eradicate any spice trees that were not in areas under direct
VOC control.[90]

In the second half of the 18th century, the Dutch commanded a large
fleet of VOC and allied indigenous warships, sailors, and soldiers for
the so-called annual Hongi expeditions. The October–December 1770
Hongi campaign involved 30 ships crewed by 1,671 men, including 100
VOC soldiers and 218 indigenous Indonesian notables and headmen,
led by the Dutch governor of Ambon and a handful of Dutch officers
and officials.[91] The objective was to enforce the VOC spice monopoly
by searching for and destroying spice trees, in particular clove and nutmeg. By controlling the number of trees and limiting the cultivation of
cloves and other spices to a few company-controlled islands, the VOC

was able to artificially inflate the price of cloves and other spices. A select few spice-producing islands were controlled by VOC forts and garrisons, and included Ambon, Nusa Laut, Saparua, and Haruku (see Map 7.2). Although Maluku farmers cultivated most of the spice trees on these islands, the VOC carefully monitored their activities, increasing or reducing plantings depending on the directives given by the company's directorate based in the Netherlands. Local leaders subject to the VOC or allied to the company had standing orders to root out any unauthorized plantings of spice trees.[92]

The Hongi fleet patrolled the spice islands of Maluku, inserting landing parties on select islands to search and destroy any spice trees they encountered. The local allied notables accompanying the expeditions served as guides and informants to search the hundreds of islands in the archipelago. The landing parties razed crops and villages, and cut down all fruit-bearing trees. Decimating the environmental infrastructure coerced the local population into subjecting themselves to the VOC and accepting the company's spice monopoly, or flee or perish. Moreover, the commanders of the Hongi campaigns and the landing parties had standing orders to kill any men in the villages who resisted, sparing only the women and children. Any repeat offenders who replanted spice trees or crops or rebuilt their settlements suffered the same fate, even if they had offered no resistance. When the sails of the Hongi fleet appeared on the horizon, villagers typically abandoned their homes, hiding in the forested interior of the islands. VOC soldiers, their Dutch commander, and allied headmen and their crews were entitled to any booty they captured in hostile villages or on enemy ships, except for captured spices, which the VOC claimed as its share in the loot.[93]

The 1767 campaign on the south coast of Ceram razed villages and captured smuggling ships, seizing numerous prisoners and plenty of plunder. During the 1769 campaign, its landing parties on the south coast of Ceram "attacked and subsequently reduced [six villages] to ashes and as much as possible cut and destroyed the fruit-bearing trees."[94]

Farmers sometimes planted the spice trees outside of the reach of the sea-borne patrols in remote hidden valleys or high in the mountains.

On Ceram, where the VOC had no permanent presence, the company held the local leaders personally responsible for eradicating the spice trees. But even on Hila, one of the few islands where spice growing was permitted under direct VOC supervision, illegal plantings were not uncommon. In 1770, two VOC soldiers and 30 auxiliaries destroyed 680 nutmeg and 1,240 clove trees as well as other planted and wild spice trees and plants in Hila's three villages. Eager for the bounties offered by the VOC, some of the villagers had tipped off the soldiers about their neighbors' illegal spice plantings.[95]

The VOC effectively treated Ambon and the other spice islands like war-occupied territory in Europe, exacting labor to maintain fortifications and demanding the villages provide men, provisions, and ships for the Hongi fleet, as well as building materials and other goods. The Hongi expeditions lasted for months, required large amounts of provisions, and tied up thousands of men and ships that could not be used for more productive purposes.[96] Echoing the rules of war, as in occupied territory under war contribution in Europe, the governor ordered the military commanders to ensure that their soldiers treated the VOC's subjects decently and that they did not commit any "extortions or exactions." Any complaints that soldiers might have against the local subject population were to be reported to the local VOC commander or the governor on Ambon so that the soldiers did not take the law in their own hands.[97]

The Hongi tours were executed as military campaigns with regular VOC soldiers led by military officers forming the core of the expedition and the landing parties. As in conventional 18th-century war, honor and courage counted during the expeditions. The VOC promoted Sergeant Hendrik de Waal to the rank of ensign after his exemplary soldiering and bravery during the Hongi campaigns against the Ceram villages in 1770. At the same time, his superiors despaired about the repeat deserter Anthony van Hoeven.[98]

The 1770 Hongi campaign caused the destruction of entire villages and many fruit-bearing trees, including the all-important coconut trees, a key food staple of the spice islands. Although their headman accompanied the Hongi fleet, a landing party sent to collect water and firewood found Maru and the neighboring village Tidore abandoned. The headman explained that he had told the villagers to stay in their homes but "as usual they had fled into the forest with everything they could carry for fear of the Hongi fleet."[99] On Ceram, the expedition bombarded and attacked a series of villages. The captain leading the attack on the first three villages had received explicit orders to raze all the fortifications in the villages, burn the houses, destroy all fruit-bearing trees and boats, take no prisoners, and kill everyone except the women and children. Encountering no resistance in the abandoned villages, the captain followed the orders to the letter. Next, the fleet sailed to and bombarded Ceylor, which had a reputation as a smugglers' hideout. Meeting little resistance, the landing party sacked and burned the abandoned villages and indiscriminately cut down all the fruit-bearing trees. The following day, two more abandoned villages received the same treatment.[100]

The governor of Ambon, however, determined that the 1770 Hongi campaign had not been enough of a deterrent because the villagers had fled before the attacks with everything they could carry. He ordered a smaller-scale Hongi contingent to return to Ceram in early 1771, instructing the commanding officer "to destroy by fire and sword everything living except women and children" in every village where spices were discovered. The governor also stipulated that any suspicious ships be captured, the crew killed, and the craft scuttled if it contained spices. At the same time, the governor urged the commander to "strictly prohibit all cruel torture . . . [of crews and villagers] as has occurred before and report those who commit [such acts] so that they can be rigorously punished." Captured loot could be kept by the Hongi soldiers, except for spices and gunpowder, which had to be handed over to the VOC.[101]

By the early 1780s, however, the VOC moderated the policy of ruthlessly eradicating spice trees and sacking and burning offending villages due to its weakened control over Maluku and Southeast Asia. Nuku Muhammad Amiruddin, a Tidore prince, fought a tenacious rebellion against the VOC with strong support from within the Tidore Sultanate and Papuan vassals. Nuku's raids on Saparua and other key VOC spice islands in 1781 and 1782, and his fleet's annihilation of the 1783 VOC

Hongi expedition, revealed the vulnerability of the company. The VOC feared that, under the circumstances, decimating tree crops would drive people into the camp of Nuku. The possibility was particularly an issue on Ambon and the surrounding islands where small-scale indigenous producers with narrow profit margins legally cultivated most of the cloves. The governor feared that reducing the number of trees and thereby threatening people's livelihoods would meet resistance. This concern was amplified because most of the indigenous VOC soldiers were from the very same islands, and uprooting their relatives' spice trees might unduly test their loyalty.[102] Hongi campaigns to Ceram and the other outlying islands subsequently became somewhat more restrained. During the 1784 Hongi campaign, several village headmen who previously had defied the VOC, but who agreed to submit to the company, received pardons, and the soldiers spared their villages. In several instances, landing parties encountered villages that had been abandoned, but instead of burning the houses as on previous occassions, the soldiers told the villagers to return to their homes.[103]

Not all villages were so lucky. One landing party tracked down the survivors of a Papua pirate fleet raid on Hatiling, who were hiding in their forest refuge. The Hongi soldiers torched the 15 huts that had sheltered the refugees and burned down a nearby abandoned village for good measure. Three days later, landing parties set fire to three more villages that had rebelled the previous year and that continued to refuse to submit to the VOC. To punish them, the governor ordered his military commander "to cause the utmost hurt [and] spare neither the inhabitants beyond the women and children nor [spare] their homes and fruittrees [sic]." Many of the homes recently had been rebuilt after the previous Hongi raid. The soldiers also cut down one hundred coconut trees and carried off the villagers' stores of sago, a food staple, robbing the survivors of both their food supplies and sources of food. Fearing the same fate, the leaders of the Waru district on eastern Ceram hastily submitted to the VOC. Granting them a pardon, the governor outlined the benefits: they could live quiet lives rather than scattering like birds. But he warned that disobedience would result in the destruction of their homes, plantations, trees, and indeed their entire land and people.[104]

As before, the VOC was prepared to deploy environcide and risk genocide in order to maintain its control over the spice trade and the islands
of Maluku.

Neither the rebels nor the VOC and their allies showed any restraint
in fighting on Tidore in the fall of 1783. Tidore rebels seized the VOC
forts and killed all the Dutchmen on the island. A joint VOC-Ternate
expedition that retook the island indiscriminately massacred the men,
women, and children of Gammafu, and looted the town for three days
after a bloody siege. The VOC forces next systematically burned all food
stores and captured or destroyed all boats and ships on the island.
Tidore's inhabitants depended on sago meal and other foodstuffs imported by boat from the neighboring island of Halmahere, and the loss
of their boats spelled hunger and famine. A contemporary VOC report
triumphantly noted that satisfactory revenge had been exacted for the
massacre of the Dutch garrisons because none of the inhabitants of
Tidore was left with a roof over their heads. An English source claimed
that 1,800 of Tidore's inhabitants had died in the fighting and the subsequent famine.[105] In the meantime, Papua pirates sacked and burned
the island of Bonoa (Boano), northwest of Ceram after the Hongi fleet
had set sail for the islands south of Ceram.[106] Environcidal violence thus
came from multiple sides: the VOC and its allies and their enemies.

The governor of Ambon who led the 1788 Hongi campaigns chose
not to use the term "Hongi" at all in his report. He also sought to limit
the violence and the destruction of homes, trees, and crops because the
rebel Nuku had gained widespread support throughout Maluku. In one
serious breach of protocol, the heads of Waru did not assemble on
the beach to greet the governor when his fleet arrived. A patrol found that
as on previous occasions, Waru had been entirely abandoned upon the
sighting of the fleet. The governor thereupon dispatched a full-size landing party of VOC and allied soldiers and sailors, under a Dutch ensign,
with strict orders not to damage any fruit trees. The landing party found
the doors of the houses in a neighboring small hamlet wide open along
with signs that the population quite recently had fled without harvesting the trees that were heavy with fruit. The allied soldiers fanned out
in the main village "robbing and pillaging all they found contrary to the

governor's orders." Before returning to his ship, the governor ordered the ensign to put a stop to the marauding and threatened the perpetrators with "rigorous punishment." He also instructed the ensign and his men to remain in Waru for a couple of days to search for and destroy any spice trees, and to encourage the population to return to their villages. To his great annoyance, he observed columns of smoke arising from the villages as the fleet was about to set sail. Three or four houses in Waru and several more in the neighboring hamlet had been set on fire. The ensign produced three suspects, but because the indigenous soldiers concerned vehemently denied the charge, they were sent back to their ship with orders to be kept under observation. To prevent further incidents, the governor refused to let anyone disembark at the fleet's next stop, meeting the local leaders on his ship, instead. During the remainder of the voyage, the governor issued several pardons for disobedience to the company, declined to take any punitive action against another abandoned village, and postponed military action against rebellious Goram because it was too well defended.[107]

A Century of Environcidal War

The notion of the 18th century as an age of limited war reflected a contemporary ideal that, moreover, masked the actual practices of war. Eighteenth-century warfare was marked by environcide and total war, and was not fundamentally different from the ways of war in the 16th and 17th centuries. Moreover, warfare in Europe and the practices of war in the Americas, Asia, and Africa were more similar than they were different: they relied heavily on environcidal strategies and tactics.

Environcidal warfare in 1740s–50s Java and 1760s Sri Lanka caused large-scale population displacements, famine, and deadly epidemics. On Java the VOC forces and their allies and their opponents alike lived off the land and used scorched earth tactics. The collapse of coffee production on Java and cinnamon production on Ceylon is suggestive of the wider rural destruction: it took years to return agricultural output to prewar levels. The 1770s and 1780s Hongi campaigns in the Maluku archipelago of eastern Indonesia were especially ruthless: VOC and allied soldiers had standing orders to sack and burn homes, crops, and fruit trees, and to kill the men, sparing only women and children, probably for enslavement. Villagers, however, fled as soon as the VOC ships appeared, but in the process lost their unmovable environmental infrastructure, including the spice and fruit trees that had taken years to establish and bear fruit. Warfare in West Africa's Gold Coast region similarly caused the loss of environmental infrastructure (cleared forest lands, towns, homes, fields, pastures, and gold mines) through massive population displacement and the sacking and burning of settlements. Refugees were not only vulnerable to hunger and disease but also to slave traders who sold men, women, and children en masse into the Atlantic slave trade. The heavy population losses severely restricted the availability of labor to invest in the repair and maintenance of environmental infrastructure. Clearing forest for settlements and fields, as well as maintaining the clearings and keeping paths open, was extremely labor intensive. Within less than a generation, the major export of the Gold Coast shifted from gold to humans as a war economy rendered more peaceful, productive pursuits highly dangerous and selling captives highly profitable.

Throughout the Americas, 18th-century wars encompassed the conscious and systematic targeting of environmental infrastructure, either through direct destruction or through intentional and unintentional population displacement, which was not fundamentally different from contemporary warfare in Western and Southern Europe. Hence, there was no unique "American way of war." Environcide equally marked warfare in West Africa, South Asia, and Southeast Asia. As this and the preceding two chapters demonstrate, belligerents and soldiers in and beyond Europe in the 18th century systematically ignored the rules and laws of war in practice even as the protocols served to legitimize intellectual discourses about a supposed European "civilized," conventional way of war and a non-Western, "uncivilized" or "small" type of war. Moreover, military leaders actively and increasingly opposed the transformation of the rules of war into a set of binding laws.

As a result, belligerents across the globe continued to intentionally use rural populations and their environmental infrastructure to sustain armies and the war effort. At the same time, belligerents sought to deny the same resources to the enemy through scorched earth and population displacement, inviting hunger, disease epidemics, mass trauma, and further dislocation. At times, environcidal warfare shaded into ecocide (e.g., the systematic and repeated destruction of spice and other crop trees) and even genocide (e.g., of the Chinese on Java). Despite the repeated reference to the laws or rules of war, environcide and attendant total war were therefore as prevalent in the 18th-century era of limited war as they had been in the 16th and 17th centuries.

8

Refugees, Removals, and Reservations

ENVIRONCIDE IN THE AMERICAN WEST IN THE 19TH CENTURY

It [the peace Andrew Jackson imposed in Florida] is the peace of the great charnel house . . . the peace which reigned along the Andes when the remorseless Pizarro had spread desolation over South America—the peace which pervaded Holland when the merciless Duke of Alva had deluged her fertile fields and drenched the streets of her cities with the blood of her citizens.[1]

Destroy their villages and ponies . . . kill or hang all warriors, and bring back the women and children.[2]

THE FIRST QUOTE is from an 1819 debate in the US House of Representatives. Defenders of Andrew Jackson's cross-border expedition against the Seminole in Spanish Florida argued that the general had at least brought peace to the region. Representative Storrs of New York, perhaps a descendent of Dutch settlers, sharply disagreed and compared Jackson's merciless sacking and burning of numerous Seminole villages to the inhumane campaigns of Pizarro and Alva, resurrecting the 16th-century Black Legend narrative. The second quote refers to the

279

orders that Custer received from his superior, General Sheridan, during the 1868–69 winter campaign against the Great Plains Cheyenne and the Arapaho.

Pillage, raids, and scorched earth marked 19th-century warfare in the West of North America as locals, refugees, colonists, and gold diggers contested control over the key resources of bison herds, horses, and guns, as well as gold and environmental infrastructure. The more powerful groups expanded into the Great Plains, taking control over such resources through trading and raiding. The weaker ones retreated into the mountainous regions between the Great Plains and the Pacific Coast, eking out a living through hunting and gathering, raiding, and agriculture where environmental conditions allowed. Further west still, the considerable indigenous populations along the Pacific Coast of North America collapsed rapidly as a result of violence, the gold rush, and disease.[3] Some have labeled the escalating and retaliatory violence that characterized the 19th century and that caused the decimation of the indigenous American populations as genocide.[4]

By the mid-1880s, the surviving 243,000 indigenous North Americans had been confined to 187 reservations, overwhelmingly located west of the Mississippi River. For many Western indigenous Americans, the removal to the reserves was the second or even third time that they had become refugees. Warfare and climate change in the North and East, trade and fur wars in the Great Lakes and the Great Plains, and Spanish conquest and raids in the South, Southwest, and West already had displaced many from their homes and environmental infrastructure.

The general image of Western indigenous Americans as iconic hunters and gatherers may constitute the upstreaming of a postcontact state of crisis caused by the displacement and violence that had robbed them of the environmental infrastructure that had sustained their lives.[5] In fact, many Western indigenous Americans were no longer even in their precontact environment. The Western indigenous Americans' experiences as refugees trying to make a living by any means possible is, therefore, important to emphasize.

A second theme of this chapter is to assess the extent to which the Western indigenous Americans constructed and maintained environmental infrastructure, despite having been displaced relatively recently. A final inquiry involves ascertaining the degree to which the Western indigenous Americans' environmental infrastructure was an object, subject, and instrument of violence in the 18th and 19th centuries. An explicit focus on the consequences of war and displacement not only helps to explain the overexploitation of such environmental resources as beaver and buffalo but also highlights how capturing existing environmental infrastructure from others was a critical shortcut that enabled refugees and colonists to secure new lives and livelihoods. The appropriation of environmental infrastructure was extremely violent because it pitted refugees and migrants against established populations or other refugees. Moreover, the plight of the Western indigenous Americans also demonstrates that they were simultaneously victims and agents of history: they experienced social and environmental collapse, and reinvented themselves and their environment not once, but twice or even three times during the course of a century.

Western Indigenous Americas as Refugees

Nineteenth-century explorers encountered "besieged, dependent, and fearful . . . peoples" in the Great Basin west of the Great Plains.[6] The indigenous Americans of the Great Basin were not an exception. All remaining indigenous North Americans were under siege, and most of the Western indigenous Americans had been displaced multiple times. They were refugees from war and conflict over crop land and hunting territories, water, fur, guns, horses, and slaves. They were victims of violent invaders: indigenous Americans, Europeans, or both. Yet, they were historical actors as well, having fled west and engaged in rebuilding communities and workable environments. During the 19th century, however, they were overtaken by a tsunami of total war and once again displaced to reservations, triggering yet another round of rebuilding and reinvention by those who survived.[7]

Except for the Southwestern indigenous Americans, the literature frequently depicted Western indigenous societies as archetypical (semi)nomadic hunter and gatherers who adapted to a challenging semiarid or arid climate over the course of millennia. Many, however, only relatively recently had been displaced from various other environments. Southern and Southwestern indigenous Americans had been deeply scarred by Spanish violence in the 16th and 17th centuries, and during the late 18th and early 19th centuries, Spanish soldiers subjected indigenous Californians to forced removals and violent raids for captives. The 18th-century indigenous Americans of Ohio similarly were refugees from violence in the Northeast: the Iroquois wars and settler violence. The iconic northern Great Plains bison hunters hailed from the Eastern Woodlands around the Great Lakes, and their equally iconic southern neighbors entered the grassy expanses from the west and south.

An environmentally deterministic argument underlays the classification of the Western indigenous Americans as hunter-gatherers: that the West simply was too arid for agriculture. Exceptions were few and far between, although precontact agriculture had been more common in the North American Southwest.[8] The Texas panhandle in the southern Great Plains, for example, had sustained dryland maize well into the 15th century.[9] Nevertheless, although the decline of Western indigenous American agriculture may have been related to climatic factors and to precontact violence rather than European invasion, the West's aridity did not impose a hunting and gathering lifestyle, per se.

The 1830s forced removals of the Southwestern indigenous Americans, including the Creek, the Cherokee, and the bulk of the Iroquois confederacy from the eastern part of North America completed a process of displacement that had begun much earlier. Huron and other survivors from the earlier Iroquois wars in the Northeast who fled west caused conflict deeper in the interior. The Great Lakes Dakota managed to defeat the encroaching Huron and their Algonquin allies in 1690, yet still moved further west. The displacement of the Dakota and other Sioux groups was partly a response to shifts in the fur trade as beaver hunting in the Eastern Woodlands became more contested and buffalo hunting on the Great Plains more attractive. But war and Iroquois western expansion were also major factors.[10]

The westward migrations of the Sioux in turn displaced the Omahas, Iowas, Missouri, and Poncas, among others.[11] After the mid-18th century,

Cree and Assiniboine bands moved toward the Great Plains; by the 1790s, the Assiniboine and the western Cree had reinvented themselves as horse-mounted buffalo hunters. In turn, the Salteaux moved into the areas in the Eastern Woodlands that had been vacated by the Cree.[12] The 19th-century Great Plains' buffalo hunting bands of the Comanche, Kiowa, Kiowa-Apache, southern Cheyenne, and Arapaho were all new-comers: none were indigenous to the region. The Comanche had been driven from southern Wyoming by the Sioux during the 18th and 19th centuries, and the Kiowa, who originated from the headwaters of the Missouri, had been pushed south by the Cheyenne and the Arapaho. The Cheyenne and the Arapaho, in turn, had been edged out of Wisconsin and Minnesota by the Sioux.[13] Many more Western indigenous Americans were displaced or otherwise affected by the Sioux and Comanche, who, along with their allies, created powerful empires in the Great Plains.[14]

The indigenous Americans of the Far West had been equally traumatized by conflict and displacement. The societies in the South and Southwest had experienced repeated Spanish invasions, including the utterly destructive Spanish-Pueblo Wars, as well as slave raids. Moreover, by the 19th century, the indigenous Californians' hunting and gathering lifestyle may have been more of an expedient strategy of desperation and improvisation than the result of an age-old adaption to a challenging natural environment. Spanish colonization broadcast violence deep into the interior of California and caused massive population displacement.[15] The most direct impact of the Spanish conquest was experienced along the coast. The Chumash villages first came into contact with a Spanish expedition in 1769. The first mission was established there in 1772, followed by a Spanish fort in 1804. Disease killed many Chumash during the early mission period, when missionaries initiated forced resettlement in concentrated villages while indigenous groups fought one another.[16]

The indigenous villages in the interior of California effectively were refugee settlements.[17] Spanish raiders pursued the indigenous Californians to replenish the populations of the Spanish missions on the coast. Most of the converted indigenous Americans residing at the missions were captives. The impacts of the Spanish raids and the concentration of captives at missions are clearly visible in Californian's archaeological record. Many of the territory's 4,000–5,000 archaeological sites were occupied early in the contact period but soon abandoned as its inhabitants fled or were captured.[18]

As on the East Coast of North America, violence and displacement literally created space for invasive species, new ideas, and innovative practices. The adoption of the horse, which permitted even greater mobility for buffalo hunting, is one example. But horses also imposed limitations: they required good grazing and shelter, particularly during the winter, as they were vulnerable to extreme low temperatures.[19] Refugee investment in productive environmental infrastructure may have been hindered by the perceived need to invest heavily in defensive fortifications, guns, and horses. Trauma and despair also may have rendered the displaced indigenous Americans and European settlers more likely to use violence to gain access to the environmental infrastructure of the societies they encountered. They may have become more ruthless in the exploitation of any resources that would help them to survive and re-build, be it hunting beaver or buffalo to acquire guns and horses, or raiding for livestock, food, or slaves.

Hunting and Gathering as Improvisation

Various Great Plains hunters, including Dakota-Sioux groups, had been sedentary farmers when they lived further east, but transformed themselves into specialized buffalo hunters during the 18th and 19th centuries. Nomadic buffalo hunting was heavily, but not entirely, dependent on the introduction of the horse, a postcontact innovation. Horses enabled a more mobile lifestyle; they could pull much larger loads than the dogs used before the equines' introduction.[20] The history of the Sioux demonstrates that the sharp distinction between (nomadic) hunter gatherers and (sedentary) agriculturalists is overdrawn. The mid-17th-century Eastern Sioux were less mobile than their Great Plains Sioux cousins, even as they were conventionally described as hunter-gatherers. Men hunted while women tapped sugar maples and gathered wild rice. The women may also have grown corn. Moreover, wild rice was not always "wild;" in some cases it may have been cultivated and in more recent times even considered the cultivator's property rather than a free or communal resource. After the rice harvest, the Eastern Sioux seasonally moved into the forests and river valleys of northeastern Minnesota to hunt elk and deer for the duration of the winter. In March–April, they returned to their villages to subsist on stored food supplemented with freshly caught water fowl and fish. They also hunted buffalo east of the Mississippi and stored dried meat and wild rice mixed with tallow and other foods. If they kept moving between their main village and various seasonal camps, resources usually were plentiful.[21]

In the early 18th century, the Sioux migrated from the Eastern Woodlands to the Great Plains west of the Mississippi River and increasingly came to rely on hunting buffalo. Yet, early 19th-century expeditions observed corn or bean fields near Sioux "camps" even as they described the Sioux as consummate hunters. Euro-American observers also noted that the larger settlements of the previous era had given way to smaller residential bands: larger villages are considered to be more typical for farmers while hunter-gatherers tended to live in smaller groups.[22] Moreover, the successful adoption of small-scale gardening by the Western Sioux in the 1880s (after they had been removed to reservations) was facilitated by their history of crop cultivation along the Missouri River before arriving in the Great Plains in the early 1800s. The Brulé Sioux had long continued to grow corn, and the name of the Minneconjou Sioux means "planters beside the stream."[23] Nomadic bison hunting thus was not a time-honored Plains' indigenous American tradition, but an 18th-century "improvisation."[24]

Similarly, after the Pawnee acquired horses in the 18th century, they disinvested from agriculture. While men and women alike had engaged in crop cultivation, the women now tilled small one- to three-acre fields in the soft soils along rivers or creeks. After weeding the crop, Pawnee bands temporarily abandoned their villages for the summer hunt. They returned to their villages for the harvest, stocking the winter stores in pits. Some Pawnees maintained or restored crop cultivation and storing practices into the early 19th century, as illustrated by an 1820s account that a party of European hunters had only survived a grueling winter because they had discovered a cache of stored corn at a Pawnee village. When the Pawnee residents returned to their village, the grateful hunters compensated them for the corn that they had eaten.[25]

The emphasis on the Great Plains indigenous Americans' dependence on bison overlooks both the past and the continued importance of agriculture and "wild" plants. Before the advent of European trade and the introduction of the horse, a drier climate caused a shift to greater reliance on buffalo hunting, especially in the western parts of the region, while agriculture remained more important in the eastern parts.[26]

The Mandan and Hidatsa agricultural complex on the Great Plains long predated the introduction of the horse. By the late 18th century, the Mandan and Hidatsa villages on the rich Upper Missouri bottomlands were the most northern agriculturalists. Employing a fast-ripening flint maize, they used the same fields repeatedly, preparing them with fire and growing their corn on small mounds. Among the 19th-century Hidatsa, the individual who undertook the heavy task of clearing a plot to make a field became its owner. Women owned their own farm plots that were inheritable in the maternal line. Agriculture had been much more widespread on the Great Plains during the 10th to the early 17th centuries. Archaeological research in the Western Canadian Red River region near today's Lockport, Manitoba, unearthed bell-shaped underground food storage caches, as well as pottery, hoes, grinding tools, and corn kernels dating to the 14th century. Climatic cooling around 1500 shortened growing seasons and pushed agriculture south.[27] The phenomena may have displaced some of the Northern Great Plains and Eastern Woodlands indigenous Americans and scattered them southward; along the way, some shifted to hunting, gathering, and raiding.

The history of such Great Basin groups as the Shoshone, Paiute, and Ute west of the Great Plains demonstrates the dramatic impact of population displacement. The Ute and the Shoshone were not indigenous to the Great Basin, having originated from further east. These groups repeatedly adapted to very different environments. Along with other indigenous Americans in the Great Basin, they not only engaged in hunting and gathering but also actively managed plants and entire ecosystems through burning, clearing, pruning, coppicing, tilling, and transplanting. The Shoshone, Paiute, and Ute practiced small-scale cropping. Except for the Southern Paiute, who reportedly engaged in small-scale horticulture in 1776 and in 1844, the chronology of these different pursuits is not entirely clear.[28]

It is similarly difficult to determine if the Shoshone added cultivation to their survival strategies after they had been driven off the Great Plains into the Great Basin. The Great Basin indigenous Americans gathered piñon nuts, mesquite, agave, yucca, and at least 161 kinds of small seeds. The assumption that hunting and gathering in the Great Basin was the "natural" subsistence strategy is problematic. Agriculture may have been marginal and limited, but it was practiced in all the major groups, including the Southern Paiute. Several Western Shoshone groups in central Nevada sowed "wild" seeds near springs, including lamb's quarters and Indian rice grass, after clearing the vegetation with fire. They also used fire and coppice on willow and skunk bush sumac to produce straight stems for basketry. The Death Valley Shoshone heavily pruned mesquite to optimize the production of seed pods and firewood. The evidence of agricultural practices suggests yet again that it was not necessarily environmental conditions that led them to specialize in hunting and gathering. Moreover, planting and tending irrigated "wild" plants, including agave, had long been known in the Great Basin. Agave, or American century plant, was a staple (and a stored food) for many of the Southwestern indigenous Americans, including the Apache, Comanche, and Ute.[29] The Southern Great Plains societies, in particular the Comanche who dominated the region in the 18th and 19th centuries, found themselves in a much more favorable environment for horse-mounted hunting because of the higher temperatures and the less severe winters south of the Arkansas River. Yet, they, too, were not simply nomadic hunter-gatherers. Trading (for corn and other foods as well as guns and horses) and raiding (for horses and captives) were as important to the Comanche as bison hunting, and they spent most of the winter months in large villages to which they returned every year.[30]

The Gold Rushers referred to the indigenous Californians as "diggers" as a means of evoking images of savagery: they purportedly lived hand to mouth, digging up roots.[31] California's indigenous societies still are seen to have relied more heavily on wild plants than any other indigenous North American group, except those in the Great Basin.[32] On one level, the mid-19th-century label reflected the dependency on digging roots, however, the practice may have been a recent invention resulting from war and displacement. On another level, the term "diggers" served as an ideological and legal discourse to legitimize the alienation of land and environmental resources by ruthless gold prospectors, settlers, land speculators, and officials.[33] The indigenous Californians, however, lived in hamlets and villages that in the 19th century appeared as fixed as those of the indigenous peoples of the Northeast.[34]

Still, "native life" had been deeply affected by Spanish colonization. The 15,000 indigenous American Christians living at the Californian missions in 1834 would have constituted almost 20 percent of the 80,000 indigenous Americans remaining after the deadly 1830s epidemic. Almost one-fifth of the indigenous Californians would have been nominal Christians who had at one time resided at a Spanish mission. Given that the Christianization of the indigenous Californians was steeped in violence, it is legitimate to question the extent to which they voluntarily abandoned their previous lifestyles and beliefs. The main point, however, is that they cannot simply be regarded as traditional hunters and gatherers. Moreover, missionized indigenous Californians had an impact beyond their numbers because they interacted with friends and relatives in the interior. Flight from the missions was common, and missionized indigenous Americans and their ideas penetrated the interior even before larger numbers of refugees returned to the interior villages after the Mexican authorities freed them from the missions. Up to 10 percent of all Christian indigenous Americans fled the missions permanently, and many more ran away for shorter or longer periods of time. One suggestive example of the extent to which missionized indigenous Americans had an impact is the spread of invasive weeds that were "domesticated" in the interior of California. Interviewees told ethnographers in early 20th-century central California that wild oats (*Avena fatua*), a highly valued food crop, had "always" grown in the area. But wild oat is an Old World weed that must have been introduced with grain seed at the Spanish missions. Other Californian invasive weeds may also have originated as escapees from Spanish mission fields, perhaps carried into the interior by human refugees.[35]

Not by Nature: Western Indigenous Americans and Environmental Infrastructure

Indigenous hunters had a major impact on the continent's fauna and contributed to the demise of the continent's large mammals, including the buffalo.[36] They also deeply shaped the New World's flora by the use of fire.[37] The indigenous Americans of the Pacific Northwest are often depicted as typical gatherers who lived off plants that "just grow by themselves."[38] Yet, they subjected 100 plant species or closely related groups of species to "some form of management associated with their maintenance or productivity" and engaged in the "cultivation of landscape." The list of plant resources that Pacific Northwestern indigenous Americans "sustained" included seaweed, 2 fungi species, 4 species of fern, 13 species of conifers, and 12 tree species, including yellow cedar, lodge pole and ponderosa pine, Rocky Mountain and big leaf maple, paper birch, and hazelnut.[39]

Pacific Northwestern indigenous Americans also managed berry bushes with fire and pruning, and they widely used and harvested at least 60 species in large quantities. They dried and stored the berries underground and berry remains are well-represented at archaeological village sites.[40] Thousands of trees in the Northwest show evidence of human use: sustainable bark harvesting left scars on lodgepole and ponderosa pines along the coast and red cedars at the Indian Heaven huckleberry site in Gifford Pinchot National Forest, Washington. The scars on the red cedars date as far back as three centuries.[41]

American settlers admired the open landscapes of Vancouver Island and elsewhere in British Columbia, which they regarded as natural savannas. But, in fact, the Garry Oak savanna, which was covered with Cama meadows and fern glades, was the product of centuries of burning by the indigenous Salish. European observers in 1842 similarly considered the Springback clover (*Trifolium wormsioldii*) expanses near Fort

Victoria to be wild and natural, but they very likely were carefully managed by the local Songhee. Indigenous Americans managed such important staple root plants as the ubiquitous Cama (*Camassia quamash*) and Wapato or swamp potato (*Sagittaria latifolia*) through landscape clearing, weeding, and selective harvesting.[42] European settlers discovered that Camas provided excellent fodder for their cattle, rendering the indigenous American staple highly vulnerable to foraging livestock. The destruction of the southern Vancouver Island Cama harvest by settler cattle factored into the outbreak of the 1877 Nez Perce war.[43]

Indigenous Californians practiced landscape burning to create a more open landscape and to manage vegetation. They especially subjected the brushy or chaparral areas to fire management.[44] Indigenous Americans also shaped the grass savannas of the Great Plains by fire. Regular burning favored such highly nutritious short grasses as Buffalo grass (a staple for the buffalo) and reduced the spread of less palatable long grasses and forbs.[45] Landscape burning was also used to move game. During the late summer, the Blackfeet and other Great Plains groups set fire to open grasslands to force the buffalo herds toward their winter pastures in the foothills, where they had their winter camps.[46]

Seasonal migrations usually occurred between sites with environmental infrastructure. Neither the Great Plains nor the Pacific Coastal indigenous Americans were truly nomadic. The Great Plains indigenous Americans had "favorite" winter camps, suggesting that they returned to the same locations repeatedly.[47] Northwestern Pacific indigenous Americans engaged in a seasonal pattern of movement to make optimal use of the resources available in different locations, for example fish along the coast or rivers, as well as lowland winter quarters and upland summer camps. The relatively predictable seasonal migration pattern involved a few select and fixed places that were proprietary: families typically returned to the same summer camps, where they carefully managed their own berry patches.[48] In the North Pacific Coast, individuals or groups owned specific fishing sites.[49] Particularly favorable hunting sites in California and elsewhere sometimes were also owned, although the practice was localized and dependent on the presence of such "improvements" as game fences.[50] Northern Great Plains bison hunters, including the Cree and Assiniboine, drove bison herds into elaborate hunting pounds made with brushwood where the animals could be killed in large numbers.[51] On the Northwest Pacific Coast and in California, locations with "wild" plants were also sometimes exclusionary rather than open access.[52]

Overwhelmingly, indigenous Americans, including hunter-gatherers, lived in permanent fixed abodes, framed by poles and covered by wood, bark, reed, earth, or stone. Dwellings required regular repair and maintenance, and they were occupied for at least part of the year. Many groups used more than one type of dwelling. The indigenous populations of the Missouri River Valley lived in multifamily, earth-covered lodges in villages during the farming season, and in hide-covered conical tepees, or tipis, when hunting buffalo.[53] In the (semi)arid West of North America, where protection against the summer heat was a priority, underground houses were common. Pit lodges provided coolness in scorching summers and warmth during freezing winters.[54] The English explorer Sir Francis Drake described such a pit house dwelling in 1571 in California's Bay Area.[55]

Buffalo hunters on the Great Plains used mobile homes consisting of pole frames covered by buffalo hides that could be transformed into drag sleds drawn by dogs or horses. The tepees were elaborate productions made of treated buffalo hides that were sewn together and kept the occupants warm even during the coldest weather. The mobility of such key environmental infrastructure allowed the Plains hunters to follow the migratory buffalo herds.[56]

All Western indigenous Americans depended on food stores to survive seasons of scarcity and lean years. As elsewhere, food stores were concentrated at settlements, and dwellings often doubled as food storages. The 19th-century indigenous American fishing communities on Vancouver Island and the Gulf Islands preserved large quantities of food during the summer months.[57] Societies in central California and the Gulf of Mexico region stored food in large baskets placed on a stone or wooden platform.[58] The Sioux preserved food, including fish, meat, and a variety of wild and domesticated plants and fruits.[59] For the Great Plains indigenous Americans, dried meat and pemmican were key food sources during the winter that they kept in their tents and transported on their travois.[60] The Northwestern Pacific indigenous Americans, who relied on a large-scale "storage economy" that dated back over three millennia, placed their food reserves in wooden boxes in their plank houses or their pit lodges.[61] The Yavapai of Arizona preserved food in baskets and pots in the caves where they wintered.[62] Seasonal migratory movements and raids encouraged hiding food stores. Caves or crevices were popular for food storage in the drier climates. Subterraneous, well-camouflaged storage pits and other hidden food stores were also common.[63]

Stored food was not ready-made manna from heaven. To the contrary, food for winter or dry season consumption had to be painstakingly processed and stored, requiring major investments of time, labor, and knowledge. Indigenous Americans often preserved food in pots and baskets.[64] In the more humid regions, maize had to be carefully dried over a fire or on drying racks before it could be safely stored. Fish was also dried.[65] The Great Plains' pemmican consisted of dried meat mixed with melted fat and marrow to which berry or fruit paste was added. Preparing pemmican was laborious and complicated, but it produced a compact and high-energy food that when packed in a rawhide container and properly stored could be preserved for several years, although it usually was consumed within one.[66]

Indigenous Californians' acorn staple was an abundant natural resource, but it was not naturally digestible. Containing high levels of tannic acid, acorns required laborious processing before they yielded a safe and nutritious food. After being ground with a mortar and pestle, acorns were cooked with hot stones or boiled in water to remove the tannic acid. Processing enough acorn to provide half of the daily dietary calories for a family of four took up to five hours per day. Indigenous Californians relied more heavily on stored food than either the Plateau indigenous Americans to the north or the Great Basin indigenous Americans to the east, yet their food stores sustained them for longer periods than even the Northwestern Coastal indigenous Americans. The elaborate acorn processing and their granary technology rendered the Californian indigenous Americans sedentary and able to sustain an unusually high population density for nonagriculturalists.[67]

Indigenous American Refugees and War

At times, the westward displacement of indigenous Americans led to cooperation, as evidenced by the 18th-century "multi-ethnic" villages of the Great Lakes' Pays d'en Haut. But desperate refugees also clashed with one another and with their host communities, leading to further displacement deeper into the interior prior to direct European contact. In large measure, attempts to gain or maintain control over and access to environmental infrastructure was the driving factor of violence. Refugees who had been displaced from their lands faced enormous challenges in adapting to and shaping the environments where they sought safety. The obstacles were higher still for war refugees weakened by disease and the long westward treks during which they carried only what they could save from their burning villages. Until they constructed new homes and produced or gathered food, rebuilt food stores, and constructed new tools, the refugees were exposed to the elements, as well as to hunger, thirst, and disease. The process of clearing vegetation and constructing homes and fields was enormously labor and time intensive, even with iron tools.[68] New iron tools could only be acquired through trading or raiding, and trading required furs, hides, or other valuable items. In migrating from the Eastern Woodlands to the Great Plains west of the Mississippi River, the Dakota successfully reinvented themselves as buffalo hunters. Adaptation was slow, however, and often exacted a terrible price: the Dakota population declined from an estimated 38,000 people in 1650 to 25,000 people in 1780.[69] Although Western Sioux groups migrated west to the Great Plains in the early 1700s, it was only by the 1770s—three generations later—that the Western Sioux emerged as horse-mounted buffalo hunters.[70]

By the mid-1700s, the Ute and their Comanche allies, who were refugees from the north, dominated the New Mexico perimeter. With the spoils and slaves acquired through raids, they purchased horses, guns, gun powder, and other trade goods. The new wealth and military strength allowed the Ute to consolidate into larger, more powerful groups, and Ute and Comanche raids displaced villagers along the Rio Grande, including Apache agriculturalists who abandoned their adobe homes and cornfields to seek refuge at Spanish settlements. Faced with the raiding, the Navajos retreated into the mountains. Paiute and Shoshone groups also fled their homes. The Comanche settled in abandoned Apache villages, easing their transition to the Great Plains environment, while the Ute continued their seasonal migrations between the plains and the mountains.[71]

Early in the Spanish colonial period, most of the postcontact groups were cast as hunter gatherers and at best even the (Western) Apache, who engaged in crop cultivation (maize, amaranth, squash, beans), were depicted as marginal agriculturalists. The indigenous Americans' dietary dependence on domesticates may have been limited, but it was significant—an estimated 25 percent for the Western Apache. The elderly and children who remained in the villages when the adult men and women left for seasonal hunting, gathering, trading, and raiding expeditions, cultivated the fields, and after the harvest, the villagers consumed the maize harvest on the spot, storing only a small portion as seed.[72] By the early 1700s, assisted and inspired by Pueblo refugees in their midst, Apache groups engaged in small-scale irrigated agriculture while living in flat-roofed houses.[73] In the long run, violence and displacement turned Apache groups away from agriculture and toward a more mobile livelihood that was increasingly based on raiding as they were pushed out of the valleys and, subsequently, the Great Plains.[74] Apache raiding in turn displaced others, including the Pawnees and the Wichita.[75] The competition between the Comanche and the Apache over the key environmental resources in the Great Plain's river valleys was a major factor in these changes. The Comanche coveted the river valleys for the shelter, water, grazing, and forage they needed for their winter villages. The Apache villages proved highly vulnerable to the Comanche war parties that destroyed their homes and burned their corn fields. Displacing the Apache also left the Comanche in control of extensive trade routes to exchange bison products, horses, guns, and food.[76]

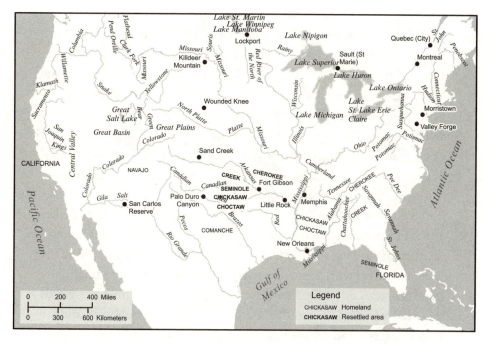

MAP 8.1. North America during the 18th and 19th centuries.

Competition for horses, guns, and bison intensified conflict on the Northwestern Plains during the 18th and 19th centuries.[77] Around 1700, the Shoshone, who had fled north, acquired horses from the south. Horses provided the Shoshone with increased mobility: they could transport and accumulate more material goods. In addition to facilitating the hunt, horses gave the Shoshone an advantage in conflicts with their northern neighbors. To keep their horses healthy, however, the Shoshone also had to relocate to different seasonal camps more often, and they had to be more selective in choosing winter camps. Moreover, neighbors seeking to acquire their own mounts increasingly turned to horse raiding. The escalating insecurity led to more cohesive bands for protection.[78]

Early in the 18th century, the newly horse-mounted Shoshones and their Crow allies dominated the Northwestern Great Plains. During the 1740s–80s, however, the Blackfeet and their allies replaced them as the dominant power because they had better access to guns through the

Cree and Assiniboine. In contrast, Mexican traders from the south supplied the Shoshone with little or no firearms. The violence and the migrations provide the context for the devastating 1781 smallpox epidemic that may have killed two-thirds of all the indigenous Americans in the Great Plains region. The epidemic struck the Blackfeet, Cree, and Assiniboine, but was especially devastating in the larger concentrated settlements of the Hidatsa and Mandan farmers.[79] The decline of the Hidatsa and Mandan, in turn, may have facilitated the rising dominance of the Great Plains horse-mounted buffalo hunters.[80]

During the precontact period, the allied Cree and Assiniboine inhabited the Eastern Woodlands north of Lake Superior, fishing the lakes and hunting caribou and moose during the winter. They became middlemen for the Hudson Bay Company fur trade in the 1670s, plying the lakes and rivers with their canoes and obtaining firearms through their trade activities. After the mid-18th century, Cree and Assiniboine bands migrated toward the Great Plains. By the 1790s, the Assiniboine and the Western Cree had reinvented themselves as horse-mounted Great Plains buffalo hunters.[81] By 1800, fortified by a steady supply of guns obtained through their Cree and Assiniboine allies, the Blackfeet increasingly drove the Shoshone and the Crow from the Northwestern Plains. The poorly armed Shoshone refugees resorted to raiding from hideouts in the mountainous margins of the Plains. Although an 1801 smallpox epidemic largely bypassed the Blackfeet, Cree, and Assiniboine, it decimated the hard-pressed Crow, who had been weakened and displaced by the incessant Blackfeet attacks.[82] Relations between the allied Cree and Assiniboine on the one hand and the Blackfeet and their allies on the other, however, soured during the first half of the 19th century and became increasingly violent as the former lost their control over the trade, and buffalo herds retreated west.[83] Initially, the huge bison herds on the Great Plains must have seemed like a bounty from the skies to those displaced by war and climate change, especially as access to the mobile resource was difficult for any single group to control. But as competition for the bison herds increased, bison hunting morphed from a source of salvation into a weapon of war.[84]

War and Settler Conquests in the 19th Century

During the last phase of the conquest in 19th-century North America, frontier warfare focused on displacing indigenous Americans, rather than enslaving, subjugating, or exploiting them. Settler communities considered the remaining indigenous Americans in the interior to be a threat and an obstacle to further European colonization. During the 1830s and 1840s, the strategy was simply to move the Eastern indigenous Americans out West across the Mississippi River into "Indian Country," in the process clearing out most of the East for white settlement. With the acquisition of US territory in the West after the US–Mexican War, and the subsequent US expansion west of the Mississippi, the policy shifted. Instead, the indigenous Americans in the West were coerced into reservations to open more land for European settlement.

The Forced Removals of the Eastern Indigenous Americans

President Thomas Jefferson adopted a policy of forced removal aimed at domesticating and civilizing the indigenous peoples by concentrating them on reservations and converting them to agriculture. The policy also would free up more land for white settlers.[85] The forced removals west of the Mississippi affected 92 percent of the Eastern indigenous Americans, and the few that remained rarely inhabited their home environments.[86] Because the Eastern indigenous Americans generally had sided with the British during the American War of Independence and the new US government saw itself as the rightful owner of all former British territories, the US liberally laid claim to the indigenous American territories on the East Coast, including Creek territories. During the 1780s, colonist and livestock encroachment on Creek lands triggered Creek raids. The publication of survey maps whet settlers' and speculators' appetites for indigenous American farmlands, which often were explicitly marked as fertile on the maps. In 1795, corrupt Georgia state representatives sold millions of acres of lands that had been earmarked by treaty as exclusive "Indian Territory."[87] During the War of 1812, various Creek leaders allied with the Red Sticks and the Seminole again supporting the British against the US forces. Villages, fields, granaries, and livestock were the main targets of destruction for the belligerents. After their 1814 defeat, many Red Stick rebels fled to the Florida Seminole towns that continued to serve as safe havens for indigenous American rebels and escaped slaves.[88] Comprised of an amalgam of first-, second-, or third-generation indigenous American war refugees from further north, escaped slaves, and free blacks, the new communities built by the Seminoles in Florida were beyond the boundaries of the US territory. In 1810 and 1811, Georgia militia men attempted to annex Florida but failed, burning down Seminole villages in the process. In 1817, during the First Seminole War, Andrew Jackson and his army of regulars, militia, and allied Creek pillaged and torched numerous Seminole settlements, disregarding international borders and forcing the inhabitants to hide in the swamps. Debating Jackson's transborder actions in the US House of Representatives, Representative Storrs of New York accused Jackson of having flaunted international law and the US Constitution. He ridiculed the argument of the general's defenders that the bloody transborder campaign had brought peace to the troubled border region. Representative Rhea of Tennessee disagreed: Jackson's actions were justified because they were directed at indigenous American groups and thus did not require a declaration of war by Congress. Rhea further argued that the Seminole were in fact refugee Creek (i.e., US subjects) who had raided the US from Spanish territory. The House eventually decided not to censor Jackson, and after the US government annexed Florida in 1818, the army drove the Seminole onto a reservation. Faced with starvation, many Seminole did not survive the first winter. The Seminole rebelled in 1835 and a guerilla war continued into 1858. In 1835 and 1836, Seminole raids on settlers in northern Florida displaced thousands of colonists and planters who sought sanctuary at army forts and in fortified villages, where they subsisted on US government rations. To force the remaining Seminole to surrender for deportation to lands west of the Mississippi, US troops systematically burned Seminole crop fields, villages, dwellings, and the property that the soldiers could not carry. The soldiers also captured or killed any livestock they encountered, causing hunger and illness among their opponents. In 1840, the army shifted from waging war only in the winter (when temperatures were lower) to campaigning in what was known as the hot summer "sickly season." Army losses due to such diseases as malaria mounted dramatically, but the soldiers persisted because the Seminole had used the summer respites in the fighting to grow crops in well-hidden fields. Lieutenant Colonel William Harney, a ruthless proponent of scorched earth, hung Seminole prisoners, raped and murdered Seminole girls, and sadistically killed any animal, domestic or wild, that crossed his path. His actions did not negatively impact his career, nor did he change his ways. A general in the 1850s, he led a massacre of Sioux men, women, and children.[89]

The best-known forced removals concern those of the southeastern Choctaw, Creek, Chickasaw, Cherokee, and Seminole. The forced migrations of such "Northern" indigenous Americans as the Shawnee, Delaware, (Huron-)Wyandot, and Potawatomis have received much less attention. All, however, were victims and refugees of ethnic cleansing by the US government, state authorities, local militias, and settler mobs (the last two were often difficult to distinguish from one another). At the same time, the indigenous Americans maintained a level of control shaping when, how, and where they moved, despite the severe constraints. They were pioneers who settled new environments in the West, under conditions that were often even more challenging than those faced by the early European colonists at Jamestown and Roanoke. The latter arrived on ships with supplies and tools, whereas most of the Eastern indigenous Americans walked for hundreds of miles with little more than they could carry.[90]

The 17th-century Iroquois Beaver Wars had pushed the Shawnee south from the Great Lakes region and the Delaware west, with some bands dispersing to seek safety at Creek and Susquehanna towns. During the American Revolutionary War, some groups crossed the Mississippi to the West, with Shawnee groups establishing agricultural villages near St. Louis. Both the Shawnee and the Delaware moved even further west in the 1820s. Like the Delaware and the Shawnee, the Potawatomi did not migrate in a single group but in smaller bands. In 1830, there were 30 Potawatomi villages around Lake Michigan with more located in southern Michigan and Indiana. Feeling threatened by incoming settlers, the villagers packed up and moved further west, exploiting family, trade, and missionary networks to ease travel and resettlement. In the fall of 1838, settler militia men destroyed various Potawatomi villages in Indiana and marched the 800 inhabitants at gunpoint over almost 700 miles to the Osage River. Three hundred forced migrants fell sick and 40 (mostly children) died during the two-month ordeal.[91]

Treaties with the US government forced the Southwestern indigenous Americans to move west of the Mississippi during the 1830s and 1840s. The treaties stipulated that the government would pay for the removal, including providing food during and after the removal as well as transport (wagons, carts, and steamboats), annuities, hunting equipment, farm implements (including plows), and land in the West. During the early removals, the US government employed private contractors to supply transportation and rations, which often arrived after delays that resulted in spoiled food and overloaded wagons and steamboats. One of the overloaded steamboats sank with a loss of over 300 indigenous American lives, making the forced migrants terrified of steamer travel. Moreover, the packed steamboats and the overcrowded assembly and transit camps at Little Rock and Memphis were incubators of such deadly diseases as cholera and dysentery. Traveling in groups of around 1,000 persons each, the forced migrants, at best, were on the trail for two to three months. Delays at transit camps, however, could add months to the travel schedule. Smaller groups that traveled on their own, choosing their own routes and camping and hunting along their way, would take even longer. All, however, were exposed to freezing cold during winter travel or dreadful epidemics if they traveled in the hot summer "sickly season," which often caused a high death toll.[92]

Early in 1831, the first group of 1,000 poorly provisioned Choctaw traveled west but ran into blistering winter weather after crossing the Mississippi, and their rations ran out. Ox wagons from the government fort at Little Rock met subsequent groups after they crossed the river. But Little Rock's transit camp lacked enough shelter for everyone who was en route to the Red River resettlement area. Many fell ill and died along the way. After the bad experience with winter travel, subsequent groups tried to avoid the cold winter months, but summer travel exposed them to cholera in the hot and humid Mississippi Valley. By early January 1833, over 3,300 Choctaw had arrived at their new Red River homeland. Another 700 who arrived in February made their own arrangements to settle in Texas. Most of the Choctaw, however, remained in the East, and it took until 1838 for the majority to be resettled west of the Mississippi. Some remained in their old territory until 1847.[93]

Violence and insecurity plagued the Creek villages in the remains of their eastern homeland in early 1830s. With the knowledge and cooperation of local magistrates, unscrupulous traders and settlers burned or occupied Creek homes and crop lands, and plundered their corn stores. Few Creek farmers dared to plant crops, resulting in food shortages and leaving the 23,000 Creek ill prepared for the removals. The first group left their homeland in December 1834 in the middle of a severe winter, traveling on foot, by wagon, and by steamer via Memphis and Little Rock to Fort Gibson in the Western Creek Agency. Only 469 of 630 Creek survived the grueling three-month exodus. Fears and tensions erupted in open war in the Creek homeland in 1836, resulting in the US Army moving in and burning more homes, crops, and possessions. Soldiers rounded up the resisters and their families, and crammed them first into detention camps and next onto steamers headed for New Orleans, where they again were placed in camps. Inadequate rations and crowded conditions invited dysentery, diarrhea, cholera, and fevers, decimating their numbers before they were deported west. Two more large groups were sent west via Memphis, filling rudimentary transit camps far above capacity as 13,000 people were packed together. Ten thousand Creek were delivered to the Fort Gibson camp during the dead of winter in 1836. The families of almost 800 Creek fighters who agreed to assist the 1836 US Army campaign against the Seminole in Florida were temporarily allowed to remain in their original territory in Alabama, where they were guarded by soldiers after individuals described by an army lieutenant as "marauders" pillaged and burned their homes. The use of the word "marauders" is significant because marauding, that is unauthorized pillaging, carried the death penalty under the laws of war. But it seems that the army did not even try to identify the culprits, let alone offer effective protection from their attacks. The Creek environmental infrastructure and their other possessions were eagerly sought after by poor settlers and rich land speculators, alike.[94]

Only too aware of the bad experiences of the Choctaw with corrupt contractors, the Chickasaw negotiated to hire their own trail leaders and guides. They also arranged for their wagon trains to be accompanied by a physician and an army officer who disbursed the government payments for travel expenses. After the deadly steamer accident, a large Choctaw wagon train of 4,000 people and 5,000 horses struggled overland through the swamplands of the Mississippi Valley, discarding much of their overweight cargo and losing 600 ponies. Smaller parties traveled west entirely on their own, camping and hunting along the way. With their well-prepared and self-organized wagon trains, the Choctaw suffered fewer human losses on the trek west than other nations. But they, too, encountered deadly disease soon after their arrival west of the Mississippi. One of their number, who had been infected during a steamer crossing of the Mississippi, brought smallpox to their new homeland, resulting in up to 500 deaths. Vaccinations stopped the epidemic, but in the ensuing panic, the crop fields were neglected, leading to food shortages and further sickness. The public health crisis paused the Choctaw removal for two years. It was resumed in 1840 and took another seven years to complete.[95]

The Cherokee removal was the deadliest, with the "Trail of Tears" taking the lives of up to 4,000 people because of army razzias, detention in overcrowded camps, the trek west itself, and having to adapt to their new environment. The first group left in April 1832 and found none of the promised provisions or money waiting for them when they arrived at their destination at the Fort Smith Cherokee Agency. Hunger marked the summer of 1833 as the bulk of the Cherokees awaited deportation. Given the insecure future, few Cherokee seriously invested in cultivating their fields. Measles and cholera hit the waiting migrants. Halfway to their destination, one group of migrants decided to leave most of its possessions temporarily at Little Rock in order to reach the Cherokee Agency on foot and avoid the rickety cholera-infested steamers. But, measles, dysentery, and upper respiratory diseases killed 80 of the 500 (more than half, children under the age of ten), and more perished after their arrival. To make matters worse, most of the possessions they had stored at Little Rock, including their plows and hoes, were stolen. Given the disastrous first experience, it is small wonder that the Cherokee removal proceeded at a snail's pace. By March 1838, only 2,000 Eastern Cherokee had moved west, leaving 15,000–17,000 still in their eastern homeland. US Army razzias drove the Cherokee from their villages into holding camps, and "rabble" looted Cherokee homes and livestock. The army moved the Cherokee west in groups of 1,000 people, on foot and by boat with those unable or too sick to walk loaded on wagons. Most of the Choctaw, Creek, and Chickasaw could at least take some of their mobile possessions with them (wagons, food, livestock). En route, they were detained in transit camps waiting for steamers and exposed to measles, fevers, drought, and the cold of winter. The first groups were guarded by soldiers, while some of the subsequent groups trekked west under their own leaders.[96]

Adapting to the new hotter and drier environment of the Eastern Great Plains proved difficult for the displaced Eastern indigenous Americans. Realizing that the Great Plains were not a land of timber and maple trees, the (Huron-)Wyandot initially refused to move from their Great Lakes homes. Many fell ill during the long trek west, and during the first three months after their arrival, 60 of the 700 Wyandot perished, mostly the young. Although in the late 1830s and 1840s Indian Affairs agents reported that the indigenous Americans were adjusting well to their new environments, their statements may have been overly optimistic. The mid-1840s were marked by heavy rains and extensive flooding along the riverbanks where the Eastern indigenous American pioneer farmers had laid out their crop fields.[97]

Unfortunately, the removal west did not mean the end of the displaced Eastern indigenous Americans' exposure to war and dislocation. As a condition for the move, both the Choctaw and the Chickasaw had requested US Army protection against their new Great Plains indigenous American neighbors, whom they considered hostile.[98] Indeed, during the 1820s and early 1830s, competition over bison caused intense conflict between the Eastern newcomer groups and Western indigenous Americans, including the Comanche and the Wichita, although the Comanche subsequently accommodated the displaced groups.[99] When conflict erupted with the Osage over hunting rights, Delaware and Shawnee bands in the 1830s allied with the first groups of removed Cherokees and the Huron-Wyandot. During the 1840s, the Delaware fought the Osages, Pawnees, and Dakota Sioux.[100] A few decades later, the resettled Eastern indigenous Americans were caught up in the US Civil War. Confederate and Union raiders, including indigenous Americans, plundered farms, fields, and livestock in "Indian Country," displacing thousands and again leaving them destitute.[101]

The US Conquest of the West

The Lewis and Clark expedition, while exploring the West for the United States in 1805, encountered the Shoshone-Bannock, a combination of Shoshone survivors of smallpox and Northern Paiute, who inhabited the arid Snake River Basin. The Shoshone-Bannock engaged in horse trade, fur hunting and trade, salmon fishing, and gathering the edible Cama bulbs. Dependent on the annual salmon run and on the winter camps where they stored preserved fish in underground caches, they were less mobile than some of their ancestors had been on the Northwestern Great Plains. In the mid-19th century, however, when the fur trade collapsed, many American settlers entered Shoshone-Bannock territory, leading to renewed conflict that escalated in the 1863 Bear Creek Massacre after the discovery of gold at Boise, Iowa. Some of the Shoshone-Bannock ended up in a refugee camp near Boise City in 1866, where they survived by begging, scavenging, prostitution, or serving as scouts for General George Crook's campaigns against other indigenous Americans. In 1869, the refugees from the Boise City camp and other Shoshone were moved to the Fort Hall reservation. Chronic food shortages plagued the 1,000–1,700 Shoshone and Shoshone-Bannock in the reservation, forcing the indigenous Americans to hunt beyond its boundaries. The authorities, in turn, attempted to keep the Shoshone on the reservation, which in 1878 led to the so-called Bannock war in which 12 percent of the population on the reservation perished.[102]

The Ute narrowly escaped annihilation by allying themselves with the settler authorities and by abandoning the Great Plains to seek refuge in the mountains.[103] Contact with the US government began violently when an 1849 punitive army raid on a Ute village resulted in the destruction of 50 lodges with all their provisions. The Ute suffered another punitive army raid in 1854, which resulted in the destruction of additional lodges and a large quantity of saddles, robes, and other materials as well as the capture of 50 women and children.[104]

Buffalo robes, an essential protection against the cold weather, and the buffalo hides that covered the tents were difficult to replace. Preparing the hide and robes was extremely labor intensive: on average, a woman tanned just ten robes per year. That bison winter robes processed by indigenous Americans were highly valued is attested to by their ability to fetch a price four to five times higher than a tanned summer hide produced by white commercial hunters.[105] By the fall of 1855, the Ute reportedly were "dying from famine" due to the loss of their homes, supplies, equipment, and the persistence of violence that inhibited harvesting and hunting.[106] Conflict and the alienation of settlement, hunting, and fishing territories by Mormon settlers in the mid-19th century transformed the Ute into desperate raiders.[107] Diplomacy and flight, however, allowed the Ute to survive: they allied themselves with the US government and retreated into the mountains, leaving the Great Plains region to growing numbers of white settlers. During the US Civil War, the Ute provided auxiliaries to the Union. At the same time, their neighbors suffered from destructive US Army scorched earth campaigns.[108]

Unlike their Ute neighbors, the Sioux engaged in direct and sustained military conflict with the settlers in the 19th century. Lack of hunting prey caused the Sioux to move west of the Mississippi River in the late 18th century, opportunistically exploiting the power vacuum left after the powerful Mandan, Arikara, and Hidatsa settlements along the Missouri River had been devastated by smallpox in the 1780s.[109]

Conflict about hunting territories between the Sioux and the Kiowa, Crow, and Shoshone marked the first half of the 19th century, until the Western Sioux bands controlled most of the region between the River Platte and Yellowstone. The 1837 smallpox epidemic and the devastating 1849 cholera, measles, and smallpox plagues that decimated the Sioux did not occur in a vacuum. Settlers and gold diggers may have carried the microbes into the Great Plains, but the dislocation caused by the massive forced removals in the 1830s and 1840s provided a major gateway for the introduction and spread of epidemics in the West. Thousands of the migrating Eastern indigenous Americans died of disease and starvation along the way.[110]

In the 1850s, the US government reservation policy in the Northwest Pacific region led to outright war. The violence spread to the Great Plains and the Southwest, and merged into the Civil War.[111] US authorities increasingly had located indigenous American reservations in wasteland and wilderness, making it unsurprising that the 1850s and 1860s were marked by drought, harvest failures, and famine for the Cherokee and other indigenous Americans on their new reservations in the West.[112] The maladministration of the reservations and the slow and inadequate disbursements of the promised subsidies and rations were major factors in the resurgence of mass violence.[113]

In the Northern Plains, indigenous American camps were the main targets of war.[114] A brutal 1861–62 winter of starvation and delayed annuity payments in the following summer led to Sioux raids on the Lower Sioux Agency, the nearby town of Ulm, and Fort Ridgeley. Although only a minority of Santee-Sioux were involved in the raids, US Army punitive expeditions in 1863 and 1864 indiscriminately attacked any indigenous Americans they considered Sioux. The 1863 expedition took place in the heat of summer and was marred by disease, foul water, scarce grazing, and wild fires. To protect their camps, the retreating Sioux skirmished with the army and intentionally set fire to the dry vegetation to hinder the army's advance. But as they fled to the Missouri River, they had to abandon food stores, buffalo hides, and lodges, which the soldiers burned, leaving the refugees without shelter and food for the winter as they hastened across the river or into Canada. Having dispersed the rebels, the army came across a large Yanktonais-Sioux hunting camp with 3,500 people engaged in scraping and drying large amounts of buffalo hides and meat. While their leaders were negotiating, the anxious Sioux women and children took the camp down and moved away with their travois laden with their lodges, dried meat, and hides. Claiming that the travois carried war booty, the army attacked, mowing down several hundred women and children. The remainder fled, abandoning all their possessions. The soldiers plundered and burned 300 lodges and destroyed 500 tons of dried meat after loading up 12 wagons of meat as provisions. The 1864 summer campaign resulted in the destruction of a large Sioux camp that counted 1,600 lodges and 8,000 inhabitants at Killdeer Mountain. Sioux warriors attempted to keep the army at a distance as artillery shells exploded among the lodges that their families were desperately taking down. When the army charged into the camp, the survivors bolted into the surrounding ravines. The soldiers pillaged the camp, appropriating buffalo robes and other goods, and stacking the remaining robes, dried berries, dried meat, and utensils on top of the lodgepoles and burning it all. They took no prisoners and shot any dogs they encountered wandering through the remains of the carnage.[115]

The Cheyenne fared no better. In 1864, after a couple of indigenous Americans were accused of horse theft, the US cavalry commander of Colorado ordered that the Cheyenne be punished severely and collectively. A cavalry unit attacked a Cheyenne village at Cedar Bluffs, killing or wounding 60 and destroying all the lodges and property. Another unit attacked an indigenous American encampment at Sand Creek and mowed down men, women, and children indiscriminately, destroying 130 lodges and capturing 500 horses and mules. An official government commission reported that fleeing women and children had been killed and that the US soldiers "tortured and mutilated in a manner that would put to shame the savage ingenuity of interior Africa."[116] A captain who participated in the campaign commented: "There was no confidence to be placed in any of these Indians. They were a bad lot. They all needed killing." Reacting to the criticism that the Sand Creek massacre had elicited from Boston humanitarians, the same captain insisted that the carnage was entirely justified.[117] During the winter of 1867, a military column destroyed a village of 300 lodges as well as large amounts of property, including buffalo robes and equipment.[118]

Following the Civil War, President Ulysses Grant's Peace Policy toward the indigenous Americans maintained the reservations policy and the use of force where necessary, but stipulated that compliant indigenous Americans would receive government annuities, including money, rations, farming equipment, and livestock. The policy aimed to keep the indigenous Americans on the reserves and allow the reserves to develop through settled agriculture. Humanitarian supporters of a peace policy toward the indigenous Americans rejected the idea of "civilizing the Indian by starving him to death" as one US representative put it in 1874. His colleague added that exterminating the bison to rob the "Indians" of their subsistence was uncivilized and unchristian. Others, however, believed the destruction of the bison to be an acceptable price to "pacify" the indigenous Americans.[119] De B. Randolph Keim, who had accompanied Sheridan's army on its 1868–69 winter campaign against the Southern Plains indigenous Americans as a *New York Herald* war correspondent, rejected the payment of annuities and food rations to keep them in the reservations as "bribes." He also disdained an 1867 measure that made it an offence to shoot indigenous Americans, countering that a "pacific course" made them "arrogant." Keim argued that the characteristic indigenous American ambushes and surprise attacks were the very opposite of "civilized war." Echoing the total war perspectives of Generals Sherman and Sheridan, Keim asserted that the indigenous Americans were on a path to "inevitable extermination."[120]

During their 1868–69 operations against the Cheyenne and the Arapaho, Generals Sherman and Sheridan intentionally campaigned during the winter, when indigenous Americans were simultaneously the least mobile and the most vulnerable because food and forage were scarce. Keim stated that the Plains indigenous Americans "were entirely governed by the use of the pony" and that during the winter they "were paralyzed" because little forage was available. With their weakened horses, the indigenous people's fighting ability was at its lowest, and they could neither quickly move their families, lodges, and other property nor save their winter food supplies. The correspondent emphasized that the best opportunity to destroy the indigenous Americans was when they were caught in the act of moving their tepee village because it forced the warriors to stand and fight to delay the enemy while the camp itself was a "scene of confusion and uproar."[121]

Sheridan built a fort in the heart of the indigenous American hunting grounds to interfere with their hunting. By establishing several supply depots for his own troops and allowing the soldiers to hunt buffalo and other game for sustenance, the general denied the indigenous Americans valuable prey, thereby practicing a form of scorched earth. Sheridan's force used Comanche auxiliaries and Osage guides to track down winter camps while Custer's 7th Cavalry had orders to destroy the indigenous villages and ponies, kill the men, and capture the women and children. In November 1868, Custer caught up with Black Kettle's camp, killing 100 people, including women and children who allegedly had joined the fight. Custer's men destroyed or captured 51 lodges, 1,000 horses and mules, 1,000 buffalo robes and buffalo skins, and other property.[122]

In December 1868, the hard-pressed indigenous Americans set fire to the grass over a wide area to hinder the army's pursuit. The scorched earth action, however, did not prevent the army from destroying another 60-lodge village that harbored tons of dried buffalo meat, hundreds of bags of (maize) meal, and other food and equipment, but the grass burning destroyed the army columns' forages as their food supplies dwindled. Having lost their food stores and being forced to remain constantly on the move, the indigenous Americans, too, soon found themselves hungry and short of forage. Disease and starvation took the lives of people and ponies alike. In May and June 1869, although the Cheyenne narrowly escaped their dogged pursuers, they lost yet more horses and supplies, including 10,000 pounds of dried meat and precious buffalo hides. In desperate straits, the Cheyenne finally agreed to move to their assigned reserve.[123]

From 1868 on, the indigenous Americans on the Northern Plains who continued to resist shifted to a largely defensive strategy. They conducted raids against US Army forts and the railroad camps, halting the

THE SEVENTH U.S. CAVALRY CHARGING INTO BLACK KETTLE'S VILLAGE AT DAYLIGHT, November 27, 1868.—[See Page 811.]

FIGURE 8.1. US cavalry attacks the village of Black Kettle in 1868, leading to the loss of life and his people's dwellings and their contents including their food supplies. (*Harper's Weekly* 12, Dec. 19, 1868, 804, accessed online at 1280px-Seventh_Cavalry_Charging_Black_Kettle_s_Village_1868wikipediacommons).

construction of the railroad through their territories. An 1875 US Army expedition against a rebel indigenous American winter camp failed because the cold weather slowed down the soldiers. Army campaigns against indigenous American villages in the spring and summer met with little success and culminated in Custer's disastrous defeat in June 1876. In late July, however, food shortages forced the militant indigenous Americans to break up their large camp and scatter in order to hunt. Low on rations and plagued by scurvy and dysentery, the US army columns could not catch up. Having succeeded in capturing an abandoned camp containing 5,000 pounds of dried meat and a supply of buffalo robes, the soldiers burned what they could not carry.[124]

General Sheridan dispatched General George Crook to lead another winter campaign. Like Sheridan, Crook made extensive use of indigenous American scouts and auxiliaries, and his strategy consisted of relentlessly pursuing his opponents with mobile columns to hinder their recovery. Crook disarmed all the indigenous Americans residing on the reservations and recruited 350 Sioux, Cheyenne, Arapaho, Shoshone, and Pawnee as scouts and auxiliaries, supplying them with horses confiscated from the Sioux chiefs. Crook also armed each of his indigenous American scouts with a gun and ammunition, promising them pay and all the horses they could capture. Launching his offensive in November 1876, Crook hoped to locate and destroy Crazy Horse's camp. His troops first stumbled upon a large Cheyenne camp in the Big Horn Mountains. The Cheyenne managed to escape with their families, their arms, and some of their horses, but the army captured buffalo robes, guns, and several hundred ponies, and burned the tepees, dried meat and pemmican stores, and clothing. Left destitute, at least 14 infants as well as an unknown number of other refugees froze or starved to death in the immediate aftermath. Only 1,000 of the 1,500 Cheyenne who escaped from Crook's attack at the Big Horn Mountains reached the safety of Crazy Horse's camp, 100 miles to the north. Crazy Horse's 3,000 people shared food, horses, and their tents with the Cheyenne survivors, greatly diminishing their own winter food supplies in the process. The army cornered Crazy Horse's camp in December. The refugees escaped but lost most of their precious winter food stores. Crazy Horse's ally, Sitting Bull, retreated across the border to Canada in February 1877. Large-scale resistance in the Northern Great Plains ended with Crazy Horse's surrender in May of 1877.[125]

The conflict in the Southern Great Plains unfolded in very similar ways. Here, too, the US Army intentionally focused on destroying the limited environmental infrastructure of the elusive indigenous Americans: dwellings and shelters, winter clothing, food stores, horses, and hunting prey. During the 1874 Red River campaign an army column encountered a large Comanche refugee village where women were drying meat and preparing pemmican. Most escaped, but the soldiers captured 120 women and children and 1,200 ponies, and destroyed 262 lodges as well as other property.[126] Later in the same year, the army located another large Cheyenne, Kiowa, and Comanche camp at Palo Duro Canyon. Soldiers destroyed all the lodges and winter stores, including quantities of sugar, flour, and dried buffalo meat, and captured 1,400 horses and mules. The army columns discovered a third camp in October and yet another in November. In both cases, the inhabitants managed to flee with their lives, but the soldiers destroyed their lodges, stores, and other property. Deprived of their winter food supplies, shelter and animals, the refugees were soon in dire straits; by March 1875, most had surrendered. An observer described the surrendered indigenous Americans as "wretched and poverty-stricken . . . bereft of lodges . . . with no ponies, half-starved . . . [and] scarcely anything that could be called clothing."[127]

Warfare against indigenous Americans was also privatized and commodified through scalp and buffalo bounty hunting. Custer's defeat in 1876 had gutted the Peace Policy of whatever substance it had left.[128] The main objective in the conflict became to drive the indigenous Americans off, resettle them in reserves, or exterminate them. Settler authorities offered bounties for indigenous American scalps in the same way that they paid for exterminating such dangerous "vermin" as mountain lions, wolves, and coyotes.[129]

Moreover, commercial hunters' extermination of the buffalo was not only an example of capitalist ecocide but also of classical scorched earth practices: it destroyed the main source of food, clothing, and shelter for the indigenous Americans. Indirectly, the US Army greatly contributed to the destruction of the buffalo: it did not enforce treaties reserving bison ranges for indigenous American hunters, and commercial white hunters operated from its forts, receiving protection and logistical assistance. During the 1870s, Plains indigenous Americans continued to leave their reservations to hunt buffalo.[130] US Army leaders were very much aware that the dependence on buffalo was the indigenous American Achilles's heel. In 1869, the *Army Navy Journal* quoted General Sherman as having said: "The quickest way to compel the Indians to settle down to civilized life was to send ten regiments of soldiers to the plains with orders to shoot buffalos until they became too scarce to support the redskins." In a 1870 book about Sheridan's 1868–69 Plains winter campaign, De B. Randolph Keim explained that, to the indigenous Americans, the bison were as essential a resource as coconut trees to the inhabitants of the tropics: "Bisons constitute the commissariat of the Indian, and govern frequently his ability for war or control his desire for peace. . . . In numbers he is evidently rapidly diminishing, though the countless herds, found during the summer along the railroads, would seem to indicate that the race is far from running out." He emphasized, however, that "recently," the "ancient customs" had been largely abandoned because "the tribes have become scattered since the rapid depletion of the buffalo." Keim himself had observed very few buffalo in the Wichita Mountains, but ample evidence of their past abundance. His guide commented that the bison scarcity "was one of the consequences of war."[131] In 1875, in the course of a debate about the slaughter of bison herds in the Texas state legislature, General Sheridan allegedly argued that only the extermination of the buffalo would bring lasting peace, and in 1881 the general wrote: "If I could learn that every Buffalo in the northern herd were killed I would be glad. . . . Since the destruction of the southern herd . . . the Indians on that section have given us no trouble."[132]

The army, however, did not need to exterminate the buffalo directly. Rather, civilian commercial hunters like Buffalo Bill decimated the buffalo herds and reduced and fragmented their habitat.[133] As such, the buffalo ecocide was the product of war as well as commercial hunting and, at the very least, aided and abetted by the US Army. In the 19th century, Great Plains buffalo hunting constituted a key component (along with raiding) of a war economy driven by considerations that surpassed any sustainability concerns from either a moral or a market economy perspective. For societies at war, the incentive was to retain access to the bison herds and deny the same to one's enemies in true scorched earth fashion, even if that meant exterminating the buffalo. That too, was basically the strategy of the Hudson Bay Company along the Canadian–US border: it created fur deserts to keep US-based hunters at bay.[134]

The US Army had earlier successfully employed the ecocidal strategy of destroying game to break indigenous American resistance elsewhere. In late January 1865, after a fruitless 12-day pursuit, General Robert B. Mitchell decided that if he could not catch his indigenous opponents, "he could at least fire the whole country and make it a lean place for them." The indigenous Americans set backfires and saved themselves, but the fire "swept the country clean" and "the game was driven out of the country [part of Colorado and the Texas panhandle]." The number of raids subsequently dropped dramatically because the lack of game made it impossible for the indigenous Americans to sustain themselves in the region throughout the winter.[135]

On the eve of Spanish colonization in 1769, California had an estimated population of 300,000 indigenous Americans. By 1860, only 32,000 indigenous Americans were left, with just 22,000 by 1900.[136] Malaria and measles were among the greatest threats. Hudson Bay Company trappers brought virulent malaria from Oregon during the 1830s, and an 1833 malaria epidemic killed 20,000 indigenous Americans, effectively depopulating California's central valleys. A decade later, collapsed houses filled with bones and skulls remained as evidence of the epidemic's deadly impact. Malaria remained endemic in the region thereafter. In 1847, a measles epidemic raged in the Sacramento Valley. Too narrow a contagion narrative, however, once again shrouds the larger context of violence and displacement. The 1847 measles epidemic struck hard at a population that had been deprived of food and livelihoods. War conditions had severely interfered with access to "wild foods" and moreover had blocked alternative wage labor opportunities at settler farms and ranches.[137]

Ironically, the stunning success of the Californian hunter-gatherers in sustaining a large population on the acorn staple made them highly vulnerable to 19th-century environcidal warfare, causing their dramatic demise. Most Californian groups in the central interior were entirely dependent on the acorn stores in their villages.[138] Once their villages and food stores had been destroyed or the villagers forced to flee from their homes, they were doomed unless they were given the opportunity to gather more acorns and painstakingly process them. But the militia and mercenary bands that the Gold Rush unleashed never provided that opportunity.

The 1840s–50s Gold Rush resulted in the loss of indigenous American hunting and fishing resources as gold diggers occupied lands and mining polluted the waters. In the 1850s, federal troops and local militias drove California's indigenous American populations into reserves that offered little protection from slave and livestock raiders. Food rations in the reserves were insufficient, the administration was disastrous, and its officials were notoriously corrupt. Most of the reserves closed in the 1860s, leaving the indigenous Americans entirely destitute. Raiding settler livestock from highland hideouts was an indigenous American survival strategy that, however, led to punitive counterraids and heightened settler hysteria about an imminent outbreak of an all-out "Indian war." Because there was no further "West" left to which to move the indigenous Americans, colonial policies oscillated between domestication and extermination. Domestication entailed "taming" the indigenous Americans by teaching them wage labor and settled life and agriculture.[139]

Sexual violence factored significantly in the decline of the indigenous American populations in California. "Indian scares" depicted indigenous American men as rapists of white women, even as white men systematically assaulted and raped indigenous American women. Moreover, the violence accompanied starvation and disease, killing thousands during the 1850s and prejudicing women's survival rates even more than men's. The 1860 census revealed that women were substantially underrepresented in every indigenous American age cohort in California.

Although women may have been undercounted because they were hiding, the California evidence nevertheless suggests strongly that the "Frontier" encounter was particularly destructive to indigenous American women.[140]

By the mid-1880s, the surviving indigenous North Americans had been concentrated in 187 reservations. They were dependent on inadequate government rations that were sometimes withheld. Hunting small game and deer for food and hides remained important. Elderly men especially turned increasingly to cultivating small gardens with corn, squash, and potato. Others engaged in cattle and horse breeding, freight hauling, and migrant labor. Still, life on the reservations in the 1880s was characterized by droughts, hunger, and disease. One of the attempts to deal with the crises was the Ghost Dance movement that led to the fateful Sioux massacre at Wounded Knee in 1890.[141]

Surviving Environcide

Eighteenth- and nineteenth-century violence displaced the indigenous Americans of the West from their lands and environmental infrastructure, exposing them to freezing cold, scorching heat, hunger, and disease, and causing unprecedented death and dramatic depopulation and displacement. By the end of the 19th century, US soldiers herded the remaining Western indigenous Americans into reservations on marginal lands. These reruns of the early 19th century forced removals were often death marches, and indigenous Americans initially were held in what were effectively concentration camps. At the reservations, US government-issue rations were insufficient and disease was rampant. In the late 18th century, the largest concentration of indigenous American populations occurred in California, which alone may have counted 300,000 people. The early 1800s forced removals added another 100,000 Eastern indigenous Americans to the indigenous populations of the West. By the late 1800s, however, 250,000 indigenous Americans remained in North America in total, fewer than the precontact indigenous population of California.

In many ways, the Western indigenous Americans were already in a precarious state by the early 1800s: they were overwhelmingly refugees or descendants of refugees, displaced by war, violence, and climate change. By the early 1900s, many Western indigenous Americans were still reconstructing societies and experimenting with new livelihoods and ways of life. Some were highly successful, building empires based on commercial hunting and raiding. But in the face of the maelstrom of violence, destruction, and displacement, none succeeded in rebuilding a sustainable environmental infrastructure. Hunting dwindling buffalo, beaver, and deer populations and gathering Cama, berry, acorn, and fish became increasingly fraught with conflict, while making war pay through slave and livestock raiding triggered only more violence.

Throughout it all, Western indigenous Americans were both victims and agents of history—at times, simultaneously.[142] Nineteenth-century war and displacement opened space for invaders, human and nonhuman, causing fundamental political, social, economic, and environmental change. The demise of the buffalo, for example, opened the Great Plains for invasive European livestock. Western indigenous Americans, however, were not merely passive victims of history. Rather, they demonstrated incredible resilience and ingenuity: despite demographic collapse and the destruction of entire societies and ways of life, the displaced rebuilt lives and livelihoods in alien environments in insecure and violent circumstances. Moreover, they survived more than one episode of environcidal war and displacement in the space of a few generations: pre-19th-century environcide, and one or two more episodes of environcide during the 19th century. In the process, sometimes out of despair and sometimes as a planned strategy, they themselves also deployed environcidal violence against neighbors and invaders, both indigenous Americans and Europeans.

9

Scorched Dutch East Indies

THE LATE 19ᵀᴴ-CENTURY COLONIAL CONQUEST OF ACEH, INDONESIA

We have attempted to identify the origins of a way of war that is so offensive to the honor of the Dutch Arms that it made Multatuli say: "A village that had just been occupied by the Dutch Army and *therefore* was burning" . . . it did not exist in the past and only has been introduced . . . some 25 years ago. . . . But now the war in the [Dutch] Indies is waged in the opposite way of what it should have been like.[1]

April 1879: "The population that is still displaced [by the war] suffers a lot in the mountains. The mortality must be quite high."[2]

June 1879, after three abandoned kampongs had been sacked and burned: "A lot of firearms and small stock were captured and a large quantity of padi [rice] destroyed."[3]

1882: "The razing of the kampongs is indeed an effective tool of punishment, but it also affects too many innocents to immediately resort to it. Only when it is absolutely necessary this extreme measure should be used."[4]

THE PROTRACTED and brutal late 19ᵗʰ-century Dutch colonial conquest of the Aceh sultanate on the Indonesian island of Sumatra took the lives of thousands of its inhabitants and resulted in the destruction of hundreds of villages with their orchards, plantations, and irrigated rice fields. Dutch scorched earth tactics left the fertile Aceh River delta a smoking ruin. Critics in the Netherlands accused their government of genocide. Although Dutch colonial soldiers summarily executed hundreds of Aceh combatants and civilians during the conflict, thousands more perished of disease and starvation because they lost their homes, fields, irrigation and drainage works, food stores, and livestock. Tens of thousands fled their homes and hid in the mountains and tropical forests; they, too, lost access to their environmental infrastructure and faced hunger, thirst, heat, cold, insects, infections, and epidemics.

The impact of the violence on Aceh society constituted environcide: the intentional destruction of environmental infrastructure and resulting population displacement triggered a humanitarian disaster. Dutch officers in the field as well as Dutch officials and politicians in the Netherlands were increasingly aware of the dire consequences of their ruthless scorched earth campaigns on Aceh society, and some were highly critical of how the war was being fought. The critics gained the upper hand in the early 1880s, instituting civilian rule, confining the military to their barracks, and ceasing scorched earth attacks. Yet, the response provided merely a brief interlude; in the face of mounting Aceh resistance, the military regained control and reintroduced scorched earth. Supporters of the scorched earth strategy believed it had been effective in the conquest of the sultanate's heartland because Aceh's armies had been entirely reliant on local food supplies.

Compared to 18th-century armies, the Dutch colonial army operating in Aceh in the 19th century was less dependent on requisitioning food supplies in the Aceh villages and on local labor. The army partly relied on food rations brought in from beyond Aceh through supply ships, and partly on locally purchased, requisitioned, or pillaged food, including cattle and small stock. In fact, when access to local fresh vegetables and fruits ceased during the early 1880s, the reliance on nutritionally deficient imported military rations caused an epidemic of beri beri among the European soldiers. Forced labor required by the military and the colonial administration was largely imported from beyond Aceh, but the colonial army still sought to make war pay by imposing irregular tributes in a practice very reminiscent of the war taxes and contributions imposed by 16th- through 18th-century European armies. Aceh leaders and villagers were individually and collectively held responsible for paying the tributes. Dutch commanders threatened to burn the villages down if they failed and all too readily executed their threats.

War, Environment, and Genocide in 19th-Century Aceh

The conquest and pacification of the greater Aceh region may have cost as many as 100,000 lives. A former Dutch officer who participated in the Aceh campaigns publicly accused the Dutch government of *volkerenmoord*, the modern Dutch translation of genocide. His revelations caused a heated national debate in the Netherlands. He argued that the war constituted *volkerenmoord* (literally murdering a nation or people), both in its *impact* and *intent*, causing the depopulation of Aceh through the deliberate killing of men, women, and children on orders to exterminate all who resisted.[5] An 1896 textbook that was used to train officers for the Dutch colonial army emphasized that effective resistance against the Dutch conquest stemmed from the enemy's ability to live off the land and that denying access to standing crops and village food stores— that is, neutralizing the environmental infrastructure of Aceh even though it caused famine and the displacement of the population—was the recipe to Dutch success.[6]

The contemporary and modern debates about the Aceh war and genocide typically focus on the actions of Dutch security forces during the 1890s and early 1900s, when the evidence of deliberate mass killings is undeniable. The key period for assessing the nature of the war and its impact, however, occurs in the earlier phase of the conflict. The atrocities of the 1890s followed the catastrophic environcidal warfare of the late 1870s and 1880s. The 1870s–80s in the Aceh Valley are marked by total warfare: the Dutch colonial army intentionally targeted the civilian population and systematically destroyed homes, food stores, crop fields, orchards, plantations, and entire villages and districts. Dutch military and civilian leaders were willing to completely destroy the Aceh nation in order to conquer the territory.

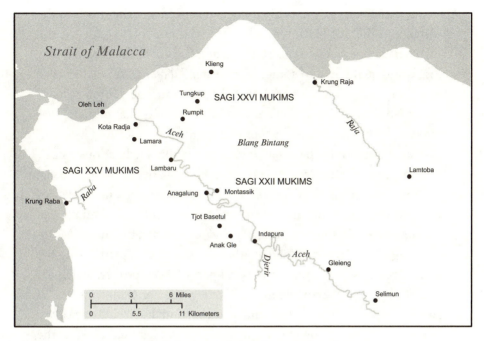

MAP 9.1. Aceh, Sumatra, Indonesia during the late 19th century.

Scorched Earth: Aceh, 1873–79

The Dutch conquest of the Aceh sultanate on Sumatra was protracted, violent, and utterly destructive. The first two Dutch invasions in 1873 were failures. The March 1873 invasion was overwhelmed by a monsoon and took the lives of its commander and fifty-some colonial soldiers. After two weeks of heavy fighting, the Dutch withdrew. A second invasion followed in December of the same year. Sent by ship from the Netherlands and led by General Jan van Swieten, the expeditionary force consisted of 8,500 soldiers, 5,000 servants and forced laborers, 75 cannons, and 2 machine guns. Yet, it took nearly a month for the army to occupy the Aceh sultan's palace, located only a few miles inland. Cholera spread faster than the Dutch advance, claiming the life of the Aceh sultan, but neither disease nor the Dutch cannons managed to quell Aceh resistance.[7]

The Aceh sultanate was highly decentralized and the death of the sultan and the occupation of his palace did not spell victory as the Dutch had hoped. Aceh consisted of federations of *mukims*, each led by highly independent and sometimes rival *hulubalangs*. A *mukim* was a group of villages or kampongs that shared a mosque. Dutch officials identified federations of *mukims* by a lower-case Roman numeral that referred to the number of *mukims* that originally constituted its membership, for example, the ix *mukims*. Multiple allied federations constituted a *sagi*, identified by capital Roman numerals, for example, the *sagi* XXV *mukims* or the XXV *mukims* for short.[8] A *panglima* or war leader led each *sagi*. The war leader of the various *sagi* and a small number of other princes (also with the title of *panglima*) elected the sultan. Moreover, the Aceh River coastal delta that the Dutch occupied during the early 1870s was only a relatively small part of Aceh proper, which extended all the way up the Aceh River Valley. Greater Aceh consisted of Aceh proper plus dependencies and allies beyond the Aceh River Valley, and included Pedir. The Dutch garrison that was left behind when the main expeditionary army withdrew in April 1874 had little control even in the Aceh River Delta. Effective Dutch control was limited to the location of the sultan's palace, which was renamed Kota Radja (modern Banda Aceh), and a few forts scattered through the valley along the Aceh River.[9]

From 1874 to 1876, despite the commitment of virtually the entire colonial army of the Dutch colony of the Netherlands Indies (modern Indonesia), all attempts to quell the Aceh resistance failed miserably. The Dutch government mounted a new pacification campaign only eight months after the withdrawal of the expeditionary force led by General van Swieten. Delayed by the onset of the monsoon season and the flooding of the Aceh River, the campaign commenced in January 1875. The Dutch forces advanced in three columns over narrow, slippery, and winding dikes, through a sea of flooded sawahs. Every village proved a deadly obstacle with dense fences of razor-sharp bamboo sticks and bush that the soldiers had to climb while facing intense gunfire. The campaign continued into 1876, when Aceh operations tied up 8,000 soldiers and 3,000 forced laborers. Losses due to violence and disease were enormous: 1,400 soldiers and 1,500 forced laborers died in 1876 alone. Moreover, 7,500 soldiers had to be evacuated due to illness or injuries. The Dutch divided their forces over 50 military posts and forts. Except for the transport between the harbor at Oleh Leh and Kota Radja, where a narrow-gauge railway had been built, the forced laborers had to carry all materials and supplies between the Dutch positions. The supply columns often had to fight their way through; in an early 1876 ambush, the attackers killed 45 out of a 60-man military escort near the Dutch main base at Kota Radja.[10]

Aceh resistance became increasingly well coordinated after the early 1876 return of Habib Abdurrahman Zahir, who had been the adviser, guardian, and prime minister of the late sultan of Aceh. He raised a large army in Pedir, the most powerful of the states that formed part of the Greater Aceh sultanate. Next, he crossed the mountains between Pedir and Aceh and descended into the Aceh River Valley to Indapura, choosing Montassik as his base. The *hulubalangs* elected him *panglima Perang Besar*, or supreme war leader, which was confirmed by the sultan-elect Mohammed Daoud, who was still a young boy. Teungku di Tiro, a well-known and influential religious leader (*ulama*) from Pedir, and other *ulamas* added their support, lending the conflict the aura of a holy war.[11]

In June 1878, Habib Abdurrachman Zahir's men invaded the *sagi* XXV *mukims* and laid siege to Krung Raba, the principal Dutch fort in northwestern Sumatra. The leading *hulubalangs* subsequently crowned the seven-year-old Muhammad Daud as the sultan of Aceh. The governor-general of the Netherlands Indies, who in 1877 had publicly declared victory in Aceh, was forced to eat his words. Having boasted that he would be able to withdraw most of the army from Aceh in 1878, he actually had to send reinforcements. The governor-general impressed upon the governor of Aceh that Dutch national prestige had been damaged and could only be restored by the absolute subjugation of Greater Aceh.[12]

General K. van der Heijden executed the governor-general's orders to the letter by unleashing total war. He formed a 2,000-man mobile column supported by 1,000 porters that relieved the besieged Dutch fort at Krung Raba, conquered Habib Abdurrahman Zahir's main base at Montassik, then relentlessly pursued the Aceh forces throughout the *sagi* XXII and XXVI *mukims*.[13] Using scorched earth tactics to annihilate the resistance as quickly as possible was at the core of the Dutch operations. During a two-week campaign in late July and early August, the mobile column destroyed all kampongs in the *sagi* XXII *mukims* that offered any resistance or appeared to support the rebels in any way. Subsequently, Dutch units also torched any kampongs that fired shots at military supply columns. Dutch forces partly lived off the land during the campaign. At least twice, commanders sent details to Lambaru to forage, exact food supplies from villagers, or impound food stores left in abandoned kampongs. Most of the kampongs the Dutch forces encountered had been so hastily abandoned that the inhabitants had been unable to take their possessions with them.[14]

The onset of the monsoon rains made the wetland rice fields surrounding the villages impassable, confining troops and supply columns to the higher ground, where villages typically were located. The forced laborers cut makeshift roads through the village orchards and plantations to open up supply routes. To reduce vegetation cover for Aceh ambush parties, the army's contingents of forced laborers also cleared wide swaths of trees and bushes on either side of the roads, further destroying orchards and plantations. Dutch engineers cut many valuable trees in and around their forts in order to lay out fields of fire and to construct palisades and living quarters in Dutch camps, posts, and forts.[15] Although it had the appearance of a swampy jungle to many Dutch soldiers, the Aceh River Valley's floodplain was covered by irrigated rice fields intersected by narrow dikes, drainages, and bridges while villages, orchards, plantations, and pastures covered the higher ground. Thus, the Dutch soldiers and their forced laborers not only razed homes and storage facilities but their actions also destroyed entire orchards, plantations, and groves of fruit and other important trees. Deprived of shelter and food, the displaced in and from the *sagi* XXII *mukims* were soon in dire straits. A girl captured a few weeks after her village had been torched confessed to her Dutch interrogators that people were going hungry as rice prices soared. She revealed that disease was decimating the displaced and that many hapless refugees were only

FIGURE 9.1. Dutch soldiers atop one of the narrow dikes marking the irrigated fields in the Aceh Valley bottom. The dikes are connected to the villages with narrow small bridges. Dense tree and bush cover in the background indicate the edges of a village with plantations and orchards (Nationaal Archief/National Archives, the Hague, the Netherlands, NL-HaNA_2.20.46_850_15).

surviving on (tree) fruit. Indeed, a desperate search for fruit had caused her to venture too close to the Dutch positions, leading to her imprisonment.[16]

The ruthless Dutch total war strategy appeared to work. On October 13, 1878, the leader of the Aceh resistance, Habib Abdurrahman Zahir, and 20 members of his family surrendered.[17] Fighting immediately subsided, and during the last quarter of 1878, thousands of refugees returned to their kampongs in the areas under Dutch control. Smaller or larger groups of refugees surrendered to Dutch military posts in the frontline every day, begging for permission to return home. A Dutch report noted with satisfaction that at the current rate the deserted ix *mukims* soon would be repopulated.[18] Some of the groups of returnees consisted mainly of men, however, suggesting that people still had security concerns that warranted keeping women and children in hiding. Incidents bore out that not all was safe. At the end of October, a small group of returnees consisting of two men, four women, and three children complained that they had been robbed of their bush knives, bags of rice, and jewelry by men from the *hulubalang* Tuku Muda Baid, who earlier had surrendered.[19]

The refugees were in a terrible state. One report stressed that "the returnees, in particular the women and children, bear the evidence of intense suffering." To make matters worse, many had nothing to which to return: soldiers had reduced many villages to ashes and clear-cut their orchards and plantations. Dutch camps, forts, and posts usually were located on the high ground where mosques, kampongs, and orchards previously had been situated in the densely settled Aceh River Valley. The mosque of Bilul, for example, had been repurposed as a Dutch fort. The practice of clearing all trees and bush alongside roads and around Dutch fortifications to deprive attackers of cover also continued. The monsoon-induced flooding of the Aceh River in mid-November, forced the Dutch to abandon all their temporary camps on lower ground and to relocate to higher ground, which subsequently displaced many returnees yet again from their homes and villages.[20]

On December 11, the *hulubalang* of the v *mukims*, Tuku Solyman Iris, surrendered to the Dutch, which markedly increased the number of refugees returning to their villages. On December 19, a patrol observed what appeared to be "families loaded with all kinds of goods and herding along cattle moving home" approaching the *sagi* XXVI *mukims* from the north and northeast.[21] Yet occasionally, fierce fighting erupted. On December 24, three locally recruited guides led a Dutch force toward a fortified mosque less than one kilometer from the Dutch fort at Lamjong that had gone entirely undetected because it was ingeniously camouflaged by houses and village orchards. The Dutch troops took heavy fire as they stormed its earthen wall. In retaliation, they obliterated the houses, fruit trees, and other vegetation around the mosque.[22]

But hopeful that the war was ending, and in an attempt to entice the refugees to return, the Dutch tried to limit the destruction of villages and homes in the areas they had occupied. In January 1879, an unidentified kampong close to the Montassik mosque narrowly escaped the torch after a group of Aceh fighters retreated into the kampong and wounded a Dutch officer and several Aceh women. The governor of Aceh took the presence of the women and children in the kampong as evidence that the inhabitants had not been involved in the attack and ordered the kampong to be spared.[23] Earlier during the campaign, any village from which shots were fired immediately had been razed to the ground.

Beyond the occupied areas, however, the Dutch projected little effective power. Patrols that operated in enemy territory frequently got lost or bogged down in flooded rice fields, saving villages considered hostile from a scorched earth fate. The challenges to operating in unknown terrain during the monsoon season led the Dutch commander to increasingly recruit local guides and allies.[24] Limiting scorched earth in the occupied territories facilitated forging alliances with select Aceh leaders who accepted Dutch rule. The head of Hoho and two of his village headmen guided a Dutch patrol through their part of the v *mukims*, forewarning the soldiers of an ambush. A patrol on a two-day reconnaissance to the Klieng area, which the Dutch considered hostile territory, found the terrain swampy and difficult to traverse, but the population was welcoming, perhaps because the patrol had not engaged in scorched earth.[25]

Through the patrols and the intelligence provided by allied Aceh leaders, Dutch Governor Van der Heijden learned that by mid-March the wet rice fields in the enemy-held east of the *sagi* XXII *mukims* were drying out and would soon be passable for his troops. The patrols also reported that the irrigated rice harvest was in full swing.[26] The reports on the "drying out" of the wet rice fields and the rice harvest were closely related: typically, farmers drained wet rice fields before the harvest. The rice harvest therefore created an excellent opportunity for the Dutch: passable rice fields meant that the troops were no longer sitting ducks moving on the narrow and slippery dikes between the villages. Attacking immediately would also deny the rice harvest to the inhabitants of the unoccupied regions and, by extension, the rebel forces. Some of the rice was still being harvested, and much of what already had been harvested was being sun dried before it could be stored, hidden, sold, or otherwise distributed or moved. Taking advantage of the vulnerability of the rice farmers and the rebels who relied on them, Governor Van der Heijden immediately resumed his offensive operations.

On March 23, two Dutch columns advanced deep into the Aceh Valley toward Indapura in the *sagi* XXII *mukims*. Led by Aceh guides and advisers, each column carried enough food supplies to last for several days.[27] Van der Heijden ordered his commanders to consult the friendly Aceh leaders accompanying them so as to identify which villages were hostile rather than continuing to indiscriminately destroy all kampongs they encountered.[28] The advance was slow and torturous in the face of fierce resistance across the swampy terrain. But, when the Dutch forces approached their objective Indapura, its *hulubalang* surrendered without a fight. Indapura's leader agreed to pay a heavy tribute, handed over 350 operable firearms, and promised to make his subjects return to their villages. The *hulubalang* explained that "livestock, rice, and goods had been carried to Datu Setegul south of the main road by the population" but that they would return to their villages when ordered. He warned, however, that the population further up the Aceh River Valley would continue to resist.[29]

The Dutch established their main camp next to the Indapura mosque. They erected palisades there and at various smaller posts, and cut fields of fire around their positions, once more destroying villages, orchards, and plantations in the process. To inundate the western approaches to Indapura and hinder the Dutch advance, the inhabitants blocked the drainage channels of the rice fields surrounding the village, flooding the road. The Dutch commander ordered the dams in the channels to be cut open, which drained the water from the *sawahs*. The irony that the flooded earth strategy that had saved Leiden and the Dutch rebel cause in the 1570s was used against his troops seems to have escaped Van der Heijden. In another unintentional flashback to the Dutch Revolt, the Dutch commander threatened to burn all the villages that resisted unless they paid a large sum of money within three days. Only the headman of the village of Anak Gle complied. The populations of the other villages fled and hid in the mountains surrounding the Aceh River Valley. Marching along the edge of Anak Gle, one of the patrols discovered several huts on a nearby hill where the villagers had stored their valuables for fear that the Dutch would burn their homes.[30]

Early in April, making good on the threat to burn the villages that failed to produce the imposed war tax, Dutch patrols destroyed four villages in the area. At Djeruk they burned 255 houses and at Grut 170 homes and two mosques. They also cut down the fruit trees at both villages.[31] Instead of burning the remaining three villages that had not paid the war tribute, the Dutch took hostages to make the inhabitants comply. The strategy failed at Lamaru because all the men had already departed for the lower slopes of the mountains to cultivate dryland ladang fields, leaving the women and children behind. The next day, however, a patrol found Lamaru entirely abandoned.[32] The inhabitants of the Indapura region en masse sought sanctuary on Sumatra's West Coast. Before leaving, they sold their rice supplies at very low prices for fear that the food would otherwise be destroyed with their villages. Dutch patrols observed women, children, and men carrying large packs of rice to their villages west of the Indapura region.[33] The villagers were likely the lucky buyers. They were fortunate because the Dutch scorched earth campaign had destroyed food supplies and villages throughout the region, and the war conditions had prevented many farmers from working their fields.

Population flight was not limited to the Indapura war zone. The population of the *sagi* XXVI *mukims* to the north of Indapura also abandoned their villages for fear of a further Dutch advance.[34] At the end of April, Governor Van der Heijden reported that "the still displaced population is suffering a lot in the mountains; the mortality must be rather considerable," demonstrating that he was well aware that the refugees were already highly vulnerable. He called on the leaders of the *sagi* XXII *mukims* to surrender: "All of you have suffered a lot of damage because of your own fault; you do not really understand the objective of the [Dutch] government. It wants to make you happy without making any changes in your country's institutions. . . . I am sad to have learned the extent of the suffering of the people and I want to make every effort to save it from these dire conditions." Leaders from the *mukims* east of Indapura assured the governor that the principal heads of the *sagi* XXII *mukims* were loyal to the Dutch government. But they also warned that if the Dutch continued to torch homes and mosques, everyone would flee and "the [*sagi*] XXII *mukims* will be as depopulated as the [*sagi*] XXV *mukims*."[35]

When the Aceh leaders refused to heed the ultimatum to surrender, the Dutch resumed their unlimited warfare. It is clear that not only Van der Heijden but also other Dutch commanders were very conscious of the humanitarian crisis their scorched earth strategy caused. Yet, they continued to target Aceh's environmental infrastructure, driving the population into the mountains to face disease and starvation not only in areas that already had been occupied but also in enemy territory. In May, after encountering further resistance in the presumably already pacified v *mukim* south of Indapura, Dutch patrols torched every abandoned village they encountered. After receiving information that the population of the middle and upper Aceh Valley had moved its possessions further upstream to Djanteh, a Dutch officer approvingly noted, "The punishment of the v mukims must have left a deep impression upon the enemy." On May 31, the Dutch advanced under standing orders: "Kampongs from which our forces are fired on, will be punished." An Aceh guide proved invaluable to the Dutch advance by indicating an alternative crossing over the Djerir River, which brought the colonial soldiers behind the Aceh fortifications that were blocking the route that originally had been planned. The Dutch reduced at least 30 kampongs to ashes during the two-week campaign; all of them had been abandoned before the Dutch arrival, a situation routinely read as a hostile act and entirely in line with war practices throughout the 16th through 19th centuries in Europe, the Americas, and Asia. The fierce resistance highlighted in the Dutch reports may have been exaggerated at times to legitimize putting villages to the torch—soldiers ransacked the homes before setting fire to them, and burning the villages erased any evidence of the soldiers' plundering and pillaging. The population of one village that the Dutch had spared in order to use the dwellings as their quarters managed to carry part of their paddy rice stores with them, hiding the remainder so well that the soldiers could not find it. In other cases, villagers narrowly escaped with their lives, leaving their food stores behind: soldiers often encountered large stores of rice and small stock in the otherwise deserted villages. At one village, under a hail of Dutch bullets, the inhabitants barely managed to get out with their water buffalo and what they could carry before the soldiers burned everything to the ground. At the main kampong Gleieng, the Dutch captured not only 24 cannons and ammunition but also a large quantity of small stock and fowl, as well as two large sheds filled with rice. The inhabitants had fled with their cattle and any other possessions they could carry only days earlier. The soldiers destroyed the rice stores and presumably ate the small stock and fowl.[36]

On July 1, after destroying the *sagi* XXII *mukims* and chasing its population into the mountains, the Dutch forces swung northward into the *sagi* XXVI *mukims*, converging on the region's heartland and burning all kampongs in their path. Initial resistance was fierce but soon crumbled, leaving the soldiers to wield the firebrand more frequently than their firearms. One column advanced at a snail's pace through a maze of rice fields across narrow winding dikes. That the rice fields were inundated in postharvest July indicates that the villagers intentionally flooded them to slow down the Dutch troops. Discovering large amounts of paddy rice buried under the houses, the soldiers torched both. All the villages were abandoned, some in great haste. At the large and prosperous-looking Lamgut kampong, weapons, gunpowder, and bullets lay scattered throughout the village, and most houses contained stores of rice. Soldiers destroyed over 200,000 pounds of paddy rice in addition to the contents of three large paddy rice sheds in the neighboring village of Tungkup. Fowl was also among the booty. Accompanied by their mobile large livestock, the majority of the *sagi* XXVI *mukim's* population fled into the mountains in the far north of the XXVI *mukims* to ultimately trek southward toward Selimun in the upper Aceh Valley. Only three kampongs formally surrendered. The destruction of one of the three, Ghani, was narrowly averted after most of the village's women and children surrendered at the Dutch camps. To deny the Aceh rebels food and ammunition, soldiers thoroughly destroyed all but the three surrendered villages of the region. The governor elaborated that the destruction of the villages "could have the most decisive impact on the surrender of the leaders and the population who fled to Selimun and therefore on the ending of the war."[37]

Again, Van der Heijden used starvation as a conscious weapon of war, by having ordered his troops to systematically destroy villages and their food stores. Executing the governor's environcidal orders, the patrols fanned out into the outlying districts of the *sagi* XXVI *mukims* over three days, torching homes and rice stores and capturing the fowl roaming the deserted villages. A patrol searching the forests in the foothills of the mountains framing the Aceh Valley stumbled across several abandoned refugee camps, one of which was littered with a large amount of rice, goods, and a couple of guns. The patrol took potshots at remote "enemies" in the mountains, some of whom were carrying loads, and captured a man and his wife and child who had been lost in the forest for five days. In total, the patrol destroyed over 12,000 pounds of rice.[38]

The Dutch patrols clearly made no distinction between armed rebels and desperate refugees: the camps in the hills were more likely refugee camps, rather than rebel bases. A patrol searching the deserted Blang Bintang grass plain found the remnants of a camp stocked with 21 bags of rice, cooking equipment, clothes, and construction materials, as well as the tracks of cattle and horses. Taking up pursuit, the patrol identified seven more abandoned camp sites before stumbling upon ten men and a number of women and children with their possessions and five head of cattle. The men immediately surrendered their weapons stating that they had been abandoned by their leaders and had been wandering through the wilderness for days. The men emphasized "that they were tired of the war," stressing that many others hiding in the mountains felt the same way. One of the captives identified himself as Wakil Ma-in, a low-ranking kampong leader. Wakil Ma-in explained that the people the patrol observed in flight higher up in the mountains were afraid of the Dutch and no longer wanted to fight. The patrol brought the people to the camp, assigning them to the few remaining houses.[39]

The Dutch commander subsequently sent Wakil Ma-in back into the mountains to talk more refugees into returning to their villages, assuring them that the Dutch meant them no harm if they quietly stayed in their kampongs. A further patrol sent from the same camp reported more refugees in the mountains and discovered yet another abandoned camp site. Refugees carrying white flags stopped running when the Dutch did not open fire, but still kept their distance from the patrol. To encourage refugees to return, the local Dutch commander halted the routine destruction of villages. The change of tactics worked almost immediately. The next day, headman Wakil Ma-in reappeared at the Dutch camp, accompanied by a group of men, women, and children loaded with their possessions and driving along their cattle and water buffalo. The commander issued them a pass to return home to their village in the west of the *sagi* XXVI *mukims*. Hearing about the success, the governor ordered the soldiers to stop the wholesale destruction of villages and to only burn individual dwellings from which gun shots had been fired. The order came in time to save at least some of the villages in the *sagi* XXVI *mukims*. Subsequently, groups of refugees with their possessions descended from the mountains to return to the Aceh Valley. Crisscrossing the *sagi* XXVI *mukims*, patrols made sometimes surprising discoveries that illustrated people's desperate attempts to survive. Near the abandoned kampong of Lampudja, a patrol found a group of 18 unarmed men, women, and children who had made a hideout in dense bush vegetation with a well-camouflaged shed, replete with rice and grain. Originating from Rumpit, the group had discovered the food store in Lampudja and hid it at their shelter. Another patrol in the mountains came across an abandoned camp where 40 bags of rice were concealed. The patrol carried the rice back to its own camp, thereby depriving the refugees of their only means of survival.[40]

Refugees captured by Dutch patrols in the mountains around the Aceh Valley confessed that many leaders and commoners from the *sagi* XXVI and XXII *mukims* had fled to Lamtoba, deeper into the mountains east of the *sagi* XXVI *mukims*. Lamtoba's population consequently had swelled to 1,000 people, and the kampong allegedly boasted a large supply of rice sufficient to sustain the population for a year, as well as abundant arms and ammunition. Probing the area, Dutch patrols found that as previously the village populations quickly returned if the soldiers did not destroy villages or homes. The patrols also found that the old road from their base at Lepong to Oleh Karang had been intentionally inundated by breaching the dikes between the sawahs and damming the small creeks descending from the mountains, blocking any Dutch advance. The patrols scoured the hills and mountain slopes on the eastern edge of the *sagi* XXVI *mukims* for huts, food stores, and weapons, destroying many campsites and capturing 210 bags of grain and 20 bags of rice. The patrols distributed the captured food supplies among the populations of local kampongs that had returned and therefore were considered "friendlies." The distribution of captured food supplies in turn made returnees more likely to inform the Dutch about refugee camps and hidden food stores in the surrounding areas. It also made it easier to recruit local guides. Except for occasional exchanges of gunfire that caused no casualties, the patrols encountered no resistance. Nevertheless, especially the women and children refugees were too afraid to return to their homes, and most of the villages remained deserted.[41] Some returnees claimed that resistance leaders had prevented the refugees from returning to their villages.[42] Deprived of their homes, food stores, fields, and orchards, hunger spread among the refugees in the mountains.

In July, one of the columns operating in the *sagi* XXVI *mukims* returned to Kota Radja and shipped to Lampanas with orders to destroy Lamtoba, where many refugees from the *sagi* XXVI *mukims* had gathered. The column disembarked near Krung Raja, where it encountered a few Aceh men in poor small fisherman's homes who "stated that they were suffering because the enemy had carried all food into the mountains." When the soldiers marched inland, the imam of Lamtoba surrendered and explained that the refugees from the *sagi* XXVI *mukims* had fled to Selimun in the far upper Aceh Valley. On August 1, accompanied by two Aceh guides supplied by the imam, the Lamtoba-based Dutch column marched across high mountain ranges and through deep ravines toward interior Selimun. The kampong was abandoned, but the Dutch were fired upon from the mountains. After destroying the 30 houses in the village, the column returned to its Lamtoba base because of a lack of potable water. Patrols sent deeper into the mountains only encountered a handful of isolated mountain farmers and 15 refugees from the Lamtoba Valley, who were ordered to return to their village within 24 hours. The patrols found no signs of the refugee concentrations that allegedly originated from the Aceh Valley *sagi* XXVI *mukims*.[43]

At the same time, patrols from the main colonial force stationed in the Aceh River Valley's eastern *sagi* XXII and XXVI *mukims* continued to harass the refugees in the mountains, keeping them on the run. One patrol caught a small group of refugees hiding at a small house stacked with bags of *gabo* grain. In a deep ravine close by, the same patrol surprised a camp consisting of a few dwellings and took 8 men and 15 women prisoner. The skirmish alerted a nearby undetected camp, allowing a larger group of refugees to escape. The patrol razed the refugees' shelters, returning to base with 79 prisoners and 200 bags of *gabo* grain, 40 guns, 3 head of cattle, and 3 water buffalo. Following these actions, several hundred refugees surrendered to Dutch military posts in the *sagi* XXII *mukims*.[44]

Soon after the Dutch had marched on Lamtoba from the north, the military administrator in the *sagi* XXII *mukims* received a letter signed by several prominent resistance leaders offering to surrender. The leaders, explaining that they were motivated by "the great misfortune that the war had presently brought upon the land," promised to bring their people back into the Aceh Valley from their mountain forest hideouts. To force the issue, on August 13 the governor sent a column to Selimun in the far east of the *sagi* XXII *mukims* with orders to destroy the region but to spare any villages that offered no resistance. He also ordered the Lamtoba column to resume its advance to Selimun from the north, cutting off refugee escape. The Lamtoba column commander received orders that each village should provide five hostages and pay a war tax of 8 dollars for each wooden dwelling and 3 dollars for each bamboo home. The column's surprise raid on a village that previously had appeared abandoned netted 67 inhabitants and their livestock. The soldiers did not destroy the kampong's houses because it was unclear whether the prisoners were local or refugees from the *sagi* XXVI *mukims*. At Lamtoba, the Panglima Banten identified 11 of the prisoners as refugees from the *sagi* XXVI *mukims*, whereupon the Dutch commander issued the refugees a pass to return to their homes after warning them they would be summarily shot if they were ever found in the Lamtoba region again. Some of the captured men, women, and children suffered from smallpox, and the disease reportedly spread to other villages. To decrease the risk of contaminating the troops, the soldiers halted foraging in the kampongs and minimized social contact with the local population. Meanwhile, the southern column, meeting resistance along the way, reached Selimun after the prominent local leader Tuku Muda Daud, surrendered to save his kampongs from destruction. The Lamtoba column from the north reached Selimun only a day later after having had to fight its way through several roadblocks and kampongs along a difficult mountain path.[45] With the fall of Lamtoba and Selimun in August 1879, the principal remaining leaders of the resistance retreated across the mountains to Pedir.[46]

By all appearances, the Dutch finally had conquered the entire core of the Aceh sultanate. Once again, the governor-general of the Dutch Indies declared victory. In a book he published in 1879, however, General Jan Van Swieten, who had led the second expedition to Aceh in 1873–74, sharply criticized how the Aceh war had been fought. Van Swieten estimated that 30,000 Achnese had been killed between 1874 and 1879 and that 400–500 kampongs had been reduced to ashes. He alleged that 230 of the kampongs indicated on a map of Greater Aceh produced in March 1876 had been utterly destroyed, asserting that in order to hide the devastating impact of the scorched earth tactics, the language of the reports had used the term "punishment" as a euphemism for burning the dwellings, destroying the harvests, and cutting down fruit trees and entire orchards. Van Swieten argued that the Dutch in their southeast Asian colonies had shifted back to a barbarous way of war fought by fire and the sword, breaching the laws of war by reducing Aceh to ruins and turning the survivors into bitter enemies in the process.[47] The prewar population of Aceh had been estimated at 300,000–400,000 people, but by 1880, only 50,000 remained in the Dutch-occupied territory. While the figures may be inflated, it seems clear that the mortality was high and that many survivors had fled the region.[48]

Some appearance of normalcy returned with the start of the early 1880 rice cultivation season. In the Indapura region, the population no longer fled when Dutch patrols approached, and the villagers attempted "to meet their needs by cultivating their fields." [49] Many refugees returned to upstream areas of the *sagi* XXII *mukims*. They lacked food, and at the urging of their leaders, the governor allowed the distribution of large quantities of rice.[50] In mid-March, the irrigated rice harvest in the *sagi* XXII *mukims* looked promising, although the harvest partially had failed in the villages of the v and vii *mukims*.[51]

The return of the displaced population was much slower in the *sagi* XXVI *mukims*. Several leaders and their followers returned to their abandoned villages in the first months of 1880.[52] Fifteen hundred refugees from the *sagi* XXVI *mukims* were stranded in Krung Raja. The long overland route through the mountains to the *sagi* XXVI *mukims* was made dangerous by marauders. In late April, the colonial administration sent a steamship, offering to repatriate the refugees by sea, but they declined, explaining that they had permanently resettled in the Krung Raja region. The refugees may have felt that they had little to return to because many villages had been razed in 1879. They also may have deemed the *sagi* XXVI *mukims* too dangerous.[53]

The refugees lived in small huts on the coastal plain surrounding Krung Raja. Only a few prominent men had constructed the fenced, large houses elevated on poles typical of preinvasion Aceh villages. The refugees prepared sugarcane gardens, worked the nearby saltpans, and fished. Neither the refugees nor the permanent inhabitants had the plowing animals or the energy to cultivate the expanse of abandoned wet rice fields on the western side of the bay. Livestock and rice were scarce. A single herd of 30 water buffalo in the plain was used for breeding rather than plowing; the reporting officer noted that the decision made sense "in a country, where livestock has virtually disappeared." The immense value of livestock—especially the water buffalo that were so critical to irrigated rice cultivation—is illustrated by a bloody cattle raid on the Blang Blintang, where the animals pastured. Despite being confronted by 50 attackers from the *sagi* XXVI *mukims* armed with guns, the refugee owners of eight water buffalo from the *sagi* XXII *mukims* defended their animals to the death. The scarcity of cattle and the key role of water buffalo in irrigated rice cultivation to a large extent explain why livestock thefts figure very prominently in 1880. Whereas many Aceh villagers were famished, the Dutch troops stationed at Krung Raja suffered no shortage of firewood, fish, and fruit, which the refugees and the local population readily offered in exchange for rice.[54]

Lamara had been rebuilt seven months after it had been destroyed during the fighting in the *sagi* XXVI *mukims*. The village consisted of a new mosque and 30 new houses built with betel nut palm (*Pinang* or *Areca catechu*) poles, bamboo sides, and a roof made of the leaves of the mangrove palm (*atap* or *Nypa fruticans*). Tragically, a cooking fire at the back of one of the new houses blazed out of control and reduced most of the homes to ashes in less than one hour. Only the mosque and seven houses were spared because they stood at some distance from the fire. One man suffered burns saving his young daughter from the flames. Fortunately, the inhabitants had been working in the rice fields beyond the village when the fire occurred, and most of their cattle and water buffalo had been pasturing outside the village. One head of cattle and a water buffalo were wounded in the fire and six goats burned to death, reflecting the practice of stabling livestock under the elevated houses. The total damage was estimated at 700 dollars. For comparison: the Dutch administration at the time paid locally hired laborers one dollar per day.[55] The incident illustrates both the resilience of the refugees, who rebuilt their homes in seven months, and the enormous destruction that the Dutch scorched earth practice caused: using the torch totally and rapidly destroyed not only Aceh homes but anything left in or under them, including food stores and livestock.

The May–June 1880 wet rice harvest was poor in most of Dutch-occupied Aceh.[56] The new agricultural season had commenced by September. The villages of colonial loyalist Tuku Njak Mohamad in the ix *mukims* (in the *sagi* XXII *mukims*) were the first to have their sawahs planted with rice. Because substantial numbers of refugees had not yet returned, however, households were short of field labor, and water buffalo were still scarce. As a result, only the sawahs closest to the inhabited kampongs throughout Aceh were under cultivation. The more remote sawahs and the fields around deserted kampongs remained fallow. In the XXVI *mukims*, in particular, villages and rice fields lay bare. To address the food shortages, the governor of Aceh proposed introducing the cultivation of manioc.[57]

Concerned about the labor shortages during the agricultural season, the Dutch administration allowed villagers in the "loyalist" villages of the ix *mukims* to postpone fulfilling their newly imposed labor obligation to maintain the colonial roads so that they could complete the demanding task of transplanting the rice in their sawahs. Dutch officials also took into consideration the fact that labor simultaneously was being diverted to rebuilding homes and villages in a region that had suffered greatly from scorched earth tactics. In another gesture meant to encourage reconstruction, the colonial army supplied the Dutch official in the *sagi* XXII *mukims* with 300 hoes to sell at cost to villagers.[58]

The start of the wet rice cultivation season encouraged more refugees to return home. In addition, given that the onset of the rainy season made the mountain refuges even less hospitable, the returnees might also simply have been running out of food. In early October, a Dutch steamer transported a group of 109 returnees from their refuge in Pedir back to Aceh. The group included 25 women; upon disembarking in Oleh Leh, they carried their possessions back to their home villages up the Aceh Valley in the *sagi* XXV and XXVI *mukims*.[59] Simultaneously, several hundred returnees arrived back in the *sagi* XXVI *mukims* on foot from the mountainous interior forests.[60] Most of the refugees from the devastated *sagi* XXVI mukims, however, failed to return, many choosing to remain in exile in Pedir.[61]

The Dutch had required Aceh leaders to surrender formally in order to receive a collective pass that allowed each leader and his followers to return to their village without interference by the Dutch troops. When the *sagi* XXVI *mukims* heads refused to surrender, the Dutch administration shifted to issuing safe conduct passes to individual adult males that covered them and their immediate family members. Just days after the shift in policy, Dutch officers issued 100 passes to men from the kampongs Krung Kali, Lam Hassan, Tjot Lamé, Lam Guguh, and

Rumpit alone. One officer commented that "almost all are married and have wife and children in the kampong." In the kampong Lam Ara, groups of 25 returnees established a work shift system in which only one of the groups worked on the village at a time to rebuild their homes.[62] The villagers of Lam Ara obviously feared that the Dutch might take hostages. All the kampongs in the area had been razed in 1879. Although the cultivation season had already begun, the 1,000 or so returnees to the *sagi* XXVI *mukims* previously mentioned could still hope to grow irrigated rice and secondary crops. Irrigated rice on Sumatra could yield up to 60 times the seeded quantity, while dryland *ladang* cultivation produced 40 times the seeded quantity.[63] With the onset of the rainy season, tree fruit also became available except where the village orchards had been cut down by the Dutch.

The decision by the Dutch administration to allow the inhabitants of the ix *mukims* villages to concentrate on their fields before exacting forced road labor paid off. In December, the irrigated rice stood a foot high in the ix *mukims*, promising a better harvest than in the previous year. The high number of recent returnees had facilitated the cultivation and planting of many additional fields. Elsewhere in the *sagi* XXII *mukims*, harvest prospects varied. In the v *mukims* Indapura villages, especially on the western side of the Aceh River, "all fields have been planted already and the rice stands one or two feet [high and appears] very good." In the vii *mukims* villages, the rice seedlings had not yet all been transplanted from the seed beds to the sawahs. In the v *mukims* Montassik, only the fields of a few kampongs had been planted, and in the Montassik area itself, virtually no planting had occurred.[64]

After the wet rice had been transplanted, the returnees cleared the roads and the upland dryland fields or *ladangs*.[65] By early February 1881, only part of the irrigated rice had been harvested in the *sagi* XXVI *mukims*, but, standing taller than a man's height, most of it was close to ripening. Both well-cultivated rice fields and areas with (partially) fallow fields marked the region.[66] The irrigated rice harvest in Aceh continued well into March and April 1881.[67]

The governor of Aceh's efforts to boost the rural economy with the introduction of coffee and silk cultivation in 1881 offers further insights into the medium-term impact of the scorched earth campaign that had occurred three years earlier. The governor argued that coffee could be grown as a cash crop on the fenced higher ground in and immediately around the villages by clear-cutting the "wilderness" that thrived there. As a bonus, he stressed that eradicating the wilderness areas around the kampongs would also enhance security because it would remove the dense vegetation cover that Aceh guerillas had used to set ambushes.[68]

The fenced areas in and around the villages that the governor quali-fied as wilderness, however, had been home gardens, orchards, and tree plantations before their destruction or abandonment. Moreover, the Aceh defenders in 1879 intentionally had "re-wilded" the approaches to the villages by adding sharpened bamboo sticks and other obstructions to the existing fences, which consisted of living bamboo fences and bush. In razed villages that had not yet been rebuilt, weedy vegetation rapidly choked orchards and plantations, and the living fences grew ever wilder and denser, invading the village grounds. Even in villages that had been spared from the torch or that had been rebuilt, the inhabitants would have been more preoccupied with building new homes and growing rice than with restoring or maintaining their living fences, gar-dens, orchards, and plantations. While many village spaces may have appeared to be impenetrable wilderness, their condition was the out-come of the destructive war and the displacement of the population and the resulting degradation of environmental infrastructure.

Rampant disease was another consequence of the flight, exposure, hunger, and trauma that had been caused by the scorched earth cam-paigns. Intestinal diseases, fevers, and smallpox grew to epidemic pro-portions in 1880.[69] Livestock, too, had suffered in the forested mountain hideouts because grazing had been in short supply. In peacetime, villa-gers took great care of their precious water buffalo and cattle; their owners stabled the animals under their homes at night and at times stall-fed them, carrying cut grass to the villages. The villagers also used fire to burn off old vegetation in the grass plains to foster young growth and maintain nutritious pastures.[70] Eventually, rinderpest struck the Aceh Valley, probably introduced from the West Coast by returnees' livestock. In March 1881, infected cattle and water buffalo in the *sagi* XXII *mukims* died in a matter of days; they had stopped eating and suffered from bloody diarrhea. Goats also fell victim to the disease.[71] Livestock losses were particularly heavy in the v *mukims* villages. The loss of plowing animals greatly jeopardized rice cultivation during the 1881/1882 agricultural season. The scarcity of livestock made the cattle used in Dutch supply transports an even greater prize, and cattle thefts spiked. After the rinderpest onslaught, the Dutch garrisons had to guard their cattle not only at night but also in broad daylight.[72]

Discouraged by the deadly plagues, a large number of the refugees from the v *mukims* chose not to return to the ruins of their villages. The entire population of the razed kampong Lihon and most of the inhabitants of the kampongs Riki and Lamdir cleared dryland *ladang* fields in the foothills beyond the valley. Instead of returning to their old homes, the refugees constructed an entirely new village on the upper Djerir River at a six hours' walk from the Dutch fort at Glé Kambing. Thus, the refugees maintained a safe distance between their new abodes and the nearest Dutch troops. Named Manga, the village counted 30 "fairly good" houses. Upon orders from their imam, part of Lamara's population, including most of the inhabitants of the kampong Anaglé, returned to the mountains to lead "a wandering existence." The imam made the decision after a work party constructing a colonial road past the village had removed a large quantity of gravel from the local river, destroying the hydraulic infrastructure of Lamara's rice lands. As a result of the Dutch engineering, water from the river could no longer flow into the ditches that fed the sawahs.[73]

"Civil" Pacification through Starvation

The March 1881 appointment of A. Pruys van der Hoeven as governor of a civilian administration ended military rule in Aceh and was meant to extend regular colonial administration over the territory. Van der Hoeven confined the military to its bases, relying instead on a newly created police force for routine security. Dutch officials and loyalist Aceh leaders locally recruited and headed the police force. With gifts and the promise of salaries, the civilian governor enticed many Aceh leaders to work with his administration, instituting a system of indirect rule through the *hulubalangs*. Civilian rule proved short-lived and did not deliver peace. In March 1883, almost immediately after succeeding van der Hoeven as governor of Aceh, his successor, P. F. Laging Tobias, requested military reinforcements.[74] In 1884, Laging Tobias replaced two of his senior civilian administrators with military officers, partially reversing his predecessor's policy of confining the army to the barracks.[75]

The dependency on Aceh allies to help pacify the region was not an entirely new strategy. That the army had neither Aceh guides nor reliable maps contributed greatly to the debacles of the early 1870s Dutch campaigns. In contrast, in his 1878 and 1879 campaigns, Van der Heijden systematically used Aceh guides and spies. The guides were not only important for their knowledge of the terrain but also because they spoke the language and could separate out hostiles from the general population to facilitate more selective punishment.[76] That individuals and groups sided with the Dutch gave the continued Aceh war aspects of a civil war, pitting regions, villages, headmen, and even brothers against one another. In 1882, Si Isa, an Aceh colonial policeman from the *sagi* XXII *mukims*, accused his own brother and fellow police officer of conspiring with the Aceh resistance to have Si Isa assassinated. The accused denied the allegations but acknowledged that "hostiles" on occasion visited his home kampong to see their relatives. Reassured, the investigating Dutch officer dismissed the case. Two weeks later, however, Si Isa was dead and his home reduced to ashes. A Dutch patrol subsequently torched the homes of the suspects in retaliation.[77]

Dutch administrators grew extremely frustrated by what they perceived as the "treacherous" nature of the Acehnese. Individual Aceh leaders and entire villages and *mukims* seemed to play both sides, and to change sides easily. Like villages in early 1570s Holland or early 17th-century Brabant, however, 1880s frontline Aceh kampongs had to hedge their bets because neither side could offer the villagers real protection from the exactions from the other. In 1880s Aceh, Dutch patrols roamed by day, Aceh rebels by night. Living in the vicinity of Dutch posts and

forts offered no protection; to the contrary, rebels increasingly conducted night raids on Dutch bases to which the garrisons responded
with indiscriminate volleys of gun and artillery fire, making the surroundings of the forts killing zones.[78]

Tuku Njak Hassan, the most successful Aceh guerilla leader and his
men ambushed Dutch supply columns and attacked Dutch positions,
robbing and killing village leaders who supported the colonial administration. Tuku Njak Hassan also exacted war taxes that financed the
resistance, and his 50–60 men lived off the land, forcing villagers to provide them with food and shelter. Both the Dutch and the Aceh resistance exacted tributes from villages. But whereas in true 16th-century
fashion the Dutch threatened to burn down the whole village upon
noncompliance, Njak Hassan and other leaders of the resistance selectively victimized village headmen, robbing or torching their homes
while sparing other villagers and their possessions.[79] In early 1882, Njak
Hassan sent written requests to several kampong heads of the *sagi* XXVI
mukims asking for contributions for the holy war against the Dutch colonial rulers.[80]

With the civilian governors confining the military to their bases, and
fewer military patrols, rebel bands could operate more freely across
Aceh. During 1882, Dutch officials increasingly identified Teungku di
Tiro, a highly respected *ulama* with a long history of supporting the resistance, as a serious threat because he systematically depicted the conflict in terms of a holy war. Governor Pruijs van der Hoeven warned that
the administration should be careful not to escalate the conflict, ventur-
ing that Teungku di Tiro probably had ties with the wider Islamic world,
where predictions were circulating about the return of the *Madhi* in the
then current Islamic year 1300. The governor worried that if the administration was thought to be fighting Teungku di Tiro, the defender of
Islam, "then the consequences will be enormous, and the struggle can
evolve into a new war."[81] The governor's fears were real enough: an Aceh
employee in the Dutch colonial offices at Anagalung was overheard telling the heads of the v *mukims* Montassik that the *Madhi* had risen, that
the Europeans in Egypt had been exterminated, and that the *Madhi*
would come to Aceh the following year.[82]

In June and July 1882, attacks on Dutch targets increased, with escalating Dutch losses. One of those killed was the Dutch commander of the Aceh indigenous police, who was massacred along with a number of his men. Reluctantly, the governor gave the military free rein in the *sagi* XXVI *mukims*, but with some important qualifications: there would be no punitive destruction of kampongs; kampong searches had to be conducted in consultation with the civil administration officers; and punishing kampongs collectively for "passive" support of Aceh rebels should be limited.[83] Aceh guerilla tactics greatly frustrated Dutch civilian and military officials. In an 1882 report, the governor lamented that the Aceh guerillas never stood their ground when pursued by Dutch patrols.[84] The Aceh Report for April 1, 1882, noted that the Panglima Njag Bintang was said to have arrived in the v *mukim* Montassik with the authorization "to wage the small war against us [i.e., the Dutch]," that is, to lead a guerilla war against the Dutch.[85]

In mid-1882, punitive shelling of kampongs by Dutch artillery became the routine response to a series of infractions, including firing at Dutch posts or patrols and the failure to pay fines or tributes. In one case, a garrison shelled a kampong at the request of two "friendly" heads, drawing the Dutch into what may have been local rivalries.[86] The governor of Aceh concluded that the shelling "keeps the population in a constant state of nervousness and restlessness, and could prevent it from quietly cultivating the fields, and the agricultural season is approaching."[87] While the governor approved of the impact of the shelling, he clearly was aware of the potentially negative effects on food production and the physical and mental well-being of the population.

The long-serving district officer in the *sagi* XXII *mukims*, L. K. Turk, proposed a more radical strategy to end what was increasingly becoming a full-blown guerrilla war. Turk argued for the reintroduction of starvation as a weapon to force the population to end their support for the Aceh resistance. Rather than what he labeled as a crude practice of burning kampongs and their food supplies, he suggested maintaining strict control over the sale of rice, dried and salted fish, and other food products in the markets and at the Chinese settlements that had sprung up across Dutch-occupied Aceh. The pro-Dutch districts of the ix and vii *mukims* not only had become self-sufficient in terms of rice production, but traders also had been marketing their surplus in the interior beyond the zone under Dutch control, effectively sustaining the rebel areas. Turk emphasized that limiting the export supply to the rebel areas would drive up food prices, thereby undercutting rebel support. He pointed to strong evidence in the Dutch military journals that acute rice shortages triggered by the scorched earth tactics had been a key factor in forcing the surrender of many Aceh leaders during the 1873–80 conquest campaigns. Turk also emphasized that starvation provided an effective means of ensuring that kampongs paid the administrative fines for disobeying colonial regulations and policies: kampongs with outstanding fines could be prohibited from planting rice. Acceding that the policy would be harsh, Turk argued nevertheless that stopping the rice trade entirely until Teungku di Tiro and his war leaders had left the area would cause the population to hold the rebels responsible for their sad plight. Pointing to historical precedents, Turk concluded that "hunger is a sharp sword and soon tames even the most evil." He noted that the Dutch had subjugated the upland Dayak of Borneo by prohibiting salt imports, as the Romans in antiquity and the French in 19th-century North Africa had subdued opponents by cutting off their water supplies. In Turk's estimation, only the unrestrained use of food warfare would prevent the pacification of Aceh from becoming a chronic guerilla war that in the long run would be costly both financially and in terms of human lives. An unidentified commentator (probably the head of the Netherlands Indies army or one of his staff officers) scribbled in the margin of Turk's report: "this is an important report" pointing to the Vendee, which the French revolutionaries had pacified in the late eighteenth 18th century by using unrestrained scorched earth tactics. The commentator noted: "every village [in the Vendee] that resisted or where the inhabitants were armed was *burned*."[88]

Encouraged by the initial success of the reintroduction of military actions, Governor P. F. Laging Tobias gave free rein to the military, with the understanding that the act of burning kampongs had to be explicitly approved by him personally. In the governor's report about the murder of the Dutch police commander of Aceh, he concluded that in truth everything outside our forts is the enemy, and only those who live in the immediate vicinity of our forts will not openly resist for fear of punishment, but there is hardly any kampong in the [*sagi*] XXV, XXVI, and XXII mukims that does not count one or more members amongst the enemy gangs. . . . We face a people that hates us indiscriminately . . . that considers the war against us as a holy war. . . . [Moreover,] we are up against a people that does not shy away from using any means in this war . . . [while] we must remain utterly civilized and can only use legitimate weapons of war.[89]

Here, Governor Laging Tobias argues that as a civilized people the Dutch were bound to fight a limited war, while the Aceh rebels fought a total war. To support his claim, the governor noted that, according to his spies, Aceh sultan Muhammad Daud had authorized the destruction of kampongs and orchards and threatened that anyone who refused to actively join the war against the Dutch oppressor would be killed.[90] In making the argument that the Aceh rebels were fighting a total war, the governor ironically identified their alleged use of the very scorched earth tactics that the Dutch army had used to subdue Aceh a few years earlier.

In April–May 1883—directly after the irrigated rice harvest—Tuku Njak Hassan issued threats to burn kampongs and took several kampong heads hostage to force the inhabitants to supply his men with food.[91] He also shifted his operations to the districts of the iv and vi *mukims* where the approaching wet rice harvest looked very promising, no doubt to secure sufficient food supplies for his men.[92] Other groups of Aceh fighters foraged in *sagi* XXII *mukims*, dispersing into smaller cells when the Dutch intensified their patrols in the region.[93] The rebels stored part of the rice and other food they requisitioned at selected kampongs. At the end of 1883, the rebel food supply "on the hoof" at Mureu included 150 goats. Believing that rebel activity in the *sagi* XXVI *mukims* had been limited because there simply was not enough food in the district to sustain the burden of feeding the guerrillas, the Dutch concluded that the rebels could only sustain themselves where the population still had rice stores.[94]

Acting upon the recommendations of Turk, the Dutch authorities continued or reinstated their control over the trade and transport of food in order to starve their opponents. Larger quantities of rice could only be transported with a permit; colonial soldiers and police arrested anyone transporting rice without a permit and impounded their load. The colonial authorities also restricted the trade and transport of other foodstuffs, including dried fish, but smuggling continued.[95] In turn, Aceh rebel leaders prohibited the population from selling food in the Dutch-controlled colonial markets near the forts.[96] In January 1884, a rebel leader advised dryland *ladang* farmers in the foothills surrounding the Aceh Valley in the iv *mukims* to harvest their rice and bring it to safety before he and his men started attacks in the area.[97] The warning demonstrates the extent to which the Dutch had built a reputation for targeting food supplies and crops. Dutch patrols traversing the foothills routinely destroyed the seasonal small dwellings, crops, and food stores they found at the *ladangs*, considering them to be "enemy camps."[98] The mix of hunger, exposure, and violence released a deadly pack of diseases. Smallpox and rinderpest reappeared in the Aceh Valley in 1883, joined by epidemic cholera, which persisted well into 1884, causing much suffering.[99]

The rebels also did not shy away from using hunger as a weapon against their Dutch opponents. Dutch food transports had been a major target for several years, and the intensity of attacks on supply columns increased in 1884. While the rebels never managed to destroy a Dutch food transport or to starve out any of the Dutch outposts, the colonial army nevertheless spent an inordinate amount of time and resources defending its supply lines. A June 1884 attack on a Dutch military transport between the Anagalung and Tjot Basetul forts illustrates the tremendous effort required in defending the Dutch supply lines against increasingly sophisticated ambushes. The Dutch had to deploy their combat engineers to clear obstacles across a bridge, fill in trenches dug across the road, remove a road block consisting of felled trees, and disarm an improvised explosive device made from a Dutch artillery shell, all the while under heavy rebel fire, and at the cost of heavy casualties.[100]

Frustrated in their ultimate objective of establishing full control over the Aceh Valley, the Dutch reverted to destroying "selected" kampongs, combining "exemplary punitive action" with the strategy of using food, food stores, and crops as a weapon. Soldiers increasingly found that kampongs along the major supply routes had been evacuated, leading the Dutch to believe that the villagers were complicit in and had prior knowledge of the rebel ambushes.[101]

On February 12, 1884, after having encountered heavy resistance during an operation against the rebels in the iv and vi *mukims* (in the *sagi* XXII *mukims*) and the vii *mukims* Baid, the Dutch meted out "exemplary punishment" in several villages. The timing again is of note: the irrigated rice harvest was in full swing in February, and by early March the rice was being stored in sheds. In between, it would have been laid out to dry in the sun. A column operating in the same area a week later received two orders: to protect a food transport and "to destroy the enemy's supply of food in the kampongs southwest of the road." This column and others that converged on the region encountered an unusually large number of enemies. The "rebels" in this case probably included the hapless farmers who had lost their homes and food stores during the previous week and the desperate villagers whose homes and food stores were threatened by the advancing column. The Dutch column completed the destruction that had begun a week earlier: "All that was left standing in the kampongs Luthu, Sepong and in the other kampongs they had punished on the 12th [of February] was burned and large supplies of padi [rice] were sacrificed to the flames."[102] In early March, soldiers razed the Klieng kampong to the ground after shots were fired on a passing Dutch column.[103] On March 21, when a Dutch column encountered opposition in what little was left of the kampong Luthu (largely destroyed a month earlier), the soldiers captured and burned large quantities of rice that had escaped destruction during the earlier raid, perhaps because it had not yet been harvested.[104]

For all the destruction, the Dutch military operations failed to establish real control in the areas beyond a narrow perimeter around each of their forts. Dutch patrols crisscrossed the contested areas in the lower and upper Aceh Valley by day, but by night, the soldiers returned to their barracks, save for occasional night time patrols. At nightfall the Aceh guerillas descended from the mountains into the kampongs to seek shelter; to collect food, supplies, and information; to exact war taxes; to raid; and to kill collaborators.[105] Large-scale operations subsided seasonally in June–July for rice planting in the sawahs.[106]

Scorched Earth and Strategic Retreat

In September 1884, Aceh formally returned to military rule when Colonel H. Demmini took over as governor.[107] The transfer probably also involved a de jure or de facto state of war or state of siege, that is, the imposition of special military jurisdiction that abrogated whatever limited rights the local population might have enjoyed during the brief interim of civilian rule.[108] To reduce the cost of the colonial administration in Aceh, which had ballooned due to the large size of the military operations, the ministry of colonies and the governor-general of the Netherlands Indies shifted to a defensive strategy. Dutch forts and posts were to be withdrawn to a new, easily defensible "concentrated line" that would seal off the heartland of Aceh around Oleh Leh and Kota Radja from rebel incursions. The new strategy, however, was not purely economically motivated. In international and imperial terms, the transformation of the Aceh capital and heartland into a Dutch fortress signaled effective occupation in the spirit of the 1884 Berlin Africa conference.[109] It also heralded the end of a short-lived experiment with civilian indirect rule that had relied heavily on the Aceh ruling elite. The creation of the defensive line further undermined the environmental infrastructure that sustained Acehnese livelihoods and the lives of friends, foes, and neutrals alike, both inside and outside the defensive perimeter, bringing Aceh society and the environment that sustained it to the brink of collapse.

Constructing the new defensive line took almost two years, from August 1884 to April 1886.[110] The line consisted of a string of separate larger and smaller forts. At the sites selected for the forts, soldiers and forced labor razed kampongs, orchards, and fields. Any building, artifact, vegetation, or terrain feature that could provide cover for attackers in the

vicinity was removed.[111] The Dutch were aware that destroying the vegetation, especially trees and orchards near and in the kampongs, caused
financial losses for the inhabitants. The creation of a new infrastructure
of roads and railways to improve logistics and communications between
the forts led to a significant loss of environmental resources. Engineers
connected all the principal forts to one another by expanding the existing narrow-gauge railroad that ran from Oleh Leh's port to Kota Radja.
Engineers and laborers constructed the railroad on top of a dike to ensure that it would remain above the wet monsoon flood levels in order
to keep open communications at all times. By December 1885, the dike
for the railroad reached the required height over a 3-mile distance.
A system of additional roads with gravel surfaces radiated out from Kota
Radja to the various forts. Work on a few large bridges continued after
the railroad and the road network largely had been completed in
April 1886. [112]

Laborers, often working under heavy fire, cleared a 0.6-mile-wide
free-fire zone along the entire 7-mile length of the rail line.[113] At Lam-
reng in the ix *mukims* district, the railroad dike ran just along the edge
of the village, cutting straight through fenced gardens, orchards, and
irrigated rice fields. The railroad dike is likely to have affected the irrigation pattern of the sawahs. Heavy October 1885 rains caused the sawahs
to flood as the water was pushed up against the railroad dike between
Ketapan Daoud and Lamdjama. The engineers expanded the number
of pipes in the dike to diminish its impact on preexisting water drainage
patterns, but with little success. Unprecedented flooding in the Aceh
and Krung Daru Rivers at the end of January 1886 damaged the railroad
dike at several locations, inundating the terrain on either side of the
railroad. The flooding also damaged the new elevated roads and several
bridges.[114]

The defensive line and the clear-cut free-fire zone became highly contested areas marred by frequent exchanges of gun and cannon fire. The
impact of the insecurity along the line was apparent as early as April 1885;
large swaths of irrigated rice fields along the line and in the security zone
remained uncultivated. Dutch maps from the 1890s indicate almost all
kampongs on the far edge of the free-fire zone as having been

abandoned and also note that irrigated rice cultivation within and directly adjacent to the line had ceased entirely. Many locations that had been identified on Dutch maps before the mid-1880s as irrigated rice fields were labeled on 1890s maps as swamps, overgrown by invasive *alang alang* grass, or marked as only "partly cultivated."[115]

Renewed violence and displacement were soon followed by disease: smallpox reappeared in September 1884.[116] Two months later, cholera struck the kampongs Lampisang and Lamku.[117] In August 1885, cholera returned to the Aceh dependencies and a cattle disease (probably rinderpest, as in 1883) struck the *sagi* XXII *mukims*. Villagers in the neighboring Anagalung region drove their animals into the mountains to protect them from the contagion.[118] Early in 1886, cholera again spread to the Dutch-occupied zone after very heavy flooding. The epidemic affected Aceh men, women, and children; Europeans; as well as indigenous and Chinese laborers. Thirty-six people fell ill, 27 of whom died during the last two weeks of February alone. By April, the epidemic had spread throughout Aceh, exacting a heavy toll; the disease hit the long-suffering vi and ix *mukims* especially hard.[119]

Security concerns led to additional clearings within the small Dutch-occupied zone, causing further destruction of the environmental infrastructure. The Dutch response to ambushes and attacks within the concentrated line was the knee-jerk razing of homes, trees, and other vegetation along the roads or railroads to remove any cover that rebel attackers might use. By 1886, most of the 18 miles of main roads are likely to have had the vegetation cleared over a width of 100 yards on each side of the road, amounting to a total devegetated surface of up to 2.3 square miles. Clearing the vegetation on either side of the 9 miles of railroad added another 1.2 square miles. These clearings alone may have rendered almost 20 percent of the total surface area within the concentrated line practically off-limits for productive or residential purposes. In addition, military and civilian colonial installations, including fortifications, factories, storage areas, and residential areas for European personnel, Chinese shopkeepers, Chinese contract laborers, and forced laborers occupied a significant share of the land surface within the line.

The installations were located on the higher ground that was less prone to flooding, competing directly with space the Aceh population used for villages, orchards, and plantations. The concentrated line thus greatly reduced the space for the local population to produce food. The loss of valuable crop land for annual and perennial (tree) crops may have contributed to flight from the area under Dutch control. In addition, fewer and fewer locally produced fruit and vegetables were available in the markets. Beri beri consequently became a major scourge, reaching epidemic proportions in early 1886. The disease largely affected European and indigenous soldiers and forced laborers who were issued military food rations. The soldiers' women and children and the Chinese laborers who had to purchase their own food at local markets were spared the disease because their diet included a variety of fresh foods. In early March 1886 alone, beri beri hospitalized 328 soldiers in a garrison of 6,600 and struck down 79 of 1,017 forced laborers.[120] After the concentrated line had been completed, soldiers could no longer purchase fruits and vegetables in the colonial markets, nor could they extort or steal fruits and vegetables from the villagers during patrols or when they were on campaign. Under the civilian administration, the garrisons had been fed rations that included fresh meat supplied by civilian contractors. Under the military administration, the garrisons received wartime military rations consisting mainly of preserved foods that caused malnutrition, making them vulnerable to such diseases as beri beri.

Under the defensive strategy, the colonial army left the pro-Dutch Aceh heads and any of their followers located beyond the new Dutch defensive perimeter to fend for themselves. The inhabitants of pro-Dutch Tolango (or Polangu), just outside the defensive line, repulsed a nighttime attack by rebels in June 1885. The Dutch military did not offer any assistance, although the fighting was clearly visible and audible.[121] Given the public display of "Dutch courage," a considerable number of Acehnese chose to flee the Dutch zone. In June 1885, the entire population of Geco fled to the area beyond the line.[122] While some left the Dutch-occupied zone for the unoccupied interior, others fled deeper into the Dutch zone, away from the forts that constituted the line. On a

June morning in 1886, "hostiles" shot at the inhabitants of Rumpit in the Dutch zone while they were at work in their irrigated rice fields, whereupon Dutch artillerists fired four shells at the assailants, driving them away.[123] The routine shelling of kampongs beyond the Dutch zone must have created a deep sense of insecurity among the villagers. In 1885 and 1886, the shelling was relatively low in volume, usually consisting of a few shells lobbed into one or two kampongs. Still, it was indiscriminate—certainly in the eyes of its victims if not in the perception of the Dutch military—and deadly, abruptly ending lives and disrupting livelihoods. Although little was reported about the direct impact of the shelling, intelligence revealed that an October 1886 episode of shelling by the Dutch navy had resulted in 31 casualties in the vi *mukims*, including 4 wounded women.[124]

Entering the line from the outside became extremely dangerous as the Dutch military set up ambushes to stop guerilla infiltration, but more often than not, they caught women and men carrying food. One evening in early February 1886, soldiers observed some people entering the line "probably to get food." The guards opened fire, killing an Aceh woman. A nightly ambush in May 1886 led to the shooting death of yet another woman. Two wounded men managed to escape. In the morning, the ambushers found no guns; instead the woman's body and four bags of rice marked the site of the tragedy.[125] Another evening, in September 1886, a patrol surprised a group of 15 women carrying vegetables and fruit into the Dutch zone. The women jettisoned their loads, narrowly escaping with their lives, perhaps because it was still light enough for the soldiers to clearly identify them as food smugglers rather than hostiles.[126] Crossing the line during the day was permitted but controlled. At times, the soldiers closed the line to traffic. For example, in July 1885, the Dutch military sealed off the Western Line at the vi *mukims* while the Dutch navy shelled the kampongs near the beach. The shelling ceased, and the line reopened two days later when the local leader, the imam of Lampager, agreed to put a stop to the hostile actions that were being launched from his area.[127]

Although the objectives of the concentrated line were to provide greater security to Dutch citizens and colonial subjects, and to economize

Dutch rule, in some ways it accomplished the opposite. Constructing the line cost yet more people their homes, fields, and orchards, and reduced local food availability even for the Dutch soldiers, contributing to the increase of beri beri. It also drove many to leave the Dutch-controlled area because the razing of homes, fields, and orchards destroyed their livelihoods. Still, because the defensive strategy effectively concentrated the violence and destruction to a narrow frontline, it relieved the pressure on Aceh communities in the interior regions, allowing them to rebuild their kampongs, farms, orchards, and lives beyond the reach of the Dutch cannons. With hindsight, however, the respite was only brief. In the late 1890s, the Dutch again changed their strategy, abandoning the defensive line and initiating another bloody all-out campaign to conquer Aceh. The new offensive campaign was led by Major J. B. van Heutsz, who in 1898 became the governor of the province. Van Heutsz's conquests and pacification methods, including the total extermination of select individual kampongs that resisted Dutch rule, led a former police officer who served in Aceh to accuse the Dutch government of genocide (*volkerenmoord*) in 1907.[128] According to Dutch official reports, during the 1899–1909 periods that Van Heutsz was governor of Aceh and subsequently governor of the Netherlands Indies, almost 22,000 inhabitants (4 percent of the population) were killed.[129] At the time, genocide did not yet exist as a legally defined crime and even the English term was yet to be coined. But the environcidal warfare of the 1870s and 1880s may have killed and displaced many more.

Environcide in Aceh

The mid-19th-century Aceh Valley was a densely settled region marked by an elaborate environmental infrastructure of villages, orchards, plantations, irrigated rice fields (*sawahs*), dikes, dams, *alang alang* pastures, and dryland fields (*ladangs*) on the lower slopes of the mountains surrounding the valley. Systematic and brutal scorched earth warfare during the 1870s and 1880s destroyed much of the environmental infrastructure. As in southern Holland during the late 16th-century Dutch

Revolt, population flight and continued violence greatly hindered reconstruction. Contemporaries argued that the Dutch warfare in Aceh
was inhumane, contrary to the norms of civilized nations and thus constituted a war crime.[130]

Although the current evidence about the extent to which the colonial
Aceh wars in Indonesia were genocidal in *outcome* is suggestive, *intent*
can perhaps be a bit more clearly discerned. Military commanders and
soldiers at the very least can be expected to have known that destroying
a population's homes, orchards, fields, and food stores, or forcibly removing people from their environmental infrastructure, would expose
them to famine, disease, and death, and risk the collapse and extermination of the Aceh nation.

In fact, late 19th-century military manuals explicitly recommended
destroying a population's rural environmental infrastructure in order to
quickly and decisively end a war. Evironcide therefore was a general and
accepted practice in the late 19th century. Moreover, the Dutch quite
consciously employed starvation as a weapon of war and were very
much aware of its disastrous impact. This is apparent in the cases of
Governor Van der Heijden and the district officer Turk. Other Dutch
commentators were even more explicit. General van Swieten condemned the Dutch way of war in Aceh and elsewhere in the Dutch
colony as an abomination and a breach of the laws of war and international law. In an 1876 publication, a Dutch senator warned that in a
people's war, as in the case of Aceh, "brute force is powerless; at best it
leads to the extermination or forced migration of the population." In
1881, during a parliamentary debate, the same Dutch senator criticized
the minister of colonies for waging "an extermination war so bloody that
the population [of Aceh] was reduced to a quarter [of what it had been
before]."[131] In 1894, a former colonial official proposed to deport the
Aceh population from the Aceh River Valley, and if they continued to
resist civilization thereafter, "they would share the fate of the redskins
of North-America."[132] Julius Jacobs, a medical officer during the Aceh
wars who was commissioned by the Dutch government to write an eth-
nography of Aceh, argued that the destructive war had caused the

physical and moral decline of the Acehnese ethnic group, leaving them with little resistance against devastating epidemics.[133]

The majority of victims in the Aceh wars died from disease or starvation because soldiers, and sometimes neighbors, intentionally deprived them access to the environmental infrastructure that they depended on for their livelihoods and their survival. Before 1881 and again after 1883, Dutch military strategy in Aceh legitimized environcidal and therefore total war, bent on utterly destroying Aceh's environmental infrastructure. Total war unleashed famine and deadly epidemics (rinderpest, smallpox, cholera, and beri beri) that killed thousands and displaced tens of thousands. The Dutch further legitimized their ruthless scorched earth practices on the basis that the Aceh rebels lived off the land, exacting money, food, and shelter from the villagers. By 1884, most of the Aceh heartland within and adjacent to the Dutch defensive line had become a green desert of weed-overgrown abandoned villages, stumped orchards, and sawahs-turned-marshes. The destruction of Aceh society was a price of conquest that many Dutch imperialists were willing to pay, and the 1870s and 1880s environcidal warfare set the stage for the subsequent rounds of ruthless war and pacification in the 1890s that led to the accusations of *volkerenmoord*—the appropriate formal and legal equivalent of the English term, "genocide."

10

Scorched African Savannas

COLONIAL CONQUEST AND THE FIRST WORLD WAR IN EARLY 20ᵀᴴ-CENTURY ANGOLA AND NAMIBIA

The country was in an unsettled state because of the war and people from one village were attacking people from another village to find food. Some people came from far, others came from nearby and attacked people in other villages to rob their millet. Some people who had millet took their grain storage baskets to the forest and hid them in holes dug in the ground. This is what my father did and how we survived. Nobody could keep their grain storage baskets in their homesteads then, because people would come and take everything. The robbers were from everywhere: Amboellas and [Ou]Kwanyamas did it. [Ou]Kwanyamas were also robbing [Ou]Kwanyamas. My father had three grain storage baskets, but one was taken by the robbers. Our cattle were all taken.[1]

THUS, TIMOTHEUS NAKALE described the tragedy of famished people fighting over food in the Ovambo floodplain in Southern Africa in an era when he and his family endured no less than two major humanitarian and environmental disasters in quick succession. The famine that Timotheus Nakale recounts, which even turned neighbors against one another, was directly related to war. Raiding, colonial conquest, and the

First World War conspired with disease and famine to cause a demographic collapse, perhaps killing up to half of the population of the northern floodplain between 1900 and 1917. The warfare saw the widespread use of scorched earth and massive refugee displacement. The loss of environmental infrastructure through destruction or displacement exposed people to drought, disease, and death.

The second disaster was the 1928–31 Famine of the Dams, which resulted in massive livestock losses, displaced thousands, and caused an unknown number of human deaths due to disease and starvation. A more devastating outcome was narrowly averted by large-scale imports of grain from Angola and because people fled to seek aid elsewhere. At first glance, the Famine of the Dams appears entirely a function of environmental factors: regional and global drought conditions. But the 1928–31 famine was equally a long-term effect of the 1900–1917 environcidal wars and in particular the devastation and displacement caused by the First World War. The famine was initially confined to the South African-occupied southern half of the Ovambo floodplain, where large numbers of war refugees had been unable to reconstruct a viable environmental infrastructure of villages, farms, fields, pastures, and water sources in advance of the late 1920s drought. The famine conditions therefore were in part a legacy of the war that had devastated the border region a decade earlier. The situation recalls the plight of indigenous Americans displaced to the North American West by climate change, European invasions, and conflicts over beaver, bison, horses, and guns. The story of the Famine of the Dams therefore provides additional insights into the challenges refugees in the Americas and elsewhere faced (and continue to face) in reconstructing environmental infrastructure in new environments in the aftermath of conflict.

The Famine of the Dams demonstrates that in the process of rebuilding homes, developing water and food sources, and creating new communities in a "wilderness" with little or no environmental infrastructure war refugees were highly vulnerable to political and environmental challenges, including war and climate dynamics. The tragedy of the Famine of the Dams highlights the medium- and long-term impacts environcidal war had on the countryside and the subsequent loss of environmental infrastructure. It also once again demonstrates how victimhood and historical agency are closely interwoven. The countryside did not recover organically from the impact of destructive war; lives, livelihoods, and rural production relied on heavy and sustained investment in creating, repairing, and maintaining water holes, dams, wells, farms, fences, fields, food stores, and trees, that is, they required refugee agency. Only by the 1950s and 1960s, fully a generation later, had the refugees and their descendants managed to successfully restore a viable environmental infrastructure that provided a measure of resilience.

Under the name of German South West Africa, modern Namibia, gained notoriety in global history as the laboratory where German total and genocidal warfare was developed. The 1904–8 German war against the Herero and Nama of central Namibia foreshadowed the Second World War Holocaust that came to define the very concept of genocide. The "German way of war," however, was neither uniquely German nor was it confined to 1904–8 Namibia, or First or Second World War Europe. During the era of colonial conquest in Africa, the "German" way of war was the golden rule rather than the exception. While Germany waged its genocidal war in central Namibia, killing up to 80 percent of the Herero, the 1900–1917 Portuguese conquest of the Ovambo floodplain on Namibia's northern border caused the death of up to 50–75 percent of the population.[2] Moreover, the early 20th century German Herero-Nama War and the Portuguese wars in the Ovambo floodplain were part of a long genealogy of environcidal and total wars stretching back to not only the 19th-century Aceh and Plains Indian Wars but to early modern wars across the globe, including the European Wars of Conquest in the Americas and the Thirty Years War.

The Portuguese invaders of the Ovambo floodplain did not employ concentration camps or mass executions, and their leaders did not issue explicit orders to exterminate the "Ovambo" as a people, but the early 1900s wars still constituted environcide. Invading armies intentionally targeted the population through its environmental infrastructure, systematically destroying homes, fields, crops, fruit trees, and food and water reserves. Moreover, the perpetrators of the violence drove the population from their homes and villages, exposing them to hunger, thirst, and the elements. Since the Portuguese did not explicitly intend to annihilate the population, their actions do not constitute genocide or ethnocide in legal terms. Intentionally displacing the population and destroying the environment on which they depended, however, risked both ecocide and genocide. Massive displacement from parts of the floodplain in the early 1900s caused immediate humanitarian catastrophes. The displacement also transformed the floodplain environment into "bush," or wilderness that was incapable of sustaining large human societies. Bush encroachment and the deterioration of environmental infrastructure in the medium term greatly hindered postwar reconstruction, with long-term impacts on human health, environment, and society.

Environmental Infrastructure in the Bush

Often considered the last wilderness continent, the persisting influence of the Nature–Culture dichotomy perhaps is nowhere felt more than in the study of Africa. Africans in rural Africa were held to thrive on Nature's bounty in good years or perish in times of scarcity. Even in peace time, the Ovambo floodplain was a highly challenging environment. Except for where it abuts the Kunene River in the northwest, the floodplain lacks any *natural* permanent sources of surface water. Before the 1960s construction of a canal and pipeline system that carried water from the Kunene River, human-made waterholes sustained year-round habitation. Because harvest failures were common, households sought to build up food stores. Sun drying was the most commonly used method to preserve foods. Farmers dried grains, fruits, nuts, and leafy vegetables (Ovambo spinaches or cabbages) before storing them in huge grain storage baskets (sing. *omaanda*, pl. *eemaanda*) lined on the inside and sealed at the top with clay. The *omaanda* was raised off the ground on three wooden legs to protect the basket from humidity, fungi, rodents, and insects, and it was shielded from the rain by a roof. As long as the basket lining and the seal remained unbroken, the millet could be safely stored and preserved for three to five years. Households kept the grain storage baskets secure in the center of the palisaded homesteads.[3]

FIGURE 10.1. The large basket type of granary (*omaanda/eemaanda*) found in every household in the early 20ᵗʰ century was still widely used in northern Namibia in the 1990s. They were sealed with clay on the interior and could preserve grain and dried fruit and vegetables for up to three years (Photo author, 1993).

A single homestead consisted of various sets of connected structures designated for sleeping, living, working, storage, and guests, some walled in, some open and consisting solely of a roof. The entire complex contained 10–20 or more dwellings and roofs and was enclosed by a sturdy palisade, giving the homesteads the appearance of small forts. The homesteads offered protection against human and animal predators as well as a sheltering microenvironment for poultry, garden crops, and budding fruit trees. At intervals of 5–10 years, households recycled part of the wood from the old homestead to construct a new homestead close by. The old homestead site became a highly prized crop field, enriched by decaying wood and household debris. Farmers also distributed livestock manure and the ashes of household fires in their fields and burned crop debris and weed on their fields. Floodplain farmers therefore created fertile dark earths in much the same way as many indigenous American farmers did, and they continue to do so, whereas the process in the Americas ended soon after contact. Floodplain villagers shaped the land beyond the homesteads by cutting, coppicing, burning, and deploying their browsing and grazing livestock.[4]

During the early 1900s, most farms had a waterhole or shared one with several neighboring households. The waterholes, which drew on highly localized mini-aquifers fed by the annual rains, had a limited yield and capacity. An average water hole, at best, could sustain a few households through the long dry season. Households first relied on the surface water left by the rains and floodwaters from the north that filled the flood channels and pans during the rainy season. When the surface water ran out, cattle owners relocated their herds from the floodplain villages to remote cattle posts for the dry season to preserve the water stored in the village waterholes. Without the thousands of waterholes that dotted the Ovambo floodplain, the extreme semiarid environment could not have sustained the high population densities characteristic of the immediate precolonial and colonial eras. The long dry season was not the only reason that the floodplain constituted a highly challenging environment. During the rainy season, the lower areas of the floodplain often became inundated as a result of heavy local rains and floodwaters that flowed from the north; the floodplain slopes gently downward from the mountains of southcentral Angola toward the Etosha Pan in the south. Settlement and crop cultivation were limited to the low ridges that lined the north-south flood channels. Rainfall was concentrated in the months of December–March, and heavy downpours caused flooding in the fields on the slopes of the ridges. To manage flooding, farmers each year rebuilt raised fields consisting of large mounds up to a foot high, intersected by a system of drains, a highly labor-intensive undertaking. The wet season and the flooding isolated villages and homesteads and exposed people to insects and disease. Malaria in particular was rampant in the floodplain.[5]

Loss of the environmental infrastructure was disastrous in the semiarid floodplain. During the wet season, it meant exposure to cold, humidity, and disease. During the dry season, it meant hunger, thirst, and blistering heat. Environcide was not unique to the early 20th-century Ovambo floodplain. Late 19th-and early 20th-century wars of colonial conquest, and violent "pacification" campaigns intersected with the

First World War, with armies living off the land; extracting labor, food, and other resources; scorching savanna and forest villages and farms; recruiting thousands of young men for military service on the continent and Europe, and displacing millions across the continent. Famine and epidemics accompanied and followed the wars resulting in massive losses of life.[6]

Colonial Wars and the First World War

During the first decade of the 20th century, Germany extended its control from central to northern Namibia, establishing military posts at Namutoni and Okaukuejo. The Namutoni and Okaukuejo forts, on the eastern and western edges of the Etosha Pan, respectively, straddled the two main trading routes from central Namibia to the Ovambo floodplain. In 1901, the Catholic missionary Erneste Lecomte reported that the Oukwanyama King Weyulu Hedimbi planned to evacuate the population of the southernmost district of his territory to stave off any German aggression.[7] Most of the territory of the preconquest Kingdom of Oukwanyama was located north of the modern Angolan-Namibia boundary. Fear of a German invasion dissipated between 1904 and 1907 because the Germans were preoccupied with the Herero and Nama wars in central Namibia. The Germans never managed to establish any formal control in the Ovambo floodplain itself: the forts at Namutoni and Okaukuejo remained the northernmost outposts of German colonialism. Although the failure to control the Ovambo floodplain may have saved its inhabitants from German genocidaires, it did not protect them from environcidal warfare.[8]

Repeated Portuguese invasions of the Ombadjas launched from across the Kunene River failed in 1901 and 1904, but the invaders succeeded in gaining a foothold east of the Kunene by constructing Fort Roçadas in 1906.[9] In 1907, the Portuguese captured the heartlands of the two Ombadja kingdoms, but fierce resistance prevented them from consolidating their control. Even in their newly established forts in the Ombadjas, the Portuguese were not secure. Ombadja guerilla bands

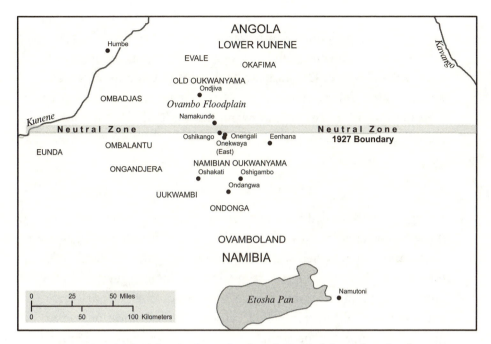

MAP 10.1. Ovambo floodplain, Southern Africa (Angola-Namibia) during the early 20th century.

harassed their patrols and supply lines. Short of food, Portuguese forces lived off the land, raiding Ombadja villages for provisions and to mete out exemplary punishment. The destructive raiding warfare continued into 1910, when famine conditions overpowered the capabilities and will of many to resist. The situation enabled the Portuguese to subjugate the remainder of the Ombadjas, leaving only the large Oukwanyama kingdom outside of Portuguese control.[10]

The outbreak of the First World War, however, spectacularly reversed Portuguese successes. Late in 1914, German forces chased the Portuguese garrison out of Fort Naulila in Ombadja along the Kunene River, encouraging the Ombadjas and Evales to rebel. Forces from Oukwanyama joined the rebels, and the Portuguese garrisons in the remaining forts were massacred or beat a hasty retreat across the Kunene River. In response, Portugal sent a large expeditionary army from Lisbon to the northern Ovambo floodplain in 1915, which regained the lost territories and invaded Oukwanyama. At the same time, British-South African forces conquered German South West Africa and occupied the southern Ovambo floodplain, meeting no resistance from the Ondonga, Uukwambi, Ombalantu, Ongandjera, Uukwaluthi, Onkolonkathi, and Eunda polities. Intermittent warfare in the region continued until the defeat and death of the Oukwanyama King Mandume Ndemufayo (King Nande's successor) at Oihole in 1917.[11]

War and Famine

Droughts compounded the effects of war during the early 1900s. The threat of Portuguese invasions and raids caused Ombadja villagers to abandon their farms, fields, and cattle posts along the fertile banks of the Kunene River and migrate deeper into the interior, away from the only natural permanent water source in the floodplain. The 1904 Portuguese invasion, although repelled, caused further dislocation and aggravated the impact of the drought, culminating in a famine.[12] The 1907 full-scale Portuguese invasion of the two Ombadja kingdoms led to the systematic destruction of farms and fields, displacing many from their homes, fields, and water sources, and burdening Oukwanyama with large numbers of desperate refugees.[13] The influx of refugees aggravated food shortages, causing a terrible famine in 1908.[14]

The 1910–11 rainy season was interrupted by a drought that coincided with the unrest caused by the sudden death of the Oukwanyama King Nande. Both events impacted agricultural field work.[15] The Portuguese made use of the confusion to occupy the Okafima polity (north of Oukwanyama) and the inland regions of the Ombadjas, as well as Dombondola and Onkwankwa directly south of Ombadja. Famine reigned through February 1912, aggravated by the failure of the key marula (*Sclerocarya birrea*) tree fruit harvest.[16] The German Rhenish Mission Society (RMS) mission stations were a safe haven for many because the missionaries distributed food that had been provided by the German colonial administration in Central Namibia. The 1912 harvest proved average, relieving immediate hunger but insufficient to accumulate any substantial food stores.[17]

The 1912–13 cropping season brought another poor harvest. By May 1913, many Christians from the RMS congregations at Ondjiva, Omupanda, and Omatemba in Oukwayama left to look for food or to seek work down south in the German colony.[18] The next year's harvest was somewhat better in Oukwanyama and ended the famine, but was again too meager to fill the granaries and rebuild food reserves.[19]

Whereas the immediate food emergency was over, the rains were too scant to recharge the aquifers that fed the water holes. The RMS missionaries reported that immediately after the 1914 May–June harvest, the female members of their Ondjiva congregation deepened the mission's source of water while most of the young men left to seek work in the German colony.[20] By October 1914, water was so scarce in the Ombadjas that the Portuguese garrisons relied entirely on dirty and brackish water from local water holes.[21] It was under these already precarious conditions that the floodplain was drawn into First World War, condemning its inhabitants to unprecedented levels of dislocation, disease, and hunger. In oral histories recorded during the last decade of the 1900s and the first decade of the 2000s, the 1915–16 vortex of war, flight, and famine was identified by multiple names that captured different aspects of the humanitarian disaster. Interviewees distinguished the *Ekuuku* or *(N)Ekomba* ("Sweeper Famine"); the *Ondjala yOwaala* (the "Famine of the War"), during the Portuguese invasion in August–September 1915; and the *Okapololo*, the "return" or "replay" of the *Ekuuku*, which lasted until March 1916. Others made no such distinctions: for Paulus Wanakashimba, who originated from Ombadja, the entire period from the 1907 invasion of Ombadja to the 1915 famines appeared a single, drawn-out Hieronymus Bosch-like tableau of mayhem and despair.[22]

Even in years of good rainfall and harvests, the latter part of the dry season (September–November) was a period of nutritional stress in the villages as people subsisted on a monotonous diet of grain porridge with perhaps some dried fruit. Highly nutritional fresh fruits (marula and birdplum) and vegetables (Ovambo spinaches) only became available after the rainy season was well underway in January–March. Men also herded the cattle back to the villages from the remote cattle posts at this time, adding dairy to the diet. The fresh foods bridged the period until the harvest of the main field crops (grains, beans, melons) in May or June. During typical years, tree fruit was a key nutritional supplement; in times of scarcity, it was a lifesaver. The valuable fruit trees, however, were found only on farms and fields in established older villages. There were no fruit trees in new refugee settlements because the trees were human-propagated and it took 10–15 years before the trees matured and started bearing fruit. Late in 1914, continued water shortages for human and animal consumption and scorched pastures indicated that the rains were late in southern Angola.[23] When the rains finally arrived, they were sufficient to cause at least some of the millet seed to germinate. On the RMS communal fields, which had been well weeded, harvest prospects seemed promising.[24]

Insect plagues, however, accompanied the rains and severely damaged the fruits of the birdplum fruit tree early in 1915.[25] Voracious caterpillars known as army worms consumed the young grain plants, wiping out entire fields in mere days.[26] With the staple crop destroyed by insects, little to no food reserves, and a partial tree fruit harvest, at best, and only in the older villages, people resorted to gathering "wild" fruits and roots.[27] The 1915 grain harvest was a failure across the entire region of southern Angola.[28] In early May, a Portuguese official urgently requested supplies of maize, millet, and sorghum to prevent starvation among the African population of the Huila district, west of the Kunene River.[29] The South African invasion of the German colony foreclosed any prospects for German food aid via the RMS missions.[30] Existing food stores at the RMS missions ran out quickly and could not be replenished. By August, mission activities ground to a halt as famished children abandoned the schools to look for food. Many deserted the German mission stations in Oukwanyama to seek sanctuary in central Namibia.[31]

In 1915, Shemange Abraham's family found itself in the path of the advancing Portuguese army at Mongwa, on the far northwestern outskirts of Oukwanyama. Although very few people lived at Mongwa at the time, it was known to herdsmen and travelers for its well-filled waterholes. Advancing during the dry season when water was extremely scarce, the Portuguese took the strategic waterholes and fortified their position at the site. When King Mandume's forces counterattacked and surrounded Mongwa, Shemange Abraham's family fled north across the Kunene to Humbe.[32] On September 3, 1915, after a fierce three-day battle at Mongwa, and with his army running low on food and ammunition, King Mandume retreated. He burned his palace at Ondjiva and fled south to seek refuge in the South African-occupied southern floodplain. Thousands followed his lead.[33] Desperate for food and perhaps hoping for some relief, refugees informed the Portuguese army entrenched at Mongwa that King Mandume had ended the siege and fled south.[34] Only then did the Portuguese become aware that they had won the Mongwa battle.

Famine and war fueled one another. Refugees from Ombadja, Evale, and northern and central Oukwanyama scattered north, northeast, and especially southward to seek the protection of the British–South African forces that had marched into the southern floodplain. Simeon Hangula Haikali's father was among the refugees that fled the violence of war, only to face starvation.[35] Fearful of the Portuguese advance and the deepening famine, the German RMS missionaries evacuated all but their southernmost missions at Namakunde and Omatemba.[36] In December 1915, the RMS missionary Welsch reported from Omatemba that the famine had reached unprecedented levels.[37] Those who still had some food left hid it or fought off starving refugees and neighbors to defend it.[38]

A missionary report from April 1916 noted that 45 deaths due to dysentery occurred in the immediate surroundings of the RMS mission at Namakunde alone, despite the distribution of grain and beef to the needy.[39] Around April there still would have been standing water in the flood channels and pans, but it would have been stale and polluted, creating the ideal conditions for the spread of dysentery and other intestinal diseases. The RMS missionaries despaired that they could not even save their own congregations: many of their adherents starved to death or fled further south to Ondonga or central Namibia.[40] Desperate for food, people en masse turned to cutting down palm trees to eat the tree marrow, nearly exterminating the adult palm trees in Oukwanyama, another example of how desperate refugees may be driven to ecocide.[41]

The British–South African occupation forces sold nearly 86,000 pounds of maize meal as food aid in the southern-most parts of Oukwanyama and throughout the southern floodplain. Such a quantity would have been enough to feed approximately 3,000 people for a month or 12,000 for a week. Most of the maize meal was sold for cattle.[42] The onset of the rainy season in December 1915 somewhat eased the food and water shortages. In southern Oukwanyama, however, refugees who had lost everything could only plant their fields after the South African official stationed at Namakunde distributed free millet seed. By early 1916, the ripening on-farm tree fruit and vegetables relieved the famine conditions for those who had access to them.[43] Ines Ndewiteko Kanana and her siblings survived the famine at her father's remote cattle post by subsisting on their cows' milk. Her mother had stayed behind in their Oshiede village and miraculously lived to see the spinaches sprout on her fields. The availability of the spinaches, which grew only on crop fields, allowed the children to return home, where they found Portuguese soldiers with ox wagons stationed at their village.[44]

Uprooted by the war, weakened by the famine, and short of seeds and tools, refugees only managed to prepare very small and inadequate fields.[45] The dark shadow of famine lingered as a continuous stream of refugees entered the far southern Oukwanyama, where South African troops were based. By April 1916, so many refugees had arrived that a German missionary feared that there would be not enough land available to allocate everyone even a small crop field.[46]

War, Refugees, and Demographic Collapse

The enormous dislocation makes it difficult to assess the human cost of the 1915 and 1916 years of war and famine. Oral histories attest to the horrifying magnitude of the crisis; the naming of the "Sweeper" (*Ekuukuu* and *Ekomba*) famines conveys the extent of their devastating impact: the famine swept people away. Survivors underscored the dramatic loss of life. In the household where Helemiah Hamutenya grew up, 3 adults and 2 children of the family of 17 perished during the years of 1915 and 1916.[47] Magdalena Malonde, who was about 20 years old during the sweeper famines, evokes a sobering image: "In some home-steads you would find the head of the household dead in the *olupale* [the area where guests were received] and his wife dead in the *epata* [the "kitchen," a wife's separate living quarters]."[48] The *Ekuukuu* occurred the year after João Baptista Lungameni Paulo was born in Otananga, near Oshigambo (in Ondonga). His parents told him that people survived by eating not only flower bulbs, but even their own leather clothing. Several of his siblings perished during the *Ekuuku*, which he was told felled young and old indiscriminately. Tree fruit was scarce, the skies were dry, and the dead bodies of people and cattle lay scattered on the land.[49] Mwulifundja Linekela Haiyaka and Natalia Shihewa were the only young children to survive the famine in their respective villages.[50] Sondjali Nsio, whose younger brother was born during the year of the sweeper famine, emphasized that famine and war killed many.[51] As Ines Ndewiteko Kanana recounted, the Portuguese wars caused great misery, taking the lives of many of the older people, including her maternal grandfather, the blacksmith Shevajena. The *Ekuukuu*, she stressed, claimed lives in almost every household.[52]

The RMS missionary Welsch estimated a 45 percent mortality rate in the Oukwanyama areas that he personally had visited on the South African-occupied side, concluding that the mortality was as high as 75 percent in some of the Portuguese-occupied areas.[53] One large household of 40 people fled to Welsch's Omatemba village, where King Mandume assigned them a homestead close to the mission. Soon thereafter, another refugee family moved into the same homestead, which had become vacant because the initial family had been wiped out. Welsch noted that the mortality rate of people who remained on their own homesteads in the areas occupied by the Portuguese was lower than the rate among people who fled southward, abandoning their homes and villages. He attributed the greater survival rate to the ability of those who remained on their farms and in their villages "to gather wild fruits."[54]

Welsch's "wild fruits" referred to the fruit of the marula and birdplum trees, which actually were cultivated in the Oukwanyama villages and only occurred on farms and in fields, constituting key environmental

infrastructure. Those who remained on their farms in central Oukwanyama retained access to the vitamin-rich fruits when they ripened as
well as to the "wild" spinaches that grew on the fields after the first rains.
In February 1915, when the famine ended, 20 percent of the members of
the Ondjiva and Omatemba RMS congregations had died. The statistic
is particularly telling because the RMS converts were a relatively privileged group that benefited from missionary patronage and food aid.[55]

Portuguese officials estimated mortality at 80 percent for the southern Angolan district of Huila, which included the Ombadja and Oukwanyama polities. The figures may have been inflated because they
served to support Portuguese claims for war indemnity from Germany
at the post-First World War Versailles peace negotiations. Still, the Portuguese estimates echo the appraisals of the oral histories, missionary
documents, and British–South African reports that the mortality rate
was staggering.[56]

The Portuguese figures stated that the Ombadjas lost 70 percent of
their pre–First World War population of 60,000; Evale lost half its population of 19,000; and Oukwanyama lost 30 percent of its population of
119,000.[57] Thus, of a prewar population of 200,000 in the northern
floodplain polities, 88,000 people perished based on the figures provided by Portuguese officials. In 1925, the Portuguese-occupied northern Ovambo floodplain, which included most of the territories of preconquest Ombadjas, Oukwanyama, Evale, and Okafima, contained
35,000 inhabitants. In 1928, with the transfer of the formerly contested
border strip known as the "Neutral Zone" to Portuguese rule, the Portuguese estimated that 50,000 Oukwanyamas lived in their territory and
only 8,000 on the South African side in Ovamboland. A 1933 count by
the colonial headmen of Namibian Oukwanyama, however, enumerated
41,000 people on the South African side, an increase of 33,000 people
in five years. The South African officials counted anyone in what they
considered Namibian Oukwanyama as Oukwanyamas, although the
population included a large number of refugees from the Ombadjas and
Evale. Another Portuguese internal report, based on a 1913 tax assessment, provides a figure of 26,000 inhabitants for the Ombadjas. At first
glance, this figure appears to discredit entirely the Portuguese war

damages claim that the pre-1915 Ombadja population was 60,000. In the context of the massive destruction, death, and displacement that the Portuguese invasions and raids had caused before 1913, however, it is not unlikely that the Ombadjas had lost a considerable percentage of their populations before the tax assessment. Indeed, the issue with the Portuguese reports may be less about inflated figures than about their strategy to shift responsibility to the First World War period in order to blame the Germans for the demographic collapse. The strategy no doubt was facilitated by the British-authored *Blue Book* of 1918, which accused the Germans of mass atrocities during their war against the Herero and Nama. The *Blue Book* was intended to support the British claim that the Germans were unfit to rule colonies because they did not abide by the laws of war that bound civilized nations.[58] In the long run, the strategy proved very successful. The genocidaire image stuck to the Germans, and the Portuguese got away with mass murder.

Even if the numbers were exaggerated and considerably fewer than 88,000 people perished between 1901 and 1916, the more reliable later figures nevertheless suggest that the number of people displaced by the wars and famines was enormous. Portuguese sources indicate that the Ombadjas alone contained 26,000 inhabitants in 1913; in 1925, however, the population of the entire Portuguese-occupied northern floodplain was only 35,000. The larger share of the 35,000 would have been inhabitants of Portuguese-occupied Oukwanyama. The 1933 South African colonial census counted 41,000 inhabitants in Namibian Oukwanyama, the large majority being refugees from the northern floodplain. Most had settled south of the border after the Portuguese invasion in 1915. A 1904 map of the Kingdom of Oukwanyama, produced by a missionary who had lived in the area, showed less than 10 percent of the more than 300 identified villages in what is modern Namibia.[59] Although refugees founded a small number of new villages south of the modern Angolan-Namibian border between 1905 and 1915, the total population of the villages in the far southern districts of Oukwanyama is unlikely to have been more than 2,000–3,000 souls. The remainder, up to 39,000 of the 41,000 inhabitants that were counted in Namibian Oukwanyama in 1933, consisted of refugees from the northern floodplain who arrived after 1915.[60]

Refugees and Postwar Reconstruction

Many fled not once, but twice. Most refugees from the northern flood-plain initially resettled in the Neutral Zone, a 6-mile-wide strip of disputed territory coadministered by a South African and a Portuguese official stationed at Namakunde after 1915. The Portuguese soldiers and policemen could not operate in the demilitarized Neutral Zone, making it a haven for refugees from Angola. The transfer of the Neutral Zone to the Portuguese colony of Angola in 1926 consequently caused great unrest among the refugees who had resettled there. The agreement between South Africa and Portugal about the transfer allowed the inhabitants of the Neutral Zone a two-year window to decide whether to move across the border into South African-controlled territory or remain and become Portuguese subjects. The South African officials stationed in the area that were eager to secure more laborers for colonial Namibia's white farms and mines strongly encouraged the refugees to move once again. The refugees were fearful of Portuguese retaliation and tax and labor exactions, and by 1928, many of the inhabitants of the Neutral Zone chose to move into the South African colony. As a result, the South African territory ended up with approximately 40,000 refugees from the Ombadjas, Oukwanyama, Evale, and Okafima. Northern floodplain refugees who had fled to southern floodplain villages beyond the Portuguese territories during the war also resettled in the new Oukwanyama, which was being carved out south of the border.[61]

The farms and fields north of the border, which the refugees had abandoned in the 1910s and in the 1920s, were a bounty to those who had remained or who chose to return to the old heartlands of the northern floodplain after the war, just like abandoned or captured indigenous American environmental infrastructure in Eastern North America had provided a shortcut to European settlers. Having temporarily sought safety in Humbe during the 1915 invasion, Shemange Abraham's family during the 1920s moved to Omupupu village. At the village, his family found many abandoned and burned homesteads. Once they built make-shift temporary dwellings, their resettlement was greatly facilitated by the environmental infrastructure of waterholes, fertile soils, and fruit trees that remained among the ruins.[62] In the Ombadjas, the depopulation due to death and flight was so severe that entire districts that before the 1904 Portuguese invasion had been described as densely populated lands of villages, farms, and fields were empty and overgrown bush wilderness by the 1930s, completely lacking the environmental infrastructure to sustain permanent human habitation.[63]

The refugees who settled south of the border had to construct new homesteads and new villages from scratch. The impact on the environment south of the border was dramatic. During the late 1910s, 1920s, and 1930s, the refugees transformed the sparsely populated bushlands of the middle floodplain into a densely settled landscape sustained by an environmental infrastructure of farms, fields, fallows, and pastures, a new Oukwanyama. Missionaries who witnessed the process in the 1920s and early 1930s warned that the wholesale destruction of the woodlands would cause desertification.[64] Between 1915 and 1933, the thousands of refugees established 6,000 new homesteads in the middle floodplain, clear-cutting 6,000–12,000 hectares for their farms and fields, and cutting large amounts of larger and smaller trees beyond the clearings to construct homes, storage facilities, palisades, and fences. The resulting deforestation was dramatic.[65]

Outbreaks of epidemic disease plagued the refugees' postwar reconstruction efforts. In 1925, influenza killed over 200 people in Namibian Oukwanyama's refugee settlements, four times as many as in neighboring Ondonga, which had not witnessed the same levels of displacement. The virus had spread from central Namibia to the north in 1924; by November, it had sickened thousands. The flu recurred during the late 1920s Famine of the Dams, killing large numbers of people in October 1928, notably children and the elderly, and again in 1931 and 1932. In 1932, it spread to the isolated refugee settlements east of the floodplain, killing one of its principal leaders, Hamkoto Kapa. Smallpox spread across the border from Angola in 1927, but a hasty colonial vaccination campaign prevented it from becoming an epidemic south of the border.[66]

The refugees had ready access to wood to construct new homes in the 1920s and 1930s middle floodplain because the region had been thinly populated. Clearing land from trees and bush, and building homes, palisades, and fences to keep wild and domestic animals out of the fields, however, was highly labor intensive. The refugees initially built very basic dwellings and cleared small fields, and over the years, they gradually expanded the homesteads and their fields. Digging new water holes was a high priority. Refugees preferred to settle next to missions, the residences of wealthy leaders, administrative posts, established villages, and the sites of old abandoned villages because they offered a rudimentary infrastructure, especially water sources. Deeper wells were rare and often confined to missions or administrative posts, but they offered higher water yields than the shallow waterholes that typically supplied most households. In addition to sources of water, existing villages and old abandoned villages also boasted precious fruit trees that boosted nutritional resources. Moreover, established villages provided social support, labor, and local environmental knowledge, and were a source of seeds, domestic animals, and emergency food supplies. Ohamwaala, Onengali, Oyongo, and Okatale, for example, were older villages with key environmental infrastructure and in the 1930s witnessed rapid population growth with the influx of refugees.[67] Remnants of environmental infrastructure in the Okalongo region in Namibia associated with the historic kingdom of Haudanu, abandoned during a 19th-century war, greatly facilitated the resettlement of Ombadja refugees from Angola during the 1920s. In the Okalongo region, refugees discovered fruit trees and repaired silted up water sources. Once they had built rudimentary dwellings, their wives and children joined them.[68]

Missions offered spiritual security to traumatized refugees as well as key resources. The competing Anglican and Finnish Missions sponsored refugee resettlement to gain converts. The missions served as safe havens throughout the early 1900s war period and as bases from where groups of converted refugees established new villages after the war ended. Paulus Haufiku Hamutenya, his brother Aalon Hamutenya, and their cousin Elia Weyulu were adherents of the German RMS mission. When the Portuguese authorities expelled the German Mission from the Neutral Zone, the trio led their followers across the border into northern Namibia and founded the villages of Edundja, Ondanda, and Eenhana. In 1933, less than a decade later, Edundja alone had 353 inhabitants, mostly Christians.[69]

If older villages were nearby, the inhabitants of new villages could make use of the established villages' water sources when water was scarce. During her 1920s childhood, Nahango Hailonga spent nearly half of every day carrying water from the neighboring village of Oshululu to her home in the refugee settlement of Onamahoka. During the dry seasons, the first refugee-settlers at Okalongo drew water from neighboring established villages across the border. To accommodate the refugees between 1926 and 1928, South African officials had three large water reservoirs constructed south of the new border.[70] The first groups of refugees who settled east of the floodplain in Namibia relied on preexisting water holes created and maintained by hunters or cattle herdsmen. In turn, the villages created at these sites served as bases for groups of men to dig water holes and wells that supported the founding of yet other villages.[71]

The Famine of the Dams

That the refugees were still in the process of constructing the new environmental infrastructure in the late 1920s and early 1930s is reflected in the spatially differentiated impact of the 1920s Famine of the Dams. The older established villages of Angolan Oukwanyama were barely affected while the rudimentary war refugee villages south of the border suffered severely. Climate was a factor in the famine: global climate dynamics exposed Southern Africa and Namibia to severe drought conditions that also contributed to the Dustbowl in North America. Southern floodplain Ondonga, which was always more vulnerable to drought and famine, was severely hit, and Ondonga famine refugees fled to Namibian Oukwanyama villages. The influx of drought refugees proved too much of a burden for many of the new villages in the middle floodplain: they were short of water sources to begin with and soon ran out of food as well. The newest refugee settlements east of the floodplain could not cope because they were too isolated to help one another and were abandoned. The drought did not trigger a famine in Oukwanyama north of the border; in fact, famine-stricken inhabitants of Namibian Oukwanyama acquired large amounts of water and millet from the villages in Angola.

Whereas the Famine of the Dams features dramatically in historical accounts south of the border in Namibian Oukwanyama, it hardly left an impression in the historical memory north of the border. Oral histories from north of the border stressed that the Famine of the Dams was an exclusively Namibian experience. Born in the late 1920s, Emilia Kulaumone Namadi was told that people in Namibia dug dams in exchange for maize and that Namibians crossed into southern Angola en masse to buy grain.[72] Natalia Tulipomwene Jonas was born in Namibia's Onaminda in the early 1910s; she and other members of her family, who were all war refugees from Evale, worked on the dams and received millet rations in return.[73] The colonial boundary between the two Oukwanyamas coincided with an environmental infrastructural fault line that was unveiled during the early stages of the famine: the new Oukwanyama south of the border became a recipient of food aid, while the old Oukwanyama north of the border was the source of the food aid. The existing elaborate environmental infrastructure north of the border rendered households resilient to the drought. South of the border, however, the shortage of environmental infrastructure translated into a lack of resilience, and famine ensued.

The 1926–28 exodus to the South African-occupied side after the transfer of the Neutral Zone to the Portuguese colony placed an enormous and immediate burden on the meager water and grazing resources in the refugee villages. With the loss of the Neutral Zone, "refugee" Oukwanyama shrunk in size almost overnight, while its human and livestock population tripled. In crossing the border, the refugees lost access to most of the territory of the southernmost districts of the old Oukwanyama and its environmental infrastructure. Even without a meteorological drought, the massive 1926–28 migration from the Neutral Zone in and of itself might have caused a serious "drought" by depleting available dry season pasturage and water sources. In fact, confronted by scarcity in their rudimentary villages south of the border, a substantial

number of refugees returned to the Angolan side during the late 1920s.
Some migrated back to Angola even before the onset of severe drought
conditions.[74] By September 1928, severe water and grazing shortages
south of the border caused conflicts between herdsmen over pasturage
and water.[75] The picture was grim:

> All over the country one sees emaciated cattle, unable to move
> lying down. The owners . . . build shelters to protect the beasts
> from the heat. It all depends on the owner whether he is prepared
> to carry food and water, anything from five to seven miles, to these
> animals.[76]

By early 1929, cattle owners in refugee Oukwanyama had lost over 5,500
out of an estimated total of 20,000 animals.[77]

Kalolina Naholo explained that rainfall and harvests north of the border had been much better during the late 1920s than further south.[78] It
is possible that localized rainfall north of the border had indeed been
more abundant, but her statement may also reflect a sense that the
drought had less of an immediate impact north of the border because
the environmental infrastructure in that area made society more resilient. South of the border, only Oshikango districts and parts of Omhedi
and Onengali districts had been settled before 1915. The five other districts of Namibian Oukwanyama were entirely the product of the refugee exodus from the northern floodplain and the Neutral Zone between
1915 and 1928. The first four Namibian Oukwanyama districts to appeal
urgently for food aid were Onenghali, Omhedi, Ohaingu, and Onanime.
The first two contained several established villages, but, as a result they
also may have attracted the bulk of the refugees. Onenghali's headman
Hamkoto Kaluvi supported the Oukwanyama Queen Ndilokelwa and
her entire entourage in his village.[79] Hosting large numbers of refugees
and their cattle may have overtaxed the Omhedi district's water and
pasture resources, explaining why the district reported the highest number of cattle losses during the 1928–29 drought: Omhedi lost 3,234 cattle,
nearly three times as much as in the next most severely affected district
of Ohaingu. Ohaingu had virtually no established villages and very little
environmental infrastructure.[80] January 1929 brought only patchy rains

that delayed seeding, and at the end of the month, many fields still lay fallow. Although some households had access to ripening tree fruit, the fruit harvest in western Ovamboland failed. Moreover, the fearsome army worms that had ravished the millet fields in 1915 reappeared. Fortunately, sustained rains in February brought flocks of migratory birds that quickly contained the voracious insects.[81]

To the south of Namibian Oukwanyama, Ondonga was affected the most. The colonial administration initiated limited food distribution at the end of January 1929, with the intention of helping the neediest to bridge the hunger season until the expected May harvest.[82] When the harvest proved very poor, many Ondongas abandoned their farms and sought refuge at neighboring communities. In Ombalantu, they were turned away. "Large numbers" of famished Ondonga migrated to Omulunga, east of Oshiede in Angolan Oukwanyama, where land and water were abundant, because many farms had been abandoned by people who had earlier fled southward into Namibia. Others fled deeper into southern Angola, as far as Ombadja and Humbe. Hundreds stayed closer to home and sought shelter in Oukwanyama villages south of the border. The influx of the drought refugees was an additional burden on already scarce food and water supplies in Namibian Oukwanyama.[83] Earlier in 1929, the South African administration sold food aid grain at subsidized prices that were payable in cattle, but soon shifted to cash-only transactions in order to cut costs. The shift forced people short of food on the Namibian side to sell their cattle across the border in southern Angola. Portuguese officials used the new dependence on grain from their colony to entice refugees who had settled in Namibian Oukwanyama to return to their side of the border.[84]

In July 1929, the South African administration introduced food-for-work programs in Ondonga but not in the refugee resettlement region of Oukwanyama. The program mobilized women, youth, and men to dig shallow reservoirs by hand to improve the dry season water storage capacity.[85] As the famine persisted, the number of reservoir projects was expanded. The reservoirs were referred to as "dams," thence the name for the famine: the "Famine of the Dams." The South African officer in charge of the Namibian Oukwanyama region, H.L.P. Eedes, worried about the growing crisis among the resettled refugees. He surveyed the 135 village leaders in his region during the same month that food aid was introduced in the neighboring Ondonga region. All but one headman in Namibian Oukwanyama reported that their villages were affected by famine, and with the exception of three, all reported a poor harvest.[86] Pastures were very poor, and most of the cattle already had been driven from the villages to remote cattle posts in Angola to save scarce water resources at the villages.[87]

The survey also indicated the shocking fact that half of the villages were without any sources of water. Almost one out of every three villages west of the old Ondangwa-Oshikango road, where the bulk of the refugee villages was located, relied on water sources that were 1 to 5 miles away. East of the road, the inhabitants of almost half of the villages drew water from similar distances. All affected villagers relied on water sources from beyond their own farms or that of their neighbors, and many must have relied on the resources of another village.[88] The drought caused large-scale population displacements. Forty-two percent of all Oukwanyama villages counted Ondonga resident households, and 30 percent reported having Ondonga refugee households squatting in their villages in makeshift shelters. Moreover, one-fourth of all the villages had lost households that had moved back to the Portuguese side of the border to escape the famine conditions.[89]

The South African administration was loath to expand its famine relief program because of the high anticipated cost. Only after the headmen and chiefs in Ovamboland acceded to the colonial demand to pay taxes as compensation for the food aid and future programs did the administrator for South West Africa, the highest South African official in Namibia, reluctantly agree.[90] Still, it was not until October 1929, after the Portuguese administration restricted cross-border food trade and grain shortages increased, that the food aid program was expanded to the refugee Oukwanyama region. The Portuguese authorities prohibited the grain trade in order to force Oukwanyama refugee households on the South African side to return to Angola.[91] Few people, however, initially signed up for food-for-work rations at the single Etale Dam (Etale is the local word for "dam") in Namibian Oukwanyama because the October rains seemed promising, and farmers instead chose to cultivate their own fields. Most adult men had left the villages to barter for food, herd cattle, or look for work in central Namibia. Only in December, after the first attempts to seed the millet staple clearly had failed, did the food-for-work project at Etale attract sufficient laborers, and by mid-month, the dam was completed using only hand tools.[92] Primarily women, girls, boys, and older men worked on the dam. The rations that the workers received as payment for their labor differed: young children only received half a pound of millet grain, older girls received one pound, older boys and adult women 1.5 pounds, and headmen and their assistants received 2.25 pounds per day.[93] While the food-for-work program in Oukwanyama ended at the dam's completion and the onset of the rainy season, the dam construction program in Ondonga continued.[94]

By December, the few herdsmen who optimistically had guided their cattle back to their villages after the promising October rains had again returned to the remote cattle posts in Angola. Water scarcity became so acute that it forced refugees to evacuate several of the most recently settled villages south of the border. The refugee-settlers at Eenhana, east of the floodplain, and Okalongo, on the western edges of the new Oukwanyama, only survived by importing potable water in drums from Angola or from Oshikango, 25 miles west of Eenhana, probably using ox wagons. The Ombadja refugee-settlers around Okalongo all relied for their drinking water on a single mission well.[95]

In December 1929, the headmen of the villages of Onekwaya and Ohalushu reported the first cases of starvation in Namibian Oukwanyama. The ripening of marula tree fruit in January 1930 checked the spread of starvation in Onekwaya, an older village that had been part of the pre-1915 Oukwanyama kingdom.[96] In addition to fruit trees, the Oshikango district's villages and farms contained another life-saving tree: the Real Fan Palm. Like marula trees, palms were closely associated with human settlements and propagated by farmers. Villagers who tapped the trunks for palm wine could consume the drink themselves to relieve their hunger and thirst, or "gift" the fermented beverage to headmen in exchange for grain, effectively creating or renewing social networks with the rich and powerful. Because it killed the plants, headmen normally restricted tapping. The desperate conditions of the last months of 1929, however, led to an unbridled surge of tapping, virtually eradicating the palm species in the border region.[97]

For some, patronage eased the burden of the droughts. Elisabeth Ndemutela's household weathered the Famine of the Dams thanks to the generosity of her "uncle," headman Nuyoma Moshipandeka, the son of a former king who was close to the South African administration. Headman Jikuma, who also had close ties to local colonial officials, donated food to recently widowed Mwulifundja Linekela Haiyaka, who lived with her mother and grandmother in an all-female household.[98] When patrons were unwilling or unable to meet requests for help, tensions arose. Food thefts rose sharply as social networks frayed:

> The natives who own a small supply of corn or dried melon pits are afraid to sleep at night and spend their time patrolling their kraals. The principal headmen will on no account assist their subjects and remind me of a lot of ghouls in the way they guard their grain baskets.[99]

Isolated refugee communities lacked the safety net of wider social networks and patrons, and many households simply were too impoverished to purchase food in Angola. Twemuna Shifedi's family had helped pioneer the settlement of Ondaanya, east of the already remote village of Edundja in the 1920s. When the drought struck, all but two of the village's households were forced to leave.[100]

The mounting tensions concerning mutual obligations and the unevenness of the impact of the crisis are captured in an alternative name for the famine: *Ondjala yokoyolangudja*, the "Enriching Famine." The name is a scathing commentary about people who took advantage of the shortage of food by selling grain at a high price. The profiteers included headmen in the new Oukwanyama who assisted colonial officials with the distribution of food aid.[101] Portuguese traders, African traders, and farmers in the Old Oukwanyama across the border were also implicated. The crop fields in Angolan Oukwanyama were the principal source of the large quantities of millet purchased by individual and institutional buyers from Namibia's Ovamboland.[102]

In January 1930, Assistant Native Commisioner Eedes, stationed at Oshikango in the heart of Namibian Oukwanyama and the instigator of the earlier famine survey, openly urged his superior, C.H.L. Hahn, to introduce food aid in Oukwanyama. Hahn refused, and when Eedes refused to back down, Hahn had Eedes sacked.[103] Before the famine, Hahn had engineered the massive refugee resettlement in Namibian Oukwanyama to enlarge the colony's limited black labor supply. Famine and flight from Namibian Oukwanyama threatened to expose the refugee resettlement project as a colossal failure and a callous gamble with the lives of 40,000 refugees. Fearing for his reputation, Hahn downplayed the extent of the impact of the famine in Namibian Oukwanyama, refusing to acknowledge any problems, and delayed the implementation of famine aid.

In May 1930, the administrator of colonial Namibia sent his director of works to Ovamboland to assess the extent of the food crisis in Oukwanyama, suggesting that he had lost confidence in both Eedes and Hahn. The director's staff encountered "considerable resentment" when breaking open the grain storage baskets in 172 randomly selected households in Ovamboland and measuring their contents. The survey found that the baskets were empty in 25 percent of the households in Oukwanyama and 50 percent of the households in Ondonga. Some households did not have a single grain of millet left, surviving on watermelon pits alone. In June 1930, extrapolating from the sample findings, and based on a monthly consumption of 30 pounds of grain per person, the director of works concluded that 25 percent of households in Namibian Oukwanyama had no food supplies left. Far worse was that only 25 percent had ten or more months of grain stored, meaning 75 percent of households would be out of food before the next harvest, which was ten months away. The situation was even more desperate in Ondonga: only one out of every 13 households had enough grain stores to last until the next harvest.[104]

The director of work's report concluded that the successive droughts, that is, climatic factors, were entirely responsible for the famine.[105] There was no mention of the massive refugee displacement that immediately had preceded the famine and that had strained the grain storage system to the breaking point. Moreover, even if the granaries had been filled to the brim, the grain storage infrastructure would have sustained at most a population of 5,000–10,000 before the massive migration triggered by the transfer of the Neutral Zone and could not have been expected to support 30,000 or more newly arrived refugees. The report, therefore, seemingly willfully obscured the responsibility of Native Commissioner Hahn and the South African administration in creating the humanitarian crisis in Namibian Oukwanyama, even as it exposed the famine as real.

Unsurprisingly, in light of his predecessor's fate and the cover-up perpetuated by the report of the director of works, Eedes's successor sounded rather cautious in his first report on conditions in the refugee villages. The new assistant native commissioner wrote in July 1930 that there were "no real cases of hardship up to the present. There are undoubtably [sic] a number of families who have very little food, for whom some relief must be afforded in the coming months. I am of [the] opinion that the majority are not so bad off as might be expected."[106] His tone was much less upbeat in his next report, after touring the region and meeting with anxious headmen who told him that more and more households had crossed the border back into Angola. He stated that "numbers of the poorer people are at the end of their resources and will expect food assistance very soon." Perhaps to appease his volatile superior, the assistant native commissioner hastened to explain: "[It is] difficult . . . to gauge the food supply, natives naturally make the position much worse than it really is. . . . . Mr. Hahn informs me that he has the question of corn and mealie [maize] meal well in hand and as any sudden emergency can be met there is no cause for anxiety."[107] Only in August 1930, 8 months after Eedes's appeal to Hahn and 20 months after the refugees' leaders first had requested food aid, did the administration finally introduce large-scale food aid distribution in Namibian Oukwanyama. The assistant native commissioner noted in his August report that the food aid "released the tension and re-established confidence in the Administration," possibly a tacit acknowledgement that the situation had been far more critical than his superior, Hahn, had been willing to admit.[108]

Most government food aid was either sold at a subsidized price or distributed through food-for-work programs aimed at improving the water infrastructure. Over 120,000 pounds of grain were sold during the seven months between August 1930 and the program's end in April 1931. Presuming that each individual required 30 pounds of grain per month, 4,000 person months of government famine aid were distributed through subsidized sales. The lion's share was sold at the assistant native commissioner's office at Oshikango in refugee Oukwanyama. Although the data are incomplete, it appears that a small number of individuals, including headmen, bought fairly large quantities of food, obviously for resale or redistribution. By far the most food aid per capita was sold in the eastern part of Namibian Oukwanyama, which lacked any pre-1915 environmental infrastructure, because it was the area that most recently had been settled by the refugees.[109] The projects aimed primarily to employ women, and in September 1930, many more men had been involved than the administration deemed advisable.[110] Migrant labor opportunities for men, however, had declined steeply due to the impact of the worldwide economic depression.[111] Since food was distributed in a limited number of locations, people routinely walked long distances to receive it, sometimes on a daily basis. Although her relatives provided her with some food, Pauline worked at the Onenghali Dam food-for-work project, almost 5 miles from her village. Salome Tushimbeni Haihambo, a girl from a single-parent household that recently had fled from Angola to Namibian Oukwanyama, also worked at Onenghali Dam; her new home in Omataku was 12 miles away.[112]

The South African administration suspended free distribution and food-for-work aid in January 1931, except in central Oukwanyama. Between August and December 1930, the total amount of grain distributed free or through food-for-work programs was approximately 350,000 pounds or roughly 12,000 person months, based on a monthly consumption per person of 30 pounds.[113] The food distribution data echoes the pattern indicated by the qualitative narratives: households in the older villages in central Oukwanyama that contained established environmental infrastructure were more resilient to the famine than new refugee villages with limited environmental infrastructure.

If the 4,000 person months of food aid that was sold is included, the total government food aid distributed in Namibian Oukwanyama was the equivalent of 16,000 person months. That is, 16,000 out of a total of 41,000 people or so may have relied entirely on food distribution for an entire month. The data closely matches the projections that the director of works made based on the sample survey of granaries, suggesting that one-third of the inhabitants of Namibian Oukwanyama had endured acute famine conditions for at least a month. As before, the food distributed through the government centers south of the border had been purchased in Angola. In addition, many households located near the Angolan border bought grain directly from producers or traders in Angolan Oukwanyama. In fact, supplying the high demand for grain in northern Namibia ultimately depleted food stores in southern Angola. By September 1930, food shortages immediately north of the border were as acute as they were in Namibia's Ovamboland. Sales by Portuguese traders dropped in October because the Portuguese administration restricted the purchase of grain from producers in districts where supplies were running low.[114]

The Portuguese administration in southern Angola, however, lacked both the means and the will to enforce its policies. In September 1930, large numbers of inhabitants of Namibian Oukwanyama, in particular those from "the wealthier class," reportedly were buying food from farmers and traders across the border. By December 1930, Portuguese traders once more were conducting a brisk trade, although they only accepted payment in the form of breeding stock. The increase in the price of grain—in September 1929 a heifer could be exchanged for 40 pounds of millet, whereas in December 1930 it only yielded 25 pounds— should therefore be seen as a reflection of both an increased demand in the new Oukwanyama south of the border and a decreased supply in old Oukwanyama north of the border.[115] At the latter price, the 120,000 pounds of grain that was sold by the colonial administration as food aid during the seven months between August 1930 and April 1931 would have cost the inhabitants of Namibian Oukwanyama 4,800 head of cattle. This is equivalent to the number of cattle that the refugees had lost early during the drought in 1928. Losses to drought and sales of cattle to purchase food therefore may have cut total cattle holdings in Namibian Oukwanyama in half over three years, an enormous loss, especially for refugees. Cattle were not only a source of food but also of animal power (plowing and transport) and manure to maintain soil fertility in the crop fields. On the other hand, households in Angolan Oukwanyama that sold grain during the famine would have made a handsome profit and may have seen their wealth in cattle grow substantially.

Good rains in December 1930 and January 1931 greatly improved food availability throughout Ovamboland, as highly nutritious vegetables and tree fruit became available in the established villages. In Namibian Oukwanyama, the rains allowed millet to be sown as early as October 1930. Seed shortages prompted the Oshikango-based South African officer to supply small quantities of seed to the "poorest."[116] In 1931, when the famine was over, the colonial administration also distributed "food aid" to 30 Oukwanyama headmen who had been especially helpful during the famine because "they had great difficulty in meeting demands for food, which their status [as patrons] obliged them to supply and at the same time they did not want to ask for free food."[117] The colonial authorities in Oukwanyama distributed 50,000 pounds of grain during the first four months of 1931, most of it for free.[118] The distribution of food aid to the Oukwanyama headmen in part may have been an attempt by Native Commissioner Hahn and the administration to restore relations with the refugee leaders whose appeals for famine aid earlier had been so blatantly ignored. Not only Hahn's reputation had been at stake but also that of the South African administration.

In Ondonga, food-for-work programs continued until early March. The remaining famine supplies were sold or issued to the "very old and indigent natives who will have no means of subsistence until they reap their own crops." By the end of March, abundant rains not only had filled waterholes and pans but also the newly constructed dams. In early April, for the first time in three years, the semiannual flood or *Efundja*, fed by rains upstream in Angola, submerged the lower lying areas in the Ovambo floodplain on either side of the colonial boundary.[119]

Conditions improved more radically in Namibian Oukwanyama than elsewhere in Ovamboland: by January, all fields had been planted. Ovambo spinaches, melons, and tree fruit became available in January and abounded in February in the older villages. Abundant rains, however, also increased weed growth. With many people physically weakened because of the famine, weed control was difficult. The colonial official instructed the headmen "to keep a watchful eye on field owners who may neglect to keep the fields free from weeds."[120] The 1931 harvest in Namibian Oukwanyama was above average; the headmen estimated that the millet supplies would last for two years.[121] For the first time in several years, the cattle herds were brought back to the villages from the remote cattle posts and paraded at the customary cattle fests. In September, conditions had improved to the extent that clan elders and headmen allowed women's initiation ceremonies (*Efundula*) to take place. The ceremonies paved the way for bridewealth exchanges and marriages, symbolizing that the crisis was over, and normal life could resume.[122]

With its inhabitants weakened by years of drought and famine, however, bubonic plague invaded Ovamboland. First discovered in January 1932, shipments of food aid from South Africa introduced the disease into the region. Between early 1932 and mid-1933, the plague infected 300 people, killing 61. Half of the cases occurred in Ondonga, mostly in remote villages. In 1934, 1935, and 1936, all laborers recruited in Ovamboland received prophylactic vaccinations against the plague. The disease remained endemic in the region, killing 27 of the 175 infected people in 1935.[123] Plague was preceded and accompanied by influenza in 1928, 1931, 1932, and 1935, and measles in 1928 and 1938, although the official reports provided little or no details.[124] One factor in the lack of data about disease undoubtedly is that a single colonial officer covered Namibian Oukwanyama. Still, Native Commissioner Hahn may have intentionally underreported the occurrence of disease before, during, and in the aftermath of the famine in order to downplay the extent of the humanitarian crisis. Following the dramatic removal of his predecessor, Eedes, the new officer may have felt compelled to tow Hahn's line. Commenting on health conditions in July 1930, the officer vaguely reported that "[a] number of death[s] of old . . . natives occurred." In October 1930, he attributed additional deaths to "poverty." That "poverty" might have been a euphemism for "starvation" can also be inferred from the officer's explanation for livestock losses during the height of the famine in September–November 1930: "death from poverty."[125]

Disease and starvation took their toll among the resettled war refugees in the Oukwanyama district in the South African colony in the late 1920s and 1930s. Officials underreported their number to hide the failure of their migration project. Poor communications also played a role; refugee communities were isolated and scattered widely across a region that was largely devoid of environmental and conventional infrastructure. But although livestock losses were high and a significant number of famine refugees migrated across the border into Portuguese territory where environmental infrastructure (abandoned just a few years earlier) was plentiful, a tragedy comparable to the 1915–17 crisis was only narrowly averted.

In the early 1930s, the inhabitants returned to the remote rudimentary villages that they had abandoned during the height of the Famine of the Dams. During the 1930s, 1940s, and 1950s, all the refugee settlements south of the border grew into villages with a robust environmental infrastructure of farms, fields, fruit trees, and food and water stores. The villages subsequently provided bases for colonizing the wilderness areas west, south, and especially east as the population increased through migration from Angola as well as natural increase. By the 1960s, the war refugees from the northern floodplain had created an entirely new Oukwanyama, replenished with villages, farms, and fields south of the border in what in 1900 had been in local terms *ofuka* (wilderness). In many respects, the new landscape of villages seemed the same as the environment they had abandoned in the 1910s, and there was much continuity, but many innovations, as well. Water holes in 1960 Namibian Oukwanyama were the principal source of dry season household water, just as they had been in the old Oukwanyama in 1915, but deeper wells constituted a new source of water. Millet continued to be the main staple crops and stored food, but by 1960 most farmers prepared their fields with an ox- or donkey-draught plow. The use of the name of Ouk-wanyama for the new district suggested societal and cultural continuity but hid the fact that a substantial part of its inhabitants fled across the border from the preconquest Ombadjas and other neighboring polities. The historical agency of the refugees, making choices about what elements of the social and environmental infrastructure (including their identity) to retain and where to innovate again recalls the situation of the indigenous American refugees displaced to and in the North American West, although the indigenous Americans moved over much larger distances into radically different environments. It took the war refugees in the Ovambo floodplain a generation or more to develop a new viable environmental infrastructure using both local and extra local resources and investments, including resources gained through migrant labor.[126] Their experience lends perspective to the ingenuity and resilience of the indigenous American refugees, highlighting the great challenges they faced and overcame, and the high cost they paid in creating new lives, livelihoods, and ways of life in the American West and, subsequently, on the reservations.

Environcide in the Floodplain

The Portuguese invaders of the Ovambo floodplain destroyed entire villages including farms and granaries to terrorize the population into submitting, punish those who resisted, and secure water supplies for their men as well as water and grain supplies for their horses. The invasions occurred during the dry season to minimize losses of men to malaria and animals to horsesickness. Because in the semiarid floodplain, all dry season food, forage, and water stores were concentrated at people's homes and farms, the Portuguese invaders made Ovambo villages a key object and weapon of war. The direct destruction of environmental infrastructure was particularly critical in the Ombadjas. In its larger and smaller neighbors, including the Oukwanyama kingdom, war and drought caused the massive displacement of the population from their environmental infrastructure, exposing people to famine and disease. Survivors fled to the southern floodplain polities that were not affected by the Portuguese invasion or hid in the woodlands beyond the villages. Some survived because they fled to remote cattle posts where the villagers sent their cattle during the dry season to preserve the water stores at their farms and villages. As the violence and insecurity continued, those who returned to their farms may have fared better than those who remained in the wilderness because the former had access to on-farm ripening fruit and vegetables. Thousands or tens of thousands perished due to starvation and disease during the war and drought-ridden years from 1915 to 1917. Food and water stores had been low even before the Portuguese invasion and losing access to key environmental infrastructure for such a sustained period was often fatal.

As insecurity persisted in the Portuguese-controlled northern floodplain, many refugees sought to rebuild farms and fields in the South African middle and southern floodplain. Existing villages with their environmental infrastructure of granaries, fruit trees, fields, and water sources facilitated refugee resettlement. But the decision to transfer the middle floodplain to the Portuguese colony of Angola in 1926 left many war refugees who had resettled in the territory insecure about their future. The South African colonial authorities, eager to maintain the refugees' labor pool for their own economy, played on local fears of Portuguese violence and exactions (tribute/taxation and labor), strongly encouraging the resettled refugees to move once again, this time into an uninhabited stretch of wilderness with little or environmental infrastructure. They promised to supply the refugees with new sources of water, which were virtually absent in the resettlement area. Tens of thousands of the refugees originally displaced during the First World War, once more abandoned their homes and fields and moved between 1926 and 1928. But when a severe drought descended upon the floodplain in 1928, they had not yet been able to build any semblance of a resilient environmental infrastructure with food and water stores to face droughts. The refugees suffered dramatic livestock losses, disease and starvation reemerged, and a repeat of the massive death and displacement that marked the 1915–17 humanitarian crisis was narrowly averted by importing food from the northern floodplain in Angola.

Thus, the late 1920s Famine of the Dams was not merely a natural disaster, but just as much the long-term consequence of the war and refugee displacement that occurred in the 1910s. South African officials callously gambled with the lives of over 30,000 war refugees, enticing them into a wilderness on their side of the border that had little or no infrastructure to sustain them, risking another humanitarian crisis in a highly drought-prone region. Many of the refugee leaders and ultimately the refugees themselves decided to go along, showing once more how victimhood and historical agency can intersect and blur.

Conclusion

ENVIRONCIDE AS A CRIME AGAINST HUMANITY AND NATURE

THE IMPACT of war on the society and the environment nexus is underestimated, and as a result, the challenges of postconflict reconstruction are underappreciated. This is partly due to the Nature–Culture dichotomy, which continues to frame analyses of human–environment processes. In segregating the realms of Nature (and natural physical and biological processes) and human Culture (the physical and metaphysical creations of humans including, artifacts, art, and technology), the dichotomy obscures the synergy between the two. In addition, the relationships between war and society and war and the environment are not only symbiotic but also reciprocal: in destroying or damaging environmental infrastructure, war simultaneously erodes societal infrastructure. This book analyzes the interactions between war, society, and the environment in terms of the impact of armed conflict, violence, and population displacement on society *and* environment, in other words, environcide.

The Nature–Culture dichotomy especially, but not only, downplays the extent of the interplay of war, society, and the environment in contexts that are regarded as premodern or non-Western. Because modern "Western" societies are defined by their use of technology and science, they are presumed to have control over Nature: Nature and the environment have been subjugated or domesticated. Artifacts and domesticates are a product of human ingenuity and action; their destruction in war is therefore a direct attack on human society and thus a war crime or a crime against humanity. In contrast, non-Western and premodern societies are defined by their inability to master the environment and control Nature; when peoples are depicted as being dependent on and living in and by Nature, the impact of war effectively is cast as war against Nature. As the chapters demonstrate, however, premodern and non-Western societies, including the proverbial indigenous hunter-gatherer nations of the North American Great Plains, the Great Basin, and the Pacific Coast, did not live in and by Nature. Rather, they relied heavily on their dwellings, settlements, and elaborate food stores in order to survive and thrive in challenging environments. Creating and maintaining key environmental infrastructure was based on substantial, sustained investments. Preparing buffalo hides for tents, fur for winter coats, and pemmican stores, and maintaining sedentary villages to store and process the acorn staple, for example, were all extremely labor-intensive activities that were essential for the ways of life and livelihoods of the indigenous societies of the Great Plains and California, respectively.

Environcide and Total War

The Nature–Culture dichotomy also influences how the impact of war is evaluated and judged. War against human Culture and its manifestations is the domain of humanitarian concerns, war crimes, crimes against humanity, and genocide. Wartime crimes against the environment and Nature, however, even in the modern West are the subject of an entirely separate body of international law. As a result, the indigenous American demographic collapse is attributed to biological processes in a contagion model that largely ignores the context of war. War and displacement, however, exposed indigenous Americans to diseases both old and new, and fostered the optimal conditions for the epidemics. People, animals, goods, and microbes migrated to towns and villages over large distances, originating from disease-ridden European cities as well as similarly disease-ridden slave ships from Africa. Many migrants from Europe and all forced migrants from Africa were the product of war and violence. Soldiers on the move and their animals, especially when massed in armies, constituted major incubators for disease and deadly sources of contagion. East Coast indigenous American refugees carried diseases inland to interethnic Ohio towns in the 1700s. Disease often followed displacement: plague in the towns of the 16th- and 17th-century war-torn Low Countries; smallpox and measles in the villages of 16th-century Spanish America and the 17th- and 18th-century fortified towns of North America; smallpox in 18th-century Ghana; rinderpest in 18th-century Western and Southern Europe; smallpox and rinderpest in 19th-century Sumatra; and influenza, measles, and the plague in early 20th-century Namibia and Angola.

Assessing the impact of war and displacement on societies' environmental infrastructure highlights both the direct and indirect impact of war. The direct destruction of environmental infrastructure triggers societal collapse. Before the 1860s US Civil War, settlers and soldiers in North America systematically targeted indigenous American settlements, food stores, and the surrounding fields and orchards during campaigns and raids. Often, settlers timed raids during or shortly after the harvest so that they could destroy or capture standing or reaped crops, maximizing damage to their opponents and optimizing opportunities for capturing food. Indigenous Americans used the same tactics against settlers, burning their farms and fields.[1]

Sherman and Sheridan's scorched earth operations during the Civil War were not new. They carried on a practice of environcidal warfare targeting human society *and* Nature that marked conflicts across the globe throughout the 16th, 17th, and 18th centuries. Sherman, Sheridan, and Crook innovated by using scorched earth tactics against the indigenous Americans of the Plains during the winter, when the latter were at their least mobile and most vulnerable. Destroying indigenous Americans' dwellings, food stores, winter furs, and horses brought them to the brink as surely as conventional scorched earth practices had against sedentary opponents. But during the 16th and 17th centuries, sieges continued during the winter, and in the 1740s, French Field Marshall Saxony campaigned in the winter, taking Brussels by surprise. Dutch forces in 1880s Aceh timed campaigns to coincide with the immediate post-harvest period when the staple irrigated rice crop was drying in the fields and villages could be easily destroyed or captured before the food could be supplied to the rebels. Early 20th-century Portuguese colonial campaigns took place during the dry season because rainy season operations exposed soldiers and horses to such debilitating diseases as malaria and horsesickness, and the swampy terrain and the dense vegetation hindered movements and facilitated enemy ambushes. Like winter warfare on the North American Plains, dry season warfare increased the vulnerability of Ovambo floodplain farmers because the limited remaining food and water stores, as well as most of the population, was concentrated in the villages.

The separation of war and society on the one hand and war and the environment on the other as discrete fields of inquiry also misses the indirect repercussions of war on society and the environment through population displacement. When war or the threat of war displaces populations from the environmental infrastructure they maintain and depend on, then the absence of human consumption, use, and management cannot be regarded merely in terms of an automatic restoration of a natural ecosystem in an antagonistic Nature–Culture framework. Moreover, it equally highlights how forced removals and war-induced migrations robbed populations of their livelihoods and means of survival, exposed them to disease, trauma, and death.

War-displaced populations also produced a multiplier effect that impacted three spaces: the home environment, the refuge environment, and the space in between. The three spaces are difficult to distinguish because locals and newcomers defined them differently depending on their perspective. For many early European settlers in the East of North America, who had lost their homes, livelihoods, and ways of life as refugees from war and religious violence, North America seemed a secure haven and a new home at the same time.

In the "home" area (the area that a group of refugees had permanently or temporarily abandoned), population displacement led to the deterioration and the eventual collapse of environmental infrastructure such as occurred in much of central and south America in the 1520s–40s, in Holland in the 1570s, in Brabant and the Huron-Wendat homeland in the 1630s and 1640s, and the Great Plains and Aceh in the 1870s.

Such newcomers as European settlers and displaced indigenous Americans might profit from abandoned environmental infrastructure, as demonstrated by the systematic alienation or capture of indigenous American food stores, livestock, villages, farms, fields, and park landscapes. European colonists and displaced indigenous Americans preferred to settle at or near sites of current or abandoned old settlements because of the presence of sources of water, clearings, fertile dark earths, and fruit- or nut-bearing trees or shrubs.

The newcomers' use of temporary or permanently abandoned environmental infrastructure relied on the same principle as armies living off the land: the exploiting of local environmental infrastructure. Tapping into and appropriating indigenous American infrastructure was critical in the early stages of the European conquest and settlement of the New World: The De Soto expedition could not operate beyond the densely settled American interior of the southern half of North America because there was no adequate indigenous American environmental infrastructure to sustain it, and the destructive impact of its own scorched earth practices prevented Spanish colonization of much of the southern half of North America. De Soto's soldiers' scorched earth tactics had been so effective that many indigenous American towns along its inward bound route had been entirely abandoned, leaving the Spaniards short of food and shelter.

Newcomer refugees might trigger conflict over existing environmental infrastructure with the local or other displaced populations once they reached an area of safety. The Great Plains became a battleground between different groups of migrants and refugees in the 18th and 19th centuries. Holland towns denied rural refugees services (access to the hospital in the case of Amsterdam) or entry to the town (in the case of Gouda to all but the wealthiest). These refugees, moreover, had little or no recourse to the law once behind the town walls and often saw their cattle impounded. Hunger and cramped unhygienic conditions resulted in towns becoming tinderboxes and plague-infested death traps. Ironically, refugees (and their descendants) from Brabant and Flanders may have played key roles in the Dutch Republic's waging of environcidal and total war in Brabant and Flanders in the 17th century.

Alternatively, locals and newcomers might cooperate to create new workable environments and societies in safe havens. Mid-17th-century Huron-Wendat villages welcomed and generously accommodated war refugees from the Iroquian Neutral Nation of the Wenro from Lake Erie as well as Algonquian groups displaced from the St. Lawrence Valley. Different groups of refugees from the East Coast collaborated to create the new interethnic indigenous American Ohio towns of the Pays d'en Haut in the 1700s. Refugees from different polities of the northern Ovambo floodplain (in modern Angola) created a new Oukwanyama in the southern Ovambo floodplain (in modern Namibia) after war, drought, and famine had displaced them in the early 1900s.

The in-between places along the routes from the refugees' original homes to their new homes are equally difficult to define because, with the hindsight of history, they may appear temporary even as they perhaps were considered permanent from a contemporary perspective. Neutral-Wenro and St. Lawrence Valley Algonquians found only temporary safety in the Huron-Wendat villages in the 1640s; in 1648, many fled with their hosts to French Quebec. A number of Huron-Wendat subsequently were forcibly removed in the early 19th century to west of the Mississippi River. Refugees from further east drove the Comanche and other groups from the Eastern Woodlands onto the Great Plains. The Sioux, Comanche, and their allies subsequently managed to found powerful empires on the Great Plains. Instances of cooperation and conflict overlapped as groups created alliances and fought to gain access to such resources as buffalo herds, horses, guns, and gunpowder. Those who lost out, including the Shoshone, moved off the Great Plains into the highlands further west, but not before having shaped and having been shaped by the environmental and societal dynamics on the Great Plains.

The Five Nations Iroquois displaced many other groups, gaining control over the fur and gun trades before the US government forcibly removed the Iroquois in the 1830s. In 18th-century Florida and California, Spanish soldiers hunted down escapees from Spanish missions; raids for captives typically helped to maintain mission populations. During the 19th century, US authorities increasingly concentrated indigenous

Americans on reservations, in marginal environments that could not sustain their populations. The reservations were little better than concentration camps: confined to the areas by guards, living in poor shelters, and malnourished because of inadequate government-issued rations, indigenous Americans suffered high incidences of diseases and mortality. Similarly, Aceh refugees who sought safety in the forested mountains surrounding the Aceh River Valley resided in rudimentary shelters near their dryland *ladang* crop fields. Without access to their permanent homes, irrigated rice fields, orchards, and food stores, the displaced were highly vulnerable to the weather, malnutrition, and disease. Smallpox struck down displaced indigenous Americans in the 17th- to 19th- century Americas, Washington's Continental Army's soldiers in their inadequate winter quarters, famished Asante soldiers in the Gold Coast, and displaced Aceh refugees in the forests and mountains of Sumatra alike.

While armies and arms technology changed dramatically between the 1500s and the early 1900s, environcide remained at the core of the practice of war. Revolutionary technology brought ever more advanced firearms and other weapon systems. Ongoing innovation produced increasingly sophisticated warfare, including Vauban forts, trench warfare, and aerial bombing. National armies based on forced mass conscription replaced warrior castes, mercenaries, and local militias. The emphasis on military mass conscription as a radical break between early modern and modern warfare, however, overlooks the heavy burden pre-mass conscription armies imposed on civilian labor directly (for example as pioneers and transport drivers) and indirectly (by living off the land).[2] Overall, revolutionary change *and* deep continuities marked the practices of war and its impact on the society-environment nexus. Although soldiers became less motivated by and dependent on plunder and extortion, the opponent's population and environmental infrastructure remained a main target, objective, and means in war.

War targeted environmental infrastructure through the effects of armies living off the land; cutting off enemy resources; displacing populations; and plunder, theft, and extortion of property, wealth, and means of livelihood. Prior to the development of extensive logistical capabilities during the course of the 19th century, armies lived off the land by necessity. In 16th- to 19th-century Europe, troops billeted or quartered in towns and the countryside during military campaigns. Host families were required to provide meals, fuel, and shelter to the soldiers and to supply forage and straw for their horses. In addition, local populations had to pay war taxes, and soldiers routinely extorted civilians and robbed and pillaged homes, villages, and towns. In this respect, 16th-century Spanish soldiers in the Americas and in the Low Countries behaved no differently than 17th- and 18th-century Dutch, French, English, Italian, German. Austrian, Javanese, Asante, or indigenous American combatants.

By and large, late 19th- and 20th-century armies relied on their own logistical apparatuses. Soldiers received food rations during campaigns and billeting became less common. US Army soldiers who fought against the indigenous Great Plains societies, Dutch soldiers who combated Aceh rebels, and Portuguese soldiers who clashed with Oukwanyama and Ombadja fighters resided in forts that stored food and munition supplies. Yet, for horse fodder, the US cavalry continued to be dependent on the availability of pastures, and soldiers hunted buffalo to supplement their rations. Moreover, during its 1870s winter campaigns, US Army forces often ran out of food and consequently resorted to foraging. The Dutch forces engaged in the Aceh war were largely supplied from overseas. Supply columns transported the food rations to the different posts. The Dutch army imported meat on the hoof, although Dutch foragers also robbed cattle from Aceh villages. The soldiers also captured and consumed small stock found at the villages, especially chickens. Moreover, to a significant degree, the soldiers appear to have been dependent on vegetables and fresh fruits that they or their camp followers purchased at Aceh markets, or took from villages. Beri beri became epidemic when the soldiers' direct access to vegetables and fruits declined as the Dutch retreated within the concentrated line and the soldiers could no longer forage. Portuguese soldiers who invaded the Ovambo floodplain in the early 1900s brought their own rations but depended on local sources for drinking water. The soldiers also raided villages to plunder granaries to feed their horses and captured livestock.

Only in the second half of the 19th century were armies and soldiers no longer entirely and directly dependent on extorting food, shelter, money, and services while in the field. Yet, environcidal warfare continued into the 20th century. In fact, denying sustenance and resources to the enemy by cutting off supply lines and disabling the logistical apparatus remained a key principle of war in practice. At a tactical level, it meant incapacitating the enemy during battles, sieges, and campaigns by starving the enemy of food and supplies. At a strategic level, it meant destroying or capturing the opponent's resources and productive infrastructure to win the war. Thus, whereas living off the land disappeared from the military manuals, scorched earth remained central to how war was waged. During the Dutch Revolt, Spanish and rebel commanders alike went to extreme lengths to destroy any resources that their opponents could use. Between the late 1400s to the late 1800s, Spanish, French, Italian, Spanish, German, Dutch, English, and indigenous American forces in the Americas and in Europe used the same principle, as did Dutch soldiers and their indigenous opponents in 18th-century Java, Sri Lanka, and Maluku, 19th-century Aceh, and Portuguese invaders in the early 20th-century Ovambo floodplain.

Environcide constituted total war because the violence was not limited to the opponent's combatants and military infrastructure alone. Although the late 18th-century Dutch VOC Hongi campaigns sought to enforce the company's monopoly of spice tree production, the VOC soldiers and their allies burned all the fruit trees, crops, and entire villages, and had standing orders to massacre the men and spare only women and children. The environmental infrastructure that sustained human populations was intentionally targeted. Destroying that infrastructure directly or indirectly by denying access to it both through scorched earth practices or forced removals resulted in famines and plagues as lethal and debilitating as such modern weapons of mass destruction as nuclear warheads, napalm, mustard gas, and Zyklon B.

Risking Genocide

Genocide as a crime is a modern phenomenon only insofar as it was legally defined as such in the 1940s and 1950s. Since genocide requires the intent to exterminate a people, culture, society, or group, annihilating a group as collateral damage, or by accident, environcide does not fit the narrow legal definition of genocide. Yet the orders given by such commanders as the Duke of Alva during the Dutch Revolt, Governor-General Valkenier during the Java Wars, or Sherman and Sheridan during the "Indian Wars" that, respectively, all Protestants rebels, all Chinese rebels, and all male indigenous Americans be killed constitute inferred intent. As such their commands are comparable to Von Trotha's extermination order during the German Herero-Nama wars, the Nazi Wannsee Protocol, and the broadcasts by radio Mille Collines calling for the mass killing of Tutsi Rwandese.

Moreover, the policy of starving a population into submission by denying food and shelter, as employed by rebels and royalists during the Dutch Revolt, by settler militias and indigenous Americans in 17th- and 18th-century North America, by Sri-Lankan and Chinese insurgents against VOC settlements in 18th-century Asia, by the US cavalry in the Great Plains, and by Dutch soldiers in Aceh, was both planned and intentional. Starvation and deprivation by destroying environmental infrastructure, including burning or impounding homes, villages, towns, food and water stores, crops, and fields was often premeditated at the highest level of command and systematically implemented in the field. Generals and soldiers surely must have been aware that destroying and denying access to food could result in mass starvation and death. For example, Turk, a Dutch district officer in Aceh, pointed to the success of earlier scorched earth campaigns in Aceh and celebrated Roman famine warfare as a model to be emulated. A senior Dutch military officer noted in the margins of Turk's recommendations that he agreed with the proposals. Moreover, the officer pointed to the case of the French revolutionary armies' success in quelling the Vendee rebellion through starvation. Half a century later, British–South African Native Commissioner Hahn refused to acknowledge that encouraging several tens of thousands of war refugees to migrate en masse and virtually overnight into a wilderness lacking shelter, water, and food resources might trigger a humanitarian crisis in a highly drought-prone environment. When the evidence of famine among the refugees became irrefutable, Hahn obstinately delayed the distribution of food aid. That another episode of mass starvation so narrowly was averted might be interpreted as high-ranking British–South African officials consciously accepting the likelihood that their (in)decisions might result in a humanitarian catastrophe.

Soldiers and armies also lived off the land for their own profit and sometimes for survival. In the process, they not only wrecked environmental infrastructure but also displaced populations from their homes and livelihoods. While their actions may not have been motivated by an intent to exterminate a human society, an animal or plant species, or an entire ecosystem, depriving a population of its environmental infrastructure and exposing it to hunger, thirst, the elements, disease, and other circumstances that threaten a community's survival constitutes environcide and risks ecocide and genocide. Through personal experience perpetrators were well aware of the likely impact of environcidal warfare. They understood that by destroying and appropriating environmental infrastructure and displacing populations from their homes and habitats, they were wielding deadly weapons.

Early during the Dutch Revolt, rebel leader William of Orange and his Spanish counterparts Alva and Requesens knew that large-scale inundations would devastate Holland's countryside. Experts on the water boards who had experienced massive flooding in 1570 warned that the farmers would be ruined and their lands might be forever lost to the seas. Spanish conquistadors, landowners, and officials continued their destructive violence in the Americas despite witnessing the demographic collapse of the indigenous American populations, ignoring the warnings of De Las Casas and the New Laws introduced to limit the conquistadors' depredations. Protestant European settlers in North America, despite their exposure to the Black Legend propaganda, emulated the Spanish conquistadors even as they vilified them for their inhumanity. Many of the settlers were either war, religious, or political refugees from Europe and therefore victims of total war or genocidal violence in Europe, or war veterans from the Wars of Religion, the Dutch Revolt, the Thirty Years War, the English Civil War, or the English wars of Conquest in Ireland.

Military officers of the 17th and 18th centuries were schooled in the classics, and their models were not only Roman and Greek army organization but also the total war practices of Rome's armies that sought to destroy their opponents through scorched earth, starvation, extermination, and enslavement. Rulers and commanders disseminated the rules of war to the armies and civilian authorities through published pamphlets that were distributed in towns and the countryside, military manuals, and orders posted at military camps and garrisons where they were read out to the troops. The rules prohibited unauthorized plunder and pillage, abuse of civilians, damage of civilian property, and extortion: all offences condemned as marauding and punishable by death. The rules also stipulated that soldiers and their officers had to pay for any of the food, goods, shelter, and services civilians had provided them. The articles' main purpose was to maintain discipline and prevent the destruction of the countryside.

During the so-called age of limited war in the 18th century, the rules of war were institutionalized as a model set of laws that humanized and rationalized the ways of war, even as commanders in the field increasingly and openly rejected their use in the practice of war. That revolutionary and Napoleonic-era generals, Civil War Union commanders, and their German counterparts in 20th-century Africa and Europe swept aside the rules of war and preached total war instead is thus not entirely remarkable. Although the rules of war resurfaced during the second half of the 19th century in international and humanitarian legal debates, they continued to have little impact on the actual practice of war. During the 1860s and 1870s Indian Wars and the contemporary Aceh Wars, commanders both preached and practiced total war and scorched earth. The United States and Dutch generals intentionally and consciously risked the extermination of their opponents, whom they considered to be on the losing side of history: the indigenous Americans and Acehnese should either submit, or be obliterated. During the German Wars of Unification, the late 19th- and early 20th-century colonial wars of conquest in Africa and Asia, and the First World War, the practices of war that marked warfare since the late 16th century continued unabated: total war and environcide ruled throughout the "civilized" world during the premodern and the modern eras, risking ecocide and genocide. Thus, environcidal warfare, total war, ecocide, and genocide were often connected.

Unlike genocide, environcide did not necessarily involve spectacular acts of mass violence, although it often did. Like ecocide, environcide may use the everyday violence of war to gradually grind away at the structural integrity of the environmental infrastructure that sustains human and nonhuman communities. In the 18th century, massacres and the pillaging of cities were formally frowned upon—the French sacking of Bergen op Zoom was regarded as an aberration—but armies and soldiers continued to live off and exploit the countryside because kings and generals were unable or unwilling to sustain their troops in the field. In the 18th century, too, soldiers often went unpaid and had to support themselves at the expense of the rural populations. In Western and Southern Europe, the impact of armies living off the land and exacting war contributions and other goods and services may have tripled or quadrupled peacetime state exactions (taxes), a burden that was entirely unsustainable. Kings and generals were aware that their exactions and their soldiers' pillaging risked the collapse of rural societies and their environments, rendering the countryside unable to provide taxes and sustenance.

Even when soldiers did not systematically rape, torture, burn, and kill, the violence loomed inexorably: environcidaires were armed soldiers ready and willing to use spectacular mass violence at a moment's notice. Noncompliance with soldiers' demands for money, food, forage, lodging, horses, and wagons resulted in swift and brutal retribution in the form of military execution and exemplary punishment. Failure to meet armies' demands was considered a hostile act and meant that the soldiers could treat the noncompliers as the enemy.

A major shortcoming of the articles of war was that they only applied to villages and farmers that were considered friendly because they were part of home, allied, or neutral territory, or to occupied enemy territory that was paying taxes and providing food and lodging to the occupation army. Nonoccupied enemy territory could be extorted at will. "Others" were per definition enemies and therefore not protected by the laws of war, although "others" could also be intimates, as was the case during the 16th-century Dutch Revolt when neighbors turned against one another. As new ethnic, racial, and other identities were shaped in the 16th through the 20th centuries, European invaders increasingly defined indigenous African and Asian populations that did not immediately submit as enemies by default. Hence war in their lands was not subject to the laws of war. Overseas territories were treated as lands under military occupation and subject to contributions, tributes, forced labor, extortions, plunder, scorched earth, and military execution. Because Holland during the late 16th century and Brabant and Flanders during the early 17th and early 18th centuries were contested between belligerents, the provinces had an ambiguous status. Armies and soldiers exploited the ambiguity to justify extortions, pillage, and worse by claiming that villagers and farmers either did not meet their demands or supplied contributions and provisions to the enemy, which constituted hostile acts and made the villagers and farmers fair game. In turn, rural communities tried to use the ambiguous status of their war-contested region to petition for the reduction of armies and soldiers' exactions. In the war zones of the 16th- to 18th-century Low Countries and 18th-century France and Italy, rural communities typically tried to comply with the taxes and extortions of all the armed parties in the conflict, which constituted an enormous burden on the countryside. Brabant (and Flanders) carried this burden for almost two centuries from the 1570s to the 1750s, throughout the Dutch Revolt, Thirty Years War, the French Wars, and the Wars of the Spanish and Austrian Succession. The exposure to incessant environcidal war was a major factor in transforming Brabant from one of the richest into one of the poorest provinces of the Low Countries. Ironically, part of the responsibility for the wartime impoverishment of Brabant during the 17th and 18th centuries was borne by refugees from Brabant or their descendants, who repopulated Holland's towns in the aftermath of the devastating 1570s warfare.

Like their counterparts in Europe, indigenous American attackers sacked and burned enemy villages and towns that resisted. Aztec chronicles recount that rulers selectively sacked and burned cities they conquered and massacred the populations of any that resisted. In their 17th-century wars against the Huron and their allies, the Five Nations Iroquois sacked and burned villages that resisted, massacring the adult male defenders and taking the survivors captive. The point is not that the sacking and burning was somehow justified, but to highlight that such excessive violence was a widespread practice in Europe, the Americas, Africa, and Asia.

The Mystic massacre similarly followed the storming of an actively defended indigenous American fortified village, and the French sacking and burning of Schenectady ensued when the village resisted. French soldiers and their allies, too, routinely sacked and burned Five Nations' villages and the surrounding fields and farms in the 17th century. Settlers and indigenous Americans sacked and burned one another's villages and farms. When attacked by European armies, indigenous American populations typically abandoned their villages just before an imminent attack, although they often tried to ambush the attackers before they reached a major village. The sacking and burning of abandoned villages in such circumstances was therefore in line with the war practices of indigenous Americans and Europeans alike. Moreover, the abandonment of a settlement before it could be occupied was considered a hostile act, and thus resulted in the suspension of any protection under the articles of war. Abandoned homes and villages were consequently highly vulnerable to being pillaged, with any contents, doors, window frames, and even walls ripped out and sold or used as fuel. Soldiers also routinely used abandoned buildings as their quarters, causing substantial damage.[3]

Sacking and burning towns and villages, whether accompanied by the massacring and/or taking the survivors captive of or not, served to punish communities that did not immediately meet demands for tributes, contributions, provisions, and other goods and services, and to terrorize and intimidate the enemy into compliance. The proceeds were distributed to the officers and soldiers, comparable to shares of booty allotted to the crew in privateering warfare after capturing an enemy ship. The highly destructive pillage and burn strategy was also used for raids in territory that an army could not effectively control, as a means of denying the enemy any available resources or extorting contributions deep into enemy territory, as was common in warfare in the Low Countries, France, Italy, and Spain during the first half of the 18th century.

Although the threat of pillage and burn destruction always loomed large, in the 17th century and early 18th century, belligerents sought to regularize the exactions they imposed upon the populations by limiting soldiers' private extortions, provided the rural communities supplied their armies with contributions (to pay the armies and officers), fed and billeted the soldiers, and provided forage, transport, and labor services. During the 18th-century Wars of the Spanish and Austrian Succession, the belligerents sought to quarter their armies in contested or occupied enemy territory to place the burden of sustaining their forces on the enemy. The strategy accomplished the same as scorched earth in that it captured resources and denied them to the enemy, making war pay and making the enemy pay for the war.

The belligerents had an interest in preserving rural communities because of their logistical dependency on them. But many different army units operated in war zones, and not all were motivated by long-term strategic and logistical considerations, especially if their main operational area was elsewhere. Armies just passing through had an incentive to make a quick profit by pillaging and looting enemy, neutral, or even allied territories. Moreover, princes and generals had limited control over their own officers and soldiers. Even Prince Maurice of Orange-Nassau, a general who is hailed as transforming the Dutch forces from rebel rabble into a highly disciplined model army in the 1620s, was unable to fully control the depredations his soldiers imposed upon the prince's own private domains. Moreover, any commander faced a dilemma: if he and his men did not loot a village, another commander, possibly even an opponent, might deplete the area of any resources. Finally, unpaid and hungry soldiers and their commanders often did not play by any rules.

Crimes against Humanity and Nature

What also remained remarkably constant throughout the 16th- to early 20th-century period is that in practice armed conflicts were largely resource wars if only because destroying, displacing, and appropriating environmental infrastructure was and remained central to wars and warfare. During the Dutch Revolt, mercenaries plundered and extorted farmers to survive and make a living as they were paid only intermittently.

Spanish conquistadors, American colonial militiamen, and indigenous American and African raiders lived off the proceeds of plunder and enslavement. Old Regime soldiers, officers, and entire armies lived off the land in enemy territory, opportunistically but systematically stealing goods, valuables, and livestock from their local hosts. Jacques Antoine Hippolyte de Guibert held up Rome's Julius Caesar, Dutch Prince Maurits of Orange-Nassau, Swedish King Gustavus Adolphus XII, and Prussian King Frederick the Great as model commanders because they made war pay for itself by living off the land in a disciplined way.[4] Late 19th- and early 20th-century soldiers in North America, Europe, Asia, and Africa were supplied by military rations, but US Army indigenous American guides, scouts, and auxiliaries were paid in plunder: captured horses. Dutch colonial soldiers in Aceh stole livestock, food, and valuables before they set fire to village houses, and Dutch generals exacted tribute from Aceh villages.

From the 16th to early 20th centuries, rulers and generals attempted to make war pay by the imposition of contributions, war taxes, and tributes in kind and in cash extorted through the threat of burn and pillage. Over time, rulers and generals increasingly managed to centralize these exactions. During the 16th, 17th, and early 18th centuries, individual officers extorted safeguards, promising to protect a village or district from pillaging soldiers in exchange for a sum of money. By the mid-18th century, this practice was no longer permissible, and only the top army commanders were authorized to exact contributions in kind and money from civilians.

In sum, the extreme violence may have been partly motivated by material gain (food, shelter, money, land, livestock) rather than an intent to exterminate, but in the process, perpetrators knowingly risked mass murder and genocide by directly and indirectly exposing people to killer famines, deadly epidemics, and massive refugee displacement. Modern mass mobilization wars of the 20th century may have had a leveling effect on income distribution within societies because the top 1 percent of the wealthy carried a larger share of the costs of war, and "the rich simply had more to lose."[5] But, leveling, as in a more equitable distribution of wealth, is not what comes to mind when Dutch, Spanish, French, and English soldiers plundered and displaced indigenous American or European villagers and farmers. Survivors of total war during the 16th to early 20th centuries emerged greatly impoverished, while the dividend for the common perpetrators of environcide, mostly soldiers and militiamen, typically varied from articles of clothing or some tools to a plot of land. Only a very small minority made huge war profits, including the Spanish elites in the 16th and 17th centuries, the urban elites of Holland in the 17th century, Old Regime elites and the North American settler elite during the 18th and 19th centuries, the Dutch colonial and metropolitan elite during the 19th century, and South Africa's colonial elite in the early 20th century.

Intent and planning, and the question of who decided how war was waged, highlights historical agency. Genocide, environcide, ecocide, mass killing, displacement, and forced removals raise questions about the roles of perpetrators and victims. A major issue within discussions about the nature of war, the origins of total war, and genocide is the identification of perpetrators, victims, and bystanders. Identification as a perpetrator or victim has repercussions in terms of moral responsibility, legal guilt, and justice. It also has implications in terms of acknowledging or denying historical agency and ultimately intent. For example, some historians emphasize that viewing indigenous Americans as victims of invasive settlers, animals, plants, diseases, commodification, capitalism, Christianity, land alienation, and genocide facilitates the erasure of indigenous Americans from history. These historians not only stress resistance and the rise of powerful indigenous empires during contact but also highlight the resilience of the indigenous societies and cultures that survive to this day. Detailing the history of indigenous Americans integrates an indigenous perspective into the history of the Americas, thereby raising awareness about past injustices and overlooked contributions.

Moreover, studies about total war, mass killings, and genocide in the 20th century have demonstrated that the dividing lines between perpetrators and victims are not always clear. The perpetrators of the Rwandan genocide themselves had been victims of past genocidal violence. Royalist and rebel leaders and their soldiers alike engaged in mass killing, scorched earth, total war, and environcide in the 16th-century Low Countries with both sides indiscriminately destroying villages and hamlets in the countryside. Some desperate victims themselves chose to become bandits, rebels, raiders or, soldiers, continuing the cycle by violating others. In the Americas, until well into the 19th century, indigenous Americans fought indigenous Americans as readily as Europeans fought Europeans. The Iroquois Five Nations' destructive mourning wars targeted other indigenous peoples, and the 18th- and early 19th-century wars for domination over the Great Plains were indigenous conflicts. East Coast indigenous Americans also repeatedly launched what appear to have been genocidal campaigns against specific settler groups. The Powhatans attempted to exterminate the English settlers in the Virginia colony in the 1620s and 1640s, the Munsee sought to drive the Dutch settlers from the Hudson Valley in the 1640s. During the 1670s and again during the 1740s, English settlers abandoned large regions in New England because of indigenous American raids. In all these cases, the indigenous Americans used scorched earth practices to destroy environmental infrastructure and perpetrated mass killings.

From the early 1500s to the late 1800s, European conquerors and settlers in America included former victims and perpetrators of total war and environcide in Europe. The characteristic Spanish, Dutch, and English settlers' treatment of indigenous Americans as being uncivilized was mirrored in interactions between the Spanish and the loyalists on one hand and the Protestant rebels on the other during the Dutch Revolt. Similar dynamics also were present in conflicts between settlers in the Americas: Protestant Virginians and Catholic Marylanders warred with one another, reproducing the religious strife they had fled in Britain. During the American Revolution, loyalists and rebels had no qualms about destroying one another's homes and properties. Indigenous Americans waged total war and environcide against Europeans and against one another. The categories of perpetrator and victim thus are neither fixed nor predetermined, and refugees and the war-displaced can be victims of history and historical actors, simultaneously and/or consecutively.

Agency and intent can also be read in the face of knowledge about risks and consequences. De las Casas publicly exposed the massive death toll of the Spanish way of war, yet Spanish officials and commanders in the Old and New Worlds continued to employ scorched earth, pillage, and forced removals, even as these practices breached newly imposed laws, including Charles V's New Laws. Dutch and English settlers in the Americas not only emulated the conquistadors but also introduced practices from contemporary war-torn Europe. Eighteenth-century armies continued to use environcidal practices, ignoring, breaching, and dismissing "scientific" and "rational" rules or laws of war that had been explicitly designed to limit the destructive impact of warfare on town and countryside. The 18th-century rules and laws of war defined soldiers' violent extortions of civilians as marauding, which was punishable by death.

Yet, as officers of ranks high and low failed or refused to enforce the rules of war, they were as complicit as their soldiers, as tracts concerning the rules of war at times acknowledged. The origins of the rules of war lay in the articles of war, which in the late 16th-century Low Countries was in essence a temporary, ad hoc, and unique contract between a prince or commander and a group of (mercenary) soldiers. In stipulating the payment, terms, and benefits the soldiers could expect to receive, the articles of war included rules concerning their behavior toward civilians. In the 17th century, the articles of war developed into a set of more or less standard rules incorporated into military orders, treaties, and ordinances that were widely disseminated with each outbreak of war. The 18th-century Age of Reason witnessed a trend to rationalize and formalize the rules of war into laws of war in order to universally and permanently regulate war and warfare impact on civilians and their homes, lands, and property. The project failed on the campaign trails and in the salons as officers and commanders opposed it passively (by ignoring the rules) or actively by their deeds and writings (Field Marshall Saxony). The disconnect also effectively set a precedent for the 19th and 20th centuries: even as the rules of war found their way into formal laws of war, their fundamental applicability during warfare remained deeply contested in the theory of war and ignored in the practice of war until the end of the First World War. In the US and the Netherlands alike, military commanders and politicians debated flagrant breaches of the rules of war by their own forces, yet neither US General Andrew Jackson, nor Dutch General K. van der Heijden, nor any other generals in either army were reprimanded for their actions. At Versailles, Germany lost its colonies because it was held responsible for war atrocities, that is, for breaching the rules of war, but such an outcome remained an exception until the war crimes tribunals following the Second World War. Pre- and post-Enlightenment officers and soldiers, kings and princes were not alone in being implicated in continuing the practice of environcidal and total war. Indigenous American guides, interpreters, porters, auxiliaries, and allies played important roles in the European conquests of the Americas, from Cortés's dependence on the interpreter Maria and his allies to Crook's deployment of hundreds of Sioux, Cheyenne, Arapaho, Shoshone, and Pawnee to fight the indigenous Americans of the Great Plains. The first two Dutch invasions of Aceh in the early 1870s failed because they had neither local guides nor allies. The subsequent Dutch successes can at least in part be attributed to having used both. In addition, during the early 1880s, the Dutch actively sought Aceh allies. Allied Aceh leaders often had their own agendas and painted rivals as rebels in order to use the Dutch army against them. In Namibia, Native Commissioner Hahn is unlikely to have been as successful in convincing the 20,000–30,000 refugees in the Neutral Zone to move into the wilderness on the South African side of the border had he not secured the support of the refugees' leaders. Hahn rewarded the loyalty of the refugee leaders after the famine by distributing the leftover government food stocks to them.

The ipso facto categorization of groups of people as victims or perpetrators because they are Western or non-Western, pre-modern or modern, civilized or uncivilized, indigenous or colonized, or because they are aliens, is ahistorical, teleological, and the product of a linear, developmentalist history. Neither genocide, nor environcide, nor total war are products of settler colonialism, in particular. Victims can become killers and vice versa. Bereft of their environmental infrastructure, populations displaced by war were in desperate straits while on the run as well as when they began to resettle in a new environment. When host populations were unable or unwilling to share their resources and environmental infrastructure, conflict was likely.

Similarly, war-displaced refugees, especially in an unfamiliar environment, are likely to exploit any available resources to survive, even to the brink of extinction. In the deserted countryside of 1570s Holland, peat represented precious heat, fuel, and money even as peat mining flooded fertile fields and pastures, which, in the long run, impoverished and literally shrank the countryside. Displaced and desperate indigenous Americans overhunted beaver, deer, and buffalo. European settlers all but exterminated buffalo, wolves, coyotes, and the passenger pigeon. European settlers in 17th-, 18th- and 19th-century North America also contributed to other destructive environmental practices. For example, in constructing fortifications, dwellings, and farms, newly arrived European settlers in the New World, caused severe deforestation. The massive early 20th-century displacement of refugees from the northern Ovambo floodplain in modern Angola to the southern floodplain in modern Namibia similarly raised the specter of deforestation and desertification. Commodification and capitalism were key factors in overhunting and extinctions but so were the urgent needs for food and income by those deprived of homes and livelihoods by war and displacement. Displacement thus caused or contributed to not only the unrestrained violence against humans but also the destruction of entire species or ecosystems—ecocide.

Resilience in the face of humanitarian or natural disasters effectively emphasizes the agency of the victims and thus frequently is used to dilute the heavy environmental determinism inherent in discussing the impact of climate change in the past and present. Resilience is often understood at the systems level. That is, the focus is on the resilience of societies, polities, communities, or ecosystems. But such systems as nations, states, cities, or ethnic groups may prove resilient by continuing to exist, despite catastrophic individual losses and trauma. At issue is that focusing on the system may suggest more continuity than might be warranted. During the Dutch Revolt, Leiden and Haarlem emerged phoenix-like from the war, boasting larger populations, and the devastated rebel territory of Holland grew into the heartland of the prosperous and powerful Dutch Republic in half a century. Dutch history celebrates how victims transformed into historical agents, with the republic ultimately ruling the seven seas in its 17th-century Golden Age. Yet, many of those who populated Leiden, Haarlem, and southern Holland in the early 1570s were not the same individuals as those who peopled the towns and countryside of southern Holland in the late 1580s. Many of those original inhabitants had perished during the war or they had been displaced from their homes, lands, and livelihoods. They were replaced by refugees from elsewhere in the Low Countries as the war moved beyond the province of Holland. Moreover, physically, the system as measured by the total size of the polder lands, shrank during the 1570s and thereafter as the Water Wolf gobbled up farms and fields. As systems, the rebel towns and rebel Holland proved highly resilient, but in the process, they went through dramatic societal and environmental changes. A focus on the system glosses over the deep human and physical destruction caused by the war and camouflages the collapse of village communities, households, livelihoods, lives, and ways of life.

The war-caused crises in the Ovambo floodplain raise similar issues. Between the late 1920s and the early 1960s, the refugees from the Portuguese-controlled northern floodplain (in modern Angola) created a new Oukwanyama on the South African-controlled side of the border (in modern Namibia), which in many ways was modeled after the villages they had abandoned. The villages, farms, and fields seemed interchangeable, with the same type of waterholes, palisades, dwellings, granaries, crops, and fruit trees. They also used the same names for their region (Oukwanyama after the old kingdom they fled) and for a number of the villages (e.g., Omupanda). But many of the inhabitants were not from the old kingdom, having originated from neighboring polities and communities. The new Oukwanyama was not the same as the old Oukwanyama: there was continuity and discontinuity, and emphasizing the former shrouds a dramatic history of war, displacement, and reconstruction at both community and individual levels. The examples demonstrate the difficulties of navigating between histories that emphasize agency and those that highlight victimhood, especially where the analytical distinctions between the two are blurred.

Even as early 16th- to early 20th-century conquerors and armies silenced their adversaries and displaced refugees in the Americas, Europe, Asia, and Africa, victims made history by refusing to be erased by environcide, ecocide, and even genocide. Their words and deeds testify to the resilience (and its limits) of the human- and non-human-shaped environmental infrastructure that sustains human societies and non-human communities, despite being a prime target and instrument of war across the globe since at least the early 16th century. Environcidal war was total war that triggered famine, disease epidemics, massive population displacements, and the devastation of people's livelihoods and ways of life, and was as destructive to humanity as it was to Nature. The history of total war as environcide highlights how and why such practices as scorched earth and armies living off the land, which culminated in the deliberate destruction of the human-shaped environment, should be condemned as a crime against humanity *and* Nature.

NOTES

Introduction: Environcide, Society, and Total War

1. Julian P. Robinson, *The Effects of Weapons on Ecosystems* (Oxford: Pergamon Press, 1979); Arthur H. Westing, *Warfare in a Fragile World: Military Impact on the Human Environment* (London: Taylor & Francis, 1980); Arthur H. Westing, *Herbicides in War: The Long-term Ecological and Human Consequences* (London: Taylor & Francis, 1984); Bengt Danielsson and Marie-Thérèse Danielsson, *Poisoned Reign: French Nuclear Colonialism in the Pacific* (New York: Penguin, 1986); Susan D. Lanier-Graham, *Ecology of War: Environmental Impacts of Weaponry and Warfare* (New York: Walker and Company, 1993); David Zierler, *The Invention of Ecocide: Agent Orange, Vietnam, and the Scientists Who Changed the Way We Think about the Environment* (Athens: University of Georgia Press, 2011); T. M. Hawley, *Against the Fires of Hell: The Environmental Disaster of the Gulf War* (New York: Hartcourt, 1992).

2. See, for example, Edmund Russell, *War and Nature: Fighting Humans and Insects with Chemicals from World War I to Silent Spring* (Cambridge: Cambridge University Press, 2001); Richard Tucker and Edmund Russell, eds., *Natural Enemy, Natural Ally: Toward an Environmental History of War* (Corvallis: Oregon State University, 2004); Charles E. Closmann, ed., *War and the Environment: Military Destruction and the Environment* (College Station: Texas A&M University Press, 2009); Jurgen Brauer, *War and Nature: The Environmental Consequences of War in a Globalized World* (Lanham: Altamira Press, 2009); J. R. McNeill, *Mosquito Empires: Ecology and War in the Greater Caribbean, 1620–1914* (Cambridge: Cambridge University Press, 2010); Lisa M. Brady, *War Upon the Land: Military Strategy and the Transformation of Southern Landscapes during the American Civil War* (Athens: University of Georgia Press, 2012); Geoffrey Parker, *Global Crisis: War, Climate Change and Catastrophe in the Seventeenth Century* (New Haven: Yale University Press, 2014 [2013]); Micah S. Muscolino, *The Ecology of War in China: Henan Province, The Yellow River, and Beyond, 1938–1950* (Cambridge: Cambridge University Press, 2015); Dagomar Degroot, *The Frigid Golden Age: Climate Change, The Little Ice Age, and the Dutch Republic, 1560–1720* (Cambridge: Cambridge University Press, 2018).

3. On the rejection of the Nature–Culture dichotomy, see D. Worster, *Rivers of Empire: Water, Aridity, and the Growth of the American West* (New York: Oxford University Press, 1985); R. White, *The Organic Machine: The Re-Making of the Columbia River* (New York: Hill and Wang, 2000); W. Cronon, *Nature's Metropolis: Chicago and the Great West* (New York: W. W. Norton, 1991). See also Emmanuel Kreike, *Deforestation and Reforestation in Namibia: The Global Consequences of Local Contradictions* (Princeton: Markus Wiener, 2010).

4. Rosemary Rayfuse, introduction to *War and Environment: New Approaches to Protecting the Environment in Relation to Armed Conflict*, ed. Rosemary Rayfuse (Leiden: Brill, 2014), 1–10; Cordula Droege and Marie-Louise Tougas, "The Protection of the Natural Environment in Armed Conflict: Existing Rules and Need for Further Legal Protection," in Rayfuse, *War and Environment*, 11–43.

5. Emmanuel Kreike, *Environmental Infrastructure in African History: Examining the Myth of Natural Resource Management in Namibia* (Cambridge: Cambridge University Press, 2013).

6. Exceptions are Emmanuel Kreike, *Re-Creating Eden: Land Use, Environment, and Society in Southern Angola and Northern Namibia* (Portsmouth: Heinemann, 2004), and Muscolino, *Ecology of War in China*.

7. William H. McNeill, *Plagues and Peoples* (New York: Anchor Books, 1998 [1976]); William C. Jordan, *The Great Famine: Northern Europe in the Early Fourteenth Century* (Princeton: Princeton University Press, 1996); and John M. Barry, *The Great Influenza: The Story of the Deadliest Pandemic in History* (New York: Penguin Books, 2009 [2004]).

8. Charles G. Roland, *Courage under Siege: Starvation, Disease, and Death in the Warsaw Ghetto* (New York: Oxford University Press, 1992); Harrison E. Salisbury, *The 900 Days: The Siege of Leningrad* (New York: Harper & Row Publisers, 1969); Zena Stein, Mervyn Susser, Gerhart Saenger, and Francis Marolla, *Famine and Human Development: The Dutch Hunger Winter of 1944–1945* (Oxford: Oxford University Press, 1975); and Henri A. van der Zee, *The Hunger Winter: Occupied Holland 1944–1945* (Lincoln: University of Nebraska Press, 1998 [1982]); Ancel Keys, Josef Brozek, and Austin Henschel, *The Biology of Human Starvation*, vol. 2 (Minneapolis: University of Minnesota Press, 1950), 1002–39; Janam Mukherjee, *Hungry Bengal: War, Famine and the End of Empire* (London: Hurst and Company, 2015).

9. See, for example, Barry S. Levy and Victor W. Sidel, eds., *War and Public Health* (New York: Oxford University Press, 1997); E. Wayne Nafziger, Thomas Steward, and Raimo Vayrynen, eds., *War, Hunger and Displacement: The Origins of Humanitarian Emergencies* (Oxford: Oxford University Press, 2000); Joanna Macrae and Anthony Zwi, eds., *War and Hunger: Rethinking International Responses to Complex Emergencies* (London: Zed Books, 1994); Matthew Smallman-Raynor and Andrew Cliff, *War Epidemics: An Historical Geography of Infectious Diseases in Military Conflict and Civil Strife, 1850–2000* (Oxford: Oxford University Press, 2004); Andrew Cunningham and Ole Peter Grell, *The Four Horsemen of the Apocalypse: Religion, War, Famine and Death in Reformation Europe* (Cambridge: Cambridge University Press, 2000); Friedrich Prinzing, *Epidemics Resulting from Wars*, ed. Harald Westergaard (n.p.: Forgotten Books, 2012 [originally Oxford: Clarendon Press, 1916]); Guido Alfani and Mario Rizzo, "Politiche Annonarie, Provvedimenti Demografici e Capitale Umano nelle Città Assediate dell'Europa Moderna," in *Nella Morsa della Guerra: Assedi, Occupazioni Militari e Saccheggi in Età Preindustriale*, ed. Alfani and Rizzo (Milano: FrancoAngeli, 2013), 15–45; and Lauro Martines, *Furies: War in Europe, 1450–1700* (New York: Bloomsbury Press, 2013), 150–60. On Rinderpest, see C. A. Spinage, *Cattle Plague: A History* (New York: Springer Science, 2003), 3, 9, 65, table 1 (82–84), 81–150. Diseases also, of course, deeply shaped armies and wars, see P. D. Curtin, *Disease and Empire: The Health of European Troops in the Conquest of Africa* (Cambridge: Cambridge University Press, 1998); and McNeill, *Mosquito Empires*.

10. See, for example, Eric D. Weitz, *A Century of Genocide: Utopias of Race and Nation* (Princeton: Princeton University Press, 2006 [2003]); and Ben Kiernan, *Blood and Soil: A World*

History of Genocide and Extermination from Sparta to Darfur (New Haven: Yale University Press, 2007).

11. John Morgan Dederer, *War in America to 1775: Before Yankee Doodle* (New York: New York University Press, 1990); John Grenier, *The First Way of Making War: American War Making on the Frontier* (Cambridge: Cambridge University Press, 2005); Gary C. Anderson, *Ethnic Cleansing and the Indian: The Crime That Should Haunt America* (Norman: University of Oklahoma Press, 2014); Hans Koning, *The Conquest of America: How the Indians Lost Their Continent* (New York: Monthly Review Press, 1993); Walter L. Hixson, *American Settler Colonialism: A History* (New York: Palgrave Macmillan, 2013); Ian K. Steele, *Warpaths: Invasions of North America* (New York: Oxford University Press, 1994); and Frank Chalk and Kurt Jonassohn, *The History and Sociology of Genocide: Analyses and Case Studies* (New Haven: Yale University Press, 1990), 4, 14–16, 23–27, 35–36, 107–203. Compare Chris Mato Nunpa, "Historical Amnesia: The 'Hidden Genocide' and Destruction of the Indigenous Peoples of the United States," in *Hidden Genocides: Power, Knowledge, Memory*, ed. Alexander Laban Hinton et al. (New Brunswick: Rutgers University Press, 2014), 96–108.

12. E. Fenn, *Pox Americana: The Great Smallpox Epidemic of 1775–1782* (New York: Hill and Wang, 2001); A. W. Crosby, *Ecological Imperialism: The Biological Expansion of Europe, 900–1900* (Cambridge: Cambridge University Press, 1986).

13. A. W. Crosby, *The Columbian Exchange: The Biological and Cultural Consequences of 1492* (Westport, CT: Greenwood Press, 1972); Crosby, *Ecological Imperialism*; E. K. Melville, *A Plague of Sheep: Environmental Consequences of the Conquest of Mexico* (Cambridge: Cambridge University Press, 1997); J. Diamond, *Guns, Germs, and Steel: The Fates of Human Societies* (New York: Norton and Company, 1999); Fenn, *Pox Americana*. For a critique of the contagion model, see Donald A. Grinde and Bruce E. Johansen, *Ecocide of Native America: Environmental Destruction of Indian Lands and Peoples* (Santa Fe: Clear Light Publishers, 1995), 48.

14. David E. Stannard, *American Holocaust: Columbus and the Conquest of the New World* (New York: London University Press, 1992); Andrew Woolford, Jeff Benvenuto, and Alexander L. Hinton, eds., *Colonial Genocide in Indigenous North America* (Durham: Duke University Press, 2014); and Nunpa, "Historical Amnesia," 96–108. For critiques of the use of genocide, see Anderson, *Ethnic Cleansing and the Indian*, and Alex Alvarez, *Native America and the Question of Genocide* (Lanham: Rowman and Littlefield, 2014).

15. Weitz, *Century of Genocide*, 1–52; Kiernan, *Blood and Soil*, 1–40. See also Ervin Staub, *The Roots of Evil: The Origins of Genocide and Other Group Violence* (Cambridge: Cambridge University Press, 1999 [1989]); Frank Chalk and Kurt Jonassohn, *The History and Sociology of Genocide: Analyses and Case Studies* (New Haven: Yale University Press, 1990); Robert Gellately and Ben Kiernan, eds., *The Specter of Genocide: Mass Murder in Historical Perspective* (Cambridge: Cambridge University Press, 2003); A. Dirk Moses, ed., *Empire, Colony, Genocide: Conquest, Occupation, and Subaltern Resistance in World History* (New York: Berghahn Books, 2008); and Alexander Laban Hinton et al., eds., *Hidden Genocides: Power, Knowledge, Memory* (New Brunswick: Rutgers University Press, 2014). On the history of the term ecocide, see David Zierler, *The Invention of Ecocide: Agent Orange, Vietnam, and the Scientists Who Changed the Way We Think about the Environment* (Athens: University of Georgia Press, 2011), 1–32. On the development of human rights ideas and institutions, see Micheline R. Ishay, *The History of Human Rights: From Ancient Times to the Globalization Era* (Berkeley: University of California Press,

2004); and L. Hunt, *Inventing Human Rights: A History* (New York: W. W. Norton and Co., 2007).

16. On "indirect genocide" to denote the impact of appalling conditions of life, see Robert Johnson and Paul S. Leighton, "African-Americans: Victims of Indirect Genocide," in *Genocide*, ed. William Dudley (San Diego: Greenhouse Press, 2001), 159–67.

17. International criminal courts' jurisprudence suggests that foreseen outcomes do not meet the requirement of genocidal intent, see Lasse Heerten and A. Dirk Moses, "The Nigeria-Biafra War: Postcolonial Conflict and the Question of Genocide," in *Postcolonial Conflict and the Question of Genocide: The Nigeria-Biafra War, 1967–1970*, ed. A. Dirk Moses and Lasse Heerten (New York: Routledge, 2018), 3–43 (27–28).

18. Kai Ambos, "What Does 'Intent to Destroy' in Genocide Mean?," *International Review of the Red Cross* 91 (2009): 876, 833–58; and *Treatise on International Criminal Law. Volume II: The Crimes and Sentencing* (Oxford: Oxford University Press, 2014), 13 and 21–27.

19. Ambos, "What Does 'Intent to Destroy' in Genocide Mean?," 833–58; and *Treatise on International Criminal Law*, 13 and 21–27.

20. Guri Larsen, "The Most Serious Crime: Eco-Genocide," in *Eco-Global Crimes: Contemporary Problems and Future Challenges*, ed. Rune Eleffsen, Ragnhild Sollund, and Guri Larsen (New York: Routledge, 2016), 33–56; Zierler, *Invention of Ecocide*; Martin Crook and Damien Short, "Marx, Lemkin and the Genocide-Ecocide Nexus," *International Journal of Human Rights*, 18 (2014): 3, 298–319; Tim Lindgren, "Ecocide, Genocide and the Disregard of Alternative Life-Systems," *International Journal of Human Rights*, 22 (2018): 4, 525–49; and Steven Freeland, *Addressing the Intentional Destruction of the Environment during Warfare under the Rome Statute of the International Criminal Court* (Cambridge: Intersentia, 2015).

21. On structural violence, see M. Watts, *Silent Violence: Food, Famine, and Peasantry in Northern Nigeria* (Berkeley: University of California Press, 1983); Allen Isaacman, *Cotton Is the Mother of Poverty: Peasants, Work, and Rural Struggle in Colonial Mozambique, 1938–1961* (Portsmouth: Heinemann, 1996), 56–60, 222–25, and 238–39 (systemic violence); and Rob Nixon, *Slow Violence and the Environmentalism of the Poor* (Cambridge: Harvard University Press, 2013 [2011]). On the structural nature of ecocide (and genocide), see Crook and Short, "Marx, Lemkin and the Genocide-Ecocide Nexus," and Lindgren, "Ecocide, Genocide and the Disregard of Alternative Life-Systems."

22. Freeland, *Addressing the Intentional Destruction*, 131–39.

23. On the compartmentalization of violence, see Abram de Swaan, *The Killing Compartment: The Mentality of Mass Murder* (New Haven: Yale University Press, 2015), 3–5, 80–81, 116–17, and 124–25.

24. Isabel V. Hull, *Absolute Destruction: Military Culture and the Practices of War in Imperial German* (Ithaca: Cornell University Press, 2006 [2005]).

25. R. Roberts, *Warriors, Merchants, and Slaves: The State and the Economy in the Middle Niger Valley, 1700–1914* (Stanford: Stanford University Press, 1987); S. Ellis, *The Rising of the Red Shawls: A Revolt in Madagascar, 1895–1899* (Cambridge: Cambridge University Press, 1985); T. C. Weiskel, *French Colonial Rule and the Baule Peoples: Resistance and Collaboration* (Oxford: Clarendon Press, 1980); R. M. Saul and P. Royer, *West African Challenge to Empire: Culture and History in the Volta-Bani Anticolonial War* (Athens: Ohio University Press, 2001); J. Lawrence, *The Savage Wars: British Campaigns in Africa, 1870–1920* (New York: St. Martin's Press, 1985);

R. Marjomaa, *War on the Savannah: The Military Collapse of the Sokoto Caliphate under the Invasion of the British Empire, 1897–1903* ([Helsinki]: Academia Sciencetarum Fennica, 1998); J. Lamphear, *The Scattering Time: Turkana Responses to Colonial Rule* (Oxford: Clarendon Press, 1992); Kreike, *Re-Creating Eden*; J. A. de Moor and H. L. Wesseling, eds., *Imperialism and War: Essays on Colonial Wars in Africa and Asia* (Leiden: Brill, 1989); M. Cocker, *Rivers of Blood, Rivers of Gold: Europe's Conquests of Indigenous Peoples* (New York: Grove, 1998); Bart Luttikhuis and A. Dirk Moses, eds., *Colonial Counterinsurgency and Mass Violence: The Dutch Empire in Indonesia* (London: Routledge, 2014); Grenier, *First Way of Making War*; Caroline Elkins, *Imperial Reckoning: The Untold Story of Britain's Gulag in Kenya* (New York: Henry Holt, 2005); P. Warwick, *Black People and the South African War, 1899–1902* (Johannesburg: Ravan Press, 1983); B. Nasson, *The South African War, 1899–1902* (London: Arnold, 1999); and F. Pretorius, ed., *Scorched Earth* (Cape Town: Human and Rousseau, 2001).

26. Mahmood Mamdani, *When Victims Become Killers: Colonialism, Nativism, and the Genocide in Rwanda* (Princeton: Princeton University Press, 2001); Caroline Elkins and Susan Pedersen, eds., *Settler Colonialism in the Twentieth Century: Projects, Practices, Legacies* (New York: Routledge, 2005); Moses, *Empire, Colony, Genocide*; Andrew Woolford, Jeff Benvenuto, and Alexander L. Hinton, eds., *Colonial Genocide in Indigenous North America* (Durham: Duke University Press, 2014). For a critique of the "colonial genocide" argument, see Elazar Barkan, "Genocides of Indigenous Peoples: Rhetoric of Human Rights," in Gellately and Kiernan, *Specter of Genocide*, 117–39.

27. Mamdani, *When Victims Become Killers*.

28. Daniel Branch, *Defeating Mau Mau, Creating Kenya: Counterinsurgency, Civil War, and Decolonization* (Cambridge: Cambridge University Press, 2009).

29. Karl Jacoby, *Shadows at Dawn: A Borderlands Massacre and the Violence of History* (New York: Penguin, 2008). On the reciprocity of genocides in East Africa, see Adam Jones, "The Great Lakes Genocides: Hidden Histories, Hidden Precedents," in Hinton et al., *Hidden Genocides*, 129–48.

30. Mamdani, *When Victims Become Killers*.

31. Jan Gross, *Neighbors: The Destruction of the Jewish Community in Jedwabne, Poland* (New York: Penguin, 2002 [2001]); Jan Tomasz Gross with Irena Grudzinska Gross, *Golden Harvest: Events at the Periphery of the Holocaust* (Oxford: Oxford University Press, 2012), 68–69; James Waller, *Becoming Evil: Ordinary People Commit Genocide and Mass Killing* (Oxford: Oxford University Press, 2007 [2002]); and Swaan, *Killing Compartments*.

32. Gross, *Golden Harvest*, 19, 58–64, and 119.

33. Social historians since the 1960s have used court records to explore the perspectives of rural societies, see Emmanuel Le Roy Ladurie, *Montaillou: Village Occitan de 1294 à 1324* (New York: G. Braziller, 1978).

34. On the use of local "War Damage" archives, see Myron P. Gutmann, *War and Rural Life in the Early Modern Low Countries* (Princeton: Princeton University Press, 1980); Leo Adriaenssen, *Staatsvormend Geweld: Overleven aan de Frontlinies in de Meierij van Den Bosch, 1572–1629* (Tilburg: Stichting Zuidelijk Historisch Contact, 2008), 13–16; Paolo Calcagno, "Guerra e Documenti, un Chiaro Rapporto di Causa-Effetto: Il Caso dell'Occupazione 'Sarda' di Savona nel 1746–49," in Alfani and Rizzo, *Nella Morsa della Guerra*, 85–110; and Clifford J. Rogers, "By Fire and Sword: Bellum Hostile and 'Civilians' in the Hundred Years' War," in *Civilians in the*

Path of War, ed. Mark Grimsley and Clifford J. Rogers (Lincoln: University of Nebraska Press, 2002), 33–78.

35. Geoffrey Parker, *Spain and the Netherlands, 1559–1659: Ten Studies* (Glasgow: Fontana, 1990 [1979]), 179.

36. On the high value of environmental infrastructure to its indigenous cocreators and to refugees and settlers, see Kreike, *Environmental Infrastructure*, 174–219.

37. On the French armies, see David A. Bell, *The First Total War: Napoleon's Europe and the Birth of Warfare as We Know It* (New York: Houghton Mifflin, 2008); and T. C. W. Blanning, "Liberation or Occupation? Theory and Practice in the French Revolutionaries' Treatment of Civilians outside France," in Grimsley and Rogers, *Civilians in the Path of War*, 111–35; and Gunther Rothenberg, "The Age of Napoleon," in *The Laws of War: Constraints on Warfare in the Western World*, ed. Michael Howard, George J. Andreopoulos, and Mark R. Shulman (New Haven: Yale University Press, 1994), 86–97. On the German army in Belgium, see Hull, *Absolute Destruction*.

38. M. Van Creveld, *Supplying War: Logistics from Wallenstein to Patton* (Cambridge: Cambridge University Press, 2005 [1977]), chapters 3–4.

39. On resource wars, see Paul Richards, *Fighting for the Rain Forest: War, Youth and Resources in Sierra Leone* (Portsmouth: Heinemann, 1996); James Fairhead, "The Conflict over Natural and Environmental Resources" in *War, Hunger, and Displacement: The Origins of Humanitarian Emergencies*, ed. E. Wayne Nafziger et al., vol. 1 (Oxford: Oxford University Press, 2000), 147–78; and David Keen, "War, Crime, and Access to Resources," in Nafziger et al., *War, Hunger, and Displacement*, 283–304; and Philippe Le Billon, *Wars of Plunder: Conflicts, Profits and the Politics of Resources* (London: Hurst and Company, 2012).

40. Gross, *Golden Harvest*, 66–67, 102–9.

41. See chapter 1.

42. See David Parrott, *The Business of War: Military Enterprise and Military Revolution in Early Modern Europe* (Cambridge: Cambridge University press 2013 [2012]). McNeill argues that wars seldom paid for themselves, with the possible exceptions of the Spanish New World possessions and the cases of the Portuguese, Dutch, and English seaborne empires, see William H. McNeill, *The Pursuit of Power: Technology. Armed Force, and Society since A.D. 1000* (Chicago: University of Chicago Press, 1982), 102–10.

43. See Nicole Graham, *Lawscape: Property, Environment, Law* (Abington, UK: Routledge, 2011), and Daniella Dam-de Jong, "From Engines for Conflict into Engines for Sustainable Development: The Potential of International Law to Address Predatory Exploitation of Natural Resources in Situations of Internal Armed Conflict," in Rayfuse, *War and Environment*, 202–27 (214–17).

44. Real or perceived hardship conditions play a key role in genocidal processes, see Staub, *Roots of Evil*, 4–6, 15–18, 35–50; Jones, "Great Lakes Genocides," Hinton el al., *Hidden Genocides*, 129–48.

45. de Swaan, *Killing Compartments*, 10–13, 18, 111, 118–19, 122–24, and 144–47.

46. Bell, *First Total War*. Others stress continuity between premodern and modern wars, see Michael Walzer, *Just and Unjust Wars: A Moral Argument with Historical Illustrations* (New York: Basic Books, 2000 [1977]), 160 and 170–71; Grenier, *First Way of Making War*; Robert Gellately

and Ben Kiernan, "The Study of Mass Murder and Genocide," in Gellately and Kiernan, *Specter of Genocide*, 3–26; and Rothenberg, "Age of Napoleon," in Howard, Andreopoulos, and Shulman, *Laws of War*, 86–97.

47. Gross, *Neighbors*, 54–63 and 80–81. See also Weitz, *Century of Genocide*.

48. For strategic bombing as scorched earth, see Mary-Wynne Ashford and Yolanda Huet-Vaughn, "The Impact of War on Women," in Levy and Sidel, *War and Public Health*, 186–96; and Mark Grimsley and Clifford J. Rogers, introduction to *Civilians in the Path of War*, ed. Grimsley and Rogers (Lincoln: University of Nebraska Press, 2002), xxii–xxiii.

49. Most of the literature on total war focuses on the mass mobilization for military service rather than including the mobilization of civilian resources for war. See for example McNeill, *Pursuit of Power*, 159–61, and Miquel A. Centeno and Elaine Enriquez, *War and Society* (Cambridge: Polity, 2016), 8, 30–31, 72, 116–17.

50. On war refugees, see Michael J. Toole, "Displaced Persons and War," in Levy and Sidel, *War and Public Health*, 197–212; Kreike, *Re-Creating Eden*; and Muscolino, *Ecology of War in China*.

51. Paul Kelton, *Epidemics and Enslavement: Biological Catastrophe in the Native Southeast, 1492–1715* (Lincoln: University of Nebraska Press, 2007).

52. On indigenous American refugee displacement, see Christopher Vecsey and Robert W. Venables, "Introduction"; Christopher Vecsey, "American Indian Environmental Religions"; Laurence M. Hauptman, "Refugee Havens: The Iroquois Villages of the Eighteenth Century"; and Robert W. Venables, "Victim versus Victim: The Irony of the New York Indians' Removal to Wisconsin," in *American Indian Environments: Ecological Issues in Native American History*, ed. Vecsey and Venables (Syracuse: Syracuse University Press, 1980), ix–xxv, 1–37, 128–39, and 140–51, respectively; and Richard White, *The Middle Ground: Indians, Empires, and Republics in the Great Lakes Region, 1650–1815* (Cambridge: Cambridge University Press, 1991), 1–48.

53. See, for example, Christopher Vecsey, "American Indian Environmental Religions," in Vecsey and Venables, *American Indian Environments*, 1–37 (especially 26).

54. On logistics in the Low Countries, see G. Parker, *The Army of Flanders and the Spanish Road, 1567–1659* (Cambridge: Cambridge University Press, 2004 [1972]); G. Overdiep, *De Groninger Schansenkrijg: De Strategie van Graaf Willem Lodewijk: Drente als Strijdtoneel* (Groningen: Wolters Noordhoff, 1970); Gutmann, *War and Rural Life*; Cunningham and Grell, *Four Horsemen of the Apocalypse*; and Van Creveld, *Supplying War*.

55. Indigenous land was a motivation to settler-genocidaires in California, see Brendan C. Lindsay, *Murder State: California's Native American Genocide, 1846–1873* (Lincoln: University of Nebraska Press, 2012), 131.

Chapter One: The Dogs of War and the Water Wolf

1. Joost van den Vondel, "Aenden Leevw van Hollant" (1641), in *De Werken van Vondel, Deel 4, 1640–1645*, ed. J. F. M. Sterck et al. (Amsterdam: De Maatschappij, 1930), 296. Author's translation. Holland here refers to the 16th–17th century Province of Holland.

2. On the Dutch Revolt, see, for example, Marjolein 't Hart, *The Dutch Wars of Independence: Warfare and Commerce in the Netherlands, 1570–1680* (London: Routledge, 2014); Leo

Adriaenssen, *Staatsvormend Geweld: Overleven aan de Frontlinies in de Meierij van Den Bosch, 1572–1629* (Tilburg: Stichting Zuidelijk Historisch Contact, 2008); Ronald de Graaf, *Oorlog, Mijn Arme Schapen: Een Andere Kijk op de Tachtigjarige Oorlog, 1565–1648* (Franeker: Van Wijnen, 2004); and Henk van Nierop, *Het Verraad van het Noorderkwartier: Oorlog, Terreur en Recht in de Nederlandse Opstand* (Amsterdam: Bert Bakker, 1999).

3. A. Brouwer and Ingena Vellekoop, *Spaans Benauwd: Strijdende Geuzen en Spanjaarden in het Maasmondgebied, 1568–1575* (Vlaardingen: Brouvelle, 1984), 6–7.

4. On the insecurity in Holland in October and November 1572, see I. H. van Eeghen, ed., *Dagboek van Broeder Wouter Jacobsz (Gualtherus Jacobi Masius)*, 2 vols. (Groningen: J. B. Wolters, 1959–60), 21–22, 37, 42, 58, 70–76, 80 (henceforth DBWJ).

5. Delfland tax for garrisons, see Oud Archief Delfland, Delft, the Netherlands (henceforth OAD) 1535, Brieven die Dijckgraven ende hooge heemraeden . . . contra de burgemrs . . . stad van delft (May 10, 1575) copie. See also DBWJ, 417.

6. DBWJ, 181.

7. DBWJ, 445 (1574) and 540 (1575).

8. DBWJ, 410 (June 3, 1574).

9. DBWJ, 183.

10. DBWJ, 215–16, 237, 242–43, 274, 277.

11. DBWJ, 280, 343, and 345.

12. Historisch Archief Westland, Naaldwijk, the Netherlands (henceforth HAW), Gemeente Monster Archief (henceforth GMA), 1449.

13. HAW, GMA, 1449, Copia, Also noodich bevonden. . . . Dordrecht, April 29, 1574.

14. HAW, GMA, 2063, Verklaring . . . voor schepene van Monster, July 12, 1575.

15. On the burdens of billeting troops, see DBWJ, 95, 334–35, 337, 544–45, 563, 591, 596–98.

16. HAW, GMA, 1449, Ten verzoucke van Adriaen Willms opden Houck, Ambachtsbewarder van Monster: Pieter Florijszn Couck, May 9, 1574, and Instructie gedaen . . . van wege die van Monster, May 1574.

17. Regionaal Archief Leiden, Leiden, the Netherlands (henceforth RAL) 512 Huisarchief Heeren van Warmond 220: Aen mijnen E. heeren der Staten slandt van Hollandt van Schout . . . van Warmondt, Den Haag, January 27, 1587, and February 1585, and statement by notary with declarations of damage caused by soldiers Noordwijck, 1577.

18. DBWJ, 321.

19. DWBJ, 141.

20. The same orders were given in Alkmaar, Hoorn, Edam, and Monnikendam, and were probably based on an announcement of the pamphlet issued by the Prince of Orange on November 29, 1572. See DWBJ, 100n4. For Leiden, see DBWJ, 108, 111; RAL, 102, Collectie Ramazzotti, 1572–74, No. 1 Verzoekschrift van de gouverneur aan de magistraat [1572]; and RAL, S. van der Paauw, Catalogus van Oudheden en Byzonderheden betreffende het Beleg en Ontzet der Stad Leyden in het Jaar 1574 [Leiden, 1824] manuscript. Manuscripten: No. 1 Afleesingh-Boek gequoteerd C. beginnende den 24 April aom 1570 eyndigende den 20 October Am. 1574. For Haarlem, DBWJ, 50, 112, and 120; and Willem Janszoon Verwer, *Memoriaelbouck: Dagboek van Gebeurtenissen te Haarlem van 1572–1581* (Haarlem: Schuyt, 1973), 9–11, 15, 37–38. In November 1572, the city of Amsterdam, fearing a siege by the rebels, also ordered the tearing down of

many houses outside the city walls, see DBWJ, 58. On Hendrick Pietersz, see Verwer, *Memoriaelbouck*, 85.

21. On the destruction of the countryside around Leiden, see DBWJ, 279, 291–92.

22. DBWJ, 92–95; Verwer, *Memoriaelbouck*, 19–23.

23. DBWJ, 96 and 105.

24. On the northern seadike, see RAL, 501A, Stadsarchief 5469: Verhandeling van Jan van Hout over de geschiedenis, de instructies en de verordeningen van het hoogheemraadschap van Rijnland (1595), ii–iii; DBWJ, 213; and Verwer, *Memoriaelbouck*, 61–62.

25. On the supply lines to Haarlem during the siege, see Verwer, *Memoriaelbouck*, 33–40, 43, 47–58, 61–98; and DBWJ, 128, 150, 175, 213, 215, 217, 219, 223, 228–33, 243, 248, 255–56, 274–75.

26. Brouwer and Vellekoop, *Spaans Benauwd*; DBWJ, 285, 292, 295–98, 301, 304, 314, 321, 331, 344.

27. DBWJ, 285.

28. DBWJ, 293, 311–15, 374, 376.

29. Brouwer and Vellekoop, *Spaans Benauwd*, 41–55.

30. DBWJ , I, 377. Not only the rebels used inundations. The inhabitants of loyalist Schoonhoven, besieged by rebels in October 1572 had inudated the surroundings of the town. See DBWJ, 39 and 41.

31. RAL, Paauw, Catalogus van Oudheden en Byzonderheden betreffende het Beleg, manuscript, 22 Augustus: Mededeeling van het ontvangen berigt, nopens het doorsteken van de Maas en de IJsseldijken.

32. For the Boshuizen sluice, see Verwer, *Memoriaelbouck*, 85.

33. OAD, 32 (1575–77) fol. 17 R and 18R–26R, Register van keuren van dijckgraaf en Hoogheemraadschap (henceforth HHR) Delfland: Aenden grave van Boussu, Delft, February 23, 1568.

34. Nationaal Archief/National Archive, The Hague, Netherlands (henceforth NL-HaNA), 3.01.04.01, Staten van Holland, 1572–1795, vol. 10, (p. 10) Acte op de doorgravinge tot het ontset der Stadt Leyden, Rotterdam, July 30, 1574. On the plague, see RAL, Paauw, Catalogus van Oudheden en Byzonderheden betreffende het Beleg, Uitreksels, Tweede Beleg, July 8, 1574.

35. S. J. Fockema Andreae, "De militaire inundatie van het vasteland van Holland in het jaar 1574," *Tijdschrift van het Koninklijk Nederlandsch Aardrijkskundig Genootschap*, 70, no. 3 (1953): 309–15, espec. 310.

36. On the royalists guarding the dikes, see C. Postma, *Het Hoogheemraadschap van Delfland in de Middeleeuwen, 1289–1589* (Hilversum: Verloren, 1989), 239–40, 389–92; Brouwer and Vellekoop, *Spaans Benauwd*, 57; Fockema Andreae, "De militaire inundatie," 310; DBWJ, 387, 426; OAD, 32 (1575–77) fol. 17 R and 18R-26 R, Register van keuren Delfland: Aenden grave van Boussu, Delft Febuary 23, 1568; and OAD, 1535, Brieven Dijckgraven ende hooge heemraeden van dell[an]t contra de burgemrs der stad van delft, copie, May 10, 1575.

37. Oud-Archief Hoogheemraadschap Schieland, Rotterdam, The Netherlands (henceforth OAHS) 654, Gemeenlandsrekeningen Schieland, May 19 to October 4, 1574.

38. See Fockema Andreae, "De militaire inundatie," 310; and Th. F. J. A. Dolk, *Geschiedenis van het Hoogheemraadschap Delfland* (The Hague: Nijhoff, 1939), 174.

39. RAL, Paauw, Catalogus van Oudheden betreffende het Beleg, manuscript, Uitreksels: Tweede Beleg, Augustus 22, 1574, Mededeeling van het ontvangen berigt, nopens het

doorsteken van de Maas en de Ijsseldijken, waardoor het water in Delfland, reeds tot 11 palmen op het land staat.

40. NL-HaNA, 3.03.01.01, Hof van Holland, 1428–1811, 382, Acte van Devoir bij den hove [van Holland] gedaen totten ontset van Leijden, September 4, 1574. On the despair in Leiden, see for example, DBWJ, 443.

41. Fockema Andreae, "De militaire inundatie," 310. On the Maas dike, see NL-HaNA, 3.03.01.01, Hof van Holland, 1428–1811, 382, Acte van Devoir bij den hove gedaen totten ontset van Leijden [folio 72], 4 September 1574; Postma, *Het Hoogheemraadschap*, 391–92; Brouwer and Vellekoop, *Spaans Benauwd*, 57.

42. NL-HaNA, 3.03.01.01, Hof van Holland, 1428–1811, 382, Acte van Devoir bij den hove [van Holland], 4 September 1574; and DBWJ, 443. On the Landscheijding dike, see also Fockema Andreae, "De militaire inundatie," 309–15.

43. NL-HaNA, 3.03.01.01, Hof van Holland, 1428–1811, 382 , Acte van Devoir bij den hove gedaen [folio 72], 4 September 1574; and Fockema Andreae, "De militaire inundatie," 312–13.

44. Fockema Andreae, "De militaire inundatie," 309–15.

45. On the southern sea dike breaches, see Brouwer and Vellekoop, *Spaans Benauwd*, 57; Fockema Andreae, "De militaire inundatie," 309–15; Postma, *Het Hoogheemraadschap*, 239–40, 389–92; and G. Van der Ham, "Schielands Gouden Eeuw 1530–1790," in *Hoge Dijken, Diepe Gronden: Land en Water tussen Rotterdam en Gouda. Een Gescheidenis van Schieland*, ed. Van der Ham (Utrecht: Matrijs, 2004), 81–126.

46. Fockema Andreae, "De militaire inundatie," 310–12; and DBWJ, 451.

47. Fockema Andreae, "De militaire inundatie," 310.

48. DBWJ, 436.

49. DBWJ, 441.

50. On Waddinxveen (Wensveen in DBWJ), see DBWJ, 435, 439n2.

51. DBWJ, 435n3, 436, 440, 442. Besieged towns sometimes expelled women, children, and elderly so that they would not consume precious supplies of food, but besiegers often would not let them pass their lines, see Guido Alfani and Mario Rizzo, "Politiche Annonarie, Provvedimenti Demografici e Capitale Umano nelle Città Assediate dell'Europa Moderna," in *Nella Morsa della Guerra: Assedi, Occupazioni Militari e Saccheggi in Età Preindustriale*, ed. Guido Alfani and Mario Rizzo (Milano: FrancoAngeli, 2013), 37–39.

52. DBWJ, 120–21.

53. DBWJ, 390 and 414.

54. DBWJ, 357; Delft's prewar population was 11,000–19,000, see S. Groenveld and J. Vermaere, eds., "Zeeland en Holland in 1569: Een Rapport voor de Hertog van Alva," Nederlands Historisch Genootschap, *Nederlandse Historische Bronnen*, vol. 2 ('s Gravenhage: Martinus Nijhoff, 1980), 103–74 (136).

55. On refugees in Haarlem, see Verwer, *Memoriaelbouck*, 133.

56. On the Haarlem region, see Verwer, *Memoriaelbouck*, 157–59, 162–63, 167–68, 175.

57. DBWJ, 324–25, 334–35, 337, 346, 439, 446, 495.

58. On the plague and poverty in Amsterdam, see DBWJ, 233, 270, 299, 321–23, 333, 458, 534.

59. DBWJ, 298.

60. On the violence and the poor legal status of rural people in the towns, see H. Van Nierop, *Het Verraad van het Noorderkwartier* (Amsterdam: Bert Bakker, 1999).

61. OAD, 1536, Poincten ende articulene die welcke de hooge heemraden van Rijnlant, Delflant ende Schielant remonstreren, [September 8, 1574].

62. OAD, 1536, President en raden in Holland to [Requesens], Utrecht, October 4, 1574.

63. OAD, 1536, Poincten . . . die welcke de hooge heemraden van Rijnlant, Delflant ende Schielant remonstreren [September 8, 1574]; OAD, 1536, Dom Luis Requesens to HHR Rijnland, Schieland en Delfland, Antwerpen, September 22, 1574; and OAD, 1536, Hoofdthesarier rekenkamer vande koning in hollandt to HHR Rijnland, Schieland end Delffland, Antwerpen, September 20, 1574.

64. On the claim for a limited impact, see Fockema Andreae, "De militaire inundatie," 312–13.

65. Oud Archief Rijnland, Leiden, the Netherlands (henceforth OAR), 9610, Documenten behoorende tot den Eerste en Leste Reekeninge van Mr. Cornelis Van Der Hooch, 1573 en 1574.

66. OAHS, 984, various accounts, January–April 1575; and Verwer, *Memoriaelbouck*, 171.

67. OAD, 1536, Remonstrantie mijne heeren den president ende raeden in hollandt overgegeven bijden hooge heemraden van Rijnlant, delflant ende schielant, March 19, 1576.

68. NL-HaNA, 3.01.04.01, Staten van Holland, 1572–1795, vol. 12, May 15, 1576.

69. OAD, 32 (1575–1577), register keuren van dijckgraaff and HHR Delfland, April 16–17, 1576.

70. NL-HaNA, 3.01.04.01, Staten van Holland, 1572–1795, vol. 12, May 15, 1576; and OAHS, 654 Gemeenlandsrekeningen Schieland, May 11, 1576, to February 23, 1577, especially June 6, 1576.

71. NL-HaNA, 3.01.04.01, Staten van Holland, 1572–1795, vol. 12, June 25 and October 5, 10, and 12, 1576.

72. OAHS, 654 Gemeenlandsrekeningen Schieland, May 11, 1576 to February 23, 1577, in particular September 17, October 9, November 12 and 18, and December 18, 1576. See also Van der Ham, "Schielands Gouden Eeuw 1530–1790," 81–126.

73. DBWJ, 669.

74. NL-HaNA, 3.01.04.01, Staten van Holland, 1572–1795, vol. 13, June 28, 1577.

75. NL-HaNA, 3.01.04.01, Staten van Holland, 1572–1795, vol. 13, June 23 (Schieland) and August 22, 1577 (Voorne); DBWJ, 669 (Schoonhoven).

76. NL-HaNA, 3.01.04.01, Staten van Holland, 1572–1795, vol. 13, May 23 (Alblasserwaard) and August 19, 1577 (eastern bank of the Schie); Noord Hollands Archief, Haarlem, the Netherlands (henceforth NHA) 1032 Ambachts- en Gemeentebestuur van Heemskerk 144, Akte van overeenkomst met het ambachtsbestuur van Uitgeest inzake . . . het gemeenschappelijke polderbeheer 1577 (Heemskerck). On the Oosterambachten (including Hof van Delft, the Vrijenban, Pijnacker, Berkel/Rodenijs) remaining inundated until well into 1578, see Brouwer and Vellekoop, *Spaans Benauwd*, 72–73.

77. On Haarlem, see Verwer, *Memoriaelbouck*, 160–71, 175, 178–81, 188, 198. On butter prices, DBWJ, 317, 323, 370, 392.

78. Pacification of Gent, Verwer, *Memoriaelbouck*, 183; and DBWJ, 649n4.

79. Verwer, *Memoriaelbouck*, 183–84.

80. On the refugees, see DBWJ, 616–17, 620, 622.

81. On rebel orders, see DBWJ, 623. On the blockade of Amsterdam and refugees, see DBWJ, 624–26, 629, 662–63, 667–68, 675–76.

82. On Haarlem, Verwer, *Memoriaelbouck*, 186–93. On Amsterdam, NL-HaNA, 3.01.04.01, Staten van Holland, 1572–1795, vol. 12, December 29, 1576; vol. 13, March 8, 1577; vol. 14, January 24, 1579; and DBWJ, 615–727.

83. DBWJ, 680–710, 693–94, 698.

84. HAW, GMA, 2064, Brief van aanbeveling door schout . . . van Monster voor de uit Vlaanderingen gevluchte linnenwever Jasper Pietersz, July 23, 1577.

85. John Desreumaux, *Leidens Weg* (Roeselaere [Belgie]: Familia et Patria: 1992), 3–40.

86. For the damaged sluices at Delfland, see OAD, 1535 Brieven die Dijckgraven ende hooge heemraeden, May 10, 1575. On the working of the sluices, see P. Van Dam, "Ecological Challenges, Technological Innovations: The Modernization of Sluice Building in Holland, 1300–1500," *Technology and Culture*, 43, no. 3 (2002): 500–520; and Petra J. E. M. Van Dam, *Vissen in Veenmeren: De Sluisvisserij op Aal tussen Haarlem en Amsterdam en de Ecologische Transformatie van Rijnland, 1440–1530* (Hilversum: Verloren, 1998).

87. OAD, 1535, Brieven die Dijckgraven ende hooge heemraeden, May 10, 1575. On the Halfweg sluices, G. 't Hart, *Rijnlands Bestuur en Waterstaat Rondom het Beleg en Ontzet van Leiden, 1570–1580* (n.p.: n.p., n.d.), 11–14.

88. OAHS, 984, various accounts, January–April 1575.

89. See http://www.janvanhout.nl, Maarleen van Amstel-Horák, schets van Spaarndam met de oude sluizen: Toestand van c. 1500, 2005, 't Vertoogh nopende het Dijckgraef en Heemraetschap van Rijnlant. Jan van Hout, Leiden, 1595; http://www.janvanhout.nl/amstelhout/kaart /A0203_spaarndam.html, Maarleen van Amstel-Horák, sluizen Sparnedam met vlnr Groote Sluis, Woerden sluis, Kolksluis and kleine haarlemmer sluis, 2005. On the damaged sluices, see NL-HaNA, 3.01.04.01, Staten van Holland, 1572–1795, vol. 12, October 5, 10, and 12, 1576. On the Woerden sluices, see OAR, 9612, Derde Rekening van Hereberts Stalpart van den Wyele heemraedt van Rhynlandt, 't zelve heemraedtschap concernerende d'Anno Xv.c ende lxxvi (1576). On the dammed sluices at Sparendam, see OAR, 21, Register van de Resolutien van Dijkgraaf, Hoogheemraden en Hooftingelanden van 1536 tot 1585, December 19, 1579; Verwer, *Memoriaelbouck*, 203–4. On the Great Haarlem sluice, see OAR, 21, February 13 and October 26, 1581. On the repair of the Woerden sluices, see OAR, 21, Register van de Resolutien van Dijkgraaf, Hoogheemraden en Hooftingelanden van 1536 tot 1585, January 28 and April 28, 1578 and December 19, 1579. On the Halfweg sluices, see OAR, 9611, Eerste en Tweede Rekeninge van Hereberts Stalpart van den Wyele heemraedt van Rhynlandt, 't zelve heemraedtschap concernerende d'Ann. Xv.c end lxxiv; www.historischhalfweg.nl/Verhalen/details.php?Id=14 and http://www .janvanhout.nl/amstelhout/kaart/A0611_halfweg.html#, Maarleen van Amstel-Horák, 2005, Halfweg en de Sluizen aldaar 1608, A. de Bruyn, [Hoogheemraadschap] Rijnland [map archive] A-0611, 't Vertoogh nopende het Dijckgraef en Heemraetschap van Rijnlant. Jan van Hout, Leiden, 1595. See also M. H. V. van Amstel-Horák, "Nieuwbouw van twee sluizen in een benarde tijd: Halfweg 1556–1558," in *Zeven eeuwen Rijnlandse uitwatering in Spaarndam en Halfweg: Van beveiliging naar beheersing*, ed. L. Giebels (Leiden: Verloren, 1994), 47–75, and Van Dam, "Ecological Challenges, Technological Innovations," *Technology and Culture*, 43, no. 3 (2002), 500–520.

90. OAD, 1535, [May 10, 1575] Brieven die Dijckgraven ende hooge heemraeden and Copie Letter Hof van Holland, Delft, July 13, 1575; Fockema Andreae, "De militaire inundatie," 310–11; and DBWJ, 451.

91. OAD, 32 (1575–77), register keuren van dijckgraff and HHR Delfland, April 16–17, 1576.

92. HAW, GMA, 14, Ingekomen stukken . . . 1575: Schout . . . van Monster, May 9, 1575.

93. OAHS, 984, rekeninghe . . . over schielant in sinte pieters schouwe anno xvc vijff-tentzeventich o[m]megeslaagen tot reparative vande lantscheijdinghe. See also NL-HaNA, 3.01.04.01, Staten van Holland, 1572–1795, vol. 12, October 5, 10, and 12, 1576; vol. 13, July 5 and August 19, 1577; and vol. 15, June 24, 1580.

94. OAR, 21, Register van de Resolutien van 1536–1585, September 21, 1577.

95. DBWJ, 112 and 120; RAL, 102, Collectie Ramazzotti, 1572–1574, No. 1 Verzoekschrift van de gouverneur aan de magistraat [1572].

96. OAHS, 654, Gemeenlandsrekeningen van het hoogheemraadschap van Schieland, September 12, 1574.

97. Many of the drainage mills in Schieland and Delfland had already been burned down by October 1574, see OAD, 1536, president en raden in Holland at Utrecht to Requesens, Utrecht, October 4, 1574; and Van der Ham, "Schielands Gouden Eeuw 1530–1790," 81–126.

98. HAW, Gemeentearchief van 's-Gravenzand, vol. 12, October 28, 1577, Octrooi van de rekenkamer van Holland voor Adriaan Duijck.

99. OAHS, 654, Gemeenlandsrekeningen Schieland, May 11, 1576, to February 23, 1577, in particular, see September 17, October 9, November 12 and 18, and December 18, 1576.

100. NHA, 1032, Ambachts- en Gemeentebestuur van Heemskerk 144, Akte van overeenkomst met het ambachtsbestuur van Uitgeest inzake te nemen maatregelen voor het gemeenschappelijke polderbeheer 1577.

101. OAD, 1631, Rechtsdag Ordinaris nae St. Jacobs schouwe [1592].

102. OAR, 4256, Stukken aangaande het afdammen van de Leede, 1521–1579. On the rebel government survey, NL-HaNA, 3.01.04.01, Staten van Holland, 1572–1795, vol. 14, March 2, 1579.

103. NL-HaNA, 3.01.04.01, Staten van Holland, 1572–1795, vol. 10, (p. 10) "Acte op de doorgravinge tot het ontset der Stadt Leyden," Rotterdam, July 30, 1574.

104. On the Ysseldijk and Gouda, see NL-HaNA, 3.01.04.01, Staten van Holland, 1572–1795, vol. 12, August 7 and 25, 1576.

105. Very few records are available for the period, see OAR, 124, Meetings HHR, and OAR, 21, Register van de Resolutien van Dijkgraaf, Hoogheemraden en Hooftingelanden van 1536 tot 1585. On the split in the water board, see 't Hart, *Rijnlands Bestuur en Waterstaat*, 3–4.

106. OAHS, 3, Heemraadsboeken, 1300–1643, 2e helft 16e eeuw and OAHS 654 Gemeenlandsrekeningen van het hoogheemraadschap van Schieland, May 11, 1576, to February 23, 1577, and February 23, 1577, to March 3, 1578.

107. The formulaic statement *"ende de spaede daer op Steecken,"* ended all rights and obligations. See OAR, 21, September 21, 1577.

108. OAD, 1535, Brieven die Dijckgraven ende hooge heemraeden van delf[lan]t appleanten contra de burgemrs . . . der stad van delft, May 10, 1575 and Copie Letter Hof van Holland agrees with appelanten, Delft, July 13, 1575.

109. NL-HaNA, 3.01.04.01, Staten van Holland, 1572–1795, vol. 12, February 28, 1576.

110. NL-HaNA, 3.01.04.01, Staten van Holland, 1572–1795, vol. 12, April 6, 1576.

111. NL-HaNA, 3.01.04.01, Staten van Holland, 1572–1795, vol. 12, April 7, 1576.

112. For Aalsmeer, see NHA, 1933, Ambachtsbestuur van Aalsmeer 348, Kohier 90, Penningen Kohieren van de 100e penning 1576–1579 en Kohier 1576, 22e Penning, November 29, 1576.

For Heemskerck, see NHA, 1032, Ambachts- en Gemeentebestuur van Heemskerk 75, Request om remissie van verpondinge en bewijs van armoede en verwoestingen aan de staten van Holland, April 18, 1586.

113. NHA, 1032, Ambachts- en Gemeentebestuur van Heemskerk 144, Akte van overeenkomst met het ambachtsbestuur van Uitgeest inzake te nemen maatregelen voor het gemeenschappelijke polderbeheer 1577.

114. NHA, 1032, Ambachts- en Gemeentebestuur van Heemskerk, 75, Stukken betreffende verzoeken aan de Staten van Holland tot vermindering van de aanslag van de ordinaries verponding. Heemskerck to Estates Holland, April 18, 1586. Rabbits were bred in the dunes in fenced compounds, see Petra van Dam, "Rabbits Swimming across Borders: Micro-Environmental Infrastructures and Macro-Environmental Change in Early Modern Holland," in *Ecologies and Economies in Medieval and Early Modern Europe: Studies in Environmental History for Richard C. Hoffman*, ed. Scott G. Bruce (Leiden: Brill, 2010), 63–91.

115. NL-HaNA, 3.01.04.01, Staten van Holland, 1572–1795, vol. 13, February 21, 1577.

116. On the beer tax, see NL-HaNA, 3.01.04.01, Staten van Holland, 1572–1795, vol. 12, October 5, 10, 12, 17, and 20, 1576; and Verwer, *Memoriaelbouck*, 194.

117. NL-HaNA, 3.01.04.01, Staten van Holland, 1572–1795, vol. 13, July 3, 1577.

118. NL-HaNA, 3.01.04.01, Staten van Holland, 1572–1795, vol. 13, April 16 and July 5, 1577. See also Fockema Andreae, "De militaire inundatie," 314–15.

119. OAR, 21, Register van de Resolutien van Dijkgraaf, Hoogheemraden . . . 1536 tot 1585, January 28, 1578.

120. NL-HaNA, 3.01.04.01, Staten van Holland, 1572–1795, vol. 13, September 2, 1578.

121. NL-HaNA, 3.01.04.01, Staten van Holland, 1572–1795, vol. 14, March 2, 1579.

122. NL-HaNA, 3.01.04.01, Staten van Holland, 1572–1795, vols. 14, May 21, 1579, and 15, April 2 and May 8, 1580.

123. NL-HaNA, 3.01.04.01, Staten van Holland, 1572–1795, vol. 12, April 6, 1576.

124. NHA, 1576, Ambachtsbesturen Haarlemmerliede en Spaarnwoude 154, Kohier 50ste en 100ste penning, 1580.

125. DBWJ, 680–710, 693–94, 698.

126. W. J. Diepeveen, *De Vervening in Delfland en Schieland tot het Einde der Zestiende Eeuw* (Leiden: Eduard Ijdo, 1950), 102–7; and RAL, 501A, Stadsarchief 5469, Verhandeling van Jan van Hout over de geschiedenis . . . van het hoogheemraadschap van Rijnland (1595).

127. Diepeveen, *De Vervening*, 102–7; and RAL, 501A, Stadsarchief 5469, Verhandeling van Jan van Hout.

128. Diepeveen, *De Vervening*, 73.

129. OAHS, 1062, Registers van de vonnissen, 1577–84, especially June 1578 to September 1580.

130. On the water boards' motivation for taxing peat, see Diepeveen, *De Vervening*, 107–8.

131. Diepeveen, *De Vervening*, 108–9.

132. On peat taxes, see NL-HaNA, 3.01.04.01, Staten van Holland, 1572–1795, vol. 14, July 24 and August 20, 1579. On the Haarlem tax, see NL-HaNA, 3.01.04.01, Staten van Holland, 1572–1795, vol. 14, October 20, 1579.

133. See, for example OAR, 1596, Stukken betreffende het onderzoek naar de afspoeling der landen aan het Haarlemmermeer, 1643–1644; RAL, 501A, Stadsarchief Leiden, 5808, Advijs van

ons Commissarissen ... beroeren[de] die van Nijeuwerckerck. Alkemade also reported land losses, see RAL, 501A, Stadsarchief Leiden, 5812, Rapporten van de landmeter Oel Koenraetsz[oon] betreffende de meting van landen in Alkemade; and OAR, 7416 and 7417, Morgenboeken van Spaarnwoude.

134. Emphasis author. OAR, 1596, Stukken betreffende het onderzoek naar de afspoeling der landen aan het Haarlemmermeer, 1643–44. Met retroacten 1550–70, Report meeting HHR, September 16, 1643.

Chapter Two: Scorched Earth, Black Legend

1. Piedro de Cieza de León, *The Discovery and Conquest of Peru: Chronicles of the New World Encounter.* Edited and translated by Alexandra Parma Cook and Noble David Cook (Durham, NC: Duke University Press, 1998), 201, accessed online at https://read-dukepress-edu.ezproxy .princeton.edu/books/book/645/. The Spanish often referred to llamas and other camelid domestic animals in South America as sheep.

2. Benjamin Schmidt, *The Dutch Imagination and the New World, 1570–1670* (Cambridge: Cambridge University Press, 2006 [2001]), 1–121. For the Act of Abjuration, see http://www .let.rug.nl/usa/documents/before-1600/plakkaat-van-verlatinghe-1581-july-26.php. For the Apology, see Stichting Gihonbron, Apologie van Willem Van Oranje (Amsterdam: Lannoo Tielt, 1980/Middelburg, 2008), 63–93, http://www.theologienet.nl/documenten/Oranje%20 Prins%20Willem%20%20Apologie.pdf. Stannard argues that the black legend was not a myth but emphasizes that it was not unique to the Spanish. See Stannard, *American Holocaust,* 97–118.

3. Bartolomé de Las Casas, *The Devastation of the Indies: A Brief Account* (Baltimore: The Johns Hopkins University Press, 1992); Cieza de León, *Discovery and Conquest of Peru*; and Pedro de Cieza de León, *The Travels of Pedro de Cieza de León, A.D. 1532–50 contained in the First Part of His Chronicle of Peru* (Antwerp: Jean Steeltz, 1553), trans. and ed. Clements R. Markham (London: The Hakluyt Society, 1864).

4. For the ecological invasion and contagion argument, see, for example, A. W. Crosby, *The Columbian Exchange: The Biological and Cultural Consequences of 1492* (Westport, CT: Greenwood Press, 1972); A. W. Crosby, *Ecological Imperialism: The Biological Expansion of Europe, 900–1900* (Cambridge: Cambridge University Press, 1986); E. K. Melville, *A Plague of Sheep: Environmental Consequences of the Conquest of Mexico* (Cambridge: Cambridge University Press, 1997); J. Diamond, *Guns, Germs, and Steel: The Fates of Human Societies* (New York: Norton and Company, 1999); E. Fenn, *Pox Americana: The Great Smallpox Epidemic of 1775–1782* (New York: Hill and Wang, 2001). For a critique of the contagion model, see Donald A. Grinde and Bruce E. Johansen, *Ecocide of Native America: Environmental Destruction of Indian Lands and Peoples* (Santa Fe: Clear Light Publishers, 1995), 48.

5. Laura Matthew, *Memories of Conquest: Becoming Mexicano in Colonial Guatemala* (Chapel Hill: University of North Carolina Press, 2012); Stephanie Wood, *Transcending Conquest: Nahua Views of Spanish Colonial Mexico* (Norman: University of Oklahoma Press, 2012 [2003]); Amber Brian, Bradley Benton, and Pablo García Loaeza, eds., *The Native Conquistador: Alva Ixtlixochitl's Account of the Conquest of New Spain* (University Park: Pennsylvania State University Press, 2015), 82–83; Matthew Restall, *Seven Myths of the Spanish Conquest* (Oxford: Oxford University

Press, 2003), 64–75 and 100–130. Super argues that postconquest diets rapidly improved because the abandoned farmlands provided pastures for the invaders' livestock and rejects the occurrence of famines. See John C. Super, *Food, Conquest, and Colonization in Sixteenth-Century Spanish America* (Albuquerque: University of New Mexico, 1988). His argument is too mechanistic and, for the 16th century, is not borne out by the literature.

6. Schmidt, *Dutch Imagination*, 68–69, 91–95. Several conquistadors who fought in Peru had served in the Italian wars, see Cieza de León, *Discovery and Conquest of Peru*, 41n16. Overall, Cieza de León attributes the extreme violence to individual commanders rather than to Spain's rulers or way of war.

7. Kris Lane, ed., *Captain Bernardo de Vargas Machuca, The Indian Militia and Description of the Indies* (Durham: Duke University Press, 2008), trans. Timothy F. Johnson from the original Spanish edition, 1599, xxxiii–xxxv (German soldiers); Pedro de Cieza de León, *Civil Wars of Peru [Part IV: Book II] The War of Chupas*, trans. ed. Clements R. Markham (London: Hakluyt Society, 1918), 8–9 (Portuguese soldier), 15–17 (French soldier); Luis L. Dominguez, ed., *The Conquest of the River Plate (1535–1555)* (Elibron Classics Replica Edition, 2005 [London: Hakluyt Society, 1891]), xxiv–xxv (Flemish and German soldiers).

8. Karen Vieira Powers, *Women in the Crucible of Conquest: The Gendered Genesis of Spanish American Society, 1500–1600* (Albuquerque: University of New Mexico Press, 2005), 15–111.

9. Lane, *Captain Bernardo de Vargas*, 26–27, 36–37, 47; Cieza de León, *Discovery and Conquest of Peru*, 136–37, 141–50, 241–45, 317–20, 322–36. McNeill emphasizes that land warfare from the 14th to mid-17th centuries very much resembled maritime war in how it was organized with captains commissioned to raise their crews/units. See William H. McNeill, *The Pursuit of Power: Technology, Armed Force, and Society since A.D. 1000* (Chicago: University of Chicago Press, 1982), 107–8.

10. Thomas M. Whitmore and B. L. Turner II, *Cultivated Landscapes of Middle America on the Eve of Conquest* (Oxford: Oxford University Press, 2001); William M. Denevan, *Cultivated Landscapes of Native Amazonia and the Andes* (Oxford: Oxford University Press, 2002 [2001]); William E. Doolittle, *Cultivated Landscapes of Native North America* (Oxford: Oxford University Press, 2000); Scott L. Fedick, ed., *The Managed Mosaic: Ancient Maya Agriculture and Resource Use* (Salt Lake City: University of Utah Press, 1996); and G. A. Bradshaw and P. A. Marquet, eds., *How Landscapes Change: Human Disturbance and Ecosystem Fragmentation in the Americas* (Berlin: Springer Verlag, 2003).

11. Whitmore and Turner, *Cultivated Landscapes*, 2.

12. Whitmore and Turner, *Cultivated Landscapes*, 165–94.

13. Cieza de León, *Discovery and Conquest of Peru*, 117, 120–21; Cieza de León, *Travels*, 99, 129–30, 212–15, 235–49, 257, 262–64, 276.

14. Denevan, *Cultivated Landscapes*, 3–26; See R. Douglas Hurt, *Indian Agriculture in America: Prehistory to the Present* (Lawrence: University of Kansas, 1987), 9, 21–23, 25, 42–50; Doolittle, *Cultivated Landscapes*, 347–409.

15. Denevan, *Cultivated Landscapes*, 16–20, 60–64, 71–72, 102–32, 163–67; Doolittle, *Cultivated Landscapes*, 219–53, 309–46, 413–27.

16. James A. Vlasich, *Pueblo Indian Agriculture* (Albuquerque: University of New Mexico Press, 2005), 12; Whitmore and Turner, *Cultivated Landscapes*, 165–94; Hurt, *Indian Agriculture*, 9; Denevan, *Cultivated Landscapes*, 22–23; Ray T. Matheny, "Northern Maya Lowland

Water-control Systems," in *Pre-Hispanic Maya Agriculture*, ed. Peter Harrison and B. L. Turner II (Albuquerque: University of New Mexico Press, 1978), 185–210; and Catherine Fowler, "'We live by them': Native Knowledge of Biodiversity in the Great Basin of Western North America," in *Biodiversity and Native America*, ed. Paul E. Minnis and Wayne J. Elisens (Norman: University of Oklahoma Press, 2000), 99–132.

17. Denevan, *Cultivated Landscapes*, 135–211.

18. Whitmore and Turner, *Cultivated Landscapes*, 145–54. T. Beach, S. Luzadder-Beach, and N. Dunning, "A Soils History of Mesoamerica and the Caribbean Islands," in *Soils and Societies: Perspectives from Environmental History*, ed. J. R. McNeill and Verena Winiwarter (Isle of Harris, UK: White Horse Press, 2006), 51–90; Noble D. Cook, *People of the Volcano: Andean Counterpoint in the Colca Valley of Peru* (Durham: Duke University Press, 2007), 74, 139–43, 245.

19. Whitmore and Turner, *Cultivated Landscapes*, 145–54.

20. Doolittle, *Cultivated*, 254–308, 309–46.

21. David Thurston and Joanne M. Parker, "Raised Beds and Plant Disease Management," in *The Cultural Dimension of Development: Indigenous Knowledge Systems*, ed. D. Michael Warren, L. Jan Slikkerveer, and David Brokensha (London: Intermediate Technologies, 1995), 140–46.

22. On raised fields in Mexico, see Denevan, *Cultivated Landscapes*, 236, 278–86; and Doolittle, *Cultivated Landscapes*, 71–72, 144, 194–216, 428–52. On raised fields in Ecuador, see Linda A. Newson, *Life and Death in Early Colonial Ecuador* (Norman: University of Oklahoma Press, 1995), 28, 34–35, 38, 75–77. On mounds in the Caribbean, see David Watts, *The West Indies: Patterns of Development, Culture and Environmental Change since 1492* (Cambridge: Cambridge University Press, 1998 [1987]), 41, 50–71. See also Whitmore and Turner, *Cultivated Landscapes*, 111–32, and T. Beach et al., "A Soils History of Mesoamerica and the Caribbean Islands," in McNeill and Winiwarter, *Soils and Societies*, 51–90.

23. Denevan, *Cultivated Landscapes*.

24. On drainage ditches, see Denevan, *Cultivated Landscapes*, 278–86.

25. Beach, "A Soils History," in McNeill and Winiwarter, *Soils and Societies*, 51–90; and Cook, *People of the Volcano*, 74, 139–43, 245.

26. Beach, "A Soils History," in McNeill and Winiwarter, *Soils and Societies*, 51–90; R. Hassig, *Trade, Tribute, and Transportation: The Sixteenth-Century Political Economy of the Valley of Mexico* (Norman: University of Oklahoma Press, 1985), 14–15, 46–53. The Florentine Codex stresses that the farmer "works the soil, stirs the soil anew, prepares the soil." See Fray Bernardino de Sahagún, *Florentine Codex: General History of the Things of Spain*, Book 10, *The People (Part XI)*, trans. Charles E. Dibble and Arthur J. O. Anderson from the Aztec text (Salt Lake City: University of Utah Press, 1981), 41–42.

27. Robert Bye and Edelmira Linares, "Relationship between Mexican Ethnobotanical Diversity and Indigenous Peoples," in *Biodiversity and Native America*, ed. Paul E. Minnis and Wayne J. Elisens (Norman: University of Oklahoma Press, 2000), 44–73.

28. See B. Glaser and W. I. Woods, eds. *Amazonian Dark Earths: Explorations in Space and Time* (Berlin: Springer, 2004); and Johannes Lehmann et al., eds., *Amazonian Dark Earths: Origin, Properties, Management* (Dordrecht: Kluwer, 2003).

29. Thomas P. Myers et al., "Historical Perspectives on Amazonian Dark Earths," and Eduardo G. Neves et al., "Historical and Socio-Cultural Origins of Amazonian Dark Earths," in Lehmann et al., *Amazonian Dark Earths*, 15–28 and 29–50, respectively.

30. Beach, "A Soils History," in McNeill and Winiwarter, *Soils and Societies*, 64–68.

31. On Amazonian bluffs, see Denevan, *Cultivated Landscapes*, 106–12, 222–35; and Thomas P. Myers et al., "Historical Perspectives on Amazonian Dark Earths," and Dirse Clara et al., "Distribution of Amazonian Dark Earths in the Brazilian Amazon," in Lehmann et al., *Amazonian Dark Earths*, 15–28 and 51–75, respectively.

32. Linda A. Newson, *Life and Death in Early Colonial Ecuador* (Norman: University of Oklahoma Press, 1995), 38.

33. Watts, *West Indies*, 50–51.

34. Ramie A. Gougeon, "Activity Areas and Households in the Late Mississippian Southeast United States," in *Ancient Households of the Americas: Conceptualizing what Households Do*, ed. John G. Douglass and Nancy Gonlin (Boulder, CO: University Press of Colorado, 2012), 141–62.

35. Catherine M. Cameron, *Hopi Dwellings: Architectural Change at Orayvi* (Tuscon: The University of Arizona Press, 1999), 10–31, 82–104; Karen R. Adams and Suzanne K. Fish, "Subsistence through Time in the Greater Southwest," in *The Subsistence Economies of Indigenous North American Societies: A Handbook*, ed. Bruce D. Smith (Washington, DC: Smithsonian Institution Scholarly Press, 2011), 147–83 (in particular 160–63). On the high maintenance of pueblo dwellings, see Ronald H. Towner, *Defending the Dinétah: Pueblitos in the Ancestral Navajo Homeland* (Salt Lake City: University of Utah Press, 2003), 146–47.

36. Luisa M. Burkhart, "Mexica Women on the Home Front: Housework and Religion in Aztec Mexico," in *Indian Women of Early Mexico*, ed. Susan Schroeder, Stephanie Wood, and Robert Haskett (Norman: University of Oklahoma Press, 1997), 25–54.

37. On the De Soto expedition dependency on captured food, see Charles Hudson, *Knights of Spain, Warriors of the Sun: Hernando de Soto and the South's Ancient Chiefdoms* (Athens: University of Georgia Press, 1997), 104, 107–8, 117, 119–21, 127, 146, 164–65, 171, 181–84, 186, 189, 201, 205, 214–18, 247, 274, 284, 288–89, 295, 311, 316, 322, 332–34, 339–41, 364–65, 368–69, 373, 375, 378–79; and Gougeon, "Activity Areas and Households," in Douglass and Gonlin, *Ancient Households*, 141–62.

38. Whitmore and Turner, *Cultivated Landscapes*, 62–63.

39. John E. Staller, "Ethnohistoric Sources on Foodways, Feasts, and Festivals in Mesoamerica," in *Pre-Columbian Foodways: Interdisciplinary Approaches to Food, Culture, and Markets in Ancient Mesoamerica*, ed. John E. Staller and Michael Carrasco (New York: Springer, 2010), 23–69 (55: Cortés and pictograms).

40. Burkhart, "Mexica Women on the Home Front," and Stephanie Wood, "Matters of Life at Death: Nahuatl Testaments of Rural Women, 1589–1801," in Schroeder, *Indian Women*, 25–54 and 165–182, respectively.

41. Harold E. Driver and William C. Massey, *Comparative Studies of North American Indians* (Philadelphia: American Philosophical Society, 1957), 248–49. By 1000 BC, Mesoamericans already stored surplus grain. See Hurt, *Indian Agriculture*, 9. On Itza granaries, see Grant D. Jones, *The Conquest of the Last Maya Kingdom* (Stanford: Stanford University Press, 1998), 368–70, 356–57.

42. On Inca storage, see Terry Y. Levine, ed., *Inka Storage Systems* (Norman: University of Oklahoma Press, 1992).

43. Linda A. Newson, *Life and Death in Early Colonial Ecuador* (Norman: University of Oklahoma Press, 1995), 138 and 126–27.

44. Driver and Massey, *Comparative Studies of North American Indians*, 248.

45. Luis L. Dominguez, ed., *The Conquest of the River Plate (1535–1555)* (n.p.: Elibron Classics Replica Edition, 2005 [London: Hakluyt Society, 1891]), 230.

46. Jeffrey P. Blomster, *Etlatongo: Social Complexity, Interaction, and Village Life in the Mixteca Alta of Oaxaca, Mexico* (Belmont, CA: Wadsworth/Thomson Learning, 2004), 75–76.

47. Driver and Massey, *Comparative Studies*, 247.

48. Hurt, *Indian Agriculture*, 50–53.

49. K. Kiple and K. Ornelas, eds., *The Cambridge World History of Food* (Cambridge: Cambridge University Press, 2000), 1248–98; and A. Brack Egg, *Perú: Diez Mil Años de Domesticación* (Lima: UNDP, 2003).

50. On cultivated and managed plants, see Driver and Massey, *Comparative Studies*, 219–23; and Doolittle, *Cultivated Landscapes*, 21–117.

51. On cultivated trees, see Lane, *Captain Bernardo de Vargas Machuca*, 182–87; Cieza de León, *Travels*, 46, 67–68, 80, 86, 90–91, 99, 103, 109, 122, 143, 174, 213, 217, 234–35, 247, 250, 262, 264; M. N. Alexiades and P. Shanley, eds., *Productos Florestales, Medios de Subsistencia y Conservación: Estudios de Caso sobre Sistemas de Manejo de Productos Florestales No Maderables: Volumen 3: America Latina* (Jakarta: CIFOR, 2004). On trees in Spain, see R. J. Harrison "Arboriculture in Southwest Europe: Dehesas as Managed Woodlands," in *The Origins and Spread of Agriculture and Pastoralism in Eurasia*, ed. D. R. Harris (Washington, DC: Smithsonian Institute, 1996), 363–67; and Juan García Latorre et al., "The Man-Made Desert: Effects of Economic and Demographic Growth on the Ecosystems of Arid Southeastern Spain," *Environmental History*, 6, no. 1 (January 2001): 75–94.

52. Cecil H. Brown, "Development of Agriculture in Prehistoric Mesoamerica: The Linguistic Evidence," in Staller and Carrasco, *Pre-Columbian Foodways*, 71–107. For central Mexican agave and fruit trees, see Bernardino de Sahagún, *Florentine Codex*, 74, 79.

53. On Ramón, see John E. Staller and Michael Carrasco, "Pre-Columbian Foodways in Mesoamerica," in Staller and Carrasco, *Pre-Columbian Foodways*, 1–20, and Whitmore and Turner, *Cultivated Landscapes*, 76n1 and 107–08n1.

54. Linda Newson, *The Cost of Conquest: Indian Decline in Honduras Under Spanish Rule* (Boulder, CO: Westview Press, 1986), 57.

55. Whitmore and Turner, *Cultivated Landscapes*, 76–110; R. Bye, "The Role of Humans in the Diversification of Plants in Mexico," in *Biological Diversity of Mexico: Origins and Distribution*, ed. T. P. Ramamoorthy et al. (New York: Oxford University Press, 1993), 701–37; Stephanie Wood, "Matters of Life at Death," in Schroeder et al., *Indian Women*, 165–82; and Stephanie Wood, "Nahua Christian Warriors in the Mapa de Cuauhtlantzinco, Cholula Parish," in Matthew and Oudijk, *Indian Conquistadores*, 254–87 (in particular 270, figure 8.23).

56. Robert Bye and Edelmira Linares, "Relationship between Mexican Ethnobotanical Diversity and Indigenous Peoples," in *Biodiversity and Native America*, ed. Paul E. Minnis and Wayne J. Elisens (Norman: University of Oklahoma Press, 2000), 44–73.

57. Wood, "Matters of Life at Death," in Schroeder et al., *Indian Women*, 165–82.

58. Robert Bye, "The Role of Humans in the Diversification of Plants in Mexico" and E. Hernandéz Xolocotzi, "Aspects of Plant Domestication in Mexico: A Personal View," in Ramamoorthy et al., *Biological Diversity of Mexico*, 701–37 (especially 715) and 733–53, respectively.

On "rewilded" trees, see N. J. H. Smith et al., *Tropical Forests and Their Crops* (Ithaca, NY: Comstock, 1992), 38–185, 240–42, 364–69, and 384–94. See also Egg, *Perú*, 17.

59. Denevan, *Cultivated Landscapes*, 68–73. Many of Columbia's fruit trees were or are cultivated or managed, see Rafael Romero Castañeda, *Frutas Silvestras de Columbia*, vol. 1 (Bogota: [San Juan Eudes], 1961).

60. Charles R. Clement et al., "Agrobiodiversity in Amazonia and Its Relationship with Dark Earths" and Laura German, "Ethnoscientific Understandings of Amazonian Dark Earths," in Lehmann et al., *Amazonian Dark Earths*, 159–77 and 179–201, respectively. See also Smith et al., *Tropical Forests and Their Crops*, 38–185, 240–42, 364–69, and 384–94.

61. Dominguez, *Conquest of the River Plate*, for example, 18, 24–25, 216–18, and 231 (the latter pages refer to "wild" fruit trees in an area that had been abandoned because of war).

62. W. Dean, *With Broadax and Firebrand: Destruction of the Brazilian Atlantic Forest* (Berkeley: University of California Press, 1997), 25–28.

63. Richard I. Ford, "Human Disturbance and Biodiversity: A Case Study from Northern New Mexico," in Minnis and Elisens, *Biodiversity*, 207–22.

64. Daniel W. Gade, *Nature and Culture in the Andes* (Madison: University of Wisconsin Press, 1999), 61–63.

65. Driver and Massey, *Comparative Studies*, 390–91.

66. Gade, *Nature and Culture*, 61–63.

67. Cook, *People of the Volcano*, 96, 100; and W. George Lovell, *Conquest and Survival in Colonial Guatemala: A Historical Geography of the Cuchumatán Highlands, 1500–1821* (Montreal: McGill/Queen's University Press, 1992 [1985]), 126, 173–75.

68. Hurt, *Indian Agriculture*, 28. On Inca use of guano, see Pedro de Cieza de León, *The Travels of Pedro de Cieza de León, A.D. 1532–50 contained in the First Part of His Chronicle of Peru* (Antwerp: Jean Steeltz, 1553), trans. and ed. Clements R. Markham (London: The Hakluyt Society, 1864), 266.

69. Elizabeth N. Arkush, *Hillforts of the Ancient Andes: Colla Warfare, Society, and Landscape* (Gainesville: University Press of Florida, 2011), 1–103.

70. Watts, *West Indies*, 41, 50–75.

71. Watts, *West Indies*, 70–111; and Stannard, *American Holocaust*, 67–73.

72. Watts, *West Indies*, 111–26.

73. Staller, "Ethnohistoric Sources," in Staller and Carrasco, *Pre-Columbian Foodways*, 23–69 (55 food Cortés).

74. Ross Hassig, *Aztec Warfare: Imperial Expansion and Political Control* (Norman: University of Oklahoma Press, 1995 [1988]), 53, 61–65, 73, 163–65, 174, 197, 226–27; and Matthew, *Memories of Conquest*, 46–47.

75. Camilla Townsend, *Malintzin's Choices: An Indian Woman in the Conquest of Mexico* (Albuquerque: University of New Mexico Press, 2006), 42–45, 57–59, 63–84; Matthew Restall, *Seven Myths of the Spanish Conquest* (Oxford: Oxford University Press, 2003), 23–24; and James Lockhart, ed., *We People Here: Nahuatl Accounts of the Conquest of Mexico*, vol. 1 (Eugene, OR: Wipf and Stock Publishers, 2004 [1993]), 86, 90, 156, 158.

76. Amber Brian, Bradley Benton, and Pablo García Loaeza, eds., *The Native Conquistador: Alva Ixtlixochitl's Account of the Conquest of New Spain* (University Park: Pennsylvania State

University Press, 2015). Ixtlixochitl stresses repeatedly that without his aid, the Spanish would have been defeated, see 38, 45, 49–50, 68.

77. On food production in the Valley of Mexico, see Staller, "Ethnohistoric Sources" and Jeffrey R. Parsons, "The Pastoral Niche in Pre-Hispanic Mesoamerica," in Staller and Carrasco, *Pre-Columbian Foodways*, 23–69 and 109–36, respectively; and Hurt, *Indian Agriculture*, 4–5. On the April/May planting season and the late summer harvest, see Hassig, *Aztec Warfare*, 53. On the siege, starvation, and disease, see Hassig, *Aztec Warfare*, 236–50; Stuart B. Schwartz, ed., *Victors and Vanquished: Spanish and Nahua Views of the Conquest of Mexico* (Boston: Bedford/ St. Martin's, 2000), 102, 182–83, 197–98; David E. Stannard, *American Holocaust: Columbus and the Conquest of the New World* (New York: London University Press, 1992), 77–79; Brian, Benton, and García Loaeza, *Native Conquistador*; Matthew, *Memories of Conquest*, 61; and Lockhart, *We People Were*, 218–19 and 240–48 (the Florentine Codex stresses the outbreak of famine and sickness, specifically dysentery). On the importance of indigenous allies, see Hassig, *Aztec Warfare*, 236–50; Restall, *Seven Myths*, 44–65; Wood, *Transcending Conquest*; Townsend, *Malintzin's Choices*; Laura E. Matthew and Michel R Oudijk, eds., *Indian Conquistadores: Indian Allies in the Conquest of Mesoamerica* (Norman; University of Oklahoma Press, 2007); and Matthew, *Memories of Conquest*. On indigenous allies as foragers and plunderers, see Michel Oudijk and Matthew Restall, "Mesoamerican Conquistadores in the Sixteenth Century," in *Indian Conquistadores*, Matthew and Oudijk, 28–63 (in particular, 41–42 and 54–55). Hassig gives an example from 1515 when the Tlaxcallans purposely destroyed the crop fields of Huexotzinco to starve the latter's inhabitants, see Hassig, *Aztec Warfare*, 234.

78. Hassig maintains that it was rare that Aztec armies sacked enemy towns, but his chapters on the military conquests of the Aztecs in the 15th and 16th centuries suggest otherwise. See Hassig, *Aztec Warfare*, 20–21, 23, 105–6, 112–13, 138, 150, 171, 173, 195, 207–8, 215, 218, 223, 226–27, 229, and 232. For the motivations of indigenous soldiers, see Hassig, *Aztec Warfare*, 36–39, 112–13, 150, 157, 200–201, 207–8, and Brian, *Native Conquistador*, 32, 45, 47, 52, 57, 59, 69, and 74–75.

79. Ida Altman, *The War for Mexico's West: Indians and Spaniards in New Galicia, 1524–1550* (Albuquerque: University of New Mexico, 2010), 169; Ida Altman, "Conquest, Coercion, and Collaboration: Indian Allies and the Campaigns in Nueva Galicia," and Bret Blosser, "'By the Force of Their Lives and the Spilling of Blood': Flechero Service and Political Leverage on a Nueva Galicia Frontier," in Matthew and Oudijk, *Indian Conquistadores*, 145–74 and 289–316, respectively.

80. John K. Chance, *Conquest of the Sierra: Spaniards and Indians in Colonial Oaxaca* (Norman: University of Oklahoma Press, 1989), 32–83.

81. Chance, *Conquest of the Sierra*, 13–83; Yanna Yannakakis, "The Indios Conquistadores of Oaxaca's Sierra Norte: From Indian Conquerors to Local Indians," in Matthew and Oudijk, *Indian Conquistadores*, 227–53.

82. John Chuchiak IV, "Forgotten Allies: The Origin and Roles of Native Mesoamerican Auxiliaries and Indios Conquistadores in the Conquest of Yucatan, 1526–1550," in Matthew and Oudijk, *Indian Conquistadores*, 175–225; and Marta Espejo-Ponce Hunt and Matthew Restall, "Work, Marriage, and Status: Maya Women of Colonial Yucatan," in Schroeder et al., *Indian Women*, 231–52. Cortés marching to Honduras in the mid-1520s encountered many pillaged and abandoned towns. See Brian, *Native Conquistador*, 85–87.

83. Jones, *Conquest of the Last Maya Kingdom.*

84. Lovell, *Conquest and Survival.* On the use of central Mexican allies, see Matthew, *Memories of Conquest,* 70–177; and Brian, *Native Conquistador,* 69–74.

85. Newson, *Cost of Conquest,* 53–64, 96–109, 120–31, 295–334.

86. Newson, *Cost of Conquest,* 53–64, 96–109, 120–31, 295–334.

87. Linda Newson, *Life and Death in Early Colonial Ecuador* (Norman: University of Oklahoma Press, 1995), 40, 43, 54–60, 119–54.

88. Piedro de Cieza de León, *The Discovery and Conquest of Peru: Chronicles of the New World Encounter,* ed. and trans. Alexandra Parma Cook and Noble David Cook (Durham, NC: Duke University Press, 1998), 136–233, accessed online at https://read-dukeupress-edu.ezproxy .princeton.edu/books/book/645/.

89. Cieza de León, *Discovery and Conquest of Peru,* 263–320; and John Hemming, *The Conquest of the Incas* (New York: MacMillan, 1970), 90 and 117.

90. Michel Oudijk and Matthew Restall, "Mesoamerican Conquistadores in the Sixteenth Century," in Matthew and Oudijk, *Indian Conquistadores,* 28–63.

91. Hemming, *Conquest,* 248–49; and Newson, *Life and Death,* 157–334.

92. Cook, *People of the Volcano,* 36–46; and Steve J. Stern, *Peru's Indian Peoples and the Challenge of Spanish Conquest: Huamanga to 1640* (Madison: University of Wisconsin Press, 1982), 28–34.

93. Cieza de León, *Travels,* 62–64, 92–94, 109, 115; Cieza de León, *Discovery and Conquest of Peru,* 265–67, 287, 313–15; Pedro de Cieza de León, *Civil Wars of Peru [Part IV: Book II] The War of Chupas,* trans. and ed. Clements R. Markham (London: Hakluyt Society, 1918), 9, 28–29; and Clements Markham, ed., *Civil Wars in Peru, The War of Las Salinas by Pedro de Cieza de León* (Burlington, VT: Ashgate, 2010 [London: The Hakluyt Society, 1923]), 230–31.

94. Cieza de León, *War of Chupas,* 4–50.

95. Cieza de León, *War of Chupas,* 19–28.

96. Cieza de León, *Travels,* 393.

97. Markham, *Civil Wars in Peru,* 60 (and n1), 194–203 (Inca Paulo), 56, 60, 62, 172, 174, 195–96.

98. Cieza de León, *War of Chupas,* 50–53, 100–115, 167–300; and Markham, *War of Las Salinas,* 45, 56–62, 94–231; Cook, *People of the Volcano,* 36–46; Stern, *Peru's Indian Peoples,* 28–34; Hemming, *Conquest,* 351; Restall, *Seven Myths,* 49.

99. Hemming, *Conquest,* 363–66; Markham, *War of Las Salinas,* 45, 184–85, 226–27; Cieza de León, *War of Chupas,* 6, 20–21, 26–27, 264–65, 306.

100. Cieza de León, *Travels,* 129–321; Hemming, *Conquest,* 347–49; Cook, *People of the Volcano,* 20; Denevan, *Cultivated Landscapes,* 144–52.

101. Terry Y. LeVine, "The Study of Storage Systems"; John R. Topic and Coreen E. Chiswell, "Inka Storage in Huamachuco"; Terence N. D'Altroy and Christine A. Hastorf, "The Architecture and Contents of Inka State Storehouses in the Xauxa Region of Peru," in Levine, *Inka Storage Systems,* 3–28, 206–33, 259–86, respectively. On the orders of Vaca de Castro, see Cieza de León, *War of Chupas,* 309. On the collapsed infrastructure, see Cieza de León, *Travels,* 147–67, 209–18, 238–41, 262, 270–71, 276, 290–91, 298, 315, 330, 361–62.

102. John Verano, "Prehistoric Disease and Demography in the Andes," in *Disease and Demography in the Americas,* ed. John W. Verano and Douglas H. Ubelaker (Washington, DC:

Smithsonian Institution Press, 1992), 15–24; Newson, *Life and Death*, 146–47; Hemming, *Conquest*, 349–50; Cook, *People of the Volcano*, 30.

103. Hemming, *Conquest*, 349–50. On the pre-Pizarro epidemic, see also Cook, *People of the Volcano*, 30.

104. Cieza de León, *Travels*, 88.

105. Cook, *People of the Volcano*, 65–66; and Stern, *Peru's Indian Peoples*, 37–48.

106. Stern, *Peru's Indian Peoples*, 90–157.

107. On Vilcabamba, see Hemming, *Conquest*, 317–18, 333, 424–34.

108. Dominguez, *Conquest of the River Plate*. The Hakluyt Society publication contains two accounts of the conquest of the region. The first is the *Voyage of Ulrich Schmidt to the Rivers La Plata and Paraguai*. Schmidt was a participant of the 1535 expedition and an opponent of Cabeza de Vaca. This account was published in 1567 in German by Protestant publishers. It does not read as a Black Legend-type accusation against Spanish colonialism, although his publishers may have meant it to be that way. Rather he portrays Cabeza de Vaca as a ruthless, cruel, and ultimately illegitimate and rogue commander who does not care about the health or welfare of his own men. The second account, *The Commentaries of Alvar Nunez Cabeza de Vaca*, were published in Spanish in 1555. On the 1542 New Laws, see Rebecca Earle, *The Body of the Conquistador: Food, Race and the Colonial Experience in Spanish America, 1492–1700* (Cambridge: Cambridge University Press, 2013 [2012]), 181–82.

109. Kris Lane, ed., *Captain Bernardo de Vargas Machuca, The Indian Militia and Description of the Indies* (Durham, NC: Duke University Press, 2008), trans. Timothy F. Johnson from the original Spanish edition, 1599, xliv–l, 3–5, 86–87 (quotes), and 245–57. Ciezo de León condemned the excessive violence but attributed it to individual greedy and cruel individuals. He claimed that several governors suspended the New Laws shortly after they had been introduced. See Cieza de León, *War of Chupas*, 20–21, 339–40, 360–62, 373.

110. See Hudson, *Knights of Spain*, 373–86; and Ian K. Steele, *Warpaths: Invasions of North America* (New York: Oxford University Press, 1994), 3–18.

111. On the importance of Amerindian porters, slaves, and guides, and Indian (mis)information, see Hudson, *Knights of Spain*, 104, 107, 115, 143, 164–65, 189, 202–3, 214–18, 332, 349–50, 363–69, 380.

112. Hudson, *Knights of Spain*, 104, 107, 115, 143, 164–65, 189, 202–3, 214–18, 332, 349–50, 363–69, 380. On the critical role of Indian allies, see Matthew and Oudijk, *Indian Conquistadores*.

113. Hudson, *Knights of Spain*, 424–25 and 436.

114. Ramie A. Gougeon, "Activity Areas and Households in the Late Mississippian Southeast United States," in *Ancient Households of the Americas: Conceptualizing what Households Do*, ed. John G. Douglass and Nancy Gonlin (Boulder, CO: University Press of Colorado, 2012), 141–62.

115. Gougeon, "Activity Areas and Households," in Douglass and Gonlin, *Ancient Households of the Americas*, 141–62.

116. Kristen J. Gremillion, "The Role of Plants in Southeastern Subsistence Economies," in *The Subsistence Economies of Indigenous North American Societies: A Handbook*, ed. Bruce D. Smith (Washington, DC: Smithsonian Institution Scholarly Press, 2011), 387–99.

117. Clark Spencer Larsen, ed., *Bioarchaeology of Spanish Florida: The Impact of Colonialism* (Gainesville: University Press of Florida, 2001), 52–81, 146–225; Mark N. Cohen and

Gillian M. M. Crane-Kramer, eds., *Ancient Health: Skeletal Indicators of Agricultural and Economic Intensification* (Gainesville: University Press of Florida, 2007), 20–34, 65–79, 92–112, 113–29; Staller and Carrasco, *Pre-Columbian Foodways*, 23–69, 315–43, 345–68. See also Newson, *Cost of Conquest*, 106–7, 121, 319.

118. James A. Vlasich, *Pueblo Indian Agriculture* (Albuquerque: University of New Mexico Press, 2005), 12–23; and Andrew Knaut, *The Pueblo Revolt of 1680: Conquest and Resistance in Seventeenth-Century New Mexico* (Norman: University of Oklahoma Press, 1995), 17–52. On the Zuni, Gregson Schachner, *Population Circulation and the Transformation of Ancient Zuni Communities* (Tucson: University of Arizona Press, 2012). On the Pueblo, see Spicer, *Cycles of Conquest*, 152–86. See also Melville, *Plague of Sheep*.

119. Stodder and Martin attribute the health decline directly to the violence of the conquest, see Ann L. W. Stodder and Debra L. Martin, "Health and Disease in the Southwest before and after Spanish Contact," in Verano and Ubelaker, *Disease and Demography*, 55–73.

120. Knaut, *Pueblo Revolt of 1680*, 152–56.

121. Denevan, *Cultivated Landscapes*, 298–99, 306.

122. See, for example, Newson, *Cost of Conquest*, 106–7, 121, 319. On wheat versus maize in contemporary eyes, see Earle, *Body of the Conquistador*, especially, 140–55.

Chapter Three: The Thirty Years War in the Dutch Republic: Environcide and the Golden Age

1. West-Brabants Archief, Bergen op Zoom, the Netherlands (henceforth WAB) 001, 3759, Supplicatie Etten to Prince of Orange [1625].

2. Geoffrey Parker, *The Thirty Years' War* (New York: Military Heritage Press, 1987 [1984]), 163–65, 190–226.

3. Peter H. Wilson, *Europe's Tragedy: A New History of the Thirty Years War* (Penguin, 2010 [2009]), 4–6, 28–29, 779–820; Parker, *Thirty Years' War*, 163–65, 190–226; Myron P. Gutmann, *War and Rural Life in the Early Modern Low Countries* (Princeton: Princeton University Press, 1980).

4. Jonathan I. Israel, *The Dutch Republic and the Hispanic World, 1606–1661* (Oxford: Clarendon Press, 1982), 97, 252, 323; William H. McNeill, *The Pursuit of Power: Technology, Armed Force, and Society since A.D. 1000* (Chicago: University of Chicago Press, 1982), 117–43. See also Marjolein 't Hart, *The Dutch Wars of Independence: Warfare and Commerce in the Netherlands, 1570–1680* (London: Routledge, 2014), 37–53, 73–74, 81–125, 112–13; Parker, *Thirty Years' War*, 199–201; Marco van der Hoeven, ed., *Exercise of Arms: Warfare in the Netherlands, 1568–1648* (Leiden: Brill, 1997), especially the contributions by: Marco van der Hoeven, "Introduction," 1–15; J. A. de Moor, "Experience and Experiment: Some Reflections upon the Military Developments in 16th- and 17th-Century Western Europe," 17–32; J. P. Puype, "Victory at Nieuwpoort, 2 July 1600," 69–112; and Gutmann, *War and Rural Life*, 31–35, 55–70, 163–68.

5. On the Dutch Golden Age and war, see Hart, *Dutch Wars of Independence*, 191–97; and Michael Howard, *War in European History* (Oxford: Oxford University Press, 1988 [1976]), 44–45.

6. Leo Adriaenssen, *Staatsvormend Geweld: Overleven aan de Frontlinies in de Meierij van Den Bosch, 1572–1629* (Tilburg: Stichting Zuidelijk Historisch Contact, 2008), 159–77, 206–8; Ronald

de Graaf, *Oorlog, Mijn Arme Schapen: Een Andere Kijk op de Tachtigjarige Oorlog, 1565–1648* (Franeker: Van Wijnen, 2004), 334, 357–60, 426–29, 552–55, 569–71; and Gutmann, *War and Rural Life.*

7. Swart and Parrott argue for much more continuity in army organization, training, discipline, and logistics; see Erik Swart, *Krijgsvolk: Militaire Professionalisering en het Ontstaan van het Staatse Leger, 1568–1590* (Amsterdam: Amsterdam University Press, 2006), 15–22, 34, 43, 53–66, 90–110; and David Parrott, *The Business of War: Military Enterprise and Military Revolution in Early Modern Europe* (Cambridge: Cambridge University Press 2013 [2012]), 165–68.

8. On pillaging overseas, see Hart, *Dutch Wars,* 126–69; and Israel, *Dutch Republic,* 109–34, 190–204, 263–82, 324–36; Ivo van Loo, "For Freedom and Fortune: The Rise of Dutch Privateering in the First Half of the Dutch Revolt, 1568–1609," in van der Hoeven, *Exercise of Arms,* 173–95.

9. Adriaenssen, *Staatsvormend Geweld,* 208–9 and 281–333.

10. On articles of war, see Swart, *Krijgsvolk,* 137–44; Adriaenssen, *Staatsvormend Geweld,* 159–68, 206–8.

11. Adriaenssen, *Staatsvormend Geweld,* 146–58, 178–79, 225–54; Parrott, *Business of War;* Alexander Gillespie, *A History of the Laws of War,* vol. 2, *The Customs and Laws of War with Regards to Civilians in Times of Conflict* (Oxford: Hart, 2011), 238–42; Lauro Martines, *Furies: War in Europe, 1450–1700* (New York: Bloomsbury Press, 2013), 41–82, 257–63.

12. Hart, *Dutch Wars,* 170–97.

13. The Republic was part of the Holy Roman Empire until 1728, see Wilson, *Europe's Tragedy,* 755.

14. Israel, *Dutch Republic,* 100–109, 162–90, 250–63; Wilson, *Europe's Tragedy,* 543–87; and Parker, *Thirty Years' War,* 47–61, 82–153.

15. Wilson, *Europe's Tragedy,* 132–45; Geoffrey Parker, "Foreword," Marco van der Hoeven, "Introduction," and de Moor, "Experience and Experiment," in Van der Hoeven, *Exercise of Arms,* ix–xi, 1–15, 17–32, respectively. See also Hart, *Dutch Wars of Independence,* 58–80, and Parker, *Thirty Years' War,* 205–7.

16. On sieges and massacres, see Wilson, *Europe's Tragedy,* 414, 467–78; Gillespie, *History of the Laws of War: Volume 2,* 110–44; and Séverin Duc, "Pavie en État de Siège (octobre 1524-février 1525)," in *Nella Morsa della Guerra: Assedi, Occupazioni Militari e Saccheggi in Età Preindustriale,* ed. Guido Alfani and Mario Rizzo (Milano: FrancoAngeli, 2013), 47–73.

17. M. Watts, *Silent Violence: Food, Famine, and Peasantry in Northern Nigeria* (Berkeley: University of California Press, 1983); Rob Nixon, *Slow Violence and the Environmentalism of the Poor* (Cambridge: Harvard University Press, 2013 [2011]).

18. On contributions (special war taxes), see Parker, *Thirty Years' War,* 133–35, 204; and Wilson, *Europe's Tragedy,* 399–409.

19. Lodovico Guicciardini, *De Idyllische Nederlanden: Antwerpen en de Nederlanden in the 16e Eeuw,* trans. Monique Jacqman (Antwerpen: C. de Vries, 1987), 89–97; Jan Bieleman, *Geschiedenis van de Landbouw in Nederland, 1500–1900* (Amsterdam: Boom Meppel, 1992), 81–82, 95–100; Adriaenssen, *Staatsvormend Geweld,* 283–335; Lucas Reijnders, *Het Boerenbedrijf in de Lage Landen: Geschiedenis en Toekomst* (Amsterdam: Van Gennep, 2002 [1997]), 57–69; Erik Thoen and Tim Soens, "The Low Countries, 1000–1750" (2015), 1–30, accessed online at https://biblio .ugent.be/publication/3104675/file/7041326.pdf. For more on the Meyerij and reclaimed

heathland, see Brabants Historisch Informatie Centrum, 's-Hertogenbosch, The Netherlands (henceforth BHIC) 2 Kwartier Peelland, 147, Aen de heeren of the drei staten 'tlants van Brabant of heure gedeputeerden [1630].

20. Guicciardini, *De Idyllische Nederlanden*, 89–97; Bieleman, *Geschiedenis van de Landbouw*, 81–82, 95–100; Adriaenssen, *Staatsvormend Geweld*, 283–335; Reijnders, *Het Boerenbedrijf*, 57–69; Thoen and Soens, "The Low Countries, 1000–1750"; BHIC 2 Kwartier Peelland, 147, Aen de heeren of the drei staten 'tlants van Brabant of heure gedeputeerden [1630]. On plaggen soils, see P. Hoppenbrouwers, "Agricultural Production and Technology in the Netherlands, c. 1000–1500," in *Medieval Farming and Technology: The Impact of Agricultural Change in Northwest Europe*, ed. G. Astill and J. Langdon (Leiden: Brill, 1997), 89–114; C. C. Bakels, "Pollen from Plaggen Soils in the Province of North Brabant, The Netherlands," in *Man-made Soils*, ed. W. Groenman-van Waateringe and M. Robinson (Oxford: B.A.R., 1988), 35–54, accessed online at https://openaccess.leidenuniv.nl/bitstream/handle/1887/10054/1_957_058.pdf?sequence=1; and Laura I. Kooistra, "Vegetation History and Agriculture in the Cover-sand Area West of Breda (Province of Noord-Brabant, The Netherlands)," *Vegetation History and Archaeobotany* 17, no. 1 (January 2008): 113–25, accessed online at https://link.springer.com/article/10.1007/s00334-007-0107-9. On heath lands as "semi-natural," see Katrien Piessens and Martin Hermy, "Does the Heathland Flora in North-western Belgium show an Extinction Debt?" *Biological Conservation*, 132, no. 3 (October 2006), 382–94, accessed online at https://www-sciencedirect-com.ezproxy.princeton.edu/science/article/pii/S0006320706001893. On fallow systems and the intensive agriculture of Flanders and Brabant, see Jan de Vries, *The Economy of Europe in an Age of Crisis* (Cambridge: Cambridge University Press, 1976), 30–83.

21. Richard Weston, *A Discours of Husbandrie used in Brabant and Flanders showing the Wonderful Improvement of Land there; and serving as a Pattern for our Practice in this Common-Wealth* (London: William du-Gard, 1650), 1–13, accessed online at https://quod.lib.umich.edu/e/eebo/A65528.0001.001?rgn=main;view=fulltext.

22. On the mixture of agriculture and industry in the countryside of eastern North Brabant, see Adriaenssen, *Staatsvormend Geweld*, 283–335.

23. Dagomar Degroot, *The Frigid Golden Age: Climate Change, The Little Ice Age, and the Dutch Republic, 1560–1720* (Cambridge: Cambridge University, 2018); Geoffrey Parker, *Global Crisis: War, Climate Change and Catastrophe in the Seventeenth Century* (New Haven: Yale University Press, 2014 [2013]). On agriculture's vulnerability, see de Vries, *Economy of Europe in an Age of Crisis*, 30–36.

24. Gutmann, *War and Rural Life*, 75–110.

25. Gutman stresses that war created a favorable environment for epidemic diseases, see Gutmann, *War and Rural Life*, 158–68. Parker and Wilson depict disease as an ecological force, see Parker, *Thirty Years' War*, 211; and Wilson, *Europe's Tragedy*, 789–95.

26. Nederlandse Liederenbank, KNAW/Meertensinstituut, recordnummer 166059, Rederijkersliederen "Liefd est fundament," 001: f5 5r (liednummer 26), Pieter Cornelisz van der Mersch, Nieuw Jaer Liedt ann 1625.

27. De Graaf, *Oorlog*, 353, 492–94.

28. Adriaenssen, *Staatsvormend Geweld*, 199–200.

29. Adriaenssen, *Staatsvormend Geweld*, 12.

30. Adriaenssen, *Staatsvormend Geweld*, 87–183, 269–307, 411–12. See also Hart, *Dutch Wars of Independence*, 108–13; De Graaf, *Oorlog*, 196–99, 278–94, 440–45; and Swart, *Krijgsvolk*, 147–54.

The 1570s massacres as examples of Spanish (Habsburg) barbarity gained renewed currency in the 1620s, see A. Cunningham and O. P. Grell, *The Four Horsemen of the Apocalypse: Religion, War, Famine and Death in Reformation Europe* (Cambridge: Cambridge University Press, 2000), 155.

31. BHIC Oorlogslasten Kwartier Peelland, 147.141 (Trancripts Henk Beijers henceforth Beijers), RANB 044.03 (1615), Stukken betreffende de rekwisitien, c. 1615.

32. BHIC, 152, statements aldermen of Breugel, November 12 and December 2; Budel, December 1; Heeze, November 12; Zesgehuchten, November 10; Geldrop, November 29; Heeze, November 12; Lieshout, November 27; and statement lord of Nuenen, November 27, 1621.

33. Geoffrey Parker, *The Thirty Years' War* (New York: Military Heritage Press, 1987 [1984]), 47–61; Wilson, *Europe's Tragedy*, 269–313.

34. BHIC, 147, Oorlogslasten Kwartier Peelland, stukken betreffende de rekitsitien . . . gedurende de 80-jarige oorlog: Letter to de Heren Staten van Brabant van de vier kwartieren, December 1619; BHIC, 147.150 (Beijers), Specificatie van de onkosten; and BHIC, 147.151 (Beijers), Specificatie van de onkosten van het transport van geschut, April 9, 1620.

35. BHIC, 152.19 (Beijers), statement aldermen of Schijndel, December 11, 1621; Adriaenssen, *Staatsvormend Geweld*, 285.

36. Jonathan I. Israel, *The Dutch Republic and the Hispanic World, 1606–1661* (Oxford: Clarendon Press, 1982), 28–42, 86–109; Hart, *Dutch Wars of Independence*, 25; Wilson, *Europe's Tragedy*, 229–38, 252–55.

37. Israel, *Dutch Republic*, 100–106; Wilson, *Europe's Tragedy*, 339–65; and Hart, *Dutch Wars of Independence*, 42–43.

38. BHIC, 152.9–26 (Beijers), statements aldermen of Erp, November 28, 1621; Geldrop, November 29, 1621; Heeze, November 12, 1621; Liempde, December 23, 1623; Son, February 3, 1622; and Nuenen, December 29, 1623.

39. Het Markiezenhof Historisch Centrum (MHC), *Bergen Belegerd 1622, Markiezenhof Bergen op Zoom 30 September tot 30 Oktober 1972* (Bergen op Zoom: Het Markiezenhof Historisch Centrum, [1972]), 4 (Exhibition catalogue); WBA, 001, 3759, Mechelman to schoutet . . . Etten, [Antwerpen], February 17, 1623.

40. BHIC, 5 Oost-, Zuid- en Westkwartier van het Markiezaat van Bergen op Zoom, 46.

41. BHIC, 152.3 (Beijers), statement of aldermen of Budel, December 25, 1628.

42. WBA, 001, 3759, De Princen van Oranien, [The Hague], December 22, 1622.

43. WBA, 001, 3759, P[rince] de Oergaigne [Oranje] to sheriffs . . . Etten, Oosterhout, Rosendael [Roosendaal], Breda, February 15, 1623.

44. WBA, 001, 3759, Authoirisatie van sijne Furst Her: tegens de moetwilligen soldaten ende heerloose knechten, October 17, 1623 (The Hague, March 1, 1623). Prince Maurice sought to spare the countryside of the Barony of Breda, see Adriaenssen, *Staatsvormend Geweld*, 214.

45. BHIC, 152.27–35 (Beijers), statements of aldermen of Someren, December 27; Bakel, December 23; Lierop, December 23; Mierlo, December 22, 1623; and Veghel, January 15, 1624.

46. BHIC, 152.33 (Beijers), statement of aldermen of Tongelre, December 26, 1623.

47. WBA, 001, 3759, Sauvegardes 1621: Sauvegarde dAnthoine JansS Verbrugghe, Brussel, June 17, 1621, and Sauvegardes pour Labourer les Cheveaux au Etten: Le Conte D'Isenburg, May 2, 1621.

48. Israel, *Dutch Republic*, 105–9; Wilson, *Europe's Tragedy*, 364–65. On the inundations, see Hart, *Dutch Wars*, 108; and De Graaf, *Oorlog*, 526.

49. WBA, 001, 3759, Justinius de Nassau to schouten . . . van Etten ende Leure, Breda, July 16, 1624.

50. WBA, 001, 3759, Spinola, Sauvegarde Etten, camp Ginneken, August 30, 1624.

51. WBA, 001, 3760, Staat van Oorlogslasten. Specificaties . . . verteerde costen, 1624, Etten, May 25, 1628.

52. WBA, 001, 3759, Den Capiteijn vand Fluytkip to Schout, Etten, September 7, 1624.

53. BHIC, 347 Collectie Verheijen 60, Attestatie Gemeijne shepene van 7 dorpen . . . van Cuijck, September 16, 1624.

54. WBA, 001, 3761, Gouverneur tot Bergen op Zoom to Schout . . . van Etten, Willemstad, October 4, 1624.

55. Israel, *Dutch Republic*, 105–9, 217–18.

56. WBA, 001, 3759, Public notice, 's-Gravenhage, September 2, 1624.

57. WBA, 001, 3759, Casimir to Schout Etten, January 20, 1625 and Concept Minuut rekwest, 1625.

58. WBA, 001, 3759, Pardon van . . . Graef Ernst voor die van Etten, Ro[o]sendaal, April 9, 1625.

59. WBA, 001, 3759, Copie Missive Comte d'Isenburg, Campe Beauchamps, Leur, May 2, 1625. Count Ernst von Isenburg was a German Catholic in the Spanish service, see William P. Guthrie, *The Later Thirty Years War: From the Battle of Wittstock to the Treaty of Westphalia* (Westport, CT: Greenwood Press, 2003), 172–74, 178.

60. Israel, *Dutch Republic*, 105–9.

61. WBA, 450 Oud Archief Klundert 1561, Plague ordinance, Nijervaert, June 28, 1625; Wilson, *Europe's Tragedy*, 789–95; De Graaf, *Oorlog*, 498–500, 505–6.

62. WBA, 001, 3759, Requeste van Surseancie der connix beden. Aen mijne E. heeren die gedeputeerden van de staten van Brabant (with response November 19, 1624); and WBA, 001, 3761 Stukken betreffende overlast en oorlogslasten tijdens de Spaanse Bezetting van Breda 1625–37, Aen mijne heeren de Baron van Batanco [Balancon] gouverneur van stadt van Breda [1630 or 1631].

63. WBA, 001, 3759, Pardon general du Marquis and [Frederick] Hendrick of Nassau, Camp Waalwijck, June 30, 1625; WBA, 001, 3761, Sauvegarde pour le village de Etten . . . Baron de Balancon, December 9, 1625. On Claude de Rye, Baron of Balançon, see https://www.geni.com/people/Claude-de-Rye-de-la-Palud-Baron-of-Valan%C3%A7on/6000000016817488126.

64. BHIC, 2 Kwartier Peelland, 150, Placcaet op't uytloopen vande Soldaten, 1625 and 1629.

65. Israel, *Dutch Republic*, 162–74; Wilson *Europe's Tragedy*, 434.

66. BHIC, 152.44 (Beijers), statement of aldermen Liempde, April 23, 1629.

67. BHIC, 152.58 (Beijers), statement of aldermen of Tongelre, April 10, 1629.

68. BHIC, 152.48 (Beijers), statement of aldermen of Lieshout, April 16, 1629.

69. Israel, *Dutch Republic*, 162–76, 217–23.

70. BHIC, 152.4 (Beijers), statement of aldermen of Budel, June, 13, 1629; BHIC, 152.36 (Beijers), statement of aldermen of Aarle Rixtel, June 14, 1629; BHIC, 152.37, statement of aldermen of Bakel, June 14, 1629; BHIC, 152.39 (Beijers), statement of aldermen of Breugel, June 18, 1629; BHIC, 152.40 (Beijers), statement of Johan Legrueff, Heusden, June 13, 1629; BHIC, 152.41 (Beijers), statement of aldermen of Deurne, June 13, 1629; BHIC, 152.42 (Beijers), statement of aldermen of Erp, June 13, 1629; BHIC, 152.45 (Beijers), statement of aldermen of Maarheeze, June 13,

1629; BHIC, 152.46 (Beijers), statement of aldermen of Tongelre, June 13, 1629; BHIC, 152.47 (Beijers), statement of aldermen of Lierop, June 13, 1629; BHIC, 152.51 (Beijers), statement of aldermen of Mierlo, June 13, 1629; BHIC, 152.52 (Beijers), statement of aldermen of Geldrop, June 13, 1629; BHIC, 152.53 (Beijers), statement of aldermen of Nederwetten, June 13, 1629; BHIC, 152.54 (Beijers), statement of aldermen of Helmond, June 13, 1629; BHIC, 152.55 (Beijers), statement of aldermen of Nuenen, June 13, 1629; BHIC, 152.56 (Beijers), statement of aldermen of Someren, June 13, 1629; BHIC 152.57 (Beijers), statement of aldermen of Stiphout, June 14, 1629; BHIC, 152.58 (Beijers), statement of aldermen of Tongelre, April 10, 1629; BHIC, 152.60 (Beijers), statement of aldermen of Vlierden, June 13, 1629; BHIC, 152.61 (Beijers), statement of aldermen of Lieshout, June 14, 1629; BHIC, 152.62 (Beijers), statement of aldermen of Son, June 18, 1629.

71. Adriaenssen, *Staatsvormend Geweld*, 281–303, 367–75; Hart, *Dutch Wars*, 69–70, 108; De Graaf, *Oorlog*, 527–32.

72. On the siege, see Israel, *Dutch Republic*, 176–77; and Wilson, *Europe's Tragedy*, 409–23. On the exactions and the threat by Frederick Hendrick, see BHIC, 2, 148, De Prince van Orange to Schout van Peellant int leger voor S Hertogenb[osch], July 12, 1629; and BHIC, 2, 153, Someren, April 14, 1642.

73. BHIC, 2, 153, Attestatie Burgemeesteren en regenten dorp van Vlierde, August 21, 1631.

74. Israel, *Dutch Republic*, 176–80; Hart, *Dutch Wars*, 112–13, 76. See also De Graaf, *Oorlog*, 462–64, 526–27 (inundations),

75. BHIC, 2, 148, Ingesetenen v/d vlecken en dorpen Peelant aen Raad van State, October 10, 1629; BHIC, 2, 150, Van ingezetenen van de vlekken en dorpen van het Kwartier Peelland to Raad van State, 1629.

76. BHIC, 2, 151, Isabel Clara Eugenia byder Gratien Godts, Infant van Spagnien, Reglement op het uyt-loopen, passagien ende logeringhe van die Soldaten ten platen lande onder contributie, Brussel 1630.

77. BHIC, 2, 147, Aen de heeren of the drei staten 'tlants van Brabant of heure gedeputeerden [1630].

78. WBA, 001, 3761, copi Raedt van State, February 14, 1630; Schout van Etten to Monsieur Catz, April 20, 1630; Denominatie vande persoonene die binnen de dorpe van etten ende op Leur sijn comen woonen, April 20, 1630; Schout . . . verclaeren dat sij de bovengestelde persoonen hebben getaxeert [1630]. For the number of households, see WBA, 001 Etten Leur 3761, Cohier van de capitaele Impositie, May 14, 1631.

79. Israel, *Dutch Republic*, 178–84; Wilson, *Europe's Tragedy*, 437–38.

80. WBA, 001 Etten Leur 3761, Om te leveren binnen Breda; Schijndel and Volgens dit cohier allen de ingesetenen daer inne genoemt . . . te gelasten, November 16, 1630, and various requisitions of carts and horses for the service of the king (all 1630) and drossaert stad Breda orders Etten to supply 40 oak trees [March 1630].

81. WBA, 001 Etten Leur 3761, magistrate Baronie van Breda to Baron van Balacon [1630 or 1631].

82. WBA, 001 Etten Leur 3761, les magistrats du pays de Breda to Baron de Balancon [1631].

83. WBA, 001, 3761, ordonnatie van de heeren schouten en schepene van Breda, May 14, 1631 (Memorij van het op Verreckening van het pluijchgelt, April 30, 1631).

84. WBA, 001, 3761, Cohier van de capitaele Impositie . . . Etten, May 14, 1631.

85. WBA, 001, 3761, Paspoort . . . om levendige sauvegarde, Leger te Halsteren, September 14, 1631.

86. WBA, 001, 3761, Alsoo den here van Balancon . . . twalf voederen hooijs, December 1, 1631.

87. WBA, 001, 3761, Specificatie van de wagendiensten gedaen bijdie van Etten inne het jaere 1631, 1632.

88. BHIC, 2 Kwartier Peelland, 148, Ordonnantie vande Raedt van State, February 11, 1631.

89. BHIC, 2, 148, Declaratie . . . byden vlecken en[de] dorpen van . . . Peelant, January 10, 1631; BHIC, 152.43 (Beijers), statement of aldermen of Geldrop, April 11, 1631.

90. Israel, *Dutch Republic*, 184–89: Parker, *Thirty Years War*, 129; Wilson, *Europe's Tragedy*, 520–23.

91. On the pest, see P. J. H. Ubachs, *Twee Heren, Twee Confessies: De Verhouding van Staat en Kerk te Maastricht, 1632–1673* (Assen: Van Gorcum, 1975), 15–18; De Graaf, *Oorlog*, 498–500, 581–82; Parker, *Thirty Years' War*, 129–33; and Wilson, *Europe's Tragedy*, 440–58, 483–86, 530–42.

92. BHIC, 2 Kwartier Peelland, 148, No. 2448.2 Staet . . . van[de] beschadicheyt . . . geleden door de trupen van Grave Johan van Nassauw, November 1632; BHIC, 2, 153, Someren, April 14, 1642, and statements of aldermen of Heeze, March 22, 1642, and aldermen of Leende, March 22, 1642. On Henry or Hendrick Casimir, see Marjolein C. 't Hart, *The Making of a Bourgeois State: War, Politics and Finance during the Dutch Revolt* (Manchester: Manchester University Press, 1993), 21.

93. BHIC, 2, 148, Staet . . . beschaedicheijt . . . geleeden door de trupen van . . . Graeff vanden Berghe, September 1632, and No. 2448.2 Staet . . . beschadicheyt . . . geleden door de trupen van Grave Johan van Nassauw, November, 1632; BHIC, 2, 153, Attestatie schepenen Breugel, Staatse voetvolk . . . van Graaf [Casimir] Hendrick, January 18, 1633.

94. BHIC, 2 Kwartier Peelland 153, Attestatie Schepenen van Baeckel [Bakel], January 24, 1633.

95. BHIC, 2, 153, Someren, April 14, 1642.

96. WBA, 001, 3761, Alsoo de heeren raden van staten bericht sijn dat de Graeff Jan van Nassau nu onlangs met des vijandts ruijterije in verscheijden quartieren het plattelandt deurreden hebbende, December 28, 1632. The documents sometimes confuse the two cousins. For John of Nassau, see Israel, *Dutch Republic*, 178, 183, 223; and Wilson, *Europe's Tragedy*, 437–38.

97. WBA, 001, 3761, Alsoo de heeren raden van staten bericht sijn dat de Graeff Jan van Nassau . . . December 28, 1632, and sheriffs and aldermen of Leur, Hage, Sundert en Rijsbergen to the [royalist] Estates of Brabant, January 17, 1633. The aldermen directed the same letter to the Dutch Council of State.

98. WBA, 001, 3761, Aen mijn . . . Heeren Staten general der verenigde Nederlanden: Geven ootmoedelijck te kennen d'Ingesetene van de heeren etten ende de Leur, April 3, 1633 (includes response by the Dutch General Estates). The beehives were probably moved seasonally from the Brabant heath lands west of Breda to the pastures of the broad river valleys of the Langstraat to the north of Breda. The Langstraat was a district of the Province of Holland but today is part of the modern Province of Brabant. For the seasonal movement of bees, see also Adriaenssen, *Staatsvormend Geweld*, 284.

99. Israel, *Dutch Republic*, 189–90.

100. BHIC, 2 Kwartier Peelland 153, statements of aldermen of Heeze, March 22, 1642, and Leende, March 22, 1642.

101. BHIC, 2 Kwartier Peelland 153, see, for example, the statements of the aldermen of Someren (Someren), November 9, 1633, and Liempden, January 24, 1633 [1634].

102. BHIC, 2 Kwartier Peelland, 148, Repartitie die het quartier van peelant vander quatiteijt van hondert mudden rogge, June 11, 1633. A Mud ranges from 301 to 430 liters, see J. M. Verhoeff, *De Oude Nederlandse Maten en Gewichten* (Amsterdam: Meertens Instituut, 1983), 35–37, 115–16.

103. BHIC, 272 (Archief van de) Kommanderij (van de Duitse Orde) Gemert 1332, Akte van attestatie van schepenen Geldrop op verzoek van Hendrik de Bije, pastor te Geldtrop, betreffende . . . de verwoestingen . . . in 1633 zijn aangericht door de Staatse en Zweedse troepen, [December 28], 1639; BHIC, 2 Kwartier Peelland 153, statement of aldermen of Geldrop, April 5, 1642. On Swedish troops, see Wilson, *Europe's Tragedy*, 522–23.

104. BHIC, 2, 153, Someren, April 14, 1642.

105. WBA, 450 Oud Archief Klundert 1305, Die Burgeme[este]r . . . der stede Nijerbaert . . . doen condt. . . . February 1, 1633.

106. Israel, *Dutch Republic*, 250–51.

107. WBA, 001, 3761, Lodora y Andneca, Antwerpen, June 24, 1634.

108. WBA, 001, 3761, Heere Alexander, Santvliet, July 2, 1634.

109. WBA, 001 Etten Leur 3761, Extracts werts boecke Leur, November 25, 1634; Specificatie van de verteeringe gedaen binnen etten, July 8, 1634; and Schouten ende schepenen van beijde [schepen]bancken tot Etten ordineren Marinusch Jan Anthois Soossch, Hoeven, September 28, 1634.

110. WBA, 001, 3761, Die Drossardt . . . van Breda . . . Bij den Coninck, Brussel July 24, 1634.

111. Israel, *Dutch Republic*, 251–55; De Graaf, *Oorlog*, 552–54.

112. WBA, 001, 3761, Duc de Bouillon . . . et comte de Turenne, Maestricht [Maastricht], September 5, 1635. On Turenne, see Hart, *Dutch Wars*, 59 and 63; Parker, *Thirty Years' War*, 147; Wilson, *Europe's Tragedy*, 605–6.

113. Israel, *Dutch Republic*, 254–58; Wilson, *Europe's Tragedy*, 659–61.

114. BHIC, 2, 153, Someren, April 14, 1642.

115. WBA, 001, 3761, Order by Frederik Hendrik van Nassau, October 7, 1637.

116. Israel, *Dutch Republic*, 258–63, 315–24, 347–74; Wilson, *Europe's Tragedy*, 588–677. For Oisterwyk's wagons, BHIC, 4, 80, Repartitie, June 3, 1638.

117. WBA, 001, 3762, Schout en schepenen van etten to rade van state [1641 or 1642].

118. BHIC, 2 Kwartier Peelland 153, statement of aldermen of Geldrop, April 5, 1642.

119. BHIC, 2, 153, Someren, April 14, 1642.

120. BHIC, 2 Kwartier Peelland 153, statements of aldermen of Heeze, March 22, 1642, and Leende, March 22, 1642.

121. WBA, 001, 3762, Den Rade van State der vereenigde Nederlanden [1642].

122. WBA 001, 3762, Doctor d'Andrade to Magistraet van Etten, Etten, June 25, 1642, and Andrade to schepenen van etten [1642].

123. BHIC 2, 149, Resitutie regeerders . . . van de quartiers van Peelant ende Kempenland tegens de regeerders . . . van het kwartier van Oisterwijck [Oisterwyk], September 12, 1644.

124. BHIC, 2, 149, Aen . . . Heeren Rade van Staten der Vereenigde Nederlanden, June 25, 1644.

125. BHIC, 2, 149, Attestien . . . by Schout Peelant, November 7, 1644, stukken aengaende militaire extortien.

126. WBA, 001, 3762, Taxatie vande peerden gesonden naer Bergen, May 31, 1645.

127. WBA, 001, 3762, Liste van de wagens . . . ten dienste van sijnne hooch[eij]h, 1646; BHIC, 4, 80, statement of Jan Egberts van der Woel, May 19, 1650.

128. Adriaenssen, *Staatsvormend Geweld*, 254.

129. Wilson, *Europe's Tragedy*, 801–6.

130. Hart, *Making of a Bourgeois State*, 45, 94–100

131. Gutmann, *War and Rural Life*, 108–10.

132. Hart, *Dutch Wars*, 81–125, 170–97.

Chapter Four: Raiders and Refugees: Environcide, Displacement, and Disease in 17th Century North America

1. Daniel K. Richter, "The Ordeal of the Longhouse: Change and Persistence on the Iroquois Frontier, 1609–1720" (PhD dissertation, Columbia University, 1984), 370.

2. Richter, "Ordeal of the Longhouse," 537.

3. *Relations des Jesuites dans la Nouvelle France* (henceforth RJ), vol. 2 (Quebec: Augustin Coté, 1888), Relations 1649, Relation Huron 1648–49, 29–31, accessed online at https://archive .org/details/relationsdesjso1jesu.

4. Ned Blackhawk, *Violence over the Land: Indians and Empires in the Early American West* (Cambridge, MA: Harvard University Press, 2006), 3–4, 7–8; W. Cronon, *Changes in the Land: Indians, Colonists, and the Ecology of New England* (New York: Hill and Wang, 1988), 12–13.

5. Nicole Graham, *Lawscape: Property, Environment, Law* (Abington, UK: Routledge, 2011), 46–50, 95–96, 100–101; Michael Witgen, *An Infinity of Nations: How the Native New World Shaped Early North America* (Philadelphia: University of Pennsylvania Press, 2012), 38.

6. On the similarities between the Spanish and English conquistadors, see Jorge Cañizares-Esguerra, *Puritan Conquistadores: Iberianizing the Atlantic, 1550–1700* (Stanford: Stanford University Press, 2006). On the Dutch, see Wim Klooster, "Marteling, Muiterij, en Beeldenstorm: Militair Geweld in de Nederlandse Atlantische Wereld, 1624–1654," in *Geweld in de West: Een Militaire Geschiedenis van de Nederlandse Atlantische Wereld, 1600–1800*, ed. Victor Enthoven, Henk den Heijer, and Han Jordaan (Leiden: Brill, 2013), 313–43; and Benjamin Schmidt, *The Dutch Imagination and the New World, 1570–1670* (Cambridge: Cambridge University Press, 2006 [2001]), 167–305.

7. Cañizares-Esguerra, *Puritan Conquistadores*, 5–34; Kathleen Donegan, *Seasons of Misery: Catastrophe and Colonial Settlement in Early America* (Philadelphia: University of Pennsylvania Press, 2014).

8. J. Diamond, *Guns, Germs, and Steel: The Fates of Human Societies* (New York: Norton, 1997), 212–13. See also Gary Clayton Anderson, *Kinsmen of Another Kind: Dakota-White Relations in the Upper Mississippi Valley, 1650–1862* (Lincoln: University of Nebraska Press, 1984), 21; Thomas M. Whitmore and B. L. Turner II, *Cultivated Landscapes of Middle America on the Eve*

of Conquest (Oxford: Oxford University Press, 2001), 3; Linda A. Newson, *Life and Death in Early Colonial Ecuador* (Norman: University of Oklahoma Press, 1995), 4–8, 278–79, 305–21. McNeill argues that in a later stage such newly introduced diseases as yellow fever and malaria turned against fresh invaders from Europe in the tropical and subtropical regions of the Americas, see J. R. McNeill, *Mosquito Empires: Ecology and War in the Greater Caribbean, 1620–1914* (Cambridge: Cambridge University Press, 2010).

9. Kelton, *Epidemics and Enslavement*, 47–48; Paul Kelton, *Cherokee Medicine, Colonial Germs: An Indigenous Nation's Fight against Smallpox, 1518–1824* (Norman: University of Oklahoma Press, 2015), 4–5; and RJ, vol. 1, Relation 1639, 39–54.

10. In isolated cases, biological warfare was used through intently spreading contaminated goods, see Elizabeth A. Fenn, *Pox Americana: The Great Smallpox Epidemic of 1775–82* (New York: Hill and Wang, 2001), 88, 129–32; Eric Hinderaker and Peter C. Mancall, *At the Edge of Empire: The Backcountry in British North America* (Baltimore: Johns Hopkins University Press, 2003), 6, 9, 15–17; Paul Kelton, *Epidemics and Enslavement: Biological Catastrophe in the Native Southeast, 1492–1715* (Lincoln: University of Nebraska Press, 2007).

11. David R. M. Beck, *Siege and Survival: History of the Menominee Indians, 1634–1856* (Lincoln: University of Nebraska press, 2002), 64; Hinderaker and Mancall, *At the Edge of Empire*, 6, 9, 15–17; Colin G. Galloway, *The Western Abenakis of Vermont, 1600–1800: War, Migration, and the Survival of an Indian People* (Norman: University of Oklahoma Press, 1990), xxiii, 22–23, 35–39.

12. Blackhawk argues that violence was the central factor in the post-Columbian encounter, but adheres to the contagion model, see Blackhawk, *Violence over the Land*, 28–29. Kelton emphasizes the war created a disease ecology that made indigenous Americans vulnerable to epidemics, see Kelton, *Epidemics and Enslavement*.

13. John Grenier, *The First Way of Making War: American War Making on the Frontier* (Cambridge: Cambridge University Press, 2005), 22–39. Fenn (over)emphasizes the contagion model; she shows that on many occasions, nutritional stress and exposure created the conditions for the outbreak of epidemics, for example, during the siege of Boston or the Quebec campaign. See Fenn, *Pox Americana*.

14. Shelley R. Saunders, Peter G. Ramsden, and D. Ann Herring, "Transformation and Disease: Precontact Ontario Iroquians," Verano and Ubelaker, *Disease and Demography*, 117–25; Kelton, *Epidemics and Enslavement*, 1–46; Hinderaker and Mancall, *At the Edge of Empire*, 33–35.

15. Gary W. Crawford, "People and Plant Interactions in the Northeast," in *The Subsistence Economies of Indigenous North American Societies: A Handbook*, ed. Bruce D. Smith (Washington, DC: Smithsonian Institution Scholarly Press, 2011), 431–47; Gayle J. Fritz, "Levels of Native Biodiversity in Eastern North America," in *Biodiversity and Native America*, ed. Paul E. Minnis and Wayne J. Elisens (Norman: University of Oklahoma Press, 2000), 223–47; W. E. Doolittle, *Cultivated Landscapes of Native North America* (Oxford: Oxford University Press, 2001 [2000]), 119–216.

16. Paul A. Otto, *The Dutch-Munsee Encounter in America: The Struggle for Sovereignty in the Hudson Valley* (New York: Berghahn Books, 2006), 16, 38–39, 64.

17. Witgen, *Infinity of Nations*, 86–96.

18. See R. Douglas Hurt, *Indian Agriculture in America: Prehistory to the Present* (Lawrence: University of Kansas, 1987), 65–66; Richter, "Ordeal of the Longhouse," 3.

19. R. Douglas Hurt, *The Ohio Frontier: Crucible of the Old Northwest, 1720–1830* (Bloomington: Indiana University Press, 1996), 39–40.

20. Jonathan E. Kerber, ed., *Archaeology of the Iroquois* (Syracuse: Syracuse University Press, 2007), the chapters by Gary A. Warrick, "The Precontact Iroquian Occupation of Southern Ontario," 124–63; Robert J. Hasenstab, "Aboriginal Settlement Patterns in Late Woodland Upper New York State," 164–88; William E. Englebrecht, "New York Iroquois Political Development," 219–33; William R. Fitzgerald, "Contact, Neutral Iroquian Transformation and the Little Ice Age," 251–68; Gary A. Warrick, "European Infectious Disease and Depopulation of the Wendat-Tionontate (Huron-Petun)," 269–84; Gary Warrick, *A Population History of the Huron-Petun, A.D. 500–1650* (Cambridge: Cambridge University Press, 2008), 3–26, 55–58, 89–103; Charles T. Gehring and William A. Starna, trans. and ed., *A Journey into Mohawk and Oneida Country, 1634–1635: The Journal of Harmen Meyndertsz van den Bogaert* (Syracuse: Syracuse University Press, 1988). For more information on the village site being transformed in fields by 1635, see RJ, vol. 1, Relation 1635, 28. French missionaries commented that Huron villages moved every decade depending on the condition of the wood used for their construction, see RJ, vol 1, Relation 1636, 131.

21. Warrick, "European Infectious Disease," 269–84; Warrick, *Population History*, 11–12, 73–77, 116–48, 192–243.

22. Dean R. Snow, in *In Mohawk Country: Early Narratives about a Native People*, ed. Dean R. Snow, Charles T. Gehring, and William A. Starna (Syracuse: Syracuse University Press, 1996), xx; Dean R. Snow, *Mohawk Valley Archaeology: The Sites* (University Park, PA: Matson Museum of Anthropology, Penn State University, 1995), Occasional Papers in Anthropology Number 23.

23. Denevan, *Cultivated Landscapes*, 236, 278–86; W. E. Doolittle, *Cultivated Landscapes of Native North America* (Oxford: Oxford University Press, 2001 [2000]), 71–72, 144, 194–216, 428–52.

24. Hurt, *Indian Agriculture*, 29, 31, 34–35.

25. Doolittle, *Cultivated Landscapes*, 119–216; David Thurston and Joanne Parker, "Raised Beds and Plant Disease Management," in *The Cultural Dimension of Development: Indigenous Knowledge Systems*, ed. D. Michael Warren, L. J. Slikkerveer, and David Brokensha (London: Intermediate Technologies, 1995), 140–46.

26. It seems that the practice was new to Byrd. See Julia E. Hammett, "Ethnohistory of Aboriginal Landscapes in the Southeastern United States," Minnis and Elisens, *Biodiversity and Native America*, 248–99. See also John R. Stilgoe, *Common Landscape of America, 1580 to 1845* (New Haven: Yale University Press, 1982), 170–82.

27. Hurt, *Indian Agriculture*, 29, 31, 34–35.

28. Hurt, *Indian Agriculture*, 29, 31, 34–35; RJ, vol. 1, Relation 1637, 79 (smoke-filled lands).

29. W. Cronon, *Changes in the Land*; S. J. Pyne, *Fire in America: A Cultural History of Wildland and Rural Fire* (Seattle: University of Washington Press, 1997 [1982]); Pyne, *World Fire*; O. S. Stewart, *Forgotten Fires: Native Americans and the Transient Wilderness*, ed. H. T. Lewis and M. K. Anderson (Norman: University of Oklahoma Press, 2002); R. Boyd, ed., *Indians, Fire and the Land in the Pacific Northwest* (Corvallis: Oregon State University Press, 1999). T. R. Vale, "The Pre-European Landscape of the United States: Pristine of Humanized?" in *Fire, Native Peoples and the Natural Landscape*, ed. Vale (Washington, DC: Island Press, 2002), 1–39.

30. Gayle J. Fritz, "Levels of Native Biodiversity in Eastern North America," Minnis and Elisens, *Biodiversity and Native America*, 223–47; Gordon G. Whitney, *From Coastal Wilderness to Fruited Plain: A History of Environmental Change in Temperate North America from 1500 to the Present* (Cambridge: Cambridge University Press, 1996 [1994]), 107–20.

31. Julia E. Hammett, "Ethnohistory of Aboriginal Landscapes in the Southeastern United States," Minnis and Elisens, *Biodiversity and Native America*, 248–99.

32. Meghan C. L. Howey, *Mound Builders and Monument Makers of the Northern Great Lakes, 1200–1600* (Norman: University of Oklahoma Press, 2012), 4–5, 80–83.

33. On floodplain cropping in the Lower Mississippi, see Hurt, *Indian Agriculture*, 15. On mounds in general, see Paul Goldberg and Richard I. MacPhail, *Practical and Theoretical Geoarchaeology* (Malden, MA: Blackwell, 2006), 225–231; and M. Bierma et al., eds., *Terpen en Wierden in het Fries-Gronings Kustgebied* (Groningen: Wolters-Noordhof/Forsten, 1988).

34. Thomas T. Waterman, *North American Indian Dwellings* (Washington, DC: GPO, 1925), 1–4; Frances Densmore, *How Indians Use Wild Plants for Food, Medicine, and Crafts* (New York: Dover Publications, 1974 [1928]), 386–90. On the missionary longhouses, RJ, vol. 1, Relation 1637, 168–77 and 1639, 53–54.

35. James D. Rice, *Nature and History in the Potomac Country: From Hunter-Gatherers to the Age of Jefferson* (Baltimore: Johns Hopkins Press, 2009), 37. Longhouses as warm and well-insulated but smoke-filled, see RJ, vol. 1, Relation 1636, 94, and 1639, 57.

36. Whitmore Turner, *Cultivated Landscapes of Middle America*, 61–63.

37. Waterman, *North American Indian Dwellings*, 1–4.

38. Driver and Massey, *Comparative Studies*, 247; Mima Kapches, "The Iroquoian Longhouse: Architectural and Cultural Identity," in *Archaeology of the Iroquois*, ed. Jonathan E. Kerber (Syracuse: Syracuse University Press, 2007), 174–88; Johannes Megapolensis Jr., "A Short Account of the Mohawk Indians (1644)," Snow, Gehring, and Starna, *In Mohawk Country*, 38–46, 43 (Mohawk pit storage); and *Journey into Mohawk and Oneida Country*, (food stores, 1634). See also RJ, vol. 1, Relation 1635, 32 (grain in longhouses Huron).

39. Howey, *Mound Builders and Monument Makers*, 98–100.

40. David R. M. Beck, *Siege and Survival: History of the Menominee Indians, 1634–1856* (Lincoln: University of Nebraska Press, 2002), 8–15.

41. Driver and Massey, *Comparative Studies*, 247, 258; and J. Leitch Wright Jr., *The Only Land They Knew: The Tragic Story of the American Indians in the Old South* (New York: Free Press, 1981), 9–10.

42. R. Douglas Hurt, *The Ohio Frontier: Crucible of the Old Northwest, 1720–1830* (Bloomington: Indiana University Press, 1996), 22–23; Hurt, *Indian Agriculture*, 9, 19, 27, 31, 34, 41, 50–61. On processing salmon, see R. White, *The Organic Machine: The Re-Making of the Columbia River* (New York: Hill and Wang, 2000 [1995]), 18–21. On nuts and berries, see Gayle J. Fritz, "Levels of Native Biodiversity in Eastern North America," Minnis and Elisens, *Biodiversity and Native America*, 223–47.

43. On the De Soto expedition using indigenous American food stores, see Charles Hudson, *Knights of Spain, Warriors of the Sun: Hernando de Soto and the South's Ancient Chiefdoms* (Athens: University of Georgia Press, 1997), 104, 107–8, 117, 119–20, 127, 146, 164–65, 171, 181–84, 186, 189, 201, 205, 214–18, 247, 274, 284, 295, 311, 316, 332–34, 339–41, 364–65, 368–69, 373, 375, 378–79.

On stored fruit, berries and nuts (and stored hickory nut oil on one occasion), see Hudson, *Knights of Spain*, 121, 201, 214–18, 288–89, 322, 339, and 340–41.

44. Driver and Massey, *Comparative Studies*, 310–13.

45. John Verano, "Prehistoric Disease and Demography in the Andes," 15–24; Jane E. Buikstra, "Diet and Disease in Late Prehistory," 87–101; George R. Milner, "Disease and Sociopolitical Systems in Late Prehistoric Illinois," 103–16; Shelley R. Saunders, Peter G. Ramsden, and D. Ann Herring, "Transformation and Disease: Precontact Ontario Iroquians," 117–25, all in John W. Verano and Douglas H. Ubelaker, eds., *Disease and Demography in the Americas* (Washington, DC: Smithsonian Institution Press, 1992); Warrick, "European Infectious Disease," Kerber, *Archaeology of the Iroquois*, 269–84. Warrick argues that the deterioration of health suggested by the analysis of skeletal remains for settled maize farmers is not the result of diets (which improved) but an effect of denser settlement and conflict, see Warrick, *Population History*, 165–89.

46. P. A. Williams, A. M. Gordon, H. E. Garnett, and L. Buck, "Agroforestry in North America and Its Role in Farming Systems," in *Temperate Agroforestry Systems*, A. M. Gordon and S. M. Newman (Wallingford, UK: Cab International, 1997), 9–84 (especially 9–11); Kristen J. Gremillion, "The Role of Plants in Southeastern Subsistence Economies," in *The Subsistence Economies of Indigenous North American Societies: A Handbook*, ed. Bruce D. Smith (Washington, DC: Smithsonian Institution Scholarly Press, 2011), 387–99. Crawford notes that fruit and nut trees were concentrated at disturbed sites, that is at forest edges or near fields, see Gary W. Crawford, "People and Plant Interactions in the Northeast," Smith, *Subsistence Economies*, 431–47 (especially 436).

47. RJ, vol. 1, Relations 1634, 36; 1636, 96; RJ vol. 2, 1649 (Relations Huron 1649–50), 1–25.

48. For information on fruit trees near indigenous American villages, see Hudson, *Knights of Spain*, 71, 104–5, 121, 171, 288–89.

49. Julia E. Hammett, "Ethnohistory of Aboriginal Landscapes in the Southeastern United States," Minnis and Elisens, *Biodiversity and Native America*, 248–99. On the association of fruit and other trees and bushes with past indigenous American village and camp sites, see Gayle J. Fritz, "Levels of Native Biodiversity in Eastern North America," Minnis and Elisens, *Biodiversity and Native America*, 223–47.

49. Robert F. Heizer and Albert B. Elsasser, *The Natural World of the California Indians* (Berkeley: University of California Press, 1980), 183; William R. Hildebrandt and Kimberley Carpenter, "Native Hunting Adaptations in California: Changing Patterns of Resource Use from the Early Holocene to European Contact," Smith, *Subsistence Economies*, 131–46.

50. Driver and Massey, *Comparative Studies*; Ernest Small, *North American Cornucopia: Top 100 Indigenous Food Plants* (Boca Raton: CRC Press, 2014), 1–49, 409–11; Doolittle, *Cultivated Landscapes of Native North America*, 65–73; Williams, Gordon, Garnett, and Buck, "Agroforestry in North America," Gordon and Newman, *Temperate Agroforestry Systems*, 9–84; Heizer and Elsasser, *Natural World of the California Indians*, 183; and Hildebrandt and Carpenter, "Native Hunting Adaptations in California"; Gremillion, "Role of Plants in Southeastern Subsistence Economies"; Crawford, "People and Plant Interactions in the Northeast"; and C. Margaret Scarry and Richard A. Yarnell, "Native Domestication and Husbandry of Plants in Eastern North America," in Smith, *Subsistence Economies*, 131–46, 387–99, 431–47, 483–501, respectively.

51. Gayle J. Fritz, "Levels of Native Biodiversity in Eastern North America," Minnis and Elisens, *Biodiversity and Native America*, 223–47.

52. Significant (modern) indigenous North American domesticated crop plants include many Rubus subspecies, Vaccinium species, grape, pecan, and wild rice. See Small, *North American Cornucopia*, 1–35.

53. Sarah Carter, *Lost Harvests: Prairie Indian Reserve Farmers and Government Policy* (Montreal: McGill-Queen's University Press, 1990), 38–40.

54. RJ, vol. 1, Relation 1635, 30. The fear of frost damaging the maize crops was discussed during a Huron council meeting during in the winter of 1645/1646, see RJ, vol. 2, Relation 1645–46, 72.

55. Richter, "Ordeal of the Longhouse," 9–20, 67–70, 75–126; Kerber, *Archaeology of the Iroquois*, the chapters by Englebrecht, "New York Iroquois Political Development," 219–33; Fitzgerald, "Contact, Neutral Iroquian Transformation," 251–68; Warrick, "European Infectious Disease," 269–84; Robert D. Kuhn, "Reconstructing Patterns of Interaction and Warfare between the Mohawk and Northern Iroquoians During the A.D. 1400–1700 Period," 321–42. See also Hinderaker and Mancall, *At the Edge of Empire*, 33–35; Warrick, *Population History*, 26, 29–31, 116–21; and Steele, *Warpaths*, 59–79.

56. RJ, vol. 1, Relations 1634, 88–91; 1635, 18, 28–30, 36; 1638, 39–54.

57. RJ, vol. 1, Relation 1640, 53–61, 72; 1641, 69–70.

58. Richter, "Ordeal of the Longhouse," 73–126, 133–36, 165–69; Kerber, *Archaeology of the Iroquois*, the chapters by Englebrecht, "New York Iroquois Political Development," 219–33; Fitzgerald, "Contact, Neutral Iroquian Transformation," 251–68; Warrick, "European Infectious Disease," 269–84; and Kuhn, "Reconstructing Patterns of Interaction," 321–42. See also Hinderaker and Mancall, *At the Edge of Empire*, 33–35; Warrick, *Population History*, 11–12, 73–77, 116–48, 192–243; Steele, *Warpaths*, 59–79; and Adriaen Cornelissen van der Donck, trans. Diederik Goedhuys, "Description of New Netherland, 1653," Snow, Gehring, and Starna, *In Mohawk Country*, 104–30 (121–22) (concerns overhunting). Indigenous Americans of the St. Lawrence River Basin expressed fears about overhunting, see RJ, vol. 1, Relation 1637, 24.

59. RJ, vol. 1, Relation 1632, 5–9; Relation 1634, 88–91; 1635, 3, 15–18, 28–30, 36. Dry summer reported in Relation 1636, 82–84.

60. RJ, vol. 1, Relation 1636, 85–86, 91.

61. RJ, vol. 1, Relation 1637, 120–167.

62. RJ, vol. 1, Relation 1636, 92, 94.

63. RJ, vol. 1, Relation 1637, 33–34, 79–80, 82, 88–89.

64. RJ, vol. 1, Relation 1638, 54; 1639, 58, 67, and 77.

65. RJ, vol. 1, Relation 1639, 55–56, 59–62. The Wenro resettlement is visible in the archaeological record thanks to a distinctive pottery style identified with the Wenro. The Jesuits named the Wenro village St. Francis Xavier. See Warrick, *Population History*, 225–26 and 219, figure 7.14.

66. RJ, vol. 1, Relation 1641, 69–70.

67. RJ, vol. 1, Relation 1639, 58, 67, 77; 1641, 58, 69–70.

68. RJ, vol. 2, Relation 1642, 45–57.

69. RJ, vol. 2, Relation 1643, 62–79; 1644–45, 35–37.

70. The camp may have been part of a more permanent village with longhouses that the Algonquians only occupied in the winter, called St. Elisabeth by the Jesuits. See RJ, vol. 1, Relation 1641, 81–83; RJ, vol. 2, Relation 1943, 100–101; and Warrick, *Population History*, 219, figure 7.14 (no. 23).

71. RJ, vol. 2, Relation 1643 (Huron Relation June 1642–June 1643), 69. This is probably the unnamed town marked as no. 25 on Warrick's map. See Warrick, *Population History*, 219, figure 7.14.

72. RJ, vol. 2, Relation 1643, 105–7.

73. RJ, vol. 2, Relation 1644–45, 18–19, 39–40; 1643, 62–67.

74. RJ, vol. 2, Relation 1644–45, 34–35; 1645–46, 3–17. The town called Ononjoté or Ouniewte in the *relations jesuites* is referred to as a "daughter." The 1565 Map of the New Netherlands lists 4 Mohawk villages south of the river, which was based on outdated information. Moreover, the map also has the name of what appears to be the name of a place or village north of the river: Onjuro. See Snow, Gehring, and Starna, *In Mohawk Country*, 111, map 4.

75. RJ, vol. 2, Relation 1644–45, 22–34; 1645–46, 3–17, 55.

76. RJ, vol. 2, Relation 1647, 1–3.

77. JR, vol. 2, Relation 1648, 2, 24.

78. JR, vol. 2, Relation 1648, 10–13, 46–47.

79. JR, vol. 2, Relation 1648, 47–48, 56–57.

80. RJ, vol. 2, Relation 1648, 50–51; 1649, 9.

81. RJ, vol. 2, Relation 1649 (relations Huron 1648–49), 1–19; Warrick, *Population History*, 219, figure 7.14.

82. RJ, vol. 2, Relation 1649 (relations Huron 1649–50), 1–25.

83. RJ, vol. 2, Relation 1649 (relations Huron 1649–50), 1–25.

84. RJ, vol. 2, Relation 1649 (relations Huron 1649–1650), 11–12.

85. RJ, vol. 2, Relation 1649 (relations Huron 1649–50), 25–29.

86. Richter, "Ordeal of the Longhouse," 73–126, 133–36, and 165–69; Kerber, *Archaeology of the Iroquois*, chapters by William E. Englebrecht, "New York Iroquois Political Development," 219–33; William R. Fitzgerald, "Contact, Neutral Iroquian Transformation and the Little Ice Age," 251–68; Gary A. Warrick, "European Infectious Disease and Depopulation of the Wendat-Tionontate (Huron-Petun)," 269–84; and Kuhn, "Reconstructing Patterns of Interaction and Warfare," 321–42. See also Hinderaker and Mancall, *At the Edge of Empire*, 33–35; Warrick, *Population History*, 11–12, 73–77, 116–148, 192–243; Steele, *Warpaths*, 59–79; Cornelissen van der Donck, "Description of New Netherland, 1653," Snow, Gehring, and Starna, *In Mohawk Country*, 104–30 (121–22) (concerns overhunting); and RJ, vol. 1, Relation 1637, 24; RJ, vol. 3, Relation 1655, 25–34, 40–42; 1656–57, 4–6.

87. Richter, "Ordeal of the Longhouse," 73–126, 133–36, and 165–69; Kerber, *Archaeology of the Iroquois*, chapters by: William E. Englebrecht, "New York Iroquois Political Development," 219–233; William R. Fitzgerald, "Contact, Neutral Iroquian Transformation and the Little Ice Age," 251–268; Gary A. Warrick, "European Infectious Disease and Depopulation of the Wendat-Tionontate (Huron-Petun)," 269–284; and Kuhn, "Reconstructing Patterns of Interaction and Warfare," 321–342; Hinderaker and Mancall, *At the Edge of Empire*, 33–35; Warrick, *Population History*, 11–12, 73–77, 116–148, 192–243; Steele, *Warpaths*, 59–79; Cornelissen van der Donck, "Description of New Netherland, 1653," Snow, Gehring, and Starna, *In Mohawk Country*, 104–30

(121–22) (concerns overhunting); and RJ, vol. I, Relation 1637, 24; RJ, vol. 3, Relation 1655, 25–34, 40–42; and 1656–57, 4–6.

88. White, *Middle Ground*, 8–48; Witgen, *Infinity of Nations*, 18–20, 29–38, 43–68, 118–67.

89. Richter, "Ordeal of the Longhouse," 123–25, 173–99, 212–27; Steele, *Warpaths*, 59–79, 137–38; Witgen, *Infinity of Nations*, 232–38; RJ, vol. 3, Relation 1664–65, 3–10; 1665–66, 6–25. On Schenectady, see Thomas E. Burke Jr., *Mohawk Frontier: The Dutch Community of Schenectady, New York, 1661–1710* (Albany: State University of New York Press, 1991), 77–79. A French missionary supported the calls to "exterminate" the Mohawk, see Jérome Lalemant, "Of the Condition of the Country of the Iroquois, and of Their Cruelties. 1659–1660" and Jérome Lalemant, "Notable Embassy of the Iroquois: 1663–1664," Snow, Gehring, and Starna, *In Mohawk Country*, 131–35 (134) and 139–143 (142), respectively.

90. Francois-Joseph le Mercier, "Of the Mission and Sainte Marie Among the Iroquois of Agnié: 1667–1668," Snow, Gehring, and Starna, *In Mohawk Country*, 149–60 (155, 158–59); RJ, vol. 3, Relation 1667–68, 1–2, 28; 1668–69, 1–12, 30–31; 1668–69, 1–3, 8; 1669–70, 3, 9–70.

91. Richter, "Ordeal of the Longhouse," 123–25, 173–99, 212–27; Steele, *Warpaths*, 59–79, 137–38; Witgen, *Infinity of Nations*, 232–38.

92. Richter, "Ordeal of the Longhouse," 227–44, 247–54, 289–304, 366–67; Burke, *Mohawk Frontier*, 62, 79, 87–108; Witgen, *Infinity of Nations*, 234–40.

93. Richter, "Ordeal of the Longhouse," 227–44, 247–54, 289–304, 366–67; Burke, *Mohawk Frontier*, 62, 79, 87–108; Witgen, *Infinity of Nations*, 234–40.

94. Richter, "Ordeal of the Longhouse," 227–44, 247–54, 289–304, 366–67; Burke, *Mohawk Frontier*, 62, 79, 87–108; Witgen, *Infinity of Nations*, 234–40.

95. Richter, "Ordeal of the Longhouse," 537.

96. Richter, "Ordeal of the Longhouse," 537.

97. Richter, "Ordeal of the Longhouse," 119.

98. D. W. Meinig, *The Shaping of America: A Geographical Perspective on 500 Years of History*, vol. 1, *Atlantic America, 1492–1800* (New Haven and London: Yale University Press, 1986), 92–95, 119–20, 146–53, 208–13; Steele, *Warpaths*, 80–87; Cronon, *Changes in the Land*, 36; Nicole Graham, *Lawscape: Property, Environment, Law* (Abington, UK: Routledge, 2011), 130–31.

99. Meinig, *Shaping America*, 248–49; Steele, *Warpaths*, 80–87; Donegan, *Seasons of Misery*, 74–79, 97–101; W. Beinart and P. Coates, *Environment and History: The Taming of Nature in the USA and South Africa* (London: Routledge, 1995), 11; A. W. Schorger, *The Wild Turkey: Its History and Domestication* (Norman: University of Oklahoma Press, 1966), 365–408.

100. Hinderaker and Mancall, *At the Edge of Empire*, 36; Whitney, *From Coastal Wilderness*, 104–5.

101. Meinig, *Shaping of America*, 92–95, 119–20, 146–53, 208–13; Galloway, 23; Wright, *Only Land They Knew*, 70–91.

102. Warrick, "The Precontact Iroquian Occupation of Southern Ontario" and "European Infectious Disease," Kerber, *Archaeology of the Iroquois*, 124–63 and 269–84, respectively.

103. On the settler rhetoric, see Whitney, *From Coastal Wilderness*, 121–30.

104. Hurt, *Indian Agriculture*, 39; Doolittle, *Cultivated*, 188–89; Scott Weidensaul, *The First Frontier: The Forgotten History of Struggle, Savagery, and Endurance in Early America* (Boston: Houghton Mifflin Harcourt, 2012), 102, 120.

105. Doolittle, *Cultivated*, 81.

106. Meinig, *Shaping of America*, 92–95, 119–20, 146–53, 208–13; John Morgan Dederer, *War in America to 1775: Before Yankee Doodle* (New York: New York University Press, 1990), 126–35; Grenier, *First Way of Making War*, 21–34; Ferling, *Wilderness of Miseries*, 10–11; Geoffrey Parker, *Spain and the Netherlands, 1559–1659: Ten Studies* (Glasgow: Fontana, 1990 [1979]), 49 (Huguenots). On Fort Orange, see Burke, "Mohawk Frontier," 120.

107. Rice, *Nature and History in the Potomac Country*, 70–192; Utley and Washburn, *Indian Wars*, 7–8, 17–24; Steele, *Warpaths*, 37–109; Donegan, *Seasons of Misery*, 69–116.

108. On the Munsee, see Otto, *Dutch-Munsee Encounter*, 106–76; Schmidt, *Dutch Imagination*, 228–99. On the Mystic Massacre and the participation of Dutch Revolt veterans, see Weidensaul, *First Frontier*, 128–45.

109. Susanah Shaw Romney, *New Netherland Connections: Intimate Networks and Atlantic Ties in Seventeenth-Century America* (Chapel Hill: University of North Carolina Press, 2014), 141–45, 175–81; Donna Merwick, *The Shame and the Sorrow: Dutch-Amerindian Encounters in New Netherland* (Philadelphia: University of Pennsylvania Press, 2006), 3, 104–5, 135–38, 157–60, 209–55; and Lynn Ceci, *The Effect of European Contact and Trade on the Settlement Pattern of the Indians in Coastal New York, 1524–1665* (New York: Garland, 1990), 120–27, 214–67.

110. Shaw Romney, *New Netherland Connections*, 18–24, 122–27, 141–45, 159–60, 175–90.

111. On the Munsee, see Otto, *Dutch-Munsee Encounter*, 106–76; Steele, *Warpath*, 110–30; Schmidt, *Dutch Imagination*, 228–99.

112. Merwick, *Shame and the Sorrow*, 3, 104–5, 135–38, 157–60, 166–79, 209–55; Shaw Romney, *New Netherland Connections*, 9–12, 129–31, 136–44, 150–68, 173.

113. Merwick, *Shame and the Sorrow*, 166–79.

114. Otto, *Dutch-Munsee Encounter*, 106–76; Steele, *Warpath*, 110–30; Shaw Romney, *New Netherland Connections*, 9, 160–61, 172–73.

115. Doolittle, *Cultivated Landscapes*, 188.

116. Hinderaker and Mancall, *At the Edge of Empire*, 46–72; Steele, *Warpath*, 55–58; Weidensaul, *First Frontier*, 149–81; Cañizares-Esguerra, *Puritan Conquistadores*; Armstrong Starkey, *European and Native American Warfare, 1675–1815* (Norman: University of Oklahoma Press, 1998), 15–35, 57–82, 87–88.

117. See Leitch Wright, *Only Land They Knew*, 84, 126–61, 215–19; Wendy Warren, *New England Bound: Slavery and Colonization in Early America* (New York: Liveright, 2016), 9–12, 35–36, 83–113.

118. Kelton, *Epidemics and Enslavement*, 101–59.

119. See Leitch Wright, *Only Land They Knew*, 84–85, 114–15, 139–46; Utley and Washburn, *Indian Wars*, 54–57, 72; Steele, *Warpaths*, 51–52; Kelton, *Epidemics and Enslavement*.

120. Rice, *Nature and History in the Potomac Country*, 70–192.

121. Rice, *Nature and History in the Potomac Country*, 70–192; Steele, *Warpath*, 53–58.

122. Isaac Jogues, "Novum Belgium and an Account of René Goupil (1644)," Snow, Gehring, and Starna, *In Mohawk Country*, 29–37 (31–32).

123. Melville, *Plague of Sheep*; compare Noble D. Cook, *People of the Volcano: Andean Counterpoint in the Colca Valley of Peru* (Durham, NC: Duke University Press, 2007), 147. For livestock damaging fields, see, for example, Susan M. Deeds, "Double Jeopardy: Indian Women in Jesuit Missions of Nueva Vizcaya," in *Indian Women of Early Mexico*, ed. Susan Schroeder, Stephanie Wood, and Robert Haskett (Norman: University of Oklahoma Press, 1997), 255–72;

Linda Newson, *The Cost of Conquest: Indian Decline in Honduras under Spanish Rule* (Boulder, CO: Westview Press, 1986), 319; Rice, *Nature and History in the Potomac Country*, 108–9; Otto, *Dutch-Munsee Encounter*, 109.

Chapter Five: Limited War and Environcide in the Age of Reason

1. John Scot, "The Remembrance: A Metrical Account of the War of Flanders, 1701–12," in *Papers Illustrating the History of the Scots Brigade in the Service of the United Netherlands, 1572–1782*, ed. James Ferguson (Charleston, SC: Nabu Press, 1912), vol. 3, part 2, 459.

2. See Reed Browning, *The War of the Austrian Succession* (New York: St. Martin's Griffin, 1995), 5–6, 13. For the classic view of 18th-century limited war, see J. F. C. Fuller, *The Conduct of War, 1789–1961: A Study of the Impact of the French, Industrial, and Russian Revolutions on War and Its Conduct* (Westport, CT: Greenwood Press, 1981 [1961]), 20–37; Michael Howard, "Temperamenta Belli: Can War be Controlled?," in *Restraints on War: Studies in the Limitation of Armed Conflict*, ed. Michael Howard (Oxford: Oxford University Press, 1979), 1–15; and Michael Howard, "Constraints on Warfare," in *The Laws of War: Constraints on Warfare in the Western World*, ed. Michael Howard, George J. Andreopoulos, and Mark R. Shulman (New Haven: Yale University Press, 1994), 1–11. See also Myron P. Gutmann, *War and Rural Life in the Early Modern Low Countries* (Princeton: Princeton University Press, 1980), 54–71; Geoffrey Best, *Humanity in Warfare* (New York: Columbia Press, 1980), 1–67; Michael Howard, *War in European History* (Oxford: Oxford University Press, 1988 [1976]); William H. McNeill, *The Pursuit of Power: Technology. Armed Force, and Society since A.D. 1000* (Chicago: University of Chicago Press, 1982), 144–84. For a critique, see Jeremy Black, *Warfare in the Eighteenth Century* (London: Cassel, 2005 [1999]), 175–76.

3. Best, who argues that 18th-century governments and thinkers did not want citizens involved in war, also argues that regulated requisitioning rather than looting marked 18th-centuy war. See Geoffrey Best, "Restraints on War by Land Before 1945," Howard, *Restraints on War*, 17–37.

4. On legitimate war and warfare, see Michael Walzer, *Just and Unjust Wars: A Moral Argument with Historical Illustrations* (New York: Basic Books, 2000 [1977]). On the limited impact of articles of war, see Alexander Gillespie, *A History of the Laws of War*, vol. 2, *The Customs and Laws of War with Regards to Civilians in Times of Conflict* (Oxford: Hart, 2011), 63–65, 135–36. Centeno and Enriquez argue that the era of the military revolution wars with its rhetoric (and practice) of limited war (and making the distinction between combatants and non-combatants) is the exception, see Miquel A. Centeno and Elaine Enriquez, *War and Society* (Cambridge: Polity, 2016), 90–91.

5. On contributions, enemy territory, and symbolic punshment, see Gutmann, *War and Rural Life*, 41–46.

6. France and the Dutch Republic imposed contributions on neutral Liège, see Gutmann, *War and Rural Life*, 45.

7. Browning, *War of the Austrian Succession*, 13. Grenier argues that the American way of war diverted from the main European model of limited war and that it showed more continuity with both earlier European ways of war and Amerindian skulking warfare. His emphasis, however, is on military tactics, rather than the impact of societies and environments. See John Grenier,

The First Way of Making War: American War Making on the Frontier (Cambridge: Cambridge University press, 2005).

8. West-Brabants Archief, Bergen op Zoom, the Netherlands (henceforth WBA), 001 Etten Leur, 1727, Placaet tegen het passeren, inlogeren, uytteeren en plegen van insolentien in de Baronnye van Breda, Lande van Cuyck, &c. by de Militaire, 's Gravenhage: Jacobus Scheltus, 1694. The rebel Dutch Republic issued a pamphlet containing 83 Articles of War as early as 1590. Article 3 threatened with death any soldier who committed murder, rape, burning, theft, and violence. The purpose of the articles was to limit the destruction in the countryside. See Articule-brieff, ofte Ordonnantie op de Discipline Militaire (Delft: Aelbrecht Heyndricxz, 1590), accessed online at http//play.google.com/reader?id=xmxJAAAACAAJ&printsec =frontcover&output=reader.

9. Zeeuws Archief, Middelburg, the Netherlands (henceforth ZA) 7 Vrije van Sluis, 1584–1796, 344, Sluijs, Reglement, Gouvernment tot Hulst, M. van Coehoorn, January 1, 1703.

10. WBA, 001 Etten Leur, 1727, Placaet tegen het passeren, inlogeren, uytteeren, 1694; WBA, 001 Etten Leur, 1727, Placcaet De Staten Generaal der Vereenigde Nederlanden: Alsoo ons dage-lijcks menichvuldige klachten voorkomen . . . over de groote schade . . . by 's lands militia ('s-Gravenhage: Jacobus Scheltus, 1673); Brabants Historisch Informatie Centrum, 's-Hertogenbosch, the Netherlands (henceforth BHIC), 342, Plakkaten, 1520–1884, 4 (1746–57), 1750, 606/211, Ordre en Reglement, 's Gravenhage, July 10, 1750.

11. BHIC, 12 Kwartiersvergadering Kempenland, 41, Vorderingen . . . Spaanse successieoor-log, 1702–11, Stapel Codde to Mijn Heer, Eindhoven, June 27, 1711. In 1714 the magistrates of De Vrije of Dutch Flanders received a 1706 reprint of the April 1704 regulations sent by the Raden van Staten. See ZA, 7 Vrije van Sluis, 339, Extract Resolutien Raden van Staten, May 7, 1716, and Extract Resolutien Raden van Staten, November 6, 1714.

12. ZA, 7 Vrije van Sluis, 1584–1796, 344, Sluijs, February 1705; Reglement waar naer de Deen-sche troupen, Hulst, December 5, 1701. See also Reglement waer naer de troupes ten lande vanden Vrijen geinquartiert sijnde Baron van Coehoorn, Sluijs, February 5, 1705; Carl Wilhelm Sparr, Commandant van Staten Vlaanderen, ordonneert, Sluijs, February 5, 1705. See also WBA, 001 Etten Leur, 3776, Patent, De Staten Generaal . . . bevelen den Capteijn, The Hague, January 8, 1708 [*sic*: 1709] and De Staten Generaal . . . bevelen den Colonel, The Hague, January 8, 1709.

13. The English had their own articles of war that were reissued at the beginning of each war. The earliest printed articles of war date to the early 17th century and culminated in the Mutiny Act of 1688–89, drawn up by King William III. The act empowered the king to draw up articles of war. See E. Samuel, *An Historical Account of the British Army: And the Law Military as Declared by the Ancient and Modern Statutes, and Articles of War for Its Government* (London: William Clowes, 1816).

14. ZA, 7 Vrije van Sluis, 339, Accoord van contributie van het land van Artois, Camp de Lens, July 29, 1708, and Extract uijt het register der resoluties, August 15, 1708.

15. Gutmann, *War and Rural Life*, 62–64; ZA, 7 Vrije van Sluis, 339, Extract Resolutions, August 29, 1708, and Charles Elisnne, Intendant . . . des armees de sa majeste, November 6, 1708, and Nous schepen Jean Helvetius, Accord Contributions de Vrije, August 1, 1708.

16. Tresoar Archief Friesland, Leeuwarden, the Netherlands (henceforth Tresoar), 7 Stadhoud-erlijk Archief, 714 Militaire orders . . . Beleg van Lille, Observantie . . . omtrent het campement.

17. BHIC, 342, Plakkaten, 4, 1750, 606/211, Ordre en Reglement van 's Lands Militie, 's Gravenhage, July 10, 1750.

18. On the French winter quarters in the Spanish Netherlands, see Archives Departmentales du Nord, Lille, France (henceforth ANDL), C 2238, Etat des quartiers et garrisons de frontier des Pays-Bas Espagnoles sur le pied des troupes qu'il y a actuellement dans le paijs [1702] and Etat des garrisons . . . pendant l'hyver de 1703.

19. James Falkner, *The War of the Spanish Succession, 1701–1714* (Barnsley: Pen & Sword Military, 2015), 1–30.

20. WBA, Gemeente Roosendaal, 391 Moerstraten 1515–1810, 2668, Lijste . . . van aller de lande dewelken inde jaeren 1700 onder water sijn geset . . . Moerstraten, July 16, 1704.

21. ZA, 7 Vrije van Sluis, 339, Den . . . gecommittteerden . . . Raden van Staten op de verpachtingen in Vlaendern [1714?]. On damage caused by inundations, ZA, 7 Vrije van Sluis, 1584–1796, 344, To Hoogh Mogende Heeren, Sluijs, July 16, 1701, and July 19, 1701, and Eersame [to the aldermen of the different villages], Sluijs, July 20, 1701.

22. ZA, 7 Vrije van Sluis, 1584–1796, 344, To Hoogh Mogende Heeren Staten Generaal. . . . Sluijs, July 16 and 19, 1701; and Eersame [to the aldermen of the different villages], Sluijs, July 20, 1701.

23. BHIC, 12, Kwartier Kempenland, 41 Vorderingen en contributies, Extract uijt Resolutien, 14 Maart 1702.

24. WBA, Rucphen 1433, Specificatie, October 13, 1706; Rucphen 1245, Specificatie, October 13, 1706; and Falkner, *War of the Spanish Succession*, 46. For Moerstraten, see WBA, Gemeente Roosendaal, 391 Moerstraten, 2668, Staetie . . . karren, February 20, 1706, and Falkner, *War of the Spanish Succession*, 49–50.

25. ZA, 7 Vrije van Sluis, 344, [aldermen Cadzand] to [General Estates, August 1, 1702] and [Burgemr. Vrijen] to Harboe, General Majoor, Sluijs, August 23, 1702; [Burgemr. Vrijen] to Staten Generaal, Sluijs, August 23, 1702; and Schlippenbach to [General Coehoorn?], Isendijck, September 8 and November 19, 1702, and Groede, January 21, 1703; Burgemr. Vrijen to Schepenen Nieuwvliet and Breskens and the various headmen, Sluijs, October 20, 1702; Reglement waer naer sig den troupen soo te Biervliet, Hulst, December 20, 1702 (signed Coehoorn); Extract uijt de Resolutien, October 13, 1702. In January 1703, Slippenbach and other officers were ordered to pay for the forage. The three Danish regiments in the region were paid by the English, which complicated matters, see ZA, 7 Vrije van Sluis, 341, Extract uijt de Resolutien, January 27, 1703.

26. On contributions to the republic, see ZA, 7 Vrije van Sluis, 339, Extract Resolutien, July 20, 1708; BHIC, 12, Kwartier Kempenland, 41 Vorderingen en contributies [1703]; BHIC, 2 Kwartiervergadering Peelland, 160 Oorlogsschade, 1702–5, Extract uijt den resolutien, Slingelandt to quartiermeester Peellandt, November 2, 1706.

27. WBA, 200 Hoeven, 1685, Extract uijt het register der resolution, September 2, 1692.

28. BHIC library 109A46.9, Jan van Helvoirt, "Diessen geplunderd in 1702: niet met de Franse Slag," *Hers en Geens dur Diessen*, 9, 37–44; and BHIC, 12 Kwartiersvergadering Kempenland, 41, Wij Schepenen der heerlijckheijt Waelre, July 7, 1703.

29. BHIC, 12, Kwartier Kempenland, 41, Lijste van de beschrijfbrieven der contributien, Eersel, July 17, 1703, and Extract uijt het schepenenregister, August 18, 1703.

30. BHIC, 9, Domeinen, 487, Philips Jacob van Boxtele to Gulliam van der Elst . . . Vertoogh van Schulden en Lasten, Boxtel (no date) and Memorie van de betalinge van de vijandelijke kontributie (no date). For other villages, see BHIC, 12, Kwartier Kempenland, 41, Lijste van carvraghten, Oirschot, August 29, 1703; Lijste van Leveranties van Haver 1702, Oirschot, August 29, 1703.

31. BHIC, 9, Domeinen, 487, Copie, Extract Resolutien, September 28, 1702.

32. BHIC, 12, Kwartier Kempenland, 41 Vorderingen en contributies . . . int jaer 1702, Oirschot, August 29, 1703.

33. BHIC, 12, Kwartier Kempenland, 41 Vorderingen en contributies, Oistelbeers, September 4, 1703. The story in Hapert was very similar; see Lijste van verteeringen van franse ende Spaensche partijen, 1703.

34. On the military operations, see Falkner, *War of the Spanish Succession*, 44–47.

35. For Tongerle, see BHIC, 9, Domeinen, 487, Memorie voor mijn heer Rentmeester and 20, Verzoekschriften . . . Extract uijt het register der resolution, April 19, 1706, and H. Moerkerken to Staten Generaal, no date [1706]. For Westerhout, see BHIC, 9, 487, Een corte lijste, 1716. For Aelst, see BHIC, 12, Wij schepenen der heerlijckheijt van Aelst, July 7, 1703. For Waelre, see BHIC, 12, 41, Wij Schepenen der heerlijckheijt Waelre, July 7, 1703. For Diessen, see Helvoirt, "Diessen geplunderd in 1702," *Hers en Geens*, 9, 37–44. For Velthoven, see BHIC, 12, 41, Memorie . . . Velthoven, no date [1704] and Corte Staet . . . Velthoven, November 7, 1704. For Wintelre, see BHIC, 12, 41, Corte specificatie . . . Wintelre, December 22, 1703. For Bergeijk, see BHIC, 9, 487, Corte ende Specifique Memorie . . . Bergeijck, March 26, 1717, and Regionaal Historisch Centrum Eindhoven, the Netherlands (henceforth RHCE), 419 Bergeijk gemeentebestuur, 1606–1930, Specificatie . . . Bergeijk, August 9, 1704. For Eersel, see BHIC, 9, 487, Lijste, Eersel, 1716. In general, see BHIC, 9, 487, Corte missive vanden toestandt vandie van Peel en Kempenlandt, July 27, 1716, and [top first page document damaged and illegible] plaetsen in t'quartier van Kemplandt hebben inden jaer 1709.

36. WBA, Gemeente Roosendaal, 390 Wouw dorpsbestuur, 1918, Extract uijt Resolutien, December 24, 1703, and various documents following document headed by name Franchoijs Pietersz, no date [1703], numbered in pencil 705b to 732b, and Staet ende Inventaris van de geledene schade . . . van Wouw.

37. WBA, 390 Wouw dorpsbestuur, 1918, Extract uijt Resolutien, December 29, 1703.

38. Nederlands Instituut voor Militaire Historie, The Hague, the Netherlands (henceforth NIMH) 511, Handschriften 47, Brieven van Willem Vleertman, s'hage [The Hague], March 23, 1703. For the war, see Falkner, *War of the Spanish Succession*, 116–19.

39. Falkner, *War of the Spanish Succession*, 60–75.

40. BHIC, 2 Kwartiervergadering Peelland, 160, Specificatie . . . Maarheeze, Zoerendonq, Gastel, February 28, 1705; Lijste van verteeringe, Gestel, August 18, 1703, October 19, 1704, and March 21, 1705; BHIC, 12 Kwartiersvergadering Kempenland, 41, Wij ondergeschreven regeerders des dorps Blarthum, October 29, 1703, and Corte specificatie . . . Oistelbeers, March 14, 1705; Specifieke state . . . Hapert, October 21, 1703, and Wij Schepenen . . . Zeelst, October 27, 1703, and Extract uijt het protocol . . . Blarthum, October 29, 1703, and Korte Staet. . . . Blarthum, November 13, 1704; Corte Specificatie Vessem, March 8, 1705; and Corte Specificatie Winterle, March 12, 1705. See also WBA, 200 Hoeven, 1863, Den ondertekende . . . Philippus van Campenhondt, 1703, and Reekeninge voor Laurens Bosch, June 20, 1703.

41. BHIC, 12, 41, Corte staet van de verteeringe . . . Middelbeers, March 12, 1705.

42. BHIC, 9, 487, Levering paarden en karren en andere schade geleden tijdens Franse oorlog, 1702–16, in particular [top first page document damaged and illegible] plaetsen in t'quartier van Kemplandt hebben inden jaer 1709, and Memorie voor mijn heer Rentmeester and 20, Verzoekschriften . . . Extract uijt het register der resolutien, April 19, 1706, and H. Moerkerken to Staten Generaal, no date [1706], and BHIC, 12 Kwartiersvergadering Kempenland, 41, Vorderingen en contributies voor in veld staande legers tijdens de Spaanse successieoolog, 1702–11, in particular, Regenten van het quartier van Kempenland to Raden van staten, December 16, 1705.

43. Scot, "Remembrance," Ferguson, *Papers*, vol. 3, part 2, 383.

44. ANDL, C2328, Traité par lesquel les etats de Tournay et Tournasis se sousmettent aux contributions de guerres ordonnés . . . par ls états generau des Provinces unies, Gand, June 13, 1706, and Traité par lequel la ville de Tournaij . . . contribution de guerres . . . des provinces unies, Gand, July 30, 1707.

45. ZA, 7 Vrije van Sluis, 339, Burgomrs Vrije, September 18, 1708, and Burgomrs . . . van Oostburg, Oostburgh, September 19, 1708, and Extract Resolutions, August 29, 1708, and Charles Elisnne, Intendant . . . des armees de sa majeste, November 6, 1708.

46. John A. Lynn, "A Brutal Necessity? The Devastation of the Platinate, 1688–1689," in *Civilians in the Path of War*, ed. Mark Grimsley and Clifford J. Rogers (Lincoln: University of Nebraska Press, 2002), 79–110 (especially, 80–81, 84–85, 92–95, 109–110n91).

47. Archives Municipales de Lille, Lille, France (henceforth AML), 396, Inventaire Ordonnances du Magistrat (1382 a l'an III), des cavaliers et soldat de l'armee, September 9, 1707 (227 verso and folio, and 228 verso).

48. AML, 1296, Etat de ce qu'il manqué au regiment du Boullonois parti du quartier de la Magdeleine, March 8, 1708, and Bordrau du dettes des officiers dues aux habitants de Lille [1708].

49. AML, 396, Ordonnance aux habitans de la campagne qui sauveront des marchandises et denrées en cette ville de donner declaration aux Commis de Porte, September 12, 1707 (229 verso through folio 231)

50. AML, AG/727/9, Estat . . . fassines . . . sur les abbaies de la chatelenie de Lille [1708].

51. Scot, "Remembrance," Ferguson, *Papers*, vol. 3, part 2, 443.

52. AML, 293, Registre aux resolutions eschevinale de la ville de Lille, commence le 26 Maij 1707: August 23 and 24, (91 verso) and August 27 (93), 1708, and AML, 1296, Le mar[che]al duc de bouffleurs, Lille, August 24, 1708; AML, AG/727/2, Extrait du process verbal . . . de la prisée et . . . valeur des moulins de l'hopital Comtesse pour l'entrée en ocupa[ti]on Jean Francois herreng et jean le Sasse [1709] and Outre Extrait . . . moulin . . . fauburg de st andre . . . le mouline de la platte forme [1709]; AML, AG/727/9, Francois Maetiij to Messieurs le Rewar, mayeur . . . de Lille [1708] and Nous le Rewar, mayeur . . . de Lille, July 24, 1708.

53. AML, AG/727/2, L'an 1709, le 24 de aout Michel de la derut a Lille declare and Dominique Couplain . . . paroisse de St Andre; AML, AG/727/9, Etat de pertes souffert par viuve de Rolf Blancher du faubourg de la Berre [1709].

54. On the shortage of grain and the garrison's provisions, see AML, 293, Registre aux resolutions eschevinale de la ville de Lille, commence le 26 Maij 1707: September 16 (101), October 2 (103 verso), October 13 (108 verso), October 15 (109 verso and 100), October 17 (110 verso),

October 20 (111 verso and 112), and October 21, 1708 (112); AML 1296, Bordrau du dettes des officiers dues aux habitants de Lille (no date); and AML, AG/727/9, Guillaume d'Obignier to Magistrats de ville de Lille, October 3, 1709.

55. Tresoar, 7 Stadhouderlijk Archief, 714 Militaire orders . . . Beleg van Lille, Memoire pour fourager demain le 14 Juin . . . Louvain, June 13, 1708 and Memoire pour faire fourager . . . le 4 d'Aoust, Werviq, August 2, 1708. On the contributions, see Memoire pour faire une course dans le pays D'Artois, July 17, 1708; Scot, "Remembrance," Ferguson, *Papers*, vol. 3, part 2, 414–15, 443; and Hervé Lépée, *Histoires et Familles du Nord: Tome 1: De Louis XIV a la Terreur* (Lille: Fleurus, 2006), 47–53.

56. Tresoar, 7 Stadhouderlijk Archief, 714 Militaire orders . . . Lille, Memoire, July 18, 1708, and Memoire de pioniers, August 15, 1708, and Memoire de faschines, August 14, 1708; and Scot, "Remembrance," Ferguson, *Papers*, vol. 3, part 2, 418.

57. Tresoar, 7 Stadhouderlijk Archief, 714 Militaire orders, Instruction pour Le Brigadier du Portal, July 19, 1708. On the destructive foraging from 1708 to 1710, see Scot, "Remembrance," Ferguson, *Papers*, vol. 3, part 2, 400–417, 451–56, 484, 527, 534, 551.

58. Tresoar, 7 Stadhouderlijk Archief, 714 Militaire orders, Memoire pour faire une course dans le Picardie, July 20, 1708; NIMH 511, 47, Brieven Vleertman, Vleertman to Burgomasters, Lens, July 31, 1708; and ANDL, 17665 [Les deputés ordinaires des Estats Generaux de Cambray et Cambresis], Cambray, July 19, 1708.

59. Lépée, *Histoires et Familles du Nord*, 47–53.

60. AML, 293, Registre aux resolutions eschevinale de la ville de Lille, commence le 26 Maij 1707: November 11 and 12, 1708 (118 verso), and December 18 (125 and 125 verso), 20 (126 verso), 22 (127), and 26, 1708 (127 verso through 129).

61. Scot, "Remembrance," Ferguson, *Papers*, vol. 3, part 2, 460–67; AML, 293, Registre aux resolutions eschevinale de la ville de Lille, commence le 26 Maij 1707: January 28, 1709 (138 verso), and December 11, 1708 (128 verso and 129 verso); and Lépée, *Histoires et Familles du Nord*, 37–53.

62. Falkner, *War of the Spanish Succession*, 159–80, and Scot, "Remembrance," Ferguson, *Papers*, vol. 3, part 2, 414–551.

63. The French Army Intendent for Cambrai, De Bernjeres claimed that most of the villages in Douai and Tournai had been pillaged, see ANDL, C 17663, De Bernjeres to Msr Cambray, Douaij, December 10, 1708.

64. ANDL, C 17662, Louis le Dreux to Msr, Douaij, December 2, 1708, and De Bernjeres to Msrs du Magistrat Cambray, Douaij, December 5, 1708; ANDL, C 17663, De Bernjeres to Msrs Cambray, Valenciennes, August 20, 1708; Jean Baptiste Lordaut, maistre de l'hotellerie le tete d'or a Cambraij to Le marquis de Bernjeres, Conseiller du Roy, Intendent de Justice, Police, Finances et des Armées de sa majesté en flandres [1708]; De Bernjeres to Cambray, Douaij, September 18, November 20, December 7, 10, 18, and 31, 1708.

65. ANDL, 17665, Cambraij, April 25, 1707 [unsigned]. The probable author of this letter is Vaticarri Demorus, the deputy Intendent for Cambraij based at Valenciennes. He had not been paid his 800 livres salary for 1708, illustrating the extent of the crisis in France, see ANDL, 17665, Vaticarri Demorus, Valenciennes, June 4, 1709.

66. Falkner, *War of the Spanish Succession*, 159–80; Scot, "Remembrance," Ferguson, *Papers*, vol. 3, part 2, 414–551.

67. ANDL, C 17661, Arrest du parlement, January 18, 1710.

68. *Il Manoscritto Borea: Chronache di Sanremo e della Liguria Occidentale* (Bordighera: Instituto Internazionale di Studi Liguri Museo Bicknell, 1970), 109.

69. ANDL, 17665, Bernieres, Intendent de la province, Cambray, May 9, 1709; [Les deputés ordinaires des Estats Generaux de Cambray et Cambresis], Cambray, June 23, 1709; Bernieres, Valenciennes, July 17, 1709; [Les deputés ordinaires des Estats Generaux de Cambray et Cambresis to Bernieres], July 20, 1709; Bernieres, Camp d'Annay, July 20, 1709 [second letter of the same place and date]; Bernieres, Douay, July 23, 1709; and Berniers, Valenciennes, August 2, 1709. Bernieres was the Intendent for the armies of the King in the Province of Cambrai from June 1708 to 1713. He accompanied the army of the king and was not initially based in Cambrai. See Paul Thomas, "Textes historiques sur Lille et le Nord de la France avant 1789 (Suite)," *Revue du Nord*, 18, no. 69 (February 1932): 30–45 (30–31).

70. ANDL, 17665, Bernieres, Camp d'Annay, July 20, 1709; ANDL, C 17659. Vesters [Conseiller pensionare de la ville de Maastrigt et directeur de contributions] to messieurs [Cambray], Tournay, August 10, 1709; De Raad van State . . . accord, Tournay, August 22, 1709; and 's Gravenhage, August 26, 1709 (signed: Slingelandt); and ANDL, C 17660, De part les etats generaux des provinces-unies, Douaij, July 31, 1710.

71. ANDL, 17665, [Cambray], July 30, 1709; Berniers, Camp de Denainle, July 31, 1709; Berniers, Camp de Dinan, August 4, 1709; Les deputés ordinaires des Estats Generaux de Cambray et Cambresis, Cambray, August 5, 1709; Berniers, Camp d'Esame, August 4, 1709; Berniers, Douay, August 14, 1709; Vapin [?] to les deputés des Etats de Cambray, Versailles, September 3, 1709; Berniers, Douay, September 3, 1709; Cambray, September 23, 1709; and Marechal duc de Boufflers, Camp de Ruesnele, October 16, 1709.

72. Scot, "Remembrance," Ferguson, *Papers*, vol. 3, part 2, 454, 458–60, 462–64, 527–51.

73. ANDL, 17665, Bernieres, Camp d'Annay, July 20, 1709; ANDL, C 17659. E[rnst] Vesters [Conseiller pensionare de la ville de Maastrigt et directeur de contributions] to messieurs [Cambray], Tournay, August 10, 1709; De Raad van State . . . accord, Tournay August 22, 1709; and 's Gravenhage, August 26, 1709 (signed: Slingelandt); ANDL, C 17660, De part les etats generaux des provinces-unies, Douaij, July 31, 1710; and ANDL, C 11313, Comians, Bavaij [Hainault], June 16, 1744, Extraict du traité de contributions reciproque entre les districts de Hollande et le Hainaut francois passé entre M. Pesters et M. Derijat le 15 Juillet 1710 and Nous soussignez Directeur de contributions pour le service des etats generaux des Provinces Unies, & Intendant pour la service de sa Majesté Trés Chrétienne (signed E. Pesters and Doujat), Binche, June 15, 1712.

74. Tresoar, 7 Stadhouderlijk Archief, 714 Militaire orders, Extract uit het Register, November 5 and 13, 1710.

75. BHIC, 9, 487, Corte missive, July 27, 1716, and Philips Jacob van Boxtele to Gulliam van der Elst . . . Vertoogh van Schulden en Lasten, Boxtel, no date; and Martin Philipsen, "Hoe een dorp steeds armer werd: Oorlogsinspanningen van Beek en Donk ten behoeve van de Spaanse Successieoorlog, 1702–1713," *D'n Tesnussik: Heemtijdschrift voor Beek en Donk*, 12 (1992), 4–17 (BHIC library T278.1992). On roaming French soldiers, see also NIMH, 511 Handschriften, 47 Brieven, W. Vleertman to Burgomasters [Amsterdam], Maastricht, January 13, 1706.

76. BHIC, 9, Domeinen, 487, Lijste . . . Eersel . . . 1702 tot 1716, Eersel, 1716.

77. WBA, 391 Moerstraten, 2671, Lijste . . . vande geledene schades, August 24, 1712, and BHIC, 9, Domeinen, 487, Extract van wegends de schade . . . van Hoogeloon, August 10–24, 1712. See also Scot, "Remembrance," Ferguson, *Papers*, vol. 3, part 2, 414–15, 451, 458.

78. ZA, 7 Vrije van Sluis, 339, Com[misaire] de Guerre M. Varcoij to mss les directeurs d' ardenburg, copie, Aerdenburgh, October 12, 1708, and Comte de la Mothe . . . commandante en Flandre, July 25, 1708.

79. ZA, 7 Vrije van Sluis, 341, Extract uijt de resolution, September 29, 1712, and De Par Le Roy . . . Il est ordonné au magistrate du Franc, October 16, 1712, and Extract uijt de resolution, October 29, 1712.

80. On war with France as a cause for the economic crisis, see NL-HaNA, 3.20.57, Archief van Jacob Surendonck, 9 Stukken betreffende de slechte financiele positie van Holland . . . Concept 1715, Consideratien tot een general redress van de vervallen finantien van Holland, February 8, 1715, and 12 'Remarques,' memorie van Jacob Surendonck betreffende de slechte financiele positie van Holland, Concept, March 11, 1720. For the Republic's postwar crisis, see T. Pfeil, "Overheidsfinancien en modernisering: Over de invloed van financiele crises op de ineenstrorting en reconstructive van staten: het geval van Nederland, 1780–1848," *Amsterdams Sociologisch Tijdschrift*, 20, no. 2 (1993): 95–122. On the general financial crisis caused by the war, see James Lacey, *Gold, Blood, and Power: Finance and War through the Ages* (Lexington: US Army War College Strategic Studies Institute, 2016), 46–48.

81. BHIC, 12, 41, Stapel Codde to Mijn Heer, Eindhoven, June 27, 1711.

82. WBA, 001, Oud Archief Gemeente Etten Leur, 1733, Johan van Rijckvoessel, Den Bosch, May 23, 1719.

83. NL-HaNA, 3.20.57, Archief van Jacob Surendonck, 9, Consideratien, February 8, 1715, and 12 'Remarques,' memorie van Jacob Surendonck betreffende de slechte financiele positie van Holland, Concept, March 11, 1720. On the Rinderpest, see J. A. Faber, "Cattle Plague in the Netherlands during the Eighteenth Century," *Mededelingen van de Landbouwhogeschool te Wageningen, Nederland* 62, no. 11 (1962): 1–7; John Broad, "Cattle Plague in Eighteenth-Century England," *Agricultural History Review* 31, no. 2 (1983): 104–15; and C. A. Spinage, *Cattle Plague: A History* (New York: Springer Science, 2003), 103–50.

84. WBA, 001 Etten Leur, 1738, various lists and documents, including Liste van de gestorve besten, no date with first listed Marinis Jacobs Geusen; Lijste van de Heerstraet van de beesten die van de besmettelijcke siekte sijn gestorven, no date: Lijste van de schade, 23 junij 1723; [List] Moleneijnde, no date [1723]; Den 24 junij anno 1723 het opschrijven van het sterven van het runtse . . . Spruudel; Den 24en junij 1723 hebben Lambregt van Eekelen, schepen, en Jacobus Plasschaart, geswore, opgeschreven de schade die de ingesetenen van Middelwijk, 1723.

85. Stress factors, including overcrowding and malnutrition, make animals vulnerable to disease, and concentrating cattle in close quarters (for example, in stables, military camps, or besieged towns) facilitates contagion, see Spinage, *Cattle Plague*, 19–20.

86. Falkner, *War of the Spanish Succession*, 35–43, 69–103, 129–42, 160–61, 180–88, 196–211.

87. Falkner, *War of the Spanish Succession*, 215–16.

88. Falkner, *War of the Spanish Succession*, 35–43, 76–93, 102–3, 129–42.

89. On Francisco (de) Caetano y Aragon, see Gregorio Colás Latorre, "Los Primeros Borbones," in *Historia General de España y América*, vol. 10, ed. Carlos E. Corona Baratech and José

Antonio Armillas Vicente (Madrid: Rialp, 1990), 335–79 (353), accessed online at https://books
.google.com/books?id=wLNVAv7N-_YC&pg=PA353&lpg=PA353&dq=Francisco+de+Caeta
no+y+Aragon&source=bl&ots=OmChoovRCS&sig=ACfU3U3oWellH1dYrE2VO6fHjX6vu
VyGYQ&hl=en&sa=X&ved=2ahUKEwiolYLY6tXjAhWjT98KHdnYAB8Q6AEwD3oECAgQ
AQ#v=onepag

90. Archivio di Stato di Napoli, Naples, Italy (henceforth ASN), Consiglio di Spagna, stanza
218, busta 256, Orders Don Raphael Lampillas, June 21, 1708, and Barcelona July 10, 1708; Concede
a Don Juan Mead, Pagador de la M[ajestad] B[ritannique] despacho para comprar granos a este
principado, Barcelona, July 3, 1708; and Demanda al Don Salvador Baldrich, Barcelona July 15, 1708.

91. ASN, Gaetani d'Aragona, stanza 168, Gaetani Carte I Parte, busta 57, Joseph de Grimaldo
to Don Francisco de Caetano y Aragon [May 1709].

92. ASN, Gaetani d'Aragona, stanza 168, Gaetani Carte I Parte, busta 57, Man de Vezondo
[?], M[adri]d, July 24, 1709, and [Proclamation by the king], Madrid, July 12, 1709; Joseph de
Grimaldi to Don Francisco de Caetano y Aragon, Madrid, July 31, 1709.

93. ASN, Gaetani d'Aragona-stanza 168, Gaetani Carte I Parte, busta 57, Joseph de Grimaldi
to Don Francisco de Caetano y Aragon, Madrid, September 13 and 18, 1709.

94. Projecto de Don Francisco de Caetano y Aragon, The[nent]e Geral de lo Ex[cercito] de
su Ma[jesta]d y Comandante del Reyno de Valencia pra quitar todos los abusos que se han
introdivindo en los quarteles de Invierno pasados con la gran destruction de los pueblos, attachment to ASN, Gaetani d'Aragona-stanza 168, Gaetani Carte I Parte, busta 57, Joseph de
Grimaldi to Don Francisco de Caetano y Aragon, Madrid, September 18, 1709.

95. ASN, Gaetani d'Aragona, stanza 168, Gaetani Carte I Parte, busta 57, Joseph de Grimaldi
to Don Francisco de Caetano y Aragon, Madrid, September 18, 1709, and September 28, 1709.

96. ASN, Gaetani d'Aragona, stanza 168, Gaetani Carte I Parte, busta 57, Joseph de Grimaldi
to Don Francisco de Caetano y Aragon, Madrid, August 13 [1709] and December 21, 1709.

97. ASN, Gaetani d'Aragona, stanza 168, Gaetani Carte I Parte, busta 57, Joseph de Grimaldi
to Don Francisco de Caetano y Aragon, Madrid, October 4, 1709.

98. ASN, Gaetani d'Aragona, stanza 168, Gaetani Carte I Parte, busta 57, Proclamation by the
king, Madrid, November 8, 1709. Soldiers' punishment earlier during the war was relatively
mild: one soldier was condemned to five years imprisonment for murder and two others to ten
years on the galleys for desertion, see Gaetani d'Aragona, stanza 168, Gaetani Carte I Parte, busta
59, Man[uel] de Zumerzuff to Don Francisco de Caetano y Aragon, Milan, September 3, 1703.

99. ASN, Gaetani d'Aragona, stanza 168, Gaetani Carte I Parte, busta 59, Man[uel] de Zumerzuff to Don Francisco de Caetano y Aragon, July 8, 1709.

100. ASN, Gaetani d'Aragona, stanza 168, Gaetani Carte I Parte, busta 57, Don Geronimo de
Solis y Santos, Marques de Odono and Le Marques, no date, no place [1709].

101. ASN, Gaetani d'Aragona, stanza 168, Gaetani Carte I Parte, busta 57, Joseph de Grimaldi
to Don Francisco de Caetano y Aragon, December 2, 1709.

102. ASN, Gaetani d'Aragona, stanza 168, Gaetani Carte I Parte, busta 59, Marques de
Co[nde?] to Don Francisco de Caetano y Aragon, September 27, 1709, and Deve to Don Francisco de Caetano y Aragon, Madrid, May 20, 1710.

103. ASN, Gaetani d'Aragona, stanza 168, Gaetani Carte I Parte, busta 59, Governadores to
Don Francisco de Caetano y Aragon, Altamira, July 14, 1709.

104. ASN, Gaetani d'Aragona, stanza 168, Gaetani Carte I Parte, busta 57, Joseph de Grimaldi to Don Francisco de Caetano y Aragon, December 8, 1709.

105. ASN, Gaetani d'Aragona, stanza 168, Gaetani Carte I Parte, busta 57, Vassalos del Mun[icipio] de Besan to Felipe V, King of Spain, Almorasbumbre, December 8, 1709.

106. ASN, Gaetani d'Aragona, stanza 168, Gaetani Carte I Parte, busta 59, El Cavallero to Don Francisco de Caetano y Aragon, Madrid, January 26, 1710.

107. ASN, Gaetani d'Aragona, stanza 168, Gaetani Carte I Parte, busta 62, A Sindico de Ribarroja, Suplica a V Ma[jestad], no date [1710].

108. ASN, Gaetani d'Aragona, stanza 168, Gaetani Carte I Parte, busta 62, Joseph de Grimaldi to Don Francisco de Caetano y Aragon, Madrid, January 1, 1710 [1].

109. ASN, Gaetani d'Aragona, stanza 168, Gaetani Carte I Parte, busta 62, Joseph de Grimaldi to Don Francisco de Caetano y Aragon, Madrid, January 22, 1710.

110. ASN, Gaetani d'Aragona, stanza 168, Gaetani Carte I Parte, busta 62, Joseph de Grimaldi to Don Francisco de Caetano y Aragon, Val[encia?], January [date illegible], 1710.

111. ASN, Gaetani d'Aragona, stanza 168, Gaetani Carte I Parte, busta 60, Jossep de Contaminas to Don Francisco de Caetano y Aragon, Valencia July 7, 1710.

112. ASN, Gaetani d'Aragona, stanza 168, Gaetani Carte I Parte, busta 62, Joseph de Grimaldi to Don Francisco de Caetano y Aragon, Cassatajades, October 28, 1710.

113. ASN, Gaetani d'Aragona, stanza 168, Gaetani Carte I Parte, busta 62, Joseph de Grimaldi to Don Francisco de Caetano y Aragon, Campo Real de Fuentes, December 13, 1710.

114. ASN, Gaetani d'Aragona, stanza 168, Gaetani Carte I Parte, busta 61, Marques de Mehon y de la Brer to Don Francisco de Caetano y Aragon, Zar[agosa], [date illegible] February 1711, and Joseph de Grimaldi to Don Francisco de Caetano y Aragon, Zaragosa, February 19, 1711 [2nd letter of same date].

115. ASN, Gaetani Carte I Parte, busta 61, Joseph de Grimaldi to Don Francisco de Caetano y Aragon, Zaragosa, February 19, 1711.

116. ASN, Gaetani d'Aragona, stanza 168, Gaetani Carte I Parte, busta 61, Joseph de Grimaldi to Don Francisco de Caetano y Aragon, Zaragosa, February 28, 1711.

117. ASN, Gaetani d'Aragona, stanza 168, Gaetani Carte I Parte, busta 61, Joseph de Grimaldi to Don Francisco de Caetano y Aragon, Zaragosa, March 1 and 5, 1711, and two more letters from same month with illegible dates, and Zaragosa, April 15, 1711.

118. ASN, Gaetani d'Aragona, stanza 168, Gaetani Carte I Parte, busta 61, Joseph de Grimaldi to Don Francisco de Caetano y Aragon, Zaragosa, May 23, 1711.

119. ASN, Gaetani d'Aragona, stanza 168, Gaetani Carte I Parte, busta 61, Joseph de Grimaldi to Don Francisco de Caetano y Aragon, Zaragosa, April 24, 1711, and Gaetani d'Aragona, stanza 168, busta 62, Joseph de Grimaldi to Don Francisco de Caetano y Aragon, Madrid, January 15, 1710.

120. ASN, Gaetani d'Aragona, stanza 168, Gaetani Carte I Parte, busta 61, Joseph de Grimaldi to Don Francisco de Caetano y Aragon, Corella, June 24, 1711.

121. ASN, Gaetani d'Aragona, stanza 168, Gaetani Carte I Parte, busta 61, Joseph de Grimaldi to Don Francisco de Caetano y Aragon, Corella, June 30, 1711.

122. ASN, Gaetani d'Aragona, stanza 168, Gaetani Carte I Parte, busta 62, Joseph de Grimaldi to Don Francisco de Caetano y Aragon, Madrid, February [illegible date], 1710.

123. ASN, Gaetani d'Aragona, stanza 168, Gaetani Carte I Parte, busta 59, Forma que considerando las actuals circunstancias y concideraciones de la tierra, y . . . para enterguer los
Miqueletes q[ue] . . . en los atentes de la ciudad de Segorve com muy graves perjuizos de presente [April 1709]; Cappelan Rodriquez de Segorbe to [Don Francisco de Caetano y Aragon],
Copia, Segorbe, April 16, 1709; Migue[l] de Pepeti to Don Francisco de Caetano y Aragon,
Campo delante a Barcelona, January, 1712; Migue[l] de Pepeti [?] to Don Francisco de Caetano
y Aragon, Campo delante a Barcelona, January 21, 1712; Migue[l] de Pepeti [?] to Don Francisco
de Caetano y Aragon, Campo delante a Barcelona, October 7, 1712; and busta 61, Joseph de
Grimaldi to Don Francisco de Caetano y Aragon, Zaragosa, May 8, 1711 [letter 2 of that date],
busta 62, Joseph de Grimaldi to Don Francisco de Caetano y Aragon, Madrid, January 8, 1710.

124. ASN, Gaetani d'Aragona, stanza 168, Gaetani Carte I Parte, busta 59, Cappelan Rodriquez de Segorbe to [Don Francisco de Caetano y Aragon], Segorbe, April 16, 1709.

125. ASN, Gaetani d'Aragona, stanza 168, Gaetani Carte I Parte, busta 62, Joseph de Grimaldi
to Don Francisco de Caetano y Aragon, Madrid, January 1 [2 different letters] and 8, and February 5, 1710.

126. ASN, Gaetani d'Aragona, stanza 168, Gaetani Carte I Parte, busta 57, Joseph de Grimaldi
to Don Francisco de Caetano y Aragon, July 16, 1709, and August 14, 1709, busta 59, Forma que
considerando las actuals circunstancias y concideraciones de la tierra, y . . . para exterguer los
Miqueletes [1709]; Cappelan Rodriquez de Segorbe to [Don Francisco de Caetano y Aragon],
Segorbe, April 16, 1709; Mayor Servidor G. Limes to Don Francisco de Caetano y Aragon,
December, 11, 1710, busta 60, Royal Placard, Madrid May 6, 1630.

127. ASN, Gaetani d'Aragona, stanza 168, Gaetani Carte I Parte, busta 61, Joseph de Grimaldi
to Don Francisco de Caetano y Aragon, Zaragosa, April 4 and April [date illegible], and June 18,
1711.

128. ASN, Gaetani d'Aragona, stanza 168, Gaetani Carte I Parte, busta 61, Joseph de Grimaldi
to Don Francisco de Caetano y Aragon, Corella, June 18, 1711 [letter 2 of that date].

129. ASN, Gaetani d'Aragona, stanza 168, Gaetani Carte I Parte, busta 61, Joseph de Grimaldi
to Don Francisco de Caetano y Aragon, Corella, June 28, 1711.

130. ASN, Gaetani d'Aragona, stanza 168, Gaetani Carte I Parte, busta 59, Migue[l] de Pepeti
to Don Francisco de Caetano y Aragon, Campo delante a Barcelona, January 21, 1712; Baron
Conde and Marquis de Mirasol, Valencia, February 18, 1712; and Campo delante a Barcelona,
October 7, 1712; Falkner, *War of the Spanish Succession*, 208–211.

131. ASN, Gaetani d'Aragona, stanza 168, Gaetani Carte I Parte, busta 59, Baron Conde and
Marquis de Mirasol, Valencia, February 18, 1712.

132. ASN, Gaetani d'Aragona, stanza 168, Gaetani Carte I Parte, busta 58, statement by Don
Antonio del Valle, Theniente General de los Exercitos de Sua Magestad . . . y Governador de
Valencia, Valencia, August 22, 1712, and attached Supplication to the king by Juana Baup[is]ta
Monrreal Pobre Biuda de Franc[is]co Monrreal Bosticarrio, y vecina do lugar de Moncada en
el reyno de Valencia [August 1712].

133. ASN, Gaetani d'Aragona, stanza 168, Gaetani Carte I Parte, busta 58, Supplication by
Don Juan Bautista Rosa to Don Francisco Caetano, Tenieto Geral del Reyno de Valencia, attached to letter Marques de Hedrasy [?] to Don Francisco de Caetano y Aragon, Madrid, September 13, 1713.

134. Gutmann, *War and Rural Life*, 47–51.

135. Falkner, *War of the Spanish Succession*, 69–75 and 143–48.

Chapter Six: Total War and Environcide during the Austrian Succession War

1. Archivio di Stato di Imperia, Imperia, Italy [henceforth ASI], Comune de Porto Maurizio, II Serie [henceforth PM II], busta 208, Carta p[er] le soldatesca que . . . austrichii, no place, no date [late 1747 or early 1748].

2. Nationaal Archief, The Hague, The Netherlands (henceforth NL-HaNA) 1.10.94, Familie Fagel: Supplement, 106, Resultats des Conferences entre les Ministres de sa Majesté Britannique, sa Majesté l'Imperatrice Reine de Hongrie et de Boheme et les Deputés de la Haute Puissance, January 9, 1747, and Brussels, June 19, 1747 [various copies to different towns].

3. Thomas Simes, *The Military Guide for Young Officers 1776* (Leeds: The Navy & Military Press, n.d. [Reprint]), 325, 329.

4. Pierre de Briquet, *Code Militaire ou Compilation des Ordonnances des Rois de France*, vol. 2 (Paris: Rollin Fils, 1741) (Kessinger Legacy Reprints), 65, 86–87, 88–89, 94.

5. Brabants Historisch Informatie Centrum, 's-Hertogenbosch, the Netherlands (henceforth BHIC), 342, Plakkaten, 1520–1884, 4, 1750, 606/211, Ordre en Reglement, July 10, 1750.

6. West-Brabants Archief, Bergen op Zoom, The Netherlands (henceforth WBA), 001 Etten Leur, 1727, Placaet tegen het . . . plegen van insolentien . . . by de Militaire ('s Gravenhage: Jacobus Scheltus, 1694) and Placcaet, De Staten Generaal: Alsoo ons dagelijcks menichvuldige klachten voorkomen ('s-Gravenhage: Jacobus Scheltus, 1673). On the limited impact of the rules of war, see Alexander Gillespie, *A History of the Laws of War*, vol. 2, *The Customs and Laws of War with Regards to Civilians in Times of Conflict* (Oxford: Hart, 2011), 63–65.

7. Simes, *Military Guide*, 91–92.

8. Gillespie, *History of the Laws of War*, 149.

9. Maurice Saxe, *Reveries, or, Memoirs Concerning the Art of War* (Edinburgh: Alexander Donaldson, 1759) (reprint ECCO Print Editions), 107–11 and 270–97. Unauthorized war-time pillaging by soldiers ("marauding") was subject to severe punishment in Louis XIV's era, see Albert A. Babeau, *La Vie Militaire sous L'Ancien Regime*, vol. 2, *Les Officiers* (Paris: Fimin-Didot et Cie, 1890) (Facsimile reprint Paris: Elibion, 2005), 152. On rape, see Gillespie, *History of the Laws of War*, 49.

10. Gillespie, *History of the Laws of War*, 140.

11. Reed Browning, *The War of the Austrian Succession* (New York: St. Martin's Griffin, 1995), 1–33.

12. Browning, *War of the Austrian Succession*, 94, 120, 164–169, 185–188, 288–289, 291–294, 296–297, and 376–378.

13. Roberto Capaccio and Bartolomeo Durante, *Marciando per le Alpi: Il Ponente Italiano durante la Guerra di Successioni Austriaca, 1742–1748* (Cavallermaggiore: Gribaudo, 1993), 24–25.

14. On the war in Italy, see Browning, *War of the Austrian Succession*; and Paolo Calcagno, "Guerra e Documenti, un Chiaro Rapporto di Causa-Effetto: Il Caso dell'Occupazione 'Sarda'

di Savona nel 1746–49," in *Nella Morsa della Guerra: Assedi, Occupazioni Militari e Saccheggi in Età Preindustriale*, ed. Guido Alfani and Mario Rizzo (Milano: FrancoAngeli, 2013), 85–110.

15. Capaccio and Durante, *Marciando per le Alpi*, 28–32.

16. Capaccio and Durante, *Marciando per le Alpi*, 20–26.

17. Browning, *War of the Austrian Succession*, 96–98, 117–20, 166–69, 185–89; Capaccio and Durante, *Marciando per le Alpi*, 39–55; Francesco Biga, *Austro Piemontesi nel Dianese: Dal Trattato di Worms alla Pace di Aquisgrana, 1743–1748* (Diano Marina: Communitas Diani-Museo Civico, 1976), 15.

18. Archives Départementales des Alpes-Maritimes, Nice, France (henceforth ADAM), E102/035, EE 4, Laurentio M: to Console e Sindice della Comita: de Lantosca, Bolena, Roccobilgliera, Belvedera, Sto Martino, Venacone, S. Dolmar, Val di Blora, Lantosca, February 26, 1745.

19. ADAM, E088, EE2, Conta . . . di pagamenti fatti dalla communitá di Boyone gli d'ordine della R[eale] delegatione che delle truppe galispane; Sindicati Trophine Berenghier, Oltre le provisoni fatte dalla comte: di Boyon alli . . . truppe tanto francesi che spagnole, September 25–December 5, 1744; and Order to supply hay and straw Regiment Fiandras, June 2, 1744; and Stato di fieno, March 4, 1744–September 18, 1745, Bouyon September 21, 1745 and [list], April 4, 1744–October 1745, Boyone, October 5, 1745.

20. ADAM, E102/035, EE 4, Chevalier Montenaits to Community of Belvedere, Contesque, September 7, 1744; Stato del Fieno . . . dalla Comita de Belvedere, Lantosca, July 12, 1745; and Consiglio (Belvedere) to Pietro Daiderij, Belvedere, May 11, 1745.

21. ADAM, E088, EE2, sindicati Trophine Berenghier, Oltre le provisoni fatte dalla comte: di Boyon, September 25-December 5, 1744; and Order to supply hay and straw Regiment Fiandras], June 2, 1744; and Stato di fieno, paglia etc alle destacimento di Lorenzo, March 4, 1744-September 18, 1745, Bouyon September 21, 1745; and [list], April 4, 1744-October 1745, Boyone, October 5, 1745.

22. ADAM, E102/035, EE 5, Dauduieu, Commandant to Levenzo, September 5, 1745.

23. ADAM, E088, EE4, Riouffe to consul Villeneuve, February 5, 1744; Estat des depenses le fourniture faites par le communaute . . . villeneufue au subjet du passage de l'armee d'Italie commande [February–July 1744]; and Rapport Du quatre may 1744 . . . faisons nous, Cezar Mougim et Jean Baptiste Fansal, Villeneuve, May 9, 1744.

24. ADAM, E004/064, EE12, Jean Antoine Boussey, Etat des grains fournis par les consuls, August 20, 1745; and Etat du foin fournis aux sept compagnies du regiment de Languedoc, St Paul, May 20, 1745.

25. ADAM, E004/064, EE12, Les Consuls de la ville de St Paul . . . concernant la pretension du payement du domage cause par les troupes d'espagne en l'année 1746, Vencele, November 13, 1756, and Varoges a Flory (Consul), to Alexander Suche le . . . premier consul . . . de St Paul, St Paul, November 17, 1746.

26. ADAM, E004/074, FF70, raport destime du bois de Mr Jean Bernardy, St Paul, August 29, 1747, and J. Abregue, montant du prix de bois coupé . . . pour le chauffage des troupes.

27. ADAM, E004/064, EE12, Les Consuls . . . de St Paul . . . concernant la pretension du payement du domage cause par les troupes d'espagne en l'année 1746, Vencele, November 13, 1756; Varoges to Suche, St Paul, November 17, 1746; Julien, St Paul to le Premier president, Aix

[no date 1747]; Nippert Supplicants of St Paul to le Premier president [1747]; Layet, consul to . . . le Premier president [1748]; and for the quote see A Suche, [1746 or 1747].

28. ADAM, E004/064, EE12, Etat de logement des geans de guerres . . . de . . . 1746 liquidée en la present année 1747, December 19, 1747, and Etat de liquidation des logements des gents de guerres . . . 1746, St Paul, January 24, 1748.

29. Browning, *War of the Austrian Succession*, 200–205, 231–40; Capaccio and Durante, *Marciando per le Alpi*, 74–84; Biga, *Austro Piemontesi nel Dianese*, 15–17; Calcagno, "Guerra e Documenti," Alfani and Rizzo, *Nella Morsa della Guerra*, 85–110.

30. ASI, PM II, busta 208, Don Fernadino de Cassigal [Caxigal] . . . Mareciallo di Campo delli de S[ua] M[ajestad] [the king of Spain] e Comandante de Oneglia e sua Provincia e del distretto di Loano, no date [1745]; Barranquet, Oneglia, September 14, 1746, June 15, 1746, and March 21, 1746; and sindico Fran[cis]co Antonio Delgrano, de la Contribuzion del Corr[en]te anno. Barranquet, Oneglia, March 6, 1746.

31. ASI, PM II, busta 208, Carlo Calsa Miglia, Oneglia, January 2, 1745; Lazaro Peijre, Delegate, Oneglia, April 11, 1745; Pedro de Villaroel, Colonello Regimento Caliciane e Comandate della Citta e Provincia, Oneglia, August 23, 1745; Don Franc[es]co Portales, December 4, 1745; Don Fernando de Caxigal, Oneglia, December 5, 1745; Don Pietro de del Maroel [Villaroel], Tenente Colonello del Regimento di Galicia, Oneglia, January 8, 1746; Man[uel] de Azave, Oneglia, January 11, 1746; Oneglia, February 24, 1746; Delegato, Oneglia, March 14, 1746; Don Fernando di Caxigal, Oneglia, March 12, 1746; Don Francisco di Agua, Commissario di Guerra di SMC [Sua Maesta Catolica], Oneglia, February 9, March 16, and April 16, 1746; Don Fernando de Caxigal, Oneglia, September 6, 1746; and Archivio di Stato di Imperia, Sezione di Sanremo, Sanremo, Italy [henceforth ASISS], Comune di Sanremo, Serie I, busta 30 (28/30), Consegna del Fieno . . . de Francesi, e Spagnoli, September 27, 1746; Gio: M:a Bosio Priera, Horas del Fieno, paglia, e legna delli Francesi, Espagnudi [September 1746]; Francesco di Aguas, Comisario di Guerra, Oneglia, November 7, 1745; and Ordine di Don Franco de Azcur, November 16, 1745.

32. In 1709, one Dutch guilder equaled 3 Venetian lires, 100 Dutch guilders equaled 9 pounds sterling, and 5 guilders equaled 6 French livres, see http://www.pierre-marteau.com/currency /converter/ita-hol.html.

33. ASI, PM II, busta 208, La Communita Supplicante, Nizza, 10 Abril 1744 [*sic*: 1745], Acuda al Intendente Marques de la Torre; Giuseppe Delgano, Sind:e del Luogo della Costa to D[on] Filippo, Infanta di Espagna, Nizza, April 12, 1745; Giuseppe Belgrano, Conto presente dai Sindici della Costa: 1745; Lazaro Calui to Podesta di Casstelvecchio [e] Delegato di . . . Don Francisco D'Ascuir, Commiss[ar]io di Guerra. . . . November 21, 1745; and Carlo Caliamighi, Console, Oneglia, November 27, 1745.

34. ASI, PM II, busta 208, Pier Luiggi Mellarede to Conte del Bettonet, Delegato de S. M., Oneglia, June 2, 1747.

35. ASI, PM II, busta 208, Franceso Antonio Belgrano, sindico to Lanery, San Remo [November 4], 1746.

36. ASI, PM II, busta 208, Don PietroVillaroel Colonello Regimento di Galizia, Oneglia, August 18, 1745 and Don Fernando de Caxigal, Oneglia [1746].

37. C. A. Spinage, *Cattle Plague: A History* (New York: Springer Science, 2003), 7–20, 104–120.

38. ASI, PM II, busta 208, de Caxigal, Oneglia, January 25, 1746.

39. Calcagno, "Guerra e Documenti," Alfani and Rizzo, *Nella Morsa della Guerra*, 88–91, 97; Browning, *War of the Austrian Succession*, 260–63, 268–69, 273–76, 287–90, 296–98; Cappacio and Durante, *Marciando per le Alpi*, 87–113; Biga, *Austro Piemontesi nel Dianese*, 17–25.

40. ASI, PM II, busta 208, Franceso Antonio Belgrano, sindico, to Lanery, San Remo, [November 4], 1746; Julius Legno to Giuseppe Belgrano, sindici, September 25, 1746; Pier Luiggi Mellarede to Conte del Bettonet, Delegato de S. M., Oneglia, June 2, 1747; Capaccio; Durante, *Marciando per le Alpi*, 87–113; Biga, *Austro Piemontesi nel Dianese*, 17–25.

41. ASISS, Comune di Sanremo, Serie I, [henceforth San Remo I] busta 30 (28/30), Falquet, Ordine de S. M., Quartiere Generale de San Remo, September 27, 1746.

42. ASI, PM II, busta 49, Ordine de Sua Maestad, Quartiere Generale di Bordighera, September 19, 1746, and ASISS, Sanremo I, busta 30 (28/30), Baudzione, Quartiere Reale de Bordighera, September 29, 1746, and Ordine de S. M., Quartiere Real Bordighiera, September 29, 1746.

43. ASISS, Sanremo I, busta 30 (28/30), Ordine de S. M., San Remo, September 28, 1746.

44. ASISS, Sanremo I, busta 30 (28/30), Ceriana, October 3, 1746, and Giacomo Rosso, Console, to Lorenso Martini, Concilire della Comunita di S [Remo], Seboica, October 6, [1746].

45. ASISS, Sanremo I, busta 30 (28/30), Ordine de S. M., San Remo, October 6, 1746; Janerij Partimonale de S. M., Ordine de S. M., San Remo, October 2 and 3 (2 different orders with the same date), 1746.

46. ASISS, Sanremo I, busta 30 (28/30), Bordighera, Quar[tier]e R[ey]te della Bordighera, October 5, 1746 (the document bears handwritten notes that seem to reflect the king's verbal responses to the requests); Il Marchese de Cravanzana, Quartier Real de Bordighera, October 5, 1746; La Regia Delegazione per la Riviera di Ponente Residente nella' Citta di Finale, Finale, February 27, 1747; ASI, CP II, busta 49, Ordini in tempo di Guerra. Alla truppa stanziata in Porto Maurizio, 1745–47, De Gubernatis, Ordine di Sua Maesta, Regolamente Generale della Tappe, April 7 and November 9, 1747; En nome de S[ignor]e Anziani, Porto Maurizio November 21, 1747; and De Gubernatis, Dolceacqua, November 20, 1747; and Calcagno, "Guerra e Documenti" Alfani and Rizzo, *Nella Morsa della Guerra*, 100–103. On de Gubernatis, see *Historia Annual, Chronologica, e Politica do Mundo e especialmente da Europa onde se fas Memoria dos Nascimentios, Desposiorios, e Morte de todos os Emperadores, Reys . . . Parte VII* (Lisbon: Pascoal da Sylva, 1721), Gazeta de Lisboa Occidental, no. 3, January 16, 1721, 28, accessed online at https:// books.google.com/books?id=eAowAAAAYAAJ&pg=PA275&dq=conde+gubernatis&hl =en&sa=X&ved=2ahUKEwi5rtzH1u_jAhWBiOAKHah-D504ChC7BTADegQIABAD#v =onepage&q=conde%20gubernatis&f=false.

47. ASISS, Sanremo I, busta158 (89/158), Libro del Magistrate di Guerra.

48. ASISS, Sanremo I, busta 30 (28/30), Carlo Emanuele, Re di Sardegna, Quartiere di Nizza, January 7, 1747.

49. ADAM, E088, EE2, Gubernatio, Copia de ordine, San Martin, January 25, 1747.

50. ASISS, Sanremo I, busta 30 (28/30), Soministranze fatte dalla Citta di St Remo all' Regimento La Regina, da 26 Genaio in 15 Giugno; and Proviste fatte . . . di S[an]Remo alli Reg[imen]ti Monfour e Pinevolo del a Anno 1747: e :1748.

51. ASI, PM II, busta 49, Conto di fieno provista alla Truppa Imperiale, 1748–49 and [Conto di fieno provista alla Truppa Imperiale] 1746.

52. Browning, *War of the Austrian Succession*, 286–98, 310–13; and *Il Manoscritto Borea: Chronache di Sanremo e della Liguria Occidentale* (Bordighera: Instituto Internazionale di Studi Liguri Museo Bicknell, 1970), 119–21.

53. ADAM, E088, EE4, Noussandre Ratte, Intendent General du Province de Comté & autres lieux . . . Grasse, December 22, 1746; Lettre circulaire, St. Paul, Villeneuve, December 30, 1747, and Communaute de Villeneuve: Etat . . . des fournitures . . . pendant les six dernieres mois de 1746 et le premier de 1747, Villeneuve, May 30, 1747.

54. ADAM, E088, EE4, Il Est ordonne a la communaute de Villeneuve, Vence, December 1746 and Communaute de Villeneuve: Etat . . . des fournitures, Villeneuve, May 30, 1747.

55. ADAM, E004/064, EE12, Ordre de Mr. Datemis, Major du Regimente de Hagenbach, Comandant de la viquerie de St Paul, January 3, 1747; quiitances . . . de St Bonnet . . . La gaude carros . . . pour les despences de l'hopital, St Paul, January 29, 1747; Consuls et communaute . . . de St Paul to Intendente General [no date]; and Les consuls . . . de St Paul to le premier president [August 1747].

56. Browning, *War of the Austrian Succession*, 286–98, 310–13, 353; and *Il Manoscritto Borea*, 119–21.

57. ADAM, E088, EE4, L'an 1747 . . . attendre la destruction faitte par les ennemis de l'etat.

58. ADAM, E088, EE4, Sur la requisition de la part de Marquis; Milhaelij [Consul], Etat de domages que les habitans . . . de Villeneufue . . . ont soufert par les ennemies, March 24, 1747; and Communaute de Villeneuve: Etat de liquidation des fournitures, Villeneuve, May 30, 1747.

59. ADAM, E088, EE4, Consuls et communaute de Villeneuve to Monseignieur le premier president and at bottom letter agreement by Besansours, April 7, 1747

60. ADAM, E088, EE4, L'an 1747 . . . attendre la destruction faitte par les ennemis de l'etat and Communaute de Villeneuve: Etat de liquidation, Villeneuve, May 30, 1747.

61. ADAM, E004/074, FF72, Supplie humblement Jeanne Daibaud [Giraud] de Mr Joseph Durbei huiser [bailiff] royal de la ville de st Paul to le Premier President [1756]; Senet, Suplie humblement Marianne Giraud, viuve de Francois Ribaud . . . to Lijmandant. Note on top left corner signed by La Tour, Aix, July 24, 1747; and La Tour to Aljiary, Aix, September 1, 1747.

62. ADAM, E088, EE4, Communaute de Villeneuve: Etat de liquidation des fournitures, Villeneuve, May 30, 1747.

63. ADAM, E088, EE4, Gurault, subdelegue de l'intendence to communaute de Villeneuve, Antibes, May 23, 1747, and Gurault to Messieurs (des communautes), Antibes, May 23, 1747.

64. ADAM, E088, EE4, Laborde to Communaute Villeneuve, Antibes, September 14, 1747, and Etats des foins . . . dans le magasin etablie . . . en Villeneufue, November 9, 1747.

65. ADAM, E004/064, EE12, Etats des logements, February 3 and 5, 1746, and February 6, 7, 9, 12, 18, 23, March 8, and April 14, 1747; "Bois que lofficiers de mtl Bonnet a pris"; Rolle du lits mondre a la cotte, March 2, 1747; and J. C. Bernard, consul [de St Paul], Memoire des fourniture, July 24, 1747.

66. ADAM, E088, EE2, Copie de l'ordre: Marechal de Bellille [Belle-Isle], nous Colonel commandant du regiment de Condé, Vence, February 5, 1747.

67. ADAM, E088, EE2, Danferret Colonel d'infanterie . . . avant garde des troupes de sa majeste . . . ordonnons a les communautres de bouillon [Bouyon], February 2, 1747; Danferret, St. Jeanne, February 5, 1747; Murraine, Suivant les orders. . . . duc de Belle [Marechal de

Belle-Isle], Grasse, February 9, 1747; Faye, St Jeannet, February 10, 1747; and Le commandant dite Bastide, Chamou, February 11, 1747.

68. ADAM, E088, EE2, Macilhas, Il est ordinne a quatre grenadiers, Gattiere, February 23, 1747; de Bailly grenadier de Medoc, Bouyon, April 29, 1747; De Vaubecourt, Il est ordonné aux consuls de Boiou [Bouyon], Levenzo, June 26, 1747; Lincé, [Bouyon], September 10, 1747; and Comte de Chevert, Boncon [Bouyon], November 16, 1747.

69. ADAM, E088, EE2, Michelis au nom de la communaute [de Bouyon] to Muraire, [July 1747].

70. ADAM, E088, EE2, Trophy Orsi, consul, Stato della fourniture, Boyone, August 21, 1747; Trophime Orsi, Etat des fournitures faites par Boyon aux troupes francoises, Bouyon, May 12, 1748; and Le Tellier, Borderau des . . . orders que la Communauté de Buyon obtenu [?] a M. LeTellier Comissaire . . . de Guerres. Nous commissaire . . . des guerres certiffions que le M. Jean Baptiste Michelis primo de Buyou nous a donne les pieces detaillés . . . que nous avons envoyé a M dela Voite . . . pour qu'il en ordonne le paiement annee ce fisciene [?: fiscale?] juilles 1748; and Etat des particuliers qui ont soufert de logemens de geans de guerre depuis l'annee de 1744 jusqu'aux premier janvier de 1748, January 2, 1748.

71. ADAM, E088, EE2, Tellis to Lesieux de la communaute de Bouyon, Gunoble [Grenoble], July 20, 1748, and Tellis to Baron de Buyon [Bouyon], Grenoble, December 3, 1748.

72. ADAM, E088, EE4, Commandant au government d'antibes to consuls Villeneuve, December 4, 1745, and Le procureur du Pays, Galear Berrisarts to Messieurs, Aix, June 22, 1745.

73. Browning, *War of the Austrian Succession*, 286–98, 310–13, 353; *Il Manoscritto Borea*, 119–21; Capaccio and Durante, *Marciando per le Alpi*, 114–38; Biga, *Austro Piemontesi nel Dianese*, 25–27.

74. ADAM, E102/035, EE 4, Chr. Danfernet, Bolenne, October 29, 1747; Comte de Langeron, Camp de Utel, October 21, 1747.

75. ADAM, E102/035, EE 4, Reggiordre del stato . . . di Belvedere, April 8, 1748.

76. ASISS, Sanremo I, busta 30 (28/30), Luis Aret: Bermudo, San Remo, July 2, 1747.

77. ASISS, Sanremo I, busta 30 (28/30), Leutrume, Quartiere Reale di Borgomare, July 27, 1747.

78. ASI, PM II, busta 49, De Gubernatis, Porto Maurizio, December 11, 1747, and Nota delle Spese fatto da me Angelo Gabrielle pro Conto della M: Communita del Porto Maurizio, September 25, 1747.

79. ASI, PM II, busta 49, Quartiere Generale de Dolceagua, October 22, 1747; Massa, Onghelia, November 12, 1747; Anziani Supplicanti of Porto Maurizio [no date] (At bottom letter added: "La Soldatesca tanto d'ordinanza che di Milizia gade in Piemonte due Terzi di legna algiorno"). On the gifts, see ASISS, Sanremo I, busta 30 (28/30), Spesa fatta per il regallo fatto al Comandate Tedesco, January 23, 1747, and Pietro Gio: Bottino, Priore, Regali fatti alli Generali Tedeschi, March 7, 1747.

80. ASISS, Sanremo I, busta 30 (28/30), d'Aponte to Sgr. Pro. Rus., Porto Maurizio, October 29, 1746.

81. ASI, PM II, busta 49, Ordini in tempo di Guerra. Alla truppa stanziata in Porto Maurizio, 1745–47, Li Anziani to V:S: Ma[estad], Porto Maurizio, August 13, 1747; De Gubernatis, Quartiere Generale di Porto Maurizio, August 4, 1747; De Gubernatis, Borgomaro, August 13, 1747;

Li Anziani, Georgio Vasallo, Porto Mau[rizi]o, September 15, 1747; Li Anziani Supplicanti to V:S:M:Ma [Imperial Majesty], Porto Maurizio, October 14, 1747; and De Gubernatis October 16, 1747.

82. ASI, PM II, busta 49, Ordini in tempo di Guerra. Alla truppa stanziata in Porto Maurizio, 1745–47, Quartiere Generale de Dolceagua, October 22, 1747.

83. ASISS, Sanremo I, busta 30 (28/30), Falques, San Remo, December 6, 1747.

84. ASISS, Sanremo I, busta 30 (28/30), Bufonio, San Remo: Visita del Fieno, San Remo, December 17, 1747.

85. ASISS, Sanremo I, busta 30 (28/30), Buffonio Comesso, Nota dei Particolari che hanno suplito in conto di questa citta il fieno ai Regimenti qui aquartierati, San Remo, [no month], 1748.

86. ASI, PM II, Elenco chronologico, Spese di Guerra e Militari 453, Ordine de Sr. de Gobernation di sei Soldati alle spese, Porto Moritio [Maurizio], January 19, 1748.

87. ASI, PM II, Elenco chronologico, Spese di Guerra e Militari 453, Paniria d'ordines Porto Mau[rizi]o, April 10, 1748; De Gubernatis, Porto Mau:o [Maurizio], March 24, 1748; Porto Morizio, Ordine de sua Maestad, April 19, 1748; de Gubernatis, Porto Morizio, April 23, 1748; and Ordine de sua Maestad, Dolcheagua, June 1, 1748.

88. Browning, *War of the Austrian Succession*, 286–98, 310–13, 353; Calcagno, "Guerra e Documenti," Alfani and Rizzo, *Nella Morsa della Guerra*, 91–92; and *Il Manoscritto Borea*, 119–21.

89. ASI, PM II, Elenco chronologico, Spese di Guerra e Militari 453, Ordine de S. M., Quartier Ge[ra]le della Bordigharse, July 18, 1748; Conrios, Porto Morizio, December 5, 1748; and Batta Molinari Anziano Priore, Obligette dalla Comm[i]ta per li Letti 400 ricecenti di Torino, Portomorizio, November 30, 1747.

90. ASI, PM II, Elenco chronologico, Spese di Guerra e Militari 453, Ordine de Sua Maestad, Quartel General de San Remo, July 26, 1748, and Ordine de Sua Maestad, Quartel General di Porto Maurizio, May 11, 1748.

91. ASI, PM II, Elenco chronologico, Spese di Guerra e Militari 453, Ordine de S. M., Cuneo, July 11, 1748.

92. ASI, PM II, Serie, Elenco chronologico, Spese di Guerra e Militari 453, Statement by Nobile Filiberto Falquet, Commissioner of War of His Majesty, Savona, September 10, 1748. One rubbo (rubi) is 25 libbri with a libbri varying by region from 0.317–0.369 kg. I used the lower value with the rub(b)o equaling approximately 8 kg. For the rubbo, see https://en.wikipedia .org/wiki/Italian.

93. ASI, PM II, busta 49, Conto di fieno per la Truppa Imperiale e Mescolanze, 1748, and Ordini, Paglia provisto en natura dalla . . . Porto Maurizio alle Truppe Piemontesi, December 1, 1748–February 3, 1749.

94. ASI, PM II, Elenco chronologico, Spese di Guerra e Militari 453, Notta di expressa fatte dalla villa di Caramagna Inferiore, 1748.

95. ASI, PM II, busta 49, Conto di fieno etc per la Truppa Imperiale e Mescolanze, 1748, and Ordini in tempo di Guerra, Paglia provisto en natura dalla . . . Porto Maurizio, December 1, 1748–February 3, 1749.

96. ASI, PM II, busta 49, Pio Felice Saccheri, Conta de San Remo, San Remo, August 1, 1748.

97. ASISS, Sanremo I, busta 30 (28/30), La Regia Delegazione per la Riviera di Ponente Residente nella' Citta di Finale, Finale, July 2, 1748, and Riparte della L[ira] 62,028 Piemonte fra de Comunita del Departimenta di San Remo per la Contribuzione stata fissata per il Messe di

9bre [Novembre] e Xbre, January 24, 1749; ASISS, busta 34 (31/34), ordine de S. M., Quartiere Generale San Remo, December 14, 1748, and ASI, PM II busta 49, Pio Felice Saccheri, Conta de San Remo, San Remo, August 1, 1748.

98. ASISS, Sanremo I, busta 34 (31/34), Ordine de S. M., San Remo, January 28, 1749.

99. See, for example, ASI, PM II, Elenco chronologico, Spese di Guerra e Militari 453, Vitala, Capt, Porto Morizio, February 11, 1748; Porto Maurizio, March 6, 1748; Ordine de sua Maestad, Quartiere General de Dolcheagua, June 1, 1748; Ordine, Soldate alle spese, Sala, San Remo, June 8, 1748; Ordine de Sua Maestad, Conrios, Porto Morizio, August 22, 1748; Sijbilla, Cdte [comandante], Porto Maurizio, September 5, 1748; Conrios, Ordine de sua Maestad: Allogio de Soldati, [October 5?, 1748]; Vitale C[apit]an, January 29, 1749 [small piece of paper is order by captain]; and Conrios, Ordine de sua Maestad, Porto Maurizio, October 1, 1748.

100. ASI, PM II, Elenco chronologico, Spese di Guerra e Militari 453, Porto Morizio, September 15, 1748; and Statto del Fieno devuto in Contanti e distibuito en natura agli Sig[nor]e Uff[izial]e del p[rim]o Battaglione Regimento Keller, November 1, 1748, signed Conrios; and Jalques, Ordini e Stabilimenti,Alassio, August 19, 1748.

101. Calcagno, "Guerra e Documenti," Alfani and Rizzo, *Nella Morsa della Guerra*, 91–92; *Il Manoscritto Borea*, 120–21; ASI, PM II, Elenco chronologico, Spese di Guerra e Militari 453, Ordine de S.M., Quartiere Generale di San Remo, November 6, 1748, and statto "Francesco Corraddo bestie grosse," [November 1748] and De Gubernatis, [n.p.] October 13, 1748; ASI, PM II, busta 49, Paglia provisto en natura dalla M:ca Com:ta di Porto Maurizio alle Truppe Piemontesi dal p[rim]o Xmbre 1748: sino al III Frebraro 1749 and Aggravij sofferti dalla M:ca Com:ta di Porto Maurizio p: allogiode soldati a sue spesi da p[rim]o xmbre 1748: sino a 11 Febraro 1749: per ritardate contribuzioni; Piazze Degl' Ufficiali Piemontesi pagate in Contanti dalla M:ca Com:ta di Porto Maurizio da p[rim]o xmbre 1748: February 11, 1749; and ASISS, Sanremo I, busta 34 (31/34), copia di Contente generali delli tre battaglione do Boegstorf, Monfort, e Leutvum: C: Halley, Tenente di Burgsdorff, San Remo, December 20, 1748; ordine de S.M., Quartiere Generale San Remo, January 24, 1749; Conti di Proviste alle Truppe Piemontesi, Letter e Supplice al Senato, Proviste e contenta di lenha, San Remo, February 2, 1749; Spleise, aiutante magiore, San Remo, February 5, 1749; de Marinozs, aide major, San Remo, February 7, 1749.

102. ADAM, E088, EE2, Conta . . . di pagamenti fatti dalla communitá di Boyone . . . che delle truppe galispane.

103. ASISS, Sanremo I, busta 34 (31/34), G. A. Cagnoli, Copia per la Regia De Megazion esecutivamente alla Lettera del Sigre Intendente M[aest]a d'Spagna, Nizza, November 1, 1748.

104. ADAM, E102/035, EE 4, Jean André Laurents, Secretaire de Belvedere to D'Andelau, Marechal de Camp des Armées du Roy, Belvedere, October 13, 1748; Laurents to Chevalier Chabo, Aide Marechal, Belvedere, October 17, 1748; Rilevo, December 27, 1748, and Role pour le logement, 1748 (Belvedere).

105. Calcagno, "Guerra e Documenti," Alfani and Rizzo, *Nella Morsa della Guerra*, 93–95.

106. ADAM, E004/064, Julien Thomaline Lagarde, procureur du Pays to consuls de St Paul, D'Aix, September 20, 1750, and ADAM, E004/064, EE12, Transtour, Consul and Giraud to le Premier president et intendent [du province] no place, no date [1747].

107. Browning, *War of the Austrian Succession*, 313–20; English Volunteer, *An Authentic Journal of the Remarkable and Bloody Siege of Bergen-op-Zoom* (London: R. Griffiths, 1747) (Reprint: ECCO Print Editions).

108. *Verfasser der Genalogische historische Nachrichten, Leben und Thaten sowohl des Grafens von Lowendahl, als der beijden herzoge Roailles und Richelieu allesamt Marschalle von Frankreich* (Leipzig: Johann Samuel Heinsius, 1749), 160–66, accessed online at https://books.google.com /books?id=bhM6AAAAcAAJ&pg=PA41&lpg=PA41&dq=general+lowendahl&source =bl&ots=WNqzfax8dt&sig=FBvizT-xtnoi4VPGjrWHe58WasA&hl=en&sa=X&ved =oahUKEwjoorHj_p7SAhXILyYKHffyAqo4ChDoAQgbMAE#v=onepage&q=general%20 lowendahl&f=false.

109. NL-HaNA, 2.21.005.41, Familie De Constant Rebecque, 12 Optekenboekje . . . betreffende zijn deelneming aan de Oostenrijkse successieoorlog, 1745–48, Extrait de l'une lettre de l'Armée Alliees eccritte du camp de Melders au depus d'Oudenaerde, July 7 [1746].

110. Browning, *War of the Austrian Succession*, 172–75; NIMH, 511 Handschriften, 20, aantekeningen betreffende de Oostenrijkse Successieoorlog (1743–48), kopie dagboek van Schlippenbach, 1743–45, No. 1 Journal de 1743, 14–15.

111. Archives Departmentales du Nord, Lille, France [henceforth ANDL], 8674, Comte de Nava to Mr [Messieur], Mons, July 16, 1744, and Mr to de Nava, Valenciennes, July 14, 1744, and Mr. to de Nava, Valenciennes, August 29, 1744.

112. Browning, *War of the Austrian Succession*, 135 and 172; Rapin de Thoyras, *Histoire d'Angleterre*, vol. 16, part 2 (The Hague: n.p., 1749), 731.

113. ANDL, C 11313, Comians, Bavaij [Hainault], June 16, 1744.

114. ANDL, 8674, Comte de Nava, Mons, September 22, 1747, and Etat contenat les noms des ville et villages du Haijnaut Autrichien ou les troupes du Roy de France ont exigé des rafraichissments . . . et enlevements and Mr. to Comte de Nava, Lt general, commandant a Mons, Valenciennes, August 29, 1744.

115. ANDL, 8674, copy of letter Comte de Estras to Comte de Nava, August 13, 1744.

116. ANDL, 8674, copy of letter Comte de Estras to Comte de Nava, August 13, 1744.

117. ANDL, 8674, Contributions en vivres et fourages exigés des paroisses du Haynaut par les hussards de la reine de hongrie [August–September 1744] and Etat des effets et denrés . . . dans les paroisses de la subdelegation de Condé depuis le 16 aout jusqu'au . . . 26 . . . septembre par les hussards enemies, Condé, 1744.

118. ANDL, 8674, copy of letter Louchier, conseiller pensionaire des etats de haijnaut autrichien to the Magistrate de Bavaij, September 23, 1744; Le magistrate de Bavaij, Valenciennes, September 26, 1744; Magistrats de Bavaij, Bavaij, September 24, 1744; Commedans in Bossu to Dono Major e scabini, Bavaij, Bossu, September 22, 1744; and Louchier conseiller penssionaire des etats de haynaut to magistrates Bavaij, Mons, September 23, 1744.

119. ANDL, 8674, Bavaij, October 1, 1744, and Etat des pertes. . . . de Bavaij and M. le Robert, Valenciennes, October 3, 1744; Hennadevares, Maubeuge, October 6, 1744, and etat des rations . . . et autres denrées que les hussarts autrichiens ont exigé . . . de Maubeuge, October 6, 1744; etat de la paroisse de Berseilles, October 24, 1744; Betteignie, estat de rations, October 3, 1744; and Etat de depenses et pilliages . . . paroisse de GognieCauchie, 1744 [no date].

120. ANDL, 8674, Etat de degas faites par les houssards de la Reyne de Hongue sur les territoirs de quelques villages dependant de Valenciennes . . . depuis le mois de May dernier, October 12, 1744.

121. Browning, *War of the Austrian Succession*, 206–13, and *Verfasser*, 81–87.

122. For the 1745 inundations and harvest losses, see ZA, 7. Vrije van Sluis, 345.2, Johannes Rombouts, hooftman van St. Baafs to Heeren Burgemeesters Vrijen te Sluijs, [December] 1747.

123. ANDL, C 11313, Etat de sommes auxquelles montent la contribution exigées en argent par force et violence dans diferentes communautes de Haynaut francois . . . 1745.

124. ANDL, C 11313, Delegou to De Sare, Du camp de Tournai, June 8, 1745; Quesnoy, Delegue to monsignieur, June 7, 1745; Le Comte Dargenson, Valenciennes, June 7 [or 17], 1745; Curé de Barbencon (n.d., n.p.); and I. Nouny, Barbencon, November 29, 1745. Maurice of Saxony at Maubeuge in April–May 1745, see Browning, *War of the Austrian Succession*, 207.

125. ANDL, C 11313, Delegou to De Sare, Du camp de Tournai, June 8, 1745; Quesnoy, Delegue to monsignieur, June 7, 1745; Le Comte Dargenson, Valenciennes, June 7 [or 17], 1745; Curé de Barbencon (n.d., n.p.); and I. Nouny, Barbencon, November 29, 1745.

126. ANDL, C 11313, Machement to Phelipier, Valenciennes, June 22, 1745; Bouval, commandant to Messieurs le Bailly, mayeur . . . liveront tout presentment la subsistence d'une detachment de l'armee de . . . marechal de saxe; Phelippes, Maubeuge, June 24, 1745; and Godemeaux (to magistrates), Maubeuge, June 24, 1745.

127. ANDL, C 11313, Jean B. Roues, mayeur Etat . . . de l'argent, meubles . . . que ont ete pris violemente par un troupe ennemis de trois compagnies franche . . . a Barbencon, Barbencon, September 14, 1745, and Nous captaine d'une compagnien franche au service . . . de la reine d'ongrie . . . qui a este depeché . . . munis de passeporte pur lever contribution dans le pays ennemis, Barbencon (collation a son original estant en Barbencon . . . trouve conform sa original, September 14, 1745, [signed] Jean B. Rouet (griffier Barbencon); and Francois, abbé de Crespin, Etat des pertes fattes a l'abbé . . . d'un partij ennemis du 22 juillet 1745 et le Sommation du de de ferru capitaine du partij, Crespin. September 17, 1745.

128. ANDL, C 11313, Etat des argents, effets et bestiaux pillés . . . dans Maubeuge par les partis de l'ennemis et des sommes payé . . . pour contribution . . . 1745; Charles Lansette, Quittance contribution to Queen of Hungary, November 3, 1745, and for village Solemier, Brussels, September 25, 1745; Etat de ce que un partit franche des etats de Mons ont pillé dans la paroisse de Villeraux, Villeraux, October 9, 1745, attached to M. Delegvue to M[essieu]r, Quesnoy, November 8, 1745; Charles Deltour, Villereaux, October 9, 1745.

129. ANDL, C 11313, Phelippes, Maubeuge, November 29, 1745.

130. Gutmann, *War and Rural Life*, 81–93, 133–73.

131. ANDL, C 11388, cahier "contributions" and on first page: "*maraudes* [mauraudes crossed out and replaced by:] *desordres et pretendiier* comises sur le pays de Liège par le corps de troupes qui etoit aux orders de M le C[om]te de Beau Soble [1745], in particular see De Samar, October 11, 1745, and M. de Sechelles, October 12, 1745.

132. Gutmann, *War and Rural Life*, 66.

133. Browning, *War of the Austrian Succession*, 259–60, 267–69; *Verfasser*, 100, 103–4.

134. ANDL, C 11313, Comte de Nava, Mons, January 11 and February 11, 1746; and Etat des contributions extraordinaires payé par les habitans . . . de Condé aux ennemis [1746].

135. ANDL, C 11313, Gillot to Messieur, Givet, July 24, 1746; ANDL 8674, Harles to Hugemontpenele, Marienbourg, August 12, 1747, and Harles, Marienbourg, August 16, 1747; St Martin to Messieur, Givet, August 13, 1747; D'huyemont, Aveses, August 27, 1747; Gillot to Mr Namur, September 15, 1747; and M[aurice] de Saxe, Camp de Tongres, September 27, 1747.

136. NIMH, 511 Handschriften, 20, kopie dagboek van Schlippenbach, No. 2 Journal de 1745, 506.

137. Regionaal Historisch Centrum Eindhoven, the Netherlands (henceforth RHCE), 15022, Stad Eindhoven en de Prinsendorpen, 2706, De Pretensie van karrevrachten . . . and Lijste van de karren door de Regenten der Stad Eindhoven . . . gelevert.

138. RHCE, 15022, Memorie van 't gene den Secretaris van Esvelt, January 14, 1750, and Lijste van Leverantien . . . aan de Engelse, Hanoverse en Hessische Troupes gedaen voor soo ver daar van geen betalinge is gekomen, October 19, 1747–July 13, 1747.

139. WBA, Bergen op Zoom, 5 Stadssecretarie 4990, Extract uijt het register der resolution, January 6, 1747. For individual villages, see WBA, 0390, Dorpsbestuur Wouw, 1926, Stukken betreffende leveranties e.d. door de inwoners aan geallieerde tropen, including Lijste . . . Wouw, March 19, 1747, and WBA, 0391, Dorpsbestuur Moerstraten, 2674, Lijsten (1747). In the 1776 military guide, foraging is included as a routine operation, Simes, *Military Guide*, 20, 45–47, 52.

140. Browning, *War of the Austrian Succession*, 304–5; NIMH, 511 Handschriften, 20, kopie dagboek van Schlippenbach, No. 2 Journal de 1745, 7; *Verfasser*, 120–21.

141. ZA, 7 Vrije van Sluis, 582, Etat de touts les Pillages . . . par les Troupes de Sa Majeste [1747]; Memorie van . . . het plucderen van mijn Hofstede . . . op den 20 april 1747; Generaale Lijst . . . den 17 April . . . Prince Willempolder, May 13, 1747; and Begrotinge van schade door de troupes van Zijne Majesteijt, Cadzand, [May, 1747].

142. *Verfasser*, 120–23.

143. ZA, 7 Vrije van Sluis, 585, Vertoog aan . . . Sechelle . . . Intendant . . . van de armeen des Konings, February 12, 1748; Het Collegie 'slands van den Vrije is debet . . . April 23, 1747; De . . . directeuren der polders in den lande van Izendijke . . . , Resolutie over de blancs de sauveguarde, May 1, 1747; Missive van de heer Beaufort to Borgemr . . . Vrije, Antwerpen, August 28, 1747; Aide d'memoire que les troupes du Roy qui se trouvent dans les villes et Pais qui etois occupe par les hollandaise servient traits de la meme maniere, Lille, January 29, 1748; Van skonings weege Jean Moreau, . . . intendant in Vlaanderen to Vrije Sluijs, Paris, January 31, 1748; Jean Moreau to Vrije Sluijs, Paris, January 31, 1748. See also *Verfasser*, 120–21; and Babeau, *La Vie Militaire*, vol. 2, 153, 158–59.

144. ZA, 7, Vrije van Sluis, 345.2 , Vertoog aan Sechelle, February 12, 1748, Resolution, February 1748 and various letters to Committee Members of the Kamer van Associate van Sluijs to and from Sechelle and Cranc, Sluijs, Gent, and Brussels, March 25 and 27, April 15 and 19, and June 4, 1748, and De Cranc to Magistrates, Gent, July 24, 1748, and Mathias de Smidt, Kamer van Associatie, Sluijs to Burgomasters Vrije, Sluijs, July 24, 1728. See also 7 Vrije van Sluis, 585, De gecommiteerde leden ter kamer van associatie, Sluijs, May 29, 1748.

145. RHCE, 15022, 2706 Stukken betreffende rekwisities . . . Franse troepen, Burgemeesters . . . Eindhoven to Rade van State, February 28, 1748. For the carts, see, RHCE, 15022, 2706, Lijste van de karren, February 10, 1750.

146. Browning, *War of the Austrian Succession*, 304–5, 313–20; *Verfasser*, 126–66. On the razing of farms, see WBA, Bergen op Zoom, 5 Stadssecretarie, 4990, Memories van schade Rijgersman; erffgenamen Santz (1747); Weduwe Frantz; Van der Mast: Nuyts (1747); erffgenamen Francois Bolcooele; Jacob Mennes; Hoeve St Jansberg and Boekweitse Hoek Hove; Aen de Hoog Mogende Heeren Staten Generaal (no date but in top left corner: "opt 6st zegel"); erffgenamen van

Juffrou Menet and Widow Perot; Lauwerijs Stevens; Widow Cornelis Koninkt, February 23, 1750.

147. Browning, *War of the Austrian Succession*, 313–20; *Verfasser*, 148–49, 159–65; ZA, 7 Vrije van Sluis, 585, Pieter Hennepan to Borgemrs Vrije, Antwerpen, August 24, 1748.

148. WBA, Bergen op Zoom, 5 Stadssecretarie 4990, C. W. Stewart to the staten general [1749].

149. WBA, Bergen op Zoom, 5 Stadssecretarie 4990, Aen de Hoog Mog. Heeren der Staten Generaal [1766]; 5 Stadssecretarie 4991, Extract uijt het register der resoluties, October 22, 1750, and April 4, 1750; and WBA, 0390, 1931, Besluit van de Staten Generaal over het herstel van de in 1747 geleden oorlogsschade, March 21, 1759.

150. On the horse carts, see WBA, 0390, 1930, Lijsten, Wouw, September 1, 1749. On the livestock, see WBA, Bergen op Zoom, 5 Stadssecretarie 4990, Uwe . . . dienaren to Doorluchtige Vorst [Prince of Orange], Bergen [op Zoom], December 30, 1749.

151. *Verfasser*, 166.

152. *Verfasser*, 131–32, 147.

153. WBA, 0390, Dorpsbestuur Wouw, 1483–1810, 1926, Extract uijt het Resolutienboek . . . Wouw, November 5, 1751 and Memorie . . . weegens karrevragten, 1747; *Verfasser*, 130.

154. WBA, Bergen op Zoom, 5 Stadssecretarie 4991, Extract uijt het register, October 22, 1750.

155. RHCE, 15022, 2706, Lijste van de karren, February 10, 1750, and Lijste van de Pioniers . . . Gestel, August 31–October 29, 1747. On the English reinforcements, see NL-HaNA 1.10.94, Familie Fagel: Supplement, 106, H. Hop to My Lord [king of Britain], London, 11/22 September 1747.

156. WBA, 0701, Dorpsbestuur Rucphen, 550 (old 558), Opgave van geleden schade en krijgslasten, 1747.

157. *Verfasser*, 164–67.

158. NIMH, 511, 20, dagboek van Schlippenbach, No. 2 Journal de 1745, 14–17; Browning, *War of the Austrian Succession*, 320–21. On the French winter quarters, see *Verfasser*, 171.

159. NL-HaNA, 1.01.50, Stadhouderlijke Secretarie, 1600–1795, 89 Staat van de inkwartiering van de Franse troepen, Pro Memoria from Corps Bavarois to the Prince of Orange, [Grave], November 13, 1747.

160. RHCE, 15022, Eindhoven, 2706, Lijste van de karren, February 10, 1750.

161. WBA, 001 Etten Leur, 3780, Regenten Etten Leur, to Raden . . . van . . . de Prince van Orangien and authorization by J. van Schinne, 's Gravenhage, October 3, 1747 and document headed by: Willem Speeck, no date and 3781, Memorie van schade . . . van de heer Cornkoper and Copie: Aan de Edele Mog. Heeren Raeden van State and notes and authorization by Raad van State in margins, J. Hop, December 9, 1749, and Specificatie van het houtwerk . . . Etten, Breda, June 13, 1748, and Specificatie van het hout.

162. Browning, *War of the Austrian Succession*, 339–53.

163. NL-HaNA, 1.01.50, Archief van de Stadhouderlijke Secretarie, 1600–1795, 89 Staat van de inkwartiering van de Franse troepen in de Zuidelijke Nederlanden, undated [1748].

164. On the poverty in France, see Browning, *War of the Austrian Succession*, 328.

165. Browning, *War of the Austrian Succession*, 346, 361–63; WBA, Bergen op Zoom, 5 Stadssecretarie, 4990, Taxatie . . . ten verzoeke van Juffrou Christine Lach and Extract, December 2, 1749.

166. NL-HaNA, 1.10.01, Familie Van Aerssen van Voshol, 1418–1910, 83 Rapport . . . besetting van Zeeland (1748).

167. WBA, 0550, Stadsbestuur Willemstad, 1773, Stukken betreffende de geleden oorlogsschade, 1748–49.

168. BHIC, 342, Plakkaten, 1520–1884, 4, 1750, 606/211, pamphlet, 's Gravenhage, November 23, 1750; J. A. Faber, "Cattle Plague in the Netherlands during the Eighteenth Century," *Mededelingen van de Landbouwhogeschool te Wageningen, Nederland* 62, no. 11 (1962): 1–7.

169. WBA, 0001, Dorpsbestuur Etten-Leur, 1430–1810, 1738, Staten van runderen, 1744–1756, and ZA, 7 Vrije van Sluis, 345.2, Stukken betreffende leveranties aan het leger, Cornelis de Jonge to [Vrije], Gent, May 24, 1748.

170. BHIC, 342, Plakkaten, 4, 1750, 606/211, Ordre en Reglement, 's Gravenhage, July 10, 1750, and Resolutie over kortingen op verponding in de Meierij om zodoende arme bevolking te stimuleren de landbouw weer met nieuwe lust en ijver aan de pakken, Den Bosch, March 18, 1750.

171. Simes, *Military Guide*, 91–92. During the early 1800s English campaigns in Spain, English commanders equally failed to stop their soldiers from plundering in friendly territory, see Samuel, *Historical Account*, 588.

172. WBA, Rucphen 560, De Raaden . . . van den doorlucthige huijze van Bergen op Zoom, July 20, 1793, and Lijst der geleedene schade . . . Rucphen, November 10, 1794.

Chapter Seven: Environcide and Genocide: A Global Comparative Perspective on 18th Century Warfare

1. Nationaal Archief, The Hague, The Netherlands (henceforth NL-HaNA, Aanwinsten [Accessions] 1902, XXVI, 115, J. Landman to Elmina, Axim, April 16, 1707.

2. NL-HaNA, 1.04.02, VOC, Stukken betreffende de Opstand van de Singalezen tegen het Bewind van de VOC 11302, Vandervoort Aan de Edele . . . bewindhebberen van de generale nederlandsche Co [VOC] . . . Kamer Middelburg, Colombo, March 4, 1760, Extract brief door den Gouverneur en Raad tot Colombo [Samland?] naar Hoog Mog: Edelheden geschreven, den March 4, 1761, translaat Singaleese ola geschreeven aan den heer Commandeur Abraham Samlandt en de verdure Hollanders die sig in het fort bevinden, door den groten Adigare den Desave van oewe, drie Mohandirame en een Batterale.

3. NL-HaNA, 1.04.02, VOC, 7940, Dag Register Hongij Vogajie gehouden rond Ceram en na de comptoiren Paparuoua, Harouka, en Hila, 1784, entry November 18, 1784 (image 223), accessed online at http://www.gahetna.nl/collectie/archief/inventaris/gahetnascan/zoekterm /VOC/eadid/1.04.02/wollig/uit/volledige-tekst/aan/gebruikersinbreng/aan/aantal/20/node /c01%3A1.c02%3A4.c03%3A4.c04%3A4.c05%3A0.c06%3A38/level/file/foto/NL-HaNA_1.04 .02_7940_0011/fotouuid/582b6f60-3d8a-2ce1-b2c1-fd43eed6202e/scan-index/.

4. McNeill argues that the western European style professional army system of organization developed by the Dutch in the 16th century and perfected during the spread of the Thirty Years' War to the rest of Europe, the New World, and India like a contagion as a byproduct of the wars of imperial expansion, see William H. McNeill, *The Pursuit of Power: Technology. Armed Force, and Society since A.D. 1000* (Chicago: University of Chicago Press, 1982), 147–48.

5. John E. Ferling, *A Wilderness of Miseries: War and Warriors in Early America* (Westport, CT: Greenwood Press, 1980), 23, 188–96.

6. Maurice Saxe, *Reveries, or, Memoirs Concerning the Art of War* (Edinburgh: Alexander Donaldson, 1759), 270–97; Jacques Antoine Hippolyte de Guibert, *Essay Général de Tactique*, vol. 2 (London: Nabu Public Domain Reprints, 1772), 87–88, 108–16, 221–50, 287–345.

7. Grenier notes that the British employed militia and during the mid-18th century created specialized Ranger units to conduct the *petite guerre*, including raiding and scorched earth. See Grenier, *First Way of War*, 53–155. On pandoers and hussars in the 1740s, see Michael Howard, *War in European History* (Oxford: Oxford University Press, 1988 [1976]), 77–79.

8. Grant D. Jones, *The Conquest of the Last Maya Kingdom* (Stanford: Stanford University Press, 1998).

9. Jones, *Conquest of the Last Maya Kingdom*.

10. Jones, *Conquest of the Last Maya Kingdom*.

11. James A. Vlasich, *Pueblo Indian Agriculture* (Albuquerque: University of New Mexico Press, 2005), 31–85; R. Douglas Hurt, *Indian Agriculture in America: Prehistory to the Present* (Lawrence: University of Kansas, 1987), 19, 50–53; Edward H. Spicer, *Cycles of Conquest: The Impact of Spain, Mexico, and the United States on the Indians of the Southwest, 1533–1960* (Tuscon: University of Arizona Press, 1976 [1962]), 152–209. On the Zuni, see Gregson Schachner, *Population Circulation and the Transformation of Ancient Zuni Communities* (Tucson: University of Arizona Press, 2012), 91–93.

12. Vlasich, *Pueblo Indian Agriculture*, 31–85; Hurt, *Indian Agriculture*, 19, 50–53; Spicer, *Cycles of Conquest*, 152–209; Schachner, *Population Circulation*, 91–93.

13. Spicer, *Cycles of Conquest*, 152–209.

14. Ronald H. Towner, *Defending the Dinétah: Pueblitos in the Ancestral Navajo Homeland* (Salt Lake City: University of Utah Press, 2003); Spicer, *Cycles of Conquest*, 210–13. See also Ned Blackhawk, *Violence over the Land: Indians and Empires in the Early American West* (Cambridge: Harvard University Press, 2006), 46–49.

15. Colin G. Galloway, *The Western Abenakis of Vermont, 1600–1800: War, Migration, and the Survival of an Indian People* (Norman: University of Oklahoma Press, 1990), 132–33.

16. Galloway, *Western Abenakis*, 22–25, 70–218, 224–50.

17. David H. Corkran, *The Cherokee Frontier: Conflict and Survival, 1740–62* (Norman: University of Oklahoma press, 1962), 207–55; Hurt, *Indian Agriculture*, 31–32; Grenier, *First Way of Making War*, 115–45.

18. Peter Silver, *Our Savage Neighbors: How Indian War Transformed Early America* (New York: Norton, 2007).

19. R. Douglas Hurt, *The Ohio Frontier: Crucible of the Old Northwest, 1720–1830* (Bloomington: Indiana University Press, 1996), 10–23, 45–48, 71–141. After 1800, many Eastern Indians turned up in the Northwestern Plains. See Theodore Binnema, *Common and Contested Ground: A Human and Environmental History of the Northwestern Plains* (Norman: University of Oklahoma Press, 2001), 172. On the heavy pillaging in contemporary Europe, see Alexander Gillespie, *A History of the Laws of War*, vol. 2, *The Customs and Laws of War with Regards to Civilians in Times of Conflict* (Oxford: Hart, 2011), 242.

20. On requisitions, billeting, and scorched earth during the American Revolution, see James A. Huston, *The Sinews of War: Army Logistics, 1775–1953* (Washington, DC: Office of the Chief of Military History United States Army, 1966), 16–17, 26–28, 31, 36–37, 44–67; and Johann Conrad Döhla, *A Hessian Diary of the American Revolution*, trans., ed., and with an introduction

by Bruce E. Burgoyne (Norman: University of Oklahoma Press, 1990), 40, 61–63, 82. 91, 101, 103–4, 110–11, 118–22, 128–30, 139, 143–44, 146, 152, 154–58, 163, 178, 183.

21. Hurt, *Ohio Frontier*, 71–141; Eric Hinderaker and Peter C. Mancall, *At the Edge of Empire: The Backcountry in British North America* (Baltimore: Johns Hopkins University Press, 2003), 174–76. On the destructive war against Amerindians in the 18th century, see also Grenier, *First Way of Making War*, 87–203.

22. Hurt, *Ohio Frontier*, 71–141.

23. John K. Thornton, *Warfare in Atlantic Africa, 1500–1800* (London: Routledge, 2003 [1999]), 33–34, 60, 69–73, 120, 130, 133–37, 151.

24. Ivor Wilks, "The State of the Akan and the Akan State: A Discursion," *Cahiers d'études Africaines*, 87–88 (1982), 22, 231–49; R. A. Kea, *Settlements, Trade and Polities in the 17th Century Gold Coast* (Baltimore: Johns Hopkins University Press, 1982), 97–98, 108–9.

25. W. Bosman, *Naauwkeurige Beschrijving van de Guineese Gout, Tand en Slave Kust* (Amsterdam, 1709), part 2, 16, 19, 73, 185–87; NL-HaNA, 1.05.14, Nederlandse Bezittingen op de Kust van Guinea (henceforth NBKG), 93, J. Maes to Elmina, Shama, June 29, 1726, and NBKG 88, entry Elmina, July 20, 1721.

26. NL-HaNA, Aanwinsten 1902, XXVI, 9, P.C. le Candel to Elmina, Shama, November 9, 1706, and 115, J. Landman to Elmina, Axim, July 31, August 16, and October 30, 1706, and February 14, March 5, April 16, and May 3, 1707; 1.05.01.02 Tweede West-Indische Compagnie (henceforth WIC), 99, J. Landman to Board of Ten, Axim, April 30, 1707.

27. NL-HaNA, Aanwinsten 1902, XXVI, 115, J. Landman to Elmina, Axim, April 16, 1707.

28. NL-HaNA, 1.05.14, NBKG 82, W. Butler to Elmina, Axim, October 2, 11, and 17, December 11, 13, 16, 22, and 31, 1715, and January 5, 11, and 27, 1716; 1.05.01.02 WIC, 102, H. Haring to Board of Ten, Elmina, November 11, 1715.

29. NL-HaNA, 1.05.14, NBKG 85, W. Butler to Van Naarssen (Axim), Elmina, November 3, 1718.

30. NL-HaNA, 1.05.14, NBKG 84, Van Alzen to Elmina, Accra, November 7, 1717, and Hendrix to Elmina, Bercou, January 7, 1718, and Elima, entry November 5, 1717; NBKG 85, W. Butler to Van Naarssen (Axim), Elmina, November 3, 1718.

31. NL-HaNA, 1.05.14, NBKG 85, Munnikxhoven to Elmina, March 21, 1718; NBKG 85, Van Alsem to Elmina, Accra, May 21, 1718.

32. NL-HaNA, 1.05.14, NBKG 85, Butler to van Naerssen (Axim), Elmina, November 3, 1718.

33. NL-HaNA, 1.05.14, NBKG 82, Butler to Elmina, Axim, January 27, 1716; NBKG 89, Entry Elmina, February 3, 1722; NBKG 88, J. van Goes to Elmina, Shama, August 4, 1721, J. Muller to Butler (Elmina), Axim, August 17, September 8, and November 20, 1721, and Butler to J. Muller (Axim), Elmina, August 20, 1721; NBKG 62, W. Butler to Board of Ten, Elmina, November 1, 1721; NBKG 88, Butler to Muller (Axim), Elmina, December 11, 1721. See also C. H. Perrot, "Le Raid d'Ebiri Moro contre Kumasi, la Capitale Ashanti (1718)," *Cultures et Développement: Revue International des Sciences du Développement*, 16, no. 3–4 (1984): 537–53. The WIC sent carpenters, blacksmiths, and masons to the new Asante King Opoku Ware to help with the rebuilding of Kumasi, see NBKG 90, A. Houtman to J. Rycxborn (Frederiksborg), Elmina, December 28, 1722, and January 11, 1723.

34. NL-HaNA, 1.05.14, NBKG 93, Munnikxhoven to Elmina, Axim, March 14, 1726; Van Hoppen to Elmina, Boutry, April 15 and 24, 1726, and Augier to Elmina, Commany, April 26,

1726, and Augier to Elmina, Taccorary, April 13 and 27, 1726, Maes to Elmina, Shama, April 27 and 30, 1726, Valckenier to Pranger (Accra), Elmina, June 15, 1726, Valkenier to Van Hoppen (Boutry), Elmina, June 17, 1726, Elet to Elmina, Cormantyn, June 19, 1726, Valckenier to Maes (Shama), Elmina, July 18, 1726, Ochers to Elmina, Mouré, July 21 and August 10, 1726, Elet to Elmina, Cormantyn, August 31, 1726, Maes to Elmina, Shama, September 10, 1726.

35. NL-HaNA, 1.05.14, NBKG 94, Van Bosch to Elmina, Shama, July 9 and September 16, 1727, and January 6, March 21, 1728; NBKG 95, Vrolijk to Elmina, Commany, May 26 and June 7, 1729, Ockers to Elmina, Axim, April 16, 1729, Augier to Elmina, Commany, December 22, 1729; NBKG 97, Bosch to Elmina, Shama, July 15 and September 20, 1730, Pranger to Bosch (Shama), Elmina, September 15 and November 14, 1730, Ockers to Elmina, Axim, January 9, 1731.

36. NL-HaNA, 1.05.14, NBKG 95, De la Planque to Elmina, Accra, August 22 and October 17, 1729, and Gawron to Elmina, Apam, October 10, 1729, and February 18, 1730; NBKG 97, De la Planque to Elmina, Accra, February 24 and October 14, 1730, Gawron to Elmina, Apam, July 10 and September 17, 1730, and Pranger to De la Planque, Elmina, November 1 and 17, 1730, and Blittersdorp to Elmina, Accra, December 23, 1730, and June 6, 1731.

37. Bosman, *Naauwkeurige Beschrijving*, 14, 74, 78–81, 85, 87–89, 177; NL-HaNA, 1.05.14, NBKG 82, H. Haring to W. Butler (Axim), Elmina, September 9, 1715; NL-HaNA, NBKG 89, P. van Schaage to Elmina, Ancober, March 5, 1722, and W. Butler to Schaage, Elmina, March 5, 1722; NL-HaNA, Aanwinsten 1902, XXVI, 115, J. Landman to Elmina, Axim, April 16, 1707; NL-HaNA, 1.05.01.02, WIC 98, W. de la Palma to Board of Ten, Elmina, September 5, 1705; WIC 99, P. Nuyts to Board of Ten, Elmina, April 19, 1706.

38. NL-HaNA, 1.05.14, NBKG 62, W. Butler to Board of Ten, Elmina, July 14, 1720.

39. NL-HaNA, 1.05.01.02, WIC 102, H. Haring to the Board of Ten, Elmina, March 4, 1714; 1.05.14, NBKG 93, A. van Bosch to Elmina, Shama, September 30 and December 11, 1726, and Maes to Elmina, Shama, September 9, 1726; NBKG 94, Norré to Gawron, Elmina, January 20 and May 28, 1728; NBKG 97, Gawron, Apam, September 17, 1730, and De la Planque, Accra, October 14, 1730.

40. For a critical assessment of the VOC sources, see M. C. Ricklefs, *Jogjakarta under Sultan Mangkubumi, 1749–1792: A History of the Division of Java* (London: Oxford University Press, 1974), xvi–xvii; Leonard Y. Andaya, *The World of Maluku: Eastern Indonesia in the Early Modern Period* (Honolulu: University of Hawaii Press, 1993), 20–22.

41. Peter Carey, "Civilization on Loan: The Making of an Upstart Polity: Mataram and Its Successors, 1600–1830," *Modern Asian Studies* 31, no. 3 (1997): 711–34; M. C. Ricklefs, "Some Statistical Evidence on Javanese Social, Economic and Demographic History in the Later Seventeenth and Eighteenth Centuries," *Modern Asian Studies* 20, no. 2 (1986): 1–32; P. Carey, "Waiting for the 'Just King': The Agrarian World of South-Central Java from Giyanti (1755) to the Java War (1825–30)," *Modern Asian Studies* 20, no. 1 (1986): 59–137. See also M. C. Ricklefs, *War, Culture, and Economy in Java, 1677–1726: Asian and European Imperialism in the Early Kartasura Period* (Sydney: Asian Studies Association of Australia, 1993), 129–202; Ricklefs, *Jogjakarta under Sultan Mangkubumi*, 14–66; and M. C. Ricklefs, *A History of Modern Indonesia, since c. 1200* (Stanford: Stanford University Press, 2008 [1981]), 99–121.

42. J. Norman Parmer, "Historical Perspectives on Chinese in Southeast Asia," in *Chinese Populations in Contemporary Southeast Asian Societies: Identities, Interdependence and*

International Influences, ed. M. Jocelyn Armstrong, T. Warwick Armstrong, and Kent Mulliner (London: Routledge, 2001), 18–54; and NL-HaNA, 1.04.17, Hoge Regering van Batavia, 1602–1827, 35 Relaas van de Oorsprong en het Verloop van de "Javanese Oorlog" tussen de Hoge Regering en Javaanse Vorsten, 1745–55, [p. 1: the page numbers provided are the author's]; Ricklefs, *History of Modern Indonesia,* 114–17.

43. NL-HaNA, 1.04.02, VOC 11226 Examinatie der verklaringen concernerende de rebellige chineese [Register Getuige en verhoren betreffende opstand Chineesen in Batavia, 1741], Relaas van de Chineesen Tsjoeki-etko, moolenaar en Tsjoet Jienko, Zuijker Riet planter aen de Zuiker-molen op Tanah Doearatoes, Batavia, January 28, 1741; and compareerende voor heeren commissarissen, Lim Sinko of Emuij, January 27, 1741.

44. Ulbe Bosma, *The Sugar Plantation in India and Indonesia: Industrial Production, 1770–2010* (Cambridge: Cambridge University Press, 2013), 13–16.

45. NL-HaNA, 1.04.02, VOC 766 Generale Resolutien des Casteels Batavia, October 21, 1740 (237); Ann Kumar, *Java and Modern Europe: Ambiguous Encounters* (London: Routledge 2015 [1997]), 32–34.

46. NL-HaNA, 1.04.02, VOC 11226 Examinatie der verklaringen concernerende de rebellige chineese, compareerende voor heeren commissarissen uijt den Raden Fiscaal . . . Jan Jans, Gabriel d'Allecroez, Israel Manuel, Joseph d'Allecroez, January 24, 1741, and Li Tsie, January 24, 1741.

47. NL-HaNA, 1.04.02, VOC 11226 Examinatie der verklaringen concernerende de rebellige chineese, compareerende voor heeren commissarissen uijt den Raden Fiscaal . . . Jan Jans, Gabriel d'Allecroez, Israel Manuel, Joseph d'Allecroez, January 24, 1741, and Li Tsie, January 24, 1741.

48. NL-HaNA, 1.04.02, VOC 766 Generale Resolutien des Casteels Batavia, October 2, 1740 (216–17), and 767 Kopie-secrete resoluties betreffende de opstand van de Chinezen 1740, October 17, 1740 (1531 verso).

49. NL-HaNA, 1.04.02, VOC 767 Kopie-secrete resoluties . . . opstand van de Chinezen 1740, October 21, 1740 (1542–47 verso).

50. NL-HaNA, 1.04.02, VOC 766 Generale Resolutien des Casteels Batavia, Register, October 25, 1740 (252–55).

51. NL-HaNA, 1.04.02, VOC 767 Kopie-secrete resoluties . . . opstand van de Chinezen 1740, October 28, 1740 (1557 verso).

52. NL-HaNA, 1.04.02, VOC 767 Kopie-secrete resoluties . . . de opstand van de Chinezen 1740, November 1, 1740 (1563 verso–1564 verso) and November 11, 1740 (1580 verso).

53. NL-HaNA, 1.04.02, VOC 767 Kopie-secrete resoluties . . . opstand van de Chinezen 1740, November 15, 1740 (1585 and verso).

54. NL-HaNA, 1.04.02, VOC 767 Kopie-secrete resoluties . . . opstand van de Chinezen 1740, November 18, 1740 (1587).

55. NL-HaNA, 1.04.02, VOC 11226 Examinatie der verklaringen concernerende de rebellige Chinese, gecompareert de gedetineerde chinees Laauw Tjeeko, January 11–12, 1741; and compareerde voor mijn . . . getuigen Jan van Thoff, January 19, 1741; and presentibus omnibus den plod: heer van Ries: de vrij Boeginees Turpia, January 11, 1741.

56. NL-HaNA, 1.04.02, VOC 766 Generale Resolutien des Casteels Batavia, Register, December 2, 1740 (329). On the sugar cane production, see Bosma, *Sugar Plantation in India and Indonesia,* 13–16.

57. NL-HaNA, 1.04.02, VOC 9526, Kopie-missive van de Raad van Justitie in Batavia aan de Heren XVII betreffende het proces tegen Valckenier 1743, Gustaaf Willem Baron van Imhoff, June 17, 1743.

58. NL-HaNA, 1.04.02, VOC 9526, Kopie-missive van de Raad van Justitie in Batavia aan de Heren XVII betreffende het proces tegen Valckenier 1743, Extract uit de notulen . . . raden van india, January 3, 1741.

59. NL-HaNA, 1.04.02, VOC 11226 Examinatie der verklaringen concernerende de rebellige chineese [Register Getuige en verhoren betreffende opstand Chineesen in Batavia, 1741], compareerende voor heeren commissarissen . . . Lim Sinko of Emuij, January 27, 1741.

60. NL-HaNA, 1.04.02, VOC 11226 Examinatie der verklaringen concernerende de rebellige chineese, compareerende voor heeren commissarissen . . . Lim Sinko of Emuij, January 27, 1741; and comparerende voor commissarissen . . . Bajaar . . . vaandrig, January 9, 1741.

61. NL-HaNA, 1.04.02, VOC 11226 Examinatie der verklaringen concernerende de rebellige Chinese, Batavia . . . Soera Marta, January 26, 1741; Buna Jaja from Cheribon, January 27, 1741; and Gabok van Bakalonga, January 27, 1741.

62. NL-HaNA, 1.04.02, VOC 11226 Examinatie der verklaringen concernerende de rebellige Chinese, comparerende voor commissarissen uijt den raad van Justitie: Sakria ook genaamd Bappa Saida, January 9 and 12, 1741; presentibus omnibus den plod: heer van Ries, January 11, 1741 and comparerende voor. . . . Bajaar, January 9, 1741.

63. NL-HaNA, 1.04.02, VOC 767, Resolutieboeken weegens der opstand der chineezen. . . . Batavia, 1 March-end July 1741, March 10, 1741 (1–2).

64. NL-HaNA, 1.04.02, VOC 767, Resolutieboeken weegens der opstand der chineezen, March 17, 1741 (14 verso).

65. NL-HaNA, 1.04.02, VOC 767, Resolutieboeken weegens der opstand der chineezen, May 19, 1741 (49).

66. NL-HaNA, 1.04.02, VOC 767, Resolutieboeken weegens der opstand der chineezen, May 19, 1741 (53).

67. NL-HaNA, 1.04.02, VOC 767, Resolutieboeken weegens der opstand der chineezen, May 26 (60–61), June 19 (73 verso–74) and 24 (91), and July 17 and 21, 1741 (137, 197).

68. NL-HaNA, 1.04.02, VOC 767, Resolutieboeken weegens der opetand der chineezen, July 13, 1741 (136).

69. NL-HaNA, 1.04.02, VOC 767, Aparte Resolutien des Casteels Batavia no 2 (starts with Register op de aparte Resolutien . . . August 1 to December 30, 1741), August 25, 1741 (23).

70. NL-HaNA, 1.04.02, VOC 767, Aparte Resolutien des Casteels Batavia no 2, August 25, 1741 (23–24).

71. NL-HaNA, 1.04.02, VOC 767, Aparte Resolutien des Casteels Batavia no 2, September 1 (40–41) and 22, 1741 (87–91).

72. NL-HaNA, 1.04.02, VOC 767, Aparte Resolutien des Casteels Batavia no 2, September 21 (73) and 28, 1741 (109).

73. NL-HaNA, 1.04.02, VOC 767, Aparte Resolutien des Casteels Batavia no 2, September 1, 1741 (43–45) and 25, 1741 (97–99).

74. Parmer, "Historical Perspectives on Chinese in Southeast Asia," Armstrong, Warwick Armstrong, and Mulliner, *Chinese Populations in Contemporary Southeast Asian Societies*, 18–54;

NL-HaNa 1.04.17 Archief van de Hoge Regering van Batavia, 1602–1827, 35 Relaas van de Oor-sprong en het Verloop van de "Javanese Oorlog" tussen de Hoge Regering en Javanese Vorsten, 1745–55. Ricklefs, *History of Modern Indonesia*, 114–17.

75. NL-HaNA, 1.04.17, Hoge Regering van Batavia, 35 Relaas [29–30, 59–60, 66–67].

76. NL-HaNA, 1.04.17, Hoge Regering van Batavia, 35 Relaas [29–30, 59–60, 66–67].

77. NL-HaNA, 1.04.17, Hoge Regering van Batavia, 35 Relaas [19–118]. Javanese peasant armies relying on local food supplies, see Ricklefs, *History of Modern Indonesia*, 115; Soemarsaid Moertono, *State and Statecraft in Old Java: A Study of the Later Mataram Period, 16th to 19th Century* (Jakarta: Equinox Publishing, 2009 [1968]), 79, 98. On the coffee figures, see Jan Bre-man, *Koloniaal Profijt van Onvrije Arbeid: Het Preanger Stelsel van Gedwongen Koffieteelt op Java, 1720–1870* (Amsterdam: Amsterdam University Press, 2010), 83, table 3.1.

78. NL-HaNA, 1.04.02, VOC 9526, Kopie-missive van de Raad van Justitie in Batavia aan de Heren XVII betreffende het proces tegen Valckenier 1743, Extract uit de notulen . . . raden van india, January 3, 1741; F. Sakeman et al to Heeren XVII, camer Middelburg, Batavia, Decem-ber 12, 1743; Declaration Gustaaf Willem Baron van Imhoff, June 17, 1743; and entry Novem-ber 20, 1743: J. Lakeman et al. to heeren. . . . XVII, Batavia, December 10, 1743.

79. On cinnamon and Ceylon, see Lodewijk Wagenaar, *Kaneel en Olifanten: Sri Lanka en Nederland sinds 1600* (Nijmegen: Uitgeverij Vantilt, 2016), 113–14; and Albert van den Belt, *Het VOC-Bedrijf op Ceylon: Een Voorname Vestiging van de Oost-Indische Compagnie in de 18e Eeuw* (Zutphen: Walberg Pers, 2008), 54–65.

80. NL-HaNA, 1.04.02, VOC Stukken betreffende de opstand van de Singalezen tegen het bewind van de VOC 11302, Thimon van Schonberg to Edele Achtbare Heeren [der VOC], Am-sterdam, November 6, 1761. Includes as attachment a letter from Consul in Aleppo T. Heemskerk with appended an extract from a letter from Bassora in English of August 1, 1761, from English consul of Ceylon stating that the writer of the letter recently received a letter from Coshin dd 17 April with report from some British warships that visited Ceylon; and 1303 rapport [from departing governor of Ceylon to VOC, 1761 or 1762].

81. NL-HaNA, 1.04.02, VOC Ceylon Missive 9935, J. Schreuder to Jacob Mossel (governor general of the Dutch Indies), Colombo, February 1 and March 4, 1761, and 11302, Vandervoort Aan de Edele . . . bewindhebberen van de generale nederlandsche Co [VOC] . . . Kamer Middelburg, Colombo, March 4, 1760, Extract brief door den Gouverneur en Raad tot Colombo [Samland?] naar Hoog Mog: Edelheden geschreven, den March 4, 1761, translaat Singaleese ola geschreeven aan den heer Commandeur Abraham Samlandt . . . door den groten Adigare den Desave van oewe.

82. NL-HaNA, 1.04.02, VOC Stukken betreffende de opstand van de Singalezen tegen het bewind van de VOC 11302, Vandervoort Aan de Edele . . . bewindhebberen van de generale nederlandsche Co [VOC] . . . Kamer Middelburg, Colombo, March 4, 1760 [discussed Decem-ber 26, 1761]: Extract brief door den Gouverneur en Raad tot Colombo naar Hoog Mog: Edel-heden geschreeven, den March 4, 1761, and Translaat Singaleese ola geschreeven op ordre van hartogt Candia aangekomen hoofd door de Jang en Zaaijmester Kahandawe Seneratne Macdeanse aan de Modlinaars van Bentotta en die van de Mahabaddi. Geschreeven op den 11 dag na de volle maand Docroetoe van het jaar Zakkewareese 1682.

83. NL-HaNA, 1.04.02, VOC Ceylon Missive 9935, J. Schreuder to Jacob Mossel (governor general of the Dutch Indies), Colombo, February 1 and March 4, 1761.

84. NL-HaNA, 1.04.02, VOC Stukken betreffende de opstand van de Singalezen tegen het bewind van de VOC 11302, Vandervoort Aan de Edele . . . bewindhebberen van de generale nederlandsche Co [VOC] . . . Kamer Middelburg, Colombo, March 4, 1760. Included the below report: Extract brief door den Gouverneur en Raad tot Colombo [Samland?] naar Hoog Mog: Edelheden geschreven, den March 4, 1761 (translaat Singaleese ola geschreeven aan den heer Commandeur Abraham Samlandt en de verdure Hollanders die sig in het fort bevinden, door den groten Adigare den Desave van oewe).

85. NL-HaNA, 1.04.02, VOC Stukken betreffende de opstand van de Singalezen tegen het bewind van de VOC 11302, 1303 rapport [from departing governor of Ceylon to VOC, 1761 or 1762] and Wagenaar, *Kaneel en Olifanten*, 115–17.

86. NL-HaNA, 1.04.02, VOC Ceylon Missive 9935, Schreuder to Mossel, Colombo, July 25, 1761.

87. NL-HaNA, 1.04.02, VOC Ceylon Missive 9935, Schreuder to Mossel, Colombo, July 25, 1761.

88. NL-HaNA, 1.04.02, VOC Ceylon Missive 9935, Scheuder to Petrus van der Parra (governor general of the Dutch Indies), Colombo, October 1, 1761.

89. Anton Muttukumaru, *The Military History of Ceylon: An Outline* (New Delhi: Navrang, 1993), 84–90; Wagenaar, *Kaneel en Olifanten*, 117–19.

90. Leonard Y. Andaya, *The World of Maluku: Eastern Indonesia in the Early Modern Period* (Honolulu: University of Hawaii Press, 1993).

91. NL-HaNa, 1.04.02, VOC Kopie-missiven en -rapporten ingekomen bij gouverneur-generaal en raden uit Ambon, 7933, Dag Register van den gedane Hongij Togt door den Heer Governeur in A[nno] 1770, entry October 17, 1770, image 267 accessed online at http://www .gahetna.nl/collectie/archief/inventaris/gahetnascan/zoekterm/VOC/eadid/1.04.02/wollig /uit/volledige-tekst/aan/gebruikersinbreng/aan/aantal/20/node/c01%3A1.c02%3A4 .c03%3A4.c04%3A4.c05%3A0.c06%3A31/level/file/foto/NL-HaNA_1.04.02_7933_0003 /fotouuid/1ebea507-5321-213b-a506-fa49959da51e/scan-index/27

92. NL-HaNA, 1.04.02, VOC 7933, Register van zodanige secretarieele papieren als er tans van hier naar Nederland verzonden werden, Amboina, September 24, 1771 (online images 27–43).

93. On booty and spices, see NL-HaNA 1.04.02, VOC 7933, Register der Marginalen Amboinese brief van September 24, 1771, H Gouverneur Amboin to Gouverneur-Generaal Indie, Dag Register van den gedane Hongij Togt door den Heer Governeur in A[nno] 1770, Instructie to narigt voor de inlandse hoofden van Waij, Ceith, Ouw, Harra, Oelath, Ema [Oma] in het bekruisen der nagul gevende compoiren, Fort Victoria, October 16, 1770 (images 466–71) and Instructie voor den capitain Hendrik van der Brink . . . gaande in expeditie naar het eijland Kessing, Boelogissen, Ceram, Laut, Satwatti, manoewoko en Goram, signed J. A. van der Voort, February 28, 1771 (online images 506–16).

94. NL-HaNA, 1.04.02, VOC 7933, Register van zodanige secretarieele papieren als er tans van hier naar Nederland verzonden werden, Amboina, September 24, 1771 (online image 43).

95. NL-HaNA, 1.04.02, VOC 7933, Register van zodanige secretarieele papieren als er tans van hier naar Nederland verzonden werden, Amboina, September 24, 1771 (online images 27–34 and 43).

96. NL-HaNA, 1.04.02, VOC 7933, Register der Marginalen Amboinese brief van September 24, 1771, Gouverneur Amboin to Gouverneur-Generaal Indie, Dag Register van den gedane Hongij Togt door den Heer Governeur in A[nno] 1770, Memorie nopens de pligten van dienaren mits[gader]s instructie voor de inlandse hoofden, Amboina, 1771 (images 443–463). On the requisitions, see Andaya, *World of Maluku*, 201–5.

97. NL-HaNA, 1.04.02, VOC 7933, Register der Marginalen Amboinese brief van September 24, 1771, Gouverneur Amboin to Gouverneur-Generaal Indie, Dag Register van den gedane Hongij Togt door den Heer Governeur in A[nno] 1770, Instructie voor den commandant van Nussalaut . . . , J.A. van der Vaart [Governor Amboin] Amboina, Fort Victoria, February 5, 1771 (images 497–506).

98. NL-HaNA, 1.04.02, VOC 7933, Register van zodanige secretarieele papieren als er tans van hier naar Nederland verzonden werden, Amboina, September 24, 1771 (online images 101–2) and Register der Marginalen Amboinese brief van September 24, 1771, Gouverneur Amboin to Gouverneur-Generaal Indie, Dag Register van den gedane Hongij Togt door den Heer Governeur in A[nno] 1770, Saparoua, November 15, 1770.

99. NL-HaNA, 1.04.02, VOC 7933, Register der Marginalen Amboinese brief van September 24, 1771, Gouverneur Amboin to Gouverneur-Generaal Indie, Dag Register van den gedane Hongij Togt door den Heer Governeur in A[nno] 1770, entry November 1, 1770 (images 322–24).

100. NL-HaNA, 1.04.02, VOC 7933, Register der Marginalen Amboinese brief van September 24, 1771, Gouverneur Amboin to Gouverneur-Generaal Indie, Dag Register van den gedane Hongij Togt door den Heer Governeur in A[nno] 1770, entries November 5–8, 1770 (images 341–69) and Instructie voor den Captain militair Patricius Baron de Mackenna ter observantie in 't attaqueeren van de negorij Ceijlor op Cerams Zuid Cust, November 6, 1770 (images 493–94) and Instructie voor den Captain militair Patricius Baron de Mackenna, on the corra corra Bonoa anchored at Tobo, November 7, 1770 (images 494–96).

101. NL-HaNA, 1.04.02, VOC 7933, Register der Marginalen Amboinese brief van September 24, 1771 (image 123), Gouverneur Amboin to Gouverneur-Generaal Indie, Dag Register van den gedane Hongij Togt door den Heer Governeur in A[nno] 1770, Instructie voor den capitain Hendrik van der Brink . . . gaande in expeditie naar het eijland Kessing, Boelogissen, Ceram, Laut, Satwatti, manoewoko en Goram, signed J. A. van der Voort, February 28, 1771 (images 506–16).

102. NL-HaNA, 1.04.02, VOC 7940, July 12–October 2, 1785; Dagregister hongitocht, October 28–December 22, 1784; bijlagen, February 28–September 15, 1785, Extract Patriasche Generale Missive . . . Heeren Seventienen to Gouverneur Generaal Batavia, Amsterdam, November 27, 1783 (images 55–57 and 80–81). On Nuku, see Andaya, *World of Maluku*, 218–37; and Piet Hagen, *Koloniale Oorlogen in Indonesie: Vijf Eeuwen Verzet tegen Vreemde Overheersing* (Amsterdam: De Arbeiderspers, 2018), 403–6.

103. NL-HaNA, 1.04.02, VOC 7940, July 12–October 2, 1785; Dagregister hongitocht, October 28–December 22, 1784; bijlagen, February 28–September 15, 1785, Extract Patriasche Generale Missive . . . Heeren Seventienen to Gouverneur Generaal Batavia, Amsterdam, November 27, 1783 (images 129–35).

104. NL-HaNA, 1.04.02, VOC 7940, Dag Register Hongij Vogajie gehouden rond Ceram en na de comptoiren Paparuoua, Harouka, en Hila, 1784, entries November 13, 16, and 18, 1784 (images 203–9, 213, 222).

105. Andaya, *World of Maluku*, 226–28; and Hagen, *Koloniale Oorlogen*, 403–6.

106. NL-HaNA, 1.04.02, VOC 7940, Dag Register Hongij Vogajie gehouden rond Ceram, 1784, entries December 8–9 and 11, 1784 (images 283 and 287–88) and Andaya, *World of Maluku*, 218–37.

107. NL-HaNA, 1.04.02, VOC 7945, Dag Register gehouden op de reijse rondom Ceram en de subaltern comptoiren onder Amboina . . . in den jaare 1788 door den wel edel achtbaare heeren Johan A. Schilling . . . gouverneur deeser provintie beginnende op 10 October, entries November 11–13, 15, and 18 (images 506–13 and 519–24). On Nuku see Andaya, *World of Maluku*, 218–37.

Chapter Eight: Refugees and Environcide in the American West

1. See US 15th Cong. 2D Sess. 1818–19 House. Debate in the House of Representatives of the United States on the Seminole War in January and February 1819 (Washington, DC: Office of the National Intelligencer, 1819), 177–293, 587–90.

2. De B. Randolph Keim, *Sheridan's Troopers on the Borders: A Winter Campaign on the Plains* (Lincoln: University of Nebraska Press, 1985 [1885]), 80–81, 103–20, 165.

3. Blackhawk argues that the role of violence has been underestimated, see Ned Blackhawk, *Violence over the Land: Indians and Empires in the Early American West* (Cambridge, MA: Harvard University Press, 2006), 6. See also Ian K. Steele, *Warpaths: Invasions of North America* (New York: Oxford University Press, 1994); and Karl Jacoby, *Shadows at Dawn: A Borderlands Massacre and the Violence of History* (New York: Penguin, 2008), 5, 13–41.

4. See, for example, Brendan C. Lindsay, *Murder State: California's Native American Genocide, 1846–1873* (Lincoln: University of Nebraska Press, 2012); and Pekka Hamalainen, *The Comanche Empire* (New Haven: Yale University Press, 2008), 292–341 (genocidal violence).

5. Early colonial documents describe postcontact conditions and were often strongly biased. See Gordon G. Whitney, *From Coastal Wilderness to Fruited Plain: A History of Environmental Change in Temperate North America from 1500 to the Present* (Cambridge: Cambridge University Press, 1996 [1994]), 16–60; and W. E. Doolittle, *Cultivated Landscapes of Native North America* (Oxford: Oxford University Press, 2001 [2000]), 7–14.

6. Blackhawk, *Violence over the Land*, 157.

7. Indigenous American agency included the perpetrating of violence against humans and animals. For the former, see Blackhawk, *Violence over the Land*, 6. For the latter, including the overhunting of deer and bison, see T. R. McCabe and R. E. McCabe, "Recounting Whitetails Past" and M. Knox, "Historical Changes in the Abundance and Distribution of Deer in Virginia," in *The Science of Overabundance: Deer Ecology and Population Management*, ed. W. J. McShea, H. B. Underwood, and J. H. Rappole (Washington, DC: Smithsonian Institution Press, 1997), 11–26 and 27–36, respectively; A. O. Isenberg, *The Destruction of the Bison* (Cambridge: Cambridge University Press, 2000); and W. Beinart and P. Coates, *Environment and History: The Taming of Nature in the USA and South Africa* (London: Routledge, 1995), 3–5.

8. Karen R. Adams and Suzanne K. Fish, "Subsistence through Time in the Greater Southwest," in *The Subsistence Economies of Indigenous North American Societies: A Handbook*, ed. Bruce D. Smith (Washington, DC: Smithsonian Institution Scholarly Press, 2011), 147–83.

9. Mary J. Adair and Richard R. Drass, "Patterns of Plant Use in the Prehistoric Central and Southern Plains," Smith, *Subsistence Economies*, 307–52; Edward H. Spicer, *Cycles of Conquest: The Impact of Spain, Mexico, and the United States on the Indians of the Southwest, 1533–1960* (Tuscon: University of Arizona Press, 1976 [1962]), viii, 9–15.

10. Clayton Anderson, *Kinsmen of Another Kind: Dakota-White Relations in the Upper Mississippi Valley, 1650–1862* (Lincoln: University of Nebraska Press, 1984), 21–74; Jeffrey Ostler, *The Plains Sioux and U.S. Colonialism from Lewis and Clark to Wounded Knee* (Cambridge: Cambridge University Press, 2004), 22; and John R. Bozell, Carl R. Falk, and Eileen Johnson, "Native American Use of Animals on the North American Great Plains," Smith, *Subsistence Economies*, 353–85.

11. Ostler, *Plains Sioux*, 22–23.

12. Sarah Carter, *Lost Harvests: Prairie Indian Reserve Farmers and Government Policy* (Montreal and Kingston: McGill-Queen's University Press, 1990), 31–33.

13. William H. Leckie, *The Military Conquest of the Southern Plains* (Norman: University of Oklahoma Press, 1963), 7–11.

14. Hamalainen, *Comanche Empire*.

15. Robert F. Heizer and Albert B. Elsasser, *The Natural World of the California Indians* (Berkeley: University of California Press, 1980), 226.

16. Philip L. Walker and John R. Johnson, "Effects of Contact on the Chumash Indians," in *Disease and Demography in the Americas*, ed. John W. Verano and Douglas H. Ubelaker (Washington, DC: Smithsonian Institution Press, 1992), 127–39.

17. Walker and Johnson, "Effects of Contact," Verano and Ubelaker, *Disease and Demography*, 127–39.

18. Heizer and Elsasser, *Natural World*, 181, 226–30.

19. On the vulnerability of horses during the winter, see Theodore Binnema, *Common and Contested Ground: A Human and Environmental History of the Northwestern Plains* (Norman: University of Oklahoma Press, 2001), 49, 141–42; Neil Van Sickle and Evelyn Rodewald, *The Indian Way: Indians and the North American Fur Trade* (North Charleston, SC: CreateSpace, 2011), 168, 175–76; and Hamalainen, *Comanche Empire*, 240–46.

20. See Thomas T. Waterman, *North American Indian Dwellings* (Washington, DC: GPO, 1925), 7–9; Mary J. Adair and Richard R. Drass, "Patterns of Plant Use in the Prehistoric Central and Southern Plains"; John R. Bozell, Carl R. Falk, and Eileen Johnson, "Native American Use of Animals on the North American Great Plains"; and Lynn M. Snyder and Jennifer A. Leonard, "The Diversity and Origin of American Dogs," Smith, *Subsistence Economies*, 307–52, 353–85, and 525–41 respectively; Sickle, *Indian Way*, 165–176.

21. Anderson, *Kinsmen of Another Kind*, 2–7; Ostler, *Plains Sioux*, 137. On ownership of locales with abundant wild rice, see Harold E. Driver and William C. Massey, *Comparative Studies of North American Indians* (Philadelphia: American Philosophical Society, 1957), 389–90.

22. Anderson, *Kinsmen of Another Kind*, 81–82 and 103–13.

23. Ostler, *Plains Sioux*, 137–38.

24. Isenberg, *Destruction of the Bison*, 2, 6–10, 31–92.

25. R. Douglas Hurt, *Indian Agriculture in America: Prehistory to the Present* (Lawrence: University of Kansas, 1987), 57–61. On the Pawnee cache, see Sickle, *Indian Way*, 257.

26. See Mary J. Adair and Richard R. Drass, "Patterns of Plant Use in the Prehistoric Central and Southern Plains," Smith, *Subsistence Economies*, 307–52.

27. Adair and Drass, "Patterns of Plant Use," Smith, *Subsistence Economies*, 307–52; Carter, *Lost Harvests*, 38–40; Gilbert L. Wilson, *Native American Gardening: Buffalobird-Woman's Guide to Traditional Methods* (Mineola, NY: Dover Publications, 2005 [1917]), 6–7, 113–18; Hurt, *Indian Agriculture*, 57–63; and Driver and Massey, *Comparative Studies*, 390.

28. Catherine S Fowler, "'We live by them' Native Knowledge of Biodiversity in the Great Basin of Western North America," *Biodiversity and Native America*, ed. Paul E. Minnis and Wayne J. Elisens (Norman: University of Oklahoma Press, 2000), 99–132.

29. Daniel E. Moerman, *Native American Food Plants: An Ethnobotanical Dictionary* (Portland: Timber Press, 2010); Adams and Fish, "Subsistence through Time in the Greater Southwest" and Catherine S. Fowler and David E. Rhode, "Plant Foods and Foodways among the Great Basin's Indigenous Peoples," Smith, *Subsistence Economies*, 147–83 and 233–69, respectively.

30. On the Comanche and their neighbors, see Hamalainen, *Comanche Empire*, 141–80, 283–85.

31. Heizer and Elsasser, *Natural World of the California Indians*, 23.

32. See Robert L. Bettinger and Eric Wohlgemuth, "Archaeological and Ethnographic Evidence for Indigenous Plant Use in California," Smith, *Subsistence Economies*, 113–29.

33. David R. Lewis, *Neither Wolf nor Dog: American Indians, Environment, and Agrarian Change* (New York: Oxford University Press, 1994), 9–10; William T. Hagan, "Justifying Dispossession of the Indian: The Land Utilization Argument," in *American Indian Environments: Ecological Issues in Native American History*, ed. Christopher Vecsey and Robert W. Venables (Syracuse: Syracuse University Press, 1980), 65–80; and Hurt, *Indian Agriculture*, 107.

34. Heizer and Elsasser, *Natural World*, 30.

35. Heizer and Elsasser, *Natural World*, 52–53, 227–28.

36. Isenberg, *Destruction of the Bison*, 9–12; Shepard Krech III, *The Ecological Indian: Myth and History* (New York: W. W. Norton and Co., 1999), 38–41; Lewis, *Neither Wolf nor Dog*, 5, 9–11; Doolittle, *Cultivated Landscapes*, 463; Hamalainen, *Comanche Empire*, 293–301; and George Colpitts, *Pemmican Empire: Food, Trade, and the Last Bison Hunts in the North American Plains, 1780–1882* (New York: Cambridge University press, 2015), 2–6, 189–218, 224–25, 248–49.

37. W. Cronon, *Changes in the Land: Indians, Colonists and the Ecology of New England* (New York: Hill and Wang, 1988 [1983]); Gordon G. Whitney, *From Coastal Wilderness to Fruited Plain: A History of Environmental Change in Temperate North America from 1500 to the Present* (Cambridge: Cambridge University Press, 1996 [1994]), 56–97, 107–20; R. Boyd, ed., *Indians, Fire and the Land in the Pacific Northwest* (Corvallies: Oregon State University Press, 1999); S. J. Pyne, *Fire in America: A Cultural History of Wildland and Rural Fire* (Seattle: University of Washington Press, 1997 [1982]); T. R. Vale, "The Pre-European Landscape of the United States: Pristine or Humanized," in *Fire, Native Peoples and the Natural Landscape*, ed. Vale (Washington, DC: Island Press, 2002), 1–39; Daniel W. Gade, *Nature and Culture in the Andes* (Madison: University of Wisconsin Press, 1999), 19, 42–55.

38. Nancy J. Turner, *Ancient Pathways, Ancestral Knowledge: Ethnobotany and Ecological Wisdom of Indigenous Peoples of Northwestern North America*, vol. 2, *The Place and Meaning of Plants*

in Indigenous Cultures and World Views (Montreal and Kingston: McGill-Queen's University Press, 2014), 147.

39. Turner, *Ancient Pathways*, vol. 2, 165, and Table 11.4 (183–92); Fiona Hamersley Chambers and Nancy J. Turner, "Plant Use by Northwest Coast and Plateau Indigenous Peoples," Smith, *Subsistence Economies*, 65–82.

40. Nancy J. Turner, *Ancient Pathways*, vol. 1, *The History and Practice of Indigenous Plant Knowledge* (Montreal and Kingston: McGill-Queen's University Press, 2014), 97, 250–52, 272–75, 295–305; and vol. 2, 189–92, 196–200.

41. Turner, *Ancient Pathways*, vol. 1, 310–13, 379–80.

42. Turner, *Ancient Pathways*, vol. 1, 43–46, 193, 221–29, 285–86; and vol. 2, 149.

43. Turner, *Ancient Pathways*, vol. 1, 221.

44. Heizer and Elsasser, *Natural World*, 73.

45. Isenberg, *Destruction of the Bison*, 71–72.

46. On hunting and burning, see Binnema, *Common and Contested Ground*, 45; Colpitts, *Pemmican Empire*, 70–71; and Whitney, *From Coastal Wilderness*, 120.

47. Isenberg, *Destruction of the Bison*, 69; Hamalainen, *Comanche Empire*, 283–85.

48. Turner, *Ancient Pathways*, vol. 2, 3–50, 86–90, 196–200.

49. Driver and Massey, *Comparative Studies*, 389. See also Turner, *Ancient Pathways*, vol. 2, 87; A. McEvoy, *The Fisherman's Problem: Ecology and Law in the California Fisheries, 1850–1980* (Cambridge: Cambridge University Press, 1990), 30–39, 56–59; R. White, *The Organic Machine: The Re-Making of the Columbia River* (New York: Hill and Wang, 2000 [1995]), 22.

50. Driver and Massey, *Comparative Studies*, 386–88.

51. Colpitts, *Pemmican Empire*, 55, 61–68.

52. Driver and Massey, *Comparative Studies*, 389–90; Heizer and Elsasser, *Natural World*, 34; and Turner, *Ancient Pathways*, vol. 2, 182, 193, 210, 221–25.

53. Driver and Massey, *Comparative Studies*, 294.

54. Heizer and Elsasser, *Natural World*, 52–53; Turner, *Ancient Pathways*, vol. 1, 389–91; vol. 2, 23–29; Waterman, *North American Indian Dwellings*, 9–13. On Comanche (summer) tepees and (winter) lodges, Hamalainen, *Comanche Empire*, 110, 311, and 334.

55. Waterman, *North American Indian Dwellings*, 9–13.

56. Waterman, *North American Indian Dwellings*, 7–9; Sickle, *Indian Way*, 165, 169.

57. Chris Arnett, *The Terror of the Coast: Land Alienation and Colonial War on Vancouver Island and the Gulf Islands, 1849–1863* (Burnabay, BC: Talonbooks, 1999), 18.

58. Driver and Massey, *Comparative Studies*, 247; Hurt, *Indian Agriculture*, 50–53.

59. Driver and Massey, *Comparative Studies*, 245.

60. Driver and Massey, *Comparative Studies*, 245; Isenberg, *Destruction of the Bison*, 8, 68.

61. Driver and Massey, *Comparative Studies*, 247; Waterman, *North American Indian Dwellings*, 18–24; Turner, *Ancient Pathways*, vol. 1, 323–29; vol. 2, 87, 96.

62. Timothy Braatz, *Surviving Conquest: A History of the Yavapai Peoples* (Lincoln: University of Nebraska Press, 2003), 27–36.

63. R. Douglas Hurt, *The Ohio Frontier: Crucible of the Old Northwest, 1720–1830* (Bloomington: Indiana University Press, 1996), 22–23; Hurt, *Indian Agriculture*, 9, 41–50; Driver and Massey, *Comparative Studies*, 247; Wilson, *Native American Gardening*, 87–97; Sickle, *Indian Way*, 257; Turner, *Ancient Pathways*, vol. 1, 323–29; vol. 2, 96.

64. Driver and Massey, *Comparative Studies*, 247; Hurt, *Indian Agriculture in America*, 50–53; Braatz, *Surviving Conquest*, 27–36.

65. Hurt, *Indian Agriculture*, 9, 41, 50–55, 57–61; Driver and Massey, *Comparative Studies*, 247.

66. Driver and Massey, *Comparative Studies*, 245; Colpitts, *Pemmican Empire*, 2–13, 58–99.

67. Bettinger and Wohlgemuth, "Archaeological and Ethnographic Evidence" and William R. Hildebrandt and Kimberley Carpenter, "Native Hunting Adaptations in California: Changing Patterns of Resource Use from the Early Holocene to European Contact," Smith, *Subsistence Economies*, 113–29 and 131–46, respectively; Heizer and Elsasser, *Natural World of the California Indians*, 84–85, 93–99, 110.

68. On the challenges of clearing land for homes and fields, see David Cheetham, "Corn, Colanders, and Cooking: Early Maize Processing in the Maya Lowlands and Its Implications," in *Pre-Columbian Foodways: Interdisciplinary Approaches to Food, Culture, and Markets in Ancient Mesoamerica*, ed. John E. Staller and Michael Carrasco (New York: Springer, 2010), 345–68; and David Watts, *The West Indies: Patterns of Development, Culture and Environmental Change since 1492* (Cambridge: Cambridge University Press, 1998 [1987]), 53–60. See also Denevan, *Cultivated Landscapes*, 115–32.

69. Anderson, *Kinsmen of Another Kind*, 21–74.

70. Ostler, *Plains Sioux*, 22–23.

71. Blackhawk, *Violence over the Land*, 18–141.

72. Adams and Fish, "Subsistence through Time in the Greater Southwest," Smith, *Subsistence Economies*, 147–83.

73. Hamalainen, *Comanche Empire*, 30–31.

74. Edward H. Spicer, *Cycles of Conquest: The Impact of Spain, Mexico, and the United States on the Indians of the Southwest, 1533–1960* (Tuscon: University of Arizona Press, 1976 [1962]), 229–67. On the Comanche-Apache wars, see Hamalainen, *Comanche Empire*, 23–106.

75. Karl Jacoby, *Shadows at Dawn*, 21–43; Hamalainen, *Comanche Empire*, 30.

76. Hamalainen, *Comanche Empire*, 30–39.

77. Binnema, *Common and Contested Ground*, 86–128; Isenberg, *Destruction of the Bison*, 50–52, 88 (bison bow hunting); Hamalainen, *Comanche Empire*, 18–140; Colpitts, *Pemmican Empire*, 76 and 112 (guns for bison hunting).

78. John W. Heaton, *The Shoshone-Bannocks: Culture and Commerce at Fort Hall, 1870–1940* (Lawrence: University Press of Kansas, 2005), 28–30. On horses and forages, see Sickle, *Indian Way*, 168, 175–76.

79. Binnema, *Common and Contested Ground*, 86–128; Heaton, *Shoshone-Bannocks*, 30–35. Fenn stresses that trade routes were key in spreading the contagion, but underplays how war, famine, and population displacement created fertile ground for the eruption of epidemics on the East Coast (the Revolutionary War) and on the Great Plains (raids and population displacements). See Elizabeth A. Fenn, *Pox Americana: The Great Smallpox Epidemic of 1775–82* (New York: Hill and Wang, 2001), 137–48, 173–263. The Eastern Comanche lost two-thirds of their population, but the Western Comanche escaped its onslaught in 1780–81, see Hamalainen, *Comanche Empire*, 111.

80. Carter, *Lost Harvests*, 38–40; Wilson, *Native American Gardening*, 6–7; Hurt, *Indian Agriculture*, 57–63.

81. Carter, *Lost Harvests*, 31–33.

82. Binnema, *Common and Contested Ground*, 130–44, 178–83.

83. Carter, *Lost Harvests*, 34–36.

84. Bison hunting as a means of survival for refugees and a source of war, see Colpitts, *Pemmican Empire*, 100–147, 189–259.

85. Hurt, *Ohio Frontier*, 316, 362–65; Hurt, *Indian Agriculture*, 107–10, 121.

86. Robert W. Venables, "Victim versus Victim: The Irony of the New York Indians' Removal to Wisconsin," Vecsey and Venables, *American Indian Environments*, 140–51.

87. Angela Pulley Hudson, *Creek Paths and Federal Roads: Indians, Settlers, and Slaves and the Making of the American South* (Chapel Hill: University of North Carolina Press, 2010), 26–29, 34–35, 41–45, 88–124.

88. Grenier, *First Way of Making War*, 204–17.

89. For the debate, see US 15th Cong. 2D Sess. 1818–19 House. Debate in the House of Representatives of the United States on the Seminole War in January and February 1819 (Washington, DC: Office of the National Intelligencer, 1819), 177–293, 587–90. For the Seminole wars, see John Missali and Mary Lou Missali, *The Seminole Wars: America's Longest Indian Conflict* (Gainesville: University Press of Florida, 2004); Grant Foreman, *Indian Removal: The Emigration of the Five Civilized Tribes of Indians* (Norman: University of Oklahoma Press, 1932), 315–85; William M. Utley and Wilcomb E. Washburn, *Indian Wars* (Boston: Mariner Books, 2002 [1977]), 130–32; Florida Memory: State Library and Archives of Florida: Thomas Sidney Jesup Diary 1836–1837, accessed online at https://www.floridamemory.com/collections/jesup/; C. S. Monaco, *The Second Seminole War and the Limits of American Aggression* (Baltimore: Johns Hopkins University Press, 2018), 30–32, 139–59 (Harney); John T. Sprague, *The Origin, Progress, and Conclusion of the Florida War* (New York: D. Appleton & Company, 1848): contains detailed descriptions of the destruction of hidden Seminole fields and dwellings, accessed online at http://gdc.galegroup.com.ezproxy.princeton.edu/gdc/artemis/MonographsDetailsPage/MonographsDetailsWindow?disableHighlighting=&displayGroupName=DVI-Monographs&docIndex=&source=&prodId=&sid=&mode=view&limiter=&display-query=&contentModules=&action=e&sortBy=&windowstate=normal&currPage=&dviSelectedPage=&scanId=&query=&search_within_results=&p=INDP&catId=&u=prin77918&displayGroups=&documentId=GALE%7CAKEPOY689117784&activityType=&failOverType=&commentary=.

90. John P. Bowes, *Exiles and Pioneers: Eastern Indians in the Trans Mississippi West* (Cambridge: Cambridge University Press, 2007), 9–15.

91. Bowes, *Exiles and Pioneers*, 17–88.

92. Grant Foreman, *Indian Removal: The Emigration of the Five Civilized Tribes of Indians* (Norman: University of Oklahoma Press, 1932).

93. Foreman, *Indian Removal*, 19–104.

94. Foreman, *Indian Removal*, 107–90.

95. Foreman, *Indian Removal*, 193–226.

96. Foreman, *Indian Removal*, 229–312.

97. Bowes, *Exiles and Pioneers*, 89–121.

98. Foreman, *Indian Removal*, 36–37, 200–202.

99. Hamalainen, *Comanche Empire*, 152–55.

100. Bowes, *Exiles and Pioneers*, 43–45, 122–51.

101. Hurt, *Indian Agriculture*, 113–18; Bowes, *Exiles and Pioneers*, 227–28.

102. Heaton, *The Shoshone-Bannocks*, 22–51.

103. Blackhawk, *Violence over the Land*, 147–209.

104. Blackhawk, *Violence over the Land*, 193–263. On hand-carved saddles, see Sickle, *Indian Way*, 169.

105. Isenberg, *Destruction of the Bison*, 47–53, 93–122; Eric Jay Dolin, *Fur, Fortune, and Empire: The Epic History of the Fur Trade in America* (New York: W. W. Norton, 2010), 299; Mari Sandoz, *The Buffalo Hunters: The Story of the Hide Men* (New York: Hastings House, 1954), 54.

106. Blackhawk, *Violence over the Land*, 193–263.

107. Lewis, *Neither Wolf nor Dog*, 36–39.

108. Blackhawk, *Violence over the Land*, 193–263.

109. Anderson, *Kinsmen of Another Kind*, 22–280; Ostler, *Plains Sioux*, 23–25.

110. Ostler, *Plains Sioux*, 36. On the trail of tears, see Utley and Washburn, *Indian Wars*, 139–40.

111. Utley and Washburn, *Indian Wars*, 193–203.

112. Hurt, *Indian Agriculture*, 107–10, 121; Isenberg, *Destruction of the Bison*, 13–30.

113. Anderson, *Kinsmen of Another Kind*, 202–80; Hamalainen, *Comanche Empire*, 309–41.

114. William H. Leckie, *The Military Conquest of the Southern Plains* (Norman: University of Oklahoma Press, 1963), 7.

115. Paul N. Beck, *Columns of Vengeance: Soldiers, Sioux, and the Punitive Expeditions, 1863–1864* (Norman: University of Oklahoma Press, 2013), 22–219.

116. Leckie, *Military Conquest of the Southern Plains*, 20–23, 38–43; Ostler, *Plains Sioux*, 44–51.

117. Eugene F. Ware, *The Indian War of 1864* (Lincoln: University of Nebraska Press, 1960), 308–9.

118. Leckie, *Military Conquest of the Southern Plains*, 20–23, 38–43.

119. Isenberg, *Destruction of the Bison*, 148–55.

120. Keim, *Sheridan's Troopers*, 58, 110, 132–33, 200, 284–97. See also Isenberg, *Destruction of the Bison*, 123–63; Russell F. Weigley, *The American Way of War: A History of United States Military Strategy and Policy* (New York: Macmillan, 1973), 157–63. There was no consensus about how the war against the indigenous Americans should be waged, see Jacoby, *Shadows at Dawn*, 115–29.

121. Keim, *Sheridan's Troopers*, 24–25, 193–94, 198–206; Binnema, *Common and Contested Ground*, 49, 141–42. Great Plains indigenous Americans' horses in the winter were entirely dependent on grass with twigs and bark as emergency food, see Sickle, *Indian Way*, 168, 175–76. On the Plains indigenous American dependency on food stores in winter, see Ostler, *Plains Sioux*; and Utley and Washburn, *Indian Wars*, 202–26. On Sheridan's winter campaigns, see Weigley, *American Way of War*, 159–63.

122. Keim, *Sheridan's Troopers*, 80–81, 103–20, 165.

123. Leckie, *Military Conquest of the Southern Plains*, 20–23, 38–43, 88–132; Utley and Washburn, *Indian Wars*, 202–14; and Ostler, *Plains Sioux*, 44–53.

124. Ostler, *Plains Sioux*, 55–83; Utley and Washburn, *Indian Wars*, 218–65.

125. Ostler, *Plains Sioux*, 55–83; Utley and Washburn, *Indian Wars*, 218–65.

126. Leckie, *Military Conquest of the Southern Plains*, 136–37, 170.

127. Leckie, *Military Conquest of the Southern Plains*, 221–30; Hamalainen, *Comanche Empire*, 292–341.

128. Isenberg, *Destruction of the Bison*, 152.

129. For predator bounties, see, for example, Whitney, *From Coastal Wilderness to Fruited Plain*, 299–323; Hurt, *Ohio Frontier*, 121–22. For bounties for Apache scalps, see Spicer, *Cycles of Conquest*, 240–41.

130. Hamalainen, *Comanche Empire*, 336.

131. Keim, *Sheridan's Troopers*, 105–7, 265.

132. Leckie, *Military Conquest of the Southern Plains*, 186–87; Dolin, *Fur, Fortune, and Empire*, 306–7; Ostler, *Plains Sioux*, 56–57; Keim, *Sheridan's Troopers*, 68, 76, 200, 207; David D. Smits in his article "The Frontier Army and the Destruction of the Bison, 1865–1883," *Western History Quarterly* (1994), 313–38, argued that the army was involved in the extermination of the Plains buffalo.

133. Blackhawk, *Violence over the Land*, 166–67; Dolin, *Fur, Fortune, and Empire: The Epic History of the Fur Trade in America* (New York: W. W. Norton, 2010), 285–92. Isenberg acknowledges that the goal of exterminating the bison was to force the indigenous Americans into the reserves, see Isenberg, *Destruction of the Bison*, 3, 123–63. On the civil war and the increased demand for buffalo products, see Sandoz, *Buffalo Hunters*, 54; and Isenberg, *Destruction of the Bison*, 130–31. On overhunting of bison on the Canadian Great Plains, see Colpitts, *Pemmican Empire*.

134. For the Canadian fur deserts, see Colpitts, *Pemmican Empire*, 48–49, 151.

135. Ware, *Indian War of 1864*, 355–57; Sandoz, *Buffalo Hunters*, 47–48. After defeating Custer at Little Big Horn in 1876, the indigenous Americans set a grass fire to cover moving their families and property to safer locations. See Utley and Washburn, *Indian Wars*, 245–46.

136. Albert L. Hurtado, *Indian Survival on the California Frontier* (New Haven: Yale University Press, 1988), 194–98.

137. Hurtado, *Indian Survival*, 46–48, 86–88, 96. On malaria, see White, *Organic Machine*, 26–27.

138. Bettinger and Wohlgemuth, "Archaeological and Ethnographic Evidence," Smith, *Subsistence Economies*, 113–29.

139. Hurtado, *Indian Survival*, 46–135, 148–54, 165.

140. Hurtado, *Indian Survival*, 154–88, 194–212.

141. Utley and Washburn, *Indian Wars*, 290–301; Ostler, *Plains Sioux*, 129–44.

142. Blackhawk identifies indigenous Americans as subjects and agents, victims and perpetrators. See Blackhawk, *Violence over the Land*, 6.

Chapter Nine: 19th Century Aceh: Genocide or Environcide?

1. Jan van Swieten, *De Waarheid over Onze Vestiging in Atjeh* (Zaltbommel: Joh. Noman, 1879), 441. Emphasis in original. Jan van Swieten was the Dutch commanding officer of the second Dutch Aceh expedition in 1873. Multatuli was the pen name of Eduard Douwes Dekker, a famous Dutch writer who criticized Dutch colonial administration in Indonesia.

2. Nationaal Archief Den Haag/National Archive, The Hague, The Netherlands (henceforth NL-HaNA), 2.10.02 Ministerie van Koloniën: Atjeh/Ministry of Colonies: Aceh (henceforth MKA), MKA 6556A (1877–79), Aceh Report April 20–27, April 22, 1879.

3. NL-HaNA, 2.10.02.

4. NL-HaNA, 2.10.02, MKA 6558B (January–May 1882), Kort Verslag Atjeh en Onder-hoorigheden, January 21–February 2, 1882, to governor general of the Netherlands-Indies (henceforth GG), Kota Radja, February 1882.

5. See Wekker, *Hoe beschaafd Nederland in de twintigste eeuw vrede en orde schept op Atjeh* ('s-Gravenhage: Avondpostdrukkerij, 1907). Two classic studies on the Aceh war are Paul Van 't Veer, *De Atjeh-oorlog* (Amsterdam: De Arbeiderspers, 1969); and Anthony Reid, *The Contest for North Sumatra: Atjeh, the Netherlands and Britain, 1858–1898* (London: Oxford University Press, 1969).

6. K. van der Maaten, *De Indische Oorlogen: een Boek ten Dienste van den jongen Officier en het Militair Onderwijs*, vol. 1 (Haarlem: De Erven Loosjes, [1896]), 81–84.

7. Van 't Veer, *Atjeh-oorlog*, 49–55 and 79–81.

8. For the Aceh terms for titles and places, I use the transcription used by Van 't Veer in *De Atjeh Oorlog* which it should be stressed is a simplified spelling that does not do full justice to the richness of the Aceh language. I replaced the Dutch–oe with the English-usage–u. See Van 't Veer, *Atjeh-oorlog*, 96.

9. Van 't Veer, *Atjeh-oorlog*, 93–103.

10. Van 't Veer, *Atjeh-oorlog*, 104–19.

11. Van 't Veer, *Atjeh-oorlog*, 110–20. On Habib Abdurrahman Zahir and di Tiro, see Reid, *The Contest for North Sumatra*, 158–85 and 206, 251–56, respectively.

12. Van 't Veer, *Atjeh-oorlog*, 122–23.

13. Van 't Veer, *Atjeh-oorlog*, 122–23.

14. NL-HaNA, 2.10.02, MKA 6556A, Journal of the Acting Column in the XXII Mukims, July 24–August 4, 1877 [1878], and Aceh Reports, August 5–9 and 10–24, September 1–10 and 11–17, 1877 [1878]. The journals held in the colonial archives in The Hague are contemporary hand-written copies of the originals that were sent to The Netherlands. The originals were kept in colonial Indonesia. The copiers appear to have mistakenly labeled the copy of the 1878 journals as dating from 1877.

15. NL-HaNA, 2.10.02, MKA 6556A, Journal of the Acting Column in the XXII Mukims, July 24–August 4, 1877 [1878], and Aceh Reports, August 5–9 and 10–24 and September 1–10 and 11–17, 1877 [1878].

16. NL-HaNA, 2.10.02, MKA 6556A, Aceh Report, September 26–October 4, 1877 [1878].

17. NL-HaNA, 2.10.02, MKA 6556A, Aceh Report, October 5–13, 1877 [1878].

18. NL-HaNA, 2.10.02, MKA 6556A, Aceh Reports, October 19–28, October 26–November 1, November 2–7, 8–11, and 12–22, and November 23–December 1, 1877 [1878].

19. NL-HaNA, 2.10.02, MKA 6556A, Aceh Reports, October 26–November 1, November 2–7, 8–11, and 12–22, and December 1–10, 1877 [1878].

20. NL-HaNA, 2.10.02, MKA 6556A, Aceh Reports, October 19–28, October 26–November 1, November 2–7, 8–11, and 12–22, and November 23–December 1, 1877 [1878].

21. NL-HaNA, 2.10.02, MKA 6556A, Aceh Reports, December 11–14, 15–22, and 23–27, 1877 [1878].

22. NL-HaNA, 2.10.02, MKA 6556A, Aceh Reports, December 23–27, 1878, and December 28, 1878–January 7, 1879.

23. NL-HaNA, 2.10.02. MKA 6556A, Aceh Report, January 13–21, 1879.

24. NL-HaNA, 2.10.02, MKA 6556A, Aceh Reports, February 10–17 and 18–22, February 23–March 2, and March 3–7, 1879.

25. NL-HaNA, 2.10.02, MKA 6556A, Aceh Reports, February 10–17 and 18–22, February 23–March 2, 1879.

26. NL-HaNA, 2.10.02, MKA 6556A, Aceh Reports, February 23–March 2, March 3–7, and 9–18, 1879.

27. NL-HaNA, 2.10.02, MKA 6556A, Aceh Reports, March 9–18, 19–22, and 23–25, 1879.

28. NL-HaNA, 2.10.02, MKA 6556A, Aceh Report, March 23–25, 1879.

29. NL-HaNA, 2.10.02, MKA 6556A, Aceh Report, March 26–31, 1879.

30. NL-HaNA, 2.10.02, MKA 6556A, Aceh Reports, March 26–31 and April 1–5, 1879.

31. NL-HaNA, 2.10.02, MKA 6556A, Aceh Reports, March 26–31, April 1–5, and 6–12, 1879.

32. NL-HaNA, 2.10.02, MKA, 6556A, Aceh Reports, April 1–5, and 6–12, 1879.

33. NL-HaNA, 2.10.02, MKA 6556A, Aceh Report, April 6–12, 1879.

34. NL-HaNA, 2.10.02, MKA, 6556A, Aceh Report, April 6–12, 1879.

35. NL-HaNA, 2.10.02, MKA 6556A, Aceh Report, April 20–27, 1879.

36. NL-HaNA, 2.10.02, MKA 6556A, Aceh Reports, May 30–31, June 1–7, 8–9, and 10–17, 1879.

37. NL-HaNA, 2.10.02, MKA 6556A, Journal of the Operations in the XXVI mukims, June 30–July 6, 1879, and Aceh Report, July 7–11, 1879.

38. NL-HaNA, 2.10.02, MKA 6556A, Aceh Report, July 7–11, 1879.

39. NL-HaNA, 2.10.02, MKA 6556A, Aceh Report, July 7–11, 1879.

40. NL-HaNA, 2.10.02, MKA 6556A, Aceh Report, July 7–11, 1879.

41. NL-HaNA, 2.10.02, MKA 6556A, Aceh Report, July 12–19, 1879.

42. NL-HaNA, 2.10.02, MKA 6556A, Aceh Reports, July 20–26 and July 27–August 4, 1879.

43. NL-HaNA, 2.10.02, MKA 6556A, Aceh Reports, July 20–26 and July 27–August 4, 1879.

44. NL-HaNA, 2.10.02, MKA 6556A, Aceh Reports, July 20–26, July 27–August 4, August 4–9 and 10–16, 1879.

45. NL-HaNA, 2.10.02, MKA 6556A, Aceh Reports, July 20–26, July 27–August 4, August 4–9 and 10–16, 1879.

46. Van 't Veer, Atjeh-oorlog, 125.

47. Van Swieten, De Waarheid and Van 't Veer, Atjeh-oorlog, 125, 129–31. The Aceh war created one of the major polemics in the Netherlands about its colonial policies. See Van 't Veer, Atjeh-oorlog, 126–33.

48. For the figures, see L. W. C. van den Berg, Review of J. Jacobs, De Atjehers, reproduced in Late Nineteenth Century and Early Twentieth Century Dutch Monographs, Pamphlets and Extracted Articles Related to Acheh, Indonesia, vol. 7 [n.p., Cornell University, n.d.], 218. Jacobs's main source is T. H. der Kinderen "De ordonnansie van 14 maart 1881 Betrekkelijk de Regtspleging onder de Inheemsche Bevolking van Groot-Atjeh (Staatsblad 1881, no. 83). Met eene Memorie van Toelichting' (Batavia: H.M. van Dork, 1881) reproduced in Late Nineteenth-Century . . . Dutch monographs . . . related to Acheh, vol. 4 [n.p., Cornell University, n.d.], 6–10. Reid supplies similar figures, probably originating in the same sources, see Reid, Contest for North Sumatra, 187–188n1.

49. NL-HaNA, 2.10.02, MKA 6557, governor of Aceh to GG, February 1, 1880.

50. NL-HaNA, 2.10.02, MKA 6557, governor of Aceh to GG, February 1, 7, and 13, 1880.

51. NL-HaNA, 2.10.02, MKA 6557, governor of Aceh to GG, March 14, 1880.

52. NL-HaNA, 2.10.02, MKA 6557, governor of Aceh to GG, January 12 and April 13, 1880.

53. NL-HaNA, 2.10.02, MKA 6557, governor of Aceh to GG, April 30, 1880, and Major Van Swieten to governor of Aceh, Krung Kali, May 5, 1880.

54. NL-HaNA, 2.10.02, MKA 6557, governor of Aceh to GG, April 30, 1880, and Major Van Swieten to governor of Aceh, Krung Kali, May 5, 1880; governor of Aceh to GG, May 22, 1880, and August 16 and October 1, 1880.

55. NL-HaNA, 2.10.02, MKA 6557, L. K. Turk to governor of Aceh, Lambaru, June 10, 1880. For houses on poles, see NA 2.10.02, MKA 6558A, Aceh Report October 27, 1881. On the salary, see governor of Aceh to GG, June 19, 1880.

56. NL-HaNA, 2.10.02, MKA 6557, L. K. Turk to governor of Aceh, Lambaru, June 10, 1880, and Governor Aceh to GG, June 26 and July 5, 1880.

57. NL-HaNA, 2.10.02, MKA 6557, governor of Aceh to GG, August 16 and 30, September 4, 18, and 25, 1880.

58. NL-HaNA, 2.10.02, MKA 6557, L. K. Turk (XXII *mukims*) to governor of Aceh, Lambaru, September 17 and October 13, 1880; De Jaager (XXVI *mukims*), Report, Krung Kali, September 29, 1880; governor of Aceh to GG, October 16, 1880. On the ix *mukims*, see MKA 6558, governor of Aceh to GG, April 2, 1881.

59. NL-HaNA, 2.10.02, MKA 6557, governor of Aceh to GG, October 10, 1880.

60. NL-HaNA, 2.10.02, MKA 6557, De Jaager, Krung Kali, October 13, 1880, and MKA 6558, governor of Aceh to GG, November 27, 1880.

61. NL-HaNA, 2.10.02, MKA 6558, governor of Aceh to GG, November 27 and December 20, 1880.

62. NL-HaNA, 2.10.02, MKA 6557, De Jaager, Krung Kali, October 13, 1880, and MKA 6558, governor of Aceh to GG, November 27, 1880.

63. For the yield ratios, NL-HaNA, 2.10.02, MKA 6558, Van Langen, Travel Report to the Southern States of the West Coast of Aceh, Malabuh, December 7, 1880.

64. NL-HaNA, 2.10.02, MKA 6558, L. K. Turk, Journal Lambaru, n.d., appended to governor of Aceh to GG, December 26, 1880.

65. NL-HaNA, 2.10.02, MKA 6558, Van Leeuwen (iv and vi *mukims*), Journal, Oleh Leh, December 24, 1880.

66. NL-HaNA, 2.10.02, MKA 6558, De Jaager, Journal Tungkup, February 10, 1881.

67. NL-HaNA, 2.10.02, MKA 6558, governor of Aceh to GG, March 5 and April 2, 1881.

68. NL-HaNA, 2.10.02, MKA 6558, governor of Aceh to GG, March 26, 1881.

69. NL-HaNA, 2.10.02, MKA 6557, governor of Aceh to GG, May 22 1880; MKA 6558, L. K. Turk (XXII *mukims*), Journal Lambaru, November 7, 1880; Van Leeuwen (iv and vi *mukims*), Journal, Oleh Leh, November 8 and 16, 1880; governor of Aceh to GG, November 27, 1880.

70. NL-HaNA, 2.10.02, MKA 6558, De Jaager (XXVI *mukims*) Journal Tungkup, January 13, 1881. Burning plains, see MKA 6558 L. K. Turk (XXII *mukims*) Journal Lambaru, November 7, 1880.

71. NL-HaNA, 2.10.02, MKA 6558, governor of Aceh to GG, January 22, March 5, and April 2, 1881; L. K. Turk (XXII *mukims*), Journal Glé Kambing, March 1, 9, and 29, 1881. An 1879–83 Rinderpest outbreak on Java killed over 200,000 animals and spread to Sumatra and other islands, see C.A. Spinage, *Cattle Plague: A History* (New York: Springer Science, 2003), p. 487.

72. NL-HaNA, 2.10.02, MKA 6558A, Aceh Reports, [August 28, 1881] and October 13, 1881.

73. NL-HaNA, 2.10.02, MKA 6559, M. T. G. Goossens, Journal, Glé Kambing, July 31, 1882.

74. Van 't Veer, *Atjeh-oorlog*, 137–42.

75. H. W. van den Doel, "Military Rule in the Netherlands Indies," in *The Late Colonial State in Indonesia: Political and Economic Foundations of the Netherlands Indies 1880–1942*, ed. Robert Cribb (Leiden: Koninklijk Instituut voor Taal-, Land- en Volkenkunde, 1994), 57–88 (especially 61–62).

76. NL-HaNA, 2.10.02, MKA 6558, De Jaager, Journal XXVI *mukims*, Krung Kali, December 19, 1880.

77. NL-HaNA, 2.10.02, MKA 6559, M. T. G. Goossens, Journal, Glé Kambing, August 8, 1882, and MKA 6559, Turk, Journal, Glé Kambing, August 18, 1882.

78. NL-HaNA, 2.10.02, MKA 6558A, Aceh Reports, July 5 and 19, 1881.

79. On collecting money to support the Aceh resistance, see NL-HaNA, 2.10.02, MKA 6556A, Aceh Report, May 28, 1879; MKA 6557, Report de Jaager, Krung Kali (XXVI *mukims*), September 29, 1880; and MKA 6558, Turk, Journal over the last 14 days [n.d.], appended to Aceh Report, January 18, 1881. On Tuku Njak Hassan's men, see MKA 6559, Aceh Report, June 25, 1882. On attacks on Aceh "collaborators," see MKA 6558, Aceh Report, November 9, 1880, and MKA 6558, Aceh Report, January 18, 1881.

80. NL-HaNA, 2.10.02, MKA 6558B, Aceh Report, March 16, 1882.

81. NL-HaNA, 2.10.02, MKA 6558B, governor of Aceh, [April 1882], following Aceh Report, April 26, 1882. Di Tiro explicitly used references to the coming of the Madhi; see MKA 6559, Aceh Report, June 25, 1882.

82. NL-HaNA, 2.10.02, MKA 6559, Van Swieten, Report to the Assistant-Resident of Greater Aceh, Anagalung, August 3, 1882. On Dutch anxieties about a global Muslim conspiracy affecting their colony, see Michael F. Laffan, "'A Watchful Eye': The Meccan Plot of 1881 and Changing Dutch Perceptions of Islam in Indonesia," *Archipel: Etudes Interdisciplinaires sur le Monde Insulindien*, 63, no. 1 (2002): 79–108.

83. NL-HaNA, 2.10.02, MKA 6559, Aceh Report, August 8, 1882.

84. NL-HaNA, 2.10.02, MKA 6558B, Aceh Report, May 31, 1882, and MKA 6559, governor of Aceh to military commander of Aceh, Kota Radja, July 2, 1882.

85. NL-HaNA, 2.10.02, MKA 6558B, April 1, 1882. The district official Turk used the word guerilla, see MKA 6559, Turk, Journal [July/August 1882], appended to Aceh Report, August 8, 1882.

86. NL-HaNA, 2.10.02, MKA 6559, Aceh Report, June 25, 1882.

87. NL-HaNA, 2.10.02, MKA 6558B, Aceh Report, May 31, 1882, and MKA 6559, Aceh Report, June 13, 1882.

88. NL-HaNA, 2.10.02, MKA 6559, Turk, Journal [July/August 1882] appendix to Aceh Report, August 8, 1882. Emphasis in original.

89. NL-HaNA, 2.10.02, MKA 6561, Aceh Reports, June 13–26 and June 27–July 14, 1883.

90. NL-HaNA, 2.10.02, MKA 6561, Aceh Reports, May 30–June 12, June 13–26, and June 27–July 14, 1883; MKA 6560, Aceh Reports, November 5 and December 4, 1882, January 1, February 18, and March 10, 1883.

91. NL-HaNA, 2.10.02, MKA 6561, Aceh Report, April 21–May 3, 1883.

92. NL-HaNA, 2.10.02, MKA 6560, Aceh Report, January 15, 1883, and MKA 6561, Aceh Reports April 21–May 3, 1883, and September 2–October 19, 1883.

93. NL-HaNA, 2.10.02, MKA 6561, Aceh Reports, October 21–November 5, November 6–20, November 20–December 2, 1883.

94. NL-HaNA, 2.10.02, MKA 6561, Aceh Reports, November 20–December 2, and December 3–18 and 19–31, 1883.

95. NL-HaNA, 2.10.02, MKA 6561B, Aceh Military Reports, October 26–November 18, November 22–30, 1883, and December 31, 1883–January 14, 1884, January [26]–February 8, and February 9–13, 1884.

96. NL-HaNA, 2.10.02, MKA 6561B, Aceh Military Report, December 31, 1883–January 14, 1884.

97. NL-HaNA, 2.10.02, MKA 6561B, Aceh Military Report, January 18–29, 1884.

98. On *ladangs*, see NL-HaNA, 2.10.02, MKA 6561B, Aceh Military Reports, January 18–29 and May 23–June 11, 1884. See also MKA 6559, Aceh Military Reports, Journal M. G. T. Goossens, July 26–31, 1882; MKA 6558, Van Langen, Report of Travel to the Southern States of the West Coast of Aceh, November 22–December 6, 1880; and MKA 6560, Aceh Report, November 21–December 3, 1882.

99. On rinderpest in the XXII *mukims*, NL-HaNA, 2.10.02, MKA 6561, Aceh Report, June 13–26, 1883. On smallpox, see MKA 6561, Aceh Report, July 15–31, 1883. On cholera, see MKA 6561, Aceh Reports, July 15–31, August 1–21, August 23–September 7, September 8–28, September 27–October 19, October 21–November 5, 1883, and December 3–18, 1883. See also MKA 6561B, Aceh Military Report, April 12–May 4, 1884.

100. See, for example, NL-HaNA, 2.10.02, MKA 6561B, Aceh Military Reports, June 28–July 2, September 23–October 20, and December 13–22, 1883, December 31, 1883–January 14, 1884, January 18–29, March 16–23, March 3–20 (Supplement), March 16–23, March 18–April 6, April 12–May 4, April 30–May 28, May 2–June 11, August 4–21, and August 22–September 3, 1884.

101. NL-HaNA, 2.10.02, MKA 6561B, Aceh Military Report, January [26]–February 8, 1884.

102. NL-HaNA, 2.10.02, MKA 6561B, Aceh Military Reports, February 9–13 and 9–24, 1884. Storing rice, see, MKA 6561 B, Aceh Military Report, March 2–15, 1884. See also MKA 6561A, Aceh Report, April 1–16, 1884.

103. NL-HaNA, 2.10.02, MKA 6561B, Aceh Military Report, March 2–15, 1884.

104. NL-HaNA, 2.10.02, MKA 6561B, Aceh Military Report, March 16–23, 1884.

105. See, for example, NL-HaNA, 2.10.02, MKA 6561B, Aceh Military Reports, August 28–September 5, 1883, and March 2–15, 1884.

106. NL-HaNA, 2.10.02, MKA 6561A, Aceh Reports, April 1–16 and 16–31, May 1–15 and 16–31, June 1–15 and 16–30, July 1–15 and 16–31, 1884.

107. NL-HaNA, 2.10.02, MKA 6561A, Bimonthly Aceh Reports, September 1–15, 1884; Van 't Veer, *Atjeh-oorlog*, 157–58; and Van den Doel, "Military Rule in the Netherlands Indies," 57–78.

108. The commander of the Netherlands Indies Army noted in the margins that the imposition of a state of war or state of siege would be an effective tool to restore order in Aceh; see NL-HaNA, 2.10.02, MKA 6561A, Aceh Report, April 1–16, 1884.

109. M. C. Piepers, "Zwaarden eischen klingen, maar ook gevesten: beschouwingen over de Atjeh-ziekte en hare genezing" (Amsterdam: S. L. van Looy, 1896) in *Late Nineteenth-Century . . . Dutch Monographs*, vol. 3 [n.p., Cornell University, n.d.], p. 22.

110. NL-HaNA, 2.10.02, MKA 6561C, Bimonthly Aceh Report, April 16–30, 1886.

111. NL-HaNA, 2.10.02, MKA 6561C, Aceh Military Reports, October 5–26, October 27–November 18, 1884.

112. On the construction of the railroads, roads, and bridges, see NL-HaNA, 2.10.02, MKA 6561A, Aceh Reports, December 1–15 and 16–31, 1884, March 16–31, April 1–15, April 16–May 1, May 16–31, August 1–5 and 16–31, September 1–15 and 16–30, November 16–30, December 1–15, 1885, March 1–15, and April 16–30, 1886.

113. NL-HaNA, 2.10.02, MKA 6561C, Aceh Military Reports, January 5–17, January 28–February 9, 1885, and October 15–17, 1885.

114. NL-HaNA, 2.10.02, MKA 6561C, Aceh Military Report, January 23–February 8, 1886, and MKA 6561A, Aceh Report, January 16–31, 1886.

115. See NL-HaNA, Ministerie van Kolonien Ministry of Colonies (henceforth NL-HaNA 4 MIKO), 1239, Map of the Occupied Territory in Greater Aceh, Surveyed January–April 1885. The same situation persists in an updated version of the same map from 1889, see NL-HaNA 4 MIKO, 1362, Map of the Occupied Territory in Greater Aceh, Surveyed January–April 1885, updated to 1889.

116. NL-HaNA, 2.10.02, MKA 6561C, Aceh Military Report, August 26–September 20, 1884.

117. NL-HaNA, 2.10.02, MKA 6561C, Aceh Military Report, October 27–November 18, 1884.

118. NL-HaNA, 2.10.02, MKA 6561C, Aceh Military Report, August 24–31, 1885.

119. NL-HaNA, 2.10.02, MKA 6561A, Aceh Reports, February 16–28, March 1–15 and 16–31, April 1–15 and 16–30, 1886.

120. NL-HaNA, 2.10.02, MKA 6561A, Aceh Reports, February 16–28, March 1–15 and 16–31, and April 1–15 and 16–30, 1886.

121. NL-HaNA, 2.10.02, MKA 6561C, Aceh Military Report, June 1–7, 1885.

122. NL-HaNA, 2.10.02, MKA 6561C, Aceh Military Report, June 8–15, 1886.

123. NL-HaNA, 2.10.02, MKA 6561C, Aceh Military Report, June 8–26, 1886.

124. NL-HaNA, 2.10.02, MKA 6561C, Aceh Military Report, October 16–21, 1886.

125. NL-HaNA, 2.10.02, MKA 6561C, Aceh Military Report, May 28–June 7, 1886.

126. NL-HaNA, 2.10.02, MKA 6561C, Aceh Military Reports, May 19–25, 1885 and August 31–September 9, 1886; MKA 6561A, Aceh Reports, June 1–15 and 16–30, 1885, and February 1–15, 1886.

127. NL-HaNA, 2.10.02, MKA 6561A, Aceh Report, July 1–15, 1885.

128. Van 't Veer, *Atjeh-oorlog*, 135–303; Van den Doel, "Military Rule in the Netherlands Indies," 72–73.

129. Van 't Veer, *Atjeh-oorlog*, 260.

130. Anonymus, "De agressieve politiek in Atjeh." *Reprint from the October-November Issues of the Tijdschrift voor Nederlandsch-Indie* (Zaltbommel: Joh. Norman, 1878), 51; and J. P. Schoenmaker, *Schetsen uit den Atjeh-oorlog* ('s-Gravenhage: W. P. van Stockum en Zoon, 1887), reproduced in *Late Nineteenth Century . . . Dutch Monographs*, vol. 1.

131. Van Swieten, *Waarheid*, 89, 302, 361, 413–15, 441–44; Meeting, December 8, 1881, *Atjeh: Parlementaire Redevoeringen van I.D. Fransen van de Putte van Februari 1873-December 1885*

[Schiedam: H. A. M. Roelants, 1886]. Reprinted in *Late Nineteenth-Century . . . Dutch Monographs*, vol. 8, 260–61; and vol. 7, 311.

132. See L. W. C. van den Berg, Review of J. Jacobs, *De Atjehers*. Reprinted in *Late Nineteenth-Century . . . Dutch Monographs*, vol. 3, 232–35.

133. See Julius K. Jacobs, *Het Familie- en Kampongleven op Groot-Atjeh: eene Bijdrage tot de Ethnographie van Noord-Sumatra* (Leiden: E. J. Brill, 1894), 307–9.

Chapter Ten: Environcide in Southern Africa: War and Refugees in the early 20th Century Ovambo Floodplain

1. Timotheus Nakale, interview by author, Olukula laKula, Namibia, February 21, 1993. Jackson Hamatwi was the interpreter for the interviews in Namibia in 1992 and 1993, and Eusebio Lilongeni was the interpreter for the interviews in Angola in 2005 and 2006.

2. On the Herero Wars, see, for example, G. Krüger, *Kriegsbewältigung und Geschichtsbewusstsein: Realität, Deutung und Verarbeitung des deutschen Kolonialkriegs in Namibia 1904 bis 1907* (Göttingen: Vandenhoeck und Ruprecht, 1999), 51–130; J.-B. Gewald, *Towards Redemption: A Socio-Political History of the Herero of Namibia between 1890 and 1923* (Leiden: Research School CNWS, 1996), 178–223, 220–24. On the 80 percent mortality, see J.-B. Gewald, *'We Thought We Would Be Free:' Socio-Cultural Aspects of Herero History in Namibia, 1915–1940* (Köln: Köppe, 2000), 22. A German missionary stationed in Oukwanyama at the time estimated that the mortality in the Portuguese-occupied larger part of Oukwanyama was up to 75 percent. See Archiv der Vereinigten Evangelischen Mission, Wuppertal-Barmen, Germany (henceforth AVEM), Rheinische Missionsgesellschaft (henceforth RMG) 2630 C/k 7, H. Welsch, "Ist ein Wiederafbau unser Ovambomission möglich," Swakopmund, May 1919, 45 verso.

3. On environmental infrastructure in the Ovambo floodplain, see Emmanuel Kreike, *Re-Creating Eden: Land Use, Environment, and Society in Southern Angola and Northern Namibia* (Portsmouth, NH: Heinemann, 2004), 15–55; and Emmanuel Kreike, *Environmental Infrastructure in African History: Examining the Myth of Natural Resource Management in Namibia* (Cambridge: Cambridge University Press, 2013).

4. Kreike, *Re-Creating Eden*, 15–55; Kreike, *Environmental Infrastructure*.

5. Kreike, *Re-Creating Eden*, 15–55; Kreike, *Environmental Infrastructure*.

6. R. Marjomaa, *War on the Savannah: The Military Collapse of the Sokoto Caliphate under the Invasion of the British Empire* ([Helsinki]: Academia Scientarum Fennica, 1998); H. Weiss, *Babban Yunwa: Hunger und Gesellschaft in Nord-Nigeria und der Nachtbarregion in der fruhen Kolonialzeit* (Helsinki: Suomen Historiallinen Seura, 1997); M. Saul and P. Royer, *West African Challenge to Empire: Culture and History in the Volta-Bani Anticolonial War* (Athens: Ohio University Press, 2001); R. Roberts, *Warriors, Merchants, and Slaves: The State and the Economy in the Middle Niger Valley, 1700–1914* (Stanford: Standford University press, 1987); Joe Lunn, *Memoirs of the Maelstrom: A Senegalese Oral History of the First World War* (Portsmouth, NH: Heinemann; Oxford: James Currey; Cape Town: David Philip, 1999); E. Howard Gorges, *Great War in West Africa* (East Sussex: Naval and Military Press, 2009); A. Meier, *Hunger und Herrschaft: Vorkoloiale und fruhe Koloniale Hungerkrisen im Nordtschad* (Stuttgart: Steiner, 1995); P. Geschiere, *Village Communities and the State: Changing Relations among the Maka of South-Eastern*

Cameroon since the Colonial Conquest (London: Kegan Paul International, 1982); A. Hochschild, *King Leopold's Ghost: A Story of Greed, Terror, and Heroism in Colonial Africa* (Boston: Houghton Mifflin, 1999); C. Miller, *Battle for the Bundu: The First World War in East Africa* (New York: Macmillan, 1974); J. Lamphear, *The Scattering Time: Turkana Responses to Colonial Rule* (Oxford: Clarendon Press, 1992); C. Brantley, *The Giriama and Colonial Resistance in Kenya, 1800–1920* (Berkeley: University of California Press, 1981); J. Iliffe, *A Modern History of Tanganyika* (Cambridge: Cambridge University Press, 1984 [1979]); G. Hodges, *Kariakor: The Carrier Corps: The Story of the Military Labour Forces in the Conquest of German East Africa, 1914–1918* (Nairobi: University of Nairobi Press, 1997); Michelle Moyd, *Violent Intermediaries: African Soldiers, Conquest, and Everyday Colonialism in German East Africa* (Athens: Ohio University Press, 2014); S. Ellis, *The Rising of the Red Shawls: A Revolt in Madagascar, 1896–1899* (Cambridge: Cambridge University Press, 1985); R. Pélissier, *Naissance de Mozambique: Résistance et Révoltes* (Orgeval: Péllissier, 1984); R. Pélissier, *Les Guerres Grises: Résistance et Révoltes en Angola, 1841–1941* (Orgeval: Pélissier, 1977); J. B. Peires, *The Dead Will Arise: Nongqawuse and the Great Xhosa Cattle-Killing Movement of 1856–7* (Johannesburg: Ravan Press, 1989); B. Maclennan, *A Proper Degree of Terror: John Graham and the Cape's Eastern Frontier* (Johannesburg: Ravan Press, 1986); P. Delius, *The Land Belongs to Us: The Pedi Polity, the Boers, and the British in the Nineteenth-Century Transvaal* (Berkeley: University of California Press, 1984); R. B. Edgerton, *Like Lions They Fought: The Zulu War and the Last Black Empire in South Africa* (New York: Ballantine, 1988); and Gewald, *Towards Redemption*.

7. E. Lecomte, "Duas Cartas do Missionário Erneste Lecomte," *Portugal em Africa*, 132 (December 1904), 742–43.

8. Kreike, *Re-Creating Eden*, 44–47.

9. Archives Générales du Congrégation du Saint Esprit, Paris, France (henceforth AGCSE) 476-A-IV, Cimbebasie ou Cubango: Situation des Missions, avec Aperçu sur la Situation 1911–20, A. Keiling, Ébauche de l'Histoire de la Préfecture Apostolique du Cubango en Angola, 1879–1929, 123–25; D. M. de Lima, *A Campanha dos Cuamatos Contado por um Soldado Expedicionário* (Lisbon: Livraria Ferreira, 1908), 21–22; Pélissier, *Les Guerres Grises*, 448–54, 465.

10. Kreike, *Re-Creating Eden*, 44–47.

11. Kreike, *Re-creating Eden*, 35–62.

12. Centro Nacional de Documentação e Investigação Histórica, Luanda, Angola (henceforth CNDIH), Avulsos, Caixa 3865 "Cubango" Capitania Môr de Ganguellas e Ambuellas, Relatório Mensal, February 29, 1904, and Caixa 5048 "Humbe," 32.1 Humbe: Administração do Concelho, Relatórios 1886–1914, Relatório Junho 1904; AGCSE 476-A-IV, Cimbebasie ou Cubango: Situation des Missions, avec Aperçu sur la Situation 1911–20, A. Keiling, Ébauche de l'Histoire de la Préfecture Apostolique do Cubango en Angola, 1879–1929, 123–25; D. M. de Lima, *A Campanha dos Cuamatos: Contada por um Soldado Expediçonário* (Lisbon: Livraria Ferreira, 1908), 21–22; Pélissier, *Guerres Grises*, 448–54, 465. See also AVEM, RMG 2517 C/h 33, A. Wülfhorst, Omupanda, September 25, 1905, and A. Wülfhorst, 4e. Quartalbericht 1906, Omupanda, January 9, 1907.

13. Interviews by author: Petrus Shanika Hipetwa, Oshiteyatemo, Namibia, June 17, 1993; Helivi Mungandjela, Olupandu (Okalongo), Namibia, June 21, 1993, and Julius Abraham, Olupito, Namibia, June 15, 1993. CNDIH, Codices 1092/252, 3-4-19, Forte Rocadas, Quartel-General, Diário da Campanha 1907, entries for September 4 and 24, October 1, 3, 5, and 20. CNDIH,

Avulsos, Caixa 4075 "Cuamato," Pasta lxxxix–1907: Operações além-Cunene-Cuamato, Registro Nº 4, Nº 309, October 4, 1907; AVEM, RMG 2517 C/h 33, A. Wülfhorst, Omupanda, October 1, 1907; Lima, *A Campanha dos Cuamatos*; Pélissier, *Guerres Grises*, 448–54 and 465.

14. Kreike, *Re-Creating Eden*, 45.

15. AVEM, RMG 2518 C/h 34, H. Gehlmann, 1e. Quartalbericht, Ondjiva, April 10, 1911; RMG 2518 C/h 34, H. Gehlmann, to Inspector, Ondjiva, January 31, 1911; and Sondjali Nsio, interview by author, Omupanda, Angola, March 23, 2005.

16. AVEM, RMG 2518 C/h 34, H. Gehlmann, 1e Quartalbericht, Ondjiva, April 12, 1912.

17. AVEM, RMG 2518 C/h 34, H. Gehlmann, Conferenzbericht, Ondjiva, n.d. (received December 23, 1912). See also interviews by author with Petrus Shanika Hipetwa, Oshiteyatemo, Namibia, June 17, 1993; Helivi Mungandjela, Olupandu, Okalongo, Namibia, June 21, 1993; and Julius Abraham, Olupito, Namibia, June 15, 1993.

18. AVEM, RMG 2517 C/h 33, A. Wülfhorst, 2nd Quartalbericht, Omupanda, July 1, 1913; RMG 2515 C/h 31, H. Welsch, 2. Quartalbericht 1913, Omatemba July 1, 1913 (E. No. 962, 1/7/13); RMG 2518 C/h 34, A. Hochstrate, Quartalbericht January 1–March 31, 1913, Ondjiva, April 1, 1913, and Konferenzbericht 1913 (received: February 26, 1914).

19. AVEM, RMG 2517 C/h 33, A. Wülfhorst, 2e Quartalbericht 1914, Omupanda, July 1, 1914. RMG 2518 C/h 34, H. Gehlmann, Konferenzbericht, Ondjiva, n.d. (1912), and 1e. and 2e. Quartalberichte, Ondjiva, May 30 and June 30, 1914; Lea Paulus, interview by author, Onandjaba, June 17, 1993. AVEM, RMG 2518 C/h 34, H. Gehlmann, 1e. Quartalbericht, Ondjiva, May 30, 1914; RMG 2517 C/h 33, A. Wülfhorst, 2e. Quartalbericht 2, 1914, Omupanda July 1, 1914.

20. AVEM, RMG 2518 C/h 34, H. Gehlmann, 1e and 2e Quartalberichte, Ondjiva, May 30 and June 30, 1914.

21. CNDIH, Avulsos, Caixa 3703 "Huila," Processo Missão de Estudos no Sul de Angola, 1914–15, Relatório do Mês de Outubro [1914].

22. Paulus Wanakashimba, interview by author, Odimbo, Namibia, February 10, 1993.

23. AGCSE 476-A-IV, Cimbebasie, Keiling, Ébauche de l'Histoire de la Préfecture Apostolique, 205–7.

24. Interviews by author: Ester Nande, Onengali, Namibia, May 20, 1993; Magdalena Malonde, Oipya, Namibia, May 28, 1993; and Helena Nailonga, Ekoka laKula, Namibia, February 23, 1993. See also AVEM, RMG 2630 C/k7, Wülfhorst, "Unsere Ovambomission vor, während und nach dem Portugiesischen Kriegs gegen Mandume," April 1916.

25. Helena Nailonga, interview by author, Ekoka laKula, Namibia, February 23, 1993. Emilia Kulaumone Namadi stressed that her mother and other elders recounted the high death rate of the Ondjala yOkapuka kaNekoto: insects ate the grain, see Emilia Kulaumone Namadi, interview by author, Onanime, Angola, August 8, 2006.

26. Interviews by author: Ester Nande, Onengali, Namibia, May 20, 1993; Magdalena Malonde, Oipya, Namibia, May 28, 1993; Helena Nailonga, Ekoka laKula, Namibia, February 23, 1993; Nahango Hailonga, Onamahoka, Namibia, February 4, 1993; and Timotheus Nakale, Olukula laKula, Namibia, February 21, 1993. See also AVEM, RMG 2630 C/k7, Wülfhorst, "Unsere Ovambomission," April 1916.

27. See Israel Hendjala, interview by author, Oshalembe, Namibia, June 3, 1993. AVEM, RMG 2630 C/k7, Wülfhorst, "Unsere Ovambomission," April 1916; CNDIH, Avulsos, Caixa 5943 "Huila" (1891–1918), Huila 31-9-4, Correspondência expedida 1902–18, Processo Nº 626,

Encarregado do Governo ao Secretária-Geral do Governo de Angola, Vila Sá da Bandeira, May 2, 1915 (Nº 62/69).

28. AVEM, RMG 2630 C/k7, Wülfhorst, "Unsere Ovambomission," April 1916.

29. AGCSE 476-A-IV, Cimbebasie: Keiling, Ébauche, 205–7. CNDIH, Avulsos, Caixa 5943 "Huila" (1891–1918), Huila 31-9-4, Correspondência expedida 1902–18, Processo Nº 626, Encarregado do Governo ao Secretária-Geral do Governo de Angola, Vila Sá da Bandeira, May 2, 1915 (Nº 62/69).

30. AVEM, RMG 2630 C/k7, Wülfhorst, "Unsere Ovambomission," April 1916.

31. AVEM, RMG 2630 C/k7, Wülfhorst, "Unsere Ovambomission," April 1916.

32. Shemange Abraham, interview by author, Omupupu, Angola, July 22, 2005.

33. Kreike, Re-Creating Eden, 52–55.

34. Shuushe Shalukeni Shoombe, interview by author, Ohacaonde, Angola, July 20, 2005.

35. Simeon Hangula Haikali, interview by author, Namacunde (Ongode yaMpolo), Angola, August 9, 2006.

36. AVEM, RMG 2630 C/k7, Wülfhorst, "Unsere Ovambomission," April 1916; RMG 2515 C/h 31, H. Welsch, Quartalbericht, Omatemba, March 30, 1916; AGCSE 476-A Mission de Cimbebasie, I. Cubango-Angola ou Haute Cimbebasie: Comptes-rendus de Visites Provinciales entre 1907–20, L. Keiling, "Situation de la Mission de l'Evale, Cimbebasie 1916"; and 476-A-IV, Cimbebasie: Keiling, Ébauche, 205–7.

37. AVEM, RMG 2515 C/h 31, H. Welsch, Quartalbericht Omatemba, December 30, 1915.

38. Interviews by author: Timotheus Nakale, Olukula laKula, Namibia, February 21, 1993; Gabriel Kautwima, Omhedi, Namibia, April 28, 1993; and Jonas Paendoambo Shimuningeni, Onanime, Angola, August 8, 2006.

39. AVEM, RMG 2630 C/k7, Wülfhorst, "Unsere Ovambomission," April 1916, and A. Hochstrate (Namakunde), "Bericht über die Ovambomission während des Krieges und ihr gegenwärtigen Stand" (1920).

40. AVEM, RMG 2630 C/k7, Wülfhorst, "Unsere Ovambomission," April 1916.

41. António Pires, "Pe. Carlos Estermann, Sangue Cuanhama," Portugal em África, 2nd series, 7 (1950), 225–26. Cf. NAN, RCO 3 [or 4] 1916/7, "Re. Proclamations by Chiefs, Notice: orders to Headmen and People."

42. NAN, UNG UA2 f. 1922–1946, "Statement Ovamboland Administration: Grain Sales, Cash, and Cattle," February 28, 1916.

43. AVEM, RMG 2515 C/h 31, H. Welsch, Quartalbericht Omatemba, December 30, 1915; NAN, RCO 9 f. 10/1916/1 (i), Union Government Representative [henceforth UGR] to Administrator of South West Africa [henceforth SWA], Namakunde, December 31, 1915; AVEM, RMG 2515 C/h 31, H. Welsch, Quartalbericht, Omatemba, March 30, 1916; CNDIH, Avulsos, Caixa 1272 "Cunene," C. E. Fairlie, "Report re. British-Portuguese Neutral Zone," February 3, 1916, appendix to Residente Português em Namakunde to Governo Geral de Angola, Relatório 20 Novembro [1916] a 10 de Abril [1917], May 8, 1917; NAN, RCO 4, 1916/1, re. FMS, Resident Commissioner Ovamboland to Deputy Secretary Protectorate, Ondonga, April 26, 1916.

44. Ndewiteko Kanana, interview by author, Oihambo, Angola, March 25, 2005.

45. AVEM, RMG 2515 C/h 31, Welsch, Quartalbericht, Omatemba, March 30, 1916; NAN, RCO 4, 1916/1, re. FMS, Resident Commissioner Ovamboland to Deputy Secretary Protectorate, Ondonga, April 26, 1916. Cf. notes by Hahn about people not making large fields or storing

supplies of grain in the past because of the insecurity, NAN, A450, 9 f. 2/39, Hahn, "Rough Notes on Tribal Customs in Ovamboland," 59 and A450, vol. 10 f. 2/40, "Political and Tribal Affairs," 3. See also interviews by author: Lea Paulus, Onandjaba, Namibia, June 17, 1993, and Elisabeth Ndemutela, Okongo, Namibia, February 16 and 17, 1993.

46. AVEM, RMG 2630 C/k7, Wülfhorst, "Unsere Ovambomission," April 1916, and Welsch, "Ist ein Wiederafbau unser Ovambomission möglich," Swakopmund, May 1919, 45 verso; RMG 2515 C/h 31, H. Welsch, Quartalbericht, Omatemba, March 30, 1916; Elisabeth Ndemutela, interview by author, Okongo, Namibia, February 16 and 17, 1993; NAN, RCO 9 f. 10/1916/1 (i), Government Representative Neutral Zone to Administrator South West Africa, Namakunde, December 31, 1915; CNDIH, Avulsos, Caixa 1272 "Cunene," Fairlie, "Report re. British-Portuguese Neutral Zone," February 3, 1916, Relatório, May 8, 1917.

47. Helemiah Hamutenya, interview by author, Omuulu Weembaxu, Namibia, July 17, 1993. Ondjala yEkomba = Ekuukuu, Joao Baptista Lungameni Paulo, interview by author, Omupanda, Angola, March 22, 2005.

48. Magdalena Malonde, interview by author, Oipya, Namibia, May 28, 1993. See also Mateus Nangobe, interview by author, Omupanda, Namibia, May 24 and 25, 1993.

49. João Baptista Lungameni Paulo, interview by author, Omupanda, Angola, March 22, 2005.

50. Mwulifundja Linekela Haiyaka, interview by author, Omhedi, Namibia, February 8, 1993. See also Jonas Paendoambo Shimuningeni, interview with author, Onanime, Angola, August 8, 2006.

51. Sondjali Nsio, interview by author, Omupanda, Angola, March 23, 2005.

52. Ndewiteko Kanana, interview by author, Oihambo, Angola, March 25, 2005.

53. AVEM, RMG 2630 C/k 7, Welsch, "Ist ein Wiederafbau unser Ovambomission möglich," Swakopmund, May 1919, 45 verso.

54. AVEM, RMG 2515 C/h 31, Welsch, Quartalbericht, Omatemba, March 30, 1916.

55. AVEM, RMG 2630 C/k 7, Welsch, "Ist ein Wiederafbau unser Ovambomission möglich." Swakopmund, May 1919, and AVEM, RMG 2515 C/h 31, Welsch, Quartalbericht, Omatemba, March 30, 1916. See also CNDIH, Avulsos, Caixa 1272 "Cunene," Fairlie, "Report re. British-Portuguese Neutral Zone," February 3, 1916, Relatório, May 8, 1917.

56. CNDIH, Avulsos, Caixa 4130 "Huila," Processo 1/y (1915), Relatório do Encarregado do Governo da Huila, António de Almeida, tenente de Cavalaria criação do Distrito de Além Cunene e Namacunde. See also "A fome, a peste e a guerra assolaram os povos do Cunene no período de 1914 a 1918." Arquivo Histórico Ultramarino, Lisbon, Portugal (henceforth AHU) 9, 590, 20, Fronteira Sul de Angola, Processo 265-E, Relatório de E. Machado, Sá da Bandeira [Lubango], January 22–February 10, 1925.

57. In the original table, Cuamato is used for Ombadja. AHU, Sala 8, Praça 115, Angola, Prejuízos causados pela guerra de 1914–18, Direcção Geral de Administração Civil, Luanda, August 14, 1919, annex to Serviço de inquérito aos prejuízos causados pela Guerra na Província de Angola Nº 22 and Correspondência expedida Nº 215, Capitão-môr dos Cuanhama, Cuamato e Evale to Delegado do Governo, Vila Sá da Bandeira [Lubango], September 26, 1919.

58. For the Portuguese claims, see CNDIH, Avulsos, Caixa 4130 "Huila," Processo 1/y (1915), Relatório do Encarregado do Governo da Huila, António de Almeida, tenente de Cavalaria criação do Distrito de Além Cunene e Namacunde. See also "A fome, a peste e a guerra assolaram os povos do Cunene no período de 1914 a 1918," AHU 9, 590, 20, Fronteira Sul de Angola,

Processo 265-E, Relatório de E. Machado, Sá da Bandeira [Lubango], January 22–February 10, 1925. For the Blue Book, see Jeremy Silvester and Jean-Bart Gewald, eds., *Words Cannot Be Found: German Colonial Rule in Namibia: An Annotated Reprint of the 1918 Blue Book* (Leiden: Brill, 2003).

59. E. Lecomte, "Duas Cartas do Missionário Erneste Lecomte," *Portugal em Africa*, 132 (December 1907): 738–749.

60. Kreike, *Re-creating Eden*, 57–155.

61. Kreike, *Re-Creating Eden*, 77–78.

62. Shemange Abraham, interview by author, Omupupu, Angola, July 22, 2005.

63. Emmanuel Kreike, *Deforestation and Reforestation in Namibia: The Global Consequences of Local Contradictions* (Princeton: Markus Wiener, 2010), 167–68.

64. Kreike, *Deforestation*, 35–40.

65. Kreike, *Environmental Infrastructure*, 128–29.

66. Kreike, *Deforestation*, 88–89. In 1945 another campaign occurred, vaccinating 54,000 people in Ovamboland against smallpox. On Hamkoto Kapa, see Kreike, *Re-Creating Eden*, 136. Another major refugee resettlement leader died around this time in the same region, Paulus Haufiku Hamutenya, see Kreike, *Re-Creating Eden*, 133.

67. On existing villages, see Kreike, *Re-Creating Eden*, 134–35.

68. Kreike, *Re-Creating Eden*, 75.

69. Kreike, *Re-Creating Eden*, 136–43.

70. On water sources, see Kreike, *Re-Creating Eden*, 75–76; and Kreike, *Environmental Infrastructure*, 105–16.

71. Kreike, *Re-Creating Eden*, 129–53. On the appropriation of San waterholes, see Kreike, *Deforestation*, 168–76.

72. Emilia Kulaumone Namadi, interview by author, Onanime, Angola, August 8, 2006. See also Jonas Paendoambo Shimuningeni, interview by author, Onanime, Angola, August 8, 2006. Valelia Nghitendeno Haiwelela was a big girl already during the Famine of the Dams (born 1922), but it did not affect them because they lived on the Angolan side, Valelia Nghitendeno Haiwelela, interview by author Oshikuku, Angola, March 19, 2005.

73. Natalia Tulipomwene Jonas, interview by author, Onamacunde, Angola, March 31, 2005.

74. AHU 9, 590, 20, Fronteira Sul de Angola, Processo No. 265-C, C. R. Machado, Chefe da Delegação Portuguesa, Oluchanja, July 23, 1927, annex: considerações de carácter reservado, to Chefe da Delegação do Governo da União; National Archives of Namibia [henceforth NAN], Native Affairs Ovamboland [henceforth NAO] 17, O/C NAO to Mr. Clarke, October 16, 1927; NAO 18 Monthly Report Oukwanyama, October 1927, June–August 1930, and Monthly Report for Ovamboland, September 1928. See also interviews by author: Ester Nande, Onengali, Namibia, May 20, 1993; Moses Kakoto, Okongo, Namibia, February 16, 1993; and Petrus Mbubi, Onanime, Namibia, February 26, 1993.

75. NAN, NAO 18, Monthly Reports for Ovamboland July–September 1928; NAO 40, "Note of interview with . . . administrator [of SWA] 9/2/29 in regard to prospective famine conditions in Ovamboland."

76. NAN, NAO 18, Monthly Report for Ovamboland, January 1929.

77. NAN, NAO 18, Monthly Report Oukwanyama, January 1929; NAO 40, Office Commanding [henceforth O/C] Oshikango to O/C NAO, Oshikango, March 11, 1929, "Stock losses:

Ukuanyama"; and "Particulars obtained from headmen in western Ukuanyama area re. famine etc."; "Particulars in regard to famine Ukuanyama areas received from headmen east of the main road from Ondonga to Oshikango"; and appendixes to O/C Oshikango to O/C NAO, Oshikango, July 31 and August 8, 1929.

78. Kalolina Naholo, interview by author, Ohamwaala, Namibia, January 26, 1993.

79. NAN, NAO 40, O/C NAO to Secretary SWA, Ondangwa, March 18, 1929; O/C Oshikango Station to O/C NAO, Oshikango, March 11, 1929 (both letters of that date); O/C Oshikango Station to O/C NAO, Oshikango, April 18, 1929; O/C Oshikango Station to O/C NAO, Oshikango, May 8 and 15, 1929; and O/C NAO to O/C Oshikango Station, Ondangwa, May 12, 1929. On Ndilokelwa, Kreike, *Re-Creating Eden*, 78.

80. NAN, NAO 18, Monthly Report Oukwanyama, January 1929; NAO 40, O/C Oshikango to O/C NAO, Oshikango, March 11, 1929, "Stock losses: Ukuanyama"; and "Particulars obtained from headmen in western Ukuanyama area re. famine etc."; "Particulars in regard to famine Ukuanyama areas received from headmen east of the main road from Ondonga to Oshikango"; and appendixes to O/C Oshikango to O/C NAO, Oshikango, July 31 and August 8, 1929.

81. NAN, NAO 18, Monthly Reports Oukwanyama, January–February 1929. On the failure of the fruit harvest, see NAO 40, O/C NAO to Secretary South West Africa, Ondangwa, January 15, 1929, and Assistant Priest St. Mary's Mission to O/C NAO, January 10, 1929.

82. NAN, NAO 41, Statement of First Consignment of 948 bags maize meal received at Ondangua from 28/1/29 to 24/4/29 for Famine Relief Ovamboland. In addition to the food bought from the colonial administration, Ondonga households from 1928 to 1930 bought millet in Oukwanyama and western Ovamboland, NAO 11, Annual Report Finnish Mission Society 1930.

83. NAO 18, Monthly Reports Oukwanyama, May–July 1929.

84. NAN, NAO 40, O/C NAO to Secretary SWA, Ondangwa, May 25 and 30, 1929; Acting Secretary SWA to O/C NAO, Windhoek, May 18, 1929; O/C NAO to Secretary SWA, Ondangwa, May 25 and June 6, 1929; and V. Alho (Finnish Mission Society) to O/C NAO, Olukonda, April 17, 1929.

85. NAN, NAO 40, Director of Works to O/C NAO, Windhoek June 17, 1929, and O/C NAO to Secretary SWA, Ondangwa, July 17 and August 10, 1929.

86. NAN, NAO 40, "Particulars obtained from headmen in western Ukuanyama area re. famine etc."; and "Particulars in regard to famine Ukuanyama areas received from headmen east of the main road from Ondonga to Oshikango"; and appendixes to O/C Oshikango to O/C NAO, Oshikango, July 31 and August 8, 1929.

87. NAN, NAO 40, "Particulars obtained from headmen in western Ukuanyama area re. famine etc."; and "Particulars in regard to famine Ukuanyama areas received from headmen east of the main road from Ondonga to Oshikango"; and appendixes to O/C Oshikango to O/C NAO, Oshikango, July 31 and August 8, 1929.

88. NAN, NAO 40, "Particulars . . . western Ukuanyama" and "Particulars . . . east of the main road," and appendixes to O/C Oshikango Station to O/C NAO, Oshikango, July 31 and August 8, 1929.

89. NAN, NAO 40, "Particulars . . . western Ukuanyama"; "Particulars . . . east of the main road"; and appendixes to O/C Oshikango to O/C NAO, Oshikango, July 31 and August 8, 1929.

90. NAN, NAO 18, Monthly Reports Oukwanyama, January–February 1929. See also NAO 40, O/C NAO to Sec. SWA, Ondangwa, January 15, 1929; Assistant Priest St. Mary's Mission

to O/C NAO, [Odibo], January 10, 1929; and "Note of interview with the administrator [d.d.] 9/2/29 in regard to prospective famine conditions in Ovamboland."

91. NAN, NAO 9, O/C NAO to Secretary SWA, September 6, 1929; NAO 18, Monthly Report Oukwanyama, September 1929.

92. NAN, NAO 18, Monthly Report Ovamboland, January 1929, and Monthly Reports Oukwanyama, September-October 1929; NAO 41, Famine Relief Ukuanyama, Works Issue Schedules, October–December 1929; NAO 40, O/C NAO to Secretary SWA, Ondangwa May 25, June 6, July 17, and August 10, 1929, and O/C Oshikango to O/C NAO, Oshikango, May 8 and 15, August 8, 1929, and O/C NAO to O/C Oshikango, Ondangwa, May 12, 1929; Pauline, interview by author, Onengali, December 15, 1992. On handtools, see NAO 40, O/C Oshikango to O/C NAO, Oshikango, July 8, 1929.

93. NAN, NAO 41, Famine Relief Ukuanyama, Works & Issue Schedules, October–December 1929.

94. On food aid, see NAN, NAO 40, O/C NAO to Secretary SWA, Ondangwa, September 5, 1929, and NAO 41, Famine Reports Ovamboland, October–December 1930.

95. NAN, NAO 18, Monthly Reports Oukwanyama, September–December 1929 and January–February 1930.

96. NAN, NAO 18, Monthly Reports Oukwanyama, September–December 1929 and January–February 1930.

97. NAN, NAO 18, Monthly Report Oukwanyama, December 1929. On the famine and social networks, see P. Hayes, "The 'Famine of the Dams:' Gender, Labour and Politics in Colonial Ovamboland, 1929–1930," in *Namibia under South African Rule: Mobility and Containment, 1915–1945*, ed. P. Hayes et al. (Oxford: James Currey, 1998), 117–46.

98. Interviews by author: Elisabeth Ndemutela, Okongo, Namibia, February 16–17, 1993, and Mwulifundja Linekela Haiyaka, Omhedi, Namibia, February 8, 1993.

99. NAN, NAO 18, Monthly Report Oukwanyama, December 1929.

100. Twemuna Shifidi, interview by author, Ondaanya, Namibia, January 28, 1993.

101. Helena Nailonga, interview by author, Ekoka laKula, Namibia, February 23, 1993, and Nahango Hailonga, interview by author, Onamahoka, Namibia, February 4, 1993.

102. NAN, NAO 41, Native Commissioner Ovamboland [henceforth NCO], Famine Reports September–October and December 1930; Union (of South Africa) Government Representative Namacunde (henceforth UNG), Union Administration 2 folder 1922–1946, UGR Oshikango, Monthly Report December 1929. NAO 40–41, Reports on Famine Relief Works: Oukwanyama, August 1930–February 1931 and Trust Fund Ovamboland, Statement for February 1930.

103. NAN, NAO 18, Monthly Reports Oukwanyama, December 1929 and January 1930; NAO 40, O/C NAO to Secretary SWA, Ondangwa, March 11, 1930; Weekly Drought Reports, Weeks ending March 22 and 29, and May 5, 1930. The Portuguese traders in southern Angola sold grain at 40 Shilling a bag, see NAO 40, Secretary SWA to O/C NAO, Windhoek September 28, 1929.

104. NAN, NAO 40, Director of Works to Secretary SWA, Windhoek, June 3, 1930.

105. NAN, NAO 40, Director of Works to Secretary SWA, Windhoek, June 3, 1930.

106. NAN, NAO 18, Monthly Reports Oukwanyama, June, July, and September–November 1930.

107. NAN, NAO 18, Monthly Reports Oukwanyama, June, July, and September–November 1930.

108. NAN, NAO 18, Monthly Report Oukwanyama, August 1930.

109. NAN, NAO 40–41, Famine Relief Reports and Issue Schedules for Oukwanyama, August 1930–April 1931.

110. NAN, NAO 41, Report on Famine Relief Works: Oukwanyama, September 1930.

111. NAN, NAO 41, Famine Relief Report Oukwanyama, December 1930.

112. Pauline, interview by author, Onengali, Namibia, December 15, 1992, and Salome Tushimbeni Haihambo, interview by author, Oipya, Namibia, June 19, 1993.

113. Data derived from NAN, NAO 40–41, Famine Relief Reports and Issue Schedules for Oukwanyama, August 1930–April 1931.

114. NAN, NAO 41, NCO, Famine Reports September–October and December 1930; NAO 18–19, Monthly Reports Oukwanyama, June-September 1930 and March 1931; and UNG, Union Administration 2 folder 1922–46, UGR Oshikango, Monthly Report December 1929.

115. NAN, NAO 41, NCO, Famine Reports September–October and December 1930; UNG, Union Administration 2 folder 1922–46, UGR Oshikango, Monthly Report December 1929.

116. NAN, NAO 41, Famine Relief Reports Oukwanyama, January–March 1931, and NAO 18–19, Monthly Reports Oukwanyama, October and December 1930 and January–February 1931.

117. See NAN, NAO 41, Famine Relief Report Oukwanyama, February 1931, Special Issues and Famine Relief Reports Oukwanyama, January–February 1931 and Famine Report Ovamboland January 1931.

118. Data derived from NAN, NAO 40–41, Famine Relief Reports and Issue Schedules for Oukwanyama, August 1930–April 1931.

119. NAN, NAO 41, Famine Relief Reports Oukwanyama, January–March 1931, and NAO 18–19, Monthly Reports Oukwanyama, October and December 1930 and January–February 1931.

120. NAN, NAO 41, Famine Relief Report Oukwanyama, January–February 1931; Famine Relief Reports Ovamboland, January 1931; NAO 18–19, Monthly Reports Oukwanyama, December 1930, January and February 1931.

121. NAN, NAO 19, Monthly Report Oukwanyama, June/July 1931.

122. NAN, NAO 19, Monthly Reports Oukwanyama, March and September 1931.

123. Kreike, *Deforestation*, 90–92.

124. Kreike, *Deforestation*, 88–89.

125. NAN, NAO 18, Monthly Reports Oukwanyama, June–July, September–November 1930.

126. On the refugees' postconflict reconstruction, see Kreike, *Recreating Eden*, 81–176.

Conclusion: Environcide as a Crime against Humanity

1. Grenier makes a strong argument for the development of an American way of war, but as this book demonstrates, the way of war he outlines was not unique to (North) America. See John Grenier, *The First Way of Making War: American War Making on the Frontier* (Cambridge: Cambridge University Press, 2005).

2. Scheidel argues modern war mobilized a far larger percentage of the population, but as is common in the military history literature, he only looks at direct mobilization of men in the

military. See Walter Scheidel, *The Great Leveler: Violence and the History of Inequality from the Stone Age to the Twenty-First Century* (Princeton: Princeton University Press, 2017), 174–46.

3. Gutman argues that villages and farmers in the 17th- and 18th-century Liège region in the Low Countries were very reluctant to leave their homes in war time because soldiers often pillaged the abandoned dwellings. This is even more significant because most of the time the Liège region was considered neutral rather than hostile territory. See Myron P. Gutmann, *War and Rural Life in the Early Modern Low Countries* (Princeton: Princeton University Press, 1980), 151–52. In Brabant during the Thirty Years War, farmers and villagers were also very hesitant to abandon their homes. See chapter 3. In Holland in the 1570s, a placard was issued to prohibit demolishing abandoned buildings to sell or reuse the building materials. Spanish and other soldiers used the timber of abandoned buildings for fuel in the winter, see chapter 1.

4. Jacques Antoine Hippolyte de Guibert, *Essai Générale de Tactique*, vol. 2 (London: Nabu Public Domain Reprints), 294–97, 306–7, 332–33.

5. Walter Scheidel, *The Great Leveler: Violence and the History of Inequality from the Stone Age to the Twenty-First Century* (Princeton: Princeton University Press, 2017), 1–22, 115–29, 130–75, 199.

INDEX

A NOTE ON THE TYPE

This book has been composed in Arno, an Old-style serif typeface in the
classic Venetian tradition, designed by Robert Slimbach at Adobe.